T0189206

Communications
in Computer and Information Science   1388

More information about this series at http://www.springer.com/series/7899

Miguel Botto-Tobar · Sergio Montes León ·
Oscar Camacho · Danilo Chávez ·
Pablo Torres-Carrión ·
Marcelo Zambrano Vizuete (Eds.)

Applied Technologies

Second International Conference, ICAT 2020
Quito, Ecuador, December 2–4, 2020
Proceedings

 Springer

Editors
Miguel Botto-Tobar ⓘ
Eindhoven University of Technology
Eindhoven, The Netherlands

Sergio Montes León ⓘ
Universidad de las Fuerzas Armadas (ESPE)
Quito, Ecuador

Oscar Camacho
Escuela Politécnica Nacional
Quito, Ecuador

Danilo Chávez
Escuela Politécnica Nacional
Quito, Ecuador

Pablo Torres-Carrión ⓘ
Universidad Técnica Particular de Loja
Loja, Ecuador

Marcelo Zambrano Vizuete ⓘ
Universidad Técnica del Norte
Ibarra, Ecuador

ISSN 1865-0929   ISSN 1865-0937 (electronic)
Communications in Computer and Information Science
ISBN 978-3-030-71502-1   ISBN 978-3-030-71503-8 (eBook)
https://doi.org/10.1007/978-3-030-71503-8

This Springer imprint is published by the registered company Springer Nature Switzerland AG
The registered company address is: Gewerbestrasse 11, 6330 Cham, Switzerland

Preface

The 2nd International Conference on Applied Technologies (ICAT) was held online during December 2nd until 4th, 2020, and it was organized jointly by Universidad de las Fuerzas Armadas ESPE, Escuela Politécnica Nacional, and Universidad Técnica Particular de Loja, in collaboration with GDEON. The ICAT series aims to bring together top researchers and practitioners working in different domains in the field of computer science to exchange their expertise and to discuss the perspectives of development and collaboration. The content of this volume is related to the following subjects:

- Communication
- Computing
- e-Government and e-Participation
- e-Learning
- Electronics
- Intelligent Systems
- Machine Vision
- Security
- Technology Trends

ICAT 2020 received 145 submissions written in English by 269 authors coming from 12 different countries. All these papers were peer reviewed by the ICAT 2020 Program Committee, consisting of 186 high-quality researchers. To assure a high-quality and thoughtful review process, we assigned each paper at least three reviewers. Based on the peer reviews, 53 full papers were accepted, resulting in a 37% acceptance rate, which was within our goal of less than 40%.

We would like to express our sincere gratitude to the invited speakers for their inspirational talks, to the authors for submitting their work to this conference, and to the reviewers for sharing their experience during the selection process.

December 2020

Miguel Botto-Tobar
Sergio Montes León
Óscar Camacho
Danilo Chávez
Pablo Torres-Carrión
José Bucheli Andrade

Organization

General Chair

Miguel Botto-Tobar   Eindhoven University of Technology, The Netherlands

Organizing Committee

Miguel Botto-Tobar	Eindhoven University of Technology, The Netherlands
Sergio Montes León	Universidad de las Fuerzas Armadas (ESPE) – Sede Latacunga, Ecuador/Universidad Rey Juan Carlos, Spain
Óscar Camacho	Escuela Politécnica Nacional, Ecuador
Danilo Chávez	Escuela Politécnica Nacional, Ecuador
Pablo Torres-Carrión	Universidad Técnica Particular de Loja, Ecuador
José Bucheli Andrade	Universidad de las Fuerzas Armadas (ESPE) – Sede Latacunga, Ecuador

Steering Committee

Miguel Botto-Tobar	Eindhoven University of Technology, The Netherlands
Ángela Díaz Cadena	Universitat de Valencia, Spain

Publication Chair

Miguel Botto-Tobar   Eindhoven University of Technology, The Netherlands

Program Chairs

Technology Trends

Miguel Botto-Tobar	Eindhoven University of Technology, The Netherlands
Hernán Montes León	Universidad Rey Juan Carlos, Spain

Computing

Miguel Zúñiga Prieto	Universidad de Cuenca, Ecuador
Lohana Lema Moreira	Universidad de Especialidades Espíritu Santo (UEES), Ecuador

Intelligent Systems

Janneth Chicaiza	Universidad Técnica Particular de Loja, Ecuador
Pablo Torres-Carrión	Universidad Técnica Particular de Loja, Ecuador
Guillermo Pizarro Vásquez	Universidad Politécnica Salesiana, Ecuador

Machine Vision

| Julian Galindo | LIG-IIHM, France |
| Erick Cuenca | Yachay Tech University, Ecuador |

Security

| Luis Urquiza Aguiar | Escuela Politécnica Nacional, Ecuador |
| Joffre León Acurio | Universidad Técnica de Babahoyo, Ecuador |

Communication

| Óscar Zambrano Vizuete | Universidad Técnica del Norte, Ecuador |
| Pablo Palacios Játiva | Universidad de Chile, Chile |

Electronics

| Ana Zambrano Vizuete | Escuela Politécnica Nacional (EPN), Ecuador |
| David Rivas | Universidad de las Fuerzas Armadas (ESPE), Ecuador |

e-Learning

| Doris Macías Mendoza | Universitat Politècnica de València, Spain |

e-Business

| Angela Díaz Cadena | Universitat de Valencia, Spain |
| Oscar León Granizo | Universidad de Guayaquil, Ecuador |

e-Goverment and e-Participation

| Vicente Merchán Rodríguez | Universidad de las Fuerzas Armadas (ESPE), Ecuador |
| Alex Santamaría Philco | Universitat Politècnica de València, Spain |

Program Committee

Andrea Bonci	Marche Polytechnic University, Italy
Ahmed Lateef Khalaf	Al-Mamoun University College, Iraq
Aiko Yamashita	Oslo Metropolitan University, Norway
Alejandro Donaire	Queensland University of Technology, Australia
Alejandro Ramos Nolazco	Instituto Tecnólogico y de Estudios Superiores Monterrey, Mexico
Alex Cazañas	The University of Queensland, Australia
Alex Santamaría Philco	Universitat Politècnica de València, Spain
Alfonso Guijarro Rodriguez	University of Guayaquil, Ecuador
Allan Avendaño Sudario	Escuela Superior Politécnica del Litoral (ESPOL), Ecuador

Alexandra González-Eras	Universidad Técnica Particular de Loja (UTPL), Ecuador
Ana Núñez Ávila	Universitat Politècnica de València, Spain
Ana Zambrano	Escuela Politécnica Nacional (EPN), Ecuador
Andres Carrera Rivera	The University of Melbourne, Australia
Andres Cueva Costales	Universidad de las Fuerzas Armadas (ESPE), Ecuador
Andrés Robles Durazno	Edinburgh Napier University, UK
Andrés Vargas González	Syracuse University, USA
Angel Cuenca Ortega	Universidad de Guayaquil, Ecuador
Ángela Díaz Cadena	Universitat de València, Spain
Angelo Trotta	University of Bologna, Italy
Antonio Gómez Expósito	University of Seville, Spain
Aras Can Onal	Tobb University of Economics and Technology, Turkey
Arian Bahrami	University of Tehran, Iran
Benoît Macq	Université Catholique de Louvain, Belgium
Bernhard Hitpass	Universidad Federico Santa María, Chile
Bin Lin	Università della Svizzera italiana (USI), Switzerland
Carlos Saavedra	Escuela Superior Politécnica del Litoral (ESPOL), Ecuador
Catriona Kennedy	Independent researcher, UK
César Ayabaca Sarria	Escuela Politécnica Nacional (EPN), Ecuador
Cesar Azurdia Meza	University of Chile, Chile
Christian León Paliz	Université de Neuchâtel, Switzerland
Chrysovalantou Ziogou	Chemical Process and Energy Resources Institute, Greece
Cristian Zambrano Vega	Universidad Técnica Estatal de Quevedo, Ecuador
Cristiano Premebida	University of Coimbra, Portugal
Daniel Magües Martinez	Universidad Autónoma de Madrid, Spain
Danilo Jaramillo Hurtado	Universidad Politécnica de Madrid, Spain
Darío Piccirilli	Universidad Nacional de La Plata, Argentina
Darsana Josyula	Bowie State University, USA
David Benavides Cuevas	Universidad de Sevilla, Spain
David Blanes	Universitat Politècnica de València, Spain
David Ojeda	Universidad Técnica del Norte, Ecuador
David Rivera Espín	The University of Melbourne, Australia
Denis Efimo	Inria, France
Diego Barragán Guerrero	Universidad Técnica Particular de Loja (UTPL), Ecuador
Diego Peluffo-Ordóñez	Yachay Tech, Ecuador
Dimitris Chrysostomou	Aalborg University, Denmark.
Domingo Biel	Universitat Politècnica de Catalunya, Spain
Doris Macías Mendoza	Universitat Politècnica de València, Spain
Edison Espinoza	Universidad de las Fuerzas Armadas (ESPE), Ecuador

Edwin Rivas	Universidad Distrital Francisco José de Caldas, Colombia
Ehsan Arabi	University of Michigan, USA
Emanuele Frontoni	Università Politecnica delle Marche, Italy
Emil Pricop	Petroleum-Gas University of Ploiesti, Romania
Erick Cuenca	Yachay Tech University, Ecuador
Fabian Calero	University of Waterloo, Canada
Fan Yang	Tsinghua University, China
Fariza Nasaruddin	University of Malaya, Malaysia
Felipe Ebert	Universidade Federal de Pernambuco (UFPE), Brazil
Fernanda Molina Miranda	Universidad de Guayaquil, Ecuador
Fernando Almeida	University of Campinas, Brazil
Fernando Flores Pulgar	Université de Lyon, France
Firas Raheem	University of Technology, Iraq
Francisco Calvente	Universitat Rovira i Virgili, Spain
Francisco Obando	Universidad del Cauca, Colombia
Franklin Parrales	University of Guayaquil, Ecuador
Freddy Flores Bahamonde	Universidad Andrés Bello, Chile
Gabriel Barros Gavilanes	INP Toulouse, France
Gabriel López Fonseca	Sheffield Hallam University, UK
Gema Rodriguez Perez	University of Waterloo, Canada
Ginger Saltos Bernal	Escuela Superior Politécnica del Litoral (ESPOL), Ecuador
Giovanni Pau	Kore University of Enna, Italy
Guilherme Avelino	Universidade Federal do Piauí (UFPI), Brazil
Guilherme Pereira	Universidade Federal de Minas Gerais (UFMG), Brazil
Guillermo Pizarro Vásquez	Universidad Politécnica Salesiana, Ecuador
Gustavo Andrade Miranda	Universidad Politécnica de Madrid, Spain
Hernán Montes León	Universidad Rey Juan Carlos, Spain
Ibraheem Kasim Ibraheem	University of Baghdad, Iraq
Ilya Afanasyev	Innopolis University, Russia
Israel Pineda Arias	Chonbuk National University, South Korea
Jaime Meza	University of Fribourg, Switzerland
Janneth Chicaiza Espinosa	Universidad Técnica Particular de Loja (UTPL), Ecuador
Javier González-Huerta	Blekinge Institute of Technology, Sweden
Javier Monroy	University of Málaga, Spain
Javier Sebastián	University of Oviedo, Spain
Jawad K. Ali	University of Technology, Iraq
Jefferson Ribadeneira Ramírez	Escuela Superior Politécnica de Chimborazo, Ecuador
Jerwin Prabu	BRS, India
Jong Hyuk Park	Korea Institute of Science and Technology, Korea
Jorge Charco Aguirre	Universitat Politècnica de València, Spain

Jorge Eterovic	Universidad Nacional de La Matanza, Argentina
Jorge Gómez Gómez	Universidad de Córdoba, Colombia
Juan Corrales	Institut Universitaire de France et SIGMA Clermont, France
Juan Romero Arguello	University of California, Davis, USA
Julián Andrés Galindo	Université Grenoble Alpes, France
Julio Albuja Sánchez	James Cook University, Australia
Kelly Garcés	Universidad de Los Andes, Colombia
Korkut Bekiroglu	SUNY Polytechnic Institute, USA
Kunde Yang	Northwestern Polytechnical University, China
Lina Ochoa	CWI, The Netherlands
Lohana Lema Moreira	Universidad de Especialidades Espíritu Santo (UEES), Ecuador
Lorena Guachi Guachi	Scuola Superiore Sant'Anna, Italy
Lorenzo Cevallos Torres	Universidad de Guayaquil, Ecuador
Luis Galárraga	Inria, France
Luis Martínez	Universitat Rovira i Virgili, Spain
Luis Urquiza-Aguiar	Escuela Politécnica Nacional (EPN), Ecuador
Maikel Leyva Vázquez	Universidad de Guayaquil, Ecuador
Manuel Sucunuta	Universidad Técnica Particular de Loja (UTPL), Ecuador
Marcela Ruiz	Utrecht University, The Netherlands
Marcelo Zambrano Vizuete	Universidad Técnica del Norte, Ecuador
María José Escalante Guevara	University of Michigan, USA
María Reátegui Rojas	Universidad Técnica Particular de Loja (UTPL), Ecuador
Maria Montoya Freire	Aalto University, Finland
Mariela Tapia-Leon	University of Guayaquil, Ecuador
Marija Seder	University of Zagreb, Croatia
Marisa Daniela Panizzi	Universidad de Morón, Argentina
Mariusz Giergiel	KRiM AGH, Poland
Markus Schuckert	University of New Oeleans, USA
Matus Pleva	Technical University of Kosice, Slovakia
Mauricio Verano Merino	Technische Universiteit Eindhoven, The Netherlands
Miguel Botto-Tobar	Eindhoven University of Technology, The Netherlands
Miguel Fornell	Escuela Superior Politécnica del Litoral (ESPOL), Ecuador
Miguel González Cagigal	Universidad de Sevilla, Spain
Miguel Murillo	Universidad Autónoma de Baja California, Mexico
Miguel Zúñiga Prieto	Universidad de Cuenca, Ecuador
Mohamed Kamel	Military Technical College, Egypt
Mohammad Al-Mashhadani	Al-Maarif University College, Iraq
Mohammad Amin	Illinois Institute of Technology, USA

Monica Baquerizo Anastacio	Universidad de Guayaquil, Ecuador
Muneeb Ul Hassan	Swinburne University of Technology, Australia
Nan Yang	Technische Universiteit Eindhoven, The Netherlands
Nathalie Mitton	Inria, France
Nayeth Solórzano Alcívar	Escuela Superior Politécnica del Litoral (ESPOL), Ecuador
Noor Zaman	Taylor's University, Malaysia
Omar S. Gómez	Escuela Superior Politécnica del Chimborazo (ESPOCH), Ecuador
Óscar León Granizo	Universidad de Guayaquil, Ecuador
Oswaldo Lopez Santos	Universidad de Ibagué, Colombia
Pablo Lupera	Escuela Politécnica Nacional, Ecuador
Pablo Ordoñez-Ordoñez	Universidad Nacional de Loja, Ecuador
Pablo Palacios	Universidad de Chile, Chile
Pablo Torres-Carrión	Universidad Técnica Particular de Loja (UTPL), Ecuador
Patricia Ludeña González	Universidad Técnica Particular de Loja (UTPL), Ecuador
Paulo Batista	CIDEHUS.UÉ-Interdisciplinary Center for History, Cultures, and Societies of the University of Évora, Portugal
Paulo Chiliguano	Queen Mary University of London, UK
Pedro Neto	University of Coimbra, Portugal
Praveen Damacharla	KineticAI, Inc., USA
Priscila Cedillo	Universidad de Cuenca, Ecuador
Quist-Aphetsi Kester	Ghana Telecom University College, Ghana
Radu-Emil Precup	Politehnica University of Timisoara, Romania
Ramin Yousefi	Islamic Azad University, Iran
René Guamán Quinche	Universidad de los Paises Vascos, Spain
Ricardo Martins	University of Coimbra, Portugal
Richard Ramirez Anormaliza	Universidad Estadal de Milagro, Ecuador
Richard Rivera	IMDEA Software Institute, Spain
Richard Stern	Carnegie Mellon University, USA
Rijo Jackson Tom	CMR Institute of Technology, India
Robert Murphy	University of Colorado Denver, USA
Roberto Sabatini	RMIT University, Australia
Rodolfo Alfredo Bertone	Universidad Nacional de La Plata, Argentina
Rodrigo Barba	Universidad Técnica Particular de Loja (UTPL), Ecuador
Rodrigo Saraguro Bravo	Escuela Superior Politécnica del Litoral (ESPOL), Ecuador
Ronald Barriga Díaz	Universidad de Guayaquil, Ecuador

Organizing Institutions

Collaborators

Contents

Intelligent Systems

Machine Vision

Security

Technology Trends

Communication

Communication

Marine Delay and Disruption Tolerant Networks (MaDTN): Application for Artisanal Fisheries

Héctor Bedón[1], Jaime Lopez Pastor[1], Edwin Cedeño Herrera[1,2]($\boxtimes$), and Carlos Miguel Nieto[3]

[1] Exponential Technology Group (GITX-ULIMA), Institute of Scientific Research (IDIC), University of Lima, Lima, Peru
hbedon@ulima.edu.pe, jrlopezp@uni.pe
[2] Faculty of Informatics, Electronics and Communication, Universidad de Panamá, Panamá, Panama
edwin.cedenoh@up.ac.pa
[3] Department of Telematic Engineering, Universidad Politécnica de Madrid, Madrid, Spain
carlos.miguel@upm.es

Abstract. The artisanal fishing activity carried out on the coasts where the production of fish can be exploited is affected by a lack of communication between the vessels in order to provide relevant information related to multiple marine sensor parameters. It is mainly due to the rugged geographic area that causes highly disruptive communication links and in which traditional IP-based communications with transport protocols such as TCP or UDP do not work properly. This paper presents and evaluates a new communications architecture to provide services to marine sensor networks using a disruption tolerant networking (DTN) based solution. We propose a new architecture that takes into account the different vessels densities. We assume a finite sensor population model and a saturated traffic condition where every sensor always has frames to transmit. The performance was evaluated in terms of delivery probabilities, delay and a DTN scenario indicator (DSI) proposed. Through simulations, this paper reveals that Low Density scenery yield greater latency, and more density of nodes has better results. We achieved a successful delivery rate of 74% and a latency of 2 h approximately. Finally indicators shows that high density of nodes is strongly recommended for fishery scenery models.

Keywords: IoT · Wireless sensor networks · Mule · Delay-Disruption tolerant networks · Epidemic routing · ONE Opportunistic network simulator

1 Introduction

In our days, it is very difficult to have a network infrastructure in a maritime environment, even in the closest miles to the coast, at an affordable price.

© Springer Nature Switzerland AG 2021
M. Botto-Tobar et al. (Eds.): ICAT 2020, CCIS 1388, pp. 3–17, 2021.
https://doi.org/10.1007/978-3-030-71503-8_1

Large vessels use systems with satellite links [9], however, their costs are very high for artisanal fishermen. The small fishermen who use the coasts to develop their activity typically use a few kilometers beyond the coasts (Lima, Caleta de Chorrillos 20 km). In this context, the coverage of wireless networks in the maritime environment is limited. Communication between artisanal fishermen is an unsolved challenge. One possible way to overcome such challenges is to provide alternative communication, through mobile nodes that allow supporting, with an opportunistic approach, the connection between isolated nodes and a network infrastructure with permanent end-to-end connectivity.

A communication alternative, for artisanal fishermen, is to equip each vessel with a node that incorporates sensors, to collect information. In addition, it includes communication capabilities at the link layer level with wireless technologies. In this way, the information collected is transmit to a base station on the ground. Then the information is transmit to a repository in the cloud, where it is processed in order to determine the best fishing areas, and to disseminate that information to the fishermen at sea. In this scenario, the vessels are considered as a network of marine mobile sensors. In addition, these form a group of network nodes, through which the information is transported to the processing center and vice versa. It is necessary to consider that the nodes are mobile, and low-cost 802.15.4 technologies offer reduced coverage ranges, therefore, communications will be possible only when they are within range. Similarly, the speed with which these vessels move and the distances they normally approach do not contribute to continuous and stable communications. In other words, these environments are characterized by disruptive, casual and short-lived communications. Research work has been carried out aimed at optimizing the transfer of messages during the contact time. Some of them have focused on proposing adaptive fragmentation mechanisms for the protocol, based on sensor density [5].

An approach is oriented towards data collection using disruption and delay tolerant networks (DTN). DTNs support disconnections and long communication delays, characteristics required by nature in the context of the challenges posed. DTNs allow data transfer where conventional network protocols cannot, because continuous end-to-end connectivity is not always available. While the Bundle Protocol (BP) has established itself as the DTN standard protocol, in many application areas such as wireless sensor networks, they often use proprietary protocols with a subset of the BP characteristics. The BP offers many capabilities required in the context of maritime networks [13]. One of the most important fact is that it uses storage persistence strategies to maintain the state of communications (Finite-State Machine FSM), allowing a bidirectional data transfer to be resumed in the previous state where it was interrupted. This functionality makes it possible to offer efficient support to event-based communication systems. Examples of this approach are systems designed under the publication/subscription paradigm, due to their natural adaptation to asynchronous communication environments, very common in the context of Wireless Sensor Networks (WSN) [20]. In this context, there may be several boats with multiple interests, in this case the concepts of the topic-base broker with multi-topic intersection support implementation model would be applied [17].

There are a plural number of application scenarios for Delay Tolerant Wireless Sensor Networks (DT-WSN), which share the same context of sensor networks deployed in maritime environments. Some representative cases from the literature and their main contributions are summarized below.

In the wildlife environment we found Seal-2-Seal [2], which consists of a delay-tolerant protocol. Mainly focused on recording the contacts between animals in their natural habitat. The protocol uses an efficient data summary mechanism to reduce the amount of information that needs to be transmitted, thus reducing power consumption. It has been implemented for Contiki, and evaluated in simulations.

Regarding the environmental issue, we have LUSTER [14], which aims to monitor environmental parameters to be analyzed by ecologists. This one uses a multi-layered approach with two separate elements. In the sensor network, LUSTER uses a log system based on the listening that the nodes carry out in the radio transmission, and saves the data in the persistent local storage. Additionally, LUSTER uses a DTN approach, for back-end connectivity, over intermittent links. This allows the back-end to query the nodes for data that was lost during the link idle time. Meanwhile, Vineyard Computing [10] presents a WSN, in which sensors in a vineyard periodically sample temperature, and data mules (i.e. workers, dogs, etc.) carry nodes to collect the data. A system based on DTN for the collection of sensor data in a farm is proposed in [8], basically the system collects data from sensors deployed in remote sites without using the network of telecommunications service operators. This considers that the sensors in the field can be separated by great distances, and that their density can be a function of the surface area, therefore the use of devices provided with satellite radio communication is prohibitive due to the cost of the equipment and of the communication service itself. The DTN approach, added to the use of the mobility of the tractors during daily work, allow the collection of data especially in isolated or remote areas, assuming that the tractors and cluster head sensors are equipped with a short-range radio device and DTN capabilities. The collecting device on board the tractor or another entity, when the cluster heads contact with it, makes use of ad-hoc communication to retrieve the data that it subsequently delivers to the data server, upon reaching the original position.

Continuous end-to-end connectivity is not always present in WSN application environments, but store-and-forward techniques use to address intermittent connectivity. An example is the proposed work Data Elevator [22], where a proprietary implementation of BP for WSN platforms is used in conjunction with BP for PC, in order to monitor the outside temperature. The Data Elevator uses the store-carry-and-forward approach, in which an elevator performs the function of a data mule (MULE - Mobile Ubiquitous LAN Extensions), to transport data from the roof to the laboratory located in another near building. This approach applies the standard BP in WSN and avoids layer three and layer four overhead.

Maritime networks can also help to reduce vessel losses in the event of damage at sea, which would lead to saving lives. A geographic location system for the safety of artisanal fishermen in Senegal [16], proposes the use of Low Power Wide Area Network (LPWAN) to deploy a communication system to rescue damaged vessels. This system would allow you to inform neighboring vessels or the control center about your situation, and provide all the information necessary for your rescue. In this same context, we find the TRITON project [1], where the use of a mesh based on WiMAX technology is explored for ship-to-ship communications on the horizon, with Delay Tolerant Network (DTN) characteristics, to provide less expensive wireless communication services at sea. The contribution of this paper is based on the evaluation of routing protocols in DTN networks, applied to this particular scenario. Another work in this regard is the design of a communication network between fishermen, based on DTN. A maritime surveillance system is presented in [4]. It focuses on the paradigm of lag-tolerant nets as a means of communication for the fisheries-based surveillance system. All fishermen can send text-like information to marine patrols or other nearby boats by using DTN.

Research work carried out in the maritime environment is focused on communication from one node to another, in many of them this communication is carried out only once. As far as we know, there is no communication system for artisanal fishing environments, where a complex data processing architecture and the return of information to fishermen are considered. Such information is relevant to your fishing activity because it will provide information on the best fishing areas according to the type of target fish. Therefore, it is necessary to provide an architecture that allows the collection of information at sea and its transmission to the cloud for processing and then disseminating the information to fishermen at sea. Figure 1 shows the basic scenario and the main elements that are considered for the system architecture.

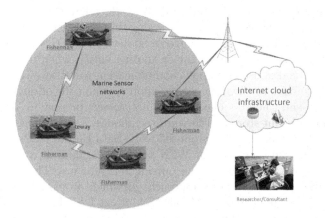

Fig. 1. System overview

2 System Model and Architecture

This paper describes the application of DTN in an artisanal fishing scenario located on the coast of the province of Lima, Peru. The architecture of its design defines several concepts that must be taken into account [7].

2.1 DTN Architecture

This part is dedicated to the interoperability between DTN Wireless Sensor Networks and other networks (in particular, IP networks) as part of the architecture proposed in Fig. 2.

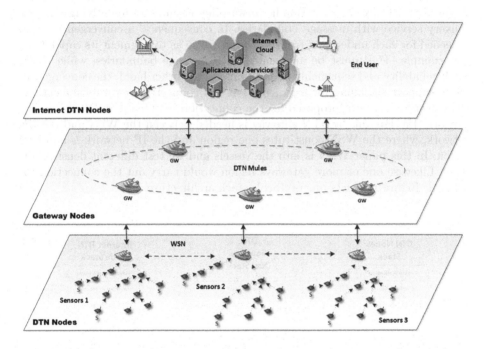

Fig. 2. Overall architecture

DTN is a specific communication protocol architecture designed for disrupted networks. These environments are characterized by high and variable end-to-end delays, potentially high bit-error rates and frequent network partitioning. Some examples are deep space communications and mobile networks with intermittent connectivity. In fact, the DTN architecture takes into account that the characteristics of end systems may include limited longevity, low duty cycle operation and limited resources, which are features encountered in WSNs. DTN creates an overlay store-and-forward message switching on top of the transport (or another) layer and is independent of the underlying bearer protocols and addressing schemes. The messages are called 'bundles'. A DTN comprises a set of regions. The devices in each region use the same protocol stack up to the transport layer within that region. The different regions share a common layer on top of the transport layer called the bundle layer. This layer is in charge of persistent storage of messages when communications links are not available, and provides also message fragmentation and optional end-to-end reliability mechanisms. The DTN architecture [6] assumes the presence of one or more DTN gateways in each region. The DTN gateway interfaces with two or more different regions and therefore supports the protocol stacks (up to the transport layer) of those regions. The DTN gateway forwards bundles between regions and maps globally significant identifiers called 'name tuples' to locally resolvable identifiers. Devices within a region can communicate between them without the need of a DTN gateway. Bundle forwarding assumes an underlying reliable delivery service with message boundaries. In consequence, a convergence layer is needed for each underlying transport protocol so as to augment its capability. For example, TCP must be augmented with message boundaries, while UDP needs reliability and sequencing in addition. On the other hand, the convergence layers support signalling for fragmentation and connection re-establishment. A DTN overlay has been proposed for the connection between a WSN and an IP network [15]. For this, a DTN gateway is needed between the WSN and the IP network, where the WSN constitutes one region and the IP network is another region. In this paper WSN is into the vessels and we test different densities of them. Likewise one or more gateways region would carry out the connection to internet. Figure 3 depicts our protocols stack architecture.

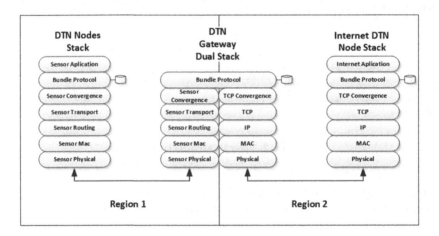

Fig. 3. DTN nodes and gateway - protocols stack

Specifically, it is formed by sensors under the sea surface in order to capture multiple oceanographic parameters for further analytical works. They are deployed in each fishery vessel. Also they have a hardware module plugged to a network interface to transmit and communicate with the nodes around their network coverage.

2.2 Maritime Communications Environment

It is the geographic area of analysis. It contains the nodes under study. It has established limits in width and depth, being 73.8 km by 20 km respectively. Within these limits we have artisanal fishing activities. In Fig. 4, we show this area and location.

Fig. 4. Geographical map of artisanal fishery

2.3 Communication Nodes and Topology

It is made up of vessels that carry out the activity of artisanal fishing, they have the function of communication nodes. The amount of vessels is defined as density. In this paper we establish three scenarios for proof of concept (PoC), densities of 50, 100 and 180 nodes within the whole defined area. The vessels also contain probes with maritime sensors that generate valuable information and form the bundles. Its topology is naturally meshed. The area is virtually subdivided into grids of every 500 m for better study and control on the positioning map.

2.4 Movement Model

The vessel movement on the sea is randomly under this premise we apply a model named RandomWayPoint (RWP) [18], this model is popular due to their simplicity [11] and due its position, speed and increasing speed change after some time. In this case maps of paths models and other related are not applicable.

2.5   Network Interface Model

For this study we have selected a network interface model based on a commercial Digi XBee S2C [1]. XBee S2C module is a RF module designed for wireless communication or data exchange. It works with medium range and low data transfer. Data rates vary from 20 kbit/s (868 MHz band) to 250 kbit/s (2.4 GHz band). This module have the following features: XBee 2mW PCB Antenna - Series 2, Outdoor RF line-of-sight range Up to 1200 m (4000 ft). We select this model based on some criteria such as the big size of the geographical area and node densities, where distances of coverage can influence in the performance metrics and at the same time trying to avoid greater overhead.

2.6   Routing Model

In this paper we propose Epidemic Routing, Epidemic Routing, where random pair-wise exchanges of messages among mobile hosts ensures eventual message delivery. The goals of Epidemic Routing are to: i) maximize message delivery rate, ii) minimize message latency, and iii) minimize the total resources consumed in message delivery [21]. Epidemic routing is flooding-based in nature [3], since nodes continuously replicate and transmit messages to newly discovered nodes that do not already possess a copy of the message.

2.7   Buffer and TTL

The buffer size of the hosts should be optimized to be what is necessary for the management of the messages (bundles). It is based on the environment to be simulated with respect to node density, simulation time and generation of events. Likewise, it will depend on the amount of information in the bundles, and the storage time of them. The buffer value we have selected is 1 MB. Also TTL value is estimated due to possible low link contact probability.

2.8   Simulation End Time

It is the typical time that the vessels take to carry out their activity. This value is variable, since each node is independent of the other in terms of its task. Typically in this artisanal fishing activity, tasks are carried out from 4 h to 14 h net, taking into account the time of transfers to certain maritime areas. We will take an average value of 12 h.

2.9   Event Generation

We adjust the simulation so that the generated events occur every 500 m, this distance determines the corresponding time value taking into account the speed of the vessels.

3   Simulation Settings

In this paper the impact of number of nodes in the proposed models are analyzed. The simulation tool we have used is ONE (Opportunistic Network Environment) in its latest version 1.6.1. This section explains the opportunistic network environment (ONE) simulator, and the environment modeling parameters.

3.1   Opportunistic Network Environment (ONE)

ONE simulator is a Java-based simulator developed by Kernenan et al. Used fr analyzing the effect of various events like tracing the movement of nodes and predicting their behaviors. Using this simulator, the trace data of nodes can be easily imported. It provides a nice GUI, which assists the user to easily visualize or emulate the real movements of nodes [12]. Each node contains a radio coverage and sends a message when any node enters into their range. ONE produces all the reports like inter-contact time, contact duration, message handling from the nodes movement among each other and keeps them in one package. In the Fig. 5, we can see a screenshot of the GUI of this specific simulation:

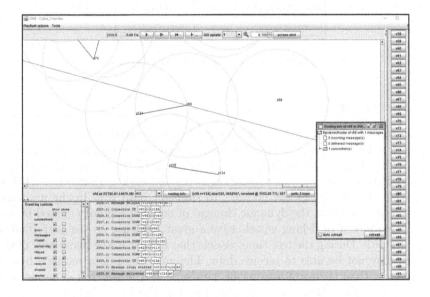

Fig. 5. GUI environment interface and a simulation

3.2   Simulation Environment Setting

In our simulation, we summarize the following environmental settings as shown in Fig. 6.

Parameter	Scenario
Number of Nodes	50, 100, 180
Groups of Nodes	1
Network Interface	Xbee S2C
Number of Interfaces per Node	1
Transmision Range (m)	1200
Duration (h)	12
Transmission Speed (kbps)	250
Buffer Size (KB)	1000
Nodes Speed (nudes)	4 to 5
Movement Model	RWP
Routing Model	Epidemic
TTL (min)	300
Warm Up Period (seg)	1000
Wait Time (min)	0 to 120
Message Size (KB)	0.5 to 1
Events Interval	each 500 m

Fig. 6. Parameter settings for simulations

3.3 Simulation

In order to evaluate this DTN system, we have carried out a test in three different scenarios of density of nodes. These scenarios are based on number of them: Low Density (50 nodes), Average Density (100 nodes) and High Density (180 nodes).

An important concept for evaluation is the Network performance. That is reflected by the ability of the network to transmit data [19]. In the maritime delay tolerant network, the dynamic changes of network topology caused by the random movement of fishing vessels have a great influence on the performance of the network. During the test time, vessels that appear in the blank area of the network may not be able to receive data. The amount of data received by the vessel is less than the total amount of data sent by the network. The network delivery ratio Q is a Delivery Probability and is defined as (Eq. 1):

$$Q = M/I \tag{1}$$

where:
      M = Number of messages delivered successfully.
      I = Number of messages generated.

4   Results and Analysis

After carrying out the simulations, we examined and compared the outcome of the three executions. The total number of messages generated, divided by the messages delivered, defines the probability of delivery of the messages. Likewise, the average latency is the time of latency that take the messages to be delivered during the total period of simulation.

4.1   Results

After the simulation, we got the following results (see Fig. 7), from MessageStatsReport class of the ONE Simulator.

KPI	Low Density	Average Density	High Density
Delivery Probability (%)	37.76	57.07	74.62

Fig. 7. Delivery probability

In the Fig. 8, we illustrate the mentioned results.

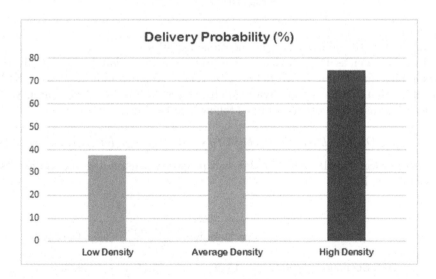

Fig. 8. Delivery probability

Also, we got Latency metrics from the reports of ONE simulator in a period of 12 h (see Fig. 9):

KPI	Low Density	Average Density	High Density
Average Time Latency (Hours)	2.7437	2.6197	2.0243

Fig. 9. Latency

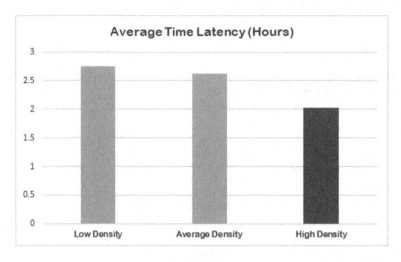

Fig. 10. Latency

In the Fig. 10, we illustrate the mentioned results.

In this paper as DTN indicator, we propose a ratio that involves Delivery Probability and Latency. We define DSI (DTN scenario indicator) as a KPI indicator, that is achieved by dividing delivery probability by average latency of bundles during a 12 h observation, as follow (see Eq. 2):

$$DSI = (Delibery\ Probability * 100)/Average\ Latency \qquad (2)$$

After processing the values of different proposed densities we got the results as follow (see Fig. 11).

KPI	Low Density	Average Density	High Density
DTN Scenario Indicator	13.76	21.79	36.86

Fig. 11. DTN scenario table

Also, We illustrate this Ratio as follow in the Fig. 12.

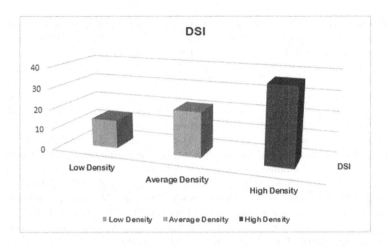

Fig. 12. DTN scenario indicator

4.2 Analysis

To compare the performance of different node densities the results are depicted in Fig. 12, where high density scenario has the best delivery probability. Then we deduced that link contact between vessels is more frequently and so the messages exchange. In this figure, we observed that Low density scenario yield greater latency, and more density of nodes has better results for the same explained reason regarding to encounters between vessels. Finally DSI indicator shows that high density of nodes is strongly recommended for fishery scenario models. This behavior was actually expected, but these simulation results can be used as a reference for future research works, that will be focused on the optimisation of this performance figures.

5   Conclusions and Future Work

In this paper, we propose and evaluate a new communications architecture based on DTN to provide data service to a network of marine sensors, using wireless communications between vessels. It assumes a finite population and saturated traffic condition. We evaluated an epidemic routing on a movement model RandonWayPoint based on delivery probability and average latency. We conclude that the proposed architecture provides simple, optimal performance for high density nodes in terms of high delivery probabilities and low latency. For future work, we plan to carry out an different routing model analysis of this proposed scenario. We will also investigate the mechanism of cluster collaboration in DTNs deployed in Marine Artisanal fishering, for end-to-end bundle transmission. The addition of a service management layer based on the information from the marine sensors disseminated an interesting area for future research. In the context of the Bundle protocol, we are also interested in implementing various levels of optimizations based on fragmentation techniques and data custody strategies.

Acknowledgement. The results of this investigation were achieved with support from the National program of innovation in fisheries and aquaculture (PNIPA) of Peru and the Institute of Scientific Research (IDIC) of the University of Lima.

References

1. XBee/XBee-PRO®s2c zigbee®RF module, p. 325 (2009)
2. Lindgren, A., Mascolo, C., Lonergan, M., McConnell, B.: Seal-2-seal: a delay-tolerant protocol for contact logging in wildlife monitoring sensor networks. In: 5th IEEE International Conference on Mobile Ad Hoc and Sensor Systems, September 2008, pp. 321–327 (2008). https://doi.org/10.1109/MAHSS.2008.4660064
3. Alnajjar, F., Saadawi, T.: Performance analysis of routing protocols in delay/disruption tolerant mobile ad hoc networks. In: Proceeding of 10th WSEAS International Conference on Electronics, Hardware, Wireless and Optical Communications, NEHIPISIC 2011. pp. 407–417. World Scientific and Engineering Academy and Society (WSEAS) (2011)
4. Basuki, A.I., Wuryandari, A.I.: Delay-tolerant-networks design and prospect on fishery communication networks. In: IEEE 4th International Conference on System Engineering and Technology (ICSET), November 2014, pp. 1–6 (2014). https://doi.org/10.1109/ICSEngT.2014.7111781
5. Bedon, H., Miguel, C., Alcarria, R., Fernández, Ruiz, F.J.: Message fragmentation assessment in DTN nanosatellite-based sensor networks. Ad Hoc Netw. **44**, 76–89. https://doi.org/10.1016/j.adhoc.2016.02.015, http://www.sciencedirect.com/science/article/pii/S1570870516300567
6. Fall, K., et al.: Delay-tolerant networking architecture (2007). https://tools.ietf.org/html/rfc4838
7. Grados, B., Bedon, H.: Software components of an IoT monitoring platform in google cloud platform: a descriptive research and an architectural proposal. In: Botto-Tobar, M., Zambrano Vizuete, M., Torres-Carrión, P., Montes León, S., Pizarro Vásquez, G., Durakovic, B. (eds.) ICAT 2019. CCIS, vol. 1193, pp. 153–167. Springer, Cham (2020). https://doi.org/10.1007/978-3-030-42517-3_12
8. Ochiai, H., Esaki, H., Ishizuka, H., Kawakami, Y.: A field experience on DTN-based sensor data gathering in agricultural scenarios. In: IEEE SENSORS, 1–4 November 2010, pp. 955–958 (2010). https://doi.org/10.1109/ICSENS.2010.5690899
9. Lin, H.M., Ge, Y., Pang, A.C., Pathmasuntharam, J.S.: Performance study on delay tolerant networks in maritime communication environments. In: OCEANS 2010 IEEE SYDNEY, May 2010, pp. 1–6 (2010). https://doi.org/10.1109/OCEANSSYD.2010.5603627
10. Burrell, J., Brooke, T., Beckwith, R.: Vineyard computing: sensor networks in agricultural production. IEEE Perv. Comput. **3**, 38–45 (2004). https://doi.org/10.1109/MPRV.2004.1269130
11. Keränen, A., Kärkkäinen, T., Ott, J.: Simulating mobility and DTNs with the ONE (invited paper). J. Commun. **5**(2), 92–105 (2010). https://doi.org/10.4304/jcm.5.2.92-105, http://www.jocm.us/index.php?m=content&c=index&a=show&catid=65&id=218
12. Keränen, A., Ott, J., Kärkkäinen, T.: The ONE simulator for DTN protocol evaluation (2009). https://eudl.eu/doi/10.4108/icst.simutools2009.5674

13. Kong, L., Yang, T., Zhao, N.: Maritime opportunistic transmission: when and how much can DTN node deliver? In: IEEE/CIC International Conference on Communications in China, 11–13 August 2019, pp. 943–948 (2019). https://doi.org/10. 1109/ICCChina.2019.8855892
14. Selavo, L., et al.: Luster: wireless sensor network for environmental research. In: The 5th International Conference on Embedded Networked Sensor Systems, pp. 103–116 (2007). https://doi.org/10.1145/1322263.1322274
15. Loubser, M.: Delay tolerant networking for sensor networks (2006). https://www. semanticscholar.org/paper/Delay-Tolerant-Networking-for-Sensor-Networks-Loubser/37254ba8b5ffaae8863a3499e1b88f1478cb0fef
16. Seye, M.R., Ngom, B., Diallo, M., Gueye, B.: Work in progress: a low cost geographical localization system for a more secure coastal artisanal fishery in Senegal. In: International Conference on Information and Communication Technologies for Disaster Management (ICT-DM), 18–20 December 2019, pp. 1–4 (2019). https:// doi.org/10.1109/ICT-DM47966.2019.9032947
17. Morales, A., Alcarria, R., Cedeño, E., Robles, T.: An extended topic-based pub/sub broker for cooperative mobile services. In: 2013 27th International Conference on Advanced Information Networking and Applications Workshops, pp. 1313–1318 (2013). https://doi.org/10.1109/WAINA.2013.119
18. Sharma, A., Diwaker, C.: Impact of node mobility and buffer space on replication-based routing protocols in DTNs. In: Kumar, A., Mozar, S. (eds.) ICCCE 2018. LNEE, vol. 500, pp. 607–613. Springer, Singapore (2019). https://doi.org/10.1007/ 978-981-13-0212-1_62
19. Shi, Y., Li, H., Du, W.C., Ma, J.X., Li, F.B.: Modeling and performance analysis of marine DTN networks with nodes-cluster in an ad hoc sub-net, pp. 182–187. Atlantis Press (2016). https://doi.org/10.2991/ceis-16.2016.36, https://www. atlantis-press.com/proceedings/ceis-16/25867854, ISSN: 2352-538X
20. Sheltami, T., Al-Roubaiey, A., Mahmoud, A., Shakshuki, E.: A publish/subscribe middleware cost in wireless sensor networks: a review and case study. In: IEEE 28th Canadian Conference on Electrical and Computer Engineering (CCECE), 11–13 August 2015, pp. 1356–1363 (2015). https://doi.org/10.1109/CCECE.2015. 7129476
21. Vahdat, A., Becker, D.: Epidemic routing for partially-connected ad hoc networks, p. 14 (2000)
22. Pöttner, W.-B., Büsching, F., Von Zengen, G., Wolf, L.: Data elevators: applying the bundle protocol in delay tolerant wireless sensor networks. In: IEEE 9th International Conference on Mobile Ad-Hoc and Sensor Systems, October 2012, pp. 218–226 (2012). https://doi.org/10.1109/MASS.2012.6502520

Computing

Computing

User Affective Experience into a Scope of Conversational Artificial Intelligence

Ligia Maza-Jiménez[1]([✉]), Pablo Torres-Carrión[1] (iD), Carina González[2],
Germania Rodríguez[1] (iD), and Silvia Vaca[1] (iD)

[1] Universidad Técnica Particular de Loja, San Cayetano Alto S/N, Loja, Ecuador
{lemaza,pvtorres,grrodriguez,slvaca}@utpl.edu.ec
[2] Universidad de La Laguna, La Laguna, Tenerife, Spain
cjgonza@ull.edu.es

Abstract. The goal of the following research is to know the User experience during the interaction into a scope of Conversational Artificial Intelligence, having "Max" the virtual assistant from Universidad Técnica Particular de Loja (UTPL) as the evaluation interface. The assessment is done through virtual form with the presence of 45 members from the university community (15 students, 15 parents and 15 external). Previously to the interaction a kind of formative initial test is applied next to the Recognition of perceived emotions, the mobile application EmoApp-Pro (EMODIANA) and the FaceApi from Microsoft Azure. The research has a mixed approach, with a concurrent and quasi-experimental design of transactional type and a descriptive scope. The obtained results show that user's affective experience is negative. Therefore, it is concluded that the must be constant feedback to the data base managed by the UTPL, precision in the addressing of answers and a mayor campaign to the society has to be done. Due to the sanitary emergency we face nowadays because of COVID-19 it will be very helpful doing academic processes that cannot be done in personal manner.

Keywords: User affective experience · Conversational Artificial Intelligence · Chatbot · University

1 Introduction

The Human Computer Interaction (HCI) is the informatics emergency area closer to the user that studies the communication produces between computers people that use them [1, 2]. In this context the User Experience (UX) refers to the felling of people when they interact with an informatics system [3] and mainly manage three dimensions or experiences: the esthetic, the significative and affective; this last is directed to measure the final user's experience through different types of emotions like: fun, anger, contempt, satisfaction, disgust, excitement, fear, guilt, pride in accomplishment, relief, sadness/anguish, sensory pleasure and shame [4].

There is a great variety in the classification of emotions being negative emotions more than positives [5] because are less frequent and there is a bigger number of threats than

© Springer Nature Switzerland AG 2021
M. Botto-Tobar et al. (Eds.): ICAT 2020, CCIS 1388, pp. 21–32, 2021.
https://doi.org/10.1007/978-3-030-71503-8_2

opportunities. According to Lazarus [6], the emotions can be classified as follow: negative emotions (fear, anger, anxiety, sadness, guilt, shame, envy, jealousy, disgust, etc., positive emotions (joy, pride, love, affection, relief, happiness) and Ambiguous emotions (surprise, hope, compassion and aesthetic emotions). Likewise, Bisquerra [7] based on the classification of the primary and secondary emotions from Goleman proposes the following psychopedagogical classification Primary negative emotions (fear, anger, sadness, joy, surprise, disgust), social negative emotions (shame), Positive emotions (joy, love, happiness) and Ambiguous emotions (surprise). Besides, he states that although there are several coincidences raised by different authors, there is no a classification that has been generally accepted.

The motions awake memories that endure and the capacity of emotional hook that can be produced becoming in this way in the user affective experience (UAX) [8].

The investigation in (UAX) like other sciences it has been enriched by the Artificial Intelligence (AI), that has allowed the establishment of interactions scopes which perceive user emotions [9]. According to Garcia [10], the AI tries to explain the mental functioning based on the development of algorithms for controlling different things, combining various fields like robotics, the expert systems among others, which have the same objective that is try to create machines that can be think by their own. The Artificial Intelligence could be divided in three wide stages [11]: a) narrow or weak limited to a functional area; b) general, which includes the power of reasoning, problem solving and abstract thinking; and, c) the super intelligence that is the maximum level when the (AI) exceeds the human intelligence. Into the week Artificial Intelligence (AI) is the Conversational, with a strong relation HCI that guaranties that simulated conversations with the computer [12], can be hold opening the space to develop empathic behavior between the machine and the user, being a great contribution in the development of User Affective Experience (UAX).

The Conversational Artificial Intelligence conferring to Nieves [13] it is responsible of the logic behind robots, that means is the brains and soul of the chatbot. Without IAC, a bot is just a heap of questions and answers. Additionally, IAC is powered by Natural Language Processing (NLP) that is centered in the interpretation of human language while the developers show the basic frame of how a normal conversation can be hold. In few words, the IAC and human being work jointly to create a virtual conversational experience.

The chatbots are programs that use natural language processing (NLP) in a system of questions and answers (QA systems) [14]. Their target is simulating a dialogue with a smart human interlocutor through text messages, a console or voice. Chatbots had their beginning since the Turing Test [15] that started in 1950 by Alan Mathison Turing. By the time until nowadays the is an interesting evolution in chatbots, the most updated are hosted in web pages in personal virtual assistants if mobile devices that become them in one of the most attractive tools for a company or institution.

As a result of the health emergency, because of the coronavirus COVID-19 expansion chatbots have gained ground providing online support with the target of keeping society informed on different topics. Therefore, this research pretends to know the UAX during the interaction with the virtual assistant "Max" UTPL property.

A mixed approach is proposed as methodology for this study with a concurrent and quasi experimental design of transactional or transversal type with a descriptive and correlational scope. The gained results show a user negative affective experience.

2 Methodology

It is proposed to know the User Affective Experience during the interaction into an active scope of Conversational Artificial Intelligence in a higher education school. "Max" the virtual assistant of the UTPL has been chosen as the interface evaluation.

2.1 Research Design

Considering what is mentioned by Hernández, Fernández and Baptista [16], this investigation has the following design (Fig. 1):

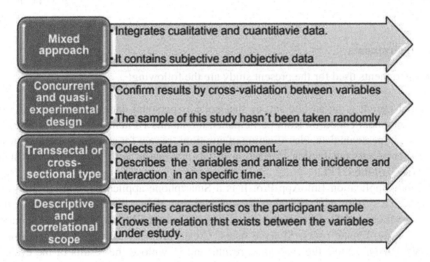

Fig. 1. Research design.

2.2 Sample

The sample is non-probabilistic type taken by the accidental technique named snowball which takes advantages of available people in a specific time for the purpose under study [17]. It has to be cleared that the type of sample was conditioned by the sanitary emergency stablished on March 17th, 2020 by Presidential Decree 1017 N° 001262020 [18] (Table 1).

Table 1. Own elaboration. Sample of participants.

Type of users	Description	n	%
Students	• Undergraduate from the Universidad Técnica Particular de Loja (English, Biochemistry, Accounting and Auditing, Medicine, Psychology, Economics and Architecture) • Postgraduate degree from the Private Technical University of Loja (Communication Sciences and Technologies) Presence and distance	15	33,33
Parents	• Between 38–60 years old • Parents of high school graduates • Parents of students from UTPL and other universities	15	33,33
External	• Between 18–36 years old • High school graduates • Students from other universities	15	33,33
TOTAL		45	100

2.3 Instruments

The instruments used for the present study are the following:

- Initial test: It is an ad-hoc survey that collects personal data and identification of the emotional condition from participants; it contains 10 items which are: informed consent; personal data, classification of emotions, reason for emotions, effectiveness, efficiency and satisfaction in relation to the interaction with the Virtual Assistant "MAX" of the UTPL.
- Mobile application EmoApp-Pro: It is a Smartphone application with an Android operative system of 4.4 versions or superior that allows the automatization of the observation tool for continuous emotional evaluation EMODIANA. The functionalities are: Create users, Manage users, Create projects, Manage projects. Apply EMODIANA, View the evaluation results and Download the results of the evaluation in.csv file format. This instrument was modified in its app version by Vicente [19], which evaluates in subjective way the user emotions (person who the test is applied) through observers (specialist in charge of the evaluation) classified in 10 emotions (joy, satisfaction, shame, sadness, boredom, seriousness, nervousness, surprise, fear and affection) from which the applier must identify entering in the App the results automatically developed.
- FaceApi from Microsoft Azure: It is developed by Microsoft allowing the user facial recognition in a smooth and safe way, it contains implemented functionalities like: face detection, easy checking and recognition of perceived emotions; detects emotions of anger, contempt, disgust, fear, happiness, neutrality, sadness and surprise [20].

2.4 Procedure

Stage 1. Interaction planning: at this stage it is specified the technology that will be used for capturing information related to user behaviour characteristics while they participate during the evaluation with IAC.

- At first instance the selection of evaluation tools is done: ad-hoc Initial test which was developed by Microsoft Forms Tool, the mobile application EmoApp-Pro (EMODI-ANA), recognition of perceived emotions FaceApi from Microsoft Azure and as IAC scope it is used the UTPL virtual assistants "Max".
- The next step was determining the sample that is divided in three groups: students, external people and parents, conformed by 15 participants each one. They have been contacted through websites WhatsApp and phone calls.
- In order to analyze the first stage, a preliminary test or piloting is done with the application of questionnaires based on a guide or application protocol to clarify, clarify and refine the method of applying instruments.

Stage 2. Execution: This stage contains three moments:

- At first, the ad-hoc test was applied in online way to know the participant's emotional state. This process had a five-minute duration approximately.
- Secondly, the participants shared screen through ZOOM the video conferences services platform and the interaction with the UTPL virtual assistant "Max" takes places for the span of two minutes recording this process. Then based on the videos during the interaction a subjective analysis will be carried out through the observation helped by two psychologists (evaluators) using the mobile application EmoAppPro (EMODIANA) for measuring emotions classifying them into: positive and negative.
- Finally, at third moment with the gained videos an analysis was done and every 5 s applying the FaceApi de Microsoft Azure the Recognition of perceived emotions took place.

Stage 3. Analysis of results: Statistical Package for the Social Sciences (SPSS) version 24.0 and Excel were applied in order to determine the statistical tests to use and it was considered the analysis objective in relation to the instruments EmoApp-Pro y FaceApi from Microsoft Azure - Recognition of perceived emotions. Regarding to the first instrument two psychologist participated with the intention of recording through the App the participants' expressed emotions. For this reason, the Cohen kappa statistical coefficient model was chosen for the analysis of results which allow adjust the azar effect in the proportion of the observed agreement (permits estimating when two or more observers agree in their measurement) for qualitative elements at this case identification of emotions [21]. Concerning to the second instrument, a data based using the obtained results was created using the application for a further creation of a descriptive matrix of positive and negative emotions demonstrated by the users.

3   Results

According to the initial test previous the interaction the emotional state of the participant was analyzed. Therefore, positive emotions results obtained 72%. Likewise, related to state of mood the answer in a mayor average related to positive emotions "That's how I am" (Fig. 2).

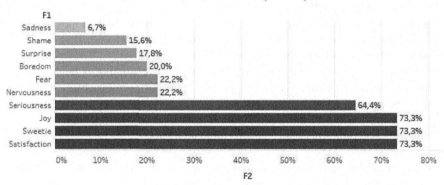

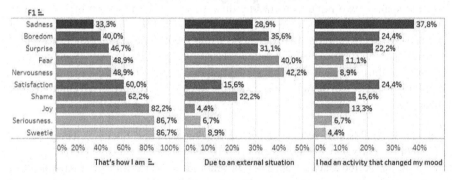

Fig. 2. Own elaboration. Emotions parameters according to the initial test.

In relation to the mobile application EmoApp-pro it was analyzed using the Cohen Kappa to compare viewers' criteria. Selecting a grade of agree from Moderate (0.41–0.60) to almost Perfect (0.81–1.00) [22], obtaining 22 cases, 4 of them with the value of 1,00 because psychologists observed during the whole process the same emotion (seriousness). Likewise, there is a significant approximation of 0,000 across the participant that means that a low value of p shows the study validity [23] (Table 2).

Regarding the classification of emotions according to EmoApp-Pro it was obtained a 63% of negative emotions (Fig. 3).

Table 2. Own elaboration. Results applying Cohen kappa.

Participants	Kappa	Asymptotic standard error[a]	T approximate[b]	Approximate significance
Student 1	0,957	0,042	23,021	0,000
Student 6	0,489	0,100	16,797	0,000
Student 8	0,531	0,100	17,467	0,000
Student 9	**1,000**	**0,000**	**23,495**	**0,000**
Student 10	0,448	0,099	16,097	0,000
Student 11	0,489	0,100	16,797	0,000
Student 12	0,785	0,084	21,000	0,000
Student 13	**1,000**	**0,000**	**23,495**	**0,000**
Student 15	0,913	0,058	22,018	0,000
External 1	0,531	0,100	17,467	0,000
External 2	0,827	0,078	21,526	0,000
External 3	0,531	0,100	17,467	0,000
External 4	0,827	0,078	21,526	0,000
External 7	0,406	0,097	15,362	0,000
External 8	0,615	0,098	18,727	0,000
Family parent 3	0,406	0,097	15,362	0,000
Family parent 4	**1,000**	**0,000**	**23,495**	**0,000**
Family parent 5	0,489	0,100	16,797	0,000
Family parent 7	0,657	0,096	19,324	0,000
Family parent 8	0,827	0,078	21,526	0,000
Family parent 12	**1,000**	**0,000**	**23,495**	**0,000**
Family parent 15	0,489	0,100	16,797	0,000

According to FaceApi from Microsoft Azure - Recognition of perceived emotions in the interaction with the virtual assistant "MAX" of the UTPL it was identified a 65% of positive emotions (Fig. 4).

As comparison method of averages from two series of measures done over the same statistics units on chart 3 are shown the results of analysis of students with sample relate to the mobile application EmoApp-Pro and FaceApi from Microsoft Azure in which was stablished the following hypothesis:

H0 = There is not significative difference into the analysis of emotions applying the EmoApp-Pro and el FaceApi from Microsoft Azure.
H_a = There is a significative experience in the analysis of emotions with the EmoAppPro and the FaceApi from Microsoft Azure.

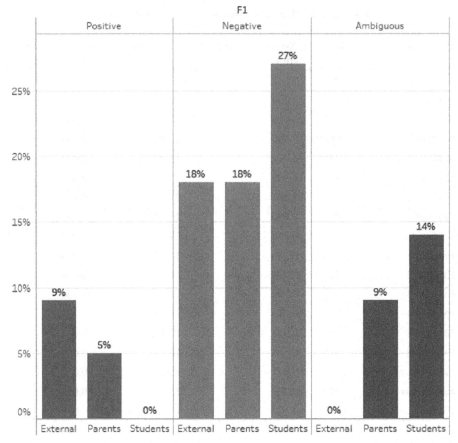

Fig. 3. Own elaboration. Classification of positive, negative and ambiguous emotions in the EmoApp-pro.

The H_o (null Hypothesis) represents the statement that there is no relation between the both studied variables and the H_a (alternative hypotheses) confirms that there is an association between the both variables under study. The "p" value shows if the association is statistically significant, a term that invades the scientific literature and is perceived as a label that supposes a "quality guarantee". This value has been arbitrarily selected and is focused in 0.05 or 0.01. A security of 95% it has an implicit $p <$ of 0.05 and a security of 99% that has an implicit $p <$ of 0.01 [24].

Since the p-value is calculated 0,266 is greater than the significance of alfa value 0,05 the alternative hypotheses is refused accepting the Null hypotheses (Table 3).

4   Discussion of Results

In this study a 72% of participants demonstrated positive emotions before they use the virtual assistant "MAX" from the UTPL being the reason of emotion "That's how I am".

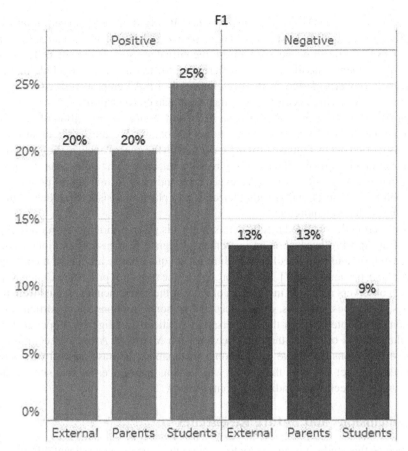

Fig. 4. Own elaboration. Classification of positive and negative emotions of the FaceApi from Microsoft Azure.

Table 3. Own elaboration. EmoApp-Pro and Microsoft Azure paired samples test.

Matched differences					t	gl	Sig. (bilateral)
Average	Deviation standard	Standard error average	95% confidence difference interval				
			Lower	Higher			
Emo-EmoAppPro tion - Azure-,136	,560	,119	−,385	,112	−1,142	21	**,266**

Likewise, referring to the mobile application EmoApp-pro at the moment of interaction it was found that a 63% of participants shown negative emotions that has a relation with a previous study carried out in Italy by Dibitonto [25], with the target of understand what kind of information and services are efficient through the chatbot "LiSA" and its personality influences along the user experience. It was obtained that user prefer to do inquiries by phone calls o in presence and the 65.4% of the respondents had never heard about "LiSA". In the drawbacks found are: the virtual assistant is repetitive. Therefore, half of the students classify her as indifferent or frustrating. They conclude that it is necessary a properly design in the personality of "LiSA" empowering empathy and sensitivity. Also, trying to emulate a human-to-human conversation.

On the other hand, the FaceApi from Microsoft Azure - Recognition of perceived emotions detected a 65% of positive emotions. The obtained results have similarity with the study carried out by Piguave [26] in Ecuador, with the goal of analyze the tool chatbot and its communicational influence on university students. Concluding, that the use of the virtual assistant offers a positive experience and easy to manage in processes of accessibility to the information without necessity of physical assistance at the institution satisfying students' requirements.

Considering the obtained results in this study it is given priority to the mobile application EmoApp-Pro because is an instrument designed to measure emotions through subjective form and tries to collects qualitative and quantitative aspects of the affective experience in participants [27]. In addition, having the statistical procedure Cohen Kappa in which observers are based in the point of view or the assessment expressed from their feelings, sensations, interests, experiences and personal opinions about participants at the moment of interact with the Conversation Artificial Intelligence scope. Different from the analysis of results through FaceApi from Microsoft Azure - Recognition of perceived emotions that make it in the objective manner, because the software is programmed to detect reality in the neutral way leaving apart the emotional site avoiding the inclusion of feelings or individual point of view.

5 Conclusions and Future Researches

To conclude this study, it is necessary to mention that there is a significant difference in the analysis of emotions with the EmoApp-Pro and the FaceApi from Microsoft Azure because it was obtained a p-value of 0,266. Thus, the Tool stability is supported by a (95%) of significant statistical variation. However, the user Affective Experience according to the obtained result from the mobile application EmoApp-Pro is negative and this might generate factors like: errors presence, difficulty when using the system, lack of friendly interface, inexact information and preference for interaction with human beings. The user negative experience (NUX) is produce by the lack of satisfaction of needs; also, the utility, obstruction, punctuality, adaptability and the learning capability during the interaction with a software product. For example, software systems of behavior change (BCSSs) [28]. Thus, the negative UAX is an element used for improving the Conversational Artificial Intelligence scope and successfully overcome the user dissatisfaction gap. This is why a constant feedback of the virtual assistant database handled by the UTPL is recommended, precision addressing answers and a better campaign to the society in general. Due to the health emergency we are facing now because of COVID-19 it would be very helpful in many academic processes that cannot be done in personal manner.

It is recommended for future investigations continue the same thematic line on Metrics for the Evaluation User Affective Experience (UAX) with Conversational Artificial

Experience through Biometric Sensors that allow the identification and recognizing emotions from other variables related to body in order to increase efficiency and decrease susceptibility to deception.

Also know the user affective experience of high school students that work with virtual academic platforms and be able to make a comparison with the traditional education in the classroom.

Likewise, in the health area it would be of great importance consider the Teleconsultation and know the user affective experience concerning to information about medical history (questioning), presumptive diagnosis and treatment of the patient.

References

1. Marcos, M.-C.: HCI (human computer interaction): concepto y desarrollo. El Prof. la Inf. **10**(6), 4–16 (2001)
2. Sears, A., Jacko, J.A.: Human-Computer Interaccion. Second (2007)
3. Boada, N.: ¿Por qué es tan importante el User Experience o Experiencia del Usuario? (2017). https://www.cyberclick.es/numerical-blog/por-que-userexperience-o-exp eriencia-del-usuario, Accessed 13 Mar 2019
4. Ekman, P.F.: Universals and cultural differences in facial expressions of emotion. J. Pers. Soc. Psychol. **19**, 208–282 (1971)
5. Nesse, R.M.: Evolutionary explanations of emotions. Hum. Nat. **1**(13), 261–289 (1990)
6. Lazarus, R.S.: Progress on a cognitive-motivational-relational theory of emotion. Am. Psychol. **46**(8), 819–834 (1991)
7. Bisquerra, R.: Psicología de las emociones, no. 1 (2003)
8. Buck, R., Khan, M., Fagan, M., Coman, E.: The user affective experience scale: a measure of emotions anticipated in response to pop-up computer warnings. Int. J. Hum. Comput. Interact. **34**(1), 25–34 (2018)
9. Mira, J.: Inteligencia artificial, emoción y neurociencia. Arbor **162**(640), 473–506 (1999)
10. Garcia, A.: Inteligencia artificial: fundamentos practica y aplicaciones. RC Libros (2012)
11. Gomes, C.C., Preto, S.: Artificial intelligence and interaction design for a positive emotional user experience. In: Karwowski, W., Ahram, T. (eds.) IHSI. AISC, vol. 722, pp. 62–68. Springer, Cham (2018). https://doi.org/10.1007/978-3-319-73888-8_11
12. Brinquis, C.: IA conversacional: conversaciones reales con un ordenador (2019). https://www.incentro.com/es-es/blog/stories/ai-conversacional-conversacionesreales-con-un-ord enador/,Accessed 13 Apr 2019
13. Nieves, B.: IA Conversacional: definición y conceptos básicos (2018). https://planetachatbot.com/ia-conversacional-conceptos-basicos-y-la-definicion107529e213c1, Accessed 04 Dec 2019
14. Fitrianie, S.: My_Eliza, A multimodal communication system. In: Proceedings of Euromedia, p. 187 (2002)
15. Turing, A.M.:Computing Machinery and Intelligence (1950)
16. Hernández, R., Fernández, C., Baptista, P.: Metodología de la investigación. Sexta, México (2014)
17. Espinosa, P., Hernández, H., López, R., Lozano, S.: Muestreo de Bola de Nieve. Departamento de Probabilidad y Estadística UNAM (2018). https://es.scribd.com/document/379661920/Pro yectofinal-Bola-de-Nieve, Accessed 15 Jul 2020
18. Constitucional, C.E.: Registro Oficial - Órgano de la República del Ecuador, Ecuador (2020)
19. Vicente, C.: Manual de usuario aplicación móvil emoAppPro, Loja (2020)

20. Microsoft. Servicios de informática en la nube|Microsoft Azure (2020)
21. Cohen, J.: A coefficient of agreement for nominal scales. Educ. Psychol. Meas. **20**(1), 37–46 (1960)
22. Richard Landis, J., Koch, G.G.: The measurement of observer agreement for categorical data. Biometrics **33**(1), 159 (1977). https://doi.org/10.2307/2529310
23. Rivas, F.: El significado de la significancia. Biomedica **18**(4), 291 (1998)
24. Rubio, M., Berlanga, V.: Cómo aplicar las pruebas paramétricas bivariadas t de Student y ANOVA en SPSS. Caso práctico. REIRE. Revista d'Innovació i Recerca en Educació **5**, 18 (2012)
25. Dibitonto, M., Leszczynska, K., Tazzi, F., Medaglia, C.M.: Chatbot in a campus environment: design of LiSA, a virtual assistant to help students in their university life. In: Kurosu, M. (ed.) HCI. LNCS, vol. 10903, pp. 103–116. Springer, Cham (2018). https://doi.org/10.1007/978-3-319-91250-9_9
26. Piguave, K.L.: Análisis de la herramienta 'chatbot' y su influencia comunicacional en los estudiantes de la carrera de comunicación social, universidad de guayaquil 2018. Universidad de uayaquil, Facultad de Comunicación Social (2019)
27. Gonzálezonzález, C.: EMODIANA: Un instrumento para la evaluación subjetiva de emociones en niños y niñas, no. September (2013)
28. Condori-Fernandez, N., Bolos, A.C., Lago, P.: Poster: discovering requirements of behaviour change software systems from negative user experience. In: Proceedings - International Conference on Software Engineering, pp. 222–223 (2018)

Virtual Reality and Haptic Devices Applied in the System of Teaching Learning with Children of Early Education Age

Marco Pilatásig[✉], Emily Tobar[✉], Lissette Paredes[✉], Zulia Sánches[✉], and Grace Naranjo[✉]

Universidad de Las Fuerzas Armadas ESPE, Sangolquí, Ecuador
{mapilatagsig,ektobar,mlparedes2}@espe.edu.ec,
zuliamaria@hotmail.com, gracenaranjo14@gmail.com

Abstract. The aim of this work is to make known the possible applicability and usefulness of new technologies such as virtual reality and haptic devices to improve the education of children of pre-school age. The aim is not only to integrate these new technologies into pre-school education but also to evaluate the improvements that this would introduce, for which a system has been designed that includes a computer and a haptic device whose shape resembles a pencil and its use is very similar to a mouse. Several virtual interfaces have been designed in which different environments are presented where the child must perform tasks designated by the teacher; the child interacts with these interfaces with the help of the haptic device that also has the ability to feedback forces that will prevent the child from performing the task incorrectly. The interfaces are designed as games to please the child, for this 3D software is used, the haptic device is a Geomagic Touch and the tasks are structures by the teacher, according to the age and skill that is intended to improve in the child. The proposals and results of two previous works carried out by the authors are presented.

Keywords: Early education · Virtual reality · Haptic devices

1 Introduction

Education in the world is a very decisive factor for the development of countries, therefore it is very important that the teaching-learning process be improved; in addition, it should be considered that in initial education the child learns based on games and begins to develop his abilities.

According to studies carried out, human intelligence will have better results if early stimulation is carried out; therefore, at this stage, the use of any resource should be focused, especially the use of new technologies applied in education to achieve the proposed objectives [1].

Education depends on many actors, however, in pre-school education, the participation of the family is a determining factor and the teacher must adequately structure the

© Springer Nature Switzerland AG 2021
M. Botto-Tobar et al. (Eds.): ICAT 2020, CCIS 1388, pp. 33–43, 2021.
https://doi.org/10.1007/978-3-030-71503-8_3

teaching-learning process, therefore it is essential to use the greatest amount of resources [2–4].

In Ecuador, attention deficit, hyperactivity, learning difficulties as well as a low level of reasoning are problems that affect children's learning and can be reduced by applying other teaching methods in which new technologies are immersed, such as computers, tablets, haptic devices, etc. [5, 6].

The new technologies with their great diversity, being attractive and attracting the attention of the child, can improve his concentration and his reasoning capacity, especially if they are applied as tools for playful games. In Ecuador, the Early Education Curriculum uses play as a tool for entertaining and meaningful learning. [7–9].

The computer has been widely used in education and now new devices such as phones and iPods can be included as teaching aids, although their misuse creates serious problems, a correct application can represent a breakthrough when it comes to encouraging the child to eager to learn, in these devices can use virtual reality and augmented reality, creating 3D environments that provide the ability to educate in an entertaining and enjoyable way, for interaction with developed environments, other devices can be used, ranging from a simple mouse to other haptic devices that present feedback of forces and integrate sensations that the child finds pleasant and at the same time can give indications for the child to correctly perform the task assigned, such as sensations that prevent him from improperly tracing a letter. [10–16].

Virtual reality (VR) allows the creation of environments with very realistic, dynamic and entertaining images and sound, where the child can feel immersed with the help of his imagination, if this is increased by a device that allows him to feel the virtual elements through touch, the sensation will be more real, pleasant and very tractive. [17, 18].

Therefore, if varied and entertaining virtual environments can be created to attract children's attention, they can be encouraged to acquire new knowledge and thus the teaching and learning process will be more effective. [20–25].

The present work presents the advances and results of the application of 3D environments realized in virtual reality helped by the use of a haptic device, in the teaching of basic concepts to children of initial education, such as: to recognize and to use colors, to recognize geometric figures, to locate objects in designated spaces, to recognize and to realize figures, finally to recognize and to write vowels. The haptic device will serve as a tool for interacting with the virtual environment, which may guide the child's hand to perform an action or stroke, or will also present a force in the child's hand to prevent the child from performing an incorrect action or drawing a stroke inappropriately, such as drawing the letter OR in the wrong direction. [26, 27].

2 Material and Method

The system has virtual environments realized with the software UNITY 3D, in addition it is possible to interact with the Geomagic Touch device, which indicates the position of the cursor and allows by means of the buttons to realize some actions like: select primary colors, combine colors, pick and place objects, also indicates when to start or finish the stroke, if the task is done correctly the haptic device does not present any force to the action performed, otherwise prevents the child from continuing until you correct the error, at the end, an audio signal will tell the child if the task was successfully performed, always with words of encouragement even when the task has not been performed correctly. Both the inputs and outputs are managed with scripts made in Visual Studio with language C, these scripts execute functions that depend on the data received from the peripheral and the virtual environment that is used. With MatLab the data management algorithms are controlled, the validation of the traces made is carried out, based on the established pattern and the data entered with Geomagic Touch. Figure shows the block diagram of the implemented system (Fig. 1).

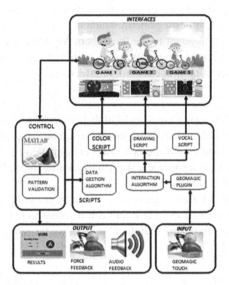

Fig. 1. Block diagram of Implemented system.

Input The device that allows giving the entries to the system is a Geomagic Touch, a haptic device that resembles the arm of a robot with six degrees of freedom and can be handled in a similar way to those of a mouse, also has the shape of a pencil, through this device the child can choose colors, draw strokes and write vowels.

Scripts

The scripts are a set of instructions programmed in language C# in Visual Studio, they are in charge of the administration of the system and specifically to deliver the outputs according to the inputs.

For the game that allows to select and locate objects, the child must choose the object with the help of the Geomagic Touch, when choosing the object he wants, thanks to the respective script the haptic device presents a feedback of forces that gives him the sensation of taking an object with a certain weight and when he moves it in places that are not allowed he has the sensation of colliding with the virtual objects that delimit this space, which gives him a sensation of realism. For the stroke game, the device opposes incorrect strokes, just as for the vowel game, it opposes the child writing in the wrong direction. In addition, the scripts turn Geomagic Touch into a teaching device, since it can move autonomously guiding the child's hand to learn how to perform the task, before performing it by himself.

Interfaces

The interfaces are environments that present everyday objects in 3D to make it more realistic and more accepted by the child, is programmed using Unity 3D software, with which you can assign properties to the objects, such as rigidity, sound and animation among others. The properties of the objects give the child an experience that is both real and attractive, since it resembles a game in which the child can interact.

The environments try to adapt to the theories of Vigotsky, that is to say they try to create environments similar to the reality of the child but with a touch of play, since in this way the teaching-learning process is more effective.

Control

The Control of the System is performed by Matlab, interacts with Unity, receives information from the interfaces and the haptic device and based on these, provides the necessary information to Unity to indicate if the task was performed correctly or can manage the Geomagic Touch to perform a specific task such as guiding the child's hand to learn how to draw a figure or write a vowel.

To validate a stroke, Matlab takes the one made by the child and compares it with a pattern, using classifiers that use the Euclidean distance to determine if the stroke is very close to the pattern. To ensure that the haptic device terminal follows a path, a PID position control is used.

Outputs

Outputs are presented in different ways:

- Graphically in the environment, to indicate the progress of the task performed.
- With sound to give auditory indications and stimulate the child while performing the task or to indicate if it was done correctly or not.
- Finally, the Geomatic Touch can deliver a force feedback that opposes the action performed by the child if it is incorrect.

2.1 Use of the System

The system currently has six games:

Primary Colors - Allows you to recognize and learn primary colors, the child must choose the color that the system asks him to choose.

Spatial Notion - To improve his spatial perception, the child must choose a particular object and place it in a set position, the device generates a force of opposition to the child's hand through the terminal of the Geomagic Touch when the trajectory he tries to follow is incorrect or when he tries to place the object in a different place from the established one (Fig. 2).

Fig. 2. Interface for learning primary colors and spatial notion.

Secondary Colors - In this case the child learns to combine two colors to form a secondary color, the system asks the child to choose the correct colors that combined serve to give color for example: a carrot or a bunch of grapes (Fig. 3).

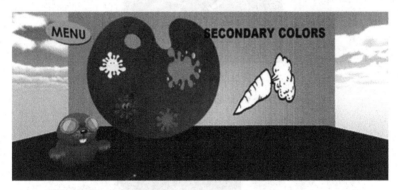

Fig. 3. Interface for learning secondary colors.

Geometric Figures - The child must recognize figures related to the environment, for example a rectangle with a door (Fig. 4).

Drawing of Figures - The aim is to improve the way the child draws a line, for this the system uses the Gemagic Touch as the hand of a teacher guiding the hand of the child, then behaves like a pencil for the child to draw the line by himself (Fig. 5).

Vowel Writing - Being a system for children in initial education, this game aims to give the notions necessary to write basic letters, in this case the vowels, in a similar way that in the previous case the system first behaves as a guide to teach the correct way to write each vowel and then allows the child to write it on its own, it is worth mentioning that in both cases if the child follows an incorrect trajectory the haptic device through force feedback will not allow him to continue until he corrects his error (Fig. 6).

Fig. 4. Interface for learning geometric figures.

Fig. 5. Interface to develop the ability to draw strokes.

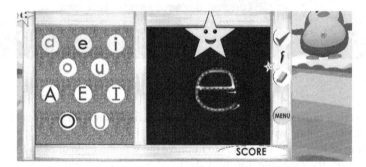

Fig. 6. Interface for learning how to write vowels.

3   Results and Discussions

3.1   Tests

The system was tested by 20 users (10 girls and 10 boys) between 6 and 9 years of age, users carried out the different activities proposed in the games under the supervision of the kindergarten teacher (Fig. 7).

Fig. 7. Children using the system.

Due to the age of the children the test is applied by means of observation and interview, during and after using the system, there is only one system due to the high cost, therefore the use is individual, nevertheless for better comfort and confidence in the children, the interview was carried out in groups of five children.

The following questions were used for the test:

Table 1. Questions to validate the implemented system.

Ord	Question	Value (1–10)
1	Are the graphics and elements used in the games pleasant?	
2	The selection of games is simple and easy to make?	
3	Are the instructions easy to follow?	
4	Are the games easy to make?	
5	Is the handling of the haptic device simple?	
6	Is the use of haptic device buttons simple?	
7	The results are easy to understand?	

Children should evaluate each question with values from 1 to 10 where 1 indicates low satisfaction and 10 indicates high satisfaction.

3.2 Results

When the child completes the tasks, the system shows the result obtained and also stores all the data so that the teacher can evaluate the performance of each child (Fig. 8).

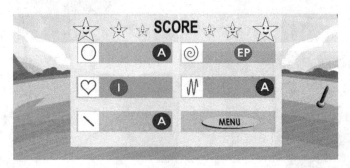

Fig. 8. Display where the results are shown.

The letters "A" indicate passed, "EP" is in the learning process but needs more practice and the letter "I" indicates that it requires more time and help to complete the task.

In general, the children had no problems performing the tasks using the system, the work was done in a versatile, cheerful and pleasant way.

By comparing the performance of the children with and without the use of the system, the following advantages were obtained:

- The children had more fun while they learned.
- Requested less help from the teacher.
- They showed greater interest because being virtual environments, children pay more attention.

The aspects mentioned above show that the system is designed properly, however to clear up doubts a test was performed on children, this test resembles a usability test with the necessary simplicity because it was applied in children. The questions applied are those shown in Table 1.

The results obtained are the following (Fig. 9).

As you can see in the results, there is a high degree of acceptance and satisfaction with the system.

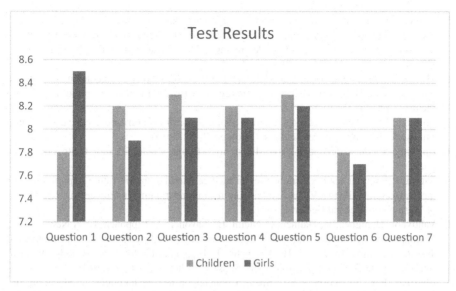

Fig. 9. Graph showing test results.

4 Conclusions

Education as the basis for the development of countries is extremely important, its improvement should always be sought and done as early as possible i.e. improvement in educational processes should begin in initial education.

Technology has the potential not only to improve an educational process but also to make it more attractive to all ages and much more so to children.

The proposed system is a very efficient alternative to improve the learning process in pre-school children, unfortunately due to its costs cannot be implemented in schools in the short term.

With the proposed system, the children learn in an entertaining way, the time they dedicate to learning is greater, on the other hand, the improvement in their abilities will be obtained in less time, in addition, the child acquires greater autonomy since although the supervision of the teacher is indispensable, the child requests less help.

References

1. Ankshear, C., Knobel, M.: New technologies in early childhood literacy research: a review of research. J. Early Child. Literacy **3**(1), 59–82 (2003)
2. Skaalvik, E., Skaalvik, S.: Teachers' perceptions of the school goal structure: Relations with teachers' goal orientations, work engagement, and job satisfaction. Int. J. Educ. Res. **62**, 199-209 (2013)
3. Blatchford, P., Kutnick, P., Baines, E.: Toward a social pedagogy of classroom group work. Int. J. Educ. Res. **39**(1–2), 153–172 (2003)
4. Méndez, R.: Investigación y planificación para el diseño de un aula de apoyo psicopedagógico y aporte de la misma al desarrollo y seguridad de la educación de niños con dificultades de aprendizaje (Tesis de Maestría). Instituto de Altos Estudios Nacionales Quito (2003)

5. Briones, M.: Guía metodológica correctiva integral neuropsicológica para dificultades específicas de lectura y escritura en niños/as de 3.er año de educación básica del Colegio Experimental El Sauce de Tumbaco" (Tesis de Pregrado), Universidad Politécnica Salesiana, Quito (2013)

6. Muñoz, X.: Representaciones y actitudes del profesorado frente a la integración de Niños/as con Necesidades Educativas Especiales al aula común. Revista Latinoamericana de Educación Inclusiva, pp. 25–35 (2008)

7. MinEduc, M.D.: Guía metodológica para la implementación del currículo de educación inicial. Ministerio de Educación del Ecuador, Quito, pp. 7–15 (2015)

8. Currículo de educación inicial 2014. Ministerio de Educación del Ecuador, Quito, pp. 12–16 (2014)

9. Satava, R.: Virtual reality: current uses in medical simulation and future opportunities & medical technologies that VR can exploit in education and training. In: Proceedings University of Washington Medical Center, USA, (2013)

10. Vahtivuori-Hänninen, S., Halinen, I., Niemi, H., Lavonen, J., Lipponen, L.: A New Finnish National Core Curriculum for Basic Education (2014) and Technology as an Integrated Tool for Learning. In: Niemi, H., Multisilta, J., Lipponen, L., Vivitsou, M. (eds.) Finnish Innovations and Technologies in Schools. SensePublishers, pp. 21–32 (2014)

11. Martínez, E.V., Villacorta, C.S.J.: Spanish policies on new technologies in education. In: Plomp, T., Anderson, R.E., Kontogiannopoulou-Polydorides, G. (eds) Cross National Policies and Practices on Computers in Education. Technology-Based Education Series, vol 1. (pp. 397–412) Springer, Dordrecht (1996) https://doi.org/https://doi.org/10.1007/978-0-585-32767-9_20

12. Wall, K., Higgins, S., Smith, H.: The visual helps me understand the complicated things': pupil views of teaching and learning with interactive whiteboards. Br. J. Educ. Technol. 36, pp. 851–867 (2005)

13. Mar, N.Y.: Utilizing information and communication technologies to achieve lifelong education for all: a case study of Myanmar. Educ. Res. Policy Pract. 3(2), 141–166 (2004) https://doi.org/10.1007/s10671-004-8241-y

14. Selwyn, N., Bullon, K.: Primary school children's use of ICT. Br. J. Educ. Technol. 31(4), 321–332 (2000)

15. Peltenburg, M., Van Den Heuvel-Panhuizen, M., Doig, B.: Mathematical power of special-needs pupils: An ICT-based dynamic assessment format to reveal weak pupils learning potential. Br. J. Educ. Technol. 40(2), 273–284 (2009)

16. Mangen, A., Walgermo, B., Bronnick, K.: Reading linear texts on paper versus computer screen: Effects on reading comprehension. Int. J. Educ. Res. 58, 61–68 (2013)

17. Dinis, F.M., Guimarães, A.S., Carvalho, B.R., Martins, J.P.P.: Development of virtual reality game-based interfaces for civil engineering education. In: Global Engineering Education Conference (EDUCON), pp. 1195–1202. IEEE (2017)

18. Elliman, J., Loizou, M., Loizides, F.: Virtual reality simulation training for student nurse education. In: Games and Virtual Worlds for Serious Applications (VS-Games), 2016 8th International Conference on, pp. 1–2. IEEE (2016)

19. Zhang, K., Liu, S.J.: The application of virtual reality technology in physical education teaching and training. In: Service Operations and Logistics, and Informatics (SOLI), 2016 IEEE International Conference on, pp. 245–248. IEEE (2016)

20. Yu, X., Zhang, M., Xue, Y., Zhu, Z.: An exploration of developing multi-touch virtual learning tools for young children. In: Education Technology and Computer (ICETC), 2010 2nd International Conference on, vol. 3, pp. V3–4. IEEE (2010)

21. Chaney, C.: Language development, metalinguistic skills, and print awareness in 3-year-old children. Appl. Psycholinguistics 13(4), 485514 (1992)

22. Clements, D., Swaminathan, S., Zeitler, M., l Sarama, J.: Young children's concepts of shape. J. Res. Math. Educ. **30**(2), pp. 192–212 (1999)
23. Achibet, M., Marchal, M., Girard, A., Kajimoto, H.: FlexiFingers: Multi-finger interaction in VR combining passive haptics and pseudo-haptics. In: IEEE Symposium on 3D User Interfaces (3DUI)/ Los Angeles, CA, USA, pp. 103–106 (2017)
24. Palluel-Germain, R., Bara, F., De Boisferon, A.H., Hennion, B., Gouagout, P., Gentaz, E.: A visuo-haptic device-telemaque-increases kindergarten children's handwriting acquisition. In: EuroHaptics Conference, 2007 and Symposium on Haptic Interfaces for Virtual Environment and Teleoperator Systems. World Haptics 2007. Second Joint, pp. 72–77. IEEE (2007)
25. Ahonen, T., O'Reilly, J.: Convergence of broadband internet, virtual reality and the intelligent home. Digital Korea, pp. 37–54 (2007)
26. Pilatásig, M., Tobar, E., Paredes, L., Silva, F., Acurio, A., Pruna, E., Sanchez, Z.: Teaching-learning system using virtual reality and haptic device to improve skills in children of initial education. In: Rocha, Á., Guarda, T. (eds.) MICRADS 2018. SIST, vol. 94, pp. 307–316. Springer, Cham (2018). https://doi.org/10.1007/978-3-319-78605-6_26
27. Pilatásig, M., et al.: Virtual system for teaching-learning of initial education using a haptic device. In: De Paolis, L.T., Bourdot, P. (eds.) AVR 2018. LNCS, vol. 10850, pp. 118–132. Springer, Cham (2018). https://doi.org/10.1007/978-3-319-95270-3_8

Interpreting Felony Acts Using Georeferenced Data. Case Study in Ambato, Ecuador

Franklin Castillo[1], Hernán Naranjo-Ávalos[2], Jorge Buele[1,3(✉)] [ID],
José Varela-Aldás[1] [ID], Yesenia D. Amaguaña[4], and Franklin W. Salazar[5] [ID]

[1] SISAu Research Group, Universidad Tecnológica Indoamérica, Ambato 180212, Ecuador
{franklincastillo,jorgebuele,josevarela}@uti.edu.ec
[2] Universidad Técnica de Ambato, Ambato 180103, Ecuador
hf.naranjo@uta.edu.ec
[3] Universidad Internacional de La Rioja, Logroño 26006, España
[4] Instituto Superior Tecnológico Riobamba, Riobamba 060106, Ecuador
yamaguana@institutos.gob.ec
[5] Universidad Autónoma de Madrid, Madrid 28049, España
franklin.salazar@estudiante.uam.es

Abstract. Georeferenced tools have made it possible to use the information collected through e-collaboration environments in a better way. Nevertheless, no study has been found on quantifying the influence of software tools over the capacity of interpreting data of victims of some kind of felony. This paper aims to validate the technology acceptance of applications georeferencing crimes using a prototype that could be useful for certain institutions to generate public policies. A web prototype is implemented to georeference data provided by felony acts victims. The application's prototype was validated by a group of 122 college students using the Technology Acceptance Model. The results were interpreted with the help of Kendall Tau-b correlation analysis where highly significant positive correlation values were obtained.

Keywords: E-government · Felony Acts · Georeferenced data · Public Policies · Technology Acceptance Model

1 Introduction

The scientific interest in the theory of crime is one of the subjects being investigated since the middle of the nineteenth century through crime maps [1, 2]. Although the possibilities and versatility of the geospatial analysis of crime have been convincingly demonstrated by criminologists and geographers, recent technology progresses require a reevaluation of established knowledge about the importance of the location where the crime occurred [3–5]. The rise of e-government has allowed collecting information in a more participative way because the communities not only provide information but become the principal actors in this new kind of government [6]. The analysis of e-government management initiatives has opened new research fields [7, 8].

© Springer Nature Switzerland AG 2021
M. Botto-Tobar et al. (Eds.): ICAT 2020, CCIS 1388, pp. 44–54, 2021.
https://doi.org/10.1007/978-3-030-71503-8_4

Google Maps provides an API for rendering a map service in a customized application. Google Maps has become one of the most important products of Google Enterprise. These benefits are justified not only by the features and performance of this product but also by its capacity to integrate different programming languages through Google Maps API to enhance the customization and exploitation of different information systems [9, 10]. Concerning the personal security, a prototype of Children Location Monitoring System (CLMS) has been developed where, using GPS and GSM technologies, the child's location is continuously emitted. This data (latitude and longitude) are received via a link to a mobile platform and shown through Google Maps. This kind of application has decreased the number of crimes against children and provides an online child location feature [4]. From the perspective of e-collaboration tools based on Google Maps, prototypes have been developed allowing to generate reminders according to the user's georeferentiation. This kind of reminders allow us to specify locations exactly and get to them quickly and efficiently [11].

The study by Worapot and Pongsak [12] is oriented to the implementation of a mobile application through which the police registers the location, images and multimedia files of committed crimes. In the implementation, HTML5 and Google Maps App were used to manage georeferenced data. This project is focused on using the same benefits from GPS devices through mobile devices. In the field of land management, the Google Maps API has been used by the Land National Agency to help the land officer and the public, to visualize the location and land limits. GPS technology is used for determining the latitude and longitude. The implementation aims to optimize resources and reduce costs in the process of collecting information. The implemented prototype works as a complement of the online maps of the abovementioned agency and can collaborate to digitally delimiting the land boundaries [13]. Earthquakes' impact is very high and, unpredictable as they are, rescue operations are difficult. For contingency situations the priority is to proceed fast, minimizing the time of response after a natural disaster. The research of [14] analyzes the Google Maps principles and its application data technologies of Google Maps in earthquakes emergency operations. Using the Google Maps data and a prototype, thematic maps were generated in emergency real operations related to earthquakes.

Other studies have focused their attention on studying the geography of delinquency in localities as New Zealand. The study analyzes the factors between the crime damage index and the priority locations index in communities and neighborhoods, having higher levels of crime. The benefits brought by this research allow the optimization of resources of the police and of the agencies responsible of reduce crime [15]. The analysis of previous works, let us affirm that in the last few years the development of applications using interactive maps for data georeferencing data is highly relevant and vital for strengthening the practices related to e-government, e-collaboration and e-democracy.

The Technology Acceptance Model (TAM) was developed by Davis and has become one of the most popular models for predicting the ease of use and acceptance of new technology and information systems [16]. According to Davis, the main aim of TAM is to identify the factors determining the use of ICT in an important context of users. TAM suggests that the perceived usefulness and ease of use are vital in the intention of an individual when using a system. From the perspective of TAM relevance, there are recent researches that confirm the importance of this model in different kinds of studies [17–19]. Considering the importance and pertinence of TAM, some authors have centered their studies proposing an enhancement of this model in the education field. Their principal purpose is to validate how their contributions to the model can bring a positive impact when analyzing the level of technology acceptance in educative digital games [19]. The relevance of TAM in the abovementioned studies, corroborate the pertinence of this methodology to validate the technology acceptance of the software prototype in our use case.

A literature review of recent works was carried out for finding the importance of the georeferenced data in crime registering systems from different perspectives of research. Nevertheless, no studies quantifying the positive or negative influence of using these tools, from the perspective of the victims of some kind of felony, were found. The aim of this study is to show the results of a quantitative evaluation of the perceived usefulness and ease of use in georeferenced crime registering tools within the area of citizen's e-collaboration. 122 persons participated in the study and an evaluation was made using the Technology Acceptance Model (TAM).

This document is made up of 4 sections, including the introduction and review of applications related to tourism management and the contribution of multiplatform frameworks in Sect. 1. The methodology used in the development of this proposal and the results and discussions is shown in Sect. 2 and Sect. 3 respectively. Conclusions and future works are described in Sect. 4.

2   Materials and Methods

2.1   Implementation of the Prototype

Taking into account that in the field where the experiment was made, no e-collaboration tools were documented for interpreting data of crimes, a web application using Google Maps API was developed, allowing to store information of two types. The first type focuses on the geographic and spatial data, related to the location where the crime was committed, as shown in Fig. 1. The second type corresponds to the victim´s information, specifying relevant variables from a statistical perspective.

This web application is based on a client–server architecture, and it is divided in three layers: client layer, business layer and the data layer. In the client layer, the map component is rendered, using Google Maps API. Collected data is then stored using the server layer.

Victim's data include: sex, race, education level and age range. Crimes data include: year, month and hour. When the felony took place, state, approximate, cost of the damage and type of felon. It is important to mention that the type of felony is typified using the most commonly committed crimes, according to the statistics of delinquency studies in Ecuador.

The application development has no technical complexity. The prototype was implemented with proprietary software (Visual Studio 2019 Community) and conceived to be used in the academic context. Nevertheless is completely feasible its migration to open-source software. Once the information has been entered to the application, a heat map of the zones of highest concentrations of crime. In Fig. 2 and Fig. 3 the obtained

Fig. 1. Crimes management system

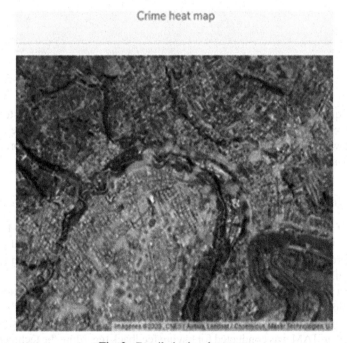

Fig. 2. Detailed crime heat map

results for the city of Ambato are shown. As can be seen in the figures, there are areas where there is a higher prevalence of crimes.

Fig. 3. Crimes heat map

From a qualitative and quantitative point of view, the information registered in the system is presented through reports as depicted in Fig. 4. The reports were developed with the Power BI tool and integrated into the web application, being processed in real-time. The user can choose from a set of 10 reports.

2.2 Experiment Design

A sample of 122 engineering students was used in the experiment. In the first phase, the students were trained in the use of the software prototype. In a second phase, the students were granted access to the tool in the places where they had been victims of some kind of felony, and they registered the corresponding information.

In a third phase, the students were asked to review the processed information through the application reports and to validate the georeferenced data of the zones of the highest concentration of crime. In the fourth phase, once the revision process was finished, a survey based on TAM was conducted for having feedback regarding the technical criteria of the participants. In the survey, demographic data was included allowing to identify the groups that might have an impact on other vulnerable groups regarding felonies.

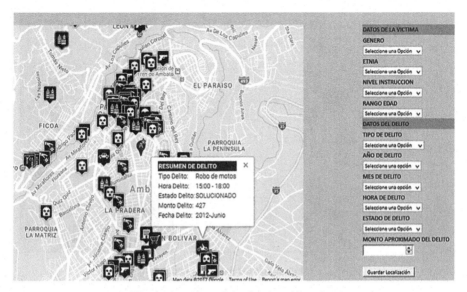

Fig. 4. Overview of the developed interface

3   Results and Discussion

3.1   Experimental Results

Based on the implementation of many other types of research and with the development of the current study, the importance of the Google Maps APIs for generating customized tools capable of georeferencing data was validated. The heat maps allow us to graphically view the concentration of georeferenced data. The registered values are displayed using color ranges identifying the zones with the highest concentration of information. The reports generated are shown in Fig. 5 and Fig. 6. Here you can quantitatively appreciate the different types of crimes that have occurred in the city. Having these data makes it easier for local law enforcement agencies to implement solutions for the crime.

The information analysis is made using the SPSS tool. For validating the pertinence of the survey results, a Cronbach-alpha test was carried out obtaining a value of 0,824, which proves the internal validity of the collected data when the survey was conducted.

To interpret the results of the survey according to the Technology Acceptance Model, a normality test was carried out showing that the results do not follow a normal distribution [20]. Then, a non-parametric correlation using Kendall Tau-b was run. The following results were obtained:

1. The greater value of correlation for information access using maps is regarding the intention of use with the crime report (correlation 4.74 significant).
2. The use of reports is strongly correlated with the perceived ease of use.
3. The perceived usefulness of the map component is strongly correlated with its capacity of enhancing the information value in the application.

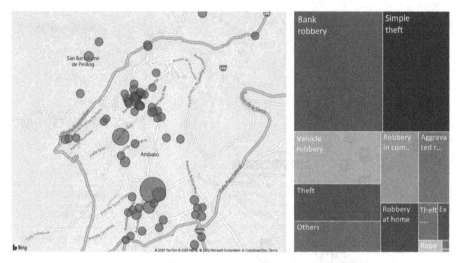

Fig. 5. Crime map obtained

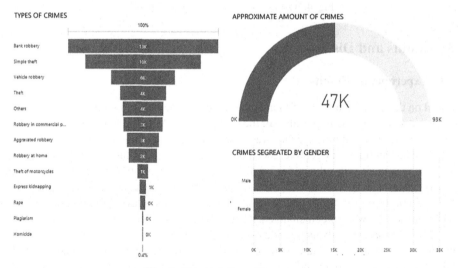

Fig. 6. Crimes information reports

4. The accessibility to the information is strongly correlated to the capacity of the report to enhance the information value. The access through the maps compliments the accessibility with a relevant positive correlation.

The results of the Tau-b from Kendall and TAM criteria are presented in Table 1 and Table 2 respectively.

Abbreviations:

Q1 Access to information through the map is made easy.

Q2 Access to information through reports is made easy.
Q3 The Map component enhances the value of the information that is managed in the application.
Q4 The reports generated to enhance the value of the information that is managed in the application.
Q5 The usefulness of the Map component is significant. CC: Correlation Coefficient. BS Bilateral Significance

Table 1. Tau-b from kendall results.

N = 122		Q1	Q2	Q3	Q4	Q5
Consider that when using the application for the recovery of information from criminal acts, it would be:	CC	,300**	,268**	,404**	,140	,363**
	BS	0,000	0,001	0,000	0,098	0,000
Do you think that when using the tool for the recovery of information from criminal acts, you would be:	CC	,266**	,186**	,196*	,341**	,255**
	BS	0,002	0,027	0,021	0,000	0,003
When analyzing the prototype of the proposed software, consider that this is:	CC	,423**	,452**	,426**	,295**	,378**
	BS	0,000	0,000	0,000	0,000	0,000
When analyzing the prototype of the proposed software, do you consider that in a short time you can become an expert user in its use?	CC	,147	,107	,222*	,047	,287**
	BS	0,091	0,212	0,010	0,580	0,001
When analyzing the prototype of the proposed software, consider that:	CC	−,279**	−,243**	−,326**	−,050	−,209*
	BS	0,001	0,003	0,000	0,535	0,011
When analyzing the prototype of the proposed software, consider that its design	CC	,144	,390**	,288**	,308**	,328**
	BS	0,092	0,000	0,001	0,000	0,000
Access to information through the map is made	CC	1,000	,288**	,313**	,273**	,333**
	BS		0,001	0,000	0,001	0,000
Access to information through reports is made	CC	,288**	1,000	,338**	,453**	,384**
	BS	0,001	0,000	0,000	0,000	0,000
The Map component enhances the value of the information that is managed in the application	CC	,313**	,338**	1,000	,131	,440**
	BS	0,000	0,000		0,000	0,000
The reports generated to enhance the value of the information that is managed in the application?	CC	,273**	,453**	,131	1,000	,205*

(*continued*)

Table 1. (*continued*)

N = 122		Q1	Q2	Q3	Q4	Q5
	BS	0,001	0,000	0,120		0,016
The usefulness of the Map component is?	CC	,333**	,384**	,440**	,205*	1,000
	BS	0,000	0,000	0,000	0,016	
Would you suggest the use of the application for information management of criminal acts?	CC	,224**	,366**	,404**	,230**	,339**
	BS	0,009	0,000	0,000	0,006	0,000
Given the experience he has had, he would use the computer application	CC	,476**	,414**	,386**	,380**	,318**
	BS	0,000	0,000	0,000	0,000	0,000
Would you use the computer application for information management of criminal acts?	CC	,221**	,443**	,327**	,301**	,270**
	BS	0,010	0,000	0,000	0,000	0,002
Would you report a criminal act of which you are a victim through an application of this type?	CC	,344**	,351**	,297**	,241**	,318**
	BS	0,000	0,000	0,001	0,005	0,000

Table 2. Statistic values of TAM criteria

TAM Criteria	Mean	Standard deviation
Usage attempt	4.67	0.29
Perceived utility	4.35	0.48
Perceived ease of use	4.52	0.31
Attitude to the use	4.33	0,51

3.2 Discussion

From the participants in the study, 53% were men. 71% of the people surveyed, were aged in a range from 20–30 years old, the other groups are distributed similarly with people between 30 to 40 years old, people over 40 and others under 20. The 85% of questioned participants are related to engineering and technology, the rest of the groups are distributed mainly in the fields of education and sciences. Concerning ethnics, 98% of the participants in the survey belong to the mestizo's ethnic group. 78% of the people surveyed live in urban sectors while 22% live in rural areas of the city. 18% comes from other cities.

The presented literature from [14–17] demonstrates the functionality of TAM as a tool widely used by several researchers and authors of relevant works. The investigations presented in [11] and [12] allow us to appreciate the use of GPS to generate operational maps in emergencies such as earthquakes; this served as a basis for this research. On the other hand, both [10] and [13] use geolocalization tools for crime management in cities. The locations of the areas with the highest levels of crime can be defined. These principles were used in this proposal, which attempts to locate areas where there are a greater number of homicides. This database will be complemented over time, offering greater results and contributing as a technological tool for the local police.

4   Conclusions and Future Works

The functionality of the software prototype in this research is relevant since it allows users to contribute, consume, rate, and promote touristic information based on personal experiences. As the project has been developed from a multiplatform perspective and with open-source technologies, allows it to broaden its spectrum of use while simplifying the maintenance processes of the application. The study shows quantitatively that users (personnel associated with tourist activities and students) agreed with the use of this type of application. The results of the TAM poll let the authors confirm that the ease of use, usage attempt, and utility are highly correlated with the handling of the tool.

The map component becomes a relevant element in the proposal. Taking into account the current post-pandemic policies and strategies for economic reactivation of the autonomous governments, it is considered that this tool can contribute significantly to the tourism promotion in the national context and easily replicated in any location.

References

1. DaViera, A.L., Roy, A.L., Uriostegui, M., Fiesta, D.: Safe spaces embedded in dangerous contexts: how chicago youth navigate daily life and demonstrate resilience in high-crime neighborhoods. Am. J. Community Psychol. **66**, 65–80 (2020). https://doi.org/10.1002/ajcp. 12434
2. Scassa, T.: Police service crime mapping as civic technology. Int. J. E-Planning Res. **5**, 13–26 (2016). https://doi.org/10.4018/ijepr.2016070102
3. Vandeviver, C., Bernasco, W.: The geography of crime and crime control. Appl. Geogr. **86**, 220–225 (2017). https://doi.org/10.1016/j.apgeog.2017.08.012
4. Sunehra, D., Priya, P.L., Bano, A.: Children location monitoring on google maps using GPS and GSM technologies. In: Proceedings - 6th International Advanced Computing Conference, IACC 2016, pp. 711–715 (2016). https://doi.org/https://doi.org/10.1109/IACC.2016.137.
5. Su Bin, O., Park, M.-H., Doo, C.: Implementation of sex crime prevention systems using the indoor location tracking system. Adv. Sci. Lett. **24**(3), 1986–1990 (2018). https://doi.org/10. 1166/asl.2018.11824
6. Galdon Clavell, G.: Exploring the ethical, organisational and technological challenges of crime mapping: a critical approach to urban safety technologies. Ethics Inf. Technol. **20**, 265–277 (2018). https://doi.org/10.1007/s10676-018-9477-1
7. Scott, M., Delone, W., Golden, W.: Measuring eGovernment success: a public value approach. Eur. J. Inf. Syst. **25**, 187–208 (2016). https://doi.org/10.1057/ejis.2015.11
8. Buele, J., Franklin Salazar, L., Altamirano, S., Abigail Aldás, R., Urrutia-Urrutia, P.: Platform and mobile application to provide information on public transport using a low-cost embedded device. RISTI - Rev. Iber. Sist. e Tecnol. Inf. 476–489 (2019)

9. Vijaya Rohini, D., Isakki, P.: Crime analysis and mapping through online newspapers: a survey. In: International Conference on Computing Technologies and Intelligent Data Engineering, ICCTIDE 2016. Institute of Electrical and Electronics Engineers Inc., pp. 1–4 (2016). https://doi.org/https://doi.org/10.1109/ICCTIDE.2016.7725331.

10. Salazar, F.W., Naranjo-Ávalos, H., Buele, J., Pintag, M.J., Buenaño, É.R., Reinoso, C., Urrutia-Urrutia, P., Varela-Aldás, J.: Prototype system of geolocation educational public transport through google maps API. In: Gervasi, O., Murgante, B., Misra, S., Garau, C., Blečić, I., Taniar, D., Apduhan, B.O., Rocha, A.M.A.C., Tarantino, E., Torre, C.M., Karaca, Y. (eds.) ICCSA 2020. LNCS, vol. 12254, pp. 367–382. Springer, Cham (2020). https://doi.org/10.1007/978-3-030-58817-5_28

11. Battin, P., Markande, S.D.: Location based reminder Android application using Google Maps API. In: International Conference on Automatic Control and Dynamic Optimization Techniques, ICACDOT 2016, pp. 649–652 (2017). https://doi.org/https://doi.org/10.1109/ICACDOT.2016.7877666

12. Jakkhupan, W., Klaypaksee, P.: A web-based criminal record system using mobile device: a case study of Hat Yai municipality. In: Proceedings, APWiMob 2014: IEEE Asia Pacific Conference on Wireless and Mobile 2014. Institute of Electrical and Electronics Engineers Inc., pp. 243–246 (2014). https://doi.org/https://doi.org/10.1109/APWiMob.2014.6920295

13. Windarni, V.A., Sediyono, E., Setiawan, A.: Using GPS and Google maps for mapping digital land certificates. In: 2016 International Conference on Informatics and Computing, ICIC 2016. pp. 422–426 (2017). https://doi.org/https://doi.org/10.1109/IAC.2016.7905756.

14. Tan, Q.Q., Luo, H.C., Ren, Z.L., Liu, Q.: Research on earthquake emergency response technology based on Google Maps data. In: Proceedings of 2016 2nd International Conference on Cloud Computing and Internet of Things, CCIOT 2016, pp. 85–88 (2017). https://doi.org/https://doi.org/10.1109/CCIOT.2016.7868308.

15. Curtis-Ham, S., Walton, D.: Mapping crime harm and priority locations in New Zealand: a comparison of spatial analysis methods. Appl. Geogr. **86**, 245–254 (2017). https://doi.org/10.1016/j.apgeog.2017.06.008

16. Leong, L.W., Ibrahim, O., Dalvi-Esfahani, M., Shahbazi, H., Nilashi, M.: The moderating effect of experience on the intention to adopt mobile social network sites for pedagogical purposes: an extension of the technology acceptance model. Educ. Inf. Technol. **23**, 2477–2498 (2018). https://doi.org/10.1007/s10639-018-9726-2

17. Islam, M.T., Hoque, M.R., Sorwar, G.: Understanding customers' intention to use ecommerce in Bangladesh: an application of the technology acceptance model (TAM). In: 19th International Conference on Computer and Information Technology, ICCIT 2016. Institute of Electrical and Electronics Engineers Inc., pp. 512–516 (2017). https://doi.org/https://doi.org/10.1109/ICCITECHN.2016.7860251.

18. Patil, K.: Retail adoption of Internet of Things: applying TAM model. In: International Conference on Computing, Analytics and Security Trends, CAST 2016. Institute of Electrical and Electronics Engineers Inc., pp. 404–409 (2017). https://doi.org/https://doi.org/10.1109/CAST.2016.7915003.

19. Dele-Ajayi, O., Strachan, R., Sanderson, J., Pickard, A.: A modified TAM for predicting acceptance of digital educational games by teachers. In: IEEE Global Engineering Education Conference, EDUCON, pp. 961–968. IEEE (2017). https://doi.org/https://doi.org/10.1109/EDUCON.2017.7942965.

20. Davis, F.D.: Perceived usefulness, perceived ease of use, and user acceptance of information technology. MIS Q. Manag. Inf. Syst. (1989). https://doi.org/10.2307/249008

Development of a Web-Based Medical Record Management Software for Digital Immigrant Users

Ricardo Celi-Párraga[1] ⓘ, Félix Fernández-Peña[2(✉)] ⓘ,
and Diana Coello-Fiallos[3] ⓘ

[1] ESIT, Universidad Nacional de la Rioja, Avda. de la Paz, 137,
26006 Logroño, La Rioja, Spain
`ricardo.celi080@comunidadunir.net`
[2] ESAI, Universidad Espíritu Santo, Km. 2,5 vía Samborondón,
092301 Guayaquil, Ecuador
`fofernandez@uees.edu.ec`
[3] Carrera de Ingeniería Civil - UTA. av. los Chasquis y Río Payamino,
Ambato, Ecuador
`dc.coello@uta.edu.ec`

Abstract. The lack of usability of automated medical record management systems holds back the quality of health care services in health institutions. This situation is especially critical with the increase of the number of patients because of the pandemic of COVID-19. In the present work, a web-based medical records management system was developed with an easy-to-use interface for digital immigrant users. For the management and development of the project, the XP (eXtreme Programming) methodology of the software life cycle was successfully applied. The system was developed using open source technologies: PHP as programming language and the Bootstrap framework for the design of user interfaces. The result was an elegant and modern user interface that provides ease of use to digital immigrant users. The system was validated through an experimental evaluation carried out at the medical center of "La Concordia", in Ecuador. This evaluation was based on Jakob Nielsen usability principles and the software product quality norms of the ISO/IEC 25010 standard. The heuristic validation of the proposal resulted in a 93% of acceptance whilst function tests where successful in 96% of times. Besides, the result of a SUS test with the participation of five digital immigrants turn out in a 91.5% of system usability. Finally, it is worth mentioning that this software is now in exploitation in a local medical center with successful results.

Keywords: Digital immigrants · Electronic medical record system · Web system usability

© Springer Nature Switzerland AG 2021
M. Botto-Tobar et al. (Eds.): ICAT 2020, CCIS 1388, pp. 55–68, 2021.
https://doi.org/10.1007/978-3-030-71503-8_5

1   Introduction

Medical information systems optimize the use of available resources for patient attention and improve the service quality and the communication with the patients [16]. By using collected data, it has been possible to increase the hepatitis C and HIV screening rates in primary care practices in more than a 20% [16]. Other studies emphasize the importance of a digitally connected healthcare system in times of pandemic [2].

Baumgart et al. also consider that the SARS-CoV-2 pandemic is accelerating the digital revolution in healthcare; they affirm that highly automated healthcare systems employing networked Electronic Medical Records (EMR) are fundamental for the success of healthcare programs [2]. This idea supports the impact that web-based platforms currently have in the implementation of medical record management systems.

Nevertheless, the reality that we found in some regions of Ecuador is that the professionals of healthcare institutions are not aware of the use of EMR. In fact, the importance of the analysis of information quality in medical service management systems has been highlighted in different studies [16, 19].

Yoo et al. consider that many health institutions are focused on increasing the efficiency and effectiveness of health attention without being familiar, let alone proficient, in advanced information technology [19]. In their research, they realm the need of taking into account specific needs of the end users of health care systems.

Doctors and nurses need access to a medical record of each patient but managing a hand-written record is inefficient and an error-prone scenario [16]. The actual problem here is that not all of the clinic staff is trained to use information systems. These users are asked to adapt to the software whilst the software should be adapted to them.

These individuals are known as digital immigrants and, unfortunately, most of senior staff, with the highest level of medical expertise, are unfamiliar with the use of automated systems.

For this reason, the aim of our work was to develop a web-based clinical records management system, with an interface designed for digital-immigrant users which lack of experience on the use of information systems. During the implementation of the system, the medical center "La Concordia", located in La Concordia municipality, in Santo Domingo de los Tsáchilas province, Ecuador, was used as study case for evaluating its applicability.

Before the implementation of the proposed system, doctors in the medical center "La Concordia" resisted to change their methodology of work whilst they kept handwritten medical records of patients and cardboard folders with tons of patient files. The clinic's staff had to deal with inefficient search of files, ink vanishing out in the documents with the passing of time, and the risk of losing all records because of a fire or any natural disaster. In terms of the patients, longer lines waiting for medical attention and confusing handwritten prescriptions of the doctors characterised the scenario that motivated our work. Nevertheless, the health care personnel made resistance to the implementation of any EMR software.

To face this situation, the development of a responsive and mobile first web application was proposed. The main difference of our proposal against other EMR software we are aware of is that the design of the application was focused on functionalities that would facilitate its use by digital immigrants.

In Sect. 2 of this paper, we discuss the results of the analysis of existing EMR software. In Sect. 3, we describe the construction of the proposed EMR software. In Sect. 4, we discuss the main practical contributions of our proposal on increasing the usability of EMR software and reducing the learning curve, mainly of valuable health care staff members who are also digital immigrants. Also, we discuss the results of the experimental validation of the proposal for small clinics. Finally, in Sect. 5 we arrive to conclusions.

2   Related Work

In Table 1, we compare different proposals of previously developed EMR software. Most of the solutions were implemented using free software platforms, being PHP the programming language used the most. This result supports our decision of choosing PHP as programming language.

Further, we see there are solutions for desktop, web environment and mobile platforms. Nevertheless, it is clear that using Bootstrap makes easier to build a responsive and mobile first application, increasing its accessibility from any device. This is why we decided to use this CSS framework to make the web application cross-platform.

Meanwhile, the eXtreme Programming software development methodology (XP) has shown to be the most common software development methodology being used in the development of EMR software in web platforms. So, we decided to use this methodology in the development of our proposal.

On the other hand, Gutarra and Quiroga determined that, with the use of the EMR software they developed, once all the staff was familiar with it, there was an increase of 56% on the information management in digital format. This result means that required time for each patient attention was reduced in 61.67%. This result corroborates the importance of shortening the learning curve for the users of our proposal.

As a general result of the analysis of the practical contribution of these solutions, we may conclude that they all have implemented the core services of an EMR software taking into account a specific scenario. However, none of them have considered the scalability of the solution for its use in other locations. Furthermore, none of them has taken into account specific functionalities for increasing the ease of use of digital immigrants.

From the result of a search of solutions in the international arena, Table 2 shows the characterization of the solutions we are aware of. All these available tools have been used for many years, and they are general EMR solutions applicable to any context. The scenario here is just the opposite to the one of previously analyzed works. Open source solutions manage so much information that they become overwhelming for small clinics. Besides, they require technical

Table 1. Characterization of related solutions found in the national arena.

Sol.	Description	Used technologies
[6]	The functionalities of the application include the generation of statistic reports of medical appointments. It is said that the reports, the tool generates, improve the decision-making process	PHP, MySQL, Apache WS and Linux OS
[17]	EMR software in mobile platform. Every doctor needs a mobile phone for using the application and the application is not available for the IPhone platform	The application was developed using XP software development metodology, Java as programming language and SQLite as database
[13]	EMR software for the medical center "San Gerardo", in Quevedo city	Desktop application developed with Visual Basic and SQL Server as database management system
[10]	EMR software for the hospital Martin Icaza, in Babahoyo city	PHP, PostgreSQL, Apache WS and Linux OS. Angular JS framework and Bootstrap were used in the client-side programming
[3]	EMR software for managing medical records in the clinic laboratory "Cedylab", in Santo Domingo de los Tsáchilas. Their objective was to reduce the time that takes the attention of the patients	The software was developed using XP software development metodology, Python as programming language, Django as software framework, PostgreSQL as database server, Nginx and Gunicorn for the server, and Bootstrap as CSS framework
[12]	EMR software for managing medical records in the health center Perú 3rd Zone. Implemented as a web application, it allows the access of users from any device. Scrum was used as software development methodology	Java was used as programming language, MySQL as database server and Apache TomCat as web server

staff for the deployment and maintenance of the system. In the case of paid solutions, the cost is not trivial.

Open source software initiatives like openEMR [11] or VistA [18] support the standardization of health care among different medical institutions. This initiatives have had big repercussion in the United States. In contrast, the situation of underdeveloped countries is quite different. Health care services need customized systems that consider the local reality. None of the solutions analyzed, take into account the needs of digital immigrants among the personnel of health care services.

None of preexisting medical record management systems were considered appropriate. The main three reasons for developing a different EMR software were the reduced experience of the health care staff with the use of technology, the complexity of available free software, and the high cost of paid systems.

3   Materials and Methods

A User Centered Design (UCD) was conducted in our work. First, the user objectives and activities were determined on interviews with the health care personnel of the clinic of "La Concordia". Managing the same language, and showing respect to the expertise of digital immigrants was a key aspect for latching their commitment to the success of the project.

For the development of the proposed EMR software, a work plan was established using the agile methodology XP (eXtreme Programming). We chose to use an agile methodology because we wanted to have a functional software to show to the potential users from the beginning of our work. The use of the XP methodology facilitated the adoption of an iterative and incremental development with emphasis in the continuous feedback of the user during the whole life cycle of the software.

After completing the implementation of the application, its usability was measured against the ISO/IEC 25010 quality standard features and according to the usability heuristics defined by Nielsen [7]. Experimental functional tests of our EMR software were performed in the medical center of "La Concordia" using data of actual patients.

This study was conducted with the participation of three experts in software development (see Table 3). Their names are not shown in the table because of personal data protection rights. The sample size corresponds to the criteria of the research group headed by Nielsen [1], who consider that the amount of experts participating in an usability test should be, no more than five, or less than three. In their research, Barnum et al. concluded that at least the 75% of usability issues are detected with this sample size. Moreover, the amount of usability issues detected do not increase with more experts involved in the study but the difficulty to solve discrepancies among them [1]. The heuristic evaluation was carried out using a questionnaire with 19 questions about the acceptance of the developed system. These questions were based on the usability heuristics of Nielsen [7] and on its enhancement, recently proposed by Ripalda et al., that established a linkage with Gestalt principles of human perception [14].

The validation of our proposal also included a usability test for which five digital immigrants, as potential users of our EMR software, filled out the System Usability Scale questionnaire of ten questions. Table 4 shows demographic data of the participants in this part of the experimental evaluation of our proposal.

Table 2. Characterization of related solutions found in the international arena.

Sol.	Description	Platform
[11]	OpenEMR is an open-source application for managing medical practice and free electronic clinical records. It is certified by the ONC (Office of the National Coordinator for Health Information Technology) and includes completely-integrated, electronic medical records; medical practice management, appointment scheduling, electronic invoicing, internationalization, free support, a vibrant community and much more	It can run on Windows, Linux and Mac OS X, because it is based on PHP and MySQL
[18]	VistA (Veterans Health Information Systems and Technology Architecture) is the most used EHR (Electronic Health Record) in the USA. It has a high compatibility with many clinic environments and healthcare systems. VistA is public and it is available free of charge, in correspondence with the Freedom of Information Act (FOIA) of the USWorldVistA [18]	The software is programmed in M programming language, uses a YottaDB database server on a Linux SO
[9]	New Open source Health Charting System (Nosh) is a free open source charting system and electronic medical record	This system is programmed in PHP, with a MySQL database, and an Apache web server. jQuery library and HTML5 are used in the implementation of the client interface. Nosh is open source with GNU licence (GPLv3)
[18]	Solismed is an open source EMR software that manages the medical records and patient data. Solismed has artificial intelligence features that contributes to the management of medical records, notifying when any test is recommended	Solismed was developed using LAMP (Linux, Apache, MySQL y PHP). Data of patients are ciphered for protection of personal data
[8]	Nimbo is another EMR software optimized for simple searches over data. Nimbo is integrated with Medi-Span and UptoDate technologies; this way, it allows a more robust management of medications. Additionally, the application has monographs of more than 3.000 drugs and products [8]. Nimbo implements a Telehealth option, which consists of virtual medical appointments that take place over a teleconference with high quality of video and audio	Nimbo is a paid service. No access to the actual code is available. With Telehealth, Nimbo receives 5% per medical virtual medical appointment
[15]	SML is a web EMR software of any medical specialty. SML is a payed application with different payment plans from $25.00 USD per month for small medical offices, up to premium plans for big hospitals thay pay $260.00 USD per month	SML is programmed using PHP language. No further information about used technologies in its construction is available at its web site
[5]	MediCloud is an EMR software in the cloud. The platform offers the possibility of connecting to different providers for the automation of service processes and to be part of a scientific Latin-American community. MediCloud offers its services with a payed plan of $ 19.99 USD per month and practitioner through a web platform	The platform was presented by Microsoft as a success example in Latin America. MediCloud was developed using Azure, a cloud computing platform provided by Microsoft

Table 3. Experts involved in the validation of our EMR software.

Id	Evaluator	Title	Experience (years)
1	Eng. X	IT Engineer	14
2	Eng. Y	IT Engineer	18
3	Eng. Z	IT Engineer	25

Table 4. Experts involved in the validation of our EMR software.

User	Sex	Age	Education
1	Masculine	52	College
2	Masculine	47	College
3	Feminine	32	High school
4	Masculine	65	College
5	Feminine	53	College

In the next section, the results of the implementation and validation of our EMR software are presented.

4 Characterization of the Proposed EMR Software

The EMR software we propose mainly complies with the data structure of ISO TC 215 [4] whilst its architecture is inspired in those open-source industrial initiatives for sharing medical records among different EMR software [11,18]. That is why, we take into account the interaction with third parties. The system architecture is shown in Fig. 1. This is a multi-user system; that is to say that all the medical staff may be using the system at the same time and the performance of the software will be not notably affected. It is also a multilevel system because users have different type of privileges: patient, doctor, nurse, assistant, and administrator.

As a result of the preliminary study of the behaviour of potential users of our EMR software, digital immigrants showed frustration if they had to wait for the software to respond. In such a situation, users used to click on the bottom for triggering the corresponding action several times instead of waiting for an answer, even when a message was notifying that the system was busy.

Because of this, we decided to make the client layer of the application as thin as possible. The decision of making use of *jquery.js* library against JS frameworks like Angular JS or React JS answers to the need of decreasing response time of the application for digital immigrants whilst the behaviour of the application is not affected.

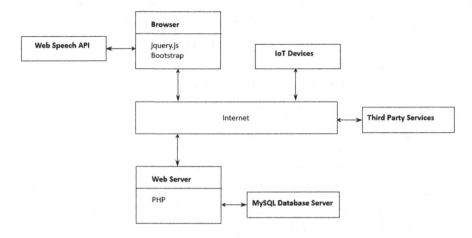

Fig. 1. Software architecture.

As part of the same preliminary study, different user interface layouts were considered but Bootstrap was the winning option. By using this CSS Framework in the implementation of our EMR software, we obtained a very simple user interface, extensively proven in the industry, with a responsive and natural look. Digital immigrant showed to value its simplicity and how intuitive its design is.

Below, we discuss our main practical contributions to the development of an EMR software, which differentiate our proposal from those that exist in the market.

4.1 Keeping the User in Control

Other EMR software implement a general search. Whilst this mechanism avoids the user to worry about defining the search fields, the amount of data which is retrieved decreases the usability of the application. One of the aspects digital immigrants value the most of the proposed EMR software is how easy it was to find any data record in the system using different criteria whislt they were always in control of what the system "was doing". Furthermore, once the user starts typing in an entry field, valid values are displayed, decreasing data entry errors. In Fig. 2, it is shown the user interface for locating a medical record by patient id or names.

When accessing the EMR software using a mobile device, the application automatically adapts to the physical characteristics of the device. Figure 3 shows the appearance of the same interface. Whilst the left menu contracts, it is evident that the user keeps in control easily knowing his/her exact location in the application and maximizing the area for data entry control.

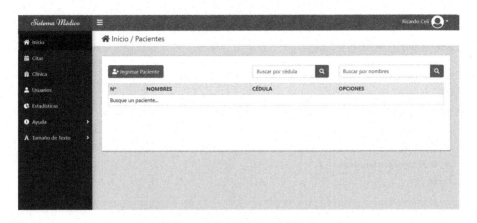

Fig. 2. Desktop interface appearance.

Fig. 3. Mobile interface appearance.

4.2 Minimizing Data Entry Errors

Another way to avoid data entry errors is by using interface components that do not require the user to type. Figure 4 shows how buttons, select controls and checkboxes are used for preventing user mistakes when entering data. Instead of using a keyboard, the user clicks or selects the options in the corresponding data form.

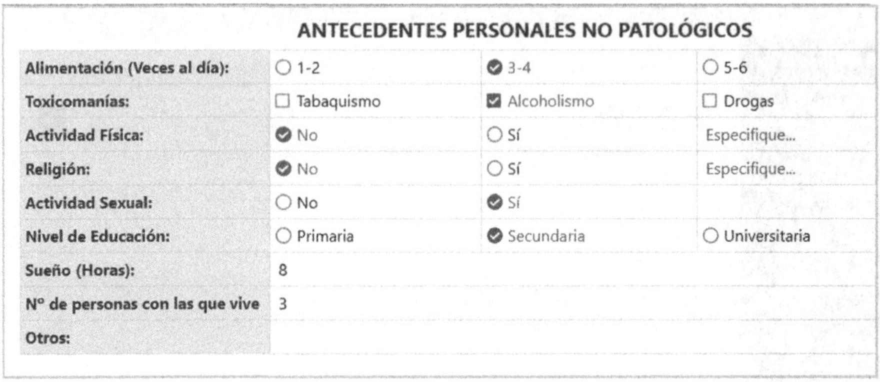

ANTECEDENTES PERSONALES NO PATOLÓGICOS		
Alimentación (Veces al día): ○ 1-2	● 3-4	○ 5-6
Toxicomanías: ☐ Tabaquismo	☑ Alcoholismo	☐ Drogas
Actividad Física: ● No	○ Sí	Especifique...
Religión: ● No	○ Sí	Especifique...
Actividad Sexual: ○ No	● Sí	
Nivel de Educación: ○ Primaria	● Secundaria	○ Universitaria
Sueño (Horas): 8		
N° de personas con las que vive 3		
Otros:		

Fig. 4. Data entry controls used in data entry forms.

4.3 Customizing Human-Computer Interface

The system also has the option for changing the font size of texts for users that have vision problems (they could be needing a bigger font size in the screen) or for users that need a broader view of data and requires to decrease font size. Figure 5 shows how the user may change font size any time just by pressing over a submenu option of the application. The preferences of the user are saved in the locale storage. This way, if this is the case, any user may have different configurations for different devices.

4.4 Customizing Human-Computer Interaction Mechanisms

Another feature added for facilitating the system use to the digital immigrant users is the voice dictation in forms where it is necessary to type a lot of text. The user can speak through the microphone and the voice recognition algorithm transforms the speech into text, as shown in Fig. 6.

Voice dictation was implemented by using the Web Speech API of JavaScript. This API provides the *SpeechRecognition* method which translates voice dictation into text in a very fast and effective way without needing any training of the algorithm.

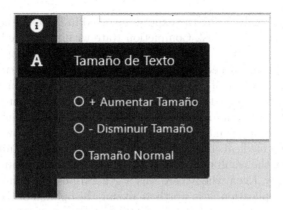

Fig. 5. Font size is easily customized by a submenu option of the proposed EMR software.

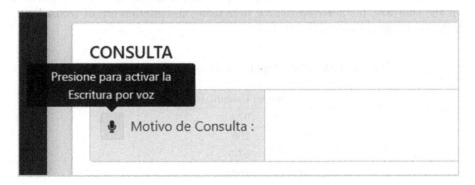

Fig. 6. Recording data entry into a text field of the application.

5   Analysis of Results

The proposed EMR software is being used at the medical center "La Concordia". This fact evidences the usability of the implemented EMR software against other solutions that exist in the market. A deeper analysis of the impact of its implementation follows, by analyzing the results of the experimental validation that we carried out after its implementation.

For quantifying the results of the heuristic evaluations based on experts criteria, the usability complying criteria was rated as follows: SI = 1 point, NO = 0 points, P = 0.5 points. The results of the evaluation of each expert, per heuristic, were accumulated and a Total Usability of the System of 93% was determined as the average value. The experts were consulted in a second phase of the experiment and they all agreed with the accuracy of this value.

Talking about the user tests, they were performed in a controlled scenario. Each participant received the assignment of tasks and time of their completion was recorded and analyzed by the experts involved in the experiment. The user tests resulted in a 96% of Task Completion Rate within expected time.

Meanwhile, the result of applying the SUS questionnaires for evaluating the usability of the system turned out into a 91.5% of acceptance by consulted digital immigrants. The number of digital immigrants participating in the study was chosen taking into account the opinion of Nielsen, who consider that a number between 5 and 9 participants is the correct number of participants in an expert evaluation [7]. This decision takes into account also that this software was mainly designed for small medical clinics in which five physicians is a significant number.

Table 5 shows the results for each of the five digital immigrants that participated in the study. Even when there was a general positive consensus with the usability of the application, it is worth analyzing the opinion of the digital immigrant that gave the lowest score for usability. It is important to mention that this specific result was attributed to the interference of technology in a human-centered health care service, and this is just an argument difficult to contest. On the contrary, further research for decreasing the interference of technology in the examination process is needed.

Table 5. Results of applying the SUS questionnaire.

Id	Score	Usability (%)
1	39	97.5
2	40	100
3	27	67.5
4	40	100
5	37	92.5

6   Conclusions

The contributions of this work are twofold. Firstly, with this work, any medical institution can now access valuable information that may help when making a decision about the automation of their processes. After the analysis of existing EMR software in the local and international arena, we conclude that tailor-made solutions characterize the local scenario whilst open source implementations looking for a standard way to share information among health care institutions are embraced in the international arena. None of the EMR solutions we found focus on making easier the use of EMR software by digital immigrants.

Secondly, an open source EMR software with an user interface conceived specifically for digital immigrants was implemented and it is now in exploitation in a local medical center with successful results. The design of this EMR software took into account the ISO TC 215 and its use is extensible to other small clinics. Finally, it is worth mentioning that the heuristic validation of the proposal resulted in a 93% of acceptance whilst function tests were successful 96% of times. Besides, the result of a SUS test with the participation of five digital immigrants turn out in a 91.5% of system usability.

Future work includes the use of biometric authentication for discouraging the use of a password that could be hard to remember even for a digital native, whilst typing would be even more discouraged. Another future research area includes the use of IoT technology for decreasing the interference of the EMR software during the examination process.

References

1. Barnum, C., Bevan, N., Cockton, G., Nielsen, J., Spool, J., Wixon, D.: The "magic number 5": is it enough for web testing? In: Conference on Human Factors in Computing Systems - Proceedings, pp. 698–699 (2003). https://doi.org/10.1145/765891.765936
2. Baumgart, D.C.: Digital advantage in the covid-19 response: perspective from canada's largest integrated digitalized healthcare system. NPJ Digit. Med. **3**(1), 1–4 (2020). https://doi.org/10.1038/s41746-020-00326-y
3. González, A.: Sistema informático para la gestión de las historias clínicas en los estudios de imagen médicas del laboratorio clínico Cedylabe en la provincia de Santo Domingo de los Tsáchilas durante el período 2017–2018. B.S. Thesis, Universidad Católica del Ecuador, Santo Domingo, Ecuador (2018)
4. ISO: Iso tc 215 (2020). http://www.himss.org/ASP/topics_ISO.asp
5. mediCloud: Medicloud - software gratuito para clínicas médicas (2020). https://medicloud.me/
6. Morales, A.: Análisis y diseño de un sistema de gestión de historias clínicas para pacientes del centro de salud Pachitea. B.S. Thesis, Universidad de Piura, Piura, Peru (2015)
7. Nielsen, J.: Usability inspection methods. In: Conference Companion on Human Factors in Computing Systems, pp. 413–414 (1994)
8. Nimbo: Software de expediente clínico electrónico moderno (2020). https://www.nimbo-x.com/clinical
9. Nosh: Nosh emr: Free, open source health charting system (2020). https://medevel.com/nosh-emr-open-source
10. Obando, G., Pérez, M.: Sistema informático para la gestión del proceso de historia clínica de los pacientes del hospital martin icaza de la ciudad de Babahoyo. B.S. Thesis, Universidad Técnica de Babahoyo, Babahoyo, Ecuador (2014)
11. openEMR: openEMR software official web page (2020). https://www.open-emr.org/
12. Gutarra, C., Quiroga, R.: Implementación de un sistema de historias clínicas electrónicas para el Centro de Salud Perú 3ra Zona. B.S. Thesis, Universidad de San Martín de Porres, Lima, Perú (2014)
13. Ramos, M.: Sistema informático para la gestión administrativa en el consultorio médico san gerardo de la ciudad de quevedo. Master's thesis, Universidad Regional Autónoma de los Andes, Ambato, Ecuador (2013)
14. Ripalda, D., Guevara, C., Garrido, A.: Relationship between gestalt and usability heuristics in mobile device interfaces. In: Karwowski, W., Ahram, T., Etinger, D., Tanković, N., Taiar, R. (eds.) IHSED 2020. AISC, vol. 1269, pp. 156–161. Springer, Cham (2021). https://doi.org/10.1007/978-3-030-58282-1_25

15. SML: Sml - software médico en línea (2020). https://smlmedico.com
16. Tapp, H., Ludden, T., Shade, L., Thomas, J., Mohanan, S., Leonard, M.: Electronic medical record alert activation increase hepatitis c and hiv screening rates in primary care practices within a large healthcare system. Prev. Med. Rep. **17**, 101036 (2020). https://doi.org/10.1016/j.pmedr.2019.101036
17. Villarruel, C.: Sistema de gestión para historias clínicas bajo la plataforma android orientado a los médicos del condominio del hospital millennium. B.S. Thesis, Universidad Técnica de Ambato, Ambato, Ecuador (2015)
18. worldVistA: Worldvista official web page (2020). http://worldvista.org/
19. Yoo, C.W., Huang, C.D., Goo, J.: Task support of electronic patient care report (epcr) systems in emergency medical services: an elaboration likelihood model lens. Inf. Manag. **57**(6), 103336 (2020). https://doi.org/10.1016/j.im.2020.103336

Ict and Creative Economy: An Analysis from Technology and Industry Enterprises 4.0, Bogota-Colombia Case

Camilo J. Peña Lapeira$^{(\boxtimes)}$ ⓘ and Liliana Vargas Puentes ⓘ

Corporación Universitaria Minuto de Dios, Bogotá, Colombia
{cjpena,Liliana.vargas}@uniminuto.edu

Abstract. In Colombia, creative and cultural industries are grouped within a sector called Orange Economy, which brings together industries such as technology, software development, information technology services. These companies are being promoted thanks to laws that favor their growth and expansion as well as the contribution of foreign investment capital. As a result of analysis, not only the impact on the country's GDP is evidenced, but the appearance of new business proposals within industry 4.0. This research proposal intends through documentary analysis and statistical analysis to show the economic impact that technology companies of order 4.0 have generated in the city of Bogota, arriving with their products in international markets as demanding as the USA and Spain, all this due to ICT and their participation in this process. As a result, it is found that not only the investment in money is necessary, but that human capital and its preparation accompany the process.

Keywords: Industry 4.0 · Creative economy · IT services · Digital business · Collaborative networks · IT training

1 Introduction

In Colombia, creative and cultural industries are grouped within a sector called Orange Economy, which brings together industries such as technology, software development, information technology services, audiovisual, film, television, performing arts, fashion, entertainment, and advertising, among others, whose dividends generate income for Bogota for more than US $ 1,250 million per year, which places this sector as one of the fastest-growing in the city, directly impacting the production of assets and services.

In Bogota, 72% of companies in the orange economy are mostly concentrated in activities related to software & IT, graphic communication, clothing, and gastronomy; This is mainly since 73% of digital content companies, 55% of video game creation studios and 65% of graphic communication companies across the country are located in the city [1].

The theme of 4.0 industries is especially enhanced in the field of animation, videogames, music, media, artificial intelligence, innovation and entrepreneurship, as

M. Botto-Tobar et al. (Eds.): ICAT 2020, CCIS 1388, pp. 69–79, 2021.
https://doi.org/10.1007/978-3-030-71503-8_6

a fundamental part of the rise of the creative and technological industry, based on the example of large companies' internationals such as Pixar, Disney, Marvel, Coursera, Cartoon Network, IBM, among many others that today move billions of dollars around the world.

This industry represents the case of the Information Technology (IT) sector, in the last 20 years, it has developed complete infrastructure remote management services through the implementation of collaborative networks, as well as the development and maintenance of applications for software for companies from different economic sectors that include the main industries [2].

The 4.0 industries are an example of how the new business models not only energize the market but also mark the path of new trends and innovation, enabling real-time exchange of information between all the actors involved in the process or that participate in the value chain, this through integration platforms designed for this purpose or the conversion of existing applications such as social networks into collaboration tools [3].

This is how the abundance in trained human resources and the first quality technological infrastructure have generated the right environment so that several local and multinational companies recognized in different mainly technological sectors have chosen Bogota as an offshore platform or platform to serve external markets.

The main business lines are software development, IT consulting, web design and development, electronic commerce, financial products and services, government and logistics, are the sectors that most demand services, leading that industry to export more than 244 million a year dollars, taking into the main US destinations. EE. UU., Ecuador, Spain, and Mexico [4].

This research proposal intends through documentary analysis to show the economic impact that technology companies of order 4.0 have generated from the creative economy to the transformation processes of the central region of Colombia, especially in the city of Bogota and the contribution that it's the national consolidated company is represented in the GDP, as an example of the influence of collaborative networks in the development of the region and as an emerging business alternative.

On the other hand, it also aims to show that the growth of this type of industry has depended mainly on the advancement of Information and Communication Technologies (ICT), and on the increase in the academic offer in programs that promote their growth and development.

1.1 Foreign Investment in Colombia

Colombia can be made through [5], contemplating a special chapter related to the technology industry, arguing that the contribution in kind of intangible assets to the capital of a company, such as technological contributions, trademarks, and patents whose exercise or exploitation can obtain economic benefits, susceptible to amortization or depreciation, which according to Colombian accounting standards, are considered under this type of investment.

The process also involves the registration in the country of said investment through the completion of the "Declaration of Exchange for International Investments", processed before the Bank of the Republic [6].

- According to the exchange balance of the Banco de la República, the arrival of foreign capital to the country reached 2,255.8 million dollars.
- 82.5% corresponded to resources that were invested in the oil, hydrocarbons and mining sectors, that is, 1,861.5 million dollars.

An example of this is that in the first quarter of 2019, foreign direct investment, according to the exchange balance of the Banco de la República, reached US 2,255.8 million, represented in sectors such as construction, electricity, water, and gas; electronic and traditional commerce, restaurants and hotels; transport and manufacturing, among others, where for the first time the representation of 4.0 industries appears as captors of much of that capital [7].

Bogota is one of the Latin American cities with the most greenfield investment attracted in creative industries, between 2007 and 2017 (Fig. 1), this mainly due to the confidence that the country gives to investors and the support that different government entities give to investment processes [8].

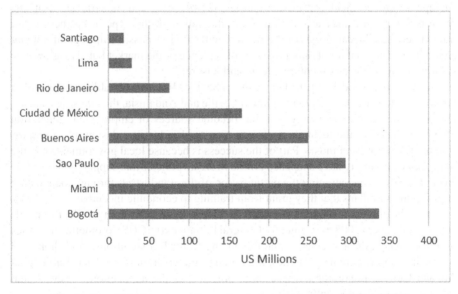

Fig. 1. Greenfield investment in creative industries, between 2007 and 2017

1.2 Background

Undoubtedly Spain represents one of the role models in terms of harnessing the potential present in the creative industries, with more than 20 years in the process of legal support, entrepreneurship potentization and adaptation to the digital era with the support of collaborative networks, without a doubt it represents a milestone for the sector, proof of this is the countless research that demonstrates its contribution to the analysis of the sector; in contrast to the Colombian case, it is hardly an incipient industry but with a lot of potentials.

In the research carried out in the city of Madrid [9], the debate is created between what is considered creative industry based on the various definitions of public and private entities at local and international level, and the concept of creativity and people creative from the bibliographic analysis and the review of the fieldwork it is identified that in the Spanish territory the creative industry, focused on cultural aspects, has been centralized in sectors near the center and the airport, this associated with the population characteristics, which allow sectors More residential and tourist.

From this, consider the term "creative cities" that encompasses the agglomeration of industries and people who work for the creative and cultural industry and are located in the sectors that must have the needs of this creative class to attract them and improve their economic development.

We discuss the concept of creativity exemplified in the case analyzed in the San Fernando Market of the City of Madrid, which is initially a central supply, and under the economic crisis of 2008, many were closing of its businesses and after several attempts by government and private entities, the recovery and modernization of this space is controlled, surgically the reflection that although this type of business is not framed between the categories of the creative industry, it is possible through of implant creativity finding that it not only preserves the essence of the market but also allows the incorporation of spaces for entertainment and leisure.

In the study carried out by the University of Seville [10], it was established that within the area of Metropolitan Agglomeration of Seville and Andalusia, the industries that are related to the creative economy and that become sources of employment generation They are related to the technological sector, cultural industries, design, photography, cinema, television, and music. Part of the success is because local governments and the European Community have deepened efforts to create policies that support and favor the creative industry, encouraging the participation of these industries through the creation of programs and plans that they grant from training to economic incentives.

From the public universities, the work developed by the University of Seville stands out, who created in 2008 the Center for Cultural Initiatives (CICUS), promoting activities of music, dance, theater, cinema, and organizing festivals, exhibitions, workshops and competitions in different specialties, highlighting the creation of the CicusLab Digital Art and Culture Laboratory, whose main objective is the application of new digital technologies to arts and culture [6].

One of the first scenarios in which the creative and cultural industries were considered was leisure, considering the space considering it as the social time/space for cultural manifestations, which will be changing according to each territory and its social relations, which entails that cultural and creative industries promote transformations in terms of values, personal preferences, lifestyles, leisure, and work, as well as the consumption profile [11], It is there that industry 4.0 gains strength by entering into a solution to these needs of the territory, through consumer products, where they would be mostly impossible without the contribution of technology.

The orange economy in Colombia has been potentiating in recent years, taking on an important role in the economy, proof of this is its participation in the GDP that is increasing every time. Concerning sustainability, the orange economy offers the possibility of involving the generation of ideas and knowledge that are adapted to the millennium changes when considering social and environmental variables for the implementation of creative and innovative ideas that allow the recovery and use of natural and cultural territories, as well as the potentization of education as a fundamental engine of the transformation and development of sustainable territories [12].

2 Materials and Method

The methodology used in this study consists of four phases, elaboration of the state of the art, construction of quantitative indicators, elaboration and application of documentary analysis instruments and analysis of the results, always preserving scientific integrity, counting on intellectual honesty, adhering to ethical codes, with transparency since there is no type of conflict or interest in such environment [13].

It is a descriptive/comparative cross-sectional study that includes the period from 2005 to 2019, based on the figures of gross domestic product, foreign investment and the contribution of creative industries to GDP; On the other hand, the data of the Colombian Ministry of Education regarding the academic offer that enhances the creation of 4.0 companies and the satisfaction of skilled labor for this type of industry are taken into account.

The historical-logical method is used for bibliographic compilation and documentary analysis on the impact of the creative economy since industry 4.0 on the country's economy. It is directed from the mixed category approach [14], who affirm that this type of educational research is molded into three elements: the conceptualization and operationalization of the variables; the degree of intervention or application by the researcher, and the nature of the objectives (contrast, describe, assess, improve).

The research instruments that were used during the research process are summarized in:

- Bibliographic matrix of documentary analysis
- Specialized analytical summaries for the construction of the theoretical framework and state of the art for the business characterization process
- Checklist and observation to document the value creation processes
- Interview format with experts on the subject
- Comparative matrix of triangulation of results

3 Results and Discussions

The existence of a growing relationship between creative economies and the economy is raised, taking up the theories of endogenous economic growth. It reflects the importance of human capital, processes of specialization, consumption, and diversity of products, where they propose a model of digital industries, all this based on the theory of endogenous growth, taking into account clusters and complementary economies, whose hypothesis to test It is if the use of technology industries as a propelling factor of the economy.

It should be taken into account then the academic offer in programs that are directly related to the development of ICT and computer systems such as programming, hardware development, mechatronics, among other related areas, become potentializing instruments for the development of Industry 4.0, concentrating their development then towards areas where there is a greater academic offer.

When analyzing the data presented by the National Information System of Higher Education in to 2019 [16], it was found that Bogota has the highest academic offer in higher education programs that range from undergraduate to doctoral level, which becomes a city attractive to the study, thus enhancing the possibility of improving training options in the workforce (Fig. 2).

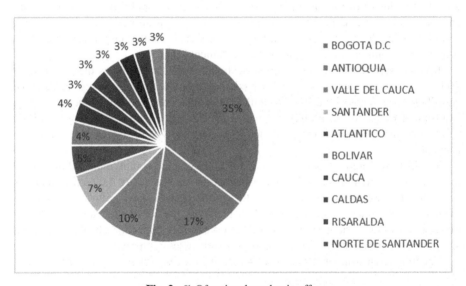

Fig. 2. % Of national academic offer

Of the total programs offered in Bogota, the largest number of these are related to Information Technology, Engineering, telematics, international business, digital marketing and related, which are the areas that feed the processes of shaping digital companies based on new technologies and innovative proposals (Fig. 3).

The Colombian Software and Information Technology market for the year 2019 was ranked as the fourth largest in Latin America, surpassed only by Brazil, Mexico, and Argentina. The combined figures from the World Bank, the ICT Ministry, and the DANE agree that, during the last 10 years, the IT market has grown at a rate of 18%; The software sector has grown 19.1% and IT services have grown 15.4%. The manufacturing industry has the highest demand for software in Colombia. Across the country, the media industry is the largest demand for ICT services, so in recent years sales have doubled to reach more than 9,500 million dollars [16].

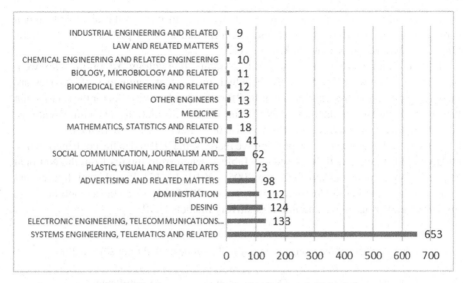

Fig. 3. Total programs offer by basic core ob Knowledge

This contrasts with the national trend of graduates in similar or related careers that has led to the increase of the competent workforce to meet the development needs of industry 4.0 (Fig. 4), trying to corroborate the theory that, at a higher level of education, the workforce increases, so it will tend to the biggest growth trend in the industry.

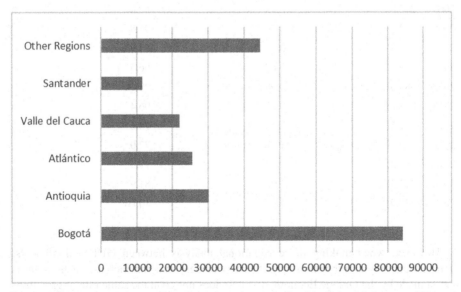

Fig. 4. Graduates in systems engineering, telematics, and related in Colombia between 2001 and 2016

Large-scale software projects are developed due, in part, to the abundant human capital of Bogota, in which the most relevant corporate software platforms such as SAP, ORACLE, Microsoft, or IBM dominate [16].

It should be taken into account that the Mature Technology Adoption Index went from 26 to 55 between 2015 and 2017, which means that companies of all sizes are increasingly aware of the importance of ICT for their productivity; As for the sectors that have best adopted mature technologies, they have been information and communications, education, financial activities, health, construction, and real estate activities.

This has to be reflected in the progressive increase in GDP and in the contribution that creative industries make to it, as seen in Table 1, wherefrom figures from the National Statistics Department - DANE between 2005 – 2019 [16, 17], World Bank figures and figures of the Chamber of Commerce of Bogota of 2019 [18], it can be corroborated that this increase is progressive and that it positively impacts GDP.

Table 1. Share of the orange economy to the national GDP from 2014 to 2019

Year	GDP colombia thousand million USD	Orange economy contribution thousands of millions USD	Contribution of bogota to GDP thousands of millions USD
2005	146,6	1,16	39,0
2006	162,6	0,98	43,3
2007	207,4	0,87	55,0
2008	244,0	0,74	64,4
2009	233,8	0,73	62,0
2010	287,0	0,70	75,8
2011	335,4	0,66	87,9
2012	369,7	0,65	96,5
2013	380,2	0,68	98,1
2014	378,2	0,87	96,4
2015	291,5	1,17	74,6
2016	280,1	1,18	72,0
2017	309,2	1,03	79,5
2018	317,5	1,01	81,9
2019	328,0	1,04	105,0

However, when making the correlational analysis between GDP Colombia vs. Orange Economy Contribution (Fig. 5), it is evident that the increase in the contribution made by the Orange Economy to GDP does not go at the same rate of growth of this, its rhythm it is a little smaller, supported by the correlation coefficient Correl (x, y) = −0.358235176, indicating a slight correlation between them.

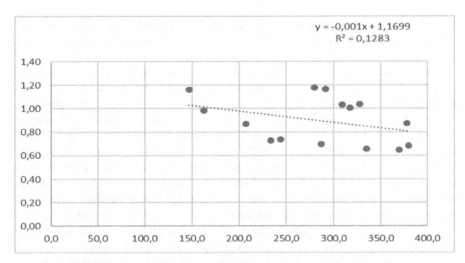

Fig. 5. Correlation GDP colombia vs orange economy contribution

When analyzing the actors of a public nature, it is identified what their tendency is towards digital markets, technology, fashion and entertainment, is a company that has emerged from entrepreneurial ideas and through participation in events Government and academics, however, depending on the development and investment they receive, they become sustainable companies or not, achieving growth and even opening up to foreign markets.

Concerning the creative economy in Latin America, it is identified that there are five (5) countries that have established policies that frame said economy: Argentina, Brazil, Chile, Colombia, and Cuba, however, there is still a tendency to only measure of these industries through their participation in the GDP and the generation of employment, omitting other variables that can help to measure the impact at socioeconomic level such as quality of life, community impact, Research & Development processes, innovation indices, Among other factors and conditions of the actors they support are industries [11].

The activity that contributed most to the growth was that of functional creations, with 61.3%, a group made up of the digital media, software, design and advertising segments [19].

4   Conclusions

It is presumed that the creative economy stimulates job creation and promotes a new economic model, through social-institutional cooperation networks that are integrated through public and private institutions [10].

This contrasts with the fact that the behavior of the Research and Development budget designated by the national government in the last 10 years, it was found that only 0.19% of the national budget was allocated for this purpose, so it is concluded that the lack of investment In this regard, the creative industry is not potentialized to the level that the market expects and generates better results contributing in greater proportions to GDP, which leads to the proposal of the creation of public policy and government plans that point to the support of The orange economy.

The increase of the academic offer in programs related to technology, innovation, creativity, electronic commerce, networks, telematics and at the end, has made the concentration of 4.0 industries be Bogotá, so much of the contribution to GDP originates in this area, representing a disadvantage to the other regions due to excessive concentration.

It is evident that the participation of ICT-related industries is higher in Bogota than in other regions of the country, this is initially because Colombian companies are weaving communication processes for the improvement of processes within them and these They are more cohesive in Bogotá because there is much more local development due to the existence of local public policies that promote it. ICTs have transformed the local industry, empowered industries 4.0, and improved technology transfer processes.

It is possible to determine that the impact of creative companies on GDP is still quite low and does not progress at the same rate as GDP does, much of this is due to variations in economic behaviors such as the Dollar and the initial start-up of support plans for the orange economy that are still in the takeoff phase.

Finally, the companies associated with the orange economy have a high potential for long-term development which would be reflected in a greater participation in the GDP, it was also possible to identify which industries such as game and toy manufacturing and production and distribution of films and videotapes, they must implement innovative strategies to improve their added value and boost the orange economy [20].

Reference

1. Garay, S.: Economía naranja colombiana en tiempos modernos. Ploutos, **7**(2), 34–41 (2018). https://journal.universidadean.edu.co/index.php/plou/article/view/1873
2. MinTIC, O.T.: Observatorio de TI-MinTIC. Caracterización del sector de Teleinformática, Software y TI en Colombia 2015 (2015). https://colombiatic.mintic.gov.co/679/articles-73973_recurso_1.pdf
3. Basco, A.I., Beliz, G., Coatz, D., Garnero, P.: Industria 4.0: Fabricando el Futuro. Inter-American Development Bank (2018). https://doi.org/10.18235/0001229
4. Portafolio. Industria del 'software' crecería 19% en el (2018). https://www.portafolio.co/neg ocios/industria-del-software-creceria-19-en-el-2018-517332
5. Presidencia de la República. DECRETO 2080 DE 2000, art 5 (2000). https://www.cancilleria. gov.co/sites/default/files/Normograma/docs/decreto_2080_2000.htm
6. Banco de la República. Inversión extranjera directa en Colombia (2012). https://www.banrep. gov.co/docum/Lectura_finanzas/pdf/ce_dcin_inversionextranjera.pdf
7. Presidencia de la República. En el primer trimestre de 2019, la inversión extranjera creció 23,3% (2019). https://id.presidencia.gov.co/Paginas/prensa/2019/190416-En-el-primer-trimestre-de-2019-la-inversion-extranjera-crecio-23-3.aspx
8. Invest in Bogotá. Industrias Creativas (2019). https://es.investinbogota.org/sites/default/files/ 2018-07/FS-IndustriasCreativas-esp-2018.pdf
9. Prada, T.J.: El debate de la creatividad y la economía en las ciudades actuales y el papel de los diferentes actores: algunas evidencias a partir del caso de estudio de Madrid. Investigaciones geográficas, Boletín, 87, 62–75 (2015). https://doi.org/10.14350/rig.40700

10. Caravana, I., Gonzalez, G., Salinas, V., García, A.: Economía creativa en la aglomeración metropolitana de sevilla: agentes, redes locales de colaboración y principales actuaciones. Boletín de la Asociación de Geógrafos Españoles (2013). https://doi.org/10.21138/bage. 1607, https://www.researchgate.net/publication/327945815_Economia_creativa_en_la_agl omeracion_metropolitana_de_Sevilla_agentes_redes_locales_de_colaboracion_y_princip ales_actuaciones

11. Gomes, C.: La economía creativa y las industrias culturales y creativas: ¿una alternativa pos-capitalista?. XV Coloquio Internacional de Geocrítica Las ciencias sociales y la edificación de una sociedad post-capitalista Barcelona, 7–12 de mayo de 2018. (2018) https://www.ub. edu/geocrit/XV-Coloquio/ChristianneGomes.pdf

12. Duque-Escobar, G.: De la economía marrón a la naranja (2018). https://bdigital.unal.edu.co/ 62321/7/delaeconomiamarronalanaranja.pdf

13. Lamas, S., y Ayuso, C.: La integridad científica como fundamento esencial de la investigación clínica: Fundamentos éticos y aspectos prácticos. In: Dal-Re, R., Carné, X., Gracia, D., (Eds.), Luces y sombras de la investigación clínica, pp. 23-38 (2014). https://www.fundaciogrifols. org/documents/4662337/4688901/cap1.pdf/005378c6-3ab6-4853-86f8-f8eae74e6df3

14. Rodríguez, D., Valldeoriola, J.: Metodología de la investigación. Universidad O. de Cataluña, España (2007)

15. Mineducación.   Información   (2018).   www.mineducacion.gov.co   ›   articles-212400_recurso_24XLS

16. República, L.: Transformación digital, clave para perdurar en el futuro (2019). https://www.lar epublica.co/alta-gerencia/transformacion-digital-clave-para-perdurar-en-el-futuro-2934476

17. DANE. Economía Naranja, Primer reporte 2019 (2019). https://www.dane.gov.co/files/inv estigaciones/pib/sateli_cultura/economia-naranja/1er-reporte-economia-naranja-2014-2018. pdf

18. DANE. Economía Naranja, Segundo Reporte 2014 – 2018 (2018). https://www.dane.gov.co/ index.php/estadisticas-por-tema/cultura/economia-naranja

19. Cámara de comercio de Bogotá. Colombia incentiva las industrias creativas con la Ley Naranja (2017). https://www.ccb.org.co/Sala-de-prensa/Noticias-Fortalezca-su-empresa/ 2017/Junio/Colombia-incentiva-las-industrias-creativas-con-la-Ley-Naranja#:~:text=A% 20prop%C3%B3sito%20de%20la%20Ley,tener%20unidades%20productivas%20m%C3% A1s%20competitivas%E2%80%9D

20. DANE. Dane reveló que las industrias de la Economía Naranja en Bogotá crecieron 1,4% en 2018 (2019). https://id.presidencia.gov.co/Paginas/prensa/2019/Dane-revelo-que-las-ind ustrias-de-la-Economia-Naranja-en-Bogota-crecieron-1-4-en-2018-190926.aspx

21. Jiménez, I.F., Millán, M.F., y Suárez, D.F.: Efecto del valor agregado del consumo cultural: una aproximación a la economía naranja en Colombia. Revista Ploutos **7**(2), 4–11 (2017). https://journal.universidadean.edu.co/index.php/plou/article/view/1870

Assessment of Two-Equation RANS Turbulence Models for High Prandtl Number Forced Convection in a Pipe

Paul S. Balcazar[✉] [iD]

The University of Manchester, Manchester M13 9PL, UK
paul.balcazarcastellanos@postgrad.manchester.ac.uk

Abstract. Turbulent, high Prandtl number (Pr), flows are widely used in industries such as automotive, renewable energy, among others. Additionally, Computational Fluid Dynamics (CFD) has a growing role in the design process, making the study of high-Pr fluids, in this scope, increasingly relevant. RANS models are computationally cheaper methods that can meet industry needs; however, their reliability for high-Pr flows requires further research.

The present work numerically investigated high-Pr pipe convection using k-ε with Enhanced Wall Treatment and k-ω Shear Stress Transport (SST) RANS turbulence models. The objective of the study was to assess model performance when applied to high-Pr flows (6.7, 18.7, 24) over the Reynolds number (Re) range $7 \times 10^3 <$ Re $< 85 \times 10^3$. Thermal predictions were validated against experimental data, while models were compared in terms of mean temperature profiles and Nusselt number (Nu) results.

Good results were obtained at the two highest Pr when compared to experimental data, while large errors were produced at Pr $= 6.7$. These discrepancies are explained by differences in mean temperature profiles between models, which were more appreciable at high Pr and low Re. On the other hand, as Re increases, they converge into a single profile.

Overall, better results were obtained with k-ε at the lower Pr, while k-ω increased in accuracy at higher Pr. Performance improved for both models as Re increased. Furthermore, the k-ω SST model showed high variability as a function of the near-wall cell y^+ at high Pr, high Re, flows; thus, caution is suggested when dealing with such flow conditions.

Keywords: Forced convection · High Prandtl number · Pipe flow · RANS · Turbulence modelling

1 Introduction

High Prandtl (Pr) working fluids in industrial applications are widely used. Heat transfer oils (Pr ≈ 100) are used in electrical devices, while engine oils (Pr ≈ 1000) are used in internal combustion engines [1]. Additionally, over the last decade the use of molten salts as the working fluid of nuclear reactors has increased, as well as solar farms and thermal storage facilities.

© Springer Nature Switzerland AG 2021
M. Botto-Tobar et al. (Eds.): ICAT 2020, CCIS 1388, pp. 80–95, 2021.
https://doi.org/10.1007/978-3-030-71503-8_7

A high Pr results from low thermal conductivity (k), and high viscosity (μ). Therefore, high-Pr fluids have a smaller conduction-dominant region—the Conduction Sublayer—compared to low-Pr fluids. The majority of the temperature gradient resultant from heat transfer occurs in this region. Thus, convection heat transfer with high-Pr fluids is dominated by thermal transport through fluid motion. Conversely, flows of low-Pr fluids, such as liquid metals, are dominated by conduction heat transfer.

1.1 Problem Definition

Advances in computational power have allowed Computational Fluid Dynamics (CFD) to take a central role in the engineering design process, with numerous approaches available for solving turbulent flows. Direct Numerical Simulation (DNS) fully resolves the governing equations down to the smallest turbulent structures, resulting in the most accurate simulation of a fluid dynamics problem. However, the computational cost associated with this approach restricts the types of flows that can be studied. The computational expense can be reduced by utilizing spatial filters. To this end, Large Eddy Simulation (LES) applies models to the smallest eddies, while fully resolving larger turbulent structures.

Solving high-Pr flows numerically requires high grid resolution in the near wall region to compute the heat transfer occurring in the Conduction Sublayer. This entails high computational requirements and limits the application of DNS and LES. On the other hand, Reynolds Averaged Navier Stokes (RANS) turbulence models compromise some of the accuracy and detail of turbulence simulations to become computationally accessible. This is achieved by modelling instantaneous turbulent motions and calculating, instead, time-averaged results.

The chosen geometry for this study is turbulent pipe convection, which is one of the most common applications in mechanical engineering, present in heat exchangers, heating, ventilation and cooling, piping systems, among others. The high grid resolution required to fully resolve high-Pr flows poses a limitation. Turbulence models and wall functions can be applied to model the near wall region and reduce the necessary gird refinement; however, their reliability for high-Pr fluids requires further study. Ensuring the accuracy of numerical approaches is essential to fuel innovation through CFD.

1.2 Literature Review

Pipe convection has been widely studied experimentally to understand the governing physical phenomena. For instance, [2] investigated turbulent flow in an electrically heated pipe using various concentrations of ethylene glycol ($2 < Pr < 40$ and $5 \times 10^3 < Re < 3 \times 10^5$). The authors concluded Re and Pr have a positive relation to the resulting Nusselt number (Nu). On the other hand, a lower heat transfer coefficient (h) is obtained from higher Pr flows.

Turbulence damping in the near wall region for fluid with $5 < Pr < 3000$ was investigated by [3]. The study concluded that the effects of kinematic viscosity—for high-Pr fluids—cannot be neglected, as it reduces eddy diffusivity in the Viscous Sublayer. Furthermore, it was observed that Pr and Re reduce the thermal entry length of the flow. The results pertaining to a shorter thermal development region of higher Pr were confirmed by [4].

Turbulent pipe convection is a common case study in CFD; however, numerical studies of high-Pr fluids are less common because of the computational cost associated with resolving the thermal field using DNS or LES. The majority of available literature of this type of flow involves low-Re channel flow. Nevertheless, some studies of high-Pr pipe flow are presented below.

[5] investigated the accuracy of different k-ε turbulence models on flows with 10^{-2} < Pr < 5×10^4 and 10^4 < Re < 10^5. The authors point out that accurate estimation of the momentum eddy diffusivity is necessary for the prediction of the turbulent Prandtl number (Pr_t) and turbulent heat transfer. Overall, it is found that Pr_t has little effect on results, and a constant value is sufficient in flows of very high Pr.

Although high-Pr turbulent flows remain a challenge for Direct Numerical Simulation (DNS), [1] performed DNS of a heated pipe to compare with RANS simulations that use a P-function. For a given Re, higher Pr causes a steeper decrease in eddy diffusivity as the flow approaches the wall. In this region, the authors concluded, Pr_t should vary, as it affects the asymptotic behavior in the near-wall region.

1.3 Aims and Objectives

The present work aims to establish the applicability of RANS two-equation turbulence models for modelling high-Pr pipe convection. To this end, thermal predictions of two RANS turbulence models for cases of Pr > 1 are compared to assess their performance.

The objectives of this investigation are the following:

- Examine the Pr sensitivity of turbulent convection in a heated pipe, with a focus on high Prandtl number cases. Three Prandtl numbers are examined (24, 18.7, 6.7) over a range of Reynolds numbers (7×10^3 < Re < 85×10^3).
- Utilize a commercial CFD code to develop thermal predictions of high-Pr forced convection. ANSYS Fluent is used, and the numerical results are validated against experimental data from the literature, and well-established heat transfer correlations.
- Assess the performance of different turbulence models when applied to high-Pr convection problems. Two turbulence models are compared: k-ε with Enhanced Wall Treatment, and k-ω Shear Stress Transport (SST).

2 Methodology

2.1 Test Cases

The studied geometry is a pipe of circular cross section, based on the experimental apparatus utilized in [2]. For the purposes of the numerical computation, a two-dimensional axisymmetric domain is used, with constant heat flux at the wall and uniform inlet velocity and temperature, as depicted in Fig. 1. The flow conditions tested, over the range Pr = 6.7, 18.7, 24 and 7×10^3 < Re < 85×10^3, are presented in Table 1, in accordance with the experimental data available.

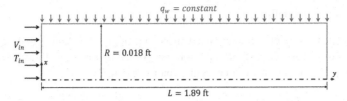

Fig. 1. Geometry and boundary conditions

Table 1. Flow conditions of investigated cases

Prandtl number (Pr)	Wall heat flux [BTU/hft^2] (q$_w$)	Inlet temperature [°F] (T$_{in}$)	Reynolds number (Re)
24	18,530	197	7,000
			10,000
			15,000
			20,000
			25,000
18.7	11,792	150	10,000
			17,000
			22,000
			25,000
			27,000
			33,000
6.7	45,484	143	17,000
			25,000
			42,000
			62,000
			85,000

2.2 Meshing

A structured grid with quadrilateral elements was applied to the fluid domain. As previously discussed, high-Pr fluids have a Conduction Sublayer completely immersed in the Viscous Sublayer, which extends to $y^+ \approx 5$. Thus, the near-wall cell was placed within $y^+ < 1$. Additionally, to accurately capture the steep temperature and velocity gradients in this region, a refinement factor was used in the radial direction. As Pr and Re affect the parameters used in calculating y^+, a new grid was generated for each test case.

2.3 Turbulence Modelling

k-ε Model. The k-ε model is the most used turbulence model. In addition to the governing equations, two additional transport equations are solved by this model: turbulent kinetic energy k (Eq. 1), and the rate of energy dissipation ε (Eq. 2).

$$\frac{\partial}{\partial t}(\rho k) + \nabla \cdot (\rho v k) = \nabla \cdot \left(\mu_{eff,k} \nabla k\right) + P_k - \rho \varepsilon \qquad (1)$$

$$\frac{\partial}{\partial t}(\rho \varepsilon) + \nabla \cdot (\rho v \varepsilon) = \nabla \cdot \left(\mu_{eff,\varepsilon} \nabla \varepsilon\right) + C_{\varepsilon 1} \frac{\varepsilon}{\kappa} P_k - C_{\varepsilon 2} \rho \frac{\varepsilon^2}{\kappa} \qquad (2)$$

The values of the constants, and definitions of the effective viscosities are available in the literature [6, 7]. This model assumes negligible molecular viscosity effects; therefore, it is best applied to high Re flows away from solid boundaries [8]. The assumptions of the k-ε model become invalid near the wall, where turbulent fluctuations, turbulent shear stress, and k, approach zero. This study uses Enhanced Wall Treatment, which models the variable profile between the wall and the first computational node.

k-ω Model. The k-ω model follows the same approach as the k-ε model, replacing ε with the transport equation for the internal thermal energy ω (Eq. 4). The model-specific equations are listed below, with values for the constants being available in the literature [7, 8].

$$\frac{\partial}{\partial t}(\rho k) + \nabla \cdot (\rho v k) = \nabla \cdot \left(\mu_{eff,k} \nabla k\right) + P_k - \beta^* \rho k \omega \qquad (3)$$

$$\frac{\partial}{\partial t}(\rho \omega) + \nabla \cdot (\rho v \omega) = \nabla \cdot \left(\mu_{eff,\omega} \nabla \omega\right) + C_{\alpha 1} \frac{\omega}{\kappa} P_k - C_{\beta 1} \rho \omega^2 \qquad (4)$$

In general, this model is considered more robust because it can be accurately applied in the vicinity of walls and is able to withstand adverse pressure gradients. Thus, k-ω is preferred when modelling of the Viscous Sublayer is important, as in the case of high-Pr flows [8].

2.4 Data Collection

Results from the numerical calculation were taken on a radial line at $x = 1.811$ ft, or $x/D = 50.3$. Two verification checks were performed: thermal development and mesh sensitivity.

Figure 2 exhibits the axial evolution of the thermal field in terms of the calculated Nu at $Pr = 18.7$, using the k-ε model. No changes in flow's thermal behavior indicate the data location is beyond the thermal entry region. This was confirmed for all test cases, using both turbulence models.

The numerical error associated with a discretization scheme is reduced with mesh refinement. A mesh independent solution is achieved when further grid refinement has no impact on the numerical result. A grid independent solution was reached for k-ε cases, but not for k-ω cases. This will be discussed further.

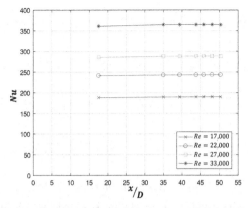

Fig. 2. Thermal development analysis for Pr = 18.7 using k-ε model

3 Results and Discussion

Thermal development and mesh sensitivity analyses were conducted as verification of the data gathered, while universal velocity profiles were produced to validate the correct modelling of the velocity field. Mean temperature profiles are shown to analyze the thermal predictions obtained from the CFD models. Finally, Nu predictions are compared to experimental data, available in [2], to evaluate the accuracy of the k-ε model with Enhanced Wall Treatment, and k-ω SST model.

3.1 Mesh Sensitivity

All k-ε solutions are mesh independent, as discussed in Sect. 2.4; however, the k-ω model exhibited a high sensitivity to the near-wall node placement. A spike in the result was observed as the mesh was refined. The magnitude of this variation increased with Pr and Re; hence, this behavior was further explored at higher Re, closer to those present in industrial applications (5×10^4 and 10^5). This is displayed in Fig. 3, where refinement in the radial direction is presented in terms of the near-wall cell y^+.

This variability calls into question the accuracy of this model in high-Pr, high-Re, flows, even in simple geometries such as pipe flow.

3.2 Mean Temperature Profile

The mean temperature profiles are plotted alongside the linear velocity profile near the wall (Eq. 5), and the logarithmic region (Eq. 6). The values of the constants are taken from [7]. This profile represents the case of Pr = 1, in which the momentum and thermal boundary layers are expected to have the same thickness.

$$U^+ = y^+ \tag{5}$$

$$U^+ = \frac{1}{\kappa} \ln y^+ + C \tag{6}$$

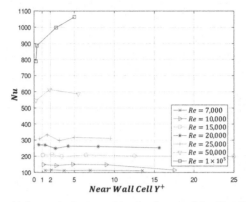

Fig. 3. Mesh sensitivity study for Pr = 24 using k-ω model with additional test cases

Turbulence Model Comparison. A comparison of the mean temperature profiles produced by both turbulence models highlights some differences in thermal modelling. As can be seen in Fig. 4 and Fig. 5, the k-ε model results in a higher temperature in the Log Region. This means the resulting Conduction Sublayer is thinner than the one obtained by the k-ω model. The difference between models decreases as Re increases. Moreover, this discrepancy is more apparent at higher Pr. Deviations in the profiles as the wall is approached may indicate a lack of mesh resolution in this region.

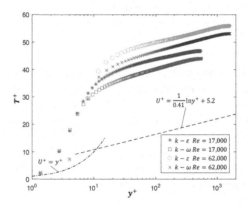

Fig. 4. Mean temperature profiles for Pr = 6.7

In contrast, a low-Pr fluid, such as air (Pr = 0.72), shows minimal variation between turbulence models, or Re (see Fig. 6).

Thus, it can be concluded that the k-ε model consistently predicts a higher mean temperature profile because of a thinner Conduction Sublayer. There is little difference between turbulence models at Pr = 0.72, but it increases with Pr. Similarly, at higher Pr, the difference caused by Re is more marked.

Reynolds Number Effects. In addition to the Re effects seen previously, the mean temperature profile shows a specific Re sensitivity. At higher Re, the magnitude of the

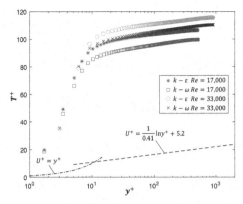

Fig. 5. Mean temperature profiles for Pr $= 18.7$

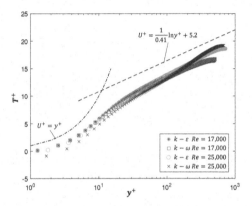

Fig. 6. Mean temperature profile for Pr $= 0.72$

temperature Log Region is greater. Higher flow velocities cause the thermal and velocity boundary layers to develop faster, making them thinner than at lower Re. Additionally, the Log Region begins at higher y^+ values and extends further into the y^+ range, as seen in Fig. 7.

Temperature profiles merge at $y^+ < 5$ with some deviations seen close to the wall. Although the near wall node of all meshes is placed at $y^+ \leq 1$, there may not be sufficient nodes within the boundary layer to adequately capture near-wall behavior.

The Re-induced behavior is maintained regardless of turbulence model. Nevertheless, the magnitude variation of T^+ is more pronounced when using the k-ω model (Fig. 8) compared to k-ε (Fig. 9). This tendency is seen at on all test cases.

Prandtl Number Effects. The Prandtl number represents the relation between the momentum and thermal boundary layer thicknesses. In the case of turbulent flow, this is observed as the size of the Conduction Sublayer relative to the Viscous Sublayer ($y^+ \approx 5$). The thickness of the Conduction Sublayer can be analyzed in terms of the ratio of thermal diffusivity ($^{\mu_t}/_{Pr_t}$) to molecular diffusivity ($^{\mu}/_{Pr}$). This parameter represents the ratio of turbulent heat flux to turbulent conduction; therefore, the Conduction

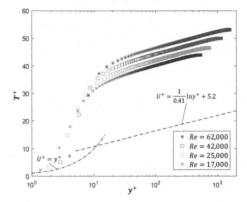

Fig. 7. Mean temperature profile for Pr = 6.7 using k-ω model

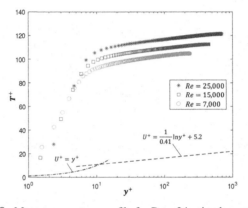

Fig. 8. Mean temperature profile for Pr = 24 using k-ω model

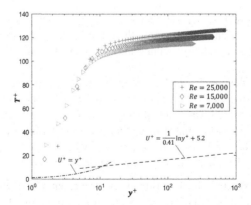

Fig. 9. Mean temperature profile for Pr = 24 using k-ε model

Sublayer is defined over the region where Eq. 7 holds true, and conduction is dominant.

$$\left(\mu_t/Pr_t \big/ \mu/Pr\right) < 1 \tag{7}$$

In fluids with $Pr < 1$, the Conduction Sublayer is thicker than the Viscous Sublayer. Conversely, fluids with $Pr > 1$ have Conduction Sublayers that develop within the Viscous Sublayer. This is exemplified in Fig. 10, where the region of dominant conduction reduces with Pr.

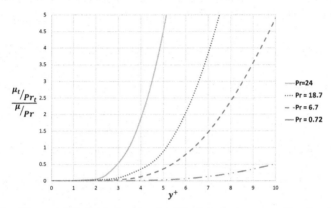

Fig. 10. Ratio of thermal diffusivity to molecular diffusivity in the near-wall region ($Re = 17{,}000$)

Moreover, the thickness of the Conduction Sublayer translates into a shift of the mean temperature profile in relation to profile of a fluid with $Pr = 1$. As illustrated in Fig. 11, an increase in Pr at constant Re results in a greater magnitude of the Log Region, and clearer transition into it.

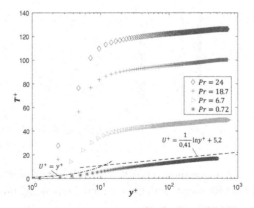

Fig. 11. Pr effect on the mean temperature profile for $Re = 25{,}000$ using the k-ε model

3.3 Nusselt Number Predictions

The previously presented results validate the correct setup and modelling of flow physics. The following is an assessment of the accuracy of the k-ε and k-ω models when modelling high-Pr forced convection, by comparing the numerical results to experimental data from [2].

Pr = 6.7. Figure 12 shows the Nu predictions as a function of Re for test cases with Pr = 6.7. Overall, both models overpredict Nu, with k-ε yielding better results over the range of Re studied. The error is quantified in Fig. 13. As can be seen, the accuracy of both turbulence models increases with Re.

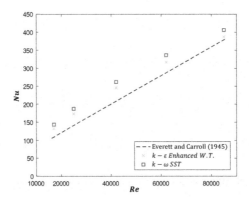

Fig. 12. Nusselt number variation with Reynolds number at constant Pr = 6.7

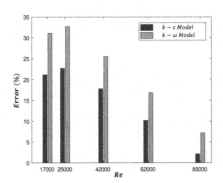

Fig. 13. Error of turbulence models in relation to experimental data (Pr = 6.7)

Pr = 18.7. Good agreement is achieved for Pr = 18.7. Both turbulence models overestimate Nu over most of the Re range, with the k-ε model producing more accurate results (see Fig. 14).

Turbulence model performance is good at this Pr, with errors lower than 11%, as seen in Fig. 15. As in the previous case, accuracy increases with Re. At Re = 33,000, the k-ε model underestimates Nu by approximately 1%.

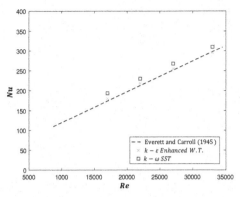

Fig. 14. Nusselt number variation with Reynolds number at constant Pr = 18.7

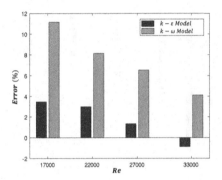

Fig. 15. Error of turbulence models in relation to experimental data (Pr = 18.7)

Pr = 24. Unlike lower Pr cases, at Pr = 24, Nu is underestimated over the range of Re. The k-ω SST model is more accurate than the k-ε model at this Pr, as seen in Fig. 16 and Fig. 17. The errors at Pr = 24 do not change linearly; however, they continue to decrease with higher Re.

Reynolds and Prandtl Number Effects. At a given Pr, Nu increases with Re due to the greater bulk transport of thermal energy. Additionally, Pr enhances the Re influence on the thermal behavior of the flow, as shown in Fig. 18.

Nu is overpredicted at Pr = 6.7 and 18.7, with the k-ε model producing better results. On the other hand, k-ω is more accurate for Pr = 24, where both models underpredict Nu. For reference, air (Pr = 0.72) is modelled at Re = 17,000 and Re = 25,000, and the results are compared to the Dittus-Boelter correlation, with good agreement. The specific Nu sensitivity to Pr is illustrated in Fig. 19 for Re = 17,000 and Re = 25,000. As can be seen, there is a positive relationship between Nu and Pr, with the constant Re lines being steeper at higher Re. Good accuracy is obtained at the high Re-high Pr end. High errors occur at Pr = 6.7. As pointed out in Sect. 3.2, higher grid resolution may be necessary to improve the accuracy of Pr = 6.7 results.

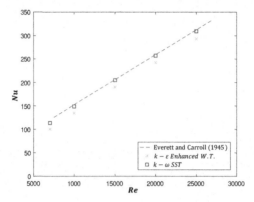

Fig. 16. Nusselt number variation with Reynolds number at constant Pr = 24

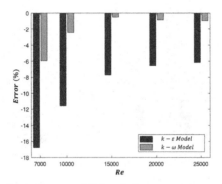

Fig. 17. Error of turbulence models in relation to experimental data (Pr = 24)

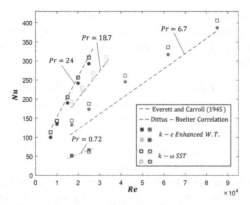

Fig. 18. Nusselt number variation with Reynolds number

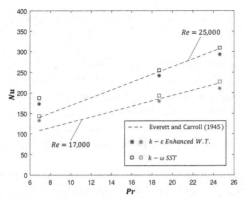

Fig. 19. Nusselt number variation with Prandtl number

4 Conclusions

Turbulent forced convection in a heated pipe at Pr = 6.7, 18.7, and 24, over the range 7 × 10³ < Re < 85 × 10³, was simulated in ANSYS Fluent using two-equation RANS turbulence models (k-ε with Enhanced Wall Treatment, and k-ω SST) to assess their accuracy when modelling high-Pr heat transfer.

4.1 Conclusions

- The effects of grid refinement, in terms of the near-wall cell y^+, were tested. Grid independent solutions were obtained when using the k-ε model, showing low variations as the mesh was refined in the radial direction. On the other hand, the k-ω model was highly sensitive to the location of the near-wall cell, particularly when y^+ < 5. The variability with grid refinement increased at higher Re and Pr. At Pr = 24, with Re = 5 × 10⁴ and Re = 10⁵, the Nu variation was too large for accurate results. Given this model's high sensitivity to near-wall cell placement, it is not recommended for high-Re, high-Pr, applications, as reliability is lost.
- The main effect of the Prandtl number is in the size of the thermal boundary layer in relation to the momentum boundary layer. The mean temperature profiles were plotted against the Law of the Wall prediction for Pr = 1. In fluids with Pr > 1, the Conduction Sublayer develops fully within the Viscous Sublayer; as Pr increases, it becomes thinner. In addition, Pr increases the magnitude of the temperature Log Region and creates a more marked transition into this region. Similarly, Re increases the magnitude, and thickness, of the Log Region.
- When the resulting mean temperature profiles of both turbulence models were compared, the k-ε model consistently yielded higher values of T^+ in the Log Region. Thus, this model predicts a thinner Conduction Sublayer than the k-ω SST model. The difference between turbulence model temperature profiles becomes more distinct at higher Pr. However, the disparity becomes minimal at higher Re, as both models were developed for high Re applications.

- Nusselt number predictions of the k-ε and k-ω models were compared to experimental data. Overall, good agreement was obtained, with numerical results generally within 15% of experimental data for Pr = 18.7 and Pr = 24. However, large errors occurred at Pr = 6.7. Nu was overpredicted at the lower Pr, with the k-ε results being more accurate. Conversely, Nu was underpredicted at Pr = 24 with k-ω producing better estimations. Additionally, the k-ω results were consistently higher than the k-ε results.
- Examining the percent error of the numerical results, it is evident that both turbulence models perform better at higher Re. Lower deviation between turbulence models occurs at these flow conditions, as was seen when comparing the mean temperature profiles.
- Overall, the k-ε model with Enhanced Wall Treatment, and k-ω SST model can be used to obtain good thermal predictions of high-Pr forced convection in a pipe with constant wall heat flux. Both models perform better when modelling higher Re flows. As Pr increases, the SST model appears to become more accurate. However, its sensitivity to near-wall grid resolution may limit its applicability at higher Pr flows than those studied here.

4.2 Future Work

Based on the results obtained in this investigation, the following are some recommendations to expand the study both within the scope of the current dissertation, and as further steps in the study of high-Pr forced convection.

- Despite ensuring the near-wall cell for all test cases was located at $y^+ < 1$, inaccurate Nu predictions were obtained at Pr = 6.7. Moreover, the universal velocity and temperature profiles illustrated deviations in modelling of the near-wall region. Thus, the number of cells within the thermal and momentum boundary layers should be examined and determine if there is a certain sensitivity to this parameter.
- Explore the high mesh sensitivity of the k-ω SST model for a wider range of Pr and Re. This should be coupled with the assessment of the number of grid cells placed inside the boundary layer. This is to determine if it is possible to reduce variability—or obtain a mesh independent solution—by placing the first cell well within $y^+ < 0.5$.
- It was well established in the Literature Review that the assumption of a constant Pr_t is acceptable for high-Pr fluids. However, those investigations used LES or DNS approaches. As Pr increases, so does the near-wall Pr_t. Investigating the effect of a variable Pr_t in RANS methods may improve their performance.

References

1. Irrenfried, C., Steiner, H.: DNS based analytical P-function model for RANS with heat transfer at high Prandtl numbers. Int. J. Heat Fluid Flow **66**, 217–225 (2017). https://doi.org/10.1016/j.ijheatfluidflow.2017.06.011
2. Everett, B., Carroll, E.: Heat-Transfer Tests of Aqueous Ethylene Glycol Solutions in an Electrically Heated Tube. Aircraft Engine Research Laboratory, Washington, Advance Restricted Report. National Advisory Committee for Aeronautics (1945)

3. Deissler, R.G.: Analysis of Turbulent Heat Transfer, Mass Transfer, and Friction in Smooth Tubes at High Prandtl and Schmidt Numbers. Lewis Flight Propulsion Laboratory, Washington, National Advisory Committee for Aeronautics (1954)
4. Malina, J.A., Sparrow, E.M.: Variable-property, constant-property, and entrance-region heat transfer results for turbulent flow of water and oil in a circular tube. Chem. Eng. Sci. **19**(12), 953–962 (1964)
5. Myong, H.K., Kasagi, N., Hirata, M.: Numerical prediction of turbulent pipe flow heat transfer for various Prandtl number fluids with the improved k-e turbulence model. JSME Int. J. **32**(4), 613–622 (1989)
6. Launder, B.E., Spalding, D.B.: The numerical computation of turbulent flows. Comput. Methods Appl. Mech. Eng. **3**(2), 269–289 (1974)
7. Pope, S.B.: Turbulent Flows. Cambridge University Press (2000). https://doi.org/10.1017/CBO 9780511840531
8. Moukalled, F., Mangani, L., Darwish, M.: The Finite Volume Method in Computational Fluid Dynamics: An Advanced Introduction with OpenFOAM® and Matlab. Springer International Publishing, Cham (2016). https://doi.org/10.1007/978-3-319-16874-6

Human-Robot Collaborative Control for Handling and Transfer Objects

Geovanny P. Moreno$^{(\boxtimes)}$, Nelson D. De la Cruz$^{(\boxtimes)}$,
Jessica S. Ortiz$^{(\boxtimes)}$, and Víctor H. Andaluz$^{(\boxtimes)}$

Universidad de Las Fuerzas Armadas ESPE, Sangolquí, Ecuador
{gpmorenol,ndde2,jsortiz4,vhandaluzl}@espe.edu.ec

Abstract. The document proposes the development of a 3D virtual environment, oriented to the common work activities between a unicycle type mobile manipulator robot and a human operator, in collaborative tasks. This strategy is focuses on the incorporation of virtual reality (VR), in which the operator will have access to visualize in an immersive way the behavior of the mobile manipulator robot in common tasks where the human being and the mobile manipulator robot interact. For the interaction between the human operator and the mobile manipulator robot, the graphic engine Unity 3D is used, which exchanges information with the mathematical software Matlab, in order to execute the control algorithm through the use of shared memories. The Novint Falcon haptic device allows human-robot interaction, which provides the operator with force feedback on what is happening in the virtual environment generated by the Unity 3D software and the interaction it has with the mobile manipulator. The HTC Vive immersion device allows the operator to visualize the virtual environment created for the execution of the task. In this work, the design and simulation of the locomotion system of a mobile manipulator robot is carried out for manipulation and object transfer tasks together with the human operator. Finally, the simulation results that validate the proposed control strategy are presented and discussed.

Keywords: Virtual reality · Mobile manipulator · Collaborative control · Matlab · Unity 3D

1 Introduction

Immersive technology, together with the development and technological advances in the last decade, focuses on different applications, in which a distributed group of users share a common 3D virtual environment [1]. It has Virtual Reality (VR) and Augmented Reality (AR) technology, where the development of virtual environments allows an intuitive interaction through input and output devices, in which several senses of human perception are used, this allows to have an immersion and interaction with the virtual environment as the manipulation of bodies, so it is possible to handle or operate different materials, with the purpose of performing tasks and meet achievable goals [2]. Within this scope, virtual reality (VR) allows to create realistic environments that acquire sensorial information for the interaction with the 3D virtual model [3].

© Springer Nature Switzerland AG 2021
M. Botto-Tobar et al. (Eds.): ICAT 2020, CCIS 1388, pp. 96–110, 2021.
https://doi.org/10.1007/978-3-030-71503-8_8

The applications of VR in different training areas motivate the user to learn new skills or get involved in different fields of knowledge, e.g., engineering where it is possible to learn different control techniques in industrial processes [4], medicine where students and doctors can practice hundreds of times a surgical intervention [5] and education where students with sensory and psychological skills improve their learning level [6], this great advance allows the development of society in different fields.

In recent years, the advance of technology has made virtual reality (VR) a completely new world [7], where the user experiences the impression of being immersed in a different environment [8], which is possible through haptic devices such as, e.g., Novint Falcon allowing the movement of the upper extremities [9], or Oculus Rift immersion technologies, HTC VIVE facilitating further perception of interaction within the virtual environment [10, 11]; these devices allow for an increased sense of human presence. In education areas it is used to train professionals in different fields, engineering [12], medicine [13], etc. this technology is used as an innovative strategy in the students' formation process, within the engineering area there are diverse applications oriented to the automation, control and instrumentation field [14], with environments where it is interacted with the measurement equipment allowing to make instrument calibration tasks, P&ID diagrams recognition, etc.

Virtual reality within robotics has generated great developments such as mapping of environmental variables [15], interfaces for mobile robots [16] and industrial manipulators [17]. Within the area of robotics there is a well-known field of service robotics that allows the introduction of autonomous robots to execute collaborative tasks with humans, such as the tele-operation of robots [18], or the cooperative control of mobile manipulators [19], making it easier for people to expand their capabilities and take on relatively heavy tasks, providing greater flexibility in production and increasing the efficiency of work done together. Virtual reality applications in collaborative tasks between different users allows the manipulation of virtual objects in the same environment, e.g., in [20]; students and surgical instructor perform collaborative training within a shared virtual environment.

As described above, this paper presents a virtual reality application developed in the Unity 3D graphic engine, as an intuitive tool that allows collaborative tasks between the human operator and mobile manipulator robot, through Novint Falcon haptic device allowing force feedback for the manipulation and transfer of objects, so the immersion device HTC Vive provides visualization of the virtual environment and human-robot interaction, the collaborative control is designed in Matlab mathematical software which allows to determine the control errors that occur when performing the common task.

This paper is divided into 5 Sections, including the Introduction. Section 2 describes the formulation of the problem. Section 3 includes the description of the virtual environment. Section 4 describes the control structure used. Section 5 discusses the experimental results obtained. Finally, Sect. 6 presents the conclusions of the implemented application.

2 Problem Formulation

Technological trends increasingly include human-robot interaction, either in a tele-operated form, i.e. the robot is controlled remotely by an operator, or the robot operates autonomously to execute a defined task. In complex tasks the integration of the mobile manipulator generates advantages thanks to the mobility offered by a mobile platform and the skill offered by the manipulator. This dedicates an unlimited workspace to the manipulator, making it possible to execute any task set by the user.

The interaction between human-robot is increasingly common in the social aspect, entertainment, among others, as the best known assistant robots, however at the time of conducting experimental tests to evaluate control algorithms in different works with a mobile manipulator robot is essential con-tar with the physical prototype, due to high investment costs in covering certain needs of the robot from the physical structure, acquisition of programming licenses and maintenance. In such a way it is added the inconveniences caused by climatic factors, where the experimental tests are carried out between the human operator and the mobile manipulator robot, the climatic conditions of the environment tend to affect significantly the tests with the robot. Under the following mentioned limitations, it is added the fact that the mobile manipulator robot is being experimented with, so it runs the risk of affecting its physical integrity and functionality. Taking into account the problems generated when performing experimental tests between man-robot, it is feasible to evaluate the control algorithm in a 3D virtual simulator, which allows to incorporate the characteristics and configurations of the mobile manipulator robot, allowing to analyze the functionality of the control algorithm, when performing collaborative man-robot tasks [21].

In the Fig. 1, describes the proposed scheme of the application from hardware and software used to the management of input/output devices Novint Falcon and HTC Vive, which provides the user to experience in a more intuitive way the immersion in the 3D virtual environment, the scenario contains 3D models that allow to create the virtual simulation environment in such a way that several elements are typical of Unity's assets, while the mobile manipulator robot is made in a CAD software (Computer Aided Design) which allows to make the 3D design of the mobile manipulator robot keeping all the mechanical characteristics of it among the most important elements are the wheels, chassis, robotic arm. The CAD design is exported to a 3D modeling, animation and rendering software, allowing to preserve all the physical characteristics of the robot before being imported to the Unity 3D graphic engine as an extension (*.fbx), the conditions of the environment are pre-established, this allows the user to have a better interaction allowing him to observe the velocities of the links that make up the robotic arm and the velocity at which the platform moves.

The Matlab mathematical software has the control algorithms that allow the mobile manipulator to correct errors during Human-Robot interaction, it receives the data sent by the graphic engine that allows the operator to perform the force feedback. The input

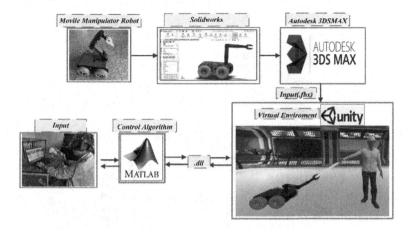

Fig. 1. Proposed outline for the development of the virtual environment

consists of Novint Falcon haptic devices that allow the operator to manipulate the virtual environment and HTC Vive that allows him to visualize the interaction with the avatar, the same one that will execute the collaborative tasks with the robot.

3 Virtual Environment

In this section describes the working methodology for the development of the application see Fig. 2, the stages that make it up are; *i) 3D Design* of the mobile manipulator robot from a CAD software, *ii) Virtual environment*, developed in the Unity 3D graphic engine, incorporating characteristics to the CAD model, *iii) Script block*, allows the control of each system block that interacts with the virtual environment, *iv) Input and output devices*, cooperate to the development of the environment, *v) Mathematical Software*, executes the control algorithm to be implemented.

3.1 CAD Design

The design is make in a CAD tool Fig. 3, so the software used in this design stage is Solidworks. It is oriented to 3D CAD design, allowing the creation of 3D solid models, assemblies, etc. It provides an easy to use design and powerful tools for engineers allowing them to create solid objects to be assembled and obtain complete 3D models. The mobile manipulator robot developed in the CAD software, has all the features and appropriate configurations that a real mobile manipulator has.

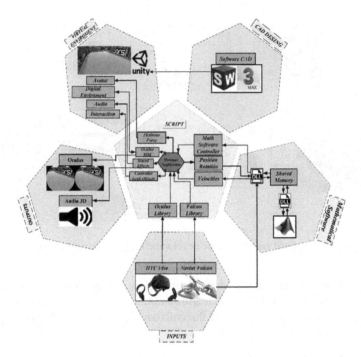

Fig. 2. Structural diagram of the interrelationship between the components

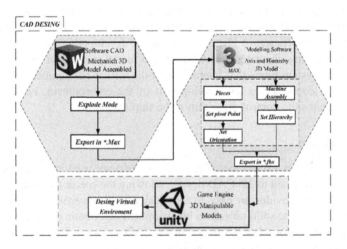

Fig. 3. Stages of CAD design

3.2   Virtual Environment Development

The virtual environment represents the attributes that make up the virtual environment developed in the Unity 3D graphic engine, among the most relevant are mentioned. *i)* *3D models*, are the objects that are loaded into the environment including the mobile manipulator; *ii*) *UI Avatar*, is responsible for interacting with the robot within the virtual environment, providing the user the ability to intervene in the tasks to be performed. *iii*) *Interaction*, allows the user to link the virtual environment, configured by Grab Object Controller. The environment created allows the sensory and motor immersion of the user in tasks to be performed in collaboration with the mobile manipulator robot. In Fig. 4, it shows the creation of the virtual environment from the migration of elements of 3DS Max and its migration to the Unity 3D graphic engine. The tool MonoDevelop which allows to use the text editor which allows to create the scripts, allowing to make the respective animations of the environment, man-robot displacement, generate environmental sounds, etc. in order to provide a more intuitive immersion to the user.

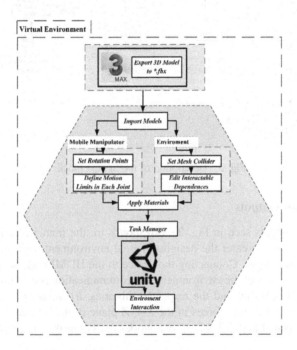

Fig. 4. Creation of the virtual environment

3.3 Block Scripts

In this stage the set of scripts is in charge of communicating Unity 3D between the input and output devices through code blocks. For the interaction with the virtual reality input device, the devices own library is used, which allows the communication with the computer to be executed to provide audio and visual feedback on the execution of the task. Finally the mathematical software by means of the use of the dynamic link library (DLL), which generates a shared memory (SM) for the exchange of data between different software. Through the SM the control actions are entered into the mobile manipulator. In Fig. 5, scheme of the script block. The data of position, rotation and velocity are read and sent to the mathematical software, later to obtain the control errors.

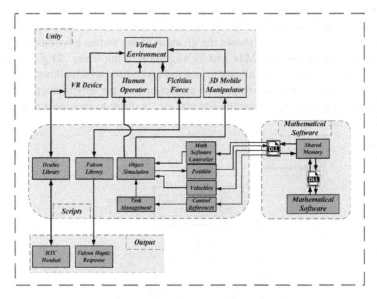

Fig. 5. Description of the Scritps block

3.4 Inputs and Outputs

The inputs and outputs seen in Fig. 2, corresponds to: the immersion device: *i) HTC Vive*, allows the user to enter the designed virtual environment, and interact with the mobile manipulator robot. Connecting the device to the HDMI port making it possible to add the visualization of the environment, the communication is established by means of the Steam VR software and the respective libraries, *ii) Novint Falcon*, is a haptic device capable of generating forces in the X-Y-Z plane of the reference system with a magnitude between 0 and 2.5 lbf, whose work area comprises a spherical region of 10 cm radius.

3.5 Mathematic Software

The mathematical software seen in Fig. 2. Structural diagram of the interrelationship between the components, has control algorithms to control the errors during the Human-Robot interaction, which receives the data sent by the graphic motor to make the calculations and determine a new value of position, orientation and velocity for the mobile manipulator robot, the signals are sent to the graphic motor causing the mobile manipulator robot to change its conditions thus obtaining an application that evolves over time.

4   Control Structure

4.1   Impedance Control

The forces that are generated at the operating end of the robot are obtained from the position of the human operator's arm Fig. 6, the mechanical impedance relationship is given in (1) between the force and velocity of the system.

$$Z(s) = \frac{F(s)}{V(s)} \tag{1}$$

Where $F(s)$ represents the external force applied to the operating end of the robot which is defined by:

$$F(s) = MXs^2 + DXs + KX \tag{2}$$

Where M is the mass, D the damping, K the stiffness and X represents the position of the system, Therefore the velocity and mechanical impedance is given by (3):

$$Z(s) = \frac{MXs^2 + DXs + KX}{Xs} = Ms + D + \frac{K}{s} \tag{3}$$

The force that feels the operating end of the robot represented by (2) allows to determine the position and desired velocity of the operating end, then the respective controller is applied, the external force **F** exerted by the human operator:

$$\mathbf{F} = \mathbf{M} \cdot \mathbf{a} \tag{4}$$

The acceleration vector is obtained from the external force applied obtaining the following one:

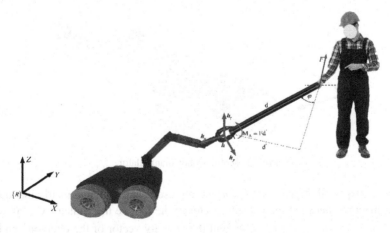

Fig. 6. Human-Robot reference system

$$\mathbf{a} = s^2 + \frac{DsX(s+K)}{M} \tag{5}$$

By integrating (5) the desired velocity of the operating end of the mobile manipulator robot is obtained:

$$\dot{\mathbf{h}}_d = s\left(s^2 + \frac{DsX(s+K)}{M}\right) \tag{6}$$

To obtain the desired position of the operating end of the robot we integrate (6):

$$\mathbf{h}_d = s^2\left(s^2 + \frac{DsX(s+K)}{M}\right) \tag{7}$$

4.2   Modeling Kinematic and Dynamic

A. Kinematic Modeling

The kinematic model of the mobile manipulator gives the location of the end effector, depending on the location of the unicycle-type dolly and the configuration of the 4DOF robot arm, as shown in Fig. 7. The mobile manipulator is guided through a u which represents the linear velocity of the moving platform; ψ represents the orientation of the vehicle with respect to $\{R\}$; angular velocity ω, represents the rotation of the dolly in relation to the axis z; l_1, l_2, l_3 y l_4 are the dimensions of the joints of the robotic arm; q_1, q_2, q_3 y q_4 are the angles of rotation for each degree of freedom of the manipulator robot [22].

$$\dot{\mathbf{h}}(t) = \mathbf{J}(\mathbf{q})\mathbf{v}(t) \tag{8}$$

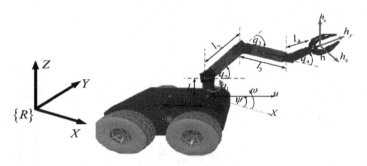

Fig. 7. Mobile robot manipulator

Where $\mathbf{J}(\mathbf{q}) \in \Re^{m \times n}$ with $m = 3$ y $n = 6$ represents the Jacobian matrix that defines a linear mapping between the velocity vector of the mobile manipulator $\mathbf{v} \in \Re^n$ where $\mathbf{v}(t) = [\, u \quad \omega \quad \dot{q}_1 \quad \dot{q}_2 \quad \dot{q}_3 \quad \dot{q}_4\,]^T$ and the velocity vector of the operating end $\dot{\mathbf{h}} \in \Re^m$ where $\dot{\mathbf{h}}(t) = [\dot{h}_x \quad \dot{h}_y \quad \dot{h}_z]^T$.

B. Dynamic Modeling

The dynamic model of the mobile manipulator robot is applied the Euler-Lagrange method, this is the energy balance equation since it is more suitable to analyze the displacements of the links that limit each other, the dynamic equation of the mobile manipulator can be represented as follows [22].

$$\mathbf{M(q)\ddot{q} + C(q, \dot{q})\dot{q} + g(q) = v}_{ref}(t) \tag{9}$$

Where $\mathbf{M(q)}$ is the inertial matrix, $\mathbf{C(q, \dot{q})}$ is the matrix of centripetal and Coriolis forces, $\mathbf{g(q)}$ represents the gravitational forces of the mobile manipulator, $\mathbf{v}_{ref}(t)$ it is the vector of the velocity control signals.

4.2.1   Kinematic Controller

The design of the kinematic controller of the mobile manipulator robot is based on the kinematics of the robot (8). The velocity (6) and position (7) required is obtained as a function of the force felt by the operating end of the robot, detected through the sensors, product of the movement of the object that is generated by the person. Therefore, the following control law is proposed for the mobile manipulator:

$$\mathbf{v_c = J^{\#}\left(\dot{h}_d + L_K \tanh(\tilde{h})\right) + \left(I - J^{\#}J\right)L_D \tanh(\eta)} \tag{10}$$

Where, $\mathbf{J^{\#} = W^{-1}J^{T}\left(JW^{-1}J^{T}\right)^{-1}}$ with $\mathbf{W}$ positive symmetrical matrix that weighs the control actions of the system, $\mathbf{\dot{h}_d}$ is the desired velocity vector of the end-effector $\mathbf{h_d}$; $\mathbf{\tilde{h}}$ it's the vector that contains the control errors $\mathbf{\tilde{h} = h_d - h}$; $\mathbf{L_K}$ and $\mathbf{L_D}$ these are defined positive diagonal gain matrices, and $\mathbf{\eta}$ is a vector allows the configuration of the arm to be at maximum manipulability [22].

4.2.2   Dynamic Compensation

Dynamic compensation controller, whose main objective is to compensate the dynamics of the mobile manipulator, thus reducing the velocity error. This controller receives as inputs the desired velocities $\mathbf{v_c}$ calculated by the kinematic controller (10), and generates velocity references $\mathbf{v_{ref}}$ for the mobile manipulator. If there is no perfect velocity tracking, the velocity error is defined as $\mathbf{\tilde{v} = v_c - v}$. Therefore, the following control law is proposed.

$$\mathbf{v_{ref} = M(q)\sigma + C(q, v)v_c + g(q)} \tag{11}$$

Where, $\mathbf{v_{ref}} = \begin{bmatrix} u_{ref} & \omega_{ref} & \dot{q}_{1ref} & \dot{q}_{2ref} & \dot{q}_{3ref} & \dot{q}_{4ref} \end{bmatrix}^{T}$ is the control action and $\mathbf{\sigma = \dot{v}_c + L_v \tanh(\tilde{v})}$ where $\mathbf{L_v}$ a defined positive matrix.

4.3   Stability Analysis

The control error $\mathbf{\tilde{h} = h_d - h}$ is analyzed assuming perfect velocity tracking $\mathbf{v \equiv v_c}$, thus substituting (10) in (8) we have:

$$\dot{\tilde{\mathbf{h}}} + \mathbf{L_K} \tanh(\tilde{\mathbf{h}}) = 0 \qquad (12)$$

The following Lyapunov function is considered for stability analysis [22]:

$$V(\tilde{\mathbf{h}}) = \frac{1}{2}\tilde{\mathbf{h}}^T\tilde{\mathbf{h}} \qquad (13)$$

Where the time derivative is located in the system trajectories is:

$$\dot{V}(\tilde{\mathbf{h}}) = \tilde{\mathbf{h}}^T \mathbf{L_K} \tanh(\tilde{\mathbf{h}}) \qquad (14)$$

The closed-loop control system (10) is asymptotically stable, so that the position error of the end-effector $\tilde{\mathbf{h}}(t) \to 0$ is asymptotically, with $t \to \infty$.

5   Experimental Results

This section presents the virtual scenarios created in the Unity 3D graphic engine, where the human operator has the option to select three test environments through the menu in Fig. 8 are *i) Laboratory, ii) Closed Hangar, iii) Factory*, in the virtual environment will perform the simulation of the collaborative task Man-robot.

Fig. 8. Start menu of the virtual environment

Once the scene is selected, the communication is linked to the Matlab software to evaluate the performance of the control algorithm applied to the mathematical model of the robot, which approaches and holds the different objects, for which the movement of the avatar's hand will be represented through a Novint Falcon haptic device that perceives the operator's input signal, the received signal is send to the virtual environment and the actuators of the haptic device are used to physically convert sensations to the human operator show in Fig. 9.

Fig. 9. Human operator interaction test

The task executed of manipulation and transport of the object, in which the avatar is interacting with the object coupled to the operative end of the robot see Fig. 10, as time passes the control evolves in such a way that the robot modifies the positions of its links to continue with the collaborative task as it is shown in Fig. 11.

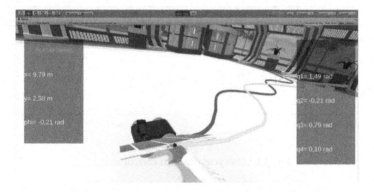

Fig. 10. Initiation of control for the collaborative task

Fig. 11. Man-robot collaborative object transport

The results obtained from the development of the collaborative task between man-robot through the interaction of the operator with the haptic device, you can see how the stability of the controller evolves over time, through the control actions of the mobile platform shown in Fig. 12, the velocities of each link of the robot arm in Fig. 13 and in Fig. 14 you can see the positioning errors of the operating end of the mobile manipulator robot.

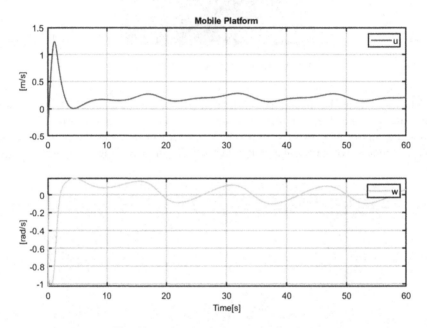

Fig. 12. Unicycle platform control actions

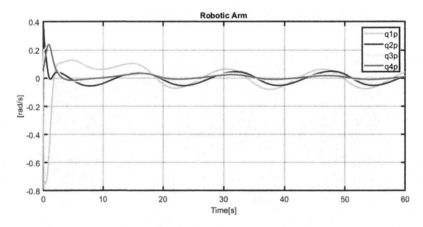

Fig. 13. Angular velocities of the robotic arm

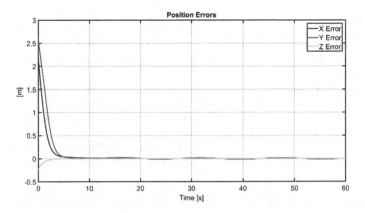

Fig. 14. Position errors of the operating end of the robot

6 Conclusions

In this paper the Human-Robot interaction carried out in Unity 3D virtual environment and the execution of the control algorithm implemented in the mathematical software allow to obtain a better interaction. In the application it allows the human operator to interact with the mobile manipulator robot through the haptic device Novint Falcon which allows to make force feedback. The development of the virtual environment in conjunction with the haptic device allows to generate an immersive environment of interaction Man-Robot and the controller implemented to meet the collaborative task.

Acknowledgements. The authors would like to thank the Corporación Ecuatoriana para el Desarrollo de la Investigación y Academia - CEDIA for their contribution in innovation, through the CEPRA projects, especially the project CEPRA-XIV-2020–08-RVA "Tecnologías Inmersivas Multi-Usuario Orientadas a Sistemas Sinérgicos de Enseñanza y Aprendizaje"; also the Universidad de las Fuerzas Armadas ESPE and the Research Group ARSI, for the support for the development of this work.

References

1. Beck, S., Kunert, A., Kulik, A., Froehlich, B.: Immersive group-to-group telepresence. IEEE Trans. Visual. Comput. Graph. **19**(4), 616–625 (2013)
2. Selzer, M., Gazcón, N., Nagel, J.T., Larrea, M., Castro, S., Bjerg, E.: Tecnologías Inmersivas Aplicadas: Realidad Virtual y Aumentada. In: XX Workshop de Investigadores en Ciencias de la Computación, pp. 366–370 (2018)
3. Pilatásig, M., Tobar, E., Paredes, L., Silva, F.M., Acurio, A., Pruna, E., Escobar, I., Sánchez, Z.: Virtual system for teaching-learning of initial education using a haptic device. Springer International Publishing AG, vol. AVR 2018, pp. 118–132 (2018)
4. Pruna, E., Rosero, M., Pogo, R., Escobar, I., Acosta, J.: Virtual reality as a tool for the cascade control learning. Springer International Publishing AG., vol. AVR 2018, pp. 243–251 (2018)

5. Gutiérrez-Maldonado, J., Alsina-Jurnet, I., Carvallo-Becíu, C., Letosa-Porta, A., Magallón-Neri, E.: Aplicaciones clínicas de la realidad virtual en el ámbito escolar. In: Medicina psicosomatica y psiquiatrica en enlace, nº 82, pp. 32–51 (2007)
6. Hilera, J.R., Otón, S., Martínez, J.: Aplicación de la realidad virtual en la enseñanza a través de internet, vol. 8, pp. 25–35 (1999)
7. Jiménez, S.M.S., Macías J.L.H., Lumbreras, M.A.M.: La Revolución Industrial a través de Realidad Virtual. Revista Iztatl Computación 13(7), 56–64 (2018)
8. Garcia, R.: Realidad virtual como herramienta en fisioterapia, ficción o realiad. ScienceDirect 40, 1–3 (2018)
9. Escobar, I., Gálvez, C., Corrales, G., Pruna, E., Pilatasig, M., Montaluisa, J.: Virtual System using haptic devicefor real-time tele-rehabilitationof upper limbs. Springer International Publishing AG., vol. AVR 2018, pp. 136–152 (2018)
10. Herrera, D.F., Acosta, S.B., Quevedo, W.X., Balseca, J.A., Andaluz, V.H.: Training for bus bodywork in virtual realityenvironments. Springer International Publishing AG., vol. AVR 2018, pp. 67–85 (2018)
11. Zhang, Y., Wang, Z.: Towards Visual Comfort: Disciplines on the Scene Structure Design for VR Contents,» Springer International Publishing AG., vol. AVR 2018, pp. 190–196 (2018)
12. Pace, F.D., Manuri, F., Sanna, A., Zappia, D.: An Augmented Interface to DisplayIndustrial Robot Faults. Springer International Publishing AG., vol. AVR 2018, pp. 403–421 (2018)
13. López, V.M., Zambrano, P.A., Pilatasig, M., Silva, F.M.: Interactive System Using Myoelectric MuscleSensors for the Strengthening Upper Limbsin Children. Springer International Publishing AG., vol. AVR 2018, pp. 18–29 (2018)
14. Ortiz, J.S., Sánchez, J.S., Velasco, P.M., Quevedo, W.X., Carvajal, C.P., Morales, V., Ayala, P., Andaluz, V.H.: Virtual Training for Industrial Automation Processes Through Pneumatic Controls. Springer International Publishing AG, vol. AVR 2018, pp. 516–532 (2018)
15. Roldán, J.J., Garcia-Aunon, P., Garzón, M., Garzón, M., de León, J., del Cerro, J., Barrientos, A.: Heterogeneous multi-robot system for mappingenvironmental variables of greenhouses. In: Centre for Automation and Robotics (UPM-CSIC), nº 1018, pp. 1–24 (2016)
16. Lin, A., Milshteyn, A., Herman, G., Garcia, M., Liu, C., Rad, K., Guillaume, D., Boussalis, H.: Virtual reality head-tracking observation system for mobile robot. In: Mediterranean Conference on Embedded Computing, nº 3, pp. 152–157 (2014)
17. Matsas, E., Vosniakos, G.-C.: Design of a virtual reality training system for human–robot collaboration in manufacturing tasks. Springer-Verlag France 2015, nº 15780, pp. 139–153 (2015)
18. Su, H., Yang, C., Ferrigno, G., Momi, E.D.: Improved human–robot collaborative control of redundant robot for teleoperated minimally invasive surgery. IEEE Robotics Autom. Lett. 4 (2), 1447–1453 (2019)
19. Andaluz, V.H., Leica, P., Roberti, F., Toibero, M., Carelli, R.: Adaptive coordinated cooperative controlof multi-mobile manipulators. Frontiers in Advanced Control Systems, pp. 163–190 (2012)
20. Chheang, V., Saalfeld, P., Huber, T., Huettl, F., Kneist, W., Preim, B., Hansen, C.: Collaborative virtual reality for laparoscopic liver surgery training. In: Conference on Artificial Intelligence and Virtual Reality (AIVR) 2019, pp. 1–9 (2019)
21. Carvajal, C.P., Méndez, M.G, Torres, D.C., Terán, C., Arteaga, O.B., Andaluz, V.H.: Autonomous and tele-operated navigation of aerial manipulator robots in digitalized virtual environments. Springer International Publishing AF, vol. AVR 2018, pp. 496–515 (2018)
22. Andaluz, V., Flavio, R., Toibero, J.M., Carel, R.: Adaptive unified motion control of mobile manipulators. Control Eng. Practice 20(12), 1337–1352 (2012)

e-Government and e-Participation

Lean Manufacturing for Optimizing Operational Processes in a Bicycle Assembly Line

Santiago Rodas[1], Lorena Siguenza-Guzman[2,3] ⓘ, and Juan Llivisaca[4(✉)] ⓘ

[1] Faculty of Chemical Sciences, Universidad de Cuenca, Cuenca, Ecuador
santiago.rodasd@ucuenca.edu.ec
[2] Department of Computer Sciences, Faculty of Engineering, Universidad de Cuenca, Cuenca, Ecuador
lorena.siguenza@ucuenca.edu.ec
[3] Research Centre Accountancy, Faculty of Economics and Business, KU Leuven, Leuven, Belgium
[4] Department of Applied Chemistry and Systems of Production, Faculty of Chemical Sciences, Universidad de Cuenca, Cuenca, Ecuador
juan.llivisaca@ucuenca.edu.ec

Abstract. Manufacturing and assembly industries are continually searching to optimize their resources and achieve improvements in their production systems. At a time when the differentiating factor is found in efficiency and competitiveness in production, Lean Manufacturing (LM) philosophy contributes to these differentiators, focusing mainly on the elimination of waste to obtain an improvement in processes, quality, and delivery times, being evident the results in a short period. This article proposes optimizing processes within a bicycle assembly plant by applying a LM tool called Value Stream Map (VSM), which presents the current production processes and their requirements, facilitating the identification of waste within the system. Regarding process mapping, the bicycle model E26 was selected for illustrative purposes. Additionally, the 5S tool was used to maintain tidiness and cleanliness within the processes for obtaining an agile production flow. The study also included the balancing of lines, getting a reduction of 14% in "cycle time" and 66% in "lead time", generating a mixed production (push and pull). Moreover, a warehouse distribution of raw material was proposed, obtaining the unification of all the materials involved in the process. Finally, the VSM future's legitimacy was confirmed through simulation, validating the results obtained from the LM tools' application.

Keywords: Lean manufacturing · Optimization · VSM · Line balancing · Lead time · 5S · Waste · Industry · Assembly · FlexSim

1 Introduction

It is common to find problems in industries that carry out their products through manufacturing and assembly lines. This is due, among other factors, to the disorganization

© Springer Nature Switzerland AG 2021
M. Botto-Tobar et al. (Eds.): ICAT 2020, CCIS 1388, pp. 113–128, 2021.
https://doi.org/10.1007/978-3-030-71503-8_9

in the supply of materials, raw materials, resources, or unnecessary movements of the worker, giving rise to downtime, a disorder in product-in-process, and the accumulation of inventories. These companies are frequently looking to implement improvements in their production chains; for example, through the elimination of waste identified as overproduction, waiting, unnecessary transportation, incorrect processing, inventories, movements, and defective products [1]. Lean Manufacturing, LM, focuses on improving the manufacturing system by eliminating waste, understanding it as anything that does not add value to the product from the customer's perspective. LM is based on the use of tools developed in Japan, inspired by Deming's principles [2], to eliminate waste that leads to improved quality and reduced production times and costs [3].

The use of LM has been more frequent due to the benefits generated and practical tools in companies of different productive nature. For example, Value Stream Mapping, VSM is a tool that graphically presents opportunities for improvement. Many authors agree that VSM is one of the most widely used tools to identify the current state of a production system, as well as its waste. For instance, Abdulmalek and Rajgopal use VSM to suggest improvements in two critical factors of a production system, production time, and in-process inventory [4]. Sundar et al. incorporate VSM for the analysis of processes within the manufacturing, achieving a simultaneous integration between the balancing of lines and the control of inventories [5]. Rohani and Zahraee combined VSM with tools such as 5S, Kanban, and Kaizen, achieving a considerable reduction in delivery time [6]. For Grewal, the analysis through VSM allowed considering the current state of small companies' production system. It revealed waste in delivery times, cycle times, and excessive inventory of products in process [7]. Choomlucksana et al. launched the application of LM tools, such as visual control, Poka-Yoke, and 5S, to identify areas of opportunity for waste reduction [8]. For Motwani [9], by implementing a "pull" production system, a significant reduction in set-up times was achieved in almost all areas of the plant (cut in half).

In this context, the current article aims to present the LM development to optimize operational processes in the assembly of bicycles. As a starting point, the use of VSM was considered to survey the current situation of the case study. Next, product selection was made to be considered in the study. The current VSM was built. Then, the identification of errors, problems, and waste was carried out for its subsequent correction and proposal of a future state. As a final point, the simulation of the optimized processes was proposed. The remainder of the paper is as follows. Section 2 presents the methodology of the optimization process. The next section reports the results obtained and the comparison of the current and future states. The implications of the changes proposed are discussed in Sect. 4. Finally, the last section concludes with a summary of the work performed and gives the most likely future research directions.

2 Materials and Methods

This work presents a process optimization proposal for a bicycle manufacturing and assembly company, by using a comparison, theoretical, descriptive, and simulation testing method. The data necessary for the study was gathered from process flow diagrams and production data collected by Rodas et al. [10]. This information allowed performing a current situation survey, analysis, correction of errors/waste, facilitating future state planning.

Through VSM, it is possible to visualize the production sequence and to determine the flow of materials and the information required from the supplier to the customer, allowing identifying the value chain and waste in the process [11]. The methodology proposed by Barcia and De Loor [12] was partially taken as a basis to develop the optimization. This generated the following sequence: mapping of the current state, measurement of indicators, identification of waste, selection of appropriate tools for each waste, mapping of the future state, and validation through simulation.

2.1 Mapping the Current State

To represent the company's current situation, a product was selected with the PROD-UCT - QUANTITY analysis. Most of the products were manufactured following the same sequence or route in the processes. For the study, the 2017's production of was considered. It should be mentioned that, the names of the models were modified for confidentiality reasons. Through a Pareto diagram and using the available production information, the E26 bicycle model was selected, highlighted in Fig. 1. Due to its limited information, F16 and C20 were discarded as they were seasonal products whose information may bias the study and the construction of the VSM.

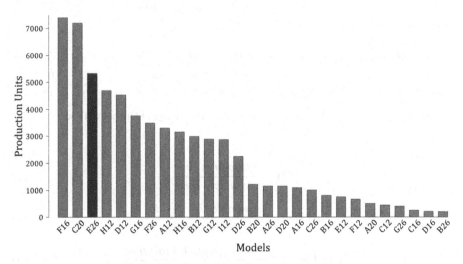

Fig. 1. Bicycle models and annual production.

The production processes of the E26 model were obtained in the process flow diagrams (Table 1), which include cycle and set-up times. With the identification of the processes, the current conditions were established. The information obtained resulted from a production of 500 bicycles, assembled in five days, with an average workday of 10 h (600 min). Several values were calculated related to the percentage of operating time (POT), "takt time" or the rate at which it should be produced, and "lead time", i.e., time required for a product to travel a process or a value chain from the beginning to end. These values were necessary for the VSM, obtained from (1), (2), and (3) [11]. As a result, a takt time corresponding to 6 min was calculated. To the lead time, five days corresponding to the initial inventory and five days for the finished product inventory were added, which provided a total of 22.5 days.

Table 1. Production processes, number of operators, CT, SUT, POT, Daily inventory, "Takt Time" and "Lead Time" for the E26 bicycle model.

Process	No. of operators	CT (min)	SUT (min)	POT	Daily inventory (units)	Takt time (min)	Lead time (days)
Cut	1	0,27	0,02	22%	280	6,00	2,8
Conformed	2	2,48	0,30	100%	220		2,2
Weld	12	25,48	2,07	100%	150		1,5
Surface treatment	2	10,00	6,78	18%	100		1
Painting	3	7,25	2,77	100%	100		1
Baking/Drying	2	120,00	0,00	100%	100		1
Full frame and pitchfork assembly	3	3,78	0,23	100%	100		1
Tire assembly	5	8,47	0,47	100%	200		2
Assemble	5	12,80	0,18	100%	0		0
Total	35	190,53	12,82			6,00	12,5

Note: CT = Cycle Time. SUT = Set-up Time. POT = Percentage of Operating Time

$$POT = \frac{Ocupation\ Time}{Available\ Time} \tag{1}$$

$$Takt\ Time = \frac{Available\ Time\ per\ day}{Daily\ demand} \tag{2}$$

$$Lead\ Time = \frac{Inventory\ Quantity * Takt\ time}{Daily\ available\ time} \tag{3}$$

The current state VSM of the E26 model describes the process sequence, as shown in Fig. 2. Starting with the weekly production order, the model begins to be manufactured, considering the reception and distribution of raw materials. Next, the manufacture of the frames is carried out. The raw material is transported from the corresponding warehouse to the different processes, i.e., cutting tubes, shaping the frames, welding, surface treatment, painting, and reinforcing the complete frame/trench and assembling. Once the process is completed, the finished product is transported to the designated area, where,

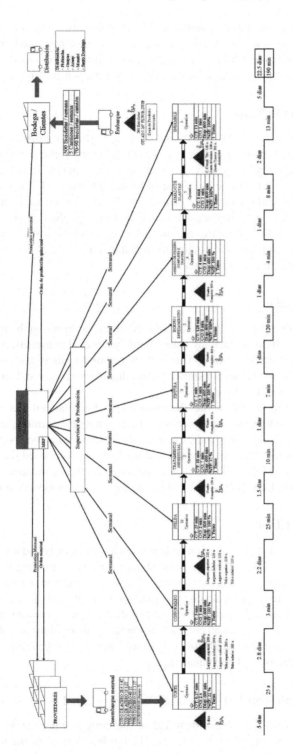

Fig. 2. VSM of the E26 current state.

later, it is transferred to the storage warehouse. The manufacture of the rings is carried out in parallel to the processes above. The total processing time presented through the VSM was 190 min for the first bicycle, going from the cutting process to the end of its assembly, while the real delivery time based on the lead time was 22.5 days.

2.2 Measurement of Indicators

Once the current state has been surveyed, the indicators are 1) the cycle time, corresponding to the time required to produce a bicycle, and 2) the takt time, representing the rate at which a bicycle must be made to satisfy the exact customer demand. The ideal production situation occurs when the cycle time is equal to the takt time [13]. The comparison between the cycle time and the takt time is made, excluding the surface treatment and baking/drying processes, since they are automated, and their production is batch-wise. The analysis shows that four processes are on takt time, which means the presence of an imbalance, causing problems for meeting the demand, unwanted activities, and over time, as well as wasting time and resources.

2.3 Waste Identification

The purpose of identifying waste (problems, shortcomings, or errors) in the production system is to reduce or eliminate them by determining, among other aspects, inventories between processes and delivery times. This is done through visits to the company to observe processes, talks with plant personnel, and production managers and thus achieve visualization of each identified waste.

As a starting point to identify waste, the unloading of raw material was taken, followed by the analysis of all production processes, from cutting to assembly, to end with the shipment of the finished product and subsequent distribution to customers. It resulted in the problems identified, the type of waste, and the LM tools proposed for their correction, as presented in Table 2. The tools are supported by the methodological study guide by Barcia and De Loor [12], which offers LM tools for each identified waste.

2.4 Selection of LM Tools

For the problem selection, a classification table was used with priority and impact. They were weighted using the Likert scale to establish a priority value ranging from 1 to 5 (null, little, medium, high, urgent), the highest value was considered the most urgent. The same concept was used to impact changes that will generate values ranging from 1 to 4 (none, low, medium, high). In addition, several direct interviews were carried out with operators, plant supervisors, and company managers to determine the stakeholders (Table 2). With the main problems identified, the tools proposed in the same table were used, i.e., plant distribution and line balancing.

2.5 Proposal to Implement LM Tools

Once the primary wastes have been identified in the current state, the 5S tool was proposed as a starting point, being the basis for the implementation of the techniques selected previously. This tool facilitates optimization through the selected LM tools by involving all the processes of the bicycle's production.

Table 2. Waste and lean manufacturing techniques, including impact analysis and improvement.

Problems/Errors	Waste	LM tool	Priority	Impact	Total
1. Transportation of raw materials from different points	Unnecessary transportation	Plant distribution	5	4	9
2. Existence of operators without performing work while waiting for the product-in process	Wait	Line balancing/Kaban	5	4	9
3. The welding process represents the bottleneck of the production system	Over Processing/Incorrect Processing	Line balancing	4	4	8
4. No area for the inventory of product-in-process and finished product	Movement	5S/Plant distribution	4	3	7
5. Accumulation of inventories of product-in-process (forming, welding, painting, tire assembly)	Inventories	Wash	4	3	7
6. High set-up times	Over Processing/Incorrect Processing	SMED/Standardization	3	4	7
7. The space of the welding area is reduced	Movement	5S	4	2	6

(continued)

Table 2. (*continued*)

Problems/Errors	Waste	LM tool	Priority	Impact	Total
8. Incorrect arrangement of the elements in the assembly line	Movement	5S	3	3	6
9. Existence of defective products in the welding process	Defective products/rework	Standardization	3	3	6
10. The bicycle frames and the automatic painting receive manual touch-ups by the operators	Defective products/rework	TPM/Line balancing	2	3	5
11. The assembly is not performed in a standardized manner	Over Processing/Incorrect Processing	Standardization	2	2	4

Note: Priority: 1 null; 2 little; 3 mean; 4 high; 5 urgent. Impact: 1 none; 2 low; 3 medium; 4 high

Proposal 5S. The 5S tool deals with the order/cleanliness within each workstation to improve its work environment and safety [14]. The proposed 5S tool analyzes the productive areas of the company and involves all staff [15]. For this, each work area initially seeks to classify and eliminate all unnecessary elements and thus achieves an adequate productive flow. To obtain an order within the processes, the frequency and sequence of each component used were taken into account, standardizing its location based on three key points: easy to find, easy to use, and easy to return. Inside the plant, there were places with elements that were not used, for which cleanliness is of great importance. For example, having a clean plant makes it more comfortable identifying sources of dirt and the machines' condition.

For the standardization of classification, order, and cleanliness, the development of policies was proposed, as well as the assignment of responsible for each process, the promotion of discipline through 5S training, its integration into daily activities, and the conduction of maintenance inspections.

Warehouse Distribution of Raw Materials. To correct the problem of transportation of raw materials, a single warehouse is proposed, currently used only with tubes and material for the cutting and forming process. Other elements involved in the assembly were found in two alternate warehouses, belonging to accessories, painting, tire materials and bicycle tires. These warehouses have the same problem; stored items occupy only a small area. Performing a redistribution, Table 3 presents current and proposed values of distances and times used to supply materials to the work stations.

Table 3. Raw material transport times and distances to its different workstations in their current state and raw material transport distances in their future state.

Process	Current state		Proposed state
	Distance traveled (m)	Total time (min)	Distance traveled (m)
Cut	144,40	3,49	144,40
Weld	118,56	12,72	57,00
Painting	130,96	19,94	88,00
Full frame and pitchfork assembly	130,96	19,94	88,00
Tire assembly	130,96	16,74	70,00
Assembly line	118,56	18,12	70,00
Total	774,40	90,95	517,40

The proposal considered a monthly quantity of raw material for all models produced. Also, a considerable space for the assembled product was taken to the finished product storage warehouse. The distribution and adaptation of the warehose were made with the following guidelines. The most frequently used items should be closer to the cellar door—the heaviest elements at the bottom. The raw material should be arranged in the order established by the production sequence. Finally, each shelf/rack of raw material should be coded, considering the material's purpose.

Line Balancing. Line balancing is performed using Meyers et al. [16] and Lopez Acosta et al. [17]. Only processes that exceed the limit set by the takt time were considered. For the balancing of lines, each process' activities, cycle times, assembly times and available time were identified, thus carrying out the analysis of workloads and operators involved.

Within this analysis, surface treatment and baking/drying processes were excluded as they are automated. The following actions were taken in organizing the activities and designating workers for each process involved in making the E26. The cutting and shaping operation continues to operate in the same manner as it is currently carried out. The welding process was divided into two processes, Weld 1 and Weld 2, reducing cycle times and increasing production at each station through the distribution of work and hiring of labor. In tire assembly, tasks were unified, and personnel was relocated, with a proposed improvement in the cycle time of 5.57 min. Likewise, for the assembly line, activities were unified, and personnel was relocated. Three workers to the line were also proposed, achieving an improvement in the cycle time to 9.02 min.

2.6 Mapping the Future State

The current VSM has a push production system, i.e., production is based on existing demand; a state that is far from an ideal situation, which would be given with the implementation of a pull production system. The future VSM proposes a mixed production system. In other words, for the initial processes of cutting, forming, welding 1, welding 2, and surface treatment, the push system would be maintained due to the existence of long waiting times between each process and the existence of a variable demand [18]. Regarding the following processes, the proposal is a pull system with a product supermarket that will have enough products (100 units) for the painting and baking/drying processes. These processes set the pace of production. Thus, the system will achieve a continuous flow, balancing production with demand [19].

The future VSM preserves the transfer batch currently handled (50 units), being implemented from the cutting process until the welding ends. After the painting, continuous production can be carried out. Thus, the VSM of the future state is represented in Fig. 3 with the improvements and leveled processes.

2.7 Simulation of the Future State

The optimization was validated through the simulation of the future VSM for the production line of the E26 model. FlexSim2018 software was used under educational license, aimed at simulation, development, visualization of systems, and activities with a dynamic flow. It allows the use of objects to visually represent the state of a production system [20]. In this software, all processes were distributed from cutting to the final assembly process, using as a template the "layout" of the existing production plant, and adding the proposal for distributing the raw material warehouse. Thus, a model was achieved with a perfect location of the processes and production areas, respecting each work area's dimensions and spaces.

The times used for the simulation resulted from making statistical distributions to preserve the variability of the production system. With the help of the "STAT:: Fit" software, the time distributions for the entire process reflected in Table 4 were obtained [21]. There were processes whose cycle and set-up times were constant because they are automated processes. The simulation's duration time was 600 min, corresponding to the average time per shift, and was run for five days of work. For the simulation of the system, when starting from scratch, García et al. recommend the use of the warmup time, with the value of one working day or one day (600 min) [21]. In addition, 30 replicas were simulated, obtaining for each simulation, an average of 653 bicycles without significant changes; this due to the variability existing in each process time.

3 Results

As a result, the optimization of the case study company's production processes was achieved through the implementation of LM tools. For the distribution of the raw material warehouse, Table 3 shows that the distance concerning the current state decreased to 517.4 m. It corresponds to a decrease of 33% in distance and a decrease in transport

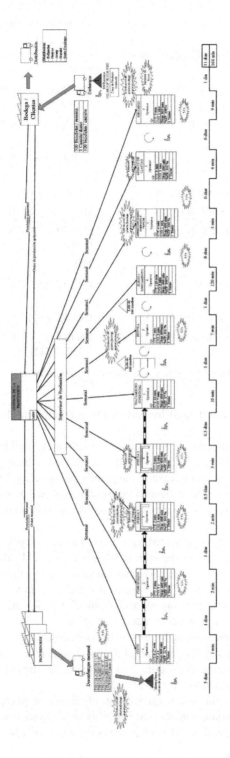

Fig. 3. Proposed VSM for the E26 model.

Table 4. Distributions for simulation times of the future state.

Process	Probability distribution	Cycle time (min)	Set-up time (min)
Cut	Normal, N (μ, σ)	N (0.203; 0.0188)	0.013
Conformed	Exponential, E (γ, μ)	E (2.32; 0.143)	0.29
Weld 1	Uniform, U (μ, h) /Normal, N (μ, σ)	U (9.47; 10)	N (0.821; 0.156)
Weld 2	Normal, N (μ, σ)	N (14.4; 1.13)	N (1.02; 0.155)
Surface Treatment	Normal, N (μ, σ)	10	N (5.48; 0.0435)
Painting	Normal, N (μ, σ)	N (6.39; 0.0549)	N (0.882; 0.0599)
Baking/Drying	–	120	0
Full frame and pitchfork assembly	Uniform, U (μ, h)	U (3.36; 3.6)	0.157
Tire assembly	Exponential, E (γ, μ)	E (6.48; 7.92)	0.3867
Assemble	Log normal, LN (γ, μ, σ)	LN (8.94; 0.333; 0.442)	0.1439

Note: μ = Average; σ = standard deviation; γ = Location; h = Average range

time. It also improves the effort used by part of the personnel in charge of the raw materials supply.

It was possible to simplify process times, organize activities, workloads, and designate its operators in terms of line balancing. Thus, it allowed reducing the cycle time of the process, and generating an increase in the plant's productivity. Figure 4 shows a more stable proposed process, where, despite the existence of two processes exceeding the takt time, a reduction in processing times was possible, as well as an increase in their production capacity.

Moreover, the total time was reduced to 176.77 min per bicycle, corresponding to a reduction of 14% compared to the current situation. Figure 4, likewise, shows a significant decrease in each process time. The bottleneck caused by the welding process was controlled, and the cycle times for tire assembly and assembly were reduced. In addition, the lead time was considerably reduced from 25 days for the current VSM to 11 days for the future VSM, representing a decrease of 66%. The future state includes implementing a product supermarket located between the surface treatment and the painting process, with inventory for one shift (100 units), to get the entire plant to start with product-in-process, eliminating waiting. Additionally, the current transfer lot was preserved, which corresponds to lots for 50 bicycles.

The simulation of 30 replicas was carried out, obtaining an average of 653 E26 bicycles as a result of the production, showing stability in the system without affecting the variability of each process time. This number results when simulating for a time of

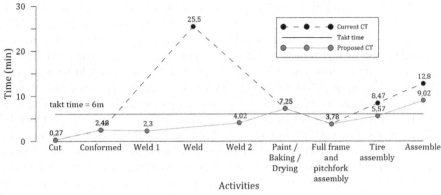

Note: CT = Cycle Time

Fig. 4. Comparison of the current state vs. Future state.

one week (3000 min). The current production of the company corresponds to 500 units assembled in five days. Through the simulation, up to 653 weekly units were achieved, representing an increase of 23.43%, corresponding to 153 additional units per week.

4 Discussion

The present study considers the methodology of Barcia and De Loor [12], following a specific guideline for the case study. The research proposal's scope contemplates obtaining a VSM of the future state for the assembly of the E26 bicycle.

From the implementation of 5S, the studies presented by Benavides et al. [22] and Gómez et al. [23] were taken as a reference. Their findings indicate an immediate improvement in aspects such as order, cleaning of the work areas, elimination of objects or waste that hinder the work, the order in the tools, reduction in processing times, achieving an increase in production, as well as, generating visual satisfaction and comfort at the time of carrying out the work. This study was applied in a company with similar characteristics to the company analyzed. Therefore, it can be inferred that the results would be similar to those proposed by the authors. Similarly, Paredes Rodríguez [24] suggests improvements through VSM following the methodology mentioned above, applying the 5S, Kanban, and plant distribution tools.

Continuing with the discussion, the identification of waste through VSM was presented, which allowed defining critical points within the production on which there was an opportunity for improvements. Regarding plant distribution, it focused on achieving the unification of raw material in a single point and reducing times and distances that the raw material travels. Results obtained a 33% decrease in the length traveled to provide raw material to the processes. To achieve the objective, it is necessary to reach an adequate organization based on the order and frequency of the stored materials.

As a value proposition, unlike the cases mentioned in the introduction, the balance of lines achieves a reduction in the cycle times of the most critical processes (welding, tire assembly, assembly). For effective line balancing, it is necessary to consider hiring personnel for the new welding processes (Weld 1, Weld 2) and assembly, also the assignment of work and new tasks. An important aspect within the future VSM is the product supermarket proposal, which represents an essential requirement for the proposed system to improve and obtain a mixed push and pull production system.

An important contribution of the study is the validation of the LM tools through simulation of the future VSM, reflecting the theoretical results in an environment close to reality. The variability existing in each process's times was taken into consideration. In Table 4, when carrying out an analysis of the distributions, it was observed that the system presents several processes with normal and uniform distributions. This simulates the real situation of the process, and the replications made of production did not show variations over time. It should be mentioned that an optimistic scenario was considered for the simulation, i.e., factors such as delays from stoppages in production due to failures, number of defective units were not considered nor the level of absenteeism of operators in the company.

5 Conclusions

This study verifies that the proposal for optimizing operational processes through the LM philosophy meets the formulated objective, showing results such as increased productivity and work leveling, which can be seen in terms of a considerable reduction in cycle times and lead time. Through the VSM, it was possible to capture the production plant's current state of operation. This was the study's primary tool, through which existing problems and waste within the production process were identified. The 5S proposal was born from the identified waste, focusing on achieving a culture of order and cleanliness. This tool is a fundamental basis for obtaining better results.

From the distribution for the raw material warehouse, significant results were obtained. For example, the unification of all the materials for the assembly of bicycles in a single point, which generates greater ease in terms of transport, a reduction in travel distances and, consequently, a considerable decrease in transport times that translates into immediate availability of raw material.

Through line balancing, the processes that were on takt time were subjected to leveling and workload allocation. Additionally, the grouping of activities to have balanced processes led to a reduction in cycle times, the most notable being the division of the welding process (weld 1, weld 2), with a total decrease of 14% in total processing time and 66% in lead time.

For the future VSM modeling, the software presented an approximation to the results obtained from the proposal. Significant productivity improvement can be verified, achieving an increase of 23.43%. In addition, the simulation demonstrated the validity of the product supermarket implementation, as a continuous flow is achieved from the painting, baking/drying process to the end of the assembly line. It must be taken into account that the variability that affects the simulation will not be the same that affects the plant's real state. This due to external factors that cannot be considered in the simulation such as absenteeism, waiting times, breaks, etc.,

As future work, the possibility of using Kanban and SMED is proposed. These tools are focused on reducing inventories of products-in-process and reducing set-up times, which are part of the problems afflicting most industries.

Acknowledgments. This study is part of the research project "Modelo de Gestión para la optimización de procesos y costos en la Industria de Ensamblaje", supported by the Research Department of the University of Cuenca (DIUC).

References

1. Villaseñor Contreras, A.: Manual de Lean Manufacturing. Guía básica. Instituto Lean Thinking Solutions, México (2017)
2. Rajadell Carreras, M.R., Sánchez García, J.L.S.: Lean Manufacturing. La evidencia de una necesidad. Ediciones Díaz de Santos (2010)
3. Valpuesta Lucena, M.: Ejemplo de aplicación de herramientas Lean en una fábrica del sector automoción (2016)
4. Abdulmalek, F.A., Rajgopal, J.: Analyzing the benefits of lean manufacturing and value stream mapping via simulation: a process sector case study. Int. J. Prod. Econ. **107**, 223–236 (2007). https://doi.org/10.1016/j.ijpe.2006.09.009
5. Sundar, R., Balaji, A.N., Kumar, R.M.S.: A review on lean manufacturing implementation techniques. Procedia Eng. **97**, 1875–1885 (2014). https://doi.org/10.1016/j.proeng.2014.12.341
6. Rohani, J.M., Zahraee, S.M.: Production line analysis via value stream mapping: a lean manufacturing process of color industry. Procedia Manuf. **2**, 6 (2015). https://doi.org/10.1016/j.promfg.2015.07.002
7. Grewal, C.: An initiative to implement lean manufacturing using value stream mapping in a small company. Int. J. Manuf. Technol. Manage. **15**, 404–417 (2008). https://doi.org/10.1504/IJMTM.2008.020176
8. Choomlucksana, J., Ongsaranakorn, M., Suksabai, P.: Improving the productivity of sheet metal stamping subassembly area using the application of lean manufacturing principles. Procedia Manuf. **2**, 102–107 (2015). https://doi.org/10.1016/j.promfg.2015.07.090
9. Motwani, J.: A business process change framework for examining lean manufacturing: a case study. Ind. Manage. Data Systs. **103**, 339–346 (2003). https://doi.org/10.1108/02635570310477398
10. Rodas, P., Guaman, R., Colina Morles, E., Peña, M., Siguenza-Guzman, L.: Mathematical model based on linear programming and fuzzy logic for time prediction in bicycle assembly industries. RISTI, pp. 581–594 (2019)
11. Hernández Matías, J.M., Vizán Idoipe, A.: Lean manufacturing: Conceptos, técnicas e implantación. Fundación EOI, Madrid (2013)
12. Barcia, K., De Loor, C.: Metodología para Mejorar un Proceso de Ensamble Aplicando el Mapeo de la Cadena de Valor (VSM). Revista Tecnológica - ESPOL. **20**, 31–38 (2007)
13. Torrents, A.S., Postils, I.A., Vilda, F.G., Postils, I.A.: Manual práctico de diseño de sistemas productivos. Ediciones Díaz de Santos (2004)
14. Sacristán, F.R.: Las 5S: Orden y limpieza en el puesto de trabajo. Fundación Confemetal Editorial, España (2005)
15. Cruz, J.: Manual para la implementación sostenible de las 5S. INFOTEP, Santo Domingo, República Dominicana (2010)
16. Meyers, F.E., Stephens, M.P., Enríquez Brito, J.: Diseño de instalaciones de manufactura y manejo de materiales. Pearson Educación, México (2006)
17. López Acosta, M., Martínez Solano, G.M., Quirós Morales, A.F., Sosa Ochoa, J.A.: 21.-Balanceo de líneas utilizando herramientas de Manufactura Esbelta. Revista El Buzón de Pacioli. 22 (2011)

18. Chapman, S.N.: Planificación y control de la producción. Pearson Educación, México (2006)
19. Arbós, L.C.: Procesos en flujo Pull y gestión Lean. Sistema Kanban: Organización de la producción y dirección de operaciones. Ediciones Díaz de Santos, Madrid (2012)
20. Casadiego Azalte, R.: Guía de usuario para el modelamiento y analisis con el Software FlexSim. Universidad Francisco de Paula Santander
21. García Dunna, E., García Reyes, H., Cárdenas Barrón, L.E.: Simulación y análisis de sistemas con ProModel. Pearson Educación, México (2006)
22. Benavides Colon, K., Castro Pájaro, P.: Diseño e implementación de un programa de 5s en industrias Metalmecánicas San Judas Ltda (2010). https://190.242.62.234:8080/jspui/handle/11227/1129
23. Gómez Gómez, L.M., Giraldo Ayala, H., Pulgarín Rojas, C.: Implementación de la metodología 5 s en el área de carpintería en la universidad de San Buenaventura. Universidad de San Buenaventura. Facultad de Ingeniería. Antioquia, Medellin-Colombia (2012)
24. Paredes-Rodríguez, A.M.: Aplicación de la herramienta Value Stream Mapping a una empresa embaladora de productos de vidrio. Entramado. **13**, 262–277 (2017). https://doi.org/https://doi.org/10.18041/entramado.2017v13n1.25103

Characteristics of Women Associated in Imbabura Province: Contributions for a Model of Edu-Communication for Women Entrepreneurs

Claudia Alicia Ruiz Chagna[1]([✉]) [iD] and Ana Iglesias Rodríguez[2] [iD]

[1] Universidad Técnica del Norte, 100150 Ibarra, Ecuador
`caruiz@utn.edu.ec`
[2] University School of Education and Tourism, University of Salamanca, 05003 Ávila, Spain
`anaiglesias@usal.es`

Abstract. To achieve gender equality in Ecuador requires more effort to improve equal access for women's employment and their integral development. To this effect, boosting entrepreneurship through training programs is required. This research characterizes women's associations in the Province of Imbabura to set a theoretical framework that builds, a posteriori, a model focused on edu-communication and non-formal education. This characterization was done by applying a mixed approach based on a field design. For this purpose, a field journal and a survey applied to 84 participants from three associations belonging to Ibarra, Urcuquí, and Cotacachi Cantons were used. The results evidence a population made up of mothers who carry out individual entrepreneurships, with less access to Information and Communication Technologies, young women with greater access to formal education; however all of them are interested in training aimed at the development of entrepreneurship competencies.

Keywords: Edu-communication · Entrepreneurship · Intercultural education · Gender equality · Andragogy · Democracy

1 Introduction

Equality is a goal that cannot be postponed by democratic governments and, hence, it must be considered in all spaces for citizens' participation. To allow and facilitate the participation of society members on equal terms, not only favors the democratic nature of a State, but also permits to move toward a sustainable economic growth, due to the existence of a negative correlation between inequality and productivity; that is to say, to greater inequality, productivity drops [1].

The analysis of the Latin American reality leads to the conclusion that "inequality is a historical and structural feature [...] which has been retained and reproduced even

The study presented in this paper is part of a Doctoral Thesis work which is being carried out within the Doctorate Program Training in the Knowledge Society at University of Salamanca.

M. Botto-Tobar et al. (Eds.): ICAT 2020, CCIS 1388, pp. 129–136, 2021.
https://doi.org/10.1007/978-3-030-71503-8_10

in growth and prosperity periods" [1]. This inequality level has been consolidated in the region through a system of privileges that emerge within a very complex socio-regional heterogeneity, which generates a system of social exclusion (of gender, class and ethnic) influencing in the socio-economic development [2]. In the case of gender inequality, this affects to the women's professional development, to the individual's advancement in the economic welfare, and to the economic development of family and society [3].

In Ecuador, sexism is a social, cultural, and political issue, which in the educational field gets especially aggravated because of the perceptions that the Ecuadorian society has about the study capabilities of every gender. This has repercussions in the university major selection done by women and in the further continuation of their studies [4].

This gender inequality condition in Ecuadorian territory has led to the development of a constitutional legal framework established in Article 11, paragraph 2, that "no one may be discriminated against, among other reasons, sex, gender identity, age, ethnicity, place of birth, sexual orientation or disabilities" [5].

In the same way, gender equality is established with regard to access to education through the Law of Education for Democracy in 2006, and in the National Plan of Good Living (2017–2021) [6].

Besides gender inequality, the Ecuadorian government must confront ethnic discrimination. The diversity of geographical areas of Ecuador has contributed to the development of different cultures in its territory throughout its history. Subsequently, as a result of the colonization process, this nation was formed in a multi-ethnic and multi-cultural melting pot, which led to the establishment of a society where "8.5% of the population is considered to be indigenous, 5.7% afro, 7.7% white, and 78.8% mestizo" [7].

This ethnic diversity has become a challenge for Ecuador. The social, political, and legal advancements have caused that through interculturality Ecuador leaves the doors open for the social system transformation; providing a new assessment for population heterogeneity, a fact that favors the social and economic development of the country. In turn, the incorporation of the interculturality concept in political thinking of the indigenous movement in Latin America, acts as a tool to define the characteristics of a new more egalitarian society [8].

Even when effort to achieve gender and ethnic equality has promoted social progress in the country, the issue about economic development still remains from a conceptual and legal framework. According to [2], the involvement of all sectors of society in the productive process drives national economy growth, as long as the appropriate economic strategies be used; including entrepreneurship.

Entrepreneurship was defined by [9] as a business strategy for the citizen empowerment and the momentum of local, regional and national economy. Therefore, entrepreneurs are a core piece within a free market economy that requires personal effort with freedom and guarantees for equal conditions and opportunities to progress; this to contribute with human development [10].

In accordance with the aforementioned assertion, entrepreneurships lead towards an economic growth and gender equality by promoting equality and economic autonomy processes, particularly of women and other vulnerable groups to social inequality. For this reason, to support the women's entrepreneurship will help to minimize the gender inequality [3], and will generate changes at individual, family, and national level; creating opportunities for the country's economic progress, through the generation of wealth and new jobs [11].

Even when in Latin America, the development of entrepreneurships has increased progressively in recent years, women continue to have a poor rate in the statistics for entrepreneurs, which decreases more when their ethnic origin is considered.

The Ministry of Economic Affairs, Development and Tourism of Chile mentions that some causes that interfere in the development of women's entrepreneurship in Latin America are related to education access [12]. In this sense, the role imposed in society and assumed by women such as early childbearing and household burden causes their disassociation from the formal educational system, which leads to a subsequent women's underemployment and economic dependency.

Thus, the gender equality can be encouraged with educational programs that provide the female population with the acquisition of competencies for the entrepreneurship development, as well as the possibility to keep up the household and take care of the family, which may be possible by entrepreneurships carried out in the household [11]. These educational programs must be accompanied by supporting processes and state funding in order to contribute to the creation of new entrepreneurships and social progress [3].

The development of Ecuadorian educational programs aimed to the acquisition of competencies for the creation and long-term maintenance of entrepreneurships must be associated with an educational model that takes into account the social dynamics of Ecuadorian women, as well as the country's ethnic diversity. This implies incorporating Information and Communication Technologies (ICT), according to educommunicative processes through non-formal education, which accepts adjusting the formation process according to the time, needs and conditions of women from various age, ethnic and social background groups.

ICT enable a very different school model, and processes of non-formal and informal education also dissimilar [13], which requires reconsideration from media because they are agents playing an intrinsic direct and indirect role in the individual's formation processes at all stages of life.

It is necessary to consider the characteristics of the target population for the creation of a training plan that brings together programs through intercultural educommunication that allows women's training in the development of entrepreneurships, Based on the vision of this training process, the research seeks to define the characteristics and the social context of women associated in Imbabura Province, Ecuador, in order to enable the generation, a posteriori, of a intercultural edu-communication model which boosts entrepreneurships and integral development.

2 Method

The study presented in this paper is part of a Doctoral Thesis work which is being carried out within the Doctorate Program Training in the Knowledge Society at University of Salamanca. The research has been conducted through a mixed approach that involves the use of characteristics from the quantitative and qualitative approaches to develop a better description of the study sample, and consolidation of results. It employed field research in order to gather information directly from the women participants from different associations selected for this study.

2.1 Study Area

This area includes three Cantons of Urcuquí, Cotacachi and Ibarra located in Imbabura Province in the northern part of the Andean region of Ecuador. The region is diverse in ecosystems, it has paramos over 3,600 m height. It also has areas with tropical climate near the Chota River basin. In accordance with the Plan of Development and Territorial Organization of Imbabura Province [14], there are nine areas of economic activity in line with the regional productive potential, highlighting the tourist undertakings, handicrafts, and traditional cuisine.

2.2 Population and Sample

The study is focused on the characterization of the women entrepreneurs associations in Imbabura Province, where the target population for this study are those associations that have an ethnic diversity constituted by women who are Quichuan, afro-descent and mestizo. Women who own active entrepreneurships, and that openly expressed their commitment to this research, through their informed consent. These inclusion criteria allowed the identification of 25 associations that together reached 90 entrepreneurships in the region.

There was an intentional sampling selected at choosing three women's associations that represent each canton in the study area; the first of them is the Association of Women Farmers "Fruits of My Land" that develops its activities in the Urcuquí Canton; the second association is the Peasant and Indigenous Women Union Organizations "Pachamama feeds us", whose scope of development is located in the Cotacachi Canton; finally, the Women's Association "The Choteñitas", made up mainly of Afro-Ecuadorian women from Chota Valley, Ibarra Canton.

It was evidenced that only 73% out of the 137 members of the organizations are active developing entrepreneurship, and this was the group considered for the research.

2.3 Techniques and Instruments

Two research techniques were applied for the diagnosis. The first one was direct observation, whose results were recorded in a field journal the objective was to describe the conditions of the associations operation area, and the outstanding features of the female entrepreneurs, which facilitated the fusion of information for a subsequent survey analysis. Secondly, a survey made up of 31 questions was applied to 84 women of the participating associations; being analyzed through descriptive statistical methods, with the purpose of getting to know the typology of associated women, the aspects related to their entrepreneurships, and access to and use of ICT. The use of both techniques enabled gathering more precise data on the context where they develop partnerships, and to know the real situation of women entrepreneurs. The informed consent was obtained from the study groups according to ethical standards of research processes before the instrument's application.

3   Results and Discussion

Several Latin American countries have adopted policies to foster economic development through associative processes of cooperatives, among others, which get adjusted to model processes of Social and Solidarity Economy [15]. This model promotes the economic development of family groups or partners for the improvement of their living conditions and the increase in equality.

In the case of gender equality, it is required to incorporate women in development processes of competencies for their economic independence, through formal and non-formal education. To do this, Information and Communication Technologies are tools which, due to their widespread deployment can allow the training of women from the ethnic groups: mestizo, Afro-Ecuadorians, and indigenous. To check for this approach, it is required to design an edu-communication model aimed to the develop women's capacities for the creation and maintenance of long-term entrepreneurships in Ibarra, Urcuqui and Cotacachi Cantons, and to improve their quality of life, along with gender, social opportunities, and labor equality.

The development of an edu-communication model with these scopes requires knowledge about the target population to be trained, in order to ensure its effectiveness.

Typology of Surveyed Women
Respondent women from participating associations of Ibarra, Urcuqui and Cotacachi Cantons in Imbabura Province are among a range of ages under 18 years and older than 55 years, where 40% is between 36 and 45 years old. If women between 26 and 35 years are added to the previous value, then the percentage rises to 67%, and it maintains the trend in Latin America [16].

This creates a majority group of women in productive age who have opted for the development of entrepreneurship as a measure to achieve greater economic stability. This age group of women coincides with the reproductive age of the Ecuadorian population, which is evident in the number of children per respondent where the 43% have between 1 and 3 children, 31% have from 4 to 6 children, and 21% over 6 children, which are higher values than the national percentages. More than 50% of women who belong to this associations have an imminent need for contributing economically in their home due to the fact the number of children is a factor that has been identified as the cause for the decline in women's economic independence, however, it is also a motivation for the development of entrepreneurships in the household; keeping in mind that the edu-communication model has as a strength to consolidate empirical knowledge in a way that over time, training turns necessity into a sustainable opportunity.

In relation to the educational level, it was noted that 6% of women do not have formal studies, 41% has only completed primary school. This situation is related to the number of children and pregnancy at an early age that causes the interruption of studies in women. An important fact is that 10% of the sample has higher education studies and they become a determining supporting factor for the organization strengthening within the women's associations because their contribution as leaders converting strategic actions into deep changes in family structures and economic independence.

Formal education has been increasingly important in Ecuador for the development of entrepreneurship, since 2015, the subject Entrepreneurship and Management was incorporated in middle and high school levels [17]. It is estimated that this education policy will generate a positive context for the new entrepreneur generations, since age group range influences the access to formal education. It can be noted that the lower levels of education are associated with older women, while the younger ones, due to access to ICT, seem to have obtained greater opportunities for study in the formal system.

An important social aspect important for gender equality is that entrepreneurship initiative by women has granted them greater respect and authority in the household. This is because of the self-recognition as heads of household from a 37% of respondents, which is a value more than 10% of the national mean in poor and non-poor households [18].

Finally, it should be highlighted that 60%, of the participants live in urban areas of the cantons being part of Imbabura Province, according to the data of entrepreneurs in the whole country it reaches 67% [19].

Forms of Organization
The entrepreneurships developed by women are, for the most part, a result of personal actions (51%), and the income goes to the home. Another way in which women develop entrepreneurships is as a family business (17%).

The conformation of alliances through associations represents only 32% of the entrepreneurships in this study, which is below the percentage of associative entrepreneurships of the Ibarra Canton that has been estimated at 55% [16]. If associations are the main organizational structure to strengthen the role of women in society, this percentage is shown as a socio-economic weakness, and more attention should be paid to the development of associative entrepreneurships in the cantons of Urcuquí and Cotacachi, considering coalitions as a strategy to reach a greater coverage of customers in markets, optimizing in this way costs in the operation, and improving their competitive capacity.

To overcome this weakness, associations can access to processes of formation through the governmental entities, and 61% of women surveyed have had access to this training through formal and non-formal education. However, course, workshops or lectures offering is scarce, it is presented in isolation, or does not respond to organizational needs nor to an integral training formation in processes for productive undertakings; that is why the edu-communication model must propose the creation of modules with common topics to achieve the entrepreneurship success.

Access to Information and Communication Technologies
It is required to determine the access to ICT, and the competencies that women from the associations of Ibarra, Urcuquí and Cotacachi Cantons have to use ICT with the aim of facilitating the training processes.

ICT enable the increase access to training through formal and non-formal education. It was determined that all respondents have access to open television, but only 32% have cable television, and slightly over (54%) has Internet connection at home.

Regarding the computers at home, in all homes there is at least one personal computer, and with the increase of cellular phones supply in the market, it is noted that 89% of respondents have access to this device. The increasing cell phone use has an impact on the knowledge of social networks (56%) accessed in a daily basis, the combination of these two factors increase the opportunities for a greater training offer. The participants prefer training processes through the television (32%), internet classes (17%) and classes by radio (6%). Nevertheless, there is a 45% of participants who prefer face-to-face training, as part of the group with no management of social networks or Internet access.

Training Interests
Due to the nature of entrepreneurships, 40% of respondents live in a rural area, the main areas of interest for training are the aspects related with basic administration (22%), improvement of their skills in the agricultural and environmental field (21%), customer service (16%), elements linked with health (12%), improvements in technological skills (13%). This coincides with the fastest growing sectors in Ecuador for rural areas [20].

4 Conclusions

The obvious differences and injustices that have characterized the living conditions of women throughout history in their various fields (family, educational, political, labor, among others), have resulted in poor access to formal education. This decoupling of the formal education system implies less possibility for economic well-being which can be remedied through the entrepreneurship development.

The entrepreneurships in Imbabura Province are led by necessity-driven women. A significant number of them are leaders of household whose instinct to protect their children supports their activity, -internal migration, family, income sources-, and that is why they require a more specific and concrete training suitable to their business needs; a training that will provide them with the entrepreneurship competencies to turn their business into optimal and long-lasting.

The presence of mass media in the Ecuadorian homes facilitates access to edu-communication programs in close coordination with the academy and its community outreach programs.

There is a need for a non-formal educational process that considers the characteristics of the population emerging from this research, a formative process aimed at the development of competencies in women from Imbabura Province that arouses an effective entrepreneurship, which educate from andragogy, interculturality and gender equity.

It is urgent the creation of programs and materials according to the interests, ages and conditions of the target population, which contribute to the development of the individual, family and associative entrepreneurships; the latter as a tool for social empowerment that offers women the possibility to benefit from the state and thus, to boost and consolidate their productive proposals.

References

1. CEPAL: Panorama Social de América Latina 2019. (LC/PUB.2019/22-P/Re v.1), Chile (2019)
2. CEPAL: Latin American Economic Outlook 2017: Youth, Skills and Entrepreneurship. OECD Publishing, Francia (2016)
3. Ilie, C., Cardoza, G., Fernández, A., Tejada, H.: Emprendimiento y Género en América Latina – 2017. INCAE Business School I (2017)

 4. Mantilla, L.M., Galarza, J.C., Zamora, A.: La inserción de la mujer en la educación superior ecuatoriana: Caso Universidad Técnica de Ambato. Revista Latinoamericana de Estudios Educativos 13(2), 12–29 (2017)
 5. Constitución de la República del Ecuador: Constitución de la República del Ecuador. Montecristi, Manabí, Ecuador: Registro oficial, septiembre de 2008
 6. Secretaría Nacional de Planificación y Desarrollo: Plan Nacional de Desarrollo 2017–2021. Toda una Vida. Quito, Ecuador (2017)
 7. FLACSO: Guía. Módulos de Capacitación. Módulo 1. Interculturalidad, derechos humanos y derechos colectivos, Quito, Ecuador: Laboratorio de interculturalidad de FLACSO Ecuador (2016)
 8. Cruz, M.R.: Construir la interculturalidad. Políticas educativas, diversidad cultural y desigualdad en Ecuador. Íconos. Revista de Ciencias Sociales (60), 217–236 (2018)
 9. Schumpeter, J.A.: The Theory of Economic Development: An Inquiry into Profits, Capital, Credit, Interest, and the Business Cycle. Transaction Publishers, 55 (1934)
10. Godoy, C., et al.: GÉNERO Y EMPRENDIMIENTO. Análisis crítico en torno a la subjetividad de emprendedores y emprendedoras de la Región Metropolitana, Chile. Antropología Experimental 18, 231–247 (2018)
11. Bizkaia: Emprendimiento con perspectivas de género: Manual de buenas prácticas 2017. Bizkaia foru aldundia diputación Foral (2017)
12. Ministerio de Economía, Fomento y Turismo: "Informe de resultados: El microemprendedor en Chile. Cuarta Encuesta de Microemprendimiento". Newsletter, vol. 29, febrero (2016)
13. Sena, W., Casillas, S., Cabezas, M., Barrientos, A.: La Educomunicación en el contexto de alfabetización de personas jóvenes y adultas en América Latina: estado de la cuestión a partir de una revisión bibliográfica sistemática. Revista Latina de Comunicación Social 74, pp. 133–171 (2019)
14. Gobierno Provincial de Imbabura: Plan de Ordenamiento y Desarrollo Territorial Imbabura. Ibarra, Ecuador (2015)
15. Coba, E., Díaz, J.: El crédito de desarrollo humano asociativo en la Economía social y solidaria de la provincia de Tungurahua-ecuadorAnalítika. Revista de análisis estadístico 7(1), 33–47 (2014)
16. Chávez, M., Coral, C., Gallar, Y.: Emprendimientos de mujeres y los entornos virtuales en Ecuador. Revista ESPACIOS 39(28) (2018)
17. Ruiz, C., Terán, C.: Emprendimiento, promotor de las economías locales en desarrollo, experiencia del cantón ibarra- imbabura ecuador. Revista Científica Ecociencia. Edición Especial, pp. 1–22 (2018)
18. CONAMU. La situación de las mujeres ecuatorianas: una mirada desde los derechos humanos, Quito, Ecuador (2008)
19. Lasio, V.: Emprendedoras. Escuela Politécnica del Litoral, Graduate School of Management. Guayaquil - Ecuador: Digital (2015)
20. Fonseca, P.: El producto interno bruto. Análisis económico (2014)

e-Learning

Gamification Within the Learning Evaluation Process Using Ardora at the Salesian Polytechnic University (Guayaquil, Ecuador)

Joe Llerena-Izquierdo$^{(\boxtimes)}$ ⓘ and Leidi Atiaja-Balseca$^{(\boxtimes)}$ ⓘ

Salesian Polytechnic University, Guayaquil, Ecuador
jllerena@ups.edu.ec, latiaja@est.ups.edu.ec

Abstract. During the pandemic months, from May to September 2020, the evaluation of emerging online learning has taken the attention of higher education educational institutions in the country, especially in the city of Guayaquil. This work presents the design and use of activities in scenarios based on interactivity for learning, through Ardora web, as a complement to the process of evaluating subjects in the Computer Engineering Career. The quasi-experimental quantitative approach study at the descriptive level is carried out to five groups of students in the subjects of Programming, Systems Modeling and Information Systems during the fully virtual academic period 56, for the purposes of the pandemic, at the Salesian Polytechnic University in the city of Guayaquil. The results of this work show that, during the online modality, teachers applied gamification for evaluation using renewable learning objects considering the quality of experience, reuse capacity and virtual context for the development of the specific learning achievement indicator within the subject's syllabus. It is further evidenced that students who passed the courses gained greater satisfaction in performing gamified activities rather than traditional activities. It is found that the level of approval in each course averaged 96% in this period compared to the previous one.

Keywords: Technology enhanced learning · Gamification · Ardora

1 Introduction

1.1 Evaluating Learning in Emerging Online Education

The effects of the covid-19 pandemic have increased globally, a rethinking of curriculum plans in education in all its modalities and at all levels [1, 2]. The evaluation of apprenticeships is part of the planning of a curriculum offered, based on the objectives to be achieved and the competencies to be acquired [3, 4], depending on this and whether the training was based on the web [5, 6] requires that it be applied continuously by fine-tuning its scope in the participants and a modification at an appropriate level according to its effectiveness.

The importance of environments or scenarios where the participant experiences the teaching and learning process [7–10] as well as the use of teacher-designed resources or

© Springer Nature Switzerland AG 2021
M. Botto-Tobar et al. (Eds.): ICAT 2020, CCIS 1388, pp. 139–150, 2021.
https://doi.org/10.1007/978-3-030-71503-8_11

objects, are in line with the new reality created by the global health crisis. The skills of teachers create activities with quality resources have confronted their skills acquired by their studies and experiences in the educational field and others, unknown but learned by the need [10, 11].

1.2 Gamification as an Evaluation Strategy

Gamification spaces with the use of emerging technologies have been expanded in different fields of study, in business, service or educational fields [12–15], and the efforts of researchers in work to evaluate the learning processes [16, 17] are now part of the set of strategies that complement different ways of performing the evaluation phase [18].

The incorporation of new technologies, and the virtual learning platforms that support them, open up the possibility of applying not only gamified activities to learn, but can be assessments of gamified learning at the quantitative level [19, 20].

2 Materials and Methods

This research work is of quantitative approach, quasi-experimental type at descriptive level aimed at two hundred students in five groups of the subjects of Programming, Modeling Systems and Information Systems of the Career of Computer Engineering, during the academic period 56 (from May to September 2020 totally virtual, for the purposes of the pandemic) at the Salesian Polytechnic University in the city of Guayaquil.

The syllabus of each subject is used in meetings of teachers (of the same subject) to perform an analysis of the contents and choose the type of learning assessment to use in common topics. Then, through a detailed design of the activity, the evaluation scenario is developed using the Web Ardora technology[1]. Instructional content is created according to the objective of learning and the feasible applicability on the part of the student to achieve the expected achievement indicator [21, 22].

Ardora uses technology for content with Hypertext Markup Language, version 5 (html5), JavaScript codes, Cascading Style Sheets (css3) and Hypertext Pre-Processor (php).

The instructional design used is based on the analysis, design, development, implementation and evaluation (ADDIE) that is carried out on the group of participants, the content developed and the environment used are according to the needs of each group [23, 24]. Renewable learning objects are sequenced with the way content is organized with a pedagogical approach [25–27]. Learning assessments are chosen from thirty-five possible options offered by Ardora[2], and that is where gamification is introduced [28, 29].

The virtual environment learning (VLE) used is Moodle version 2.0 that has the educational institutions.

---

[1] Available at https://www.webardora.net/index_cas.htm.

[2] Available at https://www.webardora.net/axuda_cas.htm.

2.1 Using Ardora for Evaluation

From the syllable of each subject, the teacher from his pedagogical and technical knowledge develops an activity that relates a learning component according to the content of a thematic unit. An interactive activity is generated that supports the learning process and evaluates the expected indicator (see Fig. 1).

This process is repeated for each learning outcome corresponding to the content and is distributed in relation to the number of activities planned in an application practices component or in the self-employed work component.

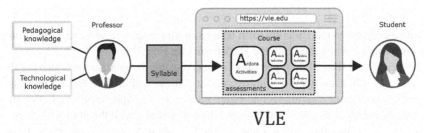

Fig. 1. Professor's competencies to create learning activities based on syllabus

According to the instructional design used in the virtual environment learning of the institution, the teacher of a subject chooses between activities of the platform (Moodle version 2.0), many of them traditional and in a "static" way, such as forums, questionnaires, essays, file upload exercises. But the use of Ardora, allows to choose activities with enriched technology (html5, css3) that transforms the content of the activity by adding visual and sound characteristics improving the perception of use by the participant (see Fig. 2).

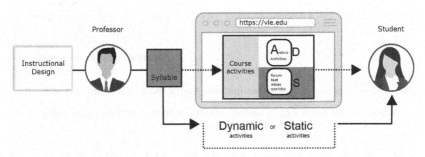

Fig. 2. Learning activities based on instructional design

The content developed is shared with teachers of the same subject or subjects that relate according to the transverse knowledge (cloister or related team). The content of the activity is improved according to the evaluation. Virtual environment learning uploads activity in two ways, through a link in the form of an integrated website to the platform for

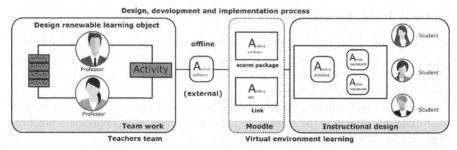

Fig. 3. Designing interactive activities and deploying to the virtual learning environment

formative evaluation and a second form using a scorn package to serve as a quantitative assessment that is integrated into the gradebook (see Fig. 3).

Ardora allows thirty-five types of activities, reusing the contents and sharing their projects with other teachers, to improve and use them within the learning process of the participants, incorporating technologies such as java scripts, html5 and css3 allow to create interactive resources and incorporation of sounds, with the ability to calculate successes and related mistakes to compute them to obtain a quantitative assessment as a result of the evaluation (Fig. 4).

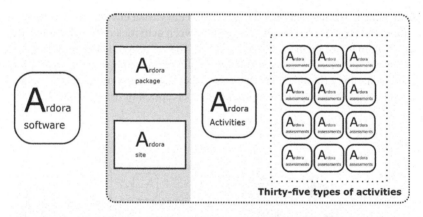

Fig. 4. Process of designing and developing evaluation activities with Ardora

Table 1 presents interactive activities according to a classification of the creators of the software. Each of these activities according to their design can be applied in a learning activity within the planning of the content of the thematic unit in a subject.

Table 1. Types of interactive activities that Ardora allows.

Type of activity	Interactive activity	Type of activity	Interactive activity
Activities with graphic	Puzzle	To complete	Words with syllables
Activities with graphic	Album	To complete	Text
Activities with graphic	Graph panel	To complete	Build words
Order	Phrases	To select	Paragraph words
Order	Paragraphs	To select	Labyrinth
Order	Images	To select	Images/Sound
Word games	Alphabet soup	Relate	Phrases-Images
Word games	Crosswords	Relate	Memory game
Word games	Hanged	Relate	Words

3   Results and Discussion

For the size of the universe of 200 students, with a margin of error of 1.1% and a confidence level of 98% the sample of 197 students was obtained. The survey technique is used for data collection. The percentage of men who participated were 37% and women 63%. The highest percentage of participants, 42% belong to the age between 20 and 22 years, 28% are over 25 years old, 22% under the age of 19 and 8% in ages 23 to 25.

Participants were asked if the resources used by teachers are motivating (see Fig. 5), resulting in only 34% thinking it is motivating and 43% that only 75% of teachers' resources are motivating, there was no value for 0%.

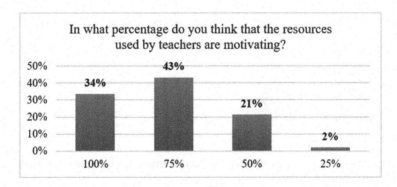

Fig. 5. Percentage of students' perception of whether teachers' resources are motivating

It also consults on how they perceive the experience when they perform an interactive activity in the virtual learning environment. As a result, 48% of participants experience interest, 30% experience motivation, 12% experience amazement, 7% experience anxiety, 2% fear and 1% stress (see Fig. 6).

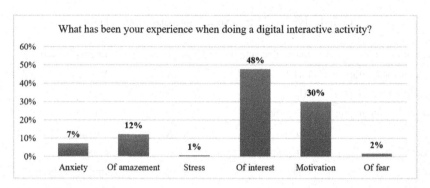

Fig. 6. Percentage of participants indicate how they perceive the experience with an interactive activity

Participants in having other subjects were consulted, if they have experienced the use of any interactive resource within more than one subject in this period, responding that 71% indicated yes, and 29% indicated no.

In other words, the heterogeneity of the ages has not been a learning factor with the use of interactive tools, in which the interest, motivation and amazement towards those learning content that their teachers were able to develop during the period 56, from May to September, is aroused.

They were consulted on what percentage of interactive resources help improve knowledge rather than traditional static resources, responding that 54% believe they help by 100%, 36% believe that by 75%, 7% by 50%, i.e. only by having the first two percentages of 100% and 75%, it is perceived that 90% think interactive resources help improve knowledge (see Fig. 7).

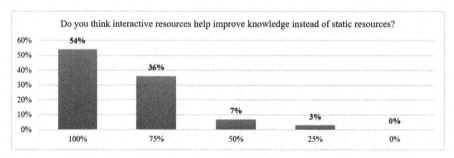

Fig. 7. Percentage of participants who think interactive activities help improve knowledge rather than traditional activities statically

They were consulted if they knew the technique of gamification, and the results were obtained from 56% did not know, and 44% indicated that they know the technique (see Fig. 8).

In the different courses activities were carried out in Ardora to form words according to concepts, use mazes according to a sequence of words that make up a theory or

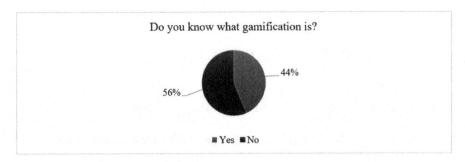

Fig. 8. Percentage of participants who know and do not know gamification

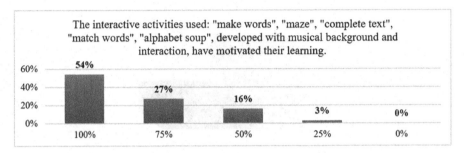

Fig. 9. Percentage of participants' motivation for using interactive activities

methodology. In addition to completing text interactively, as well as relating words, join with links (interactive lines). Put together words that represent learned concepts, all with a commensurate musical background, to create a calm, calming and motivating environment for their learning (see Fig. 9).

54% of participants indicated that activities that developed such as "create words", "mazes", "complete text", "relate words", "word soup" and others that were designed with a pleasant look (using css3 technology) and with interactivity (using html5 technology) have motivated 100% of their learnings, while 27% indicated that it motivated only 75%, 16% indicated that the motivation achieved 50% and 3% indicated that it only motivated 25%. In this response we can interpret that, although a variety of proposals were made according to the themes of the contents of the unit, there was no 0% non-motivation. It is emphasized that 81% perceive a strong motivation for the use of activities like these.

They were also asked whether, in conducting interactive activities during the academic period, the gamification technique favored their learning at different stages of the teaching process, i.e. do you think that playing learns best? Obtaining a blunt response, 93% of participants indicated yes, while 7% indicated no (see Fig. 10).

Finally, it was consulted if they think teachers found it difficult to create the resources of interactive activities. 72% said yes, and 28% said no. That is, students' perception of the teacher's work in creating the resources used was understood as a process in which the teacher must have technical skills for the resource to function properly (Fig. 11).

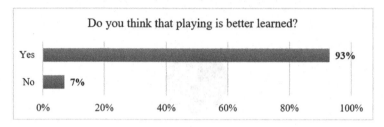

Fig. 10. Percentage of appreciation to the question if playing you learn better

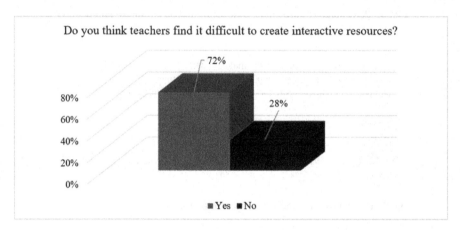

Fig. 11. Percentage of appreciation on the question that if the teacher found it difficult to create interactive resources

It should be noted that the learning of this technology is not considered within the teacher's own training, but its technical and pedagogical knowledge has allowed the design, development and evaluation of his resources. Then in their working group called cloister or team they have been able to carry prototypes suitable for implementation in virtual environments working with students. In this way, collaborative work produces renewable learning products.

It is highlighted in this work, that in the area of programming subjects two additional courses were evaluated without the use of Ardora activities and two using activities created with it. The percentage of failed assessments was 2% lower in courses that used interactive assessment activities according to the institution's final academic coordination reports. In other words, interactive evaluation activities can reduce up to 20% more from the rebukes currently obtained in a traditional objective testing scheme and benefiting the institution as the number of course losses can decrease (Fig. 12).

In addition, the tools of VLE itself (Moodle version 2.0) currently in use, its limitations and scopes, other web services for external gamification and local development applications have also been evaluated, all this has allowed a reflection throughout the institution during the time of social isolation lived. This work contributed to decisions for improvements over the following periods. Before the end of the 56th period, the

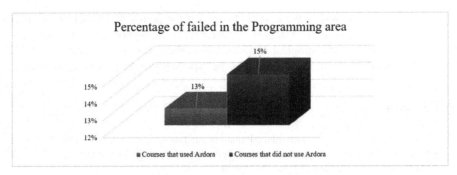

Fig. 12. Percentage difference between two courses in the scheduling area that used interactive activities with Ardora and two courses that did not.

university's teachers in the city of Guayaquil were open to the immediate use of Ardora in their activities for the new period beginning in November 2020.

4   Conclusions

In this period 56, totally online for the purposes of the pandemic and that has ended, valuable information has been collected that allows for the new period 57 (also online and especially in our city) to extend the application and use of agile tools for interaction, to the entire Salesian Polytechnic University in the city of Guayaquil, taking advantage of the benefits of its use as gamified activities. The satisfaction of the students who have passed the semester allows to identify that the strategies of creating interactive resources with gamification techniques allowed to reduce by 4% the number of students failed compared to the previous semester. Although the emerging online modality has prevented access to classrooms physically, it is visible how the skills of the teachers of the Computer Career of the Salesian Polytechnic University in the city of Guayaquil, of this study, have managed to face and creatively the teamwork for the design and development of training and evaluation activities as a complement to the teacher's own resources in face-to-face mode.

It is clear that 93% of students expect the activities of the virtual work environments of each subject to have playful components, games that allow them to develop challenges to achieve knowledge and with them improve their learning process. It is clear that having a platform with an architecture that does not allow the integration of new technologies becomes a barrier for the teacher who, although he seeks a way to integrate an activity, may not be executed by the lack of adequate infrastructure for its development.

The new challenge in the period beginning in November 2020 will allow to adjust the planning of the learning content to new virtual spaces designed from a model of interactive activities of quality and reuse in the virtual context of the student for the development of indicators of specific achievement in each subject due to evidence of the satisfaction values obtained in the results.

The university in view of the new challenge for the period 57 (November–March 2020) and the requirement of an improved platform for the support of interactive technologies and existing technological services makes the decision to upgrade the VLE platform to Moodle version 3.9 as a result of the experience of the previous 56th period.

References

1. Karadağ, E., Yücel, C.: Distance education at universities during the novel coronavirus pandemic: an analysis of undergraduate students' perceptions. Yuksekogretim Derg. **10**, 181–192 (2020). https://doi.org/10.2399/yod.20.730688
2. Kessler, A., et al.: Saving a semester of learning: MIT's emergency transition to online instruction. Inf. Learn. Sci. **121**, 587–597 (2020). https://doi.org/10.1108/ILS-04-2020-0097
3. Fujita, N.: Transforming online teaching and learning: towards learning design informed by information science and learning sciences. Inf. Learn. Sci. **121**, 503–511 (2020). https://doi.org/10.1108/ILS-04-2020-0124
4. López-Chila, R., Llerena-Izquierdo, J., Sumba-Nacipucha, N.: Collaborative work in the development of assessments on a moodle learning platform with examview. In: Botto-Tobar, M., Zambrano Vizuete, M., Díaz Cadena, A. (eds.) CI3 2020. AISC, vol. 1277, pp. 131–141. Springer, Cham (2021). https://doi.org/10.1007/978-3-030-60467-7_11
5. Schildkamp, K., Wopereis, I., Kat-De Jong, M., Peet, A., Hoetjes, I.: Building blocks of instructor professional development for innovative ICT use during a pandemic. J. Prof. Cap. Commun. (2020). https://doi.org/10.1108/JPCC-06-2020-0034
6. Llerena-Izquierdo, J., Procel-Jupiter, F., Cunalema-Arana, A.: Mobile application with cloud-based computer vision capability for university students' library services. In: Botto-Tobar, M., Zambrano Vizuete, M., Díaz Cadena, A. (eds.) CI3 2020. AISC, vol. 1277, pp. 3–15. Springer, Cham (2021). https://doi.org/10.1007/978-3-030-60467-7_1
7. Zambrano, M.E., Fuertes-Diaz, W.M., Perez-Herrera, D.D., Villacis, C.J., Perez-Estevez, E.: Production of on-line courses based on learning objects: a methodological proposal aimed at students of technical careers. Atoz-Novas Prat. Em Inf. E Conhecimento. **5**, 115–121 (2016). https://doi.org/10.5380/atoz.v5i2.49884
8. Llerena-Izquierdo, J., Valverde-Macias, A.: Google classroom as a blended learning and m-learning strategy for training representatives of the student federation of the salesian Polytechnic University (Guayaquil, Ecuador). In: Botto-Tobar, M., Zamora, W., Larrea Plúa, J., Bazurto Roldan, J., Santamaría Philco, A. (eds.) ICCIS 2020. AISC, vol. 1273, pp. 391–401. Springer, Cham (2021). https://doi.org/10.1007/978-3-030-59194-6_32
9. Campos Ortuño, R.A.: Diseño tecno-pedagógico de objetos de aprendizaje adaptados a estilos de aprender (2017). https://hdl.handle.net/10366/134377, https://doi.org/10.14201/teri.17510.
10. Ayala Carabajo, R.: Pedagogical relationship: max van manen's pedagogy in the sources of educational experience. Rev. Comput. Educ. **29**, 27–41 (2018). https://doi.org/10.5209/RCED.51925
11. Murai, Y., Muramatsu, H.: Application of creative learning principles within blended teacher professional development on integration of computer programming education into elementary and middle school classrooms. Inf. Learn. Sci. **121**, 665–675 (2020). https://doi.org/10.1108/ILS-04-2020-0122
12. Torres-Toukoumidis, A., Marin-Mateos, P., Torres-Toukoumidis, Á., Marín-Mateos, P.: Gamificación en aplicaciones móviles para servicios bancarios de España. Retos. **7**, 27 (2017). https://doi.org/10.17163/ret.n13.2017.02.

13. Llerena-Izquierdo, J., Idrovo-Llaguno, J.: Introducing gamification to improve the evaluation process of programing courses at the salesian Polytechnic University (Guayaquil, Ecuador). In: Botto-Tobar, M., Zamora, W., Larrea Plúa, J., Bazurto Roldan, J., Santamaría Philco, A. (eds.) ICCIS 2020. AISC, vol. 1273, pp. 402–412. Springer, Cham (2021). https://doi.org/10.1007/978-3-030-59194-6_33

14. Llerena, J., Andina, M., Grijalva, J.: Mobile application to promote the Malecón 2000 tourism using augmented reality and geolocation. In: Proceedings - 3rd International Conference on Information Systems and Computer Science, INCISCOS 2018, pp. 213–220 (2018). https://doi.org/10.1109/INCISCOS.2018.00038

15. Izquierdo, J.L., Alfonso, M.R., Zambrano, M.A., Segovia, J.G.: Aplicación móvil para fortalecer el aprendizaje de ajedrez en estudiantes de escuela utilizando realidad aumentada y m-learning. Rev. Ibérica Sist. e Tecnol. Informação. 120–133 (2019)

16. Barriales, A.F., Paragulla, J.V., Andrade-Arenas, L.: Gamification as part of teaching and its influence on learning computational algorithms. In: EDUNINE 2020 - 4th IEEE World Engineering Education Conference: The Challenges of Education in Engineering, Computing and Technology without Exclusions: Innovation in the Era of the Industrial Revolution 4.0, Proceedings, pp. 1–4 (2020). https://doi.org/10.1109/EDUNINE48860.2020.9149510

17. Llerena-Izquierdo, J., Ayala-Carabajo, R.: El uso de grabaciones por video como recurso de evaluación de conocimientos de aprendizajes. In: El Uso De Grabaciones Por Video Como Recurso De Evaluación De Conocimientos De Aprendizajes. Editorial Abya-Yala 8 (2018). https://www.researchgate.net/publication/327426650_El_Uso_De_Grabaciones_Por_Video_Como_Recurso_De_Evaluacion_De_Conocimientos_De_Aprendizajes

18. Aguilar, S.J.: A research-based approach for evaluating resources for transitioning to teaching online. Inf. Learn. Sci. **121**, 301–310 (2020). https://doi.org/10.1108/ILS-04-2020-0072

19. Sankaranarayanan, S., et al.: Designing for learning during collaborative projects online: tools and takeaways. Inf. Learn. Sci. (2020). https://doi.org/10.1108/ILS-04-2020-0095

20. Legaki, N.Z., Xi, N., Hamari, J., Karpouzis, K., Assimakopoulos, V.: The effect of challenge-based gamification on learning: an experiment in the context of statistics education. Int. J. Hum. Comput. Stud. **144**, 102496 (2020). https://doi.org/10.1016/j.ijhcs.2020.102496

21. Soto, C., Jiménez, W., Ibarra, M., Moreano, L., Aquino, M.: Digital educational resources to motivate environmental education in rural schools. In: Proceedings - 14th Latin American Conference on Learning Technologies, LACLO 2019. Institute of Electrical and Electronics Engineers Inc., pp. 265–271 (2019). https://doi.org/10.1109/LACLO49268.2019.00052

22. Tzelepi, M., Makri, K., Petroulis, I., Moundridou, M., Papanikolaou, K.: Gamification in online discussions: how do game elements affect critical thinking? In: Proceedings - IEEE 20th International Conference on Advanced Learning Technologies, ICALT 2020, pp. 92–94 (2020). https://doi.org/10.1109/ICALT49669.2020.00035

23. Gabriel Elías Chanchí, G., Acosta-Vargas, P., Wilmar Yesid Campo, M.: Construction of educational resources for the subject of accessibility in the course of human- computer interaction. RISTI - Rev. Iber. Sist. e Tecnol. Inf. 2019, 171–183 (2019)

24. Milosz, M., Milosz, E.: Gamification in engineering education - a preliminary literature review. In: IEEE Global Engineering Education Conference, EDUCON, pp. 1975–1979 (2020). https://doi.org/10.1109/EDUCON45650.2020.9125108

25. Verónica, A., Cecilia, S.: Learning object for the understanding of the operation merge. In: 12th Latin American Conference on Learning Objects and Technologies, LACLO 2017, pp. 1–4 (2017). https://doi.org/10.1109/LACLO.2017.8120953

26. Do Carmo, E.P., Klock, A.C.T., De Oliveira, E.H.T., Gasparini, I.: A study on the impact of gamification on students' behavior and performance through learning paths. In: Proceedings - IEEE 20th International Conference on Advanced Learning Technologies, ICALT 2020, pp. 84–86 (2020). https://doi.org/10.1109/ICALT49669.2020.00032.

27. Estrada, J.C., Nacipucha, N.S., Chila, R.L.: El uso de los códigos QR: una herramienta alternativa en la tecnología educacional. Rev. Publicando. **5**, 83–106 (2018)
28. Sáchez, S., Ávila, A., Litardo, C., Preciado, D., Chou, R., López, R.: Literature and a Facilitating Environmental Education Software. Rev. Científica la Univ. Cienfuegos. **11**, 310–317 (2019)
29. Huamani, G.T., Rodriguez, L.A., Alca, C.: Agile method and implementation of gamification in an engineering course. In: IEEE Global Engineering Education Conference, EDUCON, pp. 1815–1818 (2020). https://doi.org/10.1109/EDUCON45650.2020.9125280.

Storytelling Digital: Experience and Technology in Designs of Tele-Collaborative Projects in Higher Education

Elizabeth Ibadango-Galeano$^{(\boxtimes)}$ ⓘ, Lizarda Vargas-Chagna$^{(\boxtimes)}$ ⓘ,
Mónica Gallegos Varela$^{(\boxtimes)}$ ⓘ, Maricela Vélez-Meza$^{(\boxtimes)}$ ⓘ,
and Esteban Placencia-Enriquez$^{(\boxtimes)}$ ⓘ

Instituto de Posgrado, Universidad Técnica del Norte, Avenue 17 Julio y José Córdova 5-21,
Ibarra, Ecuador
{ejibadango,lvvargasc,mgallegos,emvelezm,emplacencia}@utn.edu.ec

Abstract. The present investigation analyzes the formative experience developed by teachers of Educational Technology and Innovation at Universidad Técnica del Norte – Imbabura-Ibarra-Ecuador, in the elaboration of a digital storytelling in the framework of the Tele-collaborative Project under ABP methodology carried out with video and stories raised from a traditional story for students of Initial Education. The degree of acquisition of skills valued at low, medium and high levels was verified; They were classified into four aspects: digital, narrative, creative and didactic competences. The construct was validated with statistical tests from RStudio where the component of experience in Tele-collaborative Projects was positively valued at 86.13%, the design Tele-collaborative Projects 80.69%, Digital Storytelling 80.47% and Level evaluation in skills 66.49%. It is concluded that a Storytelling is a useful and sustainable resource for learning because it motivates, transmits values, develops critical thinking and social skills, the experience is highly successful in teaching practice.

Keywords: ABP Tele-collaborative projects · ICT · Native and immigrant digitals · Digital skills · Storytelling

1 Introduction

Currently, there are many challenges at the educational level; the knowledge society that surrounds the human being is highly competitive, dynamic, variable and complex both in the world of work and in the academic world, so it is necessary to face the needs of society, characterized by easy and quick access to the transmission of information and knowledge (Basantes et al. 2017); In today's society, the results of technological innovation constitute sustainable technological resources that allow new pedagogical models in the teaching-learning process (Ibadango et al. 2020).

In this sense (Sevilla 2018) considers that the challenge of the current educational system has to do with the training of professionals trained to incorporate and fully participate in a society, their knowledge is the fundamental resource for socioeconomic development. Velez et al. (2019) mention that using new methodologies is vital in traditional

© Springer Nature Switzerland AG 2021
M. Botto-Tobar et al. (Eds.): ICAT 2020, CCIS 1388, pp. 151–163, 2021.
https://doi.org/10.1007/978-3-030-71503-8_12

education to modernize it. It is necessary to reach students in a new way by innovating traditionalism and replacing it with pedagogical practices that benefit student creativity (Vargas et al. 2020).

Therefore, future professionals need to develop a series of competences with an emphasis on the use of Information and Communication Technologies (ICT), which generates different skills in accessing and sharing information for the construction of knowledge.

Many authors indicate that the evolution of ICTs are efficient, safe and sustainable pedagogical strategies that facilitate the implementation of educational innovation projects to strengthen digital skills in teacher improvement and student performance, consequently including educational technology is a challenge that optimizes methods, techniques and resources in traditional activities (Guizado, Menacho, Salvatierra 2019, Rocca et al. 2019; Lion and Perosi 2019; Angelini and García-Carbonell 2019; Basantes-Andrade et al. 2020).

From this perspective, the appropriation of ICT in the pedagogical praxis of teaching staff is important, to create their own didactic resources that motivate the teaching-learning process and collaborative work.

Valuable contributions from Arango and Melissa (2019); Burgos et al. (2015); Compte and Sánchez (2019); Trujillo et al. (2019); Burden et al. (2019); Kokotsaki et al. (2016) that collaborative learning conceives group activities and has a methodology that addresses technological projects in real environments with a final product to communicate and establish dynamics of shared responsibility, strengthen skills and build problem-based learning (Thus, guarantee the active participation of students and the exchange of knowledge and the teaching role in being innovative, creative, generator of collaborative work and significant experiences in native and digital immigrants.

ABPs are strategies to encourage educational processes with technology and use communication skills through aspects of tele-collaboration (Clavel-Arroitia 2019); that turns the classroom into an active space to reinforce creativity and critical thinking supported by technological innovation and entrepreneurial activities (Gutiez 2016; Best et al. 2017); uses online communication tools where students meet and collaborate on projects under guided instruction, teacher education experiences show that web 2.0 allows collaborative work, helps promote in-depth learning, strengthens content understanding and skills development communicative and digital (Hirotani and Fujii 2019; Astall and Cowan 2016).

In this context, digital stories can support as a narrative technique that facilitates the presentation of ideas and the communication and/or transmission of knowledge with the use of technological and digital media (Del Moral et al. 2016).

Teachers say that working with a storytelling increases the participation and the sense of personal fulfillment of students, favors critical thinking and problem solving skills together with collaboration between peers, they become more creative when narrating their experiences (Dashti and Habeeb 2020). Storytelling or storytelling also allows you to experience stories that unite the present and the past, the products delivered by students become significant, capable of surprising the expectant (Dekker 2018).

Working in collaborative teams triggers a series of experiences and skills such as literacy, dramatization, imagination (Sánchez-Vera et al. 2019; Maureen et al. 2018). For this reason, the integration of technology and digital storytelling positively impacts student participation, the teaching experience is strengthened pedagogically and produces a learning experience that allows you to create your own stories, modify existing ones in a multimedia way (Liu et al. 2019). Digital storytelling favors cooperative learning in search of a common and social history that returns us to the fact that human beings are social beings par excellence and that it turns out to be something necessary for learning.

Therefore, mastering this teaching strategy requires both technological skills for the proper handling of ICT; the application of audiovisual language as well as communicative and narrative skills, in addition to didactic skills to know how to reach the student efficiently in the effective acquisition of cognitive processes (Bloome and Kim 2016).

In this way, this research seeks to identify the skills achieved in the training experience developed by teachers in Educational Technology at Universidad Técnica del Norte around the development of digital storytelling through a Tele-collaborative Project.

2   Methodology

This research is based on a descriptive, non-experimental approach that was analyzed by means of the survey and rubric of teachers from the Graduate Institute of the Technical University of the North. An intentional non-probability sampling was used, where the main inclusion criteria were teachers in the area of education and other teachers willing to collaborate in the study with the intention of observing their experience in the use of digital storytelling. The skills acquired in this Tele-collaborative Project were considered. The following phases describe the development of this proposal:

2.1   Phase 1. Definition of Competences

In this phase, the proposal that sought to identify the different skills and competences linked to the implementation of ICT through storytelling in tele-collaborative projects was analyzed, and, simultaneously, to discover the didactic possibilities of how these digital stories benefit for future professional performance. To define the competences to be developed, it was based on a study carried out by (Villalustre Martínez and Del Moral Pérez 2014); that considers 4 dimensions that are described in Table 1:

2.2   Phase 2. Process

The teachers were proposed to carry out a Tele-collaborative Project on a digital storytelling as a story that contains an educational intention and allows its pedagogical exploitation for the classroom. This proposal was intended to acquire digital, communicative, narrative and didactic skills in teachers. For this, groups of 4 people were formed who had to, among other things, fulfill certain aspects at different stages:

Approach Stage: It consisted of familiarizing the members with the possible types of history, with the characteristic elements through this adaptation of the visualization of examples or models to begin to stimulate their memory and creativity.

Table 1. Digital, narrative, creative, and didactic competences (Adapted from Villalustre Martinez and Del Moral Pérez, 2014)

Dimension	Objectives	Specific competences
Digital	Build stories from multi-format digital resources	1. Ability to master ABP and properties of audiovisual expression (use of shots, camera movements, etc.) 2. Ability to generate and manage multi-format information (soundtrack, voiceovers, special effects, images, etc.) 3. Skill for the proper use of computer programs (Movimaker, PhotoStory, Audacity, etc.)
Narratives	Develop creative narrative strategies and techniques for storytelling	1. Ability to develop written and oral compositions in digital contexts 2. Ability to select and plan a story following a previously established scheme (Visual diagram of the portrait of the story) 3. Linguistic and grammatical skills for the elaboration of dialogues and narrative sequence
Creatives		1. Ability to propose innovative and creative ideas 2. Ability to exercise critical thinking and solve problems collaboratively 3. Ability to use and exercise aesthetic sensitivity in the production of the digital story
Didactics	Discover the educational potential of digital storytelling	1. Ability to carry out artistic projects with an educational and didactic purpose 2. Ability to transmit messages and/or values through hypertextual language 3. Ability to use different didactic strategies capable of enhancing the digital and expressive resources used in the story

Source: (Villalustre Martínez and Del Moral Pérez 2014)

Conceptualization and Planning Stage Tele-collaborative Project: They were structured in Trello to plan tasks, implementation, process, execution, doubts and concerns, in addition to the assignment of roles that each student had to perform: Coordinator who organizes, manages, delegates, supervises and supports the team's activities, coordinates the integration of content, error correction and logistics of the final product. The documentary researcher identifies and coordinates the information needs for the development of the project, compiles the information. Secretary who consolidates the contributions of the team members, coordinates the systematization of the data collected. ICT expert manages the teams, multimedia resources and logistics for the development of digital Storytelling.

Storytelling Design Stage: The actors define the theme and development objective and identify the central conflict of the narrative and its structure and then develop an initial literary script to proceed with the design of the storyboard; Subsequently, the set of multimedia elements that will accompany the script is determined sequentially. This phase also consisted of executing individual and group tests that allowed to control or correct the processes before going to production using office 365 collaboration tools, created in folders in the cloud such as: Project with a final report and Resources with subfolders called: a) Documents with information from the analysis, systematization and compilation for the reinvention of stories or tales b) Images of the Storytelling c) Videos of Compilation_resources_multimedia.

Production Stage: Collect, select and create the graphic, audiovisual or symbolic elements needed for the assembly of the story (photos, drawings, videos, animations, musical tracks, sound effects, voiceovers, etc.)

Post-production Stage: Know or recognize the tools for editing the final story (programs such as Adobe Photoshop, iMovie, Macromedia Fireworks, Microsoft Photo Story, Audacity for sound, among others) and do the editing or final editing of the story in the computer, adding effects and transitions.

Dissemination and Final Evaluation Stage: The own history had to be shared and evaluated, in addition, self-evaluation exercises were carried out to identify the achievements of the project.

2.3   Phase 3. Assessment Rubric

The evaluation is an essential element that provides the teacher with the necessary information to check whether the objectives pursued have been met. Therefore, in this experience the evaluation was processed through a rubric that facilitated the assessment of the final productions prepared by the teachers, and determined the degree of competencies and skills acquired, establishing different levels of performance as presented below (Table 2):

2.4   Phase 3. Application of Instruments

To complement the data collection, a questionnaire was constructed with quantitative information measurable on the Likert scale to obtain information on the degree of acceptance of the tele-collaborative projects and competences achieved in terms of digital storytelling, by teachers. Said questionnaire provides diverse information, according to blocks of variables such as: a) individual characteristics of the students (sex, age, specialty, type of studies, professional experience.); b) Assessment of the experience in the

Table 2. Assessment rubric used to assess levels of competence in specific aspects

Aspects	Level of competence		
	Low	Medium	High
Digital uses	Little use of computer program tools with low complementary information management	Appropriate use of digital tools	The computer program is used correctly with a high use of various audiovisual tools
Narrative skill	Subject matter not adequate to the established criteria Little narrative sequence and visual	Appropriate selection of the theme Adequate narrative and visual sequence	Clearly defined theme It presents a good sequence that has coherence between the narrative structure and presentation
Creative contribution	A little creativity in digital resources	Use of different digital resources although lack of expressive capacity and initiative	It enhances the expressive capacity of the story through originality and innovation of resources
Didactic aspects	A little didactic potential. And little transmission of values and motivation	Appropriate narration for the development of skills. With little innovative teaching strategy	Enhances reflection and acquisition of values through the use of appropriate strategies

Source: Researchers

design of Tele-collaborative Projects c) Assessment of the skills acquired in the use of digital storytelling; Regarding the way the questionnaire was applied, it was anonymous using the Google Forms tool.

Subsequently, for the analysis of the data, a statistical matrix and graphs were prepared in the R Studio statistical tool, which shows the percentages and frequencies obtained in each of the questions of the applied instrument; This allowed describing the results to determine the level of acceptance of the tele-collaboration projects and the skills achieved by the teachers.

3 Results and Discussion

The results of the investigation show that the competences acquired by the teachers reached the expected level of skills, being good use of digital, narrative, creative and didactic competences for Tele-collaborative Projects. In this sense, referring to digital skills, approximately 96% have the ability to master ABP 73% and properties of audiovisual expression 85%, as well as to generate and manage multi-format information through the appropriate use of computer programs (Movimaker, 43% PhotoStory

33%, Audacity 28%, among others 9%), which leads to the efficient use of information and communication technologies. Regarding narrative competences, as 95% affirm the importance of acquiring skills to deepen the field of expression with iconic languages to be able to elaborate audio or audiovisual texts that according to (Segovia 2012) are necessary for the proper construction of the narrative speech.

On the other hand, 89% of creative skills have reached the capacity for initiative, innovation, and the imagination necessary to express their own ideas and feelings through the mastery of language and critical thinking, with novel and useful results (Chanal 2019); that were successfully exposed. Finally, 92% of the didactic competences achieved the use of adequate techniques and methods to implement digital resources and achieve effective learning, since they knew how to achieve attention and motivation (Fig. 1).

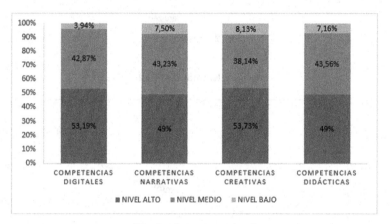

Fig. 1. Competency level

Likewise, the results of the research referring to the surveys, 4 dimensions were proposed with 22 questions and 69 surveys applied to teachers of education at the Universidad Técnica del Norte Graduate Institute, which allowed us to assess the scores of these dimensions. The results were processed in the statistical program RStudio 3.6.3 using statistical tests. Initially, normality assumptions were verified using a histogram, where the data fit a standard normal distribution. As shown in (Fig. 2). The distribution has a curve known as the Gaussian bell.

Next, the linearity assumption was verified, where the line tracks the data excellently with an increasing linear trend in the range of 2 to 2, therefore, the questions are not canceled out by adding them to each other (see Fig. 3).

In addition, the assumption of homogeneity and homoscedasticity was verified with the sphericity criterion by visualizing the Scatter Plott where the residue variation is uniform in the 4 quadrants in the interval from 2 to 2, the results are acceptable as shown in (Fig. 4).

The confirmatory factor analysis (AFC) was carried out, which is based on a statistical technique to evaluate a possible measurement model on a theoretical basis to be tested, which allows conclusions to be drawn about causality previously said, validation of

Histogram of standardized

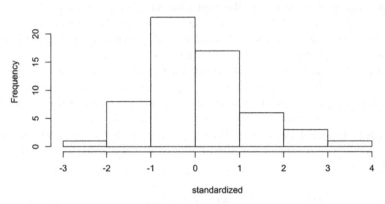

Fig. 2. Histogram

Normal Q-Q Plot

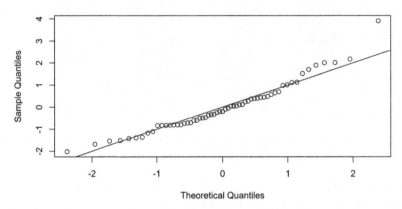

Fig. 3. QQ Plot of standardized values for quantiles

constructs, cause and effects (Fernández, 2015). Consequently, we worked with the Confirmatory Factor Analysis whose saturations are above 0.5 for each question and the positive existence of the experience in the design of Tele-collaborative projects is demonstrated. This data set allowed us to obtain the validity of the construct in the four components of: Experience with questions 2, 3, 6, 7, Design with questions 8, 9, 10, Digital storytelling with questions 11, 12, 13, Assessment questions from 1 to 12 (see Fig. 5 and 6).

Consequently, the saturations in the Tucker and Lewis index together with NNFI (Non-Normalized Fit Index) obtained results of 0.917, also the CFI was 0.941 whose results fell into an excellent category, in addition to obtaining the variance percentage for the experience and technology component in Tele-collaborative projects with 86.13%,

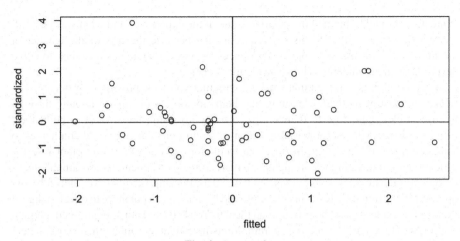

Fig. 4. Scatter plott

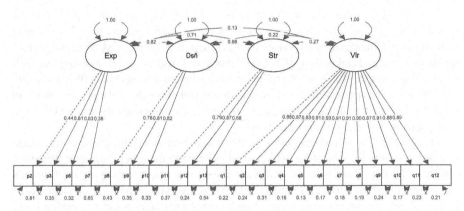

Fig. 5. Confirmatory factor analysis chart

npar	fmin	chisq	df	pvalue
23.000	0.420	49.596	32.000	0.024
baseline.chisq	baseline.df	baseline.pvalue	cfi	tli
343.564	45.000	0.000	0.941	0.917
nnfi	rfi	nfi	pnfi	ifi
0.917	0.797	0.856	0.608	0.944
rni	logl	unrestricted.logl	aic	bic
0.941	-660.549	-635.751	1367.098	1414.881

Fig. 6. Validation results

for the design of Tele-collaborative Projects with 80.69%, in Storytelling Digital 80.47% and the Assessment of levels of competences 66.49%.

In this sense, working with tele-collaborative projects strengthens innovation and teaching experience as communication strategies and collaborative work. In their results. Sánchez-Vera et al. (2019) highlight three key aspects, mainly experiences with the design of a Storytelling, a digital story through a video, in the background they disseminated the experience to serve as an example at the same time. be replicated in academic contexts and finally obtained the positive value in the experience and what was learned, consequently the results of this research coincide because the role of the teacher in teaching is to innovate and obtain experiences as positive strategies that seek to solve obstacles for their students achieve academic success.

In addition, it is obtained that working with these projects provide significant experiences because it motivates learning and helps to solve problems in a team, through the use of elements close to their reality, directly involving the student to build their own knowledge with useful learning, sustainable through challenges and challenges to achieve proposed objectives, in this area technology plays a very important role for education, by innovating traditionalism and creating environmentally sustainable technological educational resources (Vargas et al. 2020; Ibadango et al. 2020); therefore, the opportunities offered by ICT must be exploited because it is a potential to develop digital Storytelling, videos, storyboards, upload them to YouTube and other techno-pedagogical resources, where natives and digital immigrants investigate, evaluate their work, detect errors, reinforce social capacities in the exchange of ideas and agreements to improve their final result.

In the design of tele-collaborative projects, an 80.69% variance was obtained, which is considered a significant experience in higher education students as it is a reliable method to verify learning by its phases such as research, planning, task distribution, taking of decisions and elaboration of Tele-collaborative Projects, as well as empathy, work relationships, respect for respect and integrative work in various areas of knowledge, the teaching role is presented as a guide and orientation throughout the process and is in charge to introduce innovative techniques that motivate the creativity and imagination of the student, solve doubts or limitations.

80,47% 80.47% of respondents consider that digital storytelling is a useful video teaching resource for education, which, well oriented to the other curricular elements, achieves the desired skills for its elaboration, most are oriented to apply in children's stories for education initial and primary, which together with technology can learn techniques of creation and management of audiovisual language, novel for students and develop digital skills (Basantes et al. 2019). These results show that Storytelling is a significant educational resource (Dekker 2018); it favors collaborative work, content acquisition and language skills (Maureen et al. 2018); fortifies the teaching experience, increases participation and creativity (Dashti and Habeeb 2020, Liu et al. 2019). In this context, the results of (Sánchez-Vera et al. 2019); show that 73% positively valued the experience of Tele-collaborative Projects, 98% learned to develop a digital Storytelling of video with history made for boys and girls from early childhood education, 98.3% of students considered it a useful educational resource in education therefore agrees quite similarly to the results of this research.

4   Conclusion

From the results obtained, the following conclusions can be drawn: 1) The experience in Tele-collaborative Projects is significant and is valued positively in teaching teachers at the Universidad Técnica del Norte Postgraduate Institute, because it is a teaching innovation with a transversal methodology that it incorporates ICT together with activities in real contexts and serves to innovate the traditional class due to its interesting strategies that solve academic problems and cover subject objectives; 2) the application of Tele-collaborative Projects is very appropriate and of great value to promote work through collaborative tools, at the same time building knowledge until reaching a common goal, stressing the success of teamwork is the collaboration of all its members; 3) in the design of Tele-collaborative Projects, the students assume commitments for the achievement of tasks with the use of communication skills and technological tools, thus fulfilling the assignment in the established time in an effective way; 4) Consequently, it is concluded that a Digital Storytelling is a useful and sustainable video resource in learning, it constitutes the final product of the Tele-collaborative Project, which transmits digital stories with emotions, fun, suspense, creativity and values that awaken the motivation to learn, development of critical thinking, social skills, concentration, is a powerful resource in teaching work.

References

Arango, S., Melissa, L.: Nativos digitales, escuela y conocimiento. Reflexiones y Saberes **7511**, 18–24 (2019)

Astall, C., Cowan, J.: Experiences of using wiki as a participatory learning tool in teacher education. Am. J. Educ. Res. **4**(6), 459–471 (2016). https://doi.org/10.12691/education-4-6-4

Basantes-Andrade, A., Cabezas-González, M., Casillas-Martín, S.: Digital competences in e-learning. Case study: Ecuador. In: Basantes-Andrade, A., Naranjo-Toro, M., Zambrano Vizuete, M., Botto-Tobar, M. (eds.) TSIE 2019. AISC, vol. 1110, pp. 85–94. Springer, Cham (2020). https://doi.org/10.1007/978-3-030-37221-7_8

Basantes, A.V., Naranjo, M.E., Gallegos, M.C., Benítez, N.M.: Los dispositivos móviles en el proceso de aprendizaje de la facultad de educación ciencia y tecnología de la universidad técnica del norte de ecuador. Formacion Universitaria **10**(2), 79–88 (2017). https://doi.org/10.4067/S0718-50062017000200009

Best, K., Rehberg, M., Schraudner, M.: Fostering collaborative innovation: fraunhofer's participatory methodology. In: Wynarczyk, P., Ranga, M. (eds.) Technology, Commercialization and Gender, pp. 199–233. Springer, Cham (2017). https://doi.org/10.1007/978-3-319-49923-9_8

Bloome, D., Kim, M.: Storytelling: learning to read as social and cultural processes. Prospects **46**(3–4), 391–405 (2017). https://doi.org/10.1007/s11125-017-9414-9

Burden, K., Kearney, M., Schuck, S., Burke, P.: Principles underpinning innovative mobile learning: stakeholders' priorities. TechTrends **63**(6), 659–668 (2019). https://doi.org/10.1007/s11528-019-00415-0

Burgos, E., González, E., López, E.: Aprendizaje basado en proyectos. Insituto DE (2015)

Chanal, V.: La creatividad de la enseñanza en la educación superior: una perspectiva comunitaria. Aula Abierta, **48**(4), 407 (2019). https://doi.org/10.17811/rifie.48.4.2019.407-418

Clavel-Arroitia, B.: Analysis of telecollaborative exchanges among secondary education students: communication strategies and negotiation of meaning. Porta Linguarum **31**, 97–116 (2019)

Compte, M., ánchez, M.: Aprendizaje colaborativo en el sistema de educación superior ecuatoriano. Revista de Ciencias Sociales, **25**(2), 131–140 (2019). https://doi.org/10.31876/rcs.v25i2.27342

Dashti, F.A., Habeeb, K.M.: Impact of shared iPads on kindergarten students' collaboration and engagement in visual storytelling activities. Early Child. Educ. J. **48**(4), 521–531 (2020). https://doi.org/10.1007/s10643-020-01018-8

Dekker, E.: Storytelling and choice: rounded globe. J. Cult. Econ. **42**(3), 1–3 (2018). https://doi. org/10.1007/s10824-018-9325-5

Del Moral, E.M., Villalustre, L., Neira, M.: Relatos digitales: activando las competencias comunicativa, narrativa y digital en la formación inicial del profesorado. Ocnos, **15**(2), 22–41 (2016). https://doi.org/10.18239/ocnos

Fernández Aráuz, A.: Aplicación del análisis factorial confirmatorio a un modelo de medición del rendimiento académico en lectura. Revista de Ciencias Económicas, **33**(2), 39 (2015). https:// doi.org/10.15517/rce.v33i2.22216

Guizado, F., Menacho, I., Salvatierra, A.: Digital competence and professional development of teachers from two institutions of regular basic education of Los Olivos district, Lima-Peru. Hamut'Ay, **6**(2), 7 (2019). https://doi.org/10.21503/hamu.v5i2.1617

Gutiez, P.: Aulas dinámicas y telecolaborativas: desarrollo y fortalecimiento de las competencias tecnológicas para la mejora de la calidad docente. Univeridad Complutense, Madrid. Proyecto de Innovación, pp. 1–10 (2016)

Hirotani, M., Fujii, K.: Learning proverbs through telecollaboration with Japanese native speakers: facilitating L2 learners' intercultural communicative competence. Asian-Pacific J. Second Foreign Lang. Educ. **4**(1), 1–22 (2019). https://doi.org/10.1186/s40862-019-0067-5

Ibadango Galeano, E., Enríquez, E.P., Yacelga, U.Q., Rosas, W.M., Taquez, M.Q.: NEOBOOK: hypermedial language integrating knowledge in computer education. In: Basantes-Andrade, A., Naranjo-Toro, M., Zambrano Vizuete, M., Botto-Tobar, M. (eds.) TSIE 2019. AISC, vol. 1110, pp. 10–22. Springer, Cham (2020). https://doi.org/10.1007/978-3-030-37221-7_2

Kokotsaki, D., Menzies, V., Wiggins, A.: Project-based learning: a review of the literature. Improving Schools **19**(3), 267–277 (2016)

Liu, C.-C., Yang, C.-Y., Chao, P.-Y.: A longitudinal analysis of student participation in a digital collaborative storytelling activity. Educ. Tech. Res. Dev. **67**(4), 907–929 (2019). https://doi. org/10.1007/s11423-019-09666-3

Maureen, I.Y., van der Meij, H., de Jong, T.: Supporting literacy and digital literacy development in early childhood education using storytelling activities. Int. J. Early Child. **50**(3), 371–389 (2018). https://doi.org/10.1007/s13158-018-0230-z

Sánchez, M., Solano, I., Caride, S.E.: storytelling digital a través de vídeos en el contexto de la educación infantil. Revista de Medios y Educación, pixel-bit **54**, 165–184 (2019)

Segovia, B.: La adquisición de la competencia narrativa a través del cómic en la Escuela Primaria. Rev. Complutense de Educacion **23**(2), 375–399 (2012). https://doi.org/10.5209/rev_rced.2012. v23.n2.40034

Sevilla, A.: Diseño de tareas telecolaborativas para el aprendizaje de idiomas con cuentos del mundo. RIED. Revista Iberoamericana de Educación a Distancia, **21**(2), 325 (2018). https:// doi.org/10.5944/ried.21.2.20783

Trujillo, F., Salvadores, C., Gabarrón, Á.: Tecnología para la enseñanza y el aprendizaje de lenguas extranjeras: revisión de la literatura. RIED. Revista Iberoamericana de Educación a Distancia, **22**(1), 153 (2019). https://doi.org/10.5944/ried.22.1.22257

Vargas Chagna, L.V., Vargas Chagna, M.E., Navarro Chacua, R.M., Guzmán Terán, A.J., Ayala Bastidas, J.A.: Diagnosis of the use of information and communication technologies in dual training. Case study: textile confection career at "Instituto Superior Tecnólogico Cotacachi." In: Basantes-Andrade, A., Naranjo-Toro, M., Zambrano Vizuete, M., Botto-Tobar, M. (eds.) TSIE 2019. AISC, vol. 1110, pp. 72–84. Springer, Cham (2020). https://doi.org/10.1007/978-3-030-37221-7_7

Vélez Meza, E., Alexis, G.T., Mónica, G.V., Jacinto, M.U.: Digital gamification in basic general education students. In: Basantes-Andrade, A., Naranjo-Toro, M., Zambrano Vizuete, M., Botto-Tobar, M. (eds.) TSIE 2019. AISC, vol. 1110, pp. 143–156. Springer, Cham (2020). https://doi.org/10.1007/978-3-030-37221-7_13

Villalustre Martínez, L., Del Moral Pérez, M.E.: Digital storytelling: una nueva estrategia para narrar historias y adquirir competencias por parte de los futuros maestros. Revista Complutense de Educacion **25**(1), 115–132 (2014). https://doi.org/10.5209/rev_RCED.2014.v25.n1.41237

Metrics Design of Usability and Behavior Analysis of a Human-Robot-Game Platform
HRG Metrics for LOLY-MIDI

Nayeth I. Solorzano Alcivar[1,2]([⊠]) [iD], Luis C. Herrera Paltan[1,3] [iD],
Leslie R. Lima Palacios[1,3] [iD], Jonathan S. Paillacho Corredores[1,4] [iD],
and Dennys F. Paillacho Chiluiza[1,4] [iD]

[1] Escuela Superior Politécnica del Litoral, ESPOL Polytechnic University, ESPOL, Campus
Gustavo Galindo, P.O. Box 09, 01-5863 Guayaquil, Ecuador
{nsolorza,lcherrer,ldlima,jspailla,dpaillac}@espol.edu.ec
[2] Facultad de Arte, Diseño y Comunicación Audiovisual – FADCOM, Guayaquil, Ecuador
[3] Facultad de Ciencias Sociales y Humanísticas – FSCH, Guayaquil, Ecuador
[4] Facultad de Ingeniería en Electricidad Y Computación - FIEC, CIDIS, Guayaquil, Ecuador

Abstract. As an innovative technological challenge, creating and designing metrics to evaluate communication between human-robot-game interaction will benefit children's education. In humans, facial expressions or emotions are pervasive forms of communication for interaction between people. When people are trying to establish communication deploying robots and game-based learning, which are growing in popularity, expectations are that these forms of relationship will become a means through which interaction is a common tool. Although it is intuitive for a regular human being to vary their expressions and emotions, their interpretation through metrics, or results of using the game as a form of learning, is a complex task that must be carried out. This paper explains the proposed design and usability metrics testing children's use of a human-robot-game platform, identified as LOLY-MIDI. This platform promotes inclusive education, primarily those children with Autism Spectrum Disorder (ASD).

Keywords: Human-robot-game · Metrics · Dashboard · Games-based learning · EDG · Autism · ASD · SAR

1 Introduction

The development of new technologies and the emergence of skillful generations in handling them is an increasing fact. The presence of smartphones and tablets in almost every home has awakened investigators and software developers' interest in implementing many applications as learning tools. Videogames or digital games built on educational properties, identified as educational digital games (EDG) or serious games, are an excellent way of teaching content and desired behavior, creating a good impression and growing acceptance on users for grabbing the attention of children with learning purposes [1, 2]. Social Assistive Robots (SAR) also contribute to the learning process and promote user interaction and active listening [3], expecting to motivate and capture

© Springer Nature Switzerland AG 2021
M. Botto-Tobar et al. (Eds.): ICAT 2020, CCIS 1388, pp. 164–178, 2021.
https://doi.org/10.1007/978-3-030-71503-8_13

their attention. In this sense, the LOLY-MIDI project is a Human-Robot-Game platform joining a social robot (named Loly) with an EDG series (named MIDI-AM) as mobile applications. All altogether seek to enhance children's learning experience initiating primary school, mainly aiming to capture and motivate children's attention with the Autism Spectrum Disorder (ASD) for inclusive education [4]. However, more than a lesson learned needs to consider confirming HRG platforms' influence on children learning and motivating their attention.

The SAR is a new subfield in human-robot interaction (HRI), focusing on developing intelligent robots to assist with social interaction. The SAR systems have great potential for providing personalized and affordable therapeutic interventions to children with ASD. However, there are limitations in the HRI that make interpretation and an instant response difficult when the robot is not in the presence of an operator. These limitations imply that the personalization of the SAR for each user is impossible in the actual context. Children with ASD have noticeable differences in language and child-to-child variations concerning cognitive ability [5], behavioral difficulties, and social understanding [6]. Due to this variation, individuals' learning styles across the spectrum are not uniform in nature [7].

ASD is a neurological and development affection commonly diagnosed during childhood, remains for a lifetime, and influences behavior, interaction, interpersonal communication, and the learning process [8]. For decades, studies have confirmed that children with ASD have a deficiency in their social-cognitive domain and are usually averse to participate in social interactions [9]. For example, this disorder affects one in 59 children in the United States [10] and 1266 persons in Ecuador [11]. Studies reveal that SAR has already been used to educate children with ASD to play with them to evaluate their contribution to these children's learning process. Besides, studies about Human-Computer-Interaction (HCI) point out that educational videogames help reduce the apathy and distraction they have as part of their characteristic behavior. [12, 13]. This investigation aims to determine the metrics that need to be used to measure the HRG applications (Loly Robot and MIDI-AM games) usability and their influence on children's learning experience and motivation, particularly in children with ASD.

1.1 The State of Art

Research carried out by social robotics has shown the importance of studying human-machine interaction to measure the degree of attention that a person maintains with digital games [14]. It is essential to study the individual's degree of attention to know if the robot's instructions reach the person. On the other hand, according to Gros [1], digital games can produce simplification of reality for promoting challenge, problem-solving, cooperation, and other motivations to encourage learning and cooperation. As a way of technology aids focusing their design on the education environment, these games are considered appropriate for improving learning [1, 2]. Thus, both resources educational digital games - EDG, and the socially assistive robot – SAR, have been recommended for educational purposes.

MIDI-AM is a research project based on the development of EDG in mobile applications for children. This project encourages the creation of Multimedia Interactive Didactic Infantile (MIDI) productions as free mobile applications. The MIDI-AM study is seeking to generate an objective evaluation of the impact and usability of games-based learning. In 2018 as part of this study, a dashboard module was designed for MIDI-AM games. This module retrieves data from the cloud generated when the games are played. The dashboard shows a preliminary statistical graph interpretation of the data about usability and playability of the MIDI-AM games [15, 16]. However, the MIDI dashboard results are not related to the effect of using these EDGs linked to the Loly SAR.

Considering there is little to no consistency in SAR's appearance used in therapy for ASD and their scarcity for therapeutic purposes in the market, the project Loly-MIDI was undertaken to accomplish these purposes. A robotic bust named Loly was developed to work linked to MIDI EDG applications. Loly is a non-anthropomorphic robot that represents an emblematic bird of Ecuador's coast region. Loly's primary function (head and bust) is to interact with regular children and ASD patients, helping them keep focused on a single activity [4]. This robot has a frontal camera and a 7-in. LCD screen to show different aye's expressions such as happiness, sadness, anger, and enthusiasm. For the verbal interaction, Loly uses a speaker through which it expresses pre-established lines of dialogues. Loly repeats the dialogues while the MIDI games are played, encouraging them to keep going or giving them instructions. Loly's wings have two degrees of freedom that it can move to emulate a flying bird through a small engine controlled by a microcontroller [4]. More studies with similar functionality, such as the robot named KIWI of Jain, Thiagarajan, Shi, Clabaugh, and Matarić [17], can be taken as a reference for the metric design to evaluate ASD children behavior using SAR.

It is argued that all social assistive robots look to generate one or more therapeutic interactions between humans and themselves, such as promoting a specific reaction, training skills, or simply serve as some sort of training for the user's social abilities linked to specific mobile applications [17]. Loly aims to play the role of a guide in the progress of different activities within the MIDI games, and at the same time, incentivize user's development of social skills [4]. Besides, it is relevant to highlight that, even with video games' incursion as game-based learning in the classrooms, still certain distrust from educators (Serrano-Laguna et al., 2017). Therefore, it is required to show convincing data that support the effectiveness of using SAR and EDG as linked platforms such as HRG proposed by the Loly-MIDI studies. Their contribution to learning and social skills development. In which new metrics can assist in evaluating the HRI and HCI according to each case's requirement.

For collecting data from the EDG series, a JavaScript Object Notation (JSON) record is required. The data is then stored in a cloud database to be further displayed in a dashboard [15].

A facial recognition application needs to be applied to analyze a SAR interaction with children, such as OpenFace [17]. There is some open free access to facial recognition software such as OpenFace. This application allows us to identify the user's facial landmarks and collect attention metrics to measure the degrees of attention and empathy during an interaction. OpenFace can provide training and test code, helping to replay the experiments of eyes and face recognition. It operates in real-time with all the modules involved in analyzing facial behavior, which is useful for this study [18].

2   Materials and Methods

2.1   Methodology

This research has a pragmatic perspective, using a qualitative-quantitative mix method strategy [19, 20]. A methodology for the design of an evaluation of LOLY-MIDI metrics separated into three stages is applied. The first stage begins by analyzing the interaction between the user with the mobile application and the robot. The second stage includes real-time data gathering, which happens simultaneously while the Loly robot is used with the game. The third stage occurs once the interaction has ended, and data has been saved, a final report is generated on a dashboard. The designed proposed metrics need to be used to generate the outcomes for evaluations and hypotheses that need to be confirmed or rejected to the last stage.

First Stage
Focus groups with regular children and with ASD are undertaken to observe and video recording users to interact directly with the robot and the mobile application. As a play, the users completed different playing exercises and heard different stories from the EDG. At the same time, children get feedback and instructions from the robot, who serve the purpose of a guide and the interaction.

Second Stage
OpenFace application oversees monitoring and gathering real-time facial data of the user. With this data, it is possible to analyze characteristics such as emotions, head pose, and eye gaze through pre-established conditions that interpret OpenFace's output metrics.

Third Stage
During the interaction, screen reports showing performance, attention, and emotions during the interaction are finally generated in a dashboard. With the expectation to implement this platform in primary schools of inclusive education, the operability and data presented on the dashboard must be accessible to a primary school teacher and psychologist. Therefore, simple easy-to-read graphs and statistical conclusions translated to natural language constructing simple statements are also requested. The use of simple language statements is relevant to engage with most potential users and minimize human errors in analyzing and interpreting the data.

2.2   LOLY-MIDI Beneficiaries

The direct beneficiaries for which LOLY-MIDI applications are intended are children between 3 to 7 years old, but mainly for children with ASD. Other beneficiaries are the parents, guardians, psychologists, and educators of primary schools. One of the significant challenges in this research has been to find volunteers that are eligible for the focus group experiment, despite working with different educative institutes that treat ASD in Guayaquil.

Children considered for this study should meet the following criteria:

a.   The child with ASD should live in Guayaquil.

b. Should receive at least one session per week.
c. A teacher, parent, or guardian should accompany the child during the interaction with the LOLY-MIDI platform.
d. Parents and guards must sign a consent form for their child to participate in the experiment.

2.3 Research Tools Design

The robot prototype used is a parrot shaped robotic bust named Loly. The robotic bust has a camera that records a frontal view of the participants. Visual characteristics are obtained through the OpenFace software used to monitor emotions, head pose, and eye gaze. The data collected in real-time by OpenFace is intended to measure the user's degree of attention and empathy. To measure the user's attention level to the robot is expected to identify the segments on which the user's attention got lost and determine if there are significant differences in the degree of attention and empathy that Loly receives concerning the game played. Also, hypotheses are generated based on focus group experiments.

The newly proposed metrics are described as follows:

Face Detection – Emotions
There are a wide variety of available free tools that offer face detection in pictures or videos. However, few of those share their code freely. Most of them instead provide binary commands to use. Binary commands allow access to pre-established functionalities and often do not support different platforms, making their implementation almost impossible. These binary commands cause the application of facial detection tools to become a tricky task in experiments with different parameters and databases.

OpenFace applies Conditional Local Neural Fields (CLFN) [21] for facial landmark detection in real-time. CLNF is an instance of a Constrained Local Model (CLM) [22], which uses a better optimization function and more advanced expert patches. The CLNF model detects up to 68 facial landmark points (see Fig. 1). OpenFace uses this model and makes it better by training the distribution of facial landmark points in different groups (eyes, lips, and eyebrows).

Many binary variables are created from the OpenFace output that makes the identification of emotions possible. Emotions are determined based on a variation analysis of the distance between specific facial points identified and labeled by OpenFace. Distances referred to in the complementary material are tentative and will be determined with experimentation. The precision with which the distance between the facial landmark points is expected to work better is if the camera is at head level and correctly set up [24].

Head Pose
Unlike face detection, the head pose has not received the same attention from software developers. Many criteria allow for head pose estimation by using in-depth data [25]. However, they do not work appropriately on webcams. Some facial landmark detectors include the capacity of estimating head pose [26, 27], but again, most of them do not have support for webcams.

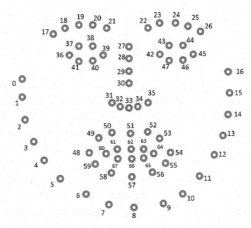

Fig. 1. OpenFace facial landmark points [23]

OpenFace can gather information about the head pose on top of facial landmark detection. These landmark detections are achieved because CLNF internally uses a 3D representation of facial landmark points, showing them on the image using an orthographic projection of the camera. The facial landmark points allow for head pose estimation once facial landmark points are correctly detected. OpenFace needs to have calibration parameters for the camera (focal distance and principal point). Without calibration parameters, OpenFace uses an estimation based on image size [18].

Binary variables are created from OpenFace's output to determine head pose. Two possible scenarios are considered, one in which the head is perpendicular and another one in which the head is tilted down (see Fig. 2). Angles proposed in the complementary material for binary variables are subject to changes in experimentation. They are expected to depend on the distance between the user's face and the camera and woks optimally if placed at head level [18].

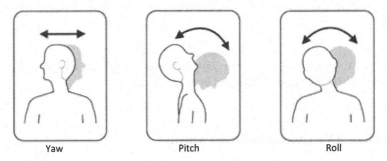

Fig. 2. OpenFace head pose [28]

Eye Gaze

There are numerous tools and commercial systems to estimate where someone is looking.

However, most of those require specialized hardware with infrared cameras or cameras set up as head-mounted cameras [29, 30]. Although, a few systems can estimate eye gaze through webcams. It is difficult for these systems to do it efficiently in real-life scenarios because it requires a meticulous calibration.

Baltrušaitis, Robinson, and Morency [18] indicate that, in contrast with other available options, OpenFace provides the training and test code, which is a significant advantage when reproducing experiments. OpenFace operates in real-time with all the modules concerning facial tracking analysis. Once the pupil and eye position has been detected, the CLFN model will use that information to generate five different outputs:

1. *gaze_0_x, gaze_0_y, gaze_0_z:* An eye gaze direction vector in world coordinates for eye 0 (normalized). The eye 0 is the last to the left in the image.
2. *gaze_1_x, gaze_1_y, gaze_1_z:* An eye gaze direction vector in world coordinates for eye 1 (normalized). Eye 1 is the last to the right in the image.
3. *gaze_angle_x, gaze_angle_y:* The direction of eye gaze is in radians. It is the world coordinates averaged for both eyes and converted into more user-friendly attention vectors.
4. *eye_lmk_x_0, eye_lmk_x_1,... Eye_lmk_x55, eye_lmk_y_1,... Eye_lmk_y_55:* The location of reference points of the 2D eye region in pixels (see example Fig. 3).

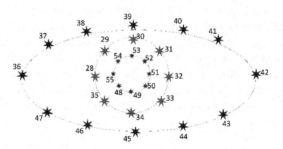

Fig. 3. Reference points to the location of the 2D eye region in pixels example [23].

5. *eye_lmk_X_0, eye_lmk_X_1,... Eye_lmk_X55, eye_lmk_Y_0,... Eye_lmk_Z_55:* The location of 3D eye region landmarks in millimeters (Fig. 4)

2.4   Additional Variables of the Robot Activity

Robot Activity
OpenFace is used to monitors in real-time the user's interaction with LOLY-MIDI EDG applications and the robotic bust. Loly collects data when it executes dialogue lines, which help evaluate its contribution to the user's interaction.

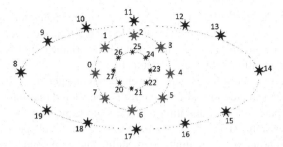

Fig. 4. Reference points location of the 3D eye region in millimeters example [23]

Four binary variables, which represent four different scenarios, are defined within the robot's programming to identify the activity it is currently on. These binary variables are based upon the line of dialogue that is being executed and whether it is talking or not: 'robot says hi,' 'robot gives instructions,' 'robot gives feedback,' 'robot is not talking.' It is worth noting that these scenarios are excluding between themselves. Binary variables will get a value depending on what line of dialogue the robot is executing to serve as conditions.

Game–Activity
A behavioral analysis of the child playing a level of the game and its activity is made, two variables are created, 'game' and 'chapter'. The first one have the name of the currently active game, for instance, Anibopi (one of the EDG of MIDI-AM series). The second one gets the name of the chapter that is active.

These variables used allows creating an analysis by game and activity. In the dashboard, the mobile application is referred to as 'game' for simplification purposes. For example, Anibopi is a game app, and one of its activities is named 'rocks. Besides making a global analysis, it is possible to filter out and analyze data for a particular game or activity satisfying the researcher's needs.

3 Results of Metric Design and Discussions

Firstly, it is necessary for data processing to determine the vectors to be analyzed concerning eye gaze and head position when the face is detected. For the eyes, the vector (gaze_angle_x, gaze_angle_y) values radians are transformed to sexagesimal degrees. For example, (3.027°, −2.718°) is obtained, understanding that they are calculated taking as a reference to the camera at (0°, 0°) [23]. In this sense, to facilitate data management, three objectives of the child's gaze are defined: robot head, Loly's bust, and tablet. The three objectives are recommended to be set as binary variables 'atent_face', 'atent_bust', 'atent_tablet', and 'atent_general'. They all take the value of 1 when the respective conditions are met and 0 if they are not.

It is considered that the child is observing the robot's head when the gaze_angle_x and gaze_angle_y angles are equal to 0°. Likewise, it is determined that the infant is looking at Loly's bust when the angle gaze_angle_x is equal to 0°, and the angle gaze_angle_y is −40°. It is established that child is looking at the tablet when: the angle gaze_angle_x is equal to 0°, and the angle gaze_angle_y is −75°. All the angles set for gaze_angle_x and gaze_angle_y can have a margin of error of 15° and 20°, respectively. Lastly, a child is considered paying attention to the interaction when variables, such as attention_face, attention_bust, or attention_tablet, are equal to 1.

If none of these conditions is true, the child is considered "not attentive". This attention metric is evaluated in real-time, and it is considered that interaction has been successful if the percentage of attention is more significant than 75% concerning the duration of the session. At least 3 h of multimodal data is collected through several sessions for each participant, including video, audio, and game preview.

3.1 Determined Correlations

Quadrant-Eye Level
The ideal position that the Loly robot camera should be placed is at the child's eye level. In this way, it is possible to capture the entire face and establish the best scenario for the use of OpenFace. This application allows us to identify the user's facial landmark, and through the collected attention metrics, it is possible to measure degrees of attention and empathy during the interaction (Fig. 5).

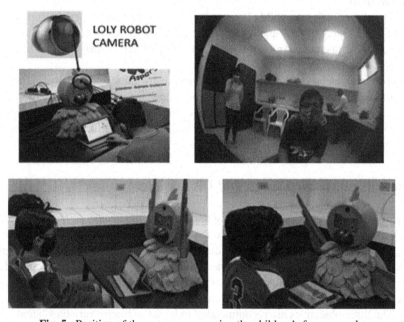

Fig. 5. Position of the camera concerning the children's face example

Empathy By identifying the 68 points that make up the facial landmark, the user's emotions are measured. For this purpose, specific facial points are taken as a reference to identify any reaction that can be found provoked (see Fig. 1).

Emotion Characteristics Vectors

Surprise: Increase the distance between facial points 21 and 39, the same as between facial points 22 and 42.

Interest (Neutral): Facial points 17 and 26 are at the same level or above facial points 18 and 25, respectively.

Happiness: At least one of the following conditions must be met.

1. Facial point 48 is above or at the same level as facial point 49.
2. Facial point 54 is above or at the same level as facial point 53.

Disinterest (Anger): For anger, the condition of Neutral/Interest mentioned above must be met. Also, the distance between points 62 and 66 increases considerably.

Sadness: Both conditions must be met.

1. Facial point 48 is at or below facial point 59.
2. Facial point 54 is at or below facial point 55.

Extra Variables

OpenFace can perform real-time monitoring when a child is interacting with LOLY-MIDI applications. Loly's influence in a child's interaction with the platform is measured when Loly executes lines of dialogue. It is necessary to define, within the programming of the robot metrics, four binary variables. These variables allow us to identify the robot's activity, taking into consideration the dialogue line executed and whether Loly is speaking or not.

The conditions established are as follows:

- Robot activity # 1: greeting $= 1$ ^ r_silence $= 0$
- Robot activity # 2: r_instruction $= 1$ ^ r_silence $= 0$
- Robot activity # 3: r_motivation $= 1$ ^ r_silence $= 0$
- Robot activity # 4: r_silence $= 1$

It is worth noting that the robot's activities are excluding. The binary variables r_greeting, r_instrution, and r_motivation must be conditioned to the dialog line's execution corresponding to the option. During activity four, to evaluate if the robot attracts the child's attention instead of playing on the tablet, three binary variables must be generated in the programming: (1) atent_loly, taking the value of 1 whenever atent_face or attention_bust is equal to 1; (2) loly_speaks, which will be 1 when r_greetings, r_instruction or r_motivation are 1; and (3) active_game, which will take the value of 1 when one of the application's games is active.

Likewise, to perform an analysis of the child's behavior by game and activity, two variables will be created, game level and chapter; the first will be the name of the active game app, for example, in Anibopi EDG. The second takes the name of the chapter that is active. Before the chapter, either of these letters will appear 'h' (game history) or 'j' (levels of the game) followed by a hyphen. These letters allow differentiating between the story part and the chapter's game. Example: 'h-rocks' or 'j-rocks'.

In the end, the outcomes presented by OpenFace generates information in 4-s intervals, as shown in the "Database" sheet (see Table 1 column 1).

Table 1. OpenFace information generated in the database Table, fragment example

Timestamp (s)	Intervention (%)	Participant	c_perpendicular	c_inc_ down	atent_face	atenc_ bust	atenc_ tablet	atenc_ general
0,00	0,00	1	1	0	1	0	0	1
4,00	0,01	1	1	0	1	0	0	1
8,00	0,01	1	1	0	0	1	0	1
12,00	0,02	1	1	0	0	1	0	1
16,00	0,03	1	1	0	0	1	0	1
20,00	0,03	1	1	0	0	1	0	1
24,00	0,04	1	1	0	0	1	0	1
28,00	0,05	1	1	0	0	0	0	1
32,00	0,05	1	0	1	0	0	1	1
36,00	0,06	1	0	1	0	0	1	1

Phonetic Analysis (Praat)

Praat makes it possible to analyze recorded audio through Loly's microphone. Praat shows not only a graphical representation of sound through audio waves but also shows various acoustic analysis: spectrograms (a representation of the high and low frequencies available in the signal); the contour of the tone (the frequency of the periodicity); and the formation of the contour (which is the main component of the spectrogram).

Using Praat, it is intended to record and analyze harmony, intensity, frequency, and tone. Although the LOLY-MIDI application does not require the user to speak, it is possible to analyze verbal reactions to specific activities within the application while Loly speaks or not (see example Table 2).

Table 2. Percentage of Loly-MIDI attention using three users' example

%Attention to Loly	P1	P2	P3	...	Total
Loly speaks	71,43%	80,00%	64,30%		71,43%
Loly does not speak	37,50%	25,00%	15,90%		37,50%

Metrics to measure the degree of the robotic bust support with the games

Metrics and hypotheses were determined at the end of the interaction once data is collected and processed. Also, it needs to be tried without the robot (see Table 3). A session will be considered successful if the child remains attentive to the interaction at least 75% of the time.

Table 3. Hypotheses for Loly-MIDI measures examples

Hypotheses	Phi coefficient interpretation example
Attention to Loly considerably increases when Loly speaks	0,3393
Attention to the tablet increases considerably when the game is active	0,7559
Recorded emotions generally occur when Loly speaks (loly_speaks = 1)	0,2826
Recorded emotions generally occur when the child hits/misses (r_motivation = 1)	0,4588

For example, to obtain the general confirmation of a hypothesis concerning the participants' attention, if all the participants had a 75% of attention to the interaction based on 86.6%, then the interactions are declared successful. An example of the formula to be applied is:

$$\%Atention = \frac{\#Secodswhentheatent\_general = 1}{\#Totalsecondsoftheinteraction} = \frac{130 * 4}{150 * 4} = \frac{520}{600} = 0.86 \approx 86.6\%$$

In this way, after piloting with real information, the collaboration of HCI and HRI in the attention and empathy that children with ASD can feel in the learning process can be verified.

4   Conclusions and Future Work

This paper explains the design and establishment of parameters that can capture the usability and impact of the LOLY-MIDI applications, making it possible to obtain accurate feedback reports and determine hypotheses that need to be confirmed or rejected for each case analyzed. Loly's robot autonomy linked to MIDI EDG used by children is possible due to the proposed implementation of OpenFace, which is a free facial recognition software. This method allows the LOLY-MIDI platform to carry on with the intervention without the need for a present real-time observer that evaluates attention and empathy levels. Data collected in real-time by OpenFace can be evaluated using pre-established conditions that dictate an intervention's success or failure.

The lessons learned through the pilot tests were carried out but could not be processed using OpenFace. However, they still contributed to the reformulation of the initial hypotheses regarding the empathy and attention of a child, along with interviews with specialized psychologists in children with ASD that helped determine the limitations of LOLY-MIDI applications, turning this work into a solid baseline on which to continue researching. Furthermore, this work can contribute to the development of metrics in different robotic platforms used to perform HRI since this work could provide a guideline to measure the degree of attention that a person can have because many times, the development of robotic platforms is truncated. After all, the user does not understand the robot's instructions due to lack of attention.

4.1 Future Work

After establishing metrics and the HRG platform's ways designed and discussed, the next stage of this research is developing a computer module; this module needs to be programmed to computerize the designed metrics to automatically present results for each evaluation. Also, the implementation of OpenFace using Loly's hardware must be exhaustively tested and calibrated to get reliable data output and make an accurate data analysis considering the pre-established conditions for all the binary variables to help us evaluate every aspect of the interaction. A thorough evaluation of the proposed LOLY-MIDI HRG platform is required. For evaluation purposes, data collection should need a representative sample size to evaluate the determined hypotheses. It is also recommended that if there is the possibility of modifying the platform to generate interaction between the child and the robot Loly, the impact will be made and measured by Praat phonetic analysis because although it is not currently part of the proposal in the short term, it is considered that it can become instrumental in learning children.

References

1. Gros, B.S.: Digital games in education: the design of games-based learning environments. J. Res. Technol. Educ. **40**(1), 23–38 (2007)
2. Plass, J.L., Homer, B.D., Kinzer, C.K.: Foundations of game-based learning. Educ. Psychol. **50**(4), 258–283 (2015)
3. Feil-Seifer, D., Mataric, M.J.: Defining socially assistive robotics. In: 9th International Conference on Rehabilitation Robotics, 2005. ICORR 2005, pp. 465–468 (2005)
4. Paillacho Chiluiza, D.F., Solorzano Alcivar, N.I., Paillacho Corredores, J.S.: LOLY 1.0: a proposed human-robot-game platform architecture for the engagement of children with autism in the learning process. In: Botto-Tobar, M., Zamora, W., Larrea Plúa, J., Bazurto Roldan, J., Santamaría Philco, A. (eds.) ICCIS 2020. AISC, vol. 1273, pp. 225–238. Springer, Cham (2021). https://doi.org/10.1007/978-3-030-59194-6_19
5. Volkmar, F.R., Paul, R., Rogers, S.J., Pelphrey, K.A.: Handbook of Autism and Pervasive Developmental Disorders, Diagnosis, Development, and Brain Mechanisms. John Wiley & Sons, 2014 (2014)
6. Rice, K., Moriuchi, J.M., Jones, W., Klin, A.: Parsing heterogeneity in autism spectrum disorders: visual scanning of dynamic social scenes in school-aged children. J. Am. Acad. Child Adolesc. Psychiatry **51**(3), 238–248 (2012)
7. Tsatsanis, K.D.: Heterogeneity in learning style in Asperger syndrome and high-functioning autism. Topics Lang. Disord. **24**(4), 260–270 (2004)
8. American-Psychiatric-Association: Diagnostic and statistical manual of mental disorders (DSM-5®). American Psychiatric Pub, 2013 (2013)
9. Sigman, M., Mundy, P., Sherman, T., Ungerer, J.: Social interactions of autistic, mentally retarded and normal children and their caregivers. J. Child Psychol. Psychiatry **27**(5), 647–656 (1986)
10. Christensen, D.L., et al.: Prevalence and characteristics of autism spectrum disorder among children aged 8 years—autism and developmental disabilities monitoring network, 11 sites, United States, 2012. MMWR Surveill. Summ. **65**(13), 1 (2018)
11. Ministerio de Salud Pública del Ecuador: Trastornos del Espectro Autista en niños y adolescentes: Detección, diagnóstico, tratamiento, rehabilitación y seguimiento. Guía de Práctica Clínica (2017)

12. Kozima, H., Nakagawa, C., Yasuda, Y.: Interactive robots for communication-care: a case-study in autism therapy. In: ROMAN 2005. IEEE International Workshop on Robot and Human Interactive Communication, pp. 341–346 (2005)
13. Contreras, R.S., Serra, A., Terrón, J.L.: Games and ADHD-ADD: a systematic mapping study. Acta Ludologica **2**(2), 4–26 (2019)
14. Yamakami, T.: From user experience to social experience: A new perspective for mobile social game design. In: 2012 9th International Conference on Ubiquitous Intelligence and Computing and 9th International Conference on Autonomic and Trusted Computing, pp. 792–796 (2012)
15. Solorzano, N.I., Carrera, D.A., Sornoza, L.I., Mendoza, M.: Developing a dashboard for monitoring usability of educational games apps for children. In: Proceedings of the 2019 2nd International Conference on Computers in Management and Business, pp. 70–75 (2019)
16. Solorzano, N.I., Sornoza, L.I., Carrera, D.A.: Adoption of children's educational video games monitored with dashboards in the cloud. Rev. Iberica Sist. Technol. Inf. **2019**(19), 146–160 (2019)
17. Jain, S., Thiagarajan, B., Shi, Z., Clabaugh, C., Matarić, M.J.: Modeling engagement in long-term, in-home socially assistive robot interventions for children with autism spectrum disorders. Sci. Robot. **5**(39) (2020)
18. Baltrušaitis, T., Robinson, P., Morency, L.-P.: Openface: an open-source facial behavior analysis toolkit. In: IEEE Winter Conference on Applications of Computer Vision (WACV), pp. 1–10. IEEE (2016)
19. Solorzano, N.I., Sanzogni, L., Houghton, L.: A pluralistic methodology for a refined selection of drivers influencing information system adoption in public organizations: the case for Ecuador (2016)
20. Creswell, J.W., Creswell, J.D.: Research design: qualitative, quantitative, and mixed methods approaches. Sage publications, 2017, Third Edition edn. (2017)
21. Baltrusaitis, T., Robinson, P., Morency, L.-P.: Constrained local neural fields for robust facial landmark detection in the wild. In: Proceedings of the IEEE International Conference on Computer Vision Workshops, pp. 354–361 (2013)
22. Cristinacce, D., Cootes, T.F.: Feature detection and tracking with constrained local models. In: Bmvc, Vol. 1, No. 2, p. 3 (2006)
23. Baltrusaitis, T.: Output Format OpenFace. In: Editor (Ed.)ˆ(Eds.): 'Book Output Format OpenFace' (edn.), pp. FaceLandmarkImg and FeatureExtraction (2019)
24. Yu, Y., Mora, K.A.F., Odobez, J.-M.: Robust and accurate 3d head pose estimation through 3dmm and online head model reconstruction. In: 12th IEEE international conference on automatic face & gesture recognition (fg 2017), pp. 711–718 (2017)
25. Fanelli, G., Gall, J., Van Gool, L.: Real-time head pose estimation with random regression forests. In: CVPR 2011, pp. 617–624. IEEE (2011)
26. Asthana, A., Zafeiriou, S., Cheng, S., Pantic, M.: Robust discriminative response map fitting with constrained local models. In: Proceedings of the IEEE Conference on Computer Vision and Pattern Recognition, pp. 3444–3451 (2013)
27. Asthana, A., Zafeiriou, S., Cheng, S., Pantic, M.: Incremental face alignment in the wild. In: Proceedings of the IEEE Conference on Computer Vision and Pattern Recognition. pp. 1859–1866 (2014)
28. https://medium.com/insights-on-virtual-reality/what-you-should-know-about-head-tra ckers-7e2289578a22. Accessed 11 Oct 2020

29. Świrski, L., Bulling, A., Dodgson, N.: Robust real-time pupil tracking in highly off-axis images. In: Proceedings of the Symposium on Eye Tracking Research and Applications, pp. 173–176 (2012)
30. Lidegaard, M., Hansen, D.W., Krüger, N.: Head-mounted device for point-of-gaze estimation in three dimensions. In: Proceedings of the Symposium on Eye Tracking Research and Applications, pp. 83–86 (2014)

Electronics

An Electronic Equipment with Face Recognition Capacity Oriented to Measuring the Alcoholic Level in People

Luis Merino, Wilson Chavesta, Guillermo Kemper$^{(\boxtimes)}$, and Kalun Lau

Universidad Peruana de Ciencias Aplicadas, Lima, Perú
{u201120490,u201217136,pcelklau}@upc.edu.pe,
guillermo.kemper@upc.pe
http://www.upc.edu.pe/

Abstract. This work proposes an equipment oriented to measuring the alcoholic level and simultaneously applying face recognition for people who enter risk places where their physical integrity can be affected due to their drunkenness state. In the state of the art, it is verified that several methods of measuring breathalyzer do not integrate the simultaneous facial recognition for the purposes of proper personnel access control and registration. It is also verified that subjective methods are applied such as the emitted smell perception, gait, the way of speaking or behavioral aspects. The proposed equipment consists of electronic devices that allow the detection of air flow and the measurement of the alcoholic level through a reduced board computer. Biometric face recognition is carried out through image processing algorithms, convolutional neural networks and support vector machines SVM, which run on a computer which is synchronized with the measurement equipment. The computer registers the recognized person in a database with the associated detected alcoholic level. For the validation of the proposed equipment, several samples of alcoholic level, delay times in the acquisition of images and the face recognition rate were evaluated. Alcohol level measurements were compared with those obtained through a certified digital breathalyzer. In this validation, Pearson's correlation coefficient was used, obtaining a value of 0.937. The maximum time delay in capturing the image during the emission of the airflow by the person was 0.067 s, while the percentage of true face recognition was higher than 95%.

Keywords: Alcohol level · Automatic detection · Face recognition · Air flow · Timing · Pearson's correlation coefficient

1 Introduction

In recent years, industrial products have had a great impact on the economy of countries [1]. This is possible thanks to the implementation of electrical devices that automate people's work. However, these companies are in constant risk of suffering economic losses and damage to their image due to accidents and damage to the infrastructure that may be caused by a worker or operator who could be intoxicated. In this context, the problem is generated many times by the limited alcohol control procedure that companies

© Springer Nature Switzerland AG 2021
M. Botto-Tobar et al. (Eds.): ICAT 2020, CCIS 1388, pp. 181–194, 2021.
https://doi.org/10.1007/978-3-030-71503-8_14

have for personnel access to areas where work is carried out that could put life or physical integrity at risk.

This has generated the motivation to develop technological tools of different scopes that can provide all the necessary information to be able to alert about the level of alcohol that a worker may have consumed.

Various methods for measuring alcoholic level and face recognition have been proposed in the state of the art.

Aiello et al. proposed, for example, an algorithm for detecting the blood alcohol level through the person's gait through the gyroscope and the accelerometer found in smart phones [2]. This system limits the maximum and minimum ranges, normalizes the characteristics (gender, height, weight and identification) and uses a j48 classifier [2]. Although the device has an accuracy of 89.45%, this is reduced by the gait of a person with fatigue or a bad mood.

Joan Aymerich et al. proposed a method that allows to measure the alcohol level in whole blood samples using LoC (Lab on a chip) portable, small and light based on smartphones [3]. The proposed method has a margin of error less than 0.009% w/v in the range of 0 to 0.5 g/L, which is comparable with sophisticated, bulky and expensive instruments [3]. However, it is an invasive method of measurement that generates a lot of discomfort if used periodically.

Some solutions and business methods can also be used. In this context, there is a personal [4] or vending [5] breathalyzer, which measure the alcoholic level by means of its concentration in the air exhaled by the person, and their difference lies in portability. However, they are not implemented because constant staff supervision is required to identify the person who has blown.

With respect to face recognition, Shah et al. proposed an automatic system that marks the presence of students by detecting their faces in front of the training group, from the image of everyone who is sitting in the classroom. It uses a cascaded classifier to detect face detection, feature extraction and recognition [6]. The proposed method has an image accuracy of 93.1%, which is lower than the results shown later.

Rao et al. proposed a facial recognition system that uses a scale invariant hybrid feature transformation (SIFT) based on a local binary pattern (LBP). The facial recognition system is pre-processed to extract SIFT and LBP based features. The scale-modified invariant feature transformation is pre-processed to extract features based on scale factors and image orientations. The proposed method is classified by the support vector machine [7]. A precision of 95.5% was obtained, which is lower than the results shown later.

In summary, the 2 main limitations found in the state of the art are: requiring the constant supervision of a staff for a correct measurement of the alcohol level and the lack of identification of the person at the time of running the test. The electronic equipment solves both limitations by integrating alcohol level detection and simultaneous face recognition. The details of this proposal are detailed in the following sections and shown in Fig. 1.

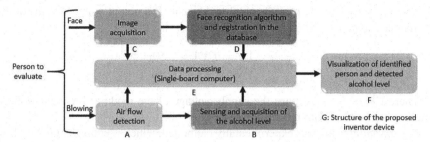

Fig. 1. Block diagram of the proposed method.

2   Description of the Proposed Method

In Fig. 1. The block diagram of the electronic equipment proposed for the measurement of alcoholic level in people with face recognition capacity is shown. The process is described in the following sections.

2.1   Air Flow Detection

Air flow detection is used to verify whether the user has blown into the equipment. For this purpose, an integrated electronic circuit with an electret microphone is used (fc-04 module) shown in Fig. 2.

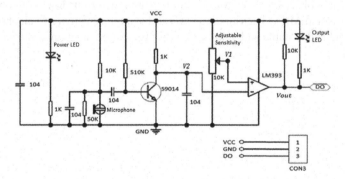

Fig. 2. Circuit diagram of the fc-04 module.

The fc-04 module was chosen due to the high signal component generated by the flow of air directed at the microphone. The advantage of using this device with respect to CO2 or O2 sensors, is based on its low cost and its independence from physical factors such as temperature or humidity, which can lead to detection errors.

The fc-04 module has a microphone that is used to detect the sound generated by the air flow. Likewise, it has a transistor polarized in the active zone that is used to amplify the voltage signal generated by the microphone to a maximum peak value of 2.53 V.

The op-amp is used to compare the amplified signal. The output voltage (Vout) of the amplifier configured as comparator is expressed in (1):

$$Vout = \begin{cases} V_{cc}, & if \ V1 > 2.50v \\ 0v, & if \ V1 < 2.50v \end{cases} \tag{1}$$

Where $V_{cc} = 5v$ constitutes the supply voltage of the module. $V1$ is the voltage subject to comparison with the 2.5 V threshold.

This threshold value was experimentally calibrated, which is equivalent to 87 dB to minimize the airflow detection error generated by ambient noise noises.

2.2 Sensing and Acquisition of the Alcohol Level

Fig. 3 shows the block diagram of the alcohol level sensing and acquisition stage. Note that the data obtained is sent to a reduced plate computer for calculations and estimations.

Fig. 3. Block diagram of the sensing and acquisition of the alcohol level.

The MQ3 electrochemical alcohol sensor coupled to an integrated electronic circuit is used for alcohol sensing. The MQ3 module is used due to its low cost compared to the MQ303-A and MR513 sensors; however, it has high sensitivity to alcohol, a short response time and is stable and long-lasting [8]. The circuit diagram is shown in Fig. 4.

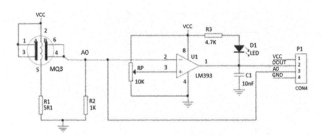

Fig. 4. Circuit diagram of the MQ3 module.

The MQ3 alcohol sensor is an electrochemical sensor which responds to changes in electrical current between pins 2 and 4 because of the presence of alcohol. That is why the 1K resistor R2 is placed to close the circuit and allow the flow of current, which will generate a voltage that is subsequently acquired and digitized. The 5.1 Ω resistor R1 is fitted to avoid long-term heating damage. The amplifier configured as a comparator for the MQ3 sensor is not used, since the A0 voltage is used as a reference for the alcohol level that will be acquired and digitized.

The digitization of the voltage that represents the alcoholic level is carried out by means of an analog-digital converter ADS1115. This converter was chosen over the MCP3008-I/P due to its configurable sample rate and higher resolution (16 bits) which allows for greater measurement precision. This converter uses the I2C interface to send data from the converter to the single board computer through the SDA and SCL pins (Fig. 3). The digitization process is divided into 3 stages that are described below:

Sampling

The analog output signal from the MQ3 is sampled at a sample rate of 128 samples/second. This frequency (fs) was chosen considering the sampling theorem and the maximum frequency (fm) of the output signal of the MQ3 module, expressed in (2):

$$fs \geq 2 \times fm \tag{2}$$

In this case, $fs = 128Hz$ or $samples/second$ was established since $fm = 2Hz$ (that is, a sampling frequency value that complies with the theorem and favors, as will be seen later, the stability of the alcohol levels measured through of the data processing algorithm that is executed in the Raspberry PI 3B + single board computer).

Quantization

The samples obtained are quantized, defining the type, the maximum and minimum values for the amplitude discretization, the resolution bits, and the quantization interval. The equation to obtain the quantization interval (Δ) is shown in (3):

$$\Delta = \frac{Xmax - Xmin}{2^r - 1} \tag{3}$$

Where $Xmax$ and $Xmin$ define the quantization range, r the quantizer resolution and Δ the quantization range.

In this case the ADS1115 uses a uniform mid-tread quantizer, with a resolution of $r = 16bits$, $Xmax = 4.096v$, $Xmin = -4.096v$ and $\Delta = 1.25 \times 10^{-4}v$, generating an error of $\pm\frac{\Delta}{2} = 0.625 \times 10^{-4}v$ which is adequate since it is very insignificant with respect to the ranges of alcoholic strength to be measured.

Coding

The quantized signal is encoded using 16-bit two's complement codes. In that sense, its binary values are between 0×8000 and $0 \times 7FFF$. These values are sent to the single board computer using the I2C communication protocol.

2.3 Image Acquisition

Image capture is performed by the Logitech C270 camera due to its high resolution and low cost.

In Fig. 5, it shows the location of the camera relative to the person and the air flow detector. In this case, 30 cm horizontally, 12.6 cm vertically and an angle of inclination of 20° was considered to achieve an adequate focus of the face at the moment of blowing. At the software level, a resolution of 500 × 480 pixels was set in RGB format (Primary components: Red, Green, and Blue) [9]. This resolution was sufficient to cover the required viewing angle for the area of interest of the face and to obtain satisfactory results in the process of recognizing the person.

The camera is connected to the single board computer for subsequent transmission to the computer where the face recognition algorithm is executed, and the database is registered.

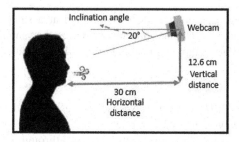

Fig. 5. Measurements for camera location that allows face registration.

To perform the synchronized capture of the face, an algorithm has been carried out in the Raspberry PI 3B + single board computer that considers the use of the air flow sensor and the web camera. The flow chart used for synchronization is shown in Fig. 6. The acquisition of images is continuous to avoid capture times greater than "1" second, which occurs each time the camera is initialized for acquisition. The program performs the continuous reading of the value of *Vout* defined in (1), which is recognized as logical "1" when $Vout = 5v$ and as logical "0" when $Vout = 0v$. The reading of this value is performed through the GPIO 4 pin of the Raspberry PI 3B +. Air flow detection occurs when $Vout = 0v$ (ie logical "0"). The image acquired at that moment is sent to the computer to be subjected to the face recognition algorithm, since the synchronization ensures that it contains the face of the person who made the breath.

2.4 Face Recognition Algorithm and Registration in the Database

This algorithm runs on the computer taking as input the image of the face sent from the Raspberry PI 3B +. This algorithm is not running on the Raspberry PI 3B + because the process would take longer than 20 s, which would be inefficient for the equipment requirements. The use of a computer also allows the information to be recorded in a database for subsequent evaluation and decision-making. In Fig. 7, the block diagram of the face recognition algorithm is shown.

HOG (Histogram of Oriented Gradients)
The RGB image is first converted to grayscale and then the HOG algorithm [10] is applied, in order to obtain the corners of the face in the digital image. For this part, this HOG algorithm is chosen due to its low computational load with respect to the convolutional neural network also used for face detection. The HOG algorithm was

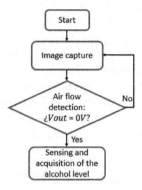

Fig. 6. Flow chart for synchronized face registration.

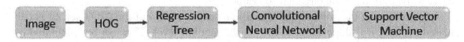

Fig. 7. Block diagram of the face recognition algorithm.

configured with a single image magnification for face search as the acquired faces occupy much of the width and height of the images.

Regression Tree

The set of regression trees [10] is used to estimate the classification points of the face, which are: the upper part of the chin, the outer edge of each eye and the inner edge of each eyebrow. This trained classifier is chosen since it is required to obtain the centralized face image, to avoid errors in recognition. It was configured to use 5 points of the face, to reduce processing time.

Convolutional Neural Network

The convolutional neural network is used to quantitatively identify the person. A pre-trained convolutional neural network [10] was used due to its good performance in recognizing people. The network was configured with an image input size of $3 \times 96 \times 96$, 13 convolution layers, 13 RELU (Rectified Linear Activation Function), 5 polling layers and 128 numerical output values that identify the person. This configuration allowed to obtain satisfactory recognition results above 95%.

Support Vector Machine

The support vector machine (SVM) is used to convert the 128 numerical values described above to characters that indicate the name of the person. For this, training has been carried out with 210 images per person to be identified. It has been configured mainly with a dimension of 128 using the radial basis function kernel due to its non-linear decision hyperplane, which allows for more robustness in the classification [10].

2.5 Data Processing

The data processing allows to obtain the alcohol level in mg/L and in %BAC (*Blood Alcohol Concentration*) from binary data obtained from the acquisition of the values. This is an algorithm developed on the Raspberry PI 3B + single board computer.

To obtain more stable and reliable alcohol levels, the values of samples acquired consecutively in a time window of 5 s (640 samples) are averaged. The computed average value is converted to an integer value (*dbits*) and with it the output voltage (V_{lea}) that the MQ3 module produced is estimated. V_{lea} is obtained through the following expression (4):

$$V_{lea} = dbits \times \frac{Xmax}{maxbits - minbits} \tag{4}$$

Where *maxbits* is equal to 32767 which constitutes the maximum positive encoded value, while *minbits* is the encoded '0' value.

After obtaining the voltage, the variable resistance (R_{sa}) of the MQ3 sensor is calculated because it is dependent on the sensed alcohol level. This can be calculated by replacing the voltage with the equation shown in (5):

$$R_{sa} = R_{lea}((V_{cc} - V_{lea})/V_{lea}) \tag{5}$$

Where R_{lea} is the load resistance of the alcohol sensor. In this case a constant value of $R_{lea} = 1K$ is considered.

From the graph of the calibration curve of the MQ3 sensor technical sheet, it was necessary to obtain the mathematical function that relates the alcohol level in mg/L and the resistances R_{sa} and R_{oa}. For this, samples of the calibration curve of the technical sheet were obtained and from potential regression the calibration function shown in Fig. 8, was obtained.

With this function it was possible to estimate the resistance ratio ($\frac{R_{sa}}{R_{oa}}$) for high levels of alcohol. In this case, an approximate relationship was obtained in (6):

$$\frac{R_{sa}}{R_{oa}} \approx 0.1 \tag{6}$$

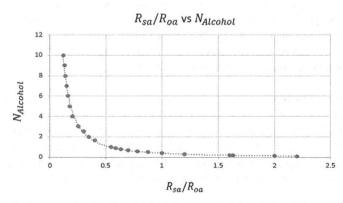

Fig. 8. Graph of the samples obtained from Alcohol (mg / L) and R_{sa} and R_{oa}.

Then with this relationship, the constant value of R_{oa} was estimated from R_{sa} for high alcohol levels. The value obtained was $R_{oa} = 2.5K$.

With the R_{oa} value obtained, it is possible to determine any level of alcohol within the range of the sensor using expression (5) and the function of the graph in Fig. 8, which can be expressed as shown in (7):

$$N_{Alcohol} = 0.4177 \cdot (R_{sa}/R_{oa})^{-1.471} \tag{7}$$

Finally, to calculate the alcoholic level in% BAC, the alcohol level in mg/L is divided by 5.

2.6 Visualization of Identified Person and Detected Alcohol Level

The registration of the person is carried out in a relational database, in which the name of the person, the detected alcohol level, the time and date on which the measurement was made is recorded. This is done by the Raspberry PI 3B +, which is integrated into the computer.

On the other hand, the face is displayed by the computer indicating the name of the person identified by each blow detection. The detected alcohol level is displayed by the Raspberry PI 3B + on an LCD screen, which is integrated through an I2C interface. The measured value and the person's name are displayed on the screen. Fig. 9 and Fig. 10 show the image of the face seen by the computer monitor and the alcoholic level (on the LCD screen) respectively.

2.7 Structure of the Proposed Device

For the design of the proposed structure, Autodesk Inventor Professional 2021 software was used. The distance of the camera from the face, the location of the "Yes" and "No" buttons, the location of the strips of LED, the distance between the sensors and the air displacement hole. The strips of LED are used to indicate whether alcohol has been detected (changing the color) and illuminate the face in a dark environments. The "Yes" and "No" buttons are used so that the person can declare before the test (for legal reasons) whether the person has ingested alcohol. The pushbutton information is acquired and recorded by the Raspberry PI 3B +.

Fig. 9. Image of a captured face (Author 2: Wilson Chavesta).

Fig. 10. Display of detected alcohol level.

The measurements of the proposed enclosure are 320 × 200 × 200 mm. In Fig. 11, the design of the proposed structure is shown and in Fig. 12, its installation on a wall or support and support surface.

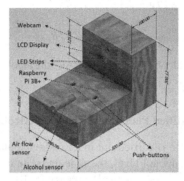

Fig. 11. Image of the design of the proposed enclosure and its general dimensions in millimeters.

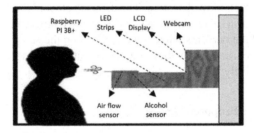

Fig. 12. Representative image of the use of the enclosure located on a wall

3   Results

For the experimental results, 532 samples have been taken. Of these, 50 samples were used to verify synchronized face registration, 450 to evaluate correct face recognition, and 32 to verify airflow detection and measurement of different alcohol levels.

Alcohol measurement tests are performed at 5 min intervals to eliminate the environment of possible presence of alcohol.

The parameter used to verify the synchronized registration of the face was the maximum image capture time for 50 samples evaluated. This parameter is used because we want to evaluate the worst case of the acquisition delay. The obtained value was 0.067 s, which for the application is quite satisfactory.

The parameters that were used to verify the correct measurement of the alcoholic level are Pearson's correlation coefficient [11] and the mean error in different ranges of alcohol level (low, moderate and high).

The alcohol measurement results in mg/L for the 32 samples were compared with those obtained with the AT-818 breathalyzer. The Pearson correlation coefficient value that was obtained was 0.937, which is a value close to 1 and therefore quite satisfactory.

To obtain the average error (ε) and the average error percentage ($\%\varepsilon$) the measurements of the proposed system were compared with those obtained with the professional digital breathalyzer AT-818. The error and the percentage error for this measurement are expressed in (8) and (9) respectively:

$$\varepsilon = \left| V_{experimental} - V_{referential} \right| \tag{8}$$

$$\%\varepsilon = \left| \frac{V_{experimental} - V_{referential}}{V_{referential}} \right| \times 100 \tag{9}$$

Where $V_{experimental}$ is the experimental value obtained from the proposed electronic equipment and $V_{referential}$ is the theoretical value obtained from the breathalyzer.

The error and percentage error were calculated in different ranges of alcohol levels of the obtained samples, then the average error and the average percentage error were calculated for each range. In [12] the ranges and values of the alcoholic level associated with the effects in humans are specified. In this reference, it is specified that level values around 0.000 and 0.199 mg/L produce little or no effect on the person, which is why it is called a low level. On the other hand, around 0.200 and 0.499 mg/L there is a decrease in reaction time, which is why it is called moderate level. Finally, values in the range of 0.500 and 1 mg/L produce difficulty in speech and vision, which is why it is called high level.

Levels greater than 1 mg/L have not been considered because 1 mg/L is the maximum measurement value of the AT-818 breathalyzer used in the measurements. The results are shown in Table 1.

Table 1. Average error and average percentage error obtained by alcohol level intervals.

Alcohol Level	Range of alcohol levels	± Average error	± Average percentage error (%)
Low	0.000 mg/L - 0.199 mg/L	0.006 mg/L	5.07
Medium	0.200 mg/L – 0.499 mg/L	0.047 mg/L	12.26
High	0.500 mg/L – 1.000 mg/L	0.059 mg/L	9.05

As can be seen in the results, the average error presents a direct relationship; that is, it increases as the level of alcohol also increases. However, this relationship is not so significant because if the results of the column "Average percentage error (%)" are averaged, a general value of all samples would be obtained equivalent to 8.79%, which would indicate to us an assertiveness for the detection of the alcohol level greater than 91%. It is worth mentioning that this percentage of correct answers is re-presented when the evaluation process by the proposed system is carried out correctly (23 samples) and is not influenced by external agents such as, for example: external noise, gaseous alcohol overload in the sensor area and soft or short puff.

The parameter used to verify the correct detection of the air flow is the percentage of success.

For this, the data obtained in the evaluation of the samples used in the measurement of the alcohol level were used. In this case, it was verified by visual inspection whether flow detection occurs in each evaluation. In each case the sound intensity was also measured in dBs.

For the latter, a digital decibel meter was used, which was located 2 cm from the electret microphone used to detect the flow.

With the obtained data, the percentage of hits (ρ_f) for flow detection was calculated, which can be defined in (10):

$$\rho_f = \frac{N_f}{N_{tf}} \times 100 \tag{10}$$

Where N_f is the total number of airflow tests detected and N_{tf} is the total number of tests.

In tests, it has been verified that the sound threshold for flow detection, applying the algorithm in Fig. 7, is equivalent to that the air flow must exceed 87 dBs for the system to be able to calculate the alcoholic level and capture the image for its recognition. With this a detection percentage of 93.7% was obtained.

Finally, the parameter used to evaluate the performance of the recognition of people is the percentage of true recognition. In this case, the person recognized by the algorithm and the person recognized by visual inspection are compared. The percentage of true recognitions ($\%P_{Vr}$) is defined in (11):

$$\%P_{Vr} = \frac{V_{rec}}{T_{img}} \times 100 \tag{11}$$

Where V_{rec} is the number of true recognitions and T_{img} is the total number of images per person.

Five people were evaluated. The convolutional network was trained with 210 images per person. For the validation, 90 images were used per person, obtaining the true recognition values shown in Table 2.

Table 2. Percentage of true recognition per person.

	Person 1	Person 2	Person 3	Person 4	Person 5	Person 6	Person 7
$\%P_{Vr}$	98.9	97.7	98.9	98.9	97.7	98.9	98.9

As can be seen in Table 2, the results are very similar and quite high (close to 100%). Which describes that in general terms the probability of identifying the person correctly is very high, if not practically exact. This is justified by the number of images on which

the convolutional network. It is worth mentioning that $\%P_{Vr}$ increase as the number of images increases, however the relationship $\%P_{Vr}$ with training time and computational load is not so favorable, that is why that amount of images was taken for training.

4 Conclusions

The proposed solution allowed the detection of the air flow, measurement of the alcohol level and the recognition of the face automatically with satisfactory results.

In airflow detection, errors sometimes occur due to loud external sounds generated near the microphone. However, the probability of their occurrence is quite low.

In the results of the measurement of the alcoholic level a maximum error of 0.159 is presented due to variation in the intensity of air flow during the tests in the AT-818 breathalyzer. In addition, the algorithm could be improved, or another alcohol sensor could be used to obtain greater precision in the measurement.

The delay in the capture time is due to delays in the control of the camera's processor for image acquisition. However, the obtained results allow the correct registration of the face since the movement of the person is not fast enough to avoid registration and subsequent recognition.

Errors in face recognition are mainly because of changes in lighting. This can be solved with the construction of an enclosure that can house the proposed equipment and isolate it from sounds and external lighting sources.

References

1. Palomino, M.: Importancia del sector industrial en el desarrollo económico: Una revisión al estado del arte. Revista Estudios de Políticas Públicas **3**(1), 139–156 (2017)
2. Aiello, C., Agu, E.: Investigating postural sway features, normalization and personalization in detecting blood alcohol levels of smartphone users. In: 2016 IEEE Wireless Health, Institute of Electrical and Electronics Engineers Inc, Bethesa, pp 73–80 (2016)
3. Aymerich, J., et al.: Cost-effective smartphone-based reconfigurable electrochemical instrument for alcohol determination in whole blood samples. Biosens. Bioelectron. **117**, 736–742 (2018)
4. LINIO Homepage. https://www.linio.com.pe/p/alcoholi-metro-digital-at818-policial-profesional-con-boquillas-negro-or94qt. Accessed 01 Aug 2020
5. CDP Homepage. https://www.cdpsa.eu/producto/alcoholimetro-a-monedas-blow-go-cdp-4500/. Accessed 02 Aug 2020
6. Shah, K., Bhandare, D., Bhirud, S.: Face recognition-based automated attendance system. In: Gupta, D., Khanna, A., Bhattacharyya, S., Hassanien, A.E., Anand, S., Jaiswal, A. (eds.) 3rd International Conference on Innovative Computing and Communication, vol. 1165, pp. 945–952. Springer, Delhi (2020) https://doi.org/10.1007/978-981-15-5113-0_79
7. Koteswara Rao, M., Veera Swamy, K., Anitha Sheela, K.: Face recognition system using a hybrid scale invariant feature transform based on local binary pattern. In: Chen, J. I.-Z., Tavares, J.M.R.S., Shakya, S., Iliyasu, A.M. (eds.) ICIPCN 2020. AISC, vol. 1200, pp. 794–804. Springer, Cham (2021). https://doi.org/10.1007/978-3-030-51859-2_72
8. Winsen Alcohol Gas Sensor. https://cdn.sparkfun.com/datasheets/Sensors/Biometric/MQ-3%20ver1.3%20-%20Manual.pdf. Accessed 15 Jan 2020

9. Alonso. M.: Espacios de color RGB, HSI y sus Generalizaciones a n- Dimensiones. PhD Thesis, Instituto Nacional de Astrofísica, Óptica y Electrónica, Puebla, México (2009)
10. Machine Learning is Fun! Part 4: Modern Face Recognition with Deep Learning Homepage. https://medium.com/@ageitgey/machine-learning-is-fun-part-4-modern-face-recognition-with-deep-learning-c3cffc121d78. Accessed 21 Nov 2016
11. Chen, H., Cui, H., He, Z., Lu, L., Huang, Y.: Influence of chloride deposition rate on rust layer protectiveness and corrosion severity of mild steel in tropical coastal atmosphere. Mater. Chem. Phys. **259**, 1–32 (2020)
12. Restrev, L., Cardona, J.: Diseño de un sistema electrónico que mide el grado de alcoholemia y comprueba por biometría la identidad del conductor de un vehículo. Thesis, Universidad tecnológica de Pereira, Pereira, Colombia (2015)

A Comparison of Linear and Nonlinear PID Controllers Reset-Based for Nonlinear Chemical Processes with Variable Deadtime

Renato Díaz and Oscar Camacho[(✉)]

Departamento de Automatización Y Control Industrial, Facultad de Ingeniería Eléctrica Y Electrónica, Escuela Politécnica Nacional, Ladrón de Guevara E11-253, Quito 170517, Ecuador
{victor.diaz,oscar.camacho}@epn.edu.ec

Abstract. This work presents an analysis, design, and comparison of the PI (Proportional and Integral) controller and control schemes PI linear and nonlinear controllers reset-based. The parameters of these control schemes have been set by trial and error to finally be tested in a nonlinear process with variable dead time. Controller performance is measured using integral square error (ISE), integral time square error (ITSE), total variations of control efforts (TVU), maximum overshoot (M_p) and settling time (t_s). The results show that reset control systems overcome fundamental limitations coming from linear control systems.

Keywords: Controllers reset-based · Nonlinear processes · Deadtime · Performance

1 Introduction

Reset systems control began to be developed sixty years ago with Clegg [1], who introduced a nonlinear integrator based on a reset action called Clegg integrator (CI). This idea was taken up in the 70s by Krishnan and Horowitz [2]; in that work, the CI's properties and its usefulness as a control element are studied. Similarly, in work by Horowitz and Rosenbaum [3], a generalization is proposed, the FORE (First-Order Reset Element). The lack of control theory, approaching basic questions such as the existence and uniqueness of solutions and continuous dependence on the initial condition (wellposedness) and stability, for several decades has put aside the further mainstream developments in reset control, both in theory and applications. However, for the last decade, several researchers have been working enthusiastically on reset control, and fortuitously, reset control has begun to be seen as a desirable control design procedure with a considerable potential for practical control applications [4].

The classical PID-type control techniques do not provide acceptable results when working with processes that present elevated delay [5] or inverse response processes [4]. It is well known that PID controllers are by far the most applied form of feedback in use. As cited in [6], more than 90% of all control loops are PID; most of them are PI since derivative action is not often used. It is generally recognized that this dominance

M. Botto-Tobar et al. (Eds.): ICAT 2020, CCIS 1388, pp. 195–206, 2021.
https://doi.org/10.1007/978-3-030-71503-8_15

of PI/PID compensation is due to its simplicity (three parameters to adjust) and its effectiveness in a wide range of applications: engines, automotive industry, flight control, food industry, for example.

As the PI/PID are linear controllers, they have fundamental limitations. These limitations could be avoided by introducing more advanced controllers. However, the introduction of other control types is challenging to implement because they are often too complicated, require much computational power, or require a good plant model. Industry wants better process control, but at the same time wants the simplicity of PID control. It is impossible to improve PID control beyond its linear limitations and, therefore, it is necessary to implement nonlinear behavior [7, 8].

The present work shows the design and simulation of two control structures: a linear PI (classical) and a nonlinear PI (NPI) with reset action applied to an industrial process with variable delay. Controllers performance is measured using integral square error (ISE), integral time square error (ITSE), total variations of control efforts (TVU), maximum overshoot (M_p) and settling time (t_s).

This work is organized as follows: Sect. 2 covers the basic concepts used to analyze the reset control schemes and the study cases' description. Section 3 presents the model identification and the values of the adjustment parameters obtained using trial and error; besides shows, the results obtained in the tracking and regulation tests in the variable deadtime process and finally, in Sect. 4 are the conclusions of this work.

2   Basic Concepts

2.1   Control Schemes

Two control schemes reset-based were used to make this document. The first is the Proportional and Integral controller, plus Clegg's Integrator (PI + CI), presented in [4]. It allows us to improve settling time and decrease the system response's maximum overshoot without sacrificing speed. The second scheme is the NPI + CI controller, defined simply by adding a Clegg integrator (CI) to an NPI controller, and the latter is presented in [9].

2.2   PI + CI Reset-Based Controller

The PI + CI controller is defined simply by adding a Clegg integrator (CI) to a PI controller (PI_{base}). The PI + CI controller will have three terms: a proportional term, an integral term, and an integral term with reset action: the integral reset term. Note that a CI term has not the attribute of eliminating the steady-state error in response to step disturbances by itself; hence, the integral term is used for that reason. The most important advantage of using the CI term is improving the system's response, being possible to get a fast response without excessive overshooting compared to its counterpart PI [10]. So the starting point is the PI_{base}, which has a transfer function depending on its proportional gain, k_p, and its integral time constant, τ_i, given by:

$$PI_{base}(s) = k_p\left(1 + \frac{1}{\tau_i s}\right) \tag{1}$$

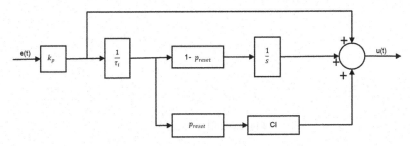

Fig. 1. PI + CI controller structure.

The structure of a PI + CI controller is shown in Fig. 1.

Where its input is the error signal $e(t)$, its output is the control signal $u(t)$, k_p the proportional gain and τ_i the integral time constant.

The new parameter named preset or reset ratio is a dimensionless constant with values preset $\in$ [0, 1] that considers the CI term's relative weight over the I term. Note that a PI + CI compensator is reduced to a PI compensator if reset is eliminated, preset $= 0$. Furthermore, on the other hand, a P + CI compensator would be obtained if preset $= 1$. However, as it was discussed above, in general, the reset should not be applied on the whole of the integral term because the fundamental asymptotic property of the integral term would be lost [4]. The distribution of the PI + CI control scheme is in the following equation.

$$PI + CI = k_p \left(1 + \frac{1}{\tau_i} \left(\frac{1 - p_{reset}}{s} + \frac{p_{reset}}{s} \right) \right) \tag{2}$$

2.3 NPID Controller

A nonlinear gain plus a classic PID controller is an NPID controller structure, as shown in Fig. 2.

The following nonlinear control law can express the plant input $u(t)$as follows:

$$u(t) = \left[k_p + k_i \int_0^t dt + k_d \frac{d}{dt} \right] \phi(e) \tag{3}$$

Where k_p, k_i and k_d are the proportional, integral, and derivative gains, and $\phi(e)$ is a nonlinear gain function. $\phi(e)$ acts on the error to produce a scaled error, that can be modified to produce a quick response. The following equation gives it:

$$\phi(e) = k(e)e(t) \tag{4}$$

Where $k(e)$ is a nonlinear gain [11].

NPID-type controllers have the advantage of a high initial gain for fast response, followed by a low gain when the output is close to the reference, to avoid oscillatory behavior.

The nonlinear gain is not exclusive or determined to a single option; the literature recommends various NPIDs controllers; this work is focused on the nonlinear PID proposed by Han [9, 12].

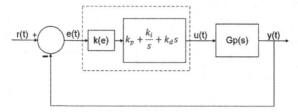

Fig. 2. NPID structure.

2.4 NPI + CI Reset-Based Controller

The NPI + CI controller was designed based on the nonlinear PI controller's combination with the Clegg integrator. The proposed design of the NPI + CI controller is seen in Fig. 3.

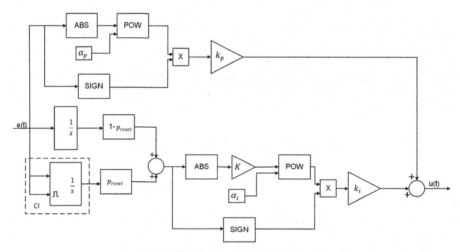

Fig. 3. Block diagram of the NPI + CI

2.5 Performance Indexes

Integral Square Error (ISE). This index allows evaluating the performance of a control scheme in the transient and stationary behavior. It is calculated using the following equation [13].

$$ISE = \int_0^\infty e^2(t)dt \tag{5}$$

Integral Time Square Error (ITSE). In this index, time appears as a factor, so, penalizes the error more at the later stages than at the beginning. It is calculated using the following equation [14].

$$ITSE = \int_0^\infty te^2(t)dt \tag{6}$$

Total Variations of Control Efforts (TVu). The TVu performance index allows us to evaluate the control actions (controller output); if the value approaches zero, it is considered that the actions of the controller are smooth. It is determined by the following equation [13].

$$TVu = \sum_{K=1}^{\infty} |u_{K+1} - u_K| \tag{7}$$

2.6 Transient Response Performance Specifications

Maximum Overshoot (M_p). It is the maximum peak value of the response curve measured from unity. The amount that the waveform overshoots the final value is also expressed as a percentage of the steady-state value. It is determined by the following equation [15].

$$M_p\% = \frac{c(t_p) - c(\infty)}{c(\infty)} \times 100 \tag{8}$$

Settling Time (t_s). It is required for the transient damping oscillations to reach and stay within ±2% or ±5% of the final or steady-state value. It is determined by the following equation [15].

3 Simulation Results

To test the proposed approaches' performance, a mixing tank is used as a model of a nonlinear system. The example is taken from Camacho and Smith [16]. In there, the equations of the mathematical model are presented, as well as the design parameters.

3.1 Mixing Tank

Consider the mixing tank shown in Fig. 4. The tank receives two streams, a hot stream, $W_1(t)$, and a cold stream, $W_2(t)$. The outlet temperature is measured at a point 125 ft downstream from the tank. The following assumptions are accepted.

- The liquid volume in the tank is considered constant
- The tank contents are well mixed.
- The tank and pipe are well insulated.

The temperature transmitter is calibrated from a range of 100 to 200 °F. The temperature of the mixture $T_3(t)$ resulting inside the tank is controlled through the opening or closing of a cold flow control valve. The magnitude of the delay time increases as the hot water flow decreases.

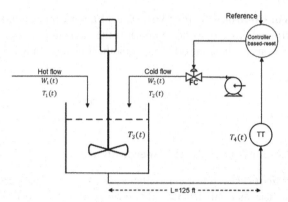

Fig. 4. Mixing tank

3.2 Process Model Identification

The previous process is approximated for the First Order Plus Dead Time (FOPDT) model for the control schemes design. The FOPDT model of the mixing tank is obtained from the reaction curve method, with a step change of ±10% in the nonlinear system [15, 16], giving, as a result, the model of Eq. (9). Figure 5 shows the comparison between the nonlinear process output and the FOPDT model output of the mixing tank.

The average FOPDT is:

$$G_p(s) = \frac{-0.858}{2.232s + 1}e^{-4.434s} \tag{9}$$

The ratio $\frac{t_0}{\tau}$, called the controllability relationship, is higher than one representing a dead time dominant process.

The parameters of each control scheme are tuned by trial and error. The values obtained are found in Table 1.

3.3 Tracking Test

Starting from the initial condition of process temperature that is 150 [°F], it is increased to 165 [°F] at 25 [min]. Then, it rises to 190 [°F] at 120 [min], and finally, at 400 [min], the process temperature is decreased to 165 [°C].

Table 1. Tuning parameters for the mixing tank

	Mixing tank						
	k_p	τ_i	p_{reset}	α_p	α_i	K_i	δ
PI	−0.293	2.232	---	---	---	---	---
PI + CI	−0.293	2.232	0.5	---	---	---	---
NPI	−0.293	2.232	---	1.1	0.775	0.725	0
NPI + CI	−0.293	2.232	0.325	1.1	0.775	0.725	0

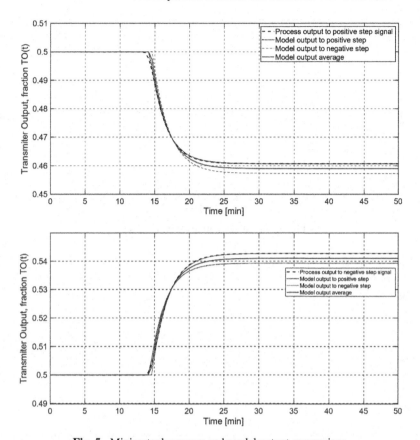

Fig. 5. Mixing tank process and model output comparison.

Radial graphs were made to compare the results obtained and to know which control scheme presents more considerable advantages from a performance viewpoint. These graphs allow us to visualize the different standardized performance indices obtained (considered 1 to the worst value). From the radial graph, it can be concluded scheme that presents the smallest area is the one that has more considerable advantages compared to the others.

Figure 6 shows the system's responses; all the controllers can follow the reference changes smoothly except for the PI due to linear control limitations. On the other hand, it can be emphasized that the proposed control schemes with reset action visually present at the most critical point of the response, that is, when there is an increase in temperature at (190°F) a significantly lower $M_p\%$ in comparison to the PI controller. NPI controller also has a significantly lower $M_p\%$.

Figure 7 shows the control signals for each control proposal; these have a control signal with reasonable oscillations (smooth signal). This means that they try to reach the reference as quickly as possible without forced action (overshoot).

To specify which controller is ideal for setpoint variations in the mixing tank, Table 2 indicates each performance index's value.

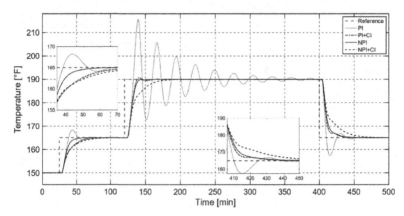

Fig. 6. Processes output (Mixing tank)

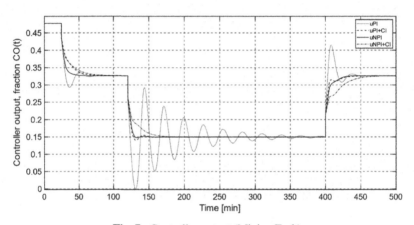

Fig. 7. Controller output (Mixing Tank)

In the next table, areas with different colors are shown. The green one represents favorable results. Meanwhile, the red indicates a poor performance for the system; there is also a yellow area, which suggests an intermediate performance value. Similarly, in the table's left part, other indicator symbols such as acceptance, exclamation mark, and disapproval indicate zones from the better until the worse performance results.

From all performance indexes, Table 2, to clarify the understanding of these indexes and criteria, they are presented in a radial graph. For the five parameters, the smallest values are those of the NPI. The best TVu index with the lowest M_p corresponds to the NPI + CI, showing the reset-term improvements. In the radial graph in Fig. 8, the PI + CI and NPI schemes present the best tracking tests in the Mixing tank.

3.4 Regulation Task

It is essential to note that for this test, disturbances are made in the hot water inlet fluid (W_1) and the range of variation of this variable is from 250 to 120 [lb/min]. Starting

Table 2. Performance indexes for setpoint changes in Mixing Tank.

CONTROL SCHEME	PERFORMANCE INDEXES				
	ISE	TVu	ITSE	Maximun overshoot M_p [%]	Settling time t_s [min]
PI	2.1900	2.4485	423.6093	13.6106	208.4333
PI + CI	1.2466	0.5439	270.2082	0.3391	77.7817
NPI	1.2610	0.5731	284.1973	0.0116	64.2484
NPI+CI	1.4909	0.5054	341.1370	0.0043	137.3329

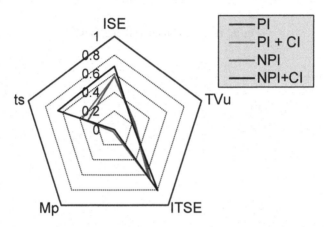

Fig. 8. Performance indexes comparison for tracking test in the Mixing tank.

with the nominal condition of 250 [lb/min], first it is changed to 215[lb/min], then it decreases to 180 [lb/min], then to 150 [lb/min] and finally it decreases to 120 [lb/min], the variations were made in the instants of 25 [min], 120 [min], 250 [min] and 500 [min] respectively.

Figure 9 shows that when the hot water flow falls to the value of 215 [lb /min] at 25 [min], the PI produces the highest M_p [%], but it is the fastest in stabilize compared to the other schemes. PI + CI compensate for the disturbance with an M_p [%] and a t_s [min] lower than its counterpart (PI). The remaining controllers do not have a maximum overshoot but an unwanted settling time.

On the other hand, when the hot water flow is reduced to its minimum value (120 [lb/min]), the superiority of the nonlinear control schemes is observed, standing out the NPI + CI controller that exhibits the lowest value M_p [%] and ideal stabilization time.

Figure 10 shows the different control actions received to the valve; all comply with the limits from 0 to 1 except for the PI controller. It should be noted that the NPI + CI controller has a control action represented by a smooth signal; this means that it tries to stabilize as soon as possible.

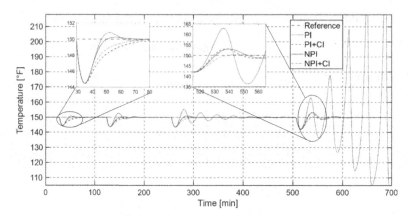

Fig. 9. Processes output (Mixing Tank)

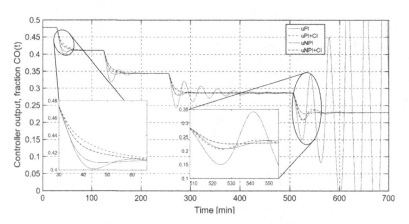

Fig. 10. Controller output (Mixing Tank)

To specify which controller is ideal for disturbances, Table 3 indicates each specification and performance indexes' value.

Table 3. Performance indexes for disturbances in Mixing Tank.

CONTROL SCHEME	PERFORMANCE INDEXES				
	ISE	TVu	ITSE	Maximum overshoot M_p [%]	Settling time t_s [min]
❌ PI	Unstable	Unstable	Unstable	Unstable	Unstable
◔ PI + CI	0.2054	0.3416	62.2182	2.1351	113.0027
◔ NPI	0.2202	0.3545	66.7677	2.1096	101.5969
✅ NPI + CI	0.2040	0.2568	65.2947	0.2601	106.6953

From the performance indexes of Table 3, Fig. 11 shows a radial graph, and from it, the NPI + CI scheme presents the best results with a lower area than the rest of the controllers.

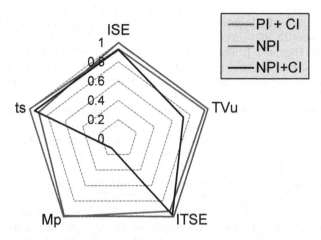

Fig. 11. Performance indexes comparison for the regulation test in the Mixing tank.

4 Conclusions

Two control schemes, reset-based using a linear and nonlinear PID structure, were presented and tested in a variable delay process.

A reset-based controller is a linear controller (base controller) that is reset in specific instants of time. Therefore, its operation is relatively simple and easily understood.

Simulink's Clegg integrator implementation is as simple as activating the external reset option in a linear integrator and introducing in this new input the signal whose zero crossings will activate the reset event.

The control schemes with reset action provide satisfactory performance despite the variable delay compared to the PI.

Programming the reset-based controller in a PLC can be easy since it has the classic control laws (PID), and it is also usual to have a variable whose activation leads to the reset action.

Acknowledgments. The authors thank PIGR-19–17 Project of the Escuela Politécnica Nacional for its sponsorship to realize this work.

References

1. Clegg, J.C.: A nonlinear integrator for servomechanisms. Trans. AIEE Part II: Appl. Ind. **77**(1), 41–42 (1958)

2. Krishnan, K.R., Horowitz, I.M.: Synthesis of a nonlinear feedback system with significant plant-ignorance for prescribed system tolerances. Int. J. Control **19**(4), 689–706 (1974)
3. Horowitz, I.M., Rosenbaum, P.: Nonlinear design for cost of feedback reduction in systems with large parameter uncertainty. Int. J. Control **21**(6), 977–1001 (1975)
4. Baños, A., Barreiro, A.: Reset Control Systems. Springer, New York (2012)
5. Camacho, O., Leiva, H.: Impulsive semilinear heat equation with delay in control and in state. Asian J. Control **22**, 1075–1089 (2020)
6. Åström, K.J., Hägglund, T.: The Future of PID. IFAC Proc. Volumes **33**(4), 205–218 (1999)
7. Kars, H.: Frequency analysis of reset systems containing a Clegg integrator. Introduction to higher order sinusoidal input describing functions. Master of Science Thesis, Delft University of Technology (2018)
8. Alfaro, V., Balaguer, P., Arrieta, O.: Robustness considerations on PID tuning for regulatory control of inverse response processes. IFAC Proc. Volumes **45**(3), 193–198 (2012)
9. Zaidner, G., Korotkin, S., Shteimberg, E., Ellenbogen, A., Arad, M., Cohen, Y.: "Nonlinear PID and its application in process control. In: 2010 IEEE 26-th Convention of Electrical and Electronics Engineers, pp. 574–577 (2010)
10. Baños, A., Vidal, A.: Definition and tuning of a PI+CI reset controller. In: 2007 European Control Conference (ECC), pp. 4792–4798 (2007).
11. Maddi, A., Guessom, A., Berkani, D.: Design of nonlinear PID controllers based on hyper-stability criteria. In: 2014 15th International Conference on Sciences and Techniques of Automatic Control and Computer Engineering (STA), pp. 736–741 (2014)
12. Han, J.: From PID to Active Disturbance Rejection Control. IEEE Trans. Ind. Electron. **56**(3), 900–906 (2009)
13. Mejía, C., Camacho, O., Chávez, D., Herrera, M.: A modified smith predictor for processes with variable time delay. In: IEEE, 4th Colombian Conference on Automatic Control (CCAC), pp. 1–6. (2019)
14. Das, S., Pan, I., Gupta, A.: A novel fractional order fuzzy PID controller and its optimal time domain tuning based on integral performance indices. Eng. Appl. Artif. Intell. **25**(2), 430–442 (2012)
15. Smith, C., Corripio, A.: Principles and Practice of Automatic Process Control, 2nd edn. Wiley, New York (1997)
16. Camacho, O., Smith, C.: Sliding mode control: An approach to regulate nonlinear chemical processes. ISA Trans. **39**(2), 205–218 (2000)

Comparison of Infinite Impulse Response (IIR) and Finite Impulse Response (FIR) Filters in Cardiac Optical Mapping Records

David Rivas-Lalaleo[1]([envelope]) [iD], Sergio Muñoz-Romero[2] [iD], Monica Huerta[3] [iD],
Víctor Bautista-Naranjo[1] [iD], Jorge García-Quintanilla[4] [iD],
Javier Moreno-Planas[5], and José Luis Rojo-Álvarez[2] [iD]

[1] Departamento de Eléctrica Y Electrónica, Universidad de Las Fuerzas
Armadas ESPE, Av. General Rumiñahui S/n, Sangolquí 171-5-231B, Ecuador
[2] Department of Signal Theory and Communications and Telematic Systems
and Computation, Universidad Rey Juan Carlos, 28933 Madrid, Spain
[3] Universidad Politécnica Salesiana, Cuenca, Ecuador
[4] Hospital Clínico San Carlos, Madrid, Spain
[5] Arrhythmia Unit, Hospital Ramon y Cajal, Ctra. de Colmenar Viejo, Madrid, Spain

Abstract. Optical cardiac mapping is an experimental method developed to record the electrical behavior of the heart, through the analysis of films filmed at high speed. Due to the conditions of the experiment along with the signal, a great amount of noise from different sources is stored. In this article, the comparison of the IIR type filters and the FIR filters is proposed, where the order of the filters, the phase difference and the application on the film have been compared. From this analysis it is determined that a 9th order IIR filter behaves in the same way as a 256 order FIR filter. Therefore, it can be determined that a 9th order IIR filter can be used for filtering this type of signal, reducing the computational costs in its application.

Keywords: Optical Mapping · Cardiac · IIR · FIR

1 Introduction

Cardiac Optical Mapping (OM) is an experimental medical imaging technique used to record the electrophysiological characteristics of the heart, which consists of recording high-resolution, high-speed images of the activation fronts on the surface of said organ [2,5]. To obtain the activation films, an **ex-vivo** heart is used, which is perfused with a voltage-sensitive contrast that binds to the outer surface of the cardiomyocyte cell membrane. This area is excited with a light, that is, with electromagnetic radiation of optical frequency. Using one or more

© Springer Nature Switzerland AG 2021
M. Botto-Tobar et al. (Eds.): ICAT 2020, CCIS 1388, pp. 207–224, 2021.
https://doi.org/10.1007/978-3-030-71503-8_16

high-speed and high-definition cameras, the light that is reflected off the surface of the heart is recorded, the intensity of which varies depending on the changes in transmembrane voltage, and in this way the technique makes it possible to evaluate the action potentials of a non-invasively in a cardiac spatial region of interest [5, 6, 10]. Some of the advantages derived from applying this experimental technique are the extraction of a greater quantity of information and the better resolution than in current bioelectric records. Furthermore, it is foreseeable that in the near future there will be systems capable of providing patients with the transmembrane potential as a three-dimensional electrical medical image that changes over time, for example, thanks to the evolution of mapping systems [6] or cardiac electrical imaging systems (ECG imaging) [1] current. Therefore, it is important to improve the quality of the records of this experimental technique from those already available today. One of the main drawbacks in current OM records is the presence of noise. This disturbance can be of different types and the following contributions can be described, according to their origin and nature:

- Gaussian noise: One of the noises that is likely to be present in most OM videos is Gaussian noise, which is usually removed by linear filtering. To date, Finite Impulse Response (FIR) convolution cores have been used for this purpose in $2D + t$, limited orders [8].
- Optical noise: this type of noise can be defined as the random appearance of dots of variable size and variations in brightness or color in the film, which generates what we will call granular artifacts [4, 13].
- Noise due to movement artifact: Another type of noise that is difficult to eliminate is movement artifact, which occurs due to the contraction and relaxation of the heart. Although several algorithms have been proposed to suppress it, this has not been solved to date through signal processing, and it is often tried to compensate by mechanically fixing the heart or canceling contractility, which can affect the observation of electrical properties [12].
- Anatomical noise: finally, the OM recordings are made on the heart, which is not a smooth muscle, but shows curvature, fibers and structures that can affect macroscopic observation [7].

Noise cancellation is not a trivial problem to solve, and that is why this chapter deals with the suppression of noise (existing in a good part of the experiments carried out with this technique) and in particular the elimination of the components of Gaussian noise, the granular optical noise and the motion artifact of the films obtained in experiments with OM. For this reason, the objective of this article is to develop exploring conventional filter techniques, performing a sharing between the Infinite Impulse Response (IIR) and Finite Impulse Response (FIR) type filters in OM registers, where it is verified what type of filter linear is more appropriate for canceling out the Gaussian noise of each pixel over time. For this, the different orders of different types of filters are contrasted, and the result of each one in the space-time domain is studied. It can be mentioned that, when working with films and since a gold standard is not available for comparison, it is necessary to pay close attention to the resulting graphs in terms of the effect that the explored filtering methods may have. Therefore, the article has a significant number of images that are taken as support at the time of presenting the results. Specifically, information on the behavior of a central pixel, of a line of pixels (vertical center) in M mode, of a representative example frame (generally containing a trigger edge), and finally of eigenvalues and eigenvectors in time and space.

2   Database of Experimental Records

In this work, 24 films have been used, which were recorded in experimental OM processes carried out at the Health Institute Carlos III and in the Clinical Hospital San Carlos (both in Madrid, España). The protocol used for taking the samples was as follows: the recording area of the heart surface was between $3,5 \times 3,5$ cm o 4×4 cm; the resolution used was 64×64 pixels; and the registration speed was between 790 a 800 frames per second, obtaining a total of 1501 frames or 2001 frames, equivalent to 1.8 s of filming and 2.5 s of footage, respectively. From the aforementioned cases, it can be mentioned that the following sets of films are available:

- Set A, in which the motion artifact is practically zero. It consists of 2 movies, which are made up of 1501 frames of 64×64 pixels.
- Sets B, C, and D, in which motion artifacts are mild, moderate, and severe, respectively, distributed in: (1) 4 movies in group B, including 2 movies of 1501 frames of 64×64 area pixels and 2 movies of 2001 frames of 64×64 area pixels; (2) 2 movies in group C, made up of 1498 frames of 64×64 pixels of area; and (3) 5 of movies in group D, made up of 2001 frames of 64×64 area pixels.
- Set E, consisting of 11 signals acquired when a lasso catheter with 13 electrodes is simultaneously attached to the heart, and with movies taken at a rate of 977 frames per second.

An example of these study groups to be examined are displayed in Fig. 1, which corresponds to group A, this graph is made up of 4 panels, so that in the upper left panel there is the representation of the pixels according to the amplitude and the number of samples, in the upper right an example table of the movie, in the lower left a frame of the movie showing the ratio of pixels and the amplitude, and in the lower right a frame of the movie delimited by borders is shown.

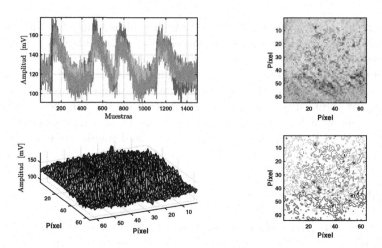

Fig. 1. Example of group A data sets without motion artifact, where pixels are represented in the upper left panel based on the amplitude and number of samples, in the upper right an example frame of the film, in the lower left a frame of the movie where the ratio of the pixels and the width is displayed, and in the lower right a frame of the movie delimited by edges.

3   Methodology

Linear filtering is one of the most widely used methods to eliminate the noise present in a signal and in this way improve its quality. This process starts from the analysis of the frequency spectrum of the signal to be filtered, which is modified by the transfer function of the filter (denoted by $|H(\omega)|$). These filters are based on linear operators and are widely used in biomedical signal processing.

FIR filters stand out for their linearity in phase, allowing the output signal to have no irregular displacements in time of each of its components. For the digital treatment of the ECG, this quality allows that the waves that belong to the cardiac complex do not distort their separation in time. From the computational point of view, a FIR filter only requires the implementation of two basic operations, which are addition and multiplication, allowing its easy implementation in real-time systems [3]. As mentioned in [9], for ECG signal filtering applications, by increasing the filter order, the distortion of the signal in the filter passband increases, but the filter execution time decreases, this is due to the increase in RMSE between the ECG and the filtered signal.

High-pass IIR filters are applied bi-directionally, managing to preserve the start (onset) and end (offset) positions of the QRS complex [11].

It is worth emphasizing that the FIR filter has a linear phase response, which implies a constant group delay for all frequencies. However, the IIR filter has a non-linear phase response, which implies a variable group delay and a possible distortion of the signal over time, which is not reflected in the frequency spectrum. It is for this reason, that despite the much higher order of the FIR filter, it is preferable to use this type of filter to eliminate the displacement of the baseline of the ECG, since it produces a level of attenuation and a distortion in the frequency spectrum acceptable and no time-filtered signal distortion occurs in the filter passband region, since the filter response is linear phase [9].

4 Experimentation

4.1 Análisis Espectral de los Píxeles Temporales

Various electrical and electronic devices are used when conducting OM experiments, so electrical noise is commonly inserted when recording videos. This noise can be described as the aggregation of all those signals that interfere with the measured signal and that have an electrical origin, such as induced currents, eddy currents, electric fields, magnetic fields or electromagnetic fields, among others. One of the most common sources of this phenomenon is caused by the electrical supply network itself, since the circulation of current through the conductors generates an electromagnetic field that affects the equipment around them. This field generally enters a component of 50 Hz or 60 Hz depending on the electrical transmission frequency of each country. In addition, voltage drops due to the connection and disconnection of higher consumption equipment are another source of this type of noise.

In order to determine and confirm the presence of this type of noise in the films recorded for our experiments, the analysis of the central pixel over time is shown. An example of this type of signal can be seen in Fig. 3(a), where the amplitudes that this pixel reaches at each instant of time are represented.

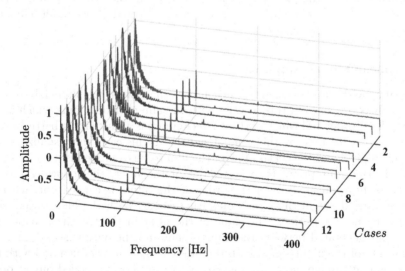

Fig. 2. Application of the FFT to the central pixel of the films recorded in the OM experimentation.

The signals to be examined are characterized by having a dimension of 1×1501 o 1×2001 points and a sample rate between 790 and 800 frames per second, as described. For this experiment, the 13 films that make up groups A, B, C and D of the database were analyzed.

The transformations carried out on this generic pixel can be represented by the function denoted by $f(t)$, which is found as a function of time. By means of this type of representations, the visualization or determination of the presence of network noise is not always immediate, therefore a transformation is carried out from the time domain to the frequency domain by applying the Fourier transform. This transformation is defined as $\mathcal{F}\{f\}$ $\xi \mapsto \hat{f}(\xi) := \int_{-\infty}^{\infty} f(t) \, e^{-2\pi i \xi x} \, dt$. To evaluate this criterion, the FFT to the central pixel of the 13 films to be processed, obtaining as a result the values displayed in Fig. 2.

In this figure you can see in M mode the FFT for each of the 13 cases corresponding to groups A, B, C and D, where the cases drawn in red correspond to a vector of 1×1501 points, while those in blue correspond to a vector of 1×2001 points. For analysis purposes, the notation $F(x, y, t)$ is used to name the acquired records and the discrete notation will be expressed as $F[r, s, n]$, so in this case we can say that the Fourier transform of each pixel was applied in time and then averaged, that is:

$$f(x, y, f, r) = \mathcal{F}(f(x, y, t, r))$$

$$T(f, r) = E_{x,y}(\mathcal{F}(x, y, f, r))$$

where r denotes the index of the film analyzed in these databases.

By analyzing the results of this experiment, the presence of a component at the frequency of 100 Hz can be determined, which is repeated in all the study cases, which shows the presence of electrical noise in the acquired films. Under these considerations, the frequency of 50 Hz was selected as the cutoff frequency of the filter to be implemented.

4.2   Linear Filters Application

Continuing with the experiments, the comparison between the filters IIR and the filters FIR is proposed in this section, with the aim of determining which is the optimal filter order and which of these 2 techniques is adjusted in a better way to the processing required by this type of signals. In this case, the visualization of the central pixel and the central line of the film to be examined is used. In order to obtain the appropriate type and order of the filter, the following process is applied: first, an analysis of the order of the filters is carried out, where a sweep is carried out in the filter's operating range; With the filter orders that present the best conditions, the slope of the filter in the transition band, the phase shift generated between the input signal and the output signal, and the relationship of the input signal with the filtered signal are verified and with the corresponding residue; next, an analysis of the residues is carried out in order to locate structures; and ends with the comparison of the filters and selection of the most suitable for this first step of preprocessing.

It is important to know the signals you are going to work with, which is why it is represented in Fig. 3(a) the behavior of the central pixel, in which the representation of the central pixel as a function of time is plotted in the upper panel and the representation of the normalized central pixel in the lower panel. The Fig. 3(b) displays potential values on the center line of pixels at a given time (upper panel) and similar information on a different spatial line (lower panel).

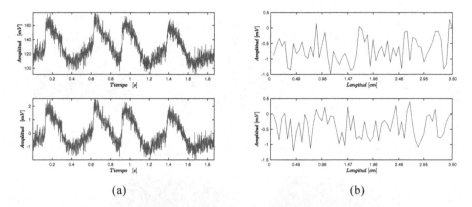

(a)   (b)

Fig. 3. Representation of: (a) amplitude-time graph of the central pixel, the upper panel represents the amplitude of the potential in the central pixel as a function of time, while the lower panel represents the same normalized signal; (b) amplitude-central pixel length graph, the upper panel represents the amplitude of the central pixel along the length of the measured frame, and the lower panel represents the normalized signal.

One way to observe the signals as a whole is the graphs in three dimensions, for example involving the variables amplitude, time and length, through a representation of the central line of the film as a function of these 2 independent variables. In Fig. 4 Panel (a) shows the representation of the central line, while panel (b) represents the normalized center line of the film to be analyzed.

Detailed processes can be summarized in Fig. 4. Under these guidelines, the nuances to be examined when applying each of the filters are included, verifying parameters such as attenuation generated by the filter, effect on the ascending and descending slope of the filtered signal, delays between the original signal and the filtered signal, or morphology of the filtered signal, among others.

4.3   Filters Application IIR

With respect to the above, it is explored below what is the proper order of a filter IIR low-pass with cutoff frequency of 50 Hz Butterworth type. This type of filter responds to the H transfer function, which must meet the condition that the $2N - 1$ first derivatives of $|H(\omega)|^2$ be zero for $\omega = 0$ y $\omega = \infty$, in which N is the order of the filter. This transfer function has only poles, and is defined as $|H(\omega)|^2 = \frac{1}{1+(\omega/\omega_c)^{2N}}$, where ω_c is the cutoff frequency and ω is the complex

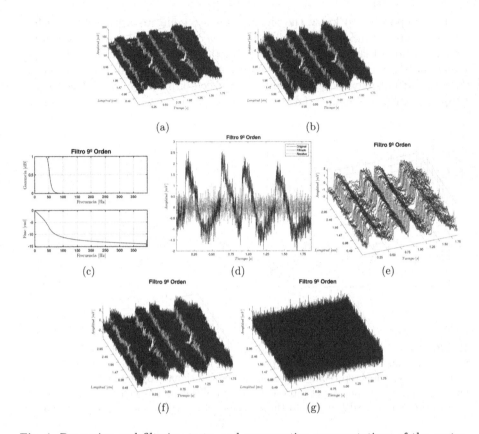

Fig. 4. Processing and filtering tests, and comparative representations of the center line: (a) original signal; (b) normalized signal. Parameters analyzed in the experiment: (c) representation of the filter design, where the slope of the filter in the transition band is observed in the upper panel, while the lag is observed in the lower panel; (d) representation of the original pixel (blue color), filtered pixel (red color), and the residue corresponding to the difference of the 2 aforementioned signals (black color); (e) representation of the signals when the filter is applied; (f) representation of the signals when the filter is applied and normalized; (g) representation of the residue between the original signal and the filtered signal. (Color figure online)

analog frequency ($\omega = jw_¿ 0$). In this case, the Matlab command *butter* has been used, which allows you to easily design a series of filters between 1° order to 25° order.

In Fig. 5 The results of applying the Butterworth filter are reviewed. Panel (a) shows the signal $f(t)$ to which a filter is applied between 1° order to 25° order, where it is determined that orders higher than 21° order distort the signal, while panel (b) shows the signal $f(t)$ to which a filter is applied between 1° command to 21° command, where you can see that the filtered signals are homogeneous.

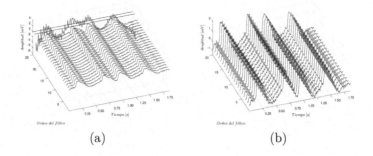

(a)   (b)

Fig. 5. Representation in M mode of the central pixel applying the IIR filter: (a) from 1° order to 25° order; (b) de 1° orden a 21° orden.

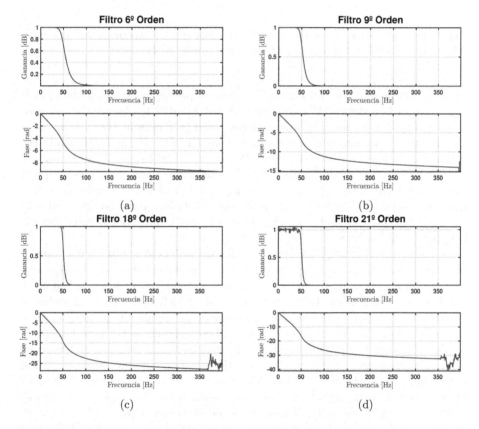

Fig. 6. Design of the IIR filters of: (a) 6° order; (b) 9° command; (c) 18° command; y (d) 21° command.

For all the above, it can be determined in this instance that the order of the filter must be from 1° to 21°.

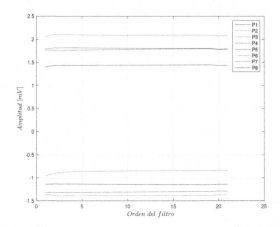

Fig. 7. Representation of the effect of an IIR filter on the maximum and minimum values of the signal, when applying filters from 1° order to 21° order.

Next, the maximum and minimum points of the signal to which the filter is applied from 1° order to 21° order are analyzed, in order to observe the behavior of these singular points. The nomenclature used to represent these values is as follows: the minimum points are denoted as $P1$, $P2$, $P3$ and $P4$; while the maximum points are denoted as $P5$, $P6$, $P7$ and $P8$. In Fig. 7 the amplitude of the maximum and minimum points is represented, and from this graph it can be determined that: between 1° order and 4° order, the amplitude values fluctuate; between 5 order to 18 order, they stabilize; and from 19° order to 21° they fluctuate again. For all the above, the study range of the filter order is between 5° order to 18° order.

Another criterion to be used to determine the order of the filter is the transfer function, a mathematical representation that is used to characterize the spectral response of a system or signal. This diagram is regularly made up of 2 figures: the first corresponds to the magnitude graph, which reflects the modulus of the transfer function as a function of frequency or angular frequency, which is drawn on a logarithmic scale; and the second corresponds to the phase diagram, which represents the phase of the transfer function as a function of frequency or angular frequency. Through this tool, the orders of the filters are evaluated below. In Fig. 6 the results obtained from the filter designs are observed: in panel (a) for 6° order; in panel (b) for 9° order; in panel (c) for 18° order; and in panel (d) 21° for order. From this graph it can be determined that between the 6° order to the 18° order there are no major changes, that is, the filter transition slope is steep and there is no disproportionate phase distortion between input signal and output signal, while in the 21° order filter there is fluctuation in the amplitude applied to the filtered signal. With the results corresponding to the filter design, it can be confirmed that a suitable value of the filter order is in the range between 6° order to 18° order.

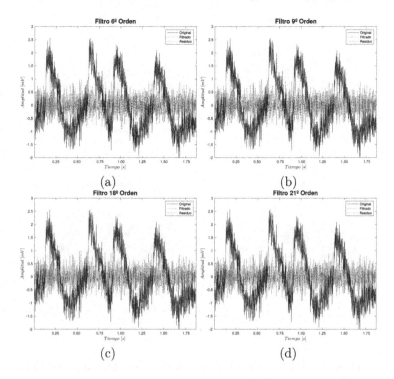

Fig. 8. Application of the IIR filters of: (a) 6° order; (b) 9° command; (c) 18° command; and (d) 21° command.

Continuing with the analysis, the original signal can be represented on the same plane in blue, the filtered signal in red and the residue in black. Figure 8 represents the result of applying the filter to the signal of the central pixel; in 6° order panel (a); in panel (b) of 9° order; in panel (c) of 18° order; and in panel (d) of the 21° order. From this graph it can be determined: that between the 6° order to the 18° order there is no phase difference between the input and output signal, the filtered signal respects the upward slope and the downward slope and the bias of the filtered signal is minimal, while in the 21° filter it presents lag and bias in the maximum and minimum peaks in the filtered signal. With the results corresponding to the analysis of the original signals with respect to the filtered signal, it can be determined that the appropriate values of the filter order are in the range between 6° order and 18° order.

To evaluate the results obtained, the central line of the analyzed film is plotted, where amplitude, length and time are related. In Fig. 9 the application to the center line of pixels of the IIR filter of: (a) 6° order, (b) 9° order, (c) 18° command, (d) 21° command. From these graphs it can be determined that between the 6° order and the 18° order, the signals are homogeneous, while in the filter of 21° order a certain distortion and skew at the maximum and

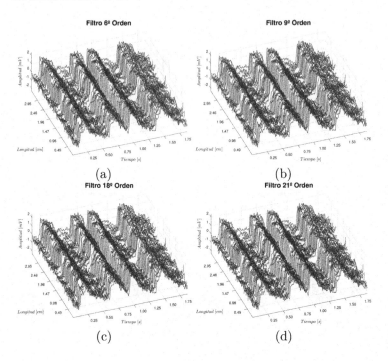

Fig. 9. Comparison application of IIR filters to the entire film applying filters of: (a) 6° order; (b) 9° command; (c) 18° command; and (d) 21° command.

minimum peaks. In this way it can be determined that the appropriate values of the filter order are in the range between 6° order to 18° order.

From the interpretation of the test results described in the previous paragraphs, it can be determined that the Butterworth filter in the range of 6° order to 18° order, is stable, respects the ascending and decent slopes, it maintains the morphology of the signal, it does not present lag, but the filter of 9° order is the one that presents the best characteristics in its frequency response, and for this reason it is selected.

4.4   Filters Application FIR

Next, and following the same criteria, a filter FIR with cutoff frequency of 50 Hz is applied to the test signals. This type of filter responds to the function

$$H(z) = \sum_{k=0}^{N-1} h(k)z^{-k}$$

in which $h(k)$, with $k = 0, 1, \ldots, N-1$, are the coefficients of the filter impulse response, $H(z)$ is the filter transfer function and N is the order of the filter. After mentioning the filter's transfer function, it allows evaluating its frequency response, and unlike the acrshort IIR filter, these structures handle a much higher order range, reaching values of 600° order.

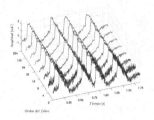

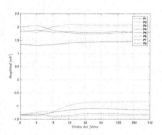

Fig. 10. M-mode representation of the central pixel applying a FIR filter from 2° order to 512° order.

Fig. 11. Representation of maximum and minimum values of the signal when applying filters FIR from 2° order to 512° order.

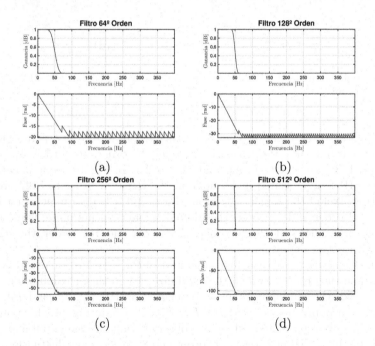

Fig. 12. Design of the FIR filters of: (a) 64° order; (b) 128° order; (c) 256° order; y (d) 512° order

For this section, the range from 2° order to 512° order is analyzed, and since it is not practical to carry out the analysis one by one, the geometric sequence

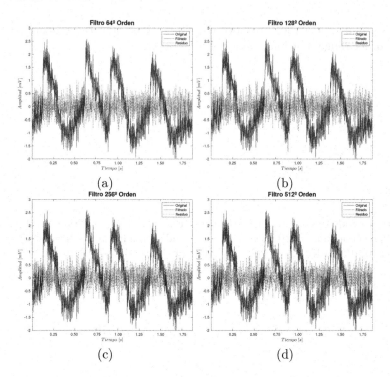

Fig. 13. Application of the FIR filters of: (a) 64° order; (b) 128° order; (c) 256° order; y (d) 512° order

that responds to the function $x = 2^i$ in order to obtain the test points. In this case, the selected ones are 2° order, 4° order, 8° order, 16° order, 32° order, 64° order, 128° order, 256° order, and 512° order. In Fig. 10 the application of the filter FIR is represented in M mode in the range 2° order to 512° order to the central pixel of the signal test. From this graph it is determined that in the 2° order, 4° order and 8° order, the filtered signal presents noise, while in 16° order, 32° order, 64° order, 128° order, 256° order and 512° order, the signal it is seen with better definition.

As in the previous case, the highs and lows of the signal are analyzed in order to determine the orders in which they stabilize. To do this, the following points are examined; the minimum points are denoted as $P1$, $P2$, $P3$ and $P4$, while the maximum points are denoted $P5$, $P6$, $P7$ and $P8$, in Fig. 11, the aforementioned points are represented, where it is observed that the values obtained when applying the filter FIR of 2° order, 4° order and 8° order, show fluctuation, while the 16° order, 32° order, 64° order and 128° order, the values show growth and decrease, and from the 256° order to 512° order they stabilize.

The next criterion to analyze is the filter design, where the frequency response diagram is used for its representation. In Fig. 12 the design of the FIR filters is observed, where: in panel (a) for 64° order; in panel (b) for 128° order; in panel

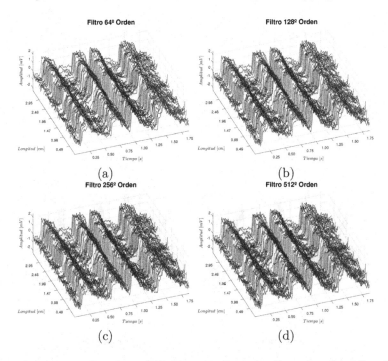

Fig. 14. Comparison of applying FIR filters to the entire film using: (a) 64° order; (b) 128° order; (c) 256° order and (d) 512° order.

(c) for 256° order; and in panel (d) for 512° order. From this graph it can be determined that between 64° order to 126° order the filter transition slope is low and does not present non-linear phase distortion, and 256° order at 512° order the filter transition slope is high and does not present non-linear phase distortion either. In this way, it can be said that in the range from 256° order to 512° order, the filter has better characteristics.

The following experiment shows the application of the filter FIR for different orders. The results are shown on the same plane, where the original signal is drawn in blue, the filtered signal is drawn in red and the residue in black, all of them in Fig. 13. It is observed in panel (a) for 64° order, in panel (b) for 128° order, in panel (c) for 256° order and in panel (d) for 512° order. From this figure it can be determined that in the range between the 64° order to 126° order, there is still the presence of noise, despite the fact that the rising and falling edges of the signal are respected , and in the range 256° order to 512° order, a greater amount of noise is eliminated, the rising and falling edges are respected and there is also a slight lag.

The results of applying this technique are also observed by examining the effects on the film's centerline of pixels. In Fig. 14 this criterion is reproduced, where it is observed in panel (a) for 64° order, in panel (b) for 128° order, in panel (c) for 256° order, and in panel (d) 512° for order. From this figure it can

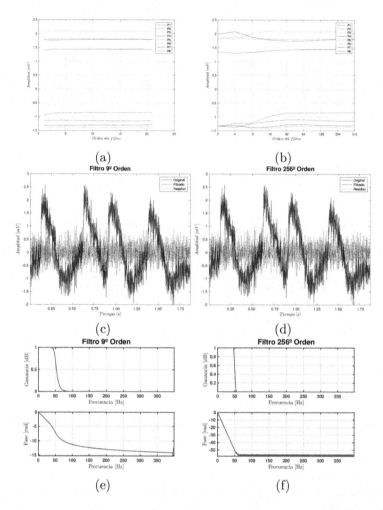

Fig. 15. Comparison of the IIR Filter of 9° order versus the FIR Filter of 256° order for: (a, b) Applying range of filters; (c, d) Application of the selected filter; (d, e) Filter design.

be determined that in the range between the 64° order to 126° order, the signals are similar and there is a significant presence of noise, while in the range of 256° order at 512° order decreases noise, rising and falling edges are respected, and there is no bias in the maximum and minimum values.

From the results obtained when applying the detailed filters, it is concluded that the order of the appropriate FIR filter is in the range between 256° order to 512° order . But in the same way as the previous case, the transfer function diagram that presents the filter design allows us to determine that the 256° order is the one that best fits the filtering requirement.

In order to determine which of the 2 filters best meets the requirements of the preprocessing of this type of signals, the results obtained when evaluating the filters IIR and the filters FIR are compared. In Fig. 15, panels (a) and (b) present the analysis of the maximum and minimum values. Panels (c) and (d) show the representation of the filter application on the central line of pixels, where the original signal in blue, the filtered signal in red and the residual of the subtraction in black. Panels (e) and (f) include the design of the filters to be compared. Panels (a), (c) and (e) correspond to the results of the filter IIR, while panels (b), (d) and (f) correspond to the results of the filter FIR. From the comparison of the results in these parameters, it can be noted that the 2 types of filters act in a similar way, characterized by not affecting the rising and falling edges, they do not generate phase shift, they do not produce biases, and that the frequency transition slope cut is high, among others.

By acting the 2 filters in a similar way, it is determined that a filter IIR of 9° order responds in a similar way as a filter FIR of 256° order, Therefore, the filter IIR of 9° is selected because it generates a lower computational cost as it is of a lower order than its similar filter of type IIR. Finally, remember that in both cases a null phase linear filtering scheme is being used, which allows a null phase distortion in both cases.

5 Conclusions

At the end of this work it can be determined that in cases of cardiac signal treatment where traditionally high order digital filters of FIR type are used, IIR filters can also be used, maintaining the same characteristics but reducing notably the computational costs in their execution.

6 Future Jobs

At the end of this analysis, the presence of additional noise is determined, so temporal, spatial or spatial-temporal analysis studies can be proposed and in this way the recovery of intrinsic electrical information in the film will be improved.

Acknowledgements. To the URJC and Universidad de las fuerzas Armadas ESPE, for the contribution to the FINALE project to the Wicom Energy Research group.

References

1. Cheniti, G., et al.: Noninvasive mapping and electrocardiographic imaging in atrial and ventricular arrhythmias (cardioinsight). Card. Electrophysiol. Clin. 11(3), 459–471 (2019). https://doi.org/10.1016/j.ccep.2019.05.004
2. Efimov, I., Nikolski, V.P., Salama, G.: Optical imaging of the heart. Circ. Res. 95(1), 21–33 (2004)
3. González, J.: Velandia, Cristian, Nieto, Johann: Implementación de filtro digital en tiempo real para detección de la onda R. Revista TecnoLógicas 18(34), 75–86 (2015)

4. Laughner, J.I., Ng, F.S., Sulkin, M.S., Arthur, R.M., Efimov, I.R.: Processing and analysis of cardiac optical mapping data obtained with potentiometric dyes. Am. J. Physiol. Heart Circulatory Physiol. **303**(7), H753–H765 (2012). https://doi.org/ 10.1152/ajpheart.00404.2012, pMID: 22821993
5. Laughner, J.I., Ng, F.S., Sulkin, M.S., Arthur, R.M., Efimov, I.R.: Processing and analysis of cardiac optical mapping data obtained with potentiometric dyes. Am. J. Physiol. Heart Circulatory Physiol. **303**(7), 753–65 (2012)
6. Lee, P., et al.: In vivo Ratiometric optical mapping enables high-resolution cardiac electrophysiology in pig models. Cardiovasc. Res. **115**(11), 1659–1671 (2019). https://doi.org/10.1093/cvr/cvz039
7. Maciejewski, M., Dzida, G.: ECG parameter extraction and classification in noisy signals. In: 2017 Signal Processing: Algorithms, Architectures, Arrangements, and Applications, pp. 243–248 (September 2017)
8. Mironov, S.F., Vetter, F.J., Pertsov, A.M.: Fluorescence imaging of cardiac propagation: spectral properties and filtering of optical action potentials. Am. J. Physiol. Heart Circulatory Physiol. **291**(1), H327–H335 (2006). https://doi.org/10.1152/ ajpheart.01003.2005, https://www.ncbi.nlm.nih.gov/pubmed/16428336
9. Monroy, N., Villamizar, J., Otero, M., Altuve, M.: Análisis del desempeño de filtros IIR y FIR para la reducción del desplazamiento de la línea de base del ECG en Matlab^{TM}. In: VI Congreso Venezolano de Bioingeniería. pp. 154–157 (2017)
10. Quintanilla, J.G. et al.: QRS duration reflects underlying changes in conduction velocity during increased intraventricular pressure and heart failure. Prog. Biophys. Mol. Biol. **130**, 394–403 (2017). https://doi.org/10.1016/j.pbiomolbio.2017.08.003
11. Taboada, A., Lorenzo, J., Lovely, D.: Algunas contribuciones a la detección de potenciales tardíos ventriculares. Ingeniería Electrónica, Automática y Comunicaciones **25**(1), 34–41 (2004)
12. Taeryoung, S., Lee, S., Lee, J.: A wearable electrocardiogram monitoring system robust to motion artifacts. In: 2018 International SoC Design Conference, pp. 241–242 (2018)
13. Wan, Y., Chen, Q.: A novel quadratic type variational method for efficient salt-and-pepper noise removal. In: 2010 IEEE International Conference on Multimedia and Expo, pp. 1055–1060 (July 2010). https://doi.org/10.1109/ICME.2010.5583306

Construction of a Low-Cost Semi-automatic Machine for Tensile Testing

José Varela-Aldás[1,2(✉)] ⓘ, Jorge Buele[1] ⓘ, and Juan Cruz[1]

[1] SISAu Research Group, Facultad de Ingeniería Y Tecnologías de La Información Y La Comunicación, Universidad Tecnológica Indoamérica, Ambato, Ecuador
{josevarela,jorgebuele,juancruz}@uti.edu.ec
[2] Department of Electronic Engineering and Communications, University of Zaragoza, Zaragoza, Spain

Abstract. Tensile tests make it possible to determine the resistance and other relevant parameters of the materials. These procedures are usually performed with equipment that is expensive and inaccessible to higher education centers with limited budgets. In the case of acquiring this hardware, the disadvantage is that this are purely manual machines that make the use and learning process difficult. That is why this document shows the construction of a machine that allows this type of testing, but using low-cost materials. The mechanical and electronic design and programming that has been used to implement and semi-automate the machine is briefly but clearly described. To validate the functionality, the respective tests have been carried out, although it is a limited version that requires improvements, the results are satisfactory. The curve obtained when carrying out tests with A36 steel has shown a similarity with the theory. Thus, students obtain a technological tool that contributes to academic training, strengthening knowledge in the study of materials.

Keywords: Semi-automatic machines · Applied technology · Material testing · Tensile tests

1 Introduction

In the structural industry metallic materials are used that must respond adequately to certain mechanical circumstances [1]. In practice, these materials are expected to demonstrate resistance and fulfill the assigned function, in addition to having well-defined physical and technical characteristics [2, 3]. Other factors to be taken into account are the type of stress, loads and mechanical stresses to which they will be subjected [4]. So it can choose the right material with the ability to withstand these conditions without breaking or distorting. To determine this resistance, various tests must be carried out under regional regulations, which simulate normal operating conditions in a real environment. The main mechanical tests carried out are traction, hardness, creep, bending, impact and fatigue [5, 6]. Regarding the types of forces that are applied to materials, there is elongation due to a tensile load, compression deformation, shear stress deformation and deformation due to torsional stress [7, 8].

© Springer Nature Switzerland AG 2021
M. Botto-Tobar et al. (Eds.): ICAT 2020, CCIS 1388, pp. 225–235, 2021.
https://doi.org/10.1007/978-3-030-71503-8_17

In particular, this document describes a tensile test, since it is a simple, low-cost and standardized procedure [9–11]. In these tests the mechanical properties of the material are measured (elongation, elastic limit or breaking load) when exposed to one or more external forces [12]. The pieces of materials used for this test are called test piece or samples and the dimensions are standardized (length of the test piece and the cross-sectional area) [11]. The test piece is held at the ends, between two accessories called grips or clamps. Gradually, the applied forces increase and in this way a stretching (elongation) can be appreciated, until the rupture occurs. The materials used must be ductile and have a certain degree of plasticity, otherwise it would not deform. All the data obtained allows to compare different materials and thus know if they will be useful in a certain application [13].

In a conventional test, the operator must manually record the force and stretch data of the test piece and thus develop a stress-elongation curve. And at the end, the final and original length are compared to determine the elongation obtained. In the same way, the reduction of the cross-sectional area is determined. The tests that are carried out manually produce greater difficulty when obtaining and analyzing the data and therefore several investigations promote optimization through the use of technological tools. In [14] they propose a universal testing machine designed to meet the maximum load (traction force), reduction of minimal physical effort and minimized losses. With it, students can test materials, adapting to limited economic possibilities. Although this prototype is a bit rustic, it allows the student to have a better understanding of the testing procedures and examine the properties of the materials.

In the work of Atanasovska et al. [15] describes the design and implementation of a universal tool to test the tensile properties of hexagonal steel wire mesh, a material that is used in the field of construction. The most relevant point of this proposal is the safety component since it prevents the wire mesh samples from slipping during loading. For other part, Jadhav et al. [16] present a prototype to evaluate the mechanical properties and characterize the properties of the materials, all based on the stress and other parameters that the user requires. By means of this tool a sinusoidal oscillating voltage is applied, this as a load. These forces are applied to the sample by means of actuators (servo-controlled electric motors) and as future work it is proposed that each of the servomotors be equipped with a load cell to measure tension and compression loads.

As has been briefly seen in the literature presented, there are various machine designs that allow evaluating different types of materials. This type of proposal allows students and researchers to have better tools to increase learning options. This is why this document describes the design, construction and implementation of a semi-automatic machine for tensile tests. This design has been made with low-cost materials, which allows it to be replicated by institutions with limited financial resources. The mechanical and electronic design and the software used are shown. In this way, an innovative proposal is made available to the reader that allows improving the technical skills of the students in the training process.

This document is divided into 4 sections, including the introduction in Sect. 1. Section 2 shows the materials and methods that have been used and Sect. 3 the tests and experimental results. Finally, the conclusions and future work are described in Sect. 4.

2 Materials y Methods

2.1 Formulation

The need for a team that allows tensile tests to be carried out on the students of a higher education center has motivated the development of this prototype in an initial version. For this reason, an applied research has been carried out, since the objective is to solve this problem, with the direct application of the experiences and knowledge of the authors of this document. As a starting point, the physical structure of the machine is formed and then certain components are automated, such as: the drive and the length reading; The rest of the variables are obtained by the user. Figure 1 presents the general design with all the elements defined. A personal computer is proposed as the central processing unit and interface device, i.e., the control and visualization of the machine is carried out from the main computer screen. The electronic components are managed by a controller card that receives the sensory information and commands the actuator. The stretching actions on the test piece are executed by a motor coupled to the traction mechanism. In addition, the machine includes a distance sensor to measure the length of the test piece. On the other hand, the mechanism works using a hydraulic component, this allows to obtain the pressure applied through a manometer so that the user can manually calculate the area and effort, entering the data into the computer to obtain the characterization of the material.

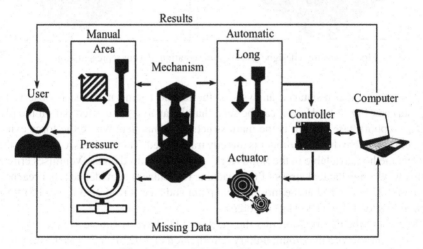

Fig. 1. General design of the proposal.

2.2 Mechanical Design

The architectural design is detailed in Fig. 2(a), which is performed using SolidWorks software, all machine measurements were modeled to scale and component colors and details are clearly identified. This design has optimized resources, since operating the machine manually or mechanically generates an 8-lb load. This value is multiplied to about 1000 kg thanks to the incorporated hydraulic system. To ensure the rigidity of the structure, it has been chosen to use A-520 steel throughout the architecture and cold-rolled 1020 steel in the jaws. In this way it is ensured that it is suitable for testing metallic materials and polymeric materials. For a better appreciation of the internal mechanisms of each system and of the pressure multiplier chamber, a sectional representation of the mechanic system components is shown in Fig. 2(b).

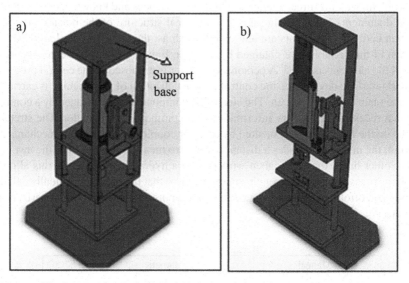

Fig. 2. Machine design: (a) full representation. (b) cut representation.

The mechanical resistance analysis of the tensile testing machine is observed in Fig. 3(a) and Fig. 3(b). Here it can be seen that the analysis is carried out on the plate called "support base" which is the main structural component where the force exiting the incorporated hydraulic cylinder is directly transmitted. This analysis, called the finite element method, available in the SolidWorks package is based on the Vonmises criteria. In this way, a mechanical stress of the machine (resistance) is evidenced that reaches a value of 2.77 E + 3 PSI at the most critical point and an effort of 2.33 E + 2 PSI for an applied load of 1 Ton (1000 kg) of force.

Regarding the deformation that the machine may have, it can be seen in Fig. 3(b). This diagram shows a maximum unitary deformation of 7,922 E-3 mm as the maximum (critical) value and a value of 1E-3 mm as the minimum value for the same load of 1 ton (1000 kg).

The drive of the machine is based on a crank crank mechanism, converting the rotational movement of a motor into linear movement of the piston in the hydraulic component. For the selection of the motor, a specific analysis of the torque (T) that enters the system is carried out, as data there is an average manual force value applied by an operator during use. It should be clarified that the applied force depends on the length of the hydraulic cylinder lever. However, for the optimization of this design, a

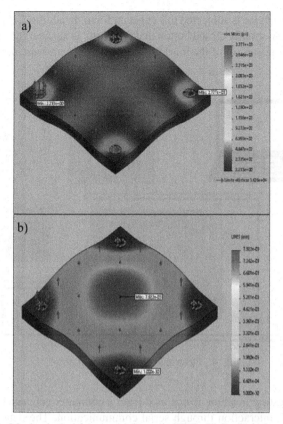

Fig. 3. Mechanical resistance (a) Stress in [PSI], (b) Strain in [mm/mm]

force of 3.63 kg and a distance of 10 cm are used, calculating as a requirement a motor with a minimum of 36.3 kg cm of torque. Said torque is calculated with (1).

$$T = F d \tag{1}$$

2.3 Electronic Design

The electronic design is based on the Arduino embedded board, this electronic development platform is characterized by low cost and a large support community on the web. Figure 4 shows the proposed electronic circuit, where the components used and the respective connections are detailed, as well as the energization of the system with a 12V DC source. To measure the length of the test piece, an ultrasonic sensor is used that obtains the distance between the upper and lower plate of the test chamber, the sensor is installed on digital pins 8 and 9. The motor is incorporated into the circuit using the L298N driver that allows speed and direction of rotation to be regulated. For this application, only one direction of rotation is required to operate the hydraulic jack, the return to the initial position is done manually by releasing the hydraulic pressure.

In this way the test piece is subjected to a constant force. In addition, the motor output is interrupted with a normally closed button that functions as an emergency stop to prevent abnormalities in the control of the machine and as a safety measure for the operator.

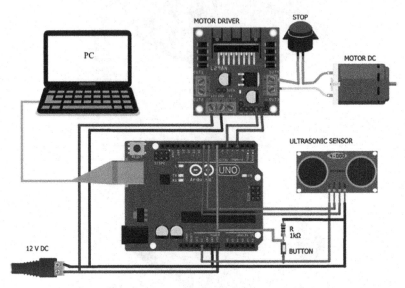

Fig. 4. Electronic circuit of the proposal.

The tensile testing machine is operated from a computer connected by USB cable, programming the interaction through serial communication. The data received by the Arduino is the activation and deactivation of the motor movement, and the distance obtained by the ultrasonic sensor is sent. Additionally, the circuit includes a button to control the motor directly as a second control option, the program is carried out in such a way that the machine is activated only when the user keeps the button pressed.

2.4   Software

Using the mathematical software MATLAB, scripts are developed that allow an intuitive graphical interface to be presented to the user. For the development of this type of applications, MATLAB offers to use its own built-in wizard or to write structured code. In this case, the *uicontrol* code is used to insert the elements of the main window. Figure 5 shows the interface already running; at the beginning the user must specify the communication port of the Arduino board and press the Connect button, then the program opens the serial communication with the specified object and enables the rest of the buttons. The reading option allows enabling and disabling the visualization of distance data in real time, generating a graph of length as a function of time. To control the motor of the machine there are two independent on and off buttons, so a digit is sent for comparison: 1 for ON and 0 for OFF.

Once the tensile test information has been collected, pressing the Continue button generates a file with an.xlsx extension with the data obtained. In this file, the user must add

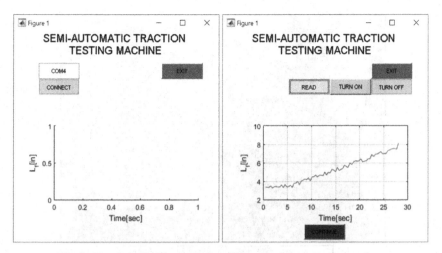

Fig. 5. User interface for control and visualization of tensile test data.

the information generated manually to characterize the material, the manual acquisition data must record the moment of reading to synchronize the information. Finally, the Exit button stops reading data, turns off the engine and closes the main program window.

3   Results and Discussions

3.1   Construction of the Machine

The designs presented in the previous section are executed, obtaining the machine shown in Fig. 6. At the side of the equipment a case is installed to contain the electronic components. The distance sensor is placed at the bottom of the test chamber, pointing towards the top. The motor with a gearbox is coupled to the hydraulic jack using the mechanical clamping elements, for this purpose a motor with a maximum torque of 40 kg.cm and a maximum current consumption of 1.5 Amps is used. The power supply used is 12 V and 2 amps. In total, the equipment requires an economic investment of 262 USD, being the mechanical structure and the motor the most expensive elements.

3.2   Experimental Results

After the physical assembly of the machine has been carried out, it is subjected to a test to identify the behavior. An A36 steel test piece is used which is subjected to a tensile test, where initially there was a section of 0.25 in. As different levels of force are applied, the material is structurally modified. The data obtained are recorded and through (2), (3), (4) and (5) the values of stress and strain are obtained that are shown in Table 1. This is presented graphically in Fig. 7 where the characterization of material can be seen in the stress plot (σ) as a function of the deformation (ε).

$$\sigma = F / A \tag{2}$$

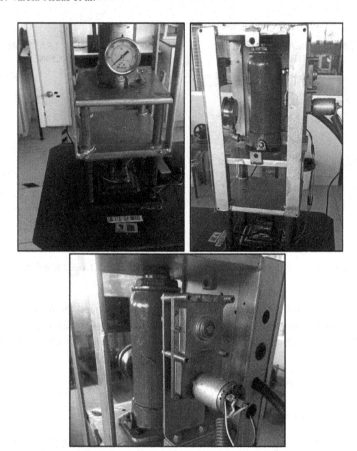

Fig. 6. Photographs of the physical implementation of the proposal.

$$\varepsilon = \Delta L / L_o \qquad (3)$$

$$A = \pi d^2 / 4 \qquad (4)$$

$$\Delta L = L_f - L_o \qquad (5)$$

This material has a rising proportional elastic behavior that reaches up to 36261.63 PSI. Afterwards, a stress concentration is observed in the material, with a minimum upward trend that reaches a value of 36977.10 PSI. Finally, a maximum resistance of the material is evidenced at 58010.21 PSI, clearly concluding that the stress and longitudinal deformation have a relationship directly proportional to the applied load and inversely proportional to the transverse deformation (diameter of the test piece).

In order to evaluate the functionality of this prototype, the data provided by ASTM A-36 are presented in Fig. 8. The elastic behavior obtained varies by 2.71% with respect to the theory and the maximum resistance does so by 0.02%. Although the data and the

Table 1. Tensile test data.

Diameter (in)	Area (in^2)	Strength (lb.)	L$_f$ (in)	L$_o$ (in)	ΔL (in)	σ (lb./in^2)	ε (in/in)
0,25	0,0490875	500	5,1	5	0,1	10185,8925	0,020
0,19	0,02835294	650	5,4	5,1	0,3	22925,3122	0,060
0,159	0,0198557	720	5,9	5,4	0,5	36261,6324	0,100
0,158	0,01960673	725	6,8	5,9	0,9	36977,1075	0,180
0,14	0,01539384	893	8	6,8	1,2	58010,2171	0,240
0,145	0,01651304	910	9.3	8	1.3	55107,9798	0,260

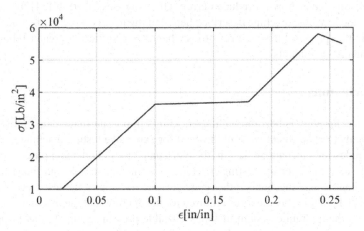

Fig. 7. Graph of stress vs strain using an A36 steel test piece.

shape of the curve are similar to those obtained, it should be noted that the resolution is limited, due to the few data recorded manually by the user.

Steel Grade	Chemical compositión % in weigh											Thickness		Physical requirements					
	C Máx.	Mn	P Máx.	S Máx.	Si Máx.	C u	Cb	V	NI	Cr	N2	Pulg.	mm	Yield limit Mín		Tensile strength		Elongation % Mín	
														KSI	MPA	KSI	MPA	EN 8"	EN 2"
ASTM A-36	0.25	0.80 - 1.20	0.040	0.050	0.40	---	---	---	---	---	---	0.180 - 0.500	4.6 - 12.7	36	250	58 - 80	400 - 550	20	21

Fig. 8. Physical and chemical requirements according to ASTM A36 Standard.

3.3 Discussion

Although there is little bibliography related to this proposal, the growing interest in applying technology to solve immediate problems with low investment and with rapid implementation stands out. In [15] the development of a machine to test the resistance of hexagonal steel wire meshes is described, although the theme is not the same as that of this proposal, it can be seen that there are several designs, which have the same purpose. Both it and the one presented here have satisfactory results focused on different types of materials (hexagonal meshes and test pieces of different materials). This approach is repeated in [16] in which a device with an innovative design with servomotors is presented, but which does not present operational tests, since it is an initial prototype. In contrast to the testing machine built in this proposal, which has been tested with steel and the results have shown a reduced error. The work described in [14] has a design similar to the low-cost machine described here, but the results show an absolute error of 6%, while this proposal has an error of less than 3%, resulting in greater reliability of the tests made by students.

4 Conclusions

Access to technology is becoming cheaper, so it is important to develop proposals that help students to experiment without the need for expensive testing machines. This proposal includes the mechanical design, the electronic circuit and a computer application for a semi-automatic tensile testing machine. The mechanical design made in Solid-Work uses an inverse mechanism that generates the traction of the test piece through a hydraulic jack, in this way the force required for the operation of the machine is reduced. In addition, the hydraulic system includes a visible pressure gauge to record pressure. The electronic system implemented with Arduino technology automates the actuation of the hydraulic jack and the reading of the length of the test piece, sharing the information with a computer for interaction with the user. The user interface developed in Matlab has a simple format, allowing to activate the engine at will and view the collected data. On the other hand, the user must record some data manually, such as pressure and diameter, to obtain effort and area, respectively.

In the execution stage, the mechanical structure is built using cutting and welding, and the electronic system is installed using physical wiring. Through the operation of the machine, the characterization of a material is obtained, observing an adequate operation of the proposed system. This allows the user to actuate the traction through the computer application and displaying the deformation data directly on the computer screen. The experimental tests carried out with A36 steel allowed to observe an absolute error of 2.71% in terms of the elastic behavior obtained and of 0.02% in the maximum resistance, comparing these values with the normalized curves. The resolution of the characteristic curve of the material is limited to the data recorded manually by the user, so that it prevents the exact observation of the change points. However, this tool has an optimized budget, being accessible to higher-level students and the general public, allowing the team to reach other institutions that wish to replicate it. As future work, the authors propose to improve the resolution of the results, adding sensors that complement the missing information and offer complete automation of the prototype.

References

1. Santos, J., Gouveia, R.M., Silva, F.J.G.: Designing a new sustainable approach to the change for lightweight materials in structural components used in truck industry. J. Clean. Prod. (2017). https://doi.org/10.1016/j.jclepro.2017.06.174

2. Estrin, Y., Beygelzimer, Y., Kulagin, R.: Design of Architectured Materials Based on Mechanically Driven Structural and Compositional Patterning (2019). https://doi.org/10.1002/adem.201900487

3. Dwivedi, S.K., Vishwakarma, M.: Effect of hydrogen in advanced high strength steel materials (2019). https://doi.org/10.1016/j.ijhydene.2019.08.149

4. Floor, J., Van Deursen, B., Tempelman, E.: Tensile strength of 3D printed materials: review and reassessment of test parameters (2018). https://doi.org/10.3139/120.111203

5. Li, H.T., Young, B.: Residual mechanical properties of high strength steels after exposure to fire. J. Constr. Steel Res. (2018). https://doi.org/10.1016/j.jcsr.2018.05.028

6. Valíček, J., et al.: Identification of upper and lower level yield strength in materials. Materials (Basel). (2017). https://doi.org/10.3390/ma10090982

7. Tilmatine, A., Alibida, A., Zelmat, S., Louati, H., Bellebna, Y., Miloua, F.: On the attraction force applied on metal pieces in a traveling wave conveyor. J. Electrostat. (2018). https://doi.org/10.1016/j.elstat.2018.10.001

8. Sedmák, P., et al.: Grain-resolved analysis of localized deformation in nickel-titanium wire under tensile load. Science (80) (2016). https://doi.org/10.1126/science.aad6700

9. Garbatov, Y., Saad-Eldeen, S., Guedes Soares, C., Parunov, J., Kodvanj, J.: Tensile test analysis of corroded cleaned aged steel test piece. Corros. Eng. Sci. Technol. (2019). https://doi.org/10.1080/1478422X.2018.1548098

10. Wang, J.Y., Guo, J.Y.: Damage investigation of ultra high performance concrete under direct tensile test using acoustic emission techniques. Cem. Concr. Compos. (2018). https://doi.org/10.1016/j.cemconcomp.2018.01.007

11. Van Der Klift, F., Koga, Y., Todoroki, A., Ueda, M., Hirano, Y., Matsuzaki, R.: 3D printing of continuous carbon fibre reinforced thermo-plastic (CFRTP) tensile test test piece. Open J. Compos. Mater. (2016). https://doi.org/10.4236/ojcm.2016.61003

12. Wang, H., Li, C., Tu, J., Li, D.: Dynamic tensile test of mass concrete with Shapai Dam cores. Mater. Struct. **50**(1), 1–11 (2016). https://doi.org/10.1617/s11527-016-0901-x

13. Centelles, X., Martín, M., Solé, A., Castro, J.R., Cabeza, L.F.: Tensile test on interlayer materials for laminated glass under diverse ageing conditions and strain rates. Constr. Build. Mater. (2020). https://doi.org/10.1016/j.conbuildmat.2020.118230

14. Ali, R., Junejo, F., Imtiaz, R., Shamsi, U.S.: Indigenous design for automatic testing of tensile strength using graphical user interface. In: MATEC Web of Conferences (2016). https://doi.org/10.1051/matecconf/20167708007.

15. Atanasovska, I., Momčilović, D., Gavrilovski, M.: Development of the universal tool for testing of tensile properties of hexagonal steel wire mesh for civil engineering. Metall. Mater. Eng. (2018). https://doi.org/10.30544/365.

16. Jadhav, A., Pillai, P. V., Jafri, S.: Development of bench top biaxial tensile testing machine. In: IOP Conference Series: Materials Science and Engineering (2020). https://doi.org/10.1088/1757-899X/810/1/012028

Carwash Station Prototype with Automatic Payment Using Intelligent Control Systems

Jorge Buele[1,3](✉) (ID), Darío Quilumba[2], David I. Ilvis[2], Fernando Saá[1],
and Franklin W. Salazar[4] (ID)

[1] SISAu Research Group, Universidad Tecnológica Indoamérica, Ambato 180212, Ecuador
{jorgebuele,fernandosaa}@uti.edu.ec
[2] Universidad Técnica de Ambato, Ambato 180103, Ecuador
{dquilumba5988,dilvis9234}@uta.edu.ec
[3] Universidad Internacional de La Rioja, Logroño 26006, España
[4] Universidad Autónoma de Madrid, Madrid 28049, España
franklin.salazar@estudiante.uam.es

Abstract. The daily activities of human being can be improved with the use of technology. Therefore, in this work we propose the design of an imperative system of automatic payment to prevent contact between people, avoiding the transmission of viruses and bacteria. Thus, new appropriate and innovative tools are created and applied to business models for the industrial and service sectors. Using and integrating communication between visual programming platforms, telecommunications (messaging) and online payments, using a programmable automaton, an HMI and a Raspberry board. The results show a robust platform framed in electronic payment technology with high performance and very reliable that uses the MQTT protocol for communication. The results show a time of 2.07 s in data writing after sending the signal and 0.80 s of reading the PLC outputs to the monitoring page.

Keywords: MQTT · Industrial Internet of Things · Automatic payment · 4.0 Industry

1 Introduction

Currently, due to the evolution of technology within the productive sector, all industries, and specifically manufacturing, face intense competition for scientific development and innovation [1–4]. To maintain high competitiveness in the market by offering its products and services [5]. Industry 4.0 and intelligent manufacturing integrated with technological aspects, provides execution of "Smart Factories" with modular structures [6, 7]. Capable of increasing production, saving costs and creating new ways of doing business, generating a value proposition towards customers [8]. In general, an Industry 4.0 is not simply a new concept but covers the main technological innovations in the automation fields, control and information technology [9, 10]. Applied to manufacturing processes with benefits in the industrial area and in the treatment of diseases such as low-cost respirator prototypes, among others [11].

© Springer Nature Switzerland AG 2021
M. Botto-Tobar et al. (Eds.): ICAT 2020, CCIS 1388, pp. 236–249, 2021.
https://doi.org/10.1007/978-3-030-71503-8_18

The application of intelligent systems focused on Industry 4.0 can be evidenced in various investigations [12]. For this reason, in the work carried out by [13] a system for a greenhouse in flower production is proposed. It includes parameters such as atmospheric humidity, temperature, CO_2 concentration, soil water content and lighting intensity that are remotely monitored from a cell phone or PC, considering the importance of data transfer and transmission in real time. Through an IoT network without having contact with sensors or other devices in the physical environment. In a similar case [14] directs her study in an automatic irrigation system to increase farmers' profits; by increasing productivity and reducing water and electricity consumption by using field-mounted humidity sensors, valves and pumps controlled by a PLC. With the system that the author proposes, users can control and monitor the irrigation procedure from a remote area with the help of SCADA or from a mobile phone using RFID technology.

The research done by [15] is mentioned that there are systems conformed with automatic conditions and with intelligent environments for the integration between people and devices or M2M through communication networks such as the Internet, RFID and NFC for the collection, processing and correct distribution of data. The authors allude to the fact that a large percentage of these systems are commercial and require payments for products or services provided; therefore, the integration of electronic payments is addressed in conjunction with the development of IoT technologies. On the other hand, [16] proposes an easy payment system based on the IoT gateway. The authors divide this system into two processes (registration of stores and orders) to communicate them through HTTP, from this system customers can request information about the products or services offered through the M2M standard, to others within This system, once the orders are placed, the servers of the stores are notified so that the client makes his corresponding payment through the IoT gate and according to the payment system.

Finally, because of the Covid-19 pandemic that our planet is experiencing currently, large health centers mainly located in China have implemented IoT systems called "Intelligent Diagnosis and Treatment Assistant Program" for monitoring patients to minimize the contact between doctors and infected people, to stop or block the transmission of diseases or infections, allowing to control its expansion as soon as possible. This system is responsible for classifying patients, updating the online database of Covid-19 in real time and guiding certain treatments for affected patients, on the other hand, this system also contributes to long-term patient follow-up by avoiding contact between people, favoring social distancing [17].

Based on the previously cited studies, in this work, an intelligent control system based on IoT networks is carried out to minimize interactions between people and prevent the spread of diseases caused by Covid-19, whose main objective is the social distancing between users of a car wash system and direct contact with money, which is a source of spread of this virus. On the other hand, coronavirus disease HE 2019 (COVID-19), caused by severe acute respiratory syndrome coronavirus 2 (SARS-CoV-2), is a pandemic that is raging the world today. The number of people infected and killed by the virus is also known to have increased quickly around the world [18]. The most likely route of transmission of COVID-19 is by contact and respiratory drops (aerosols), over short distances (1.5 m) and also by fomites contaminated by such aerosols, followed by contact with the mucosa of the mouth, nose or eyes [19]. Prolonged contact is the highest risk, contagion from casual contacts being less likely considering social distancing the best way to avoid contagion[1]. For this reason, creating innovative services in which there is no contact between customers and operators is of great importance to safeguard the health and prevent the spread of viruses or bacteria.

This document is made up as follows: the introduction is indicated in Sect. 1. Section 2 shows the materials and methods and Sect. 3 the results and discussion. Finally, Sect. 4 establishes the conclusions and future work.

2   Materials and Methods

The present work develops communication between different platforms, to avoid direct contact between people to avoid the transmission of viruses and bacteria, using a Siemens S7–1200 PLC and a KTP600 screen for the operation of a prototype, which simulates the car wash process automatically. This communication allows interaction between clients and the process control system (PLC) through the use of IoT, with additional platforms, allowing the changes in the states of the inputs and outputs of the PLC to be viewed in a web address for monitoring operation. The proposed process is integrated by actuator elements such as cleaning rollers that are powered by DC (direct current) motors, solenoid valves and a water pump, controlled by S7–1200 PLCs using the conventional MQTT protocol for IoT. Figure 1 presents the structure of the communication made. The prototype of the car wash station starts working as long as the user has paid for the service with their credit card through the online payment platform.

The development of the proposed system covers a simple structure, to program the PLC and the HMI, the SIMATIC STEP7 programming software (TIA portal V13) was used, for communication between the PLC and the Raspberry Pi, the Liberia SNAP7 is used, which determines the write and read data from all types of variables (bits, Word, Dword, Real). For the creation of the web page, the PHP language is used to visualize the states of the PLC in real time. For the alarm message, the visual flow programming NODE-RED is used, and for the automatic payment the online payment system PayPal is used, all users who require to use the system first will be stored in a database.

2.1   SNAP 7 Implementation

With the use of the Snap 7 (C++) library, it's intended to obtain data from the S7–1200 PLC by reading the internal databases of the PLC using the Raspberry Pi 3. This library uses the S7 Ethernet communication interface of Siemens for reading and writing PLC data and has three independent components: client, server and partner. The following shows the condition of the Snap 7 client for communication with the s7–1200 PLC. See listing 1.

---

[1] https://repisalud.isciii.es/handle/20.500.12105/9557

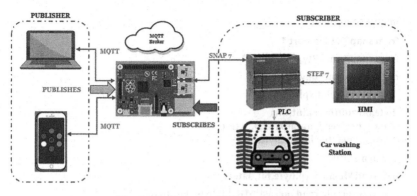

Fig. 1. Hardware architecture platform.

```
1    from time import sleep
2    import snap.client
3    from snap7.util import *
4    from snap7.snap7types import *
5
6    def WriteMemory (p,byte,bit,datatype,value):
7      result=p.read_areas['MK'],0,byte,databyte)
8        if datatype == S7WLBit:
9            set_bool (result,0,bit,value)
10     else:
11       return None
12
13   p.write_area(areas['MK'],0,byte,resul)
14   myplc = snap7.client.Client()
15   myplc.connect('192.168.0.7',0,1)
     print(myplc.get_connected())
16   WriteMemory(myplc,3,0,S7WLBit,True)
17   sleep(0.5)
18   WriteMemory(myplc,3,0,S7WLBit,False)
```

List 1. Running the Snap 7 library for the writing data.

The advantages of using the Snap 7 library are many since it's written in C++, to read the data from the Ethernet compatible PLC, as long as the requests to Ethernet are not restricted. In the work done, the data is read through bytes, Double Word, but variables of type: Word, Real can be used. Reading in the program is done through the following programming code according to listing 2.

```
1    import snap.client
2    from snap7.util import *
3    from snap7.snap7types import *
4    def ReadOutput(dev,bytebit):
5     byte,bit=bytebit.split('.')
6     byte,bit=int(byte),int(bit)
      data = dev.read_area(0x82,0,byte,1)
7     Status = get_bool(data,byte.bit)
8      return status
9    def ReadMemory (p,byte,bit,datatype):
10     result=myplc.read_areas['MK'],0,byte,databyte)
11      if datatype == S7WLDWord:
12        return get_dword (result,0)
13     else:
14        return None
15   myplc = c.Client()
16   myplc.connect('192.168.0.7',0,1)
17   print "System ON:"
18   print ReadOutput(myplc,'0.5')
19   print "Vertical rollers:"
20   print ReadOutput(myplc,'0.1')
21   print "Number of washed cars:"
22   print ReadMemory(myplc,40,0,S7WLDWord)
```

List 2. Reading of the PLC outputs.

2.2 MQTT Protocol Implementation

As MQTT is a communication protocol based on intermediaries, it needs a central entity called a broker that's in charge of managing communications (Leon et al., 2020). In this work, we will implement the Mosquitto broker using the Paho-mqtt library. Once the broker for MQTT communications has been selected, listing 3 presents the line of code to post a message on the server.

```
1    import paho.mqtt.client as mqtt
2    broker_address= "192.168.1.200"
3    client = mqtt.Client ("PLC")
4    Client.connect(192.168.1.200)
5    Client.publish("carwash/act01","OFF")
```

List 3. Posting messages to the server.

To avoid confusion between messages and their recipients, each client must use a subscription method that accepts two parameters: a topic or topics and a quality service

(QoS). In this work, we use a QoS = 1 to ensure that messages are delivered to the receiver at least once until the message is acknowledged. Listing 4 shows the creation of a client instance, the connection to the broker, the subscription to a topic, the publication of a message and the callbacks.

```
1    import paho.mqtt.client as mqtt
2    import time
3
4    def on_message(client,userdata,message):
5    print("mensaje recibido", str(message,payload.decode("utf-8")))
6    print ("Topic=", message.topic)
7    print ( Nivel de calidad=", message.qos
8    Print("Flag de retencion =", message.retain)
9
10   Broker_address= "192.168.1.200"
11   print (" Create new instance")
12   Client = mqtt.Client("PLC")
13   Client.on_message=on_message
14   print (" Connect with broker")
15   Client.connect(broker_address)
16   Client.loop_star()
17   print("Subscribing Topic", "PLC/Rollers/Vertical")
18   Client.suscribe("PLC/Rollers/Vertical")
19   print("Posting message to Topic","PLC/Rollers/Vertical")
20   Client.publish("PLC/Rollers/Vertical",OFF)
     Time.sleep(4)
     Client.loop_stop()
```

List 4. Creation of a client instance, connection to the broker, subscription to a topic and publication of a message.

2.3   Implementation of the Platform for the Alarm Message to the Mobile Phone

When any type of system failure happens, an alarm message will be sent immediately to the customer's mobile phone number. Twilio is used for this research, which is a platform that allows developers to build cloud communication applications and advanced web systems. Within this platform a number must be released with the purchase option, then with the programmable SMS icon, the linked and released number is configured and immediately the platform indicates the parameters to be used in the programming for sending the message, note Fig. 2.

The previous code is used in the Node-Red platform to carry out visual programming based on java script, in the first input block called PLC S7–1200 the IP address of the PLC is entered for communication (see Fig. 3). Besides, the variables (PLC inputs), which are used in the output blocks, are declared, when the emergency stop button is pressed from the control panel, it receives a pulse and sends a signal to the trigger.

Fig. 2. Twilio platform programming code.

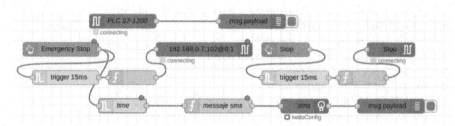

Fig. 3. S7–1200 PLC communication with Node-Red.

The configuration for sending the message to the phone number begins with the detection of an impulse (emergency button), followed by a trigger with the sending time. In Fig. 4 the blocks are exposed to the programming blocks within this platform.

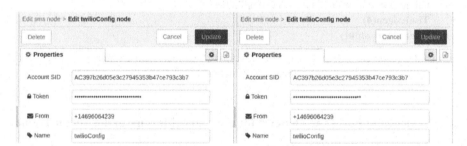

Fig. 4. Node-Red function block programming: ALERT fails in the AUTOWASH system (left). Message block, SID of the account to receive the warning message (right).

In the first block, the message that reads "ALERT in the AUTO-WASH system" is observed, which is sent once the impulse change has been detected in the emergency stop button. While in block b the data from the Twilio page is added once the first phone number is released. Enter the SID of the account, the token that comes to be the password, the number that sends and receives the warning message.

2.4 Implementation of the Platform for Automatic Payment

For the payment to be made automatically, the PayPal platform is used, which is an online payment system for sellers or people. In the SELLER TOOL, more options appear and

PayPal buttons are chosen. In Fig. 5, its configuration is observed, the type of button that the client observes is chosen, followed by the name of the article "Car Wash Station" and the article Id. The two services provided by the Autowash station are written, single wash at $ 1.50 and double wash at $ 2.00, you must also choose the type of currency. Later in the view that the client will have is the final result of the custom icon. When finished with the ready button, the platform generates a new window that contains the HTML code that is used in the development of the prototype web pages. This is shown in Fig. 5.

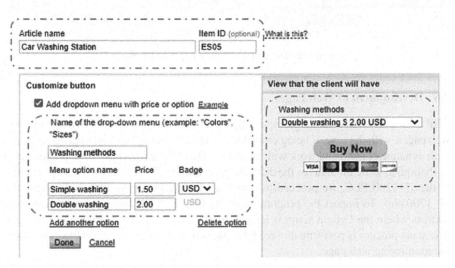

Fig. 5. Sending data from the server to different clients.

2.5 HMI Development

With the help of the functions offered by the interface of the TIA portal, the auto wash process is programmed and the main interface was designed, to monitor the variables in real time, of everything that is happening within the prototype. The structure of the main screen has the title, logo, time and date, operational commands [20].

In Fig. 6 (a), you can see the design of the main screen which consists of the following elements: Emergency stop: in case of any fault for the entire system. Start: Power on the system. Stop: System shutdown. Pilot light: Indicator that the system is on. Simple wash: first wash cycle. Double wash: Second wash cycle. Fig. 6 (b), is the real-time screen, in which the status of the actuators is observed, whether they are on or off, and the operation of the motor that is directed forward and visually is shown in a textual and visual way. Backward, also from the ignition of the lateral and horizontal rollers. The variables used within the indicators or pilot lights of each motor are the same physical outputs of the PLC.

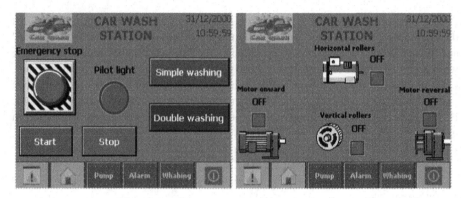

Fig. 6. HMI screens according to GUEDIS guide.

2.6 Development of Web Pages

PHP is an open-source language, especially used in the development of environments and web pages, with the ease of being embedded in HTML and allows you to generate pages with dynamic content and work with databases. Once the scripts have been programmed in Python, to write bit data for the different push buttons, both emergency, stop and start in the s7–1200 PLC, we proceed to import all the scripts in the PHP code of the file s7_1200.php. To import the programming file into the PHP code, you must enter the address where the Python script is located on the Raspberry Pi, as shown in Listing 5. The same process is performed to read the status data from the s7–1200 PLC outputs to the monitoring web page.

```
1    </body>
2    </html>
3    <?php
4    if ($_POST[Emergencia]){
5    $a- exec('sudo python /home/pi/test/button_emergency.py');
6    echo $a; }
7    if ($_POST[Stop])
8    $a- exec('sudo python /home/pi/test/button_stop.py');
9    echo $a; }
```

List 5. Import Python scripts into PHP.

Figure 7 (a) indicates the welcome to the new user, where they have to select the type of washing required and then pay with their credit card for the service. In Fig. 7 (b), the controls of the auto wash station, contains all the buttons for start, emergency and stop. The user must select the time to turn on the water pump, then turn on the system with the Start button and finally select the type of wash that was previously liquidated on the first web page.

In Fig. 8, the last web page of the system is presented where the digital data of the states of the outputs of the Siemens s7–1200 PLC are shown, which are connected to

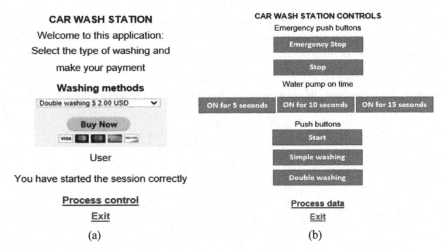

Fig. 7. Web pages to control the car wash.

the different actuators within the washing system, the status of each output will change from True = On to False = Off, also how many with a counter that shows the number of cars washed at the end of each day.

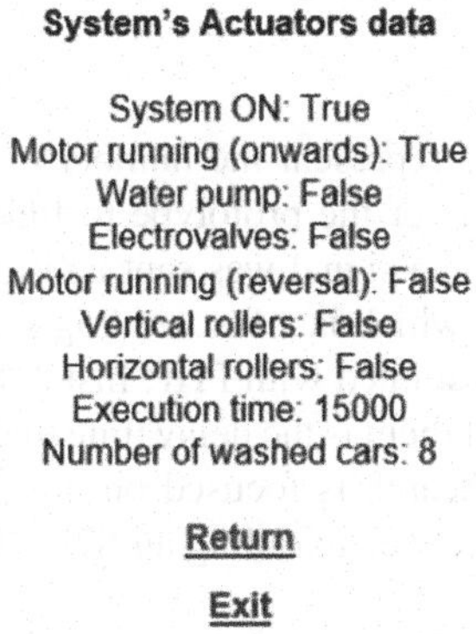

System's Actuators data

System ON: True
Motor running (onwards): True
Water pump: False
Electrovalves: False
Motor running (reversal): False
Vertical rollers: False
Horizontal rollers: False
Execution time: 15000
Number of washed cars: 8

Return

Exit

Fig. 8. Monitoring web page.

3 Results and Discussions

3.1 Delay in Movement

The tests carried out began on January 20, 2020 and ended on the 29th of the same month and year, with a total of 10 days, 30 tests were performed in 2 h and the average for each day is shown in Table 1. One of the most important factors to consider is the response time for both writing and reading data from the prototype auto-wash station. The time was taken from when one of the two washing processes is sent from the website until the prototype platform begins to move linearly, which is powered by a motor. Table 1 shows the reaction periods obtained when executing the prototype startup each day.

Table 1. Taking response times of the car wash prototype when it makes a linear movement.

Samples	Time (s)	
	Writing	Reading
1	2.24	0.73
2	2.21	0.68
3	2.21	0.91
4	2.15	0.82
5	2.09	0.69
6	2.17	0.83
7	2.16	0.89
8	2.17	0.69
9	2.17	0.85
10	2.13	0.92
Average	2.07	0.80

The 10 samples of the data represent the number of observations and the time in which the client gives an order for the prototype to function. On average 2.07 s was obtained for writing data after the signal was sent and for reading the PLC outputs to the monitoring page of 0.80 s, which is a fast reading speed when reading the Python script from the web page programmed with PHP. Instability in a system can be caused by different components, one of them is the delay time that happens in a network control system, for this reason, the research is focused on this analysis. The communication cycle corresponds to the time between sending an S7–1200 PLC from the web page to the controller.

3.2 Discussion

Due to the current health crisis, several measures have emerged to contain the Covid-19 pandemic and one of them is the limitation of contact with bills and coins since they are means where the disease-transmitting microorganisms are housed. The proposed system is characterized by being part of contactless electronic payments technology, which at the same time endows the systems with characteristics of feasibility, simplicity and speed. By means of the proposed prototype, customers or users must simply go to their computer or mobile to pay for the car wash service and start the system without having contact with people and thus take care of their state of health when contracting the service.

The performance of the prototype shows a robust system with all the elements integrated into this document, it begins with automatic payment through the customer's credit card once the type of washing has been selected, then with the START button from the website, the HMI display or the control panel turns on the system and is indicated by a pilot light, the type of washing liquidated is selected; The platform motor, the pump and the solenoid valves are turned on, allowing the water to pass through. It reaches a limit switch, it reverses the motor of the platform, the pump and solenoid valves are paid. The vertical and horizontal rollers are turned on until they reach another limit switch that indicates the end of the washing cycle. For double washing, the sequence is repeated once again, in addition to the HMI screens and web pages, the washing stages, the time of operation of the water pump, the status of the actuators in real time and the car number are shown.

4 Conclusions and Future Work

This work shows the automation of a process with an automatic payment system for a credit card and alert messages, through the use of various platforms, integrated for the control and monitoring of a prototype of a car wash station focused on the creation and innovation of new products and services, focused on safeguarding the health and integrity of people. The interaction between customers, vehicle owners and the implemented system was achieved through the design and programming of both the PLC, the HMI screen and the web pages through the MQTT communication protocol with the Raspberry Pi, which are necessary for the control and monitoring of the car wash process.

The results of the performance tests show a robust integration system between prototype, HMI, PLC and Raspberry Pi, which on average requires 2.07 s for writing data after the signal is sent and for reading the outputs from the PLC to the 0.80 s monitoring page which is a fast read speed when reading variables from the web page programmed with PHP. The programming carried out has not been shown, since it is a prototype that is with a patent in process.

When implementing automatic payment in the system set out in this document or in any other process, what is search is to frame the electronic payment technology from any mobile device, avoiding contact between the people who offer the service and customers, safeguarding the integrity and preventing the transmission of viruses and bacteria present in banknotes and coins, since they are means in which disease-transmitting microorganisms are housed. As future work, it pretends carried out an analysis of the main manufacturing industries and services that can implement an automatic payment system, through intelligent control to avoid contact between people due to the current health emergency.

References

1. Lin, J., Yu, W., Zhang, N., Yang, X., Zhang, H., Zhao, W.: A survey on internet of things: architecture, enabling technologies, security and privacy, and applications. IEEE Internet Things J. (2017). https://doi.org/10.1109/JIOT.2017.2683200

2. Reyna, A., Martín, C., Chen, J., Soler, E., Díaz, M.: On blockchain and its integration with IoT. Challenges and opportunities. Futur. Gener. Comput. Syst. (2018). https://doi.org/10.1016/j.future.2018.05.046.

3. Varela-Aldás, J., Chávez-Ruiz, P., Buele, J.: Automation of a lathe to increase productivity in the manufacture of stems of a metalworking company. In: Botto-Tobar, M., Zambrano Vizuete, M., Torres-Carrión, P., Montes León, S., Pizarro Vásquez, G., Durakovic, B. (eds.) ICAT 2019. CCIS, vol. 1195, pp. 244–254. Springer, Cham (2020). https://doi.org/10.1007/978-3-030-42531-9_20

4. Varela-Aldas, J., Andaluz, V.H., Chicaiza, F.A.: Modelling and control of a mobile manipulator for trajectory tracking. In: Proceedings - 3rd International Conference on Information Systems and Computer Science, INCISCOS 2018 (2018). https://doi.org/10.1109/INCISCOS.2018.00018.

5. Rodríguez, I.C.T., González, P.F.H., Bautista, Z.I.B.: PLC update of a computer-integrated manufacturing system. RISTI - Rev. Iber. Sist. e Tecnol. Inf. 18–35 (2018). https://doi.org/10.17013/risti.27.18-35.

6. Prinz, C., Morlock, F., Freith, S., Kreggenfeld, N., Kreimeier, D., Kuhlenkötter, B.: Learning factory modules for smart factories in industrie 4.0. In: Procedia CIRP (2016). https://doi.org/10.1016/j.procir.2016.05.105

7. Weyer, S., Meyer, T., Ohmer, M., Gorecky, D., Zühlke, D.: Future modeling and simulation of CPS-based factories: an example from the automotive industry. IFAC-PapersOnLine. (2016). https://doi.org/10.1016/j.ifacol.2016.12.168

8. Ynzunza, C., Izar, J., Bocarando, J., Aguilar, F., Larios, M.: El Entorno de la Industria 4.0: Implicaciones y Perspectivas Futuras Implications and Perspectives of Industry 4.0. Concienc. Tecnológica. 33–45 (2017)

9. Zohdi, T.I.: Modeling and simulation of laser processing of particulate-functionalized materials. Arch. Comput. Methods Eng. 24(1), 89–113 (2015). https://doi.org/10.1007/s11831-015-9160-1

10. Varela-Aldás, J., Fuentes, E.M., Ruales, B., Ichina, C.: Construction of a WBGT index meter using low cost devices. In: Rocha, Á., Ferrás, C., Montenegro Marin, C.E., Medina García, V.H. (eds.) ICITS 2020. AISC, vol. 1137, pp. 459–468. Springer, Cham (2020). https://doi.org/10.1007/978-3-030-40690-5_45

11. de Sá Carvalho, E.D.S., Filho, N.F.D.: Proposal for a mobile learning system focusing on the characteristics and applications practical of industry 4.0. RISTI - Rev. Iber. Sist. e Tecnol. Inf. 2018, 36–51 (2018). https://doi.org/10.17013/risti.27.36-51

12. Saá, F., Varela-Aldás, J., Latorre, F., Ruales, B.: Automation of the feeding system for washing vehicles using low cost devices. In: Botto-Tobar, M., León-Acurio, J., Díaz Cadena, A., Montiel Díaz, P. (eds.) ICAETT 2019. AISC, vol. 1067, pp. 131–141. Springer, Cham (2020). https://doi.org/10.1007/978-3-030-32033-1_13

13. Zou, Z., Bie, Y., Zhou, M.: Design of an intelligent control system for greenhouse. In: Proceedings of 2018 2nd IEEE Advanced Information Management, Communicates, Electronic and Automation Control Conference, IMCEC 2018 (2018). https://doi.org/10.1109/IMCEC.2018.8469309.

14. KM, S., A, M.J.: An empirical study of factors that influence HRD climate in public sector industries. Int. J. Psychosoc. Rehabil. (2019). https://doi.org/10.37200/ijpr/v23i4/pr190387

15. Tomić, N., Todorović, V.: The Future of Payments in the Internet of Things. (2017). https://doi.org/10.15308/sinteza-2017-97-104

16. Lee, H.R., Kim, W.J., Park, K.H., Cho, H.J., Lin, C.H.: Development of an easy payment system based on IoT gateway. In: International Conference on Electronics, Information and Communication, ICEIC 2018 (2018). https://doi.org/10.23919/ELINFOCOM.2018.8330665

17. Bai, L., et al.: Chinese experts' consensus on the Internet of Things-aided diagnosis and treatment of coronavirus disease 2019 (COVID-19). Clin. eHealth. (2020). https://doi.org/10.1016/j.ceh.2020.03.001

18. Shi, F., et al.: Review of artificial intelligence techniques in imaging data acquisition, segmentation and diagnosis for COVID-19. IEEE Rev. Biomed. Eng. (2020). https://doi.org/10.1109/RBME.2020.2987975

19. Trilla, A.: One world, one health: the novel coronavirus COVID-19 epidemic. Med. Clin. (Barc). (2020). https://doi.org/10.1016/j.medcli.2020.02.002

20. Buele, J., et al.: Interactive system for monitoring and control of a flow station using LabVIEW. In: Rocha, Á., Guarda, T. (eds.) ICITS 2018. AISC, vol. 721, pp. 583–592. Springer, Cham (2018). https://doi.org/10.1007/978-3-319-73450-7_55

Distribution Networks with Distributed Generation and Electric Vehicles

Wilson Jhonatan Olmedo Carrillo[1]($\boxtimes$) (iD), Andrés Santiago Cisneros-Barahona[2]($\boxtimes$) (iD),
María Isabel Uvidia Fassler[2]($\boxtimes$) (iD), Gonzalo Nicolay Samaniego Erazo[2]($\boxtimes$) (iD),
and Byron Andrés Casignia Vásconez[2]($\boxtimes$) (iD)

[1] Escuela Superior de Tecnología y Gestión, Leiria, Portugal
2192546@my.ipleiria.pt
[2] Universidad Nacional de Chimborazo, Riobamba, Ecuador

Abstract. With the continuous advancement of technology, energy systems have been gaining a greater field in the generation and distribution of renewable energies oriented to electric vehicles (EV).

The effect of both solar and wind power plants on EVs has a different behavior throughout the day, therefore, in the charging stations of these EVs, an optimal size and efficiency should be sought, with the best possible performance.

As a solution to circumstances where energy distribution needs to be improved, it has been considered that the integrated modeling of renewable energy sources is the best alternative to be used because it tries to mitigate negative effects on the sources of resource distribution towards EVs and generally, these solutions are rarely applied in a real test space.

Identifying a conventional scenario within society will be the way to simulate a study as realistic as possible to be able to demonstrate the operation of these points of the distribution network, thus being able to identify the strengths and weaknesses that a renewable energy system is connected to the distribution network may have.

Keywords: Electric vehicles · Distribution network · Renewable energy · Solar plant · Wind plant

1 Introduction

Global EV Scenario

Global EV sales have been on the rise and have increased by 50% from 2013 to 2014. According to the EVI 2015 update of its Global EV Outlook 2015, USA with a stock of EV and EVSE (Electric Vehicle Supply Team) of 276,104 and 21,814 respectively joins countries such as the Netherlands, Norway and Sweden as the only countries that have electric vehicle sales in 2014 exceeding 1% market shares. Similarly, 2014 also saw tremendous growth in electric vehicle charging infrastructure, the number of Tier 1 and Tier 2 chargers increased from 46,000 in 2012 to around 940,000 in 2014 and the number of fast chargers (Tier 3, CHAdeMo and SuperCharger) increased from 1,900

© Springer Nature Switzerland AG 2021
M. Botto-Tobar et al. (Eds.): ICAT 2020, CCIS 1388, pp. 250–260, 2021.
https://doi.org/10.1007/978-3-030-71503-8_19

in 2012 to 15,000 in 2014. According to, among all countries, the US had the highest number of PEVs (14,832 vehicles) in the first quarter of 2015 [1].

Distributed generation (DG) is becoming more and more a key component in the operation of distribution networks, this is due in part to the technological improvement of many RES (renewable energy sources) such as wind energy, photovoltaic, cells of Fuel and Heat and Power Combination (CHP), generating an environment-friendly reduction in CO_2 emissions [2].

Microgrids can potentially provide an increase in the reliability and quality of the services offered to users, with the use of distributed energy resources (DER). For this study of conditions, responses obtained from various previous investigations are used.

Currently, with fossil fuels and little concern for environmental problems, make the conventional combustion engine vehicle lose interest in favor of electric vehicles or hybrids. Taking into account that around 14% of greenhouse gas emissions are caused by transport, which progressively becomes a focus for environmental conservation [3].

The approach to a solution scenario to these problems through control strategies, pricing policies, incentives to opt for V2G (Vehicle to Grid), is the method on which the investigations of various authors carried out in this field is based, then it is essential to have a data analysis tool with which graphs can be generated and that serve to compare different control methods in the case that it cannot be applied or real implementation is not available, as in this case.

The scenario is simulated on a hypothetical group of cars using transport and charging data, each study on issues related to electric vehicle (PEV) plugs, as addressed in previous work, offers recommendations for utilities on how to optimize better integration of PEVs in the distribution network. For the analysis to be more effective and applicable, a specific approach to the system needs to be investigated.

2   Methodology

The microgrid-based field model consists of photovoltaic (PV) panels that are considered solar power plants (SPP) and EV parking lots equipped with charging stations. As in the first stage of the study, the scenario is investigated by a possible field of photovoltaic panels with their possible connections for charging stations, the existing transformers.

2.1   Intra-daily Behavior of Vehicles

The PEV charging process can be described as a process involving many uncertainties such as mileage, charging time, charge level, number and location of vehicles. Data from the National Domestic Travel Survey is used to estimate daily mileage and charging time, which is generally the time when people return home from work. And this data is used to generate the cumulative distribution functions shown in Fig. 2 with the help of MSC [4] (Fig. 1).

2.2   Load Demand

Grid performances are evaluated in terms of voltage violation, power losses, and line load due to different PEV penetration levels and load scenarios. Charging scenarios include

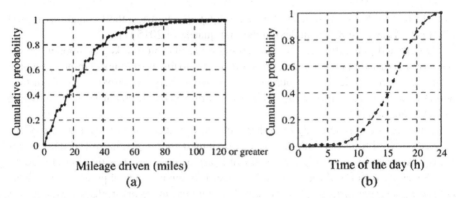

Fig. 1. Cumulative distribution functions for (a) mileage and (b) start and finish time. IEEE TRANSACTIONS ON SUSTAINABLE ENERGY [5].

normal and fast charging. The analysis starts with a base case, which is zero PEV penetration and continues to increase PEV penetration levels by up to 30%. Consequently, the performance of the distribution network is evaluated according to the violation of voltage and power losses, as well as the load levels of the lines [6].

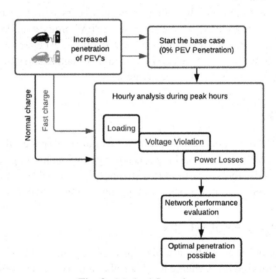

Fig. 2. Method flow chart

This section presents the simulation process of a car generation and power system together with the network, applying the proposed method to a practical distribution. It is a brief explanation of the test system, which includes a simulation model that Matlab offers then, in this simulation environment the topology, line and load data are presented. It is followed by the details of the PEV model, including the PEV characteristics and load levels.

2.3 The General Algorithm of Battery Required by an EV

1: **START**

Inputs:

E_b: Specific battery capacity

d: Daily travel in miles

ε: Specific consumption in kWh/mile

η: Charging efficiency

2: Set the vehicle to minimum SOC

$$\text{SOC}_{min} = \begin{cases} 30\% & \text{if they are type PHEV} \\ 5\%, & \text{if they are type AEV} \end{cases} \qquad (1)$$

3: Compute the energy consumed Econ

$$E_{con} = \frac{d \times \varepsilon}{E_b}. \qquad (2)$$

4: Compute battery SOC

$$\text{SOC} = \max\left\{(1 - E_{con}), \text{SOC}_{min}\right\}. \qquad (3)$$

5: Calculate the required energy

$$E_{rec} = \frac{(1 - \text{SOC})}{\eta} \times E_b. \qquad (4)$$

Output: Required energy E_{rec}

6: **END**

Fig. 3. General algorithm

The data per unit are calculated assuming the base values for the apparent power and voltage of the as in Eq. 5 and according to the Zbase, the values per unit of the branch, the parameters are obtained from the general formula (Eq. 6 and Eq. 7) [7] (Figs. 3 and 4).

$$Z_{base} = \frac{V_{base}^2}{S_{base}} \qquad (5)$$

$$R_{line} = R_{ph} \times length \Rightarrow R_{pu} = \frac{R_{line}}{Z_{base}} \qquad (6)$$

$$X_{line} = X_{ph} \times length \Rightarrow X_{pu} = \frac{X_{line}}{Z_{base}} \qquad (7)$$

Fig. 4. Equations

2.4 Basic Charge Levels

As the final stage of the SPP design, the solar radiation data is implemented in the simulation environment during the period of 6 am and 8 pm with hourly intervals. The solar radiation data of the SPPs are indicated in Table 1 (Fig. 5).

Table 1. Solar radiation data 1 day

Time	Average radiation (W/sqm)	Time	Average radiation (W/sqm)
6:00	158	14:00	907
7:00	520	15:00	889
8:00	696	16:00	855
9:00	794	17:00	798
10:00	852	18:00	704
11:00	887	19:00	534
12:00	906	20:00	185
13:00	912		

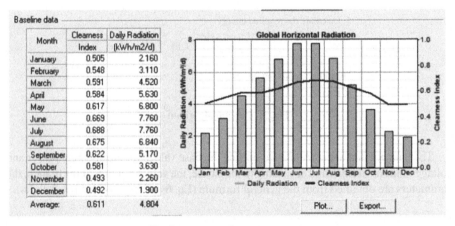

Fig. 5. Solar radiation data 1 year

The parking capacity of electric vehicles is decided according to the physical limitations of the parking area and the electrical limitations of the LV switchboard.

To maximize the number of parking spaces available, EVs should be taken into account the most common vehicles, being the following 10 brands of cars that were taken into account:

The EVs indicated in the Table 2 are modeled as a constant in Matlab since the system that offers modeling on a normal day, that is, the behavior of the energy that it may have and on which season its energy will depend the most. According to the time of day.

Table 2. EV technical data

Brand and model of car	Battery capacity kWh	kWh charging power kWh
Volkswagen E-Golf	24	7.2
BMW i3	22	6.6
Mercedes B-Class	28	10
Tesla Model – S	85	17.2
Fiat 500E	24	6.6
Ford Focus Electric	23	6.6
Kia Soul EV	27	6.6
Mitsubishi i-MiEV	16	3.3
Chevy Volt	17	3.3
Nissan LEAF	24	6.6

Finally, in this work, the following model that Matlab offers has been used to analyze the behavior and observe the impact that renewable energies can have (Fig. 6).

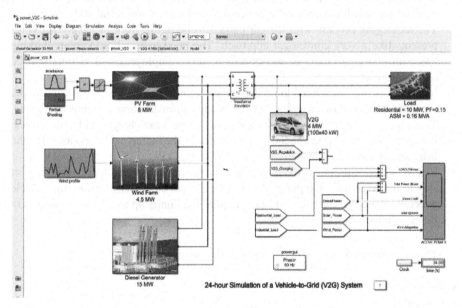

Fig. 6. Matlab simulation environment

3   Results

The simulation environment must follow the next diagram (Fig. 7).

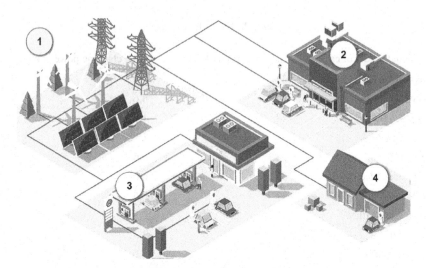

Fig. 7. Operation diagram

1. In addition to a fossil fuel energy source, low-carbon energy sources such as wind farms and photovoltaic (PV) systems convert energy from wind or light into the electricity needed to meet customer needs. Commercial, industrial and residential.
2. The recharging process with the car parked while doing work or leisure activities presents like a very convenient approach. The need to install and create parking lots with charging points in workplaces to serve employees and visitors will be increasingly important.
3. In case of people who need to recharge their vehicles at the fastest rate during the trips, the electric fast chargers and the needed infrastructure is being developed. These high-power fast chargers or super-fast chargers can charge an electric vehicle between 10 up to 30 min depending on the size of the battery and the power that the fast charger can deliver usually from 50 kW to 350 kW.
4. Finally, charging the electric vehicle at home is the most cost-effective and convenient way to recharge from the point of view of a private customer. Because the vehicle generally is parked overnight it needs regular load units up to 22 kW connected to the central metering unit.

Then a behavior that we will obtain from the power generation is:

- Total charge: blue
- Charge: yellow
- Diesel: red
- Solar: blue
- Wind: purple

It can be noticed that at night the PV or voltaic energy does not affect anything since there is no presence of the sun (Figs. 8 and 9).

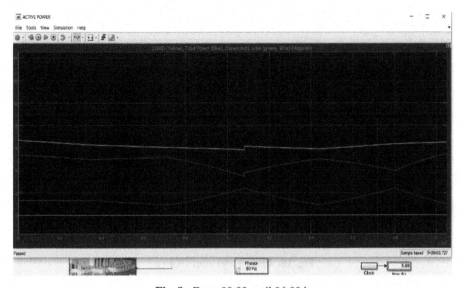

Fig. 8. From 00:00 until 06:00 h

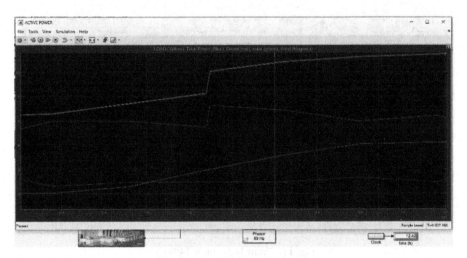

Fig. 9. From 06:00 until 12:00 h

Once having the presence of the sun, photovoltaic plants can begin to contribute to the energy of the system, however, the wind in the morning is not very considerable since this factor depends on the interaction of heat with the atmosphere and in the morning is still mild but at midday, it begins to have considerable value (Figs. 10 and 11).

Finally, when the afternoon and evening arrive, the energy of the photovoltaic plants loses power, and the wind turbine tends to rise due to the presence of wind.

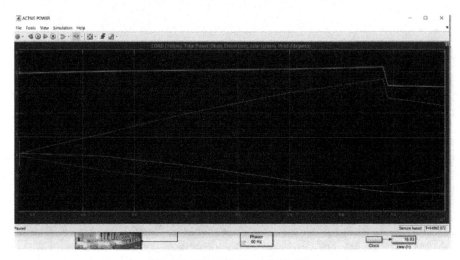

Fig. 10. From 12:00 until 18:00 h

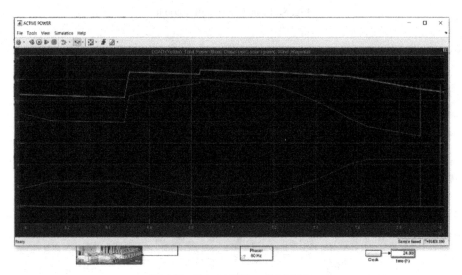

Fig. 11. From 18:00 until 24:00 h

3.1 The Energy in the Future

It is imperative to take into account that as time progresses, renewable energy tends to show a lower and lower production value, making it attractive for investors who little by little lose their power when generating energy with fossil fuels, there is currently a committee at the level called the International Renewable Energy Agency or by its acronym IRENA, generate more and more investment projects of different product categories, for their members and both Portugal and Ecuador are within this system showing the following renewable energy production data (Figs. 12 and 13).

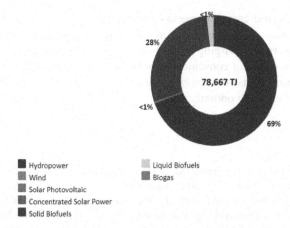

Fig. 12. Energy production in Ecuador. IRENA, Transporte [9]

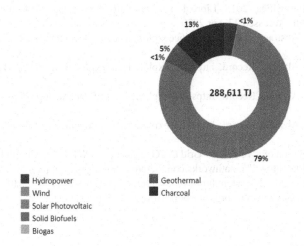

Fig. 13. Energy production in Portugal. IRENA, Transporte [9]

4   Conclusions

Actual carbon dioxide (CO_2) emission reduction trends are not yet on track. Under current policies, the world would exhaust its energy-related carbon budget in less than 20 years. Even then, fossil fuels such as oil, natural gas and coal will continue to dominate the global energy mix for decades to come, so there is a need to raise awareness about the green energy system and implementation so renewables must also expand significantly as a source for direct uses, including transportation fuels.

One helping method is battery storage systems because they are emerging as a possible solution to integrate solar and wind renewable energy into power systems around the world because they have the unique ability to rapidly absorb, retain and then reinject electricity into the transport vehicle.

Recharging electric cars at home is often the most convenient and cost-effective way to recharge, particularly since most private vehicles are generally parked overnight. In most cases, overnight charging at the home base is the cheapest time to recharge. Charging at work can be a convenient way for people to recharge their electric cars while parked during their work hours or for companies with electric fleets to provide employees with a charging option.

References

1. Fripp - Savings and Peak Reduction Due to Optimally-Timed.pdf. https://fsec.ucf.edu/en/pub lications/pdf/HI-14-17.pdf. Accessed 15 June 2020
2. Hassan, A.S., Firrincieli, A., Marmaras, C., Cipcigan, L.M., Pastorelli, M.A.: Integration of electric vehicles in a microgrid with distributed generation. In: 2014 49th International Universities Power Engineering Conference (UPEC), September 2014, pp. 1–6 (2014). https://doi. org/10.1109/UPEC.2014.6934641
3. Jornadas de Automática - 2015 - Libro de actas.pdf. https://www.ehu.eus/documents/3444171/ 4484748/36.pdf. Accessed 27 Apr 2020
4. IEEE Xplore Abstract Record. https://ieeexplore.ieee.org/document/6922582. Accessed 15 June 2020
5. IEEE Xplore Abstract Record. https://ieeexplore.ieee.org/document/6934641. Accessed 15 June 2020
6. IEEE Xplore Abstract Record. https://ieeexplore.ieee.org/document/6345583. Accessed 15 June 2020
7. IEEE Xplore Abstract Record. https://ieeexplore.ieee.org/document/6934641. Accessed 27 Apr 2020
8. 24-hour Simulation of a Vehicle-to-Grid (V2G) System - MATLAB & Simulink - MathWorks América Latina. https://la.mathworks.com/help/physmod/sps/examples/24-hour-simulation-of-a-vehicle-to-grid-v2g-system.html?s_tid=srchtitle. Accessed 18 June 2020
9. Transport. https://www.irena.org/transport. Accessed 18 June 2020

Intelligent Systems

Machine Learning Model for the Prediction of Emotions in a Mobile Application

Pablo Torres-Carrión$^{(\boxtimes)}$ ⓘ, Carlos Vicente-Tene, Yuliana Jiménez ⓘ, and Darwin Castillo ⓘ

Universidad Técnica Particular de Loja, San Cayetano Alto S/N, Loja, Ecuador
{pvtorres,acvicente,ydjimenez,dpcastillo}@utpl.edu.ec

Abstract. Emotional intelligence is a transversal axis in the integral development of the person. As a variable, in the interaction environment, research is carried out in various fields of science, reaching great advances with the contribution of artificial intelligence. The EMODIANA has been designed as a subjective emotion research tool, with an extension in the EmoAppPro mobile app. The objective is to design and put into production a machine learning model for classification and prediction from the target of emotions, to a simplification (positive, neutral and negative) in real time. The experimentation is carried out with biology students (n = 30) of the Technical Private University of Loja, during an evaluation process, capturing all the video interaction. A thesaurus of emotions is constructed, from observation of experts, with time windows (t = 20 s), applying Fleap's Kappa for label validation. The Knowledge Discovery in Databases - KDD methodology is applied in the ML process, obtaining better results with a model based on a decision tree.

Keywords: Emotions · Prediction · Machine learning

1 Introduction

Emotions represent the form through which we demonstrate different behaviors, response and adaptation, typical of human social behavior; According to the stimulus received, they can be positive or negative [1]. We constantly show emotions because they are a fundamental part of human life. In [2] an emotion is defined as a complex state of the organism characterized by an excitement or disturbance that predisposes to action; Emotions are generated in response to an external or internal event, they are present in our day-to-day lives, and are manifested based on our emotional intelligence. Daniel Goleman [3] defined as the ability to motivate ourselves, to persevere in the effort despite possible frustrations, control impulses, delay gratification, regulate our own moods, prevent anxiety from interfering with our faculties rational, and even, the ability to empathize and trust others. Taking facial expressions as input, Paul Ekman [4] exposes four categories: emotional expressions, conversational signals, facial emblems, facial manipulators; emotional expressions can be organized and placed into one of seven emotion families: anger, happiness, sadness, contempt, surprise, fear, disgust. Bizquerra [2] explains that when we are faced with a situation, be it positive as joy, or negative

© Springer Nature Switzerland AG 2021
M. Botto-Tobar et al. (Eds.): ICAT 2020, CCIS 1388, pp. 263–271, 2021.
https://doi.org/10.1007/978-3-030-71503-8_20

as danger, our emotional response is activated automatically, manifesting a reaction, it is composed of three components: neurophysiological, behavioral and cognitive. Psychology is the science that supports, from the methodological and theoretical proposal, affective computing and other sub-areas of Human Computer Interaction, and from subjective techniques supported by observation, it has been possible to validate the basic information for the realization of this investigation.

To evaluate emotional behavior, the use of qualitative resources is common, mainly sustained in observation techniques. In [5] a subjective research instrument is proposed to record the continuous observation of emotions, sustained in the EMODIANA [6]; This mobile application allows you to manage the entire methodological process of gathering information, manage projects, assign observers and manage the participants (population subject to observation). In this work a complement to this proposal is proposed, designing a prediction model of the participant's emotional behavior, in a basic range of positive, neutral or negative emotions. For this, it is proposed to apply Machine Learning techniques, supported by the Knowledge Discovery in Databases (KDD) [7] methodology, previously applied in Human-Computer Interaction (HCI) research by Holzinger [8]. The sustained classification technique is applied to two decision tree algorithms: Rpart[1] and Party,[2] available in the R language library; with these two algorithms, efficiency evaluation metrics higher than 89% were obtained. With these results, a tool to support the investigation of user emotions is proposed to the scientific community, an emerging field in HCI.

In the scientific literature, after a systematic search in the WoS and Scopus databases, no proposals were found for ML models applied to subjective tools for the analysis of emotions. These tools have been used for research purposes in several studies, to corroborate quantitative results from a qualitative context sustained in observation; Thus, in [9] instruments for direct observation of the emotional behavior of the young child and the mother are applied to validate the Pediatric Attachment Style Indicator (PASI); in [10] a methodology is exposed that complements the subjective evaluation of emotions EMODIANA [6] with sustained evaluation in software. In [11] he develops an observation tool to measure the intrapersonal emotions of youth sports coaches, resulting in 12 categories of behavioral content and eight emotion modifiers (Neutral, Happy, Affectionate, Alert, Tense, Anxious, Angry and Disappointed). In complement to these investigations, this work demonstrates the validity of complementing a digital tool EmoApp [5] for continuous emotional evaluation [12], with ML models to predict emotional behavior.

This document is organized to facilitate reading, from a general exposition of research related to the use of conventional and digital emotional assessment tools, available in the introduction. The methodology is then explained, detailing each phase of the KDD method for construction of ML models. The results of the two algorithms with the best classification results are then presented, and the main conclusions of the work are finally shared.

---

[1] Recursive Partitioning and Regression Trees.

[2] A Laboratory for Recursive Partytioning.

2   Methodology

For this research, from a general context, a mixed methodology is proposed, supported by qualitative techniques such as observation, and quantitative techniques for the construction of ML models. For the construction of models, we work with the Knowledge Discovery in Databases (KDD) methodology, which in an orderly way allows the development of an ML model; each of the phases is detailed below.

2.1   Data Selection

The data for the decision tree algorithm training were obtained by means of an application called EmoAppPro [5], which provides the functionality of applying the subjective measurement instrument of emotions, through the methodology called EMODIANA [6]. The methodology used to develop the model was divided into several phases, which are exposed from the KDD methodology.

To start this stage, use was made of a set of audiovisual material, which has as content, the recording of a group of students from the biology area of the Particle Technical University of Loja, who are developing an online evaluation. The base resource consists of 18 videos, the same ones that have an average time of 40 min. In [13] an analysis is made from the didactic context with this database.

To obtain the data, all the videos are ordered, tagging by student code. Subsequently, the subjective emotion measurement instrument is applied with the help of the EmoApp application, creating a participant-type user for each of the videos; at the end of the evaluation process, the results are exported in CSV format, making use of the export functionality of the application. The information contained in the file can then be viewed as a result of the evaluation, with sequences of time (hh:mm:ss), emotion, level and subject (Fig. 1).

Emoción	Nivel	Sujeto	Actividad	Externo	Centecima	Segundo	Minuto	Hora
alegria	4	0	1	0	73	4	0	0
alegria	2	0	1	0	18	15	0	0
alegria	4	0	1	0	12	21	0	0
seriedad	2	0	1	0	12	29	0	0
seriedad	3	0	1	0	68	54	0	0
seriedad	4	0	1	0	88	14	1	0
sorpresa	1	0	1	0	37	33	1	0
sorpresa	2	0	1	0	44	43	1	0
alegria	4	0	1	0	10	56	1	0
alegria	2	0	1	0	41	10	2	0
alegria	3	0	1	0	29	28	2	0
alegria	4	0	1	0	73	38	2	0

Fig. 1. Data obtained when exporting in .CSV format, the results of applying the EmoAppPro subjective emotion measurement instrument

2.2 Data Preprocessing

In data preprocessing, you work with two files. The first (Fig. 2a) Is obtained from the previous file (Fig. 1), grouping all the emotions that are within a set time range (t = 20 s), merging from the three variables of the timeline (hours, minutes and seconds); both emotion and level are preserved.

Rango	Emoción	Nivel
20	alegria	4
20	alegria	2
40	alegria	4
40	seriedad	2
60	seriedad	3
80	seriedad	4
100	sorpresa	1
120	sorpresa	2
120	alegria	4
140	alegria	2
160	alegria	3
160	alegria	4
180	alegria	5
180	nerviosismo	1
200	alegria	4
200	alegria	2

Rango	Valoración 1	Valoración 2	Valoración 3
20	0	0	0
40	1	1	1
60	0	0	1
80	1	1	1
100	1	1	1
120	1	1	1
140	1	1	1
160	0	0	0
180	1	1	1
200	1	1	1

Fleiss's Kappa

	-1	0	1	Total general
			3	3
			3	3
3				3
			3	3
			3	3
	1	2		3
			3	3
			3	3
			3	3
			3	3
			3	3
3				3
3				3

alpha	0,05	
tails	2	

	Total	-1	0	1
kappa	0,83406027	0,89322618	0,80370544	0,80128205
s.e.	0,05463531	0,07332356	0,07332356	0,07332356
z-stat	15,2659578	12,1819809	10,9610808	10,9280302
p-value	0	0	0	0
lower	0,72697704	0,74951464	0,65999391	0,65757052
upper	0,9411435	1,03693771	0,94741697	0,94499358

a) File 1, grouping of emotions within the 20-second range

b) File 2, data from the valuation of three observers, in positive, negative and neutral emotions.

Fig. 2. Processed data

To build the second file (Fig. 2b), we proceed by applying the qualitative methodology of continuous observation, with the collaboration of three observers, who with an established time line (t = 20 s), make a subjective appreciation of three emotional states (-1: negative; 0: neutral; 1: positive) from the original videos of the interaction; Each of the observers was given a template that was made up of two variables: range (t = +20 s) and Rating (-1; 0; 1); a stopwatch is used to guide the assessment of the emotional state according to the time range. The results of the three observers are then unified (Fig. 2b above), to carry out a technical validation of the data obtained by the observers, using the concordance technique, applying Fleiss Kappa[3] (Fig. 2b below). A data cleaning is carried out, leaving only the evaluations where their level of agreement is greater than 60%; Thus, the observations made to video 2 and video 7 are discarded, which obtained a percentage of agreement of 55% and 53% respectively, leaving 16 videos as validated work data.

---

[3] Fleiss Kappa: measures the degree of concordance of nominal or ordinal evaluations performed by multiple evaluators when evaluating the same samples.

2.3 Transformation

In this section the information is structured, from the two files built in the previous section; the data are unified in a single file, which contains the information regarding the data set made up of the range, emotions, levels and their assessment (Fig. 3 above). By having several emotions observed for each 20-s range, it was necessary to structure a single list of emotions, for each range and assessment (Fig. 3 below).

Rango	Emoción	Nivel	Valoración
20	alegria	4	1
20	alegria	2	1
40	alegria	4	1
40	seriedad	2	1
60	seriedad	3	0
80	seriedad	4	0
100	sorpresa	1	0

E1	N1	E2	N2	E3	N3	E4	N4	E5	N5	E6	N6	E7	N7	V
alegria	4	alegria	2											1
sorpresa	3	nerviosismo	5											-1
nerviosismo	5	nerviosismo	4	nerviosismo	4									-1
sorpresa	4	nerviosismo	5	nerviosismo	5	sorpresa	3	nerviosismo	5	nerviosismo	5			-1
alegria	2	nerviosismo	3	nerviosismo	4									-1
nerviosismo	3	miedo	2	satisfaccion	5	alegria	2	miedo	5	verguenza	2			-1
sorpresa	3	satisfaccion	4	seriedad	3	alegria	4							1

Fig. 3. Unified file structure of observed emotions and their level, for each range (t = 20 s) and assessment (1, 0, −1)

2.4 Data Mining

In this section the entire data mining process is carried out, making use of the tools and libraries provided by the R programming language, through its integrated development environment RStudio. The elaboration of the decision tree is used to predict the emotional state of the participant, from the data obtained in the process of applying the subjective emotion measurement instrument with the help of the application. First, the Data Set was loaded, which consists of 15 variables and a total of 1321 data. In RStudio, the data types of each variable are established as a factor. For the elaboration of the decision tree model, the variable Valuation V is taken as dependent or variable to be predicted from the set of emotions and their levels. After the corresponding experiments, it is found that the models with the highest efficiency are obtained using decision trees, using the Rpart and Party libraries available in the R libraries. The variables that most contribute to the construction of the tree are E1, E2, E3, N1 and N2, which is valid because in most of the data collection of file 1, they are observed in a range of 20 s, at least two or three emotions. The number of acceptable levels in the tree was also obtained, from which the relative error varies not significantly; thus, from size = 3 the difference is reduced, but from size = 9 the difference is close to zero (Fig. 4).

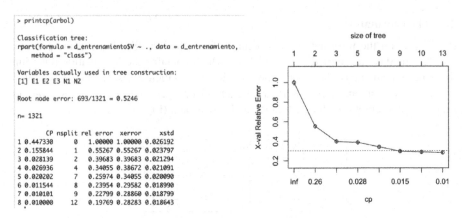

```
> printcp(arbol)

Classification tree:
rpart(formula = d_entrenamiento$V ~ ., data = d_entrenamiento,
    method = "class")

Variables actually used in tree construction:
[1] E1 E2 E3 N1 N2

Root node error: 693/1321 = 0.5246

n= 1321

        CP nsplit rel error  xerror     xstd
1 0.447330      0   1.00000 1.00000 0.026192
2 0.155844      1   0.55267 0.55267 0.023797
3 0.028139      2   0.39683 0.39683 0.021294
4 0.026936      4   0.34055 0.38672 0.021091
5 0.020202      7   0.25974 0.34055 0.020090
6 0.011544      8   0.23954 0.29582 0.018990
7 0.010101      9   0.22799 0.28860 0.018799
8 0.010000     12   0.19769 0.28283 0.018643
```

Fig. 4. Cross validation to determine the dimension of the decision tree

2.5   Integration/Evaluation

The obtained models were put into production in the EmoApp, as a cloud service, and are available as an additional service of this research tool. Product details can be reviewed at [5]. The models were put into production on a local server, using the shiny R language package, which shows the results through interactive graphics, with easy publication on any website.

3   Results

Two models were obtained by applying decision tree algorithms. In Fig. 5 the first tree obtained with the RPart algorithm is shown; and in Fig. 6 the second tree model is shown, made with the Party algorithm. Both algorithms are available in the standard R Language library.

The results of the model evaluation metrics are detailed in Table 1. The first model obtained with the Rpart library (89.78), is slightly more effective than the second obtained with the Party library (89.63). Both are valid models to put into production.

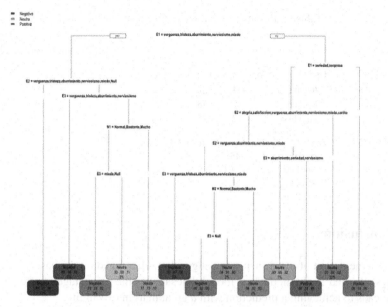

Fig. 5. Decision tree model obtained with the RPart library

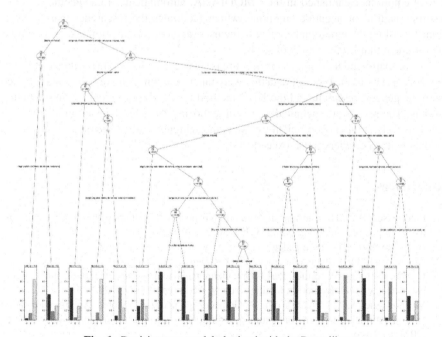

Fig. 6. Decision tree model obtained with the Party library

Table 1. Results of the metrics of the resulting models

Library	Confusion matrix				Effectiveness percentage
Rpart library	`test` `Negativa Neutra Positiva` `Negativa` 454 32 2 `Neutra` 36 568 26 `Positiva` 13 28 162				89.78
Party library	`test` `Negativa Neutra Positiva` `Negativa` 452 28 16 `Neutra` 47 574 14 `Positiva` 4 26 160				89.63

4 Conclusions

The implementation of the decision tree algorithm, elaborated on the basis of different libraries, allowed to obtain the best model that satisfies the percentage of effectiveness, which leads to achieving a prediction with a great margin of validity.

The models obtained will allow establishing a conversion from the reading of subjective emotions established in the EMODIANA, automatically to a specific range of positive, neutral or negative emotions, which facilitates the researcher making decisions regarding the emotional change in the user facing a certain stimulus, or a singular environment that is the subject of study.

A transparent methodological procedure is shared, which complies with a methodology appropriate to the types of data that were taken as input. A mixed method is applied from the general research, and the KDD method for the development of the prediction models. The results are technically proven, exposing the most relevant predictor variables, as well as the most efficient tree size; these inputs made it possible to obtain two models with an efficiency that exceeds 89%.

References

1. Fredrickson, B.L.: The role of positive emotions in positive psychology: the broaden-and-build theory of positive emotions. Am. Psychol. **56**, 218 (2001)
2. Bisquerra Alzina, R.: Psicopedagogía de las emociones, Madrid (2009)
3. Goleman, D.: Inteligencia emocional. Kairo's, Barcelona (2011)
4. Ekman, P.: Emotion Families: Part 1. Organizing facial expressions of emotion. https://www.paulekman.com/blog/emotion-families-part-1/. Accessed 01 Aug 2020
5. Vicente-Tene, A.C., Torres-Carrión, P., Gonzalez-Gonzalez, C.: Mobile App for automation of observational instrument for continuous emotional evaluation. Commun. Comput. Inf. Sci. (2021, in press)
6. González-González, C.S., Cairós-González, M., Navarro-Adelantado, V.: EMODIANA: Un instrumento para la evaluación subjetiva de emociones en niños y niñas. In: Actas del XIV Congr. Int. Interacción Pers. (2013). https://doi.org/10.13140/RG.2.1.5112.2169
7. Fayyad, U., Piatetsky-Shapiro, G., Smyth, P.: The KDD process for extracting useful knowledge from volumes of data. Commun. ACM. **39**, 27–34 (1996)

8. Holzinger, A.: Human–computer interaction and knowledge discovery (HCI-KDD): what is the benefit of bringing those two fields to work together? In: Cuzzocrea, A., et al. (eds.) IFIP International Federation for Information Processing 2013, pp. 319–328 (2013)
9. Favez, N., Berger, S.: Presentation and validation of the pediatric attachment style indicator (PASI). Devenir **24**, 215–230 (2012). https://doi.org/10.3917/dev.123.0215
10. Torres-Carrión, P., González-González, C., Carreño, A.M.: Methodology of emotional evaluation in education and rehabilitation activities for people with Down Syndrome. Presented at the (2014). https://doi.org/10.1145/2662253.2662274
11. Allan, V., Turnnidge, J., Vierimaa, M., Davis, P., Côté, J.: Development of the assessment of coach emotions systematic observation instrument: a tool to evaluate coaches' emotions in the youth sport context. Int. J. Sport. Sci. Coach. **11**, 859–871 (2016). https://doi.org/10.1177/1747954116676113
12. Torres-Carrión, P.: Metodología HCI con análisis de emociones para personas con Síndrome de Down. Aplicación para procesos de aprendizaje con interacción gestual (2017)
13. Jiménez Gaona, Y., Vivanco Galván, O., Torres-Carrión, P., Castillo Malla, D., Jiménez Gaona, M.: Artificial Intelligence in neuroeducation: the influence of emotions in the learning science. In: International Congress of Research and Innovation, Quito, Ecuador. Springer CS Proceedings (LCNS) (2020)

Is It Intelligent? A Systematic Review of Intelligence in the Most Cited Papers in IoT

Billy Grados$^{(\boxtimes)}$ [ID] and Héctor Bedón$^{(\boxtimes)}$ [ID]

Exponential Technology Group (GITX-ULIMA), Instituto de Investigación
Científica (IDIC), Universidad de Lima, Lima, Peru
{bgrados,hbedon}@ulima.edu.pe

Abstract. Artificial intelligence is a buzz word and even more when its accomplishments have challenged our intelligence. However, what is intelligence? Is there a consensus in its meaning for researchers and professionals? Is it just a sales word? What does it mean in practical terms? To answer these questions, we followed a systemic review of literature in most cited papers about intelligent systems in the Internet of Things (IoT) and discovered that only 58% were intelligent as we defined: "Intelligent Systems are systems conformed by algorithms that are programmed using some machine learning techniques and that can learn from data and perform tasks with a superior performance". The rest 42% were just traditional systems with hardware or software enhancements.

Keywords: Artificial intelligence · Intelligent systems · IoT · Machine learning

1 Introduction

Nowadays, we are witnesses of the breakthroughs of artificial intelligence that is not anymore only in science-fiction books or films. In 2020, Brown et al. [11] demonstrated the accomplishments in several tasks like translation, reading comprehension, completion, simple arithmetic operations, news article generation, poem generation, and other tasks using Generative Pre-trained Transformer (GPT-3). In 1997, IBM Deep Blue computer program beat the world chess champion Garry Kasparov [32]. In 2016, AlphaGo won against the legendary Go player Mr. Lee Sedol [18]. In 2012, AlexNet Convolutional Neural Network (CNN) significantly outperformed previous methods on the ImageNet Large-Scale Visual Recognition Challenge (ILSVRC) [39] achieving human-level performance when classifying objects in images of natural scenes [28]. Waymo, formerly called Google self-driving car project, has led the autonomous driving

Supported by the National Innovation Program in Fishing and Aquaculture (PNIPA) of Peru and the Institute of Scientific Research (IDIC) of the University of Lima.

M. Botto-Tobar et al. (Eds.): ICAT 2020, CCIS 1388, pp. 272–286, 2021.
https://doi.org/10.1007/978-3-030-71503-8_21

progress for the automobile industry since 2009 [82]. Aside from these impressive examples, we can see its ubiquity and its contribution in other examples: route-finders that display maps and offer navigation advice to drivers; recommender systems that suggest products, movies, books, and music albums based on a user's previous purchases and ratings; medical decision support systems that help doctors diagnose breast cancer [9].

In all these previous cases, we can ask: What is intelligence? Is it similar to our intelligence? What makes a machine intelligent? "Can machines think?" (from A. Turing [77]) Is our intelligence a single entity? or Is there multiple intelligence? (adapted from Gardner [26]). And even more, how can we discriminate against a traditional system from an intelligent one? Is there a consensus about these topics in the scientific community or the industries?

Answering these questions does not lead us to only satisfy our curiosity, but more importantly, they help us: 1) to have a common understanding about Artificial Intelligence (AI) as researchers and practitioners, 2) to avoid using the intelligence term as a sales word and the misuse of it, and 3) to push all the efforts in the right direction for the development of intelligent systems, 4) to find the implicit consensus about the technical or practical definition of intelligence, and 5) to define the main elements of intelligent systems. Nevertheless, we haven't found a simple explanation to solve these questions, as it is explained in the chapter "How should we define AI?" [76]: "AI means different things to different people, and AI researchers have no exact definition of AI. The field is rather being constantly redefined when some topics are classified as non-AI, and new topics emerge". We found papers that have tracked the progress of AI research through the number of published papers [22], or that have discussed "problems, challenges and opportunities in AI" [60], or that have made a detailed review of AI applied in the fashion and apparel industry [29], but they do not have an explanation of what is AI or what are the practical implications in a broader scope or other industries. For that reason, we did a systemic review of most cited papers in the topic "Intelligent Systems in the Internet of Things (IoT)" to answer these questions and to fill this gap between the theory and practice of AI in IoT.

The remaining article is organized as follows: Sect. 2 discusses the definitions of artificial intelligence. Section 3 describes the steps involved in the systemic review process. Sections 4, 5, and 6 present the results, discussion, and conclusions of the study respectively.

2   Intelligent Systems

When we talk about the intelligence of systems, we refer to artificial intelligence. Also, "intelligence: the ability to learn or understand or to deal with new or trying situations, the ability to apply knowledge to manipulate one's environment or to think abstractly as measured by objective criteria (such as tests)" [52], "artificial intelligence: the capability of a machine to imitate intelligent human behavior" [51], "the ability of a digital computer or computer-controlled robot to perform tasks commonly associated with intelligent beings" [10], "artificial intelligence: the ability of machines, computers, systems to learn and solve problems" [60]. Even though, these definitions do not help us to discriminate against a traditional system from an intelligent one, or to understand the technical aspect of intelligence. To grasp a better understanding, we condensed the history of artificial intelligence in the following subsection where we can appreciate the progress of the "artificial intelligence" concept, and then, we defined it.

2.1 History of Artificial Intelligence

In the Brief History of AI [75], under the title "Ancient History", it is mentioned conceptual achievements like the intellectual roots of AI and the appearance of intelligent artifacts in literature. In [63,75], there is an overview of the "Modern History" of artificial intelligence that is compiled in the next paragraphs.

The gestation of AI dates between 1943 and 1955 with Alan Turing's vision and its persuasive agenda in his famous article "Computing Machinery and Intelligence" [77]. A. Turing introduced the Turing Test, machine learning, genetic algorithms, and reinforcement learning. The birth of artificial intelligence was in 1955 where the term artificial intelligence was used the first time by John McCarthy, a math professor at Dartmouth who organized the seminal conference on the topic in 1956 [15,49].

Early enthusiasm and great expectations of AI comprehends from 1952 to 1969 wherein 1958, McCarthy defined the high-level language Lisp, which was to become the dominant AI programming language for the next 30 years. Nevertheless, it was eclipsed with a dose of reality (1966–1973) in the form of limitations, difficulties, and failures such as the attempt to speed up the translation of Russian scientific papers in the wake of the Sputnik launch in 1957, no progress in machine evolution (the belief of an appropriate series of small mutations to a machine-code program can generate a program with good performance for any particular task. Now called genetic algorithms), the end of support for AI research in the United Kingdom, the impossibility to recognize when two inputs were different in a two-input perceptron (a simple form of artificial neural network).

Between 1969 and 1979, we highlighted the importance of expert systems like MYCIN, a program with about 450 rules to diagnose blood infections and was able to perform as well as some experts, and considerably better than junior doctors. Since 1980, AI has become an industry, and in 1986, it was reinvented the back-propagation learning algorithm that is a key element in artificial neural networks. Since 1987, there was progress in speech recognition, machine translation, robotics, computer vision, and knowledge representation due to new techniques like hidden Markov models (HMMs), data mining, and Bayesian networks. In 1995, the intelligent agents as a whole agent have appeared as a topic to develop human-level AI, artificial general intelligence, and friendly AI. Since 2001, the availability of very large data sets and its usage has emerged as an important aspect in the building of AI algorithms. And finally, the examples of Sect. 1 enrich this history.

2.2   Definitions

As explained in the chapters "What is AI?" and "Related Fields" by The University of Helsinki [76], we tend to use suitcase words for terms that carry a whole bunch of different meanings or that encapsulate jumbled ideas or dozens of different mechanisms (Marvin Minsky, one of the greatest pioneers in AI [53]). Its course also suggests that AI is not a countable noun, it is a scientific discipline, like mathematics or biology, it is a collection of concepts, problems, and methods for solving them, and it is related to other fields. Deep Learning is part of Machine Learning (ML), ML is part of AI, AI is part of Computer Science. All these fields and Data Science have concepts and methods in common. Moreover, AI is the field devoted to building artifacts that are intelligent (operationalized through intelligence tests) [70]. AI is the ability of machines to make decisions, learn similarly as humans, and complete tasks that normally require the intelligence of humans, including speech recognition, visual perception, decision making, and language translations [48]. AI corresponds to a system, machine, or computer that thinks humanly, thinks rationally (the ideal performance), acts humanly, or acts rationally [63, 70].

In this study, when we say artificial intelligence, we mostly mean machine learning [15] because machine learning is a more appropriate concept to answer our research questions than AI. In the same manner, in "Artificial intelligence, revealed" [23], Yann LeCun, one of the fathers of Deep Learning and a winner of the 2018 ACM A.M. Turing Award [1] that is known as the "Nobel Prize of Computing" [3], explained that a machine learning algorithm "supervised learning" is a technique for adjusting parameters in a program to recognize things that are similar to what a machine has been trained on but has never seen. Additionally, another useful explanation comes from Yoshua Bengio, another winner of the same award. He said that machine learning allows computers to learn from examples, to learn from data. Bengio's mission is to discover and understand the principles of intelligence through learning [8]. His start-up Element AI [20] considers that the function of AI is defined by its ability to find patterns in enormous data sets, and to solve problems faster and more accurately than humans can [21]. Likewise, in Deep learning review, Geoffrey E. Hinton, the godfather of Deep Learning [78] and a winner of the same award, in collaboration with the two aforementioned authors, presented: the key aspect of deep learning is that the representations needed for detection or classification are learned from data using a general-purpose learning procedure, and not designed by human engineers [42]. They also noticed that the key advantage of deep learning above other techniques like linear classifiers or kernel methods is that the good representation can be learned automatically using a general-purpose learning procedure.

To summarize all the presented information and to elaborate our working definition, we consider that algorithms are the basic operational aspect of AI and its key elements are 1) Autonomy: the ability to perform tasks in complex environments without constant guidance by a user, and 2) Adaptivity: the ability to improve performance by learning from experience [76].

Definition 1. *Intelligent Systems are systems conformed by algorithms that are programmed using some machine learning techniques and that have the ability to learn from data and perform tasks with a superior performance*

This definition has the following implications: 1) the intelligence can be found on the used algorithms, 2) the definition discriminates some machine learning techniques from others, e.g. deep learning over linear classifiers, 3) the algorithms need to learn from data using a general-purpose learning procedure, and not a hand-crafted one, 4) the tasks involve input data and output results, 5) they have superior performance than traditional programming methods and sometimes better than human level, 6) examples of the tasks are speech recognition, natural language processing, image recognition (computer vision or machine vision), recommendation, anomaly detection [25, 33, 48].

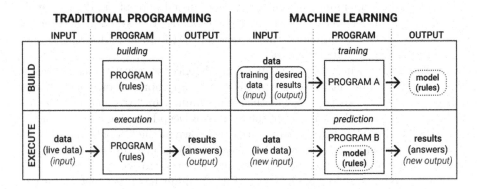

Fig. 1. Traditional programming vs. Machine learning

The Fig. 1 helps us to understand the difference between a traditional program and a machine learning program [4, 6, 17, 30, 38, 56, 66, 74]. Programming a system, machine or computer consists of building a program to execute it and output results from input data. Every program on its basis is an algorithm that establishes the steps or rules to generate the output given the input. A didactic example in traditional programming is the sum operation of two numbers where the program has a rule explicitly written by a human. This program $y = x_1 + x_2$ is able to execute the sum operation resulting in the output $y = 2$ with the inputs $x_1 = 1$ and $x_2 = 1$. On the other hand, in machine learning, the rules are the output of the training program A. These rules were not explicitly programmed by a human, and they serve to the predicting program B. Continuing the previous case, the input data in the training process is conformed by the training data $x_1 = 1$ and $x_2 = 1$, and the desired result $y = 2$ wherein the traditional programming, x_1 and x_2 are the inputs and y is the output. Then, this input data obtains the output rule $y = x_1 + x_2$, and this model serves to the program B that has a similar execution as traditional programming but with new inputs $x_1 = 2$ and $x_2 = 2$, and new output $y = 4$.

This working definition and its implications is used to classify intelligent systems from traditional systems.

3   Materials and Methods

To discover what is the true meaning of intelligent systems in practical terms, we followed a systemic review of literature about intelligent systems in the Internet of Things (IoT).

3.1   Article Retrieval

We considered computer science-related databases for article retrieval: IEEE Xplore with more than five-million documents [34], ACM [2] with 2,888,831 publications, ArXiv with 1,790,396 scholarly articles [7]. We decided to use just one large database to accelerate this process. We accessed the IEEE Xplore on March, 5th, 2020, used the query string "Intelligent systems in IoT" (the spaces were considered as OR), and filtered by IEEE as the publisher. We chose the more recent articles.

3.2   Article Selection

To select papers, we followed this strategy. We explored intelligence concepts in the titles. We used the words smart, intelligent, intelligence, machine learning, supervised learning, automation, autonomous, and other related words to tag the titles. Then, we grouped the titles by area to have sample papers in different scopes or industries. We had two ways to determine the area. One way was extracting the word that modifies that area or component in the tags with the word "intelligent", e.g. in an "intelligent transportation systems", the area was "transportation systems". The other way was writing the whole tag in the tags with the word "intelligence", e.g. in an "artificial intelligence", the area was "artificial intelligence". Finally, we selected the most cited papers. We considered 80% of the sum of the maximum article citation count per area. For example, in the vehicle area, we selected the article with 32 article citation count which is the maximum value of three papers with article citation counts of 32, 4, and 1 each, and then, we summed it with the maximum values of all other areas.

3.3   Information Extraction

The data collection process included the reading of all selected papers to determine what enables intelligence in the systems. We read the abstract, all the figures, tables, or charts, the conclusions, discussions, introductions, material and methods, and results, in that order. We collected the information in a table with these variables: Author, Year, Title, Pages, Citations, Abstract, Purpose, Scope/product/process, Explicit definition, Implicit definition, Other concepts.

Scope/product/process was the key element where the intelligence lies. The definitions were about the intelligence concept in that scope/product/process on an empirical basis. Other useful information was put on Other concepts. The analysis had two measures: type of intelligence and the detail or specification considered by the papers understudy.

All the information was collected and summarized in a Google Sheet spreadsheet [68]. The papers were downloaded in PDF format and were stored in the reference management application Mendeley [50]. We read the papers in that desktop application and we highlighted the texts that we considered relevant for the variables in the systemic review. Our database sheet had the following basic columns: Title, Authors, Publication Year, Abstract, DOI (Digital Object Identifier), Article Citation Count. We added the columns Tag, and Group Area to facilitate the selection process. Also, we used the same spreadsheet to analyze and evaluate the results classifying the documents in intelligent systems or traditional ones.

If our classification determines similar percentages, it means that there is no consensus in practical terms about traditional systems using intelligence in a different way than our definition determined from the literature.

Other used tools were Overleaf [57] to write the document, Figma [24] to elaborate diagrams, and Word Art [83] to generate a word cloud.

4   Results

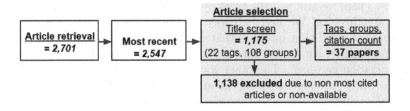

Fig. 2. Screening process

The result of the selection process is depicted in Fig. 2. First, we found *2,701* papers since 2010. Then, we included the more recent papers that were *2,547* papers representing 94% and comprehends the year range from 2017 to 2020. We found *2,547* papers using our selection criteria: 609 in 2017, 926 in 2018, 925 in 2019, and 87 in 2020.

Second, we tagged *1,175* paper titles (46% of 2,547) with 22 tags related to intelligence. Ordered by frequency in papers: smart, intelligent, intelligence, machine learning, automated, automation, cognitive, deep learning, autonomous, neural network, automatic, reinforcement learning, supervised learning, autonomic, unsupervised learning, machine intelligence, q learning, automata, automating, deep network, incremental learning, self-learnable. The top 3 tags were "smart" (627 titles = 53% of 1,175), "intelligent" (377 titles = 32%) and "intelligence" (63 titles = 5%) whose accumulated title count was 1,067 representing 91% of 1,175. There were 1,036 titles with just one tag and 139 with more than one tag: 130 with two tags and 9 with 3 tags. Examples, for two tags: "intelligent, smart"; for three tags: "deep learning, intelligent, smart".

Fig. 3. Word cloud of groups

Third, we grouped the papers by area or component and we detected *108* groups. We showed the most cited groups in Fig. 3 with the sum of article citation count represented as its word size.

Then, we obtained *37* papers choosing the ones with the maximum article citation count in its group and if they were available for us. Their sum of article citation counts was 512 representing 80% of 640 article citation counts. "fog computing" was the area with the maximum of 62 article citation count representing 9.7% of the 640. Reading these papers took us about one hour per paper.

As we show in Fig. 4, our research discovered that in practical means, there are 42% of systems that claim they are intelligent but they are traditional ones: 38% of them are hardware enhancements like adding sensors to a traditional system and 62% are software enhancements to a traditional algorithm.

In detail, we summarize the papers through a brief description of the technical aspects of systems in the following paragraphs. And, we use the word 'enhanced' to describe the improvements to a traditional system that we do not consider 'intelligent' according to our definition.

4.1 Hardware Enhanced Systems

When the authors of these papers considered intelligence, they referred to a hardware enhancement like giving sensing capabilities to a system or component. In [87], "Intelligent Things" means elements that have been optimized with sensors and were used in an infusion monitoring system (droplet count, remaining medicine). In [36], the "Intelligent Manhole Cover Management System" involves

Fig. 4. Result of intelligence in most cited papers on intelligent systems in IoT

an efficient, enhanced, and connected system that uses sensors (tilt, vibration, and location sensors) for self-perception and a traditional algorithm to perform efficient actions. "Intelligent Connected Vehicles" [88] and "Intelligent Vehicles" [71] are described as vehicles with advanced capabilities like sensing (GPS, RFID, headlight range sensor, mirror sensor, transmission sensor, and fuel level sensor) and diagnostics. In [79], "Intelligent steel inventory tracking" denotes an automatized process with the sensing ability that reads codes in RFID and performs efficiently. This ability could be used in an intelligent system that takes decisions on its own. Perhaps, in [46], the "Intelligent Agriculture Service Platform" refers to a platform that collects, monitors, senses, and makes decisions; in practice, the paper only shows the platform as a sensor-enabled one.

4.2   Software Enhanced Systems

In this subsection, intelligence is understood as a software enhancement (e.g. an improved or more efficient traditional algorithm) or enabled computing capabilities. We detail the explicit or implicit definitions in the following sentences. "Intelligent Tracking": an algorithm that is more accurate than others [80]. "Intelligent Edge": efficient, enhanced computation ability [58]. "Intelligent Transportation Systems": efficient platform in resource management [5]. "Intelligent traffic monitoring and guidance system": efficient algorithm to find the shortest path [41]. "Intelligent Parking System": efficient through traditional image processing algorithms [61]. "Intelligent security framework": an algorithm to solve a problem [69]. "Intelligent Bus Transportation System": efficient that shows more useful information and optimizes time for users [27]. "Intelligent Management System": automated, more efficient through thresholds set by a user in agricultural greenhouses [43]. "Intelligent Power Equipment Management": efficient that uses inference for a lot of information [14]. "Intelligent Data Processing": efficient and distributed way to filter data to save costs [86].

4.3   Intelligent Systems

We found intelligence as we defined in the following papers: "Intelligence in Fog Computing" [72], "Intelligent Traffic Load Prediction-Based Adaptive Channel Assignment Algorithm" [73], "Intelligent Sensor Nodes" [35], "Artificial Intelligence" [85], "Distributed Intelligence" [64], "Intelligent Personal Assistants" [65], "Intelligent Edge Computing" [44], "Intelligent IoT Traffic Classification" [19],

"Intelligent Algorithms" [81], "Intelligent Wireless Services" [12], "Threat Intelligence Scheme" [54], "Intelligent Fall Detection IoT System" [31], "Intelligent traffic light control" [45], "Intelligent vehicle commination" [67], "Ambient Intelligence Challenge" [16], "Intelligent and secure IoT edge mote" [37], "Intelligent System" [62], "Intelligent Edge Computing" [13], "Intelligent Secure Communication" [84], "Intelligent smartphone" [47], "Intelligent service fulfillment" [55], "Intelligent irrigation system" [59]. They use modern Natural Language Processing (NLP) techniques, algorithms for Self-driving Cars, or Machine Learning (ML) algorithms such as: Neural Networks (NN), Deep Learning (DL), Deep Neural Networks (DNN), Convolutional Neural Network (CNN o ConvNet), Recurrent Neural Network (RNN), Long Short-Term Memory (LSTM), Reinforcement Learning (RL), Deep Reinforcement Learning (DRL), Q-Learning, Deep Q-network (DQN), Dyna-Q, Bayes Statistics, Naive Bayes, Non-parametric Bayesian, Genetic Algorithm, K-Means, K-Nearest Neighbor (K-NN), Random Forest, Support Vector Machine (SVM), Adaptive Neuro Fuzzy Inference System (ANFIS), Beta Mixture Model (BMM), Dirichlet Mixture Models (DMM), distributed FrankWolfe (dFW), Expectation–Maximization (EM), FCBFiP (Fast Correlation Based Feature in Pieces), Gaussian Mixture Model (GMM), Hybrid RNN Occupancy Estimation Algorithm, Incremental Aggregated Gradient, Mixture-Hidden Markov Models (MHMM), Multivariate Correlation Analysis, Partial least squares regression (PLSR), Post Decision State (PDS).

5 Discussions

In the most cited papers, we found no consensus about intelligent systems because 42% of traditional systems used the word intelligence in a different way than our working definition.

Machine learning is a clear topic that reveals intelligence in its several algorithms such as Deep Learning, Reinforcement Learning, and others. Artificial intelligence is constantly evolving and some topics are classified as non-AI, and new algorithms emerge.

Our study is similar to [40] that reviewed the field of artificial intelligence and concluded no consensus nor formalism in this field. Its review is more theoretical than practical. [29] reviewed AI but only applied in the fashion and apparel industry and to find gaps in the application of AI techniques. In contrast, we considered other groups like transportation, communication, or agriculture, and to find the practical use of AI based on specific methods or techniques. This study doesn't assume a vague or colloquial definition of intelligence and challenges the technical aspect of the buzz word artificial intelligence.

We just covered one article with the maximum citation count per selected groups for time limitations. We spent about 40 h to only read the chosen papers. We also plan to research the meaning of the term smart to complement this study. Smart was also one of the most frequent tags.

6   Conclusions

It has been always said "not all that glitters is gold". In the same manner, not all that uses the word intelligence is intelligent. As we presented, only 58% of the reviewed papers were about true intelligent systems and the remainder were traditional ones. They are built upon algorithms and those that let machines to learn from data can be called intelligent ones. We consider that this insight is our main contribution and the starting point for a common understanding of artificial intelligence for researchers and professionals in a practical and detailed way.

References

1. ACM: 2018 Turing Award. https://awards.acm.org/about/2018-turing
2. ACM: ACM Digital Library. https://dl.acm.org/about
3. ACM: A.M. Turing Award. https://amturing.acm.org/
4. AI Trends: Artificial Intelligence vs. a Clever Algorithm – What's the Difference? https://www.aitrends.com/ai-software/software-development/artificial-intelligence-vs-a-clever-algorithm-whats-the-difference/
5. Al-Dweik, A., Muresan, R., Mayhew, M., Lieberman, M.: IoT-based multifunctional scalable real-time enhanced road side unit for intelligent transportation systems. In: Canadian Conference on Electrical and Computer Engineering, pp. 1–6 (2017). https://doi.org/10.1109/CCECE.2017.7946618
6. Allen, G.: Understanding AI technology. Technical report, Department of Defense Joint AI Center (2020). https://www.linkedin.com/company/dod-joint-artificial-intelligence-center/
7. arXiv. https://arxiv.org/
8. Bengio, Y.: The Rise of Artificial Intelligence through Deep Learning. https://www.youtube.com/watch?v=uawLjkSI7Mo
9. Bostrom, N.: Superintelligence: Paths, Dangers, Strategies. Oxford University Press, Oxford (2014)
10. Britannica: artificial intelligence. https://www.britannica.com/technology/artificial-intelligence
11. Brown, T.B., et al.: Language models are few-shot learners. arXiv (2020). http://arxiv.org/abs/2005.14165
12. Chen, M., Miao, Y., Jian, X., Wang, X., Humar, I.: Cognitive-LPWAN: towards intelligent wireless services in hybrid low power wide area networks. IEEE Trans. Green Commun. Netw. **3**(2), 409–417 (2019). https://doi.org/10.1109/TGCN.2018.2873783
13. Chen, S., et al.: Internet of Things based smart grids supported by intelligent edge computing. IEEE Access **7**, 74089–74102 (2019). https://doi.org/10.1109/ACCESS.2019.2920488
14. Choi, C., Esposito, C., Wang, H., Liu, Z., Choi, J.: Intelligent power equipment management based on distributed context-aware inference in smart cities. IEEE Commun. Mag. **56**(7), 212–217 (2018). https://doi.org/10.1109/MCOM.2018.1700880
15. Chojecki, P.: Artificial Intelligence Business: How You Can Profit from AI. Amazon Digital Services LLC (2020)

16. Corno, F., Russis, L.D.: Training engineers for the ambient intelligence challenge. IEEE Trans. Educ. **60**, 40–49 (2016)
17. Da Rocha, R.: What is machine learning and deep learning? https://towardsdatascience.com/what-is-machine-learning-and-deep-learning-47fe6718adec
18. DeepMind: AlphaGo - DeepMind. https://deepmind.com/research/case-studies/alphago-the-story-so-far
19. Egea, S., Rego Manez, A., Carro, B., Sanchez-Esguevillas, A., Lloret, J.: Intelligent IoT traffic classification using novel search strategy for fast-based-correlation feature selection in industrial environments. IEEE Internet Things J. **5**(3), 1616–1624 (2018). https://doi.org/10.1109/JIOT.2017.2787959
20. Element AI: About us. https://www.elementai.com/about-us
21. Element AI: Why understanding AI matters. https://www.elementai.com/news/2020/why-understanding-ai-matters
22. Erokhin, S.D.: A review of scientific research on artificial intelligence. In: 2019 Systems of Signals Generating and Processing in the Field of on Board Communications, SOSG 2019, pp. 1–4 (2019). https://doi.org/10.1109/SOSG.2019.8706723
23. Facebook Engineering: Artificial intelligence, revealed. https://engineering.fb.com/ai-research/ai-revealed/
24. Figma: Figma: the collaborative interface design tool. https://www.figma.com
25. Forbes: The Key Definitions of Artificial Intelligence (AI) That Explain Its Importance. https://www.forbes.com/sites/bernardmarr/2018/02/14/the-key-definitions-of-artificial-intelligence-ai-that-explain-its-importance/#10273034f5d8
26. Gardner, H.: Frames of Mind: The Theory of Multiple Intelligences. Basic Books (2011). https://www.amazon.com/Frames-Mind-Theory-Multiple-Intelligences-ebook/dp/B004MYFV0E
27. Geetha, S., Cicilia, D.: IoT enabled intelligent bus transportation system. In: Proceedings of the 2nd International Conference on Communication and Electronics Systems (ICCES), pp. 7–11 (2018). https://doi.org/10.1109/CESYS.2017.8321235
28. Geirhos, R., et al.: Comparing deep neural networks against humans: object recognition when the signal gets weaker. arXiv (2017). http://arxiv.org/abs/1706.06969
29. Giri, C., Jain, S., Zeng, X., Bruniaux, P.: A detailed review of artificial intelligence applied in the fashion and apparel industry. IEEE Access **7**, 95376–95396 (2019). https://doi.org/10.1109/ACCESS.2019.2928979
30. Guru99: Machine Learning Tutorial for Beginners. https://www.guru99.com/machine-learning-tutorial.html
31. Hsieh, Y.Z., Jeng, Y.L.: Development of home intelligent fall detection IoT system based on feedback optical flow convolutional neural network. IEEE Access **6**(c), 6048–6057 (2017). https://doi.org/10.1109/ACCESS.2017.2771389
32. IBM: IBM - Deep Blue. https://www.ibm.com/ibm/history/ibm100/us/en/icons/deepblue/
33. IBM: What is Artificial Intelligence (AI)? https://www.ibm.com/cloud/learn/what-is-artificial-intelligence
34. IEEE: IEEE Xplore. https://ieeexplore.ieee.org/Xplorehelp/overview-of-ieee-xplore/about-ieee-xplore
35. Javed, A., Larijani, H., Ahmadinia, A., Emmanuel, R., Mannion, M., Gibson, D.: Design and implementation of a cloud enabled random neural network-based decentralized smart controller with intelligent sensor nodes for HVAC. IEEE Internet Things J. **4**(2), 393–403 (2017). https://doi.org/10.1109/JIOT.2016.2627403

36. Jia, G., Han, G., Rao, H., Shu, L.: Edge computing-based intelligent manhole cover management system for smart cities. IEEE Internet Things J. **5**(3), 1648–1656 (2018). https://doi.org/10.1109/JIOT.2017.2786349
37. Karnik, T., et al.: A cm-scale self-powered intelligent and secure IoT edge mote featuring an ultra-low-power SoC in 14nm tri-gate CMOS. In: Digest of Technical Papers - IEEE International Solid-State Circuits Conference, vol. 61, pp. 46–48 (2018). https://doi.org/10.1109/ISSCC.2018.8310176
38. Kharkovyna, O.: Machine Learning vs Traditional Programming. https://towardsdatascience.com/machine-learning-vs-traditional-programming-c066e39b5b17
39. Krizhevsky, A., Sutskever, I., Hinton, G.E.: ImageNet classification with deep convolutional neural networks. In: Handbook of Approximation Algorithms and Metaheuristics, pp. 1–1432 (2012). https://doi.org/10.1201/9781420010749
40. Kumar, M., Sood, I.: Review on artificial intelligence techniques. J. Crit. Rev. **7**(7), 1363–1367 (2020). https://doi.org/10.31838/jcr.07.07.247
41. Latif, S., Afzaal, H., Zafar, N.A.: Intelligent traffic monitoring and guidance system for smart city. In: 2018 International Conference on Computing, Mathematics and Engineering Technologies (iCoMET), pp. 1–6 (2018). https://doi.org/10.1109/ICOMET.2018.8346327
42. LeCun, Y., Bengio, Y., Hinton, G.: Deep learning. Nature **521**, 436–444 (2015). https://www.cs.toronto.edu/ hinton/absps/NatureDeepReview.pdf
43. Li, Z., Wang, J., Higgs, R., Zhou, L., Yuan, W.: Design of an intelligent management system for agricultural greenhouses based on the Internet of Things. In: Proceedings - 2017 IEEE International Conference on Computational Science and Engineering and IEEE/IFIP International Conference on Embedded and Ubiquitous Computing, CSE and EUC 2017, vol. 2, pp. 154–160 (2017). https://doi.org/10.1109/CSE-EUC.2017.212
44. Liu, Y., Yang, C., Jiang, L., Xie, S., Zhang, Y.: Intelligent edge computing for IoT-based energy management in smart cities. IEEE Netw. **33**(2), 111–117 (2019). https://doi.org/10.1109/MNET.2019.1800254
45. Liu, Y., Liu, L., Chen, W.P.: Intelligent traffic light control using distributed multi-agent Q learning. In: 2017 IEEE 20th International Conference on Intelligent Transportation Systems (ITSC), pp. 1–8 (2017). https://doi.org/10.1109/ITSC.2017.8317730
46. Ma, Y.W., Chen, J.L.: Toward intelligent agriculture service platform with LoRa-based wireless sensor network. In: Proceedings of 4th IEEE International Conference on Applied System Innovation 2018, ICASI 2018, pp. 204–207 (2018). https://doi.org/10.1109/ICASI.2018.8394568
47. Mamun, M.A.A., Puspo, J.A., Das, A.K.: An intelligent smartphone based approach using IoT for ensuring safe driving. In: ICECOS 2017 - Proceeding of 2017 International Conference on Electrical Engineering and Computer Science: Sustaining the Cultural Heritage Toward the Smart Environment for Better Future, pp. 217–223 (2017). https://doi.org/10.1109/ICECOS.2017.8167137
48. Mc Frockman, J.: Artificial Intelligence and Machine Learning. Amazon Digital Services LLC (2019)
49. McCarthy, J.: A Proposal for the Dartmouth Summer Research Project on Artificial Intelligence (1996). http://www-formal.stanford.edu/jmc/history/dartmouth/dartmouth.html
50. Mendeley. https://www.mendeley.com
51. Merriam-Webster: Artificial Intelligence. https://www.merriam-webster.com/dictionary/artificialintelligence

52. Merriam-Webster: Intelligence. https://www.merriam-webster.com/dictionary/intelligence
53. Minsky, M.: Consciousness is a Big Suitcase. http://www.edge.org/3rd_culture/minsky/minsky_p2.html
54. Moustafa, N., Adi, E., Turnbull, B., Hu, J.: A new threat intelligence scheme for safeguarding industry 4.0 systems. IEEE Access 6(c), 32910–32924 (2018). https://doi.org/10.1109/ACCESS.2018.2844794
55. Munir, M.S., Abedin, S.F., Alam, M.G.R., Tran, N.H., Hong, C.S.: Intelligent service fulfillment for software defined networks in smart city. In: International Conference on Information Networking, pp. 516–521 (2018). https://doi.org/10.1109/ICOIN.2018.8343172
56. NO Complexity: Creating stupid software. https://nocomplexity.com/creating-stupid-software/
57. Overleaf: Overleaf, Online LaTeX Editor. https://www.overleaf.com
58. Patel, P., Intizar Ali, M., Sheth, A.: On using the intelligent edge for IoT analytics. IEEE Intell. Syst. 32(5), 64–69 (2017). https://doi.org/10.1109/MIS.2017.3711653
59. Rajkumar, M.N., Abinaya, S., Kumar, V.V.: Intelligent irrigation system - an IOT based approach. In: IEEE International Conference on Innovations in Green Energy and Healthcare Technologies - 2017, IGEHT 2017, pp. 1–5 (2017). https://doi.org/10.1109/IGEHT.2017.8094057
60. Rana, A.K., et al.: Review on artificial intelligence with internet of things - problems, challenges and opportunities. In: 2019 2nd International Conference on Power Energy Environment and Intelligent Control, PEEIC 2019, pp. 383–387 (2019). https://doi.org/10.1109/PEEIC47157.2019.8976588
61. Rane, S., Dubey, A., Parida, T.: Design of IoT based intelligent parking system using image processing algorithms. In: 2017 Proceedings of the International Conference on Computing Methodologies and Communication (ICCMC), pp. 1049–1053 (2017). https://doi.org/10.1109/ICCMC.2017.8282631
62. Rego, A., Canovas, A., Jimenez, J.M., Lloret, J.: An intelligent system for video surveillance in IoT environments. IEEE Access 6(c), 31580–31598 (2018). https://doi.org/10.1109/ACCESS.2018.2842034
63. Russell, S., Norvig, P.: Artificial Intelligence. Springer, London (2012)
64. Sahni, Y., Cao, J., Zhang, S., Yang, L.: Edge mesh: a new paradigm to enable distributed intelligence in Internet of Things. IEEE Access 5(c), 16441–16458 (2017). https://doi.org/10.1109/ACCESS.2017.2739804
65. Santos, J., Rodrigues, J.J., Casal, J., Saleem, K., Denisov, V.: Intelligent personal assistants based on Internet of Things approaches. IEEE Syst. J. 12(2), 1793–1802 (2018). https://doi.org/10.1109/JSYST.2016.2555292
66. Shah, A.: Challenges Deploying Machine Learning Models to Production. https://towardsdatascience.com/challenges-deploying-machine-learning-models-to-production-ded3f9009cb3
67. Singh, M., Kim, S.: Trust bit: reward-based intelligent vehicle commination using blockchain paper. In: IEEE World Forum on Internet of Things, WF-IoT 2018 - Proceedings, pp. 62–67 (2018). https://doi.org/10.1109/WF-IoT.2018.8355227
68. Springer. https://www.springer.com/us/about-springer
69. Sridhar, S., Smys, S.: Intelligent security framework for IoT devices. In: International Conference on Inventive Systems and Control (ICISC 2017) Intelligent, pp. 1–5 (2017)
70. Stanford Encyclopedia of Philosophy: Artificial Intelligence. https://plato.stanford.edu/entries/artificial-intelligence/

71. Sun, W., Liu, J., Zhang, H.: When smart wearables meet intelligent vehicles: challenges and future directions. IEEE Wireless Commun. **24**(3), 58–65 (2017)
72. Tang, B., et al.: Incorporating intelligence in fog computing for big data analysis in smart cities. IEEE Trans. Industr. Inf. **13**(5), 2140–2150 (2017). https://doi.org/10.1109/TII.2017.2679740
73. Tang, F., Fadlullah, Z.M., Mao, B., Kato, N.: An intelligent traffic load prediction-based adaptive channel assignment algorithm in SDN-IoT: a deep learning approach. IEEE Internet Things J. **5**(6), 5141–5154 (2018). https://doi.org/10.1109/JIOT.2018.2838574
74. TensorFlow: Machine Learning Zero to Hero (Google I/O'19). https://www.youtube.com/watch?v=VwVg9jCtqaU
75. The Association for the Advancement of Artificial Intelligence (AAAI): A Brief History of AI. https://aitopics.org/misc/brief-history
76. The University of Helsinki: Elements of AI. https://course.elementsofai.com/
77. Turing, A.M.: Computing machinery and intelligence. Mind **LIX**(236), 1–28 (1950). https://doi.org/10.1093/mind/lix.236.433. http://mind.oxfordjournals.org/cgi/doi/10.1093/mind/LIX.236.433
78. University of Toronto: How U of T's 'godfather' of deep learning is reimagining AI. https://www.utoronto.ca/news/how-u-t-s-godfather-deep-learning-reimagining-ai
79. Valente, F.J., Neto, A.C.: Intelligent steel inventory tracking with IoT/RFID. In: 2017 IEEE International Conference on RFID Technology and Application, RFID-TA 2017, pp. 158–163 (2017). https://doi.org/10.1109/RFID-TA.2017.8098639
80. Wan, L., Kong, X., Xia, F.: Joint range-doppler-angle estimation for intelligent tracking of moving aerial targets. IEEE Internet Things J. **5**(3), 1625–1636 (2018). https://doi.org/10.1109/JIOT.2017.2787785
81. Wang, D., Chen, D., Song, B., Guizani, N., Yu, X., Du, X.: From IoT to 5G I-IoT: the next generation IoT-based intelligent algorithms and 5G technologies. IEEE Commun. Mag. **56**(10), 114–120 (2018). https://doi.org/10.1109/mcom.2018.1701310
82. Waymo: Journey. https://waymo.com/journey/
83. Word Art. https://wordart.com
84. Xia, J., Xu, Y., Deng, D., Zhou, Q., Fan, L.: Intelligent secure communication for Internet of Things with statistical channel state information of attacker. IEEE Access **7**, 144481–144488 (2019). https://doi.org/10.1109/ACCESS.2019.2945060
85. Xiao, L., Wan, X., Lu, X., Zhang, Y., Wu, D.: IoT security techniques based on machine learning: how do IoT devices use AI to enhance security? IEEE Signal Process. Mag. **35**(5), 41–49 (2018). https://doi.org/10.1109/MSP.2018.2825478
86. Young, R., Fallon, S., Jacob, P.: An architecture for intelligent data processing on IoT edge devices. In: Proceedings - 2017 UKSim-AMSS 19th International Conference on Modelling and Simulation, UKSim 2017, pp. 227–232 (2018). https://doi.org/10.1109/UKSim.2017.19
87. Zhang, H., Li, J., Wen, B., Xun, Y., Liu, J.: Connecting intelligent things in smart hospitals using NB-IoT. IEEE Internet Things J. **5**(3), 1550–1560 (2018). https://doi.org/10.1109/JIOT.2018.2792423
88. Zhang, H., Zhang, Q., Liu, J., Guo, H.: Fault detection and repairing for intelligent connected vehicles based on dynamic Bayesian network model. IEEE Internet Things J. **5**(4), 2431–2440 (2018). https://doi.org/10.1109/JIOT.2018.2844287

Detection and Fault Prediction in Electrolytic Capacitors Using Artificial Neural Networks

Acélio L. Mesquita[1]([⊠]), Vandilberto P. Pinto[2]([⊠]), and Leonardo R. Rodrigues[3]([⊠])

[1] Federal University of Ceará - UFC, Sobral, Brazil
`acelioucolie@hotmail.com`
[2] University of International Integration of the Afro-Brazilian Lusophony - UNILAB,
Redenção, Brazil
`vandilberto@unilab.edu.br`, `vandilberto@ufc.br`
[3] Institute of Aeronautics and Space - IAE, São José dos Campos, Brazil
`leonardolrr2@fab.mil.br`

Abstract. Capacitors are electronic components that present a considerable variation in their characteristics during their useful life. After being submitted to several charge/discharge cycles, capacitors present losses in capacitance values and operate differently from the nominal characteristics. PHM (Prognostics and Health Monitoring) techniques can be used to monitor the evolution of a capacitor health condition and to predict its RUL (Remaining Useful Life). This paper uses artificial neural networks to monitor the degradation index of capacitors and predict the corresponding RUL. Different neural network architectures are investigated: MLP (Multilayer Perceptron), RBF (Radial Basis Function), and ELM (Extreme Learning Machine). The performances of the different architectures are compared in terms of the coefficient of determination (R^2) and the Mean Squared Error (MSE). The accuracy of RUL predictions are compared based on the Relative Accuracy (RA) indicator, which is a performance indicator proposed in the literature to evaluate PHM algorithms.

Keywords: Capacitors · Artificial neural networks · Prognostics · Health monitoring · Remaining useful life

1 Introduction

The use of electronic modules for the execution of several functionalities in systems has shown a continuous growth in recent years (Siltala and Tuokko 2009). Electronic modules have also been used to implement critical functions in systems (Lauer et al. 2013). As a result, the need arises to monitor the degradation level of electronic components, and to estimate the probable time of failure (Vichare and Pecht 2006). The failures in electronic components can be caused by a number of factors such as temperature variations, vibration, humidity, current peaks, voltage surges, among others. (FIDES Group 2004).

One way to monitor the degradation of electronic components is through the use of Prognostics and Health Monitoring (PHM) techniques, which evaluate the degradation

© Springer Nature Switzerland AG 2021
M. Botto-Tobar et al. (Eds.): ICAT 2020, CCIS 1388, pp. 287–298, 2021.
https://doi.org/10.1007/978-3-030-71503-8_22

index and estimate the remaining useful life (RUL) of electronic components from statistical data, information on the physics of system failure modes, and sensor measurements (Roemer et al. 2005).

According to Bizarria (2009), systems that do not use the PHM concept tend to waste equipment life. Proper use of PHM techniques has the following advantages:

- Reduction in maintenance, logistics, inventory, and operation costs;
- Reduction in the number of unscheduled stops (corrective maintenance);
- Increased system reliability;
- Maximization of equipment useful life.

Electronic systems have numerous components that are of vital importance for their proper operation. Among them are the capacitors, which can present changes in their capacitance over time due to the charge and discharge cycles. According to the norm MIL-C-62F (2008), the failure of a capacitor is declared when its internal resistance increases between 280 and 300% of the initial value, or when its capacitance has a reduction of 20% in its nominal value. With these values, it is possible to define the threshold values for the capacitor wear to perform its replacement. PHM techniques have been used in the area of power systems, as in the study proposed by Kulkarni et al. (2009), which addresses the degradation of capacitors in DC-DC converters. In another study, Marcos et al. (2014) use monitoring techniques to diagnose failures in hydraulic generating units with the aid of diffuse logic. In Soualhi et al. (2018), the authors use different signal processing techniques to use PHM strategies applied to the monitoring of bearings and gearboxes in industrial components. In the study proposed by Alozie et al. (2019), a model-based prognostic framework is applied to aircraft gas turbines.

Böhm (2017) used a classification strategy by means of an artificial neural network and a Support Vector Machine (SVM) to forecast the remaining useful life for an application in the railway industry. Corroborating with the previous study, Costa (2019) stated that neural networks are able to obtain satisfactory results in monitoring systems health. With the use of neural networks and PHM techniques, in Yang et al. (2018) used extreme learning machine to calculate the remaining useful life in lithium batteries.

In Duong and Raghavan (2017), the author used a Kalman filter to calculate the remaining useful life of systems subject to various types of degradation. Rodrigues et al. (2020) used particle filter heuristic to predict the RUL of lithium batteries with the presence of various degradation factors. For monitoring the condition of the equipment, Bhargava (2018) used the accelerated aging due to temperature stress to analyze the conditions of the aluminum electrolytic capacitor.

The use of PHM techniques is of vital importance for electronic systems and, through these techniques, the degradation level of components can be monitored to predict their remaining useful life. Thus, this paper aims to apply different architectures of artificial neural networks to predict the behavior of capacitor degradation up to the failure threshold, in addition to comparing the performance obtained by each of the different architectures considered.

The remaining sections of this paper are organized as described below. Section 2 presents the theoretical foundations of the different artificial neural network architectures considered in the work. Section 3 describes the performance indicators considered. In

Sect. 4, the results obtained in the numerical experiments are presented and discussed. The conclusions of the work are presented in Sect. 5.

2 Artificial Neural Networks

In this section, the principles of the neural network architectures are described, in addition to the validation technique used in the experiments.

2.1 Multilayer Perceptron (MLP)

Many methods can be used to predict failures. However, one of the most frequently used technique is the artificial neural networks. A commonly used neural network architecture is the Multilayer Perceptron (MLP), which uses the technique of learning backpropagation of the error (back-propagation). Figure 1 schematically illustrates an MLP neural network, with the input layer, the hidden layer, and the output layer.

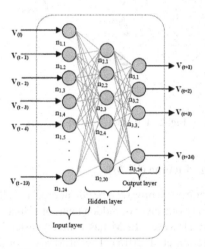

Fig. 1. Layout of an MLP network.

The neurons in the network communicate with each other through connections similar to biological synapses. They are able to analyze and learn non-linear relationships that exist between an input and an output. The error back propagation equation is defined in (1).

$$u_j(n) = \sum_{i=1}^{p} w_{ij}(n) \cdot y_j(n) \tag{1}$$

where w_{ij} are the weights of neurons, and y_j is the network output, computed according to (2).

$$y_j(n) = \varphi(u_j(n) - \theta_j(n)) \tag{2}$$

where $\phi(\cdot)$ is the activation function. In the present work, the sigmoid function is used.

2.2 Radial Basis Function (RBF)

As in MLP, the RBF network also uses techniques for learning how to propagate the error. However, the RBF network consists, in most cases, of a single hidden layer and an output layer, differently from the MLP that can contain several hidden layers (Mota et al. 2011).

Figure 2 shows a scheme that represents an RBF network. It is possible to observe the similarity between the RBF and the MLP networks. However, the RBF network has a radial base function as the activation function of the hidden layer, and in the output layer it uses linear activation functions (Mota et al. 2011).

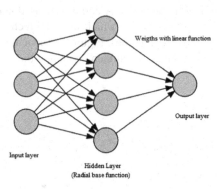

Fig. 2. Layout of an RBF network.

2.3 Extreme Learning Machine (ELM)

The ELM (Extreme Learning Machine) can be considered a feedforward neural network, without feedback, with only one layer of hidden neurons (Huang et al. 2006). ELM, like RBF, is similar to MLP. However, ELM has a much faster learning phase than the previous networks (Mesquita et al. 2015). The ELM also consists of an input layer, a hidden layer, and an output layer. Figure 3 illustrates the structure of an ELM.

The ELM is a neural network with random weights w and biases b in the hidden layer. The network output is calculated using (3).

$$\sum_{i=1}^{L} \beta_i \varphi(w_i, b_i, x_j) = t_j \tag{3}$$

where $\phi(\cdot)$ is the activation function.

Equation (3) can be represented in a matrix form, as presented in (4).

$$H\varphi = T \tag{4}$$

where:

$$H = \begin{pmatrix} G(w_1, b_1, x_1) & \dots & G(w_L, b_L, x_L) \\ \vdots & \ddots & \vdots \\ G(w_1, b_1, x_n) & \cdots & G(w_L, b_L, x_n) \end{pmatrix}_{N \times L} \tag{5}$$

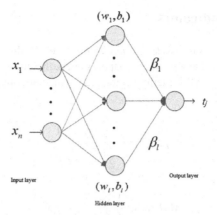

Fig. 3. Layout of an ELM network.

Then the output weight is calculated using (6).

$$\beta = H^{+}T \qquad (6)$$

Thus, it can be seen that compared to traditional networks, ELM does not contain interaction steps, which considerably reduces the computational complexity of the training process (Yang et al. 2018).

2.4 Leave-One-Out (LOO) Cross Validation Technique

The Leave-One-Out (LOO) technique consists of performing training with data and then performing the test with data that have not been used. The process is repeated, leaving each data out of the training. With leave-one-out, more consistent results can be obtained, since the technique uses almost the entire database, especially when the database is considered large (Cunha 2019). This technique has a higher computational cost, but it is indicated for situations in which there is little data to be analyzed.

2.5 Remaining Useful Life - RUL

In order to calculate the RUL, it is necessary to identify the expected End of Life (EOL) of the equipment, which is based on the failure threshold defined in (7) (Saxena et al. 2010).

$$RUL(t_p) = t_{EOL} - t_p. \qquad (7)$$

where t_{EOL} is the predicted time of failure, and t_p is the current prediction instant.

As time is a continuous variable, a linear interpolation is made to identify the time of t_{EOL}, which is defined by the moment when the degradation index reaches the failure threshold.

3 Performance Indicators

Several methods are used to assess the performance of predictions, although none is considered the standard method. In this paper, the coefficient of determination R^2 and the Mean Squared Error - MSE method were used, which are obtained from (8) and (9), respectively.

$$R^2 = 1 - \frac{\sum (y_i - \hat{y})}{\sum (y_i - \bar{y})^2} \tag{8}$$

$$MSE(i) = \frac{1}{L} \sum_{l=1}^{L} (\hat{y}_i - y_i)^2 \tag{9}$$

where y_i are the values of the observed data, $\bar{y}$ is the average of the observed data, $\hat{y}$ are the data estimated by the model, and L is the number of points observed.

In (8), a perfect forecast is obtained when R^2 it is equal to 1 (Bitencourt 2015). In (9), a perfect result is obtained when the indicator is equal to zero.

To evaluate the performance of the different network architectures in the RUL forecast, the Relative Accuracy - RA metric is used, defined in (10) (Saxena et al. 2010).

$$RA = 100(1 - \frac{|RUL * -RUL'|}{RUL*}) \tag{10}$$

The RA metric allows an evaluation of the percentage precision in relation to the value of the true RUL (RUL*). RA values of 100 represent perfect accuracy.

4 Results and Discussions

For the application of the algorithms, degradation data from electrolytic capacitors available in the NASA repository (Celaya et al. 2012) were used. This database contains data series that describe the evolution of the degradation index of six capacitors, as illustrated in Fig. 4.

In order to monitor the capacitors' health, they were subjected to accelerated aging with the use of a 10 V voltage stress between 0 and 196 h. The capacitors used in the study had a nominal capacitance of 2200 μF.

The prognostic methodology presented in this work is based on the use of artificial neural networks. All simulations were performed using the Matlab® software. The MLP and ELM networks were trained ten times, the best results will be presented.

The first 55% of the data was used as input and the remaining 45% as targets. The input data represents the accelerated aging of the capacitors during 116 h of operation, and the targets represent the values up to 196 h of operation. Both the MLP and the ELM networks used nine neurons, and for training the MLP network, 1,500 epoch times and 1,000 validations were used.

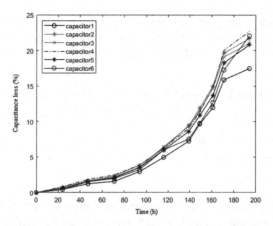

Fig. 4. Capacitor degradation data over time (h).

For a better evaluation of which neural network architecture obtained the best result, Tables 1, 2, and 3 are presented. These tables contain the computed values for the indicators R^2 and MSE for the ELM, RBF, and MLP networks, respectively. Figures 5, 6, and 7 show the best results obtained with the ELM, RBF, and MLP networks, respectively.

Analyzing Table 1, it can be seen that the best result obtained with the ELM network occurred with data from capacitor 5, which presented an R^2 coefficient equal to 0.998 and an MSE of 0.035. Figure 5 shows that the result contained in the prediction zone has a satisfactory result, since the ELM network is able to follow the real model of capacitor degradation within the 95% confidence range reaching the failure threshold almost at the same time as the real model. As capacitor 1 has not exceeded the fault threshold, it is impossible to calculate the RUL using (7) and the RA using (10) for this capacitor.

Table 1. ELM network performance indicators.

Capacitor 1		Capacitor 2		Capacitor 3		Capacitor 4		Capacitor 5		Capacitor 6	
R^2	MSE	R^2	MSE	R^2	MSE	R^2	MSE	R^2	MSE	R^2	MSE
0,562	6,294	0,996	0,091	0,830	3,305	0,957	1,133	0,998	0,039	0,987	0,349
0,740	3,745	0,994	0,124	0,795	3,983	0,956	1,151	0,998	0,035	0,990	0,276
0,113	12,745	0,997	0,075	0,640	6,990	0,940	1,157	0,998	0,044	0,987	0,345
0,831	2,435	0,995	0,106	0,605	7,682	0,952	1,264	0,998	0,042	0,987	0,345
0,850	2,151	0,995	0,108	0,847	2,982	0,950	1,304	0,998	0,058	0,988	0,338
0,922	1,116	0,994	0,126	0,844	3,027	0,944	1,463	0,997	0,100	0,989	0,298
0,767	3,344	0,995	0,115	0,974	0,564	0,942	1,533	0,995	0,061	0,988	0,339
0,832	2,411	0,995	0,096	0,987	0,256	0,954	1,205	0,997	0,067	0,988	0,325
0,724	3,971	0,995	0,112	0,952	0,929	0,956	1,162	0,997	0,063	0,988	0,336
0,924	1,086	0,995	0,109	0,797	3,948	0,960	1,042	0,997	0,063	0,989	0,309

In Table 2, it can be seen that the best result obtained with the RBF network occurred with data from capacitor 2, which presented an R^2 coefficient equal to 0.999 and an MSE of 0.029. Figure 6 shows this result following a 95% confidence interval.

Table 2. Performance indicators of the RBF network.

Capacitor 1		Capacitor 2		Capacitor 3		Capacitor 4		Capacitor 5		Capacitor 6	
R^2	MSE	R^2	MSE	R^2	MSE	R^2	MSE	R^2	MSE	R^2	MSE
−3,480	64,387	0,999	0,029	0,955	0,880	0,996	0,107	0,996	0,077	0,992	0,210

The results presented in Table 3 show that the best result obtained with the MLP network occurred with data from capacitor 5, presenting an R^2 coefficient equal to 0.998 and an MSE equal to 0.046. Figure 7 illustrates the result obtained from the simulation with a 95% confidence interval.

Table 3. MLP network performance indicators.

Capacitor 1		Capacitor 2		Capacitor 3		Capacitor 4		Capacitor 5		Capacitor 6	
R^2	MSE	R^2	MSE	R^2	MSE	R^2	MSE	R^2	MSE	R^2	MSE
0,564	6,263	0,994	0,132	0,951	0,947	0,978	0,583	0,977	0,473	0,929	1,939
0,613	5,569	0,993	0,153	0,991	0,170	0,985	0,392	0,987	0,267	0,957	1,167
0,664	4,834	0,985	0,313	0,990	0,194	0,987	0,357	0,998	0,046	0,950	1,378
0,461	7,752	0,632	7,753	0,996	0,078	0,985	0,387	0,978	0,443	0,984	0,444
0,838	2,328	0,978	0,463	0,390	11,869	0,971	0,771	0,990	0,211	0,970	0,814
0,744	3,680	0,989	0,229	0,975	0,480	0,985	0,397	0,966	0,700	0,932	1,859
0,825	2,511	0,989	0,223	0,947	1,029	0,992	0,205	0,998	0,050	0,946	1,484
0,339	9,503	0,934	1,388	0,989	0,225	0,991	0,248	0,958	0,861	0,928	1,977
0,607	5,643	0,978	0,460	0,998	0,458	0,959	1,092	0,992	0,169	0,840	4,355
0,749	3,603	0,986	0,294	0,991	0,182	0,933	1,775	0,995	0,106	0,958	1,140

Table 4 shows the estimated RUL values for each network architecture. For each of capacitors 2 to 6, the actual RUL value (RUL*) is also shown in Table 4. Table 5 shows the values of the RA indicator computed for the different network architectures in each of the capacitors from 2 to 6, according to (10).

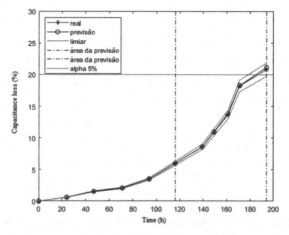

Fig. 5. Best result obtained with the ELM network for capacitor 5.

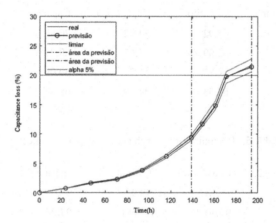

Fig. 6. Best result obtained with the RBF network for capacitor 2.

Through the results presented in Tables 4 and 5, it is possible to observe how much life remains and the forecast reliability of each capacitor. All the architectures considered in the experiments had an RA indicator above 94, which shows that they all presented satisfactory performance. The ELM network presented the best index only for capacitor 4, while the other architectures presented the best performance index for two capacitors each. If we compute the average index of each architecture considering all capacitors, the MLP network presented the best index (97.43). The best index considering only one capacitor was obtained with the ELM network for capacitor 4 (99.91).

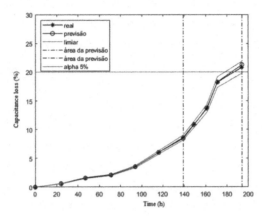

Fig. 7. Best result obtained with the MLP network for capacitor 5.

Table 4. Capacitor RUL estimates.

	Capacitor 2	Capacitor 3	Capacitor 4	Capacitor 5	Capacitor 6
RUL*	59,04	65,92	54,92	70,86	68,24
ELM	60,84	62,69	54,87	68,77	72,14
RBF	58,10	62,23	56,79	69,09	69,89
MLP	59,70	67,53	54,39	68,43	71,58

Table 5. RA indicator for each neural network architecture.

	Capacitor 2	Capacitor 3	Capacitor 4	Capacitor 5	Capacitor 6
ELM	96,95	95,10	**99,91**	97,05	94,28
RBF	98,41	94,40	96,60	**97,50**	**97,58**
MLP	**98,88**	**97,56**	99,03	96,57	95,11

5 Conclusions

The present paper presented a study on the application of different artificial neural network architectures to monitor the evolution of the degradation index and predict the remaining useful life of electrolytic capacitors. Data available on a public NASA data repository were used. Different network architectures were considered: MLP (Multilayer Perceptron), RBF (Radial Basis Function), and ELM (Extreme Learning Machine). The performance of the networks was compared in terms of the coefficient of determination R^2 and the Mean Squared Error (MSE). The accuracy of the RUL estimates were quantified by the RA (Relative Accuracy) index, which is a performance indicator proposed in the literature specifically for PHM algorithms.

Through the analysis of the results it was possible to observe that the RBF network presented a better performance in terms of both the R^2 and MSE indicators, presenting for these indices the values 0.999 and 0.029, respectively. For capacitor 1, whose data series had many outliers, the networks showed a poor performance.

The calculation of the RA index made it possible to compare the different architectures in terms of the RUL predictions. All the architectures showed good results for capacitors from 2 to 6. The ELM network obtained the best index for a single capacitor (99.91 for capacitor 4), while the MLP network had the best average index (97.43), which demonstrates the effectiveness of neural networks for PHM studies.

As a future work, we intend to implement other forecasting techniques such as the Gaussian process regression - GPR for a comparison with the results obtained with artificial neural networks.

Acknowledgments. The authors would like to acknowledge the Universidade Federal do Ceará -Campus de Sobral, the Fundação Cearense de Apoio ao Desenvolvimento Científico e Tecnológico - FUNCAP (BP3-0139-00241.01.00/18 Edital BPI 03/2018), and the Conselho Nacional de Desenvolvimento Científico e Tecnológico - CNPq (grant 423023/2018-7).

References

Alozie, O., Li, Y.-G., Wu, X., Shong, X., Ren, W.: An adaptive model-based framework for prognosis of gas path faults in aircraft gas turbine engines. Int. J. Prognostics Health Manag. **10**(2), 1–2 (2019)

Bhargava, C., Banga, V.K., Singh, Y.: Condition monitoring of aluminium electrolytic capacitors using accelerated life testing: a comparison. Int. J. Qual. Reliab. Manag. **35**(8), 1671–1682 (2018). https://doi.org/10.1108/IJQRM-06-2017-0115

Bitencourt, D.B.: Estratégias de previsão de geração de energia eólica utilizando redes neurais artificiais. Dissertação de Mestrado em Engenharia Elétrica, Universidade Federal de Sergipe, São Cristóvão, 86 f. (2015)

Bizzarria, C.O.: Prognóstico de falhas no atuador do leme da aeronave EMBRAER-190. Dissertação de Mestrado em Engenharia Aeronáutica, Instituto Tecnológico de Aeronáutica, São José dos Campos, 98f. (2009)

Böhm, T.: Remaining useful life prediction for railway switch engines using classification techniques. Int. J. Prognostics Helath Manag. **8**(Sp7), 1–5 (2017)

Celaya, J., Kulkarni, C., Biswas, G., Goebel, K.: Towards a model-based prognostics methodology for electrolytic capacitors: a case study based on electrical overstree accelerated aging. Int. J. Prognostics Health Manag. **3**(2), 1–9 (2012)

Costa, E.F.: Predição da descarga e capacidade de baterias li-íon utilizadas em vants. Dissertação de Mestrado em Engenharia Elétrica e da Computação, Universidade Federal do Ceará, Sobral, 95f. (2019)

Cunha, J.P.Z.: Um estudo comparativo das técnicas de validação cruzada aplicadas a modelos mistos. Dissertação de Mestrado em Engenharia Estatística, Universidade de São Paulo, 59 f. (2019)

Duong, P.L.T., Raghavan, N.: A metaheuristic approach to remaining useful life estimation of systems subject to multiple degradation mechanisms. In: 2017 IEEE International Conference on Prognostics and Health Management, ICPHM 2017, pp. 227–233 (2017). https://doi.org/10.1109/ICPHM.2017.7998333

FIDES Group: A Reliability Methodology for Electronic Systems. FIDES Guide Issue A (2004)

Huang, G.-B., Zhu, Q.-Y., Siew, C.-K.: Extreme learning machine: theory and applications. Neurocomputing **70**(1–3), 489–501 (2006). https://doi.org/10.1016/j.neucom.2005.12.126

Kulkarni, C.S., Biswas, G., Koutsoukos, X.: A prognosis case study for electrolytic capacitor degradation in DC-DC converters. In: Annual Conference of the Prognostics and Health Management Society, San Diego, pp. 1–10 (2009)

Lauer, M., Mullins, J., Yeddes, M.: Cost optimization strategy for iterative integration of multicritical functions in IMA and TTEthernet architecture. In: 2013 IEEE 37th Annual Computer Software and Applications Conference Workshops, Japan, pp. 139–144 (2013). https://doi.org/10.1109/COMPSACW.2013.16.

Marcos, I.P.M., Álvares, A.J., Abadia, M.R.U.: Metodologia para diagnóstico de falhas em unidades geradoras hidráulicas usando conceitos de lógica difusa. In: Congresso Nacional de Engenharia Mecânica (CONEM), Uberlândia, pp. 1–10 (2014)

Mesquita, D.P.P., Gomes, J.P.P., Rodrigues, L.R., Galvão, R.K.H.: Pruning extreme learning machines using the successive projections algorithm. IEEE Lat. Am. Trans. **13**(12), 3974–3979 (2015). https://doi.org/10.1109/TLA.2015.7404935

MIL-C-62F: General specification for capacitors, fixed, electrolytic (dc. aluminum, dry electrolyte, polarized). Military Specification, Department of Defense (2008)

Mota, J.F., Siqueira, P.H., Souza, L.V., Vitor, A.: Uma rede neural de base radial baseada em computação evolucionária. In: XXXIII Congresso Íbero Latino Americano de Métodos Computacionais em Engenharia (CILAMCE), Ouro Preto, pp. 1–15 (2011)

Rodrigues, L.R., Coelho, D.B.P., Gomes, J.P.P.: A hybrid TLBO-particle filter algorithm applied to remaining useful life prediction in the presence of multiple degradation factors. In: IEEE Congress on Evolutionary Computation, CEC 2020 - Conference Proceedings (2020). https://doi.org/10.1109/CEC48606.2020.9185898

Roemer, M.J., Byington, C.S., Kacprzynski, G.J., Vachtsevanos, G.: An overview of selected prognostic technologies with reference to an integrated PHM architecture. In: Proceedings of the First International Forum on Integrated System Health Engineering and Management in Aerospace, Big Sky, pp. 3941–3947 (2005)

Saxena, A., Celaya, J., Saha, B., Saha, S., Goebel, K.: Metrics for offline evaluation of prognostic performance. Int. J. Prognostics Health Manag. **1**(1), 1–20 (2010)

Siltala, N., Tuokko, R.: Use of electronic module descriptions for modular and reconfigurable assembly systems. In: Proceedings of the 2009 IEEE International Symposium on Assembly and Manufacturing, Suwon, pp. 214–219 (2009). https://doi.org/10.1109/ISAM.2009.5376903

Soualhi, A., Hawwari, Y., Medjaher, K., Clerc, G., Hubert, R., Guillet, F.: PHM survey: implementation of signal processing methods for monitoring bearings and gearboxes. Int. J. Prognostics Health Manag. **9**(2), 14 (2018)

Vichare, N.M., Pecht, M.G.: Prognostics and health management of electronics. IEEE Trans. Compon. Packag. Technol. **29**(1), 222–229 (2006). https://doi.org/10.1109/TCAPT.2006.870387

Yang, J., Peng, Z., Wang, H., Yuan, H., Wu, L.: The remaining useful life estimation of lithium-ion battery based on improved extreme learning machine algorithm. Int. J. Electrochem. Sci. **13**(5), 4991–5004 (2018)

Constraint Programming
for the Pandemic in Peru

Willy Ugarte$^{(\boxtimes)}$ ⓘ

Universidad Peruana de Ciencias Aplicadas (UPC), Lima, Peru
willy.ugarte@upc.pe

Abstract. Currently, the world requires techniques that match infected people and hospital beds together given various criteria such as the severity of infection, patient location, hospital capacity, etc. Deep Learning might seems to be a perfect fit for this: various configurations from a broad range of parameters that need to be reduced to a few solutions. But, this models require to be trained, hence the need for historical data on previous cases leading to a waste of time would in cleaning and consolidating a dataset and lengthy training sessions need to be performed with a variety of architectures.

Nevertheless, formulating this problem as a Constraint Satisfaction Problem (CSP), the aforementioned downsides will not be present while still optimal results, and without the need for any historical data. In this paper, a CSP model is used to search for the best distribution of COVID-19 patients with a severity of patients requiring hospitalization and patients requiring ICU beds, in hospitals in a part of Lima.

Keywords: CSP · Pandemic · CoViD · Constraint programming

1 Introduction

Many real-life problems are solved using programming algorithms, in which the user's requirements are met. For problems where it is required to obtain the optimal result(s), various techniques are used (e.g., Branch-and-bound, local search, ...). Nevertheless, when the user requires to express its preferences into the model, the best technique to apply is *Constraint Programming*. Which, as its name says, it is built based on constraints that are taken into account into the algorithm functioning. These constraints are validating rules that enable to prune the search space and furthermore to find solutions to given problems, such as ordering the guests of a wedding or obtaining the least time from a train route.

COVID-19 is an infectious disease caused due to the SARS-CoV-2 virus that presents symptoms similar to other respiratory diseases like influenza, but due to the lack of specific treatment to combat the virus, the death rate of the virus is around 0.5% to 1%[1]. At the end of May 2020, around 6 millions (resp. more

---

[1] https://www.who.int/news-room/commentaries/detail/estimating-mortality-from-covid-19.

© Springer Nature Switzerland AG 2021
M. Botto-Tobar et al. (Eds.): ICAT 2020, CCIS 1388, pp. 299–311, 2021.
https://doi.org/10.1007/978-3-030-71503-8_23

than 150 thousand) cases have been confirmed and almost 400 thousand (resp. around 4 thousand) deaths worldwide[2] (resp. for Peru[3]).

These numbers are rapidly increasing, for instance, one month later, at the end of June 2020, there are around 10 millions (resp. almost 300 thousand) cases have been confirmed and more than 500 thousand (resp. around 10 thousand) deaths worldwide (See Footnote 2) (resp. for Peru (See Footnote 3)).

Due to this situation, various approaches using artificial intelligence have been proposed to tackle problems issued from this pandemic. Most of these approaches aim to diagnosis and treatment [1], infection detection [14,24], image processing [15] and smart quarantine [12]. But, they mainly focus on making predictions with machine learning techniques.

Most of predictive models (e.g., ANN, Bayesian networks, decision trees, ...) require treating data from all kinds of sources, then a lot of training and fine tuning to be efficient. Since, there is under-reporting[4], most of these require error measurement [2] which may lead them to disproofs. Furthermore, other problems cannot be tackled directly by predictive models either by the lack (or degradation) of historical data (hence it requires a lot pre-processing or tackling under-reporting) or a variety of architectures would need to be tested with lengthy training sessions.

Nowadays, one of the main global problems is **matching infected people and hospitals**, in other words hospitals must be organized with the aim of giving treatment to most infected people by assigning beds to each infected person. This problem is known as *patient bed assignment problem*, this is finding a mapping between patients who require critical medical assistance and available beds [17].

When the demand for these resources is less than the resources available, this problem is trivial. Nevertheless, when hospitals are crowded, this assignment problem become a very complex task, which is exactly the case for this pandemic. For such assignment, many criteria must be taken into account [7] (e.g., the severity of the disease, the age and location of the patient, the capacity and equipment of the hospital, ...).

Our contribution are as follows:

- Formulating the problem of hospitals' beds assignments for CoVid infected patients as a Constraint Satisfaction Problem (CSP). The CSP model presented here is easy to understand and by using a CP toolkit[5] yields an optimal result with real data of infected people in Lima, Peru.
- This CSP model can be used as a basis on which additional constraints can be imposed, covering variants of bed assignment problem that might arise naturally in practical applications, but which cannot be accommodated easily by existing algorithms.

---

[2] COVID-19 Dashboard by John Hopkins University - https://bit.ly/3hRyIbg.
[3] Open Data Peru - https://bit.ly/309k0GI.
[4] Forbes Under-reporting of COVID-19 Deaths - https://bit.ly/3hSyhhd.
[5] OR-tools - https://developers.google.com/optimization.

- Discussing the results, for showing that CSPs are a straightforward paradigm that do not require training a model nor gathering any historical data and are an elegant way to solve this kind of problem.

This paper is organized as follows: Sect. 2 shows the background we describe all the main topics used for our proposal. Section 3 shows the description of our CSP model and our optimization criterion. Section 4 shows experiments, we demonstrate our best results and the feasibility of our approach. Section 5 shows the related works part, we analyze the most important works on the state of the art. Finally, Sect. 6 in the conclusion we analyze the results of the experimentation process.

2   Material

Nowadays, many countries face the collapsing of their health systems, in particular their bed capacity due to lack of coordination and other factors. For third world countries, like Peru[6], this situation is accentuating since their health systems were under-prepared and under-funded before the pandemic.

2.1   Problem Statement

Taking into consideration the current situation, it is essential to organize hospitals with the aim of giving treatment to most of the (seriously) infected people in the context of the COVID-19 pandemic. Assigning infected people to hospitals is not a trivial problem, since it requires satisfying various criteria. Like the capacity and equipment of the hospitals (i.e., Number of beds in each hospital), the severity of the disease (i.e., the state of infection of the patient), the location of the (possible) patient and the location of the hospitals.

Given the aforementioned criteria, it is required that as many (severely) infected people as possible be assigned to hospital beds. This problem can be simplified to two principles:

1. Infected or sick people should be assigned to the nearest hospital.
2. Sick people with a severe condition should be assigned earlier than the rest.

2.2   Constraint Programming

Definition 1 (Constraint Satisfaction Problem (CSP) [5,18]). *A Constraint Satisfaction Problem (CSP) $P = (\mathcal{X}, \mathcal{D}, \mathcal{C})$ is defined as:*

- *a finite set of variables $\mathcal{X} = \{x_1, x_2, \ldots, x_k\}$,*
- *a set of domains $\mathcal{D}$, mapping every variable $x_i \in \mathcal{X}$ to a set of values $D(x_i)$,*
- *a finite set of constraints $\mathcal{C}$.*

---

[6] El Comercio - https://bit.ly/2Pd8bcs.

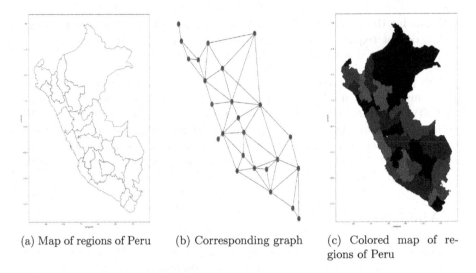

(a) Map of regions of Peru   (b) Corresponding graph   (c) Colored map of regions of Peru

Fig. 1. Map of regions of Peru (Color figure online)

The problem is to find a mapping from variables to values such that each variable x_i is mapped to a value in its domain $D(x_i)$ and such that all constraints of C are satisfied. This mapping is called a solution to the CSP.

Example 1 (Graph Coloring). *Given a graph $G = (V, E)$, Graph Coloring consists in coloring the vertices (v_i) of G such that no two adjacent vertices are of the same color. This problem can be modeled as a CSP (see Definition 1) as:*

- *$\mathcal{X} = \{c_1, c_2, \ldots, c_k\}$, where c_i is the color variable for each node v_i in G.*
- *$\mathcal{D} = \{1, 2, \ldots, m\}$, where each number represents a label for a color (e.g., 1 is blue, 2 is red, ...).*
- *$\mathcal{C} = \{c_i \neq c_j, \forall(i, j) \in E\}$, where each inequality ensures having no two adjacent vertices are of the same color.*

Figure 1a shows map of Peru distributed by regions. Figure 1b shows how this map can be represented by a graph. Figure 1c shows the colored map corresponding to the Graph Coloring of 25 regions.

Definition 2 (Constraint Optimization Problem (COP) [10,18]). *A Constraint Optimization Problem (COP) $P' = P \cup \{f\}$ where P is a CSP (see Definition 1) and f is an objective function to be optimized (either maximized or minimized).*

The problem is, besides finding mappings from variables to values, is to optimize (either maximize or minimize) these mapping with the purpose of finding the optimal mapping w.r.t an objective function f.

Example 2 *Continuing the Example 1. Let* $G = (V, E)$ *a graph, the COP (see Definition 2) for Graph Coloring* $P' = P \cup \{f\}$ *is defined as* $P = (\mathcal{X} = \{c_1, c_2, \ldots, c_k\}, \mathcal{D} = \{1, 2, \ldots, m\}, \mathcal{C} = \{c_i \neq c_j, \forall(i,j) \in E\})$ *and* $f = number\ of\ colors.$

Figure 1c shows the Graph Coloring of 25 regions with only 4 colors. This result is optimal since, it cannot be done with fewer colors.

3   Method

Modeling our problem as a CSP requires to define a triplet $(\mathcal{X}, \mathcal{D}, \mathcal{C})$ that will be treated and solved by a solver.

Variables: Let H a set of hospitals, B_i the set of beds in hospital i and P be the set of patients. The set of variables is defined as:

$$x_{ijk} \in \{0, 1\} \text{ where } (i, j, k) \in H \times B_i \times P \tag{1}$$

If in the hospital i, the bed j is taken by the person k then $x_{ijk} = 1$. In order to associate each bed of an hospital to an ill person, the goal is to find a set of variables that satisfies all of our constraints.

Constraints: Constraints are essential to a CSP model since they define whether a variable assignment is possible or the problem cannot be solved.

The core rules that hospitals must respect for this problem are:

– **There must be at most a single person assigned to each bed.** This can be modeled as:

$$\forall i \in H, \forall j \in B_i, \sum_{k \in P} x_{ijk} \leq 1 \tag{2}$$

– **There must be at most a single bed assigned to every person.** This can be modeled as:

$$\forall k \in P, \sum_{i \in H} \sum_{j \in B_j} x_{ijk} \leq 1 \tag{3}$$

Therefore, the CSP $P_{pandemic} = (\mathcal{X}, \mathcal{D}, \mathcal{C})$ for this problem is defined as:

– $\mathcal{X} = \{x_{ijk}\}$ where $(i, j, k) \in H \times B_i \times P$,
– $\mathcal{D} = \{0, 1\}$ for all variables
– $\mathcal{C} = \{\forall i \in H, \forall j \in B_i, \sum_{k \in P} x_{ijk} \leq 1\} \cup \{\forall k \in P, \sum_{i \in H} \sum_{j \in B_j} x_{ijk} \leq 1\}.$

Preferences: Also known as *soft constraints* [6], preferences are highly desired, in other words, a solution to this problem must try to satisfy them as much as possible, yet they are not essential to find a solution. Some of these rules are:

- Ideally, every sick person should have access to a hospital bed if necessary, but this is not realistic. This can be modeled as:

$$\max_{sol} \sum_{i \in H} \sum_{j \in B_i} \sum_{k \in P} x_{ijk} \qquad (4)$$

- If possible, everyone should be treated at the closest health facility. This can be modeled as:

$$\min_{sol} \sum_{i \in H} \sum_{j \in B_i} \sum_{k \in P} (x_{ijk} \times distance(i,k)) \qquad (5)$$

where $distance(i,j)$ is the distance from hospital i from patient k.
- Mostly, severe cases should be prioritized when there are not enough beds. This can be modeled as:

$$\max_{sol} \sum_{i \in H} \sum_{j \in B_i} \sum_{k \in P} (x_{ijk} \times severity_k) \qquad (6)$$

where $severity_k$ is the degree of severity of patient k.

Preferences are not modeled as a (in)equality, but a maximization or a minimization, since we would rather to satisfy them the most. These three preferences can be joint into a single objective function to be optimized as:

$$\max f = \max \sum_{i \in H} \sum_{j \in B_i} \sum_{k \in P} \left(x_{ijk} \times \left(1 - \frac{distance(i,k)}{\max_{dist}} + \frac{severity_k}{\max_{sev}} \right) \right) \qquad (7)$$

The objective function (7) is asking to maximize the overall patient attention. Note that if $x_{ijk} = 0$, then the person it is not taken into account for the sum. The distance $distance(i,k)$ (resp. the severity $severity_k$) must be normalized by dividing it by its corresponding maximum value $\max_{dist}$ (resp. $\max_{sev}$), thus we have $\frac{distance(i,k)}{\max_{dist}}$ (resp. $\frac{severity_k}{\max_{sev}}$). Nevertheless, the distance is negative since it should be minimal and f it's maximized.

Therefore, the COP is defined as $P'_{pandemic} = \{P_{pandemic} \cup f\}$.

4   Results

4.1   Data

In this case, two main sources of information were needed:

Table 1. List of 10 health centers

Id	District	Name	Latitude	Longitude	Number of beds		
					ICU	Regular	Total
H_1	Magdalena	Hospital de la Solidaridad	−12.092	−77.070	0	25	25
H_2	San Isidro	Clinic Ricardo Palma	−12.090	−77.017	18	142	160
H_3	San Isidro	Clinic Angloamericana	−12.106	−77.046	7	55	62
H_4	San Isidro	Clinic Internacional	−12.101	−77.035	10	79	89
H_5	Miraflores	EsSalud Suarez Angamos	−12.106	−77.055	0	25	25
H_6	Miraflores	Hospital Casimiro Ulloa	−12.128	−77.017	0	25	25
H_7	Miraflores	Hospital Central FAP	−12.103	−77.029	10	79	89
H_8	Miraflores	Clinic Delgado	−12.115	−77.033	6	47	53
H_9	Miraflores	Clinic Good Hope	−12.125	−77.033	7	55	62
H_{10}	Surquillo	INEN	−12.112	−76.998	10	79	89

Health Centers: The information on hospitals and clinics, and their geographical location were found on a map provided by PAHO and WHO[7], and obtained manually. For instance, for districts of Magdalena del Mar, San Isidro, Miraflores and Surquillo, the 10 principal health centers are listed in Table 1. In one hand, an ICU bed is a specially designed bed for the patients under the intensive care unit. On the other hand, a regular bed is a low-equipped bed designed to take care of non-severe patients.

Numbers of beds (ICU and regular ones) might changed tremendously, we based our estimations from press[8] and Ministry of Health of Peru (MINSA)[9]. Approximately, 11.23% of hospitalized people use mechanical ventilation, while 88.77% do not have such a resource.

Infections: From Health Ministry of Peru (MINSA)[10], we can establish 5 categories of severity of patients:

- **Asymptomatic** (20.2% of the people),
- **Weak symptoms** (34.7% of the people),
- **Strong symptoms** (25.2% of the people),
- **Hospitalization required** (13.8% of the people) and
- **ICU required** (6.1% of the people).

Furthermore, these proportions are confirmed by the *National Center for Epidemiology, Prevention and Control of Diseases of Peru* (CNEPCE)[11]. Therefore, the data regarding hospitals and infected people is supported by official sources.

---

[7] Cumulative covid-19 cases reported in the americas - https://bit.ly/39Tx9qV.

[8] Villasís, G. - "El Comercio" - https://bit.ly/2CVeLlq.

[9] MINSA - https://covid19.minsa.gob.pe/sala_situacional.asp.

[10] MINSA - https://bit.ly/33aSMBv.

[11] CNEPCE - https://bit.ly/3facgZm.

Geographic Location: Due to the National Law of Personal an Health Data of Peru, the National Authority of Personal Data Protection is protecting the geolocation data for infected people[12].

Lacking real information about the location of infected people, it was required to generate locations following their distribution in the risk map[13].

4.2   Experiments

Experimental Protocol: We first report an experimental study on this data (see Sect. 4.1). All experiments were conducted on a personal computer running a Linux operating system with an i5-8600 CPU core processor with a clock speed of 3.10 GHz and 16 GB of RAM. The implementation was carried out in OR-tools[14]. All source codes and data sets are publicly available at https://bit.ly/3mNIui0.

Numerical Results: Now, we report and discuss the numerical results on synthetic problems when comparing assignments of ICU beds (see Fig. 2a), Regular beds (see Fig. 2b) and a comparison between both of them (see Fig. 2c).

Figure 2a depicts a table with the average execution times for assigning ICU beds for a given number of hospitals at a given percentage of capacity. For instance, it takes 0.3 (resp. 2.9) seconds for 1 (resp. 10) hospital to assign the 10% of their capacity.

Figure 2b depicts a table with the average execution times for assigning regular beds for a given number of hospitals at a given percentage of capacity. For instance, it takes 3.6 (resp. 16.6) seconds for 1 (resp. 5) hospital to assign the 75% of their capacity.

Figure 2c depicts graphically a comparison between the times for assigning ICU beds and Regular beds, for given number of hospitals and a given percentage of their capacity. As expected assigning all beds takes much longer times (up to 5 times) than assigning only ICU beds. Nevertheless, all the experiments take seconds to obtain an optimal solution, with 20,000 registered patients.

Figures 3a and 3b show the location of 10 hospitals listed in Table 1, the location of infected people as colored points (the colors change according to the district) and the (ICU) bed assignments with color lines.

Now, two test scenarios will be described. For the first one, the equipment of the hospitals was limited to ICU beds, while in the second one, all beds are taken into account.

Scenario 1 (see Fig. 3a): For this case, only ICU beds will be considered in the hospital bed count with more than 20,000 registered patients. Ten execution tests were performed. An average execution time of 22.2 s was achieved, managing to take 680 patients in ICU beds.

---

[12] National Authority of Personal Data Protection - https://bit.ly/3ke9XY6.

[13] https://covid19.orcebot.com/mapa-riesgo.

[14] OR-tools - https://developers.google.com/optimization.

# Hospitals	% of Beds				
	10%	25%	50%	75%	100%
1	0.3	0.8	1.1	1.9	3.0
5	1.4	4.7	6.6	9.1	12.3
10	2.9	5.4	9.2	13.4	22.2

(a) Times for ICU beds (in seconds)

# Hospitals	% of Beds				
	10%	25%	50%	75%	100%
1	1.3	2.3	3.6	4.1	6.1
5	5.1	11.2	16.6	18.2	21.3
10	6.0	14.3	22.4	36.3	46.2

(b) Times for Regular beds (in seconds)

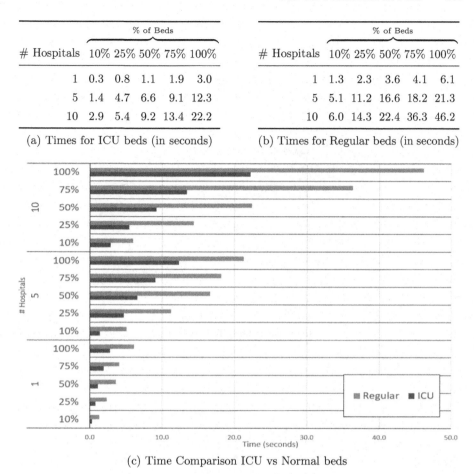

(c) Time Comparison ICU vs Normal beds

Fig. 2. Average execution time for bed assignments.

Since some hospitals do not count with ICU beds, there are no assignments for these. In Fig. 3a, we can see this for the hospital H_1 ("Hospital de la Solidaridad" in Magdalena) in the top left corner. Contrarily, H_5 ("EsSalud Suarez Angamos" in Miraflores) has various assignments.

Scenario 2 (see Fig. 3b): For this case, all beds will be considered in the hospital bed count with more than 20,000 registered patients. Ten execution tests were performed. An average execution time of 46.2 s was obtained, allowing the care of 4,010 infected people in general.

In Fig. 3b, we can see that most of the hospitals have assignments from patients nearby (e.g., red lines for hospital H_1, green lines for hospital H_6, black lines for hospital H_9, ...). Contrarily, hospitals H_3 (orange lines) and H_8 (blue

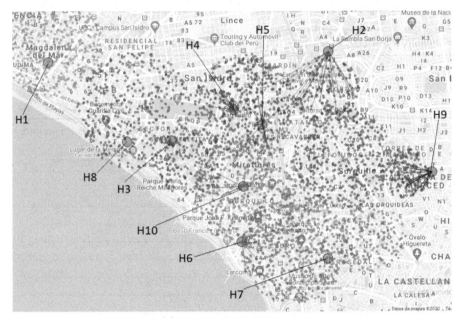

(a) Case 1: Only ICU beds.

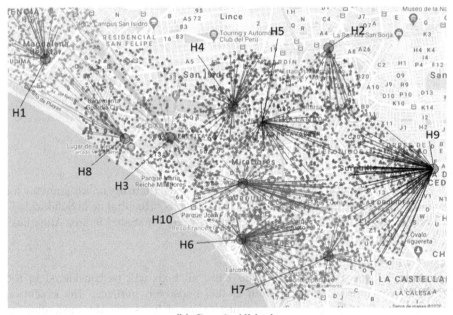

(b) Case 2: All beds

Fig. 3. Comparison of bed assignments (a) for ICU (b) for all (Color figure online)

lines) take assignments further. It might seem counter-intuitive that hospitals H_3 and H_8 take patients that are closer to hospital H_1, but it may indicate that:

- Hospital H_1 has a limited capacity.
- Infected people around hospitals H_3 and H_8 did not reach a severe level of infection.

This happens because the objective function (see Eq. (7)) tries to minimize distance and simultaneously maximize the medical attention for severe cases.

5   Discussion

Recently, combinatorial optimization, operational research, and constraint programming have been applied to patient care related problems [7].

There are mainly three types of patient scheduling tasks [8,16]: i) dynamic patient scheduling, ii) distributed patient scheduling and iii) coordinated patient scheduling. All of these focus on improving hospital resources to reduce patients waiting times [23], unlike our approach that focus on hospital attention during a pandemic

There are many propositions to solve patient bed assignment problem. Like using mixed integer-programming-based heuristics [4,20] as exact methods handling instances of the problem. However, in real world scenarios, sometimes it's allowed to violate certain constraints in order to cover others of greater relevance for their model.

Contrarily, a few works tackle this problem with other kinds of optimization algorithms (e.g., genetic algorithms, local search, . . .). For instance, in [11], the authors propose an hybrid tabu search algorithm that automatically assigning patients to beds. Another example, in [3], the authors present a two-level metaheuristic to solve the operating room scheduling and assignment problem. However, they treat all patient requirements as hard constraints, unlike our approach that takes into account preferences into the objective function.

To the best of our knowledge, none of these approaches deals with geolocation for various hospitals simultaneously as a whole, they rather used it to locate patients into a single hospital to optimize its resources and reducing the patient waiting time.

6   Conclusions

In this paper, we have shown that it is possible to model and solve a complex real-world problem through the constraint programming. The problem discussed is based on the organization of hospitals to treat infected people in the context of a pandemic. To model the problem, we use the "constraint optimization problem" paradigm. The main idea is to maximize a weighted sum of the satisfied soft constraints. It was possible to obtain data related to the hospital location and capacity, location and severity of infected people from official sources regarding the development of COVID-19 in Peru. Regarding the model, variables, domains and appropriate restrictions were defined for the problem. We have solved several instances of the patient bed assignment problem using our approach and evaluate it by several problem instances.

Applying constraint programming for this type of problem is very relevant, because it enables to obtain optimal results by modeling in a declarative way. Even if machine learning techniques may address this problem (e.g. SVM, Bayesian Networks, Artificial Neural Networks, ...), there are a number of disadvantages such as the need for historical data, the investment of time in pre-processing, the long duration of tests, among others. In this sense, the Constraint Programming, in comparison, makes it possible to obtain solutions in non-deterministic polynomial time and the need for some historical data.

The natural extension of this work is to build additional constraints on top of one of the models presented here, according to the pandemic evolution tuning/upgrading the objective function. Another possible future work is to integrate our proposal into a larger assignment optimization platform to reduce the workload of the clinical staff. Furthermore, multi-objective optimization is a promising perspective, since various criteria might need to added to our approach (e.g., skylines [9,13,22]) for getting optimal solutions w.r.t various criteria simultaneously or even test other types of soft constraints [19,21] to represent better user preferences into the model.

References

1. Abdel-Basset, M., Mohamed, R., Elhoseny, M., Chakrabortty, R.K., Ryan, M.J.: A hybrid COVID-19 detection model using an improved marine predators algorithm and a ranking-based diversity reduction strategy. IEEE Access **8**, 79521–79540 (2020)
2. Adams, R., Ji, Y., Wang, X., Saria, S.: Learning models from data with measurement error: tackling underreporting. In: ICML (2019)
3. Aringhieri, R., Landa, P., Soriano, P., Tanfani, E., Testi, A.: A two level metaheuristic for the operating room scheduling and assignment problem. Comput. Oper. Res. **54**, 21–34 (2015)
4. Ben Bachouch, R., Guinet, A., Hajri-Gabouj, S.: An integer linear model for hospital bed planning. Int. J. Prod. Econ. **140**(2), 833–843 (2012)
5. Biere, A., Heule, M., van Maaren, H., Walsh, T. (eds.): Handbook of Satisfiability. Frontiers in Artificial Intelligence and Applications, vol. 185. IOS Press, Amsterdam (2009)
6. Bistarelli, S., Faltings, B., Neagu, N.: Interchangeability with thresholds and degradation factors for soft CSPs. Ann. Math. Artif. Intell. **67**(2), 123–163 (2013)
7. Brailsford, S.C., Vissers, J.: OR in healthcare: a European perspective. Eur. J. Oper. Res. **212**(2), 223–234 (2011)
8. Cardoen, B., Demeulemeester, E., Beliën, J.: Operating room planning and scheduling: a literature review. Eur. J. Oper. Res. **201**(3), 921–932 (2010)
9. Che, M., Wang, L., Jiang, Z.: An approach to multidimensional medical data analysis based on the skyline operator. In: IEEM, pp. 1806–1810. IEEE (2018)

10. Chen, D., Deng, Y., Chen, Z., He, Z., Zhang, W.: A hybrid tree-based algorithm to solve asymmetric distributed constraint optimization problems. Auton. Agent. Multi-Agent Syst. **34**(2), 1–42 (2020). https://doi.org/10.1007/s10458-020-09476-5

11. Demeester, P., Souffriau, W., Causmaecker, P.D., Berghe, G.V.: A hybrid tabu search algorithm for automatically assigning patients to beds. Artif. Intell. Med. **48**(1), 61–70 (2010)

12. Fu, Z., Wu, Y., Zhang, H., Hu, Y., Zhao, D., Yan, R.: Be aware of the hot zone: A warning system of hazard area prediction to intervene novel coronavirus COVID-19 outbreak. In: SIGIR. ACM (2020)

13. Gavanelli, M.: An algorithm for multi-criteria optimization in CSPs. In: ECAI (2002)

14. Hu, S., et al.: Weakly supervised deep learning for COVID-19 infection detection and classification from CT images. IEEE Access **8**, 118869–118883 (2020)

15. Mahmud, T., Rahman, M.A., Fattah, S.A.: CovXNet: a multi-dilation convolutional neural network for automatic COVID-19 and other pneumonia detection from chest x-ray images with transferable multi-receptive feature optimization. Comp. Bio. and Med. **122**, 103869 (2020)

16. Marynissen, J., Demeulemeester, E.: Literature review on multi-appointment scheduling problems in hospitals. Eur. J. Oper. Res. **272**(2), 407–419 (2019)

17. Nasrabadi, A.M., Najafi, M., Zolfagharinia, H.: Considering short-term and long-term uncertainties in location and capacity planning of public healthcare facilities. Eur. J. Oper. Res. **281**(1), 152–173 (2020)

18. Rossi, F., van Beek, P., Walsh, T. (eds.): Handbook of Constraint Programming. Foundations of Artificial Intelligence, vol. 2. Elsevier, Amsterdam (2006)

19. Schiendorfer, A., Knapp, A., Anders, G., Reif, W.: MiniBrass: soft constraints for MiniZinc. Constraints Int. J. **23**(4), 403–450 (2018)

20. Turhan, A.M., Bilgen, B.: Mixed integer programming based heuristics for the patient admission scheduling problem. Comput. Oper. Res. **80**, 38–49 (2017)

21. Ugarte, W., Boizumault, P., Loudni, S., Crémilleux, B., Lepailleur, A.: Soft constraints for pattern mining. J. Intell. Inf. Syst. **44**(2), 193–221 (2013). https://doi.org/10.1007/s10844-013-0281-4

22. Ugarte, W., Loudni, S., Boizumault, P., Crémilleux, B., Termier, A.: Compressing and querying skypattern cubes. In: Wotawa, F., Friedrich, G., Pill, I., Koitz-Hristov, R., Ali, M. (eds.) IEA/AIE 2019. LNCS (LNAI), vol. 11606, pp. 406–421. Springer, Cham (2019). https://doi.org/10.1007/978-3-030-22999-3_36

23. Vermeulen, I.B., Bohte, S.M., Elkhuizen, S.G., Lameris, H., Bakker, P.J.M., Poutré, H.L.: Adaptive resource allocation for efficient patient scheduling. Artif. Intell. Med. **46**(1), 67–80 (2009)

24. Waheed, A., Goyal, M., Gupta, D., Khanna, A., Al-Turjman, F., Pinheiro, P.R.: CovidGAN: data augmentation using auxiliary classifier GAN for improved covid-19 detection. IEEE Access **8**, 91916–91923 (2020)

Detecting Xenophobic Hate Speech in Spanish Tweets Against Venezuelan Immigrants in Ecuador Using Natural Language Processing

Raúl R. Romero-Vega[1]([✉]) [iD], Oscar M. Cumbicus-Pineda[1] [iD],
Ruperto A. López-Lapo[1] [iD], and Lisset A. Neyra-Romero[2] [iD]

[1] Facultad de Energía, CIS, Universidad Nacional de Loja,
Ave. Pío Jaramillo Alvarado, La Argelia, Loja, Ecuador
`raul.romero@unl.edu.ec`
[2] Departamento de Ciencias de la Computacion y Electronica, Universidad Tecnica
Particular de Loja, San Cayetano Alto, Loja, Ecuador

Abstract. In recent reports, Ecuador and Venezuela are located as the
countries with the worst social indicators, showing ethnic and racial discrimination between both countries, one possible cause is a large number
of Venezuelan immigrants in Ecuador.

The present work has the goal of determining the existence of xenophobic content from a set of tweets collected around Venezuelan immigrants in Ecuador, using the diverse phases of the Knowledge Discovery
in Text (KDT) methodology. Identifying xenophobia by mean of Natural
Language Processing (NLP) is not an easy task; nonetheless, with the use
of techniques as Synthetic Minority Oversampling (SMOTE) and Crowdsourcing it is possible to make it. The feelings classification: xenophobic,
offensive and other are possible thanks to executing of three supervised
classification algorithms: Logistic Regression, Support Vector Machines
(SVM) and Naive Bayes.

As a result of the execution of the three algorithms, SVM algorithm
obtains a better performance with an F1-score of 98%. On the other
hand, of the 100% of data analysed, it is determinate that there exist a
5.76% of xenophobic sentiments, 31.23% of offensive emotions and 63%
contains other feelings.

Keywords: Hate speech · Natural Language Processing · Sentiment
analysis · Xenophobia · SMOTE

1 Introduction

Social networks have been a means of making the ideas and thoughts public.
According to Valdez [27], this has led to an increase in hate speech by spreading
messages of xenophobia, intolerance or pointing out others as a threat; such feelings are mostly directed towards vulnerable groups of people such as foreigners,

M. Botto-Tobar et al. (Eds.): ICAT 2020, CCIS 1388, pp. 312–326, 2021.
https://doi.org/10.1007/978-3-030-71503-8_24

causing them to be rejected in their environment and even with the possibility of being victims of hate crimes. This research raise the hypothesis: Are there tweets with xenophobic content towards Venezuelan immigrants in Ecuador?

This research starts with the carry out of a systematic literature review based on the phases of Barbara Kitchenham's methodology [15], which allows to determine the necessary steps to perform sentiment analysis, to few name: obtaining tweets, feature extraction, data pre-processing, application of supervised algorithms, evaluation [2,18,26] and graphic representation [1,12]. Based on this generic process, it considers applying a formal methodology like Knowledge Discovery in Text [1,14] that helps to achieve the goal of the research.

Based on systematic literature review is considered the use a set of tools, as below in detail: Python [23] and libraries of Machine Learning. Algorithms of Supervised Learning as Logistic Regression [1,24], Support Vector Machine [1,20,24] and Naive Bayes [1,21,24]. GoogleTrans library [4] is used to translate the content from Spanish to English by the Machine Translation technique, such technique allows to obtain the best results in terms of word processing, tweet collection and sentiment analysis; also highlighted fine-tuning techniques [11] that allowed to improve the performance of classification algorithms, such as the Synthetic Minority Oversampling Technique (SMOTE) [10], capable of reproducing synthetic samples of the minority classes, which allows to improve the learning of classification models.

This paper contains some sections to know: Methodology Sect. (2), where each of the phases of the methodology to feelings analysis is detailed. Later, in the Results Sect. (3), the interpretation and findings given by the implementation of the KDT methodology are presented. In the Discussion Sect. (4), the contribution of the present study is compared with the results of related studies. Finally, in the sections of Conclusions (5.1) and Future Work (5.2) the most relevant aspects of this study were raised, i.e., the experiences during its execution and what improvements can be made.

2   Methodology

The development of this study is carried out using the methodology KDT [9], whose stages are presented in Fig. 1.

In each phase, a series of additional tasks are carried out, such as the application of fine-tuning to the models, with the aim of improving the classification results of the applied algorithms. The tasks that are finally carried out are presented in Fig. 2, which are ordered according to the stages of the KDT methodology.

The process begin with the conceptualisation of the techniques, algorithms, metrics, and libraries that are used to perform the classification of xenophobic content successfully, and a series of additional tasks are performed to conclude each phase. The following is a presentation of the realisation of each of the phases of this methodology.

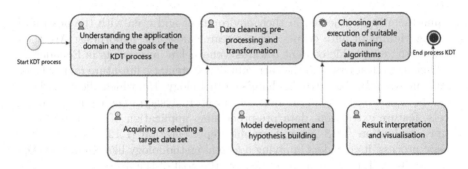

Fig. 1. Phases of the KDT methodology.

2.1 Phase 1: Understand the Application Domain and the Goals of the KDT Process

In this phase, a series of terms were defined that allowed the concepts used for the development of the methodology to be understood.

Hate Speeches. It is intended as speech to insult, offend, or intimidate a person because of some trait (such as race, religion, sexual orientation, nationality, or disability) [28].

Xenophobia. It consists of the generalised rejection of people of foreign origin, or in its case, certain groups of origin [25].

Crowdsourcing. It is the open collaboration or outsourcing of tasks, where website workers are in charge of manually sorting datasets, each observation had to be sorted by at least three people to be considered valid [6].

Machine Translation. Automatic translation has been one of the most prominent applications of artificial intelligence since its inception, there are now neural networks for automatic translation, i.e., the system can extract the patterns that allow translation from one language to another [3].

SMOTE. It is a Synthetic Minority Oversampling Technique (offered by the Imbalance-Learn library) that takes an oversampling approach to balance the original training set. This new data is created by interpolation between various minority class instances within a defined neighbourhood [10].

Fine-Tuning. The fine-tuning of a model is given by modifying its parameters or applying techniques that improve the data to be trained, to lead to a better performance of the algorithm [11].

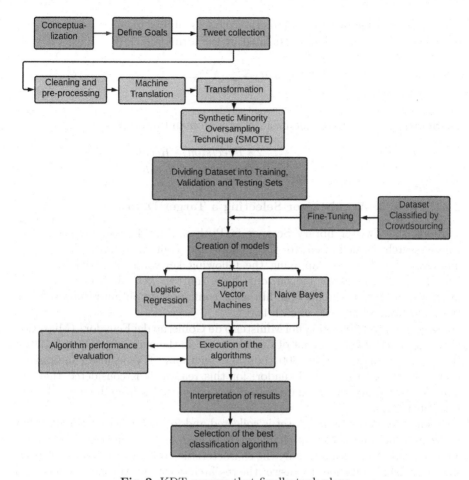

Fig. 2. KDT process that finally took place.

Accuracy. It is the proportion of the total number of correct predictions [7,17]:

$$Accuracy = \frac{\sum_{i=1}^{n} N_{ii}}{\sum_{i=1}^{n} \sum_{j=1}^{n} N_{ij}}$$

Precision. Precision is a measure of accuracy whenever a specific class has been predicted. It is defined by the formula [7,17]:

$$Precision_i = \frac{N_{ii}}{\sum_{k=1}^{n} N_{ki}}$$

Recall. It is a measure of a prediction model's ability to select instances of a particular class from a dataset, defined by the formula [7,17]:

$$Recall_i = \frac{N_{ii}}{\sum_{k=1}^{n} N_{ik}}$$

F1-Score. It is the harmonic mean of precision and recall [7,17]:

$$F1 - score_i = \frac{2 * Precision_i * Recall_i}{Precision_i + Recall_i}$$

2.2 Phase 2: Acquiring or Selecting a Target Dataset

Through the Twitter library Scraper in Python, 13,474 tweets are collected; whose search is delimited to the xenophobic content towards Venezuelan immigrants in Ecuador, applying the following keywords: Ecuador, Venezuelan, chamo/a, chamos/a, racism, out, hate, murder, xenophobia, immigrants, migrants, migration and also the library is configured to obtain results through the geolocation (Ecuador) of each tweet.

According to "Migración del Ministerio de Gobierno del Ecuador" (Migration of the Ministry of Government of Ecuador) [13], in the period from 2016 to 2019, there have been more than 300 thousand migrants of Venezuelan nationality that have stayed to live in Ecuador, for this reason, it is considered that the most feasible range for the data collection on Twitter is from January 2016 to December 2019.

Using these criteria, a dataset is collected and formed, where it is found that the texts contained irrelevant characteristics, such as their identifier, username, amount of likes, etc. Finally, only the characteristic "text" is considered relevant, since this field is sufficient to answer the research question: Are there tweets with xenophobic content towards Venezuelan immigrants in Ecuador?

2.3 Phase 3: Data Cleaning, Pre-processing and Transformation

In this phase, the cleaning, pre-processing, and transformation process are carried out to both datasets as shown in Table 1.

Table 1. Datasets used. There is the dataset that has been previously classified by crowdsourcing that was obtained from Davidson et al. study (named Dataset 1) in which he considers the classes of hate speech, offensive language or none, and that collected in the context of Venezuelan immigrants in Ecuador (Dataset 2).

Name	Context	Final size
Dataset 1	Previously classified by crowdsourcing	24,783
Dataset 2	Collected in the context of Venezuelan immigrants in Ecuador	9,888

From both datasets, the characteristics of interest are taken to carry out their cleaning and pre-processing, discarding those characters or words that do not contribute to the build of the classification model. From the Dataset 1 is taken all its 24,783 tweets and through the RegEx library, with the use of regular expressions is eliminated, unnecessary texts contained in each tweet. The regular expressions used are shown in Table 2. The same process is applicable for the Dataset 2 with its 13,474 initial tweets and later also to remove the duplicate tweets. Finally, from this last dataset, a total of 9,888 tweets is left ready to be processed in further stages.

Table 2. Use of regular expressions.

Type of text	Regular expression
User mentions	'@[\w\-]+'
Hashtag	'#[\w\-]+'
Links	'http[s]?://(?:[a-zA-Z]—[0-9]—[$-_@.& +]—' '[!*\(\),]—(?:%[0-9a-fA-F][0-9a-fA-F]))+'
Special characters and punctuation marks	'\W'
Excess spacing	'\s+'

Dataset 1 is used to train the classification models, which according to Davidson et al. [6], this classification is done through crowdsourcing by CrowdFlower workers.

Dataset 1 present an imbalance in its classes, as shown in Fig. 3, in which 19,190 tweets are classified as offensive sentiments, 1,430 tweets as hate speech, and 4,163 tweets as other sentiments, which causes a bias when training the classification models, causing a lower performance during the learning of the models. For this reason, it is applied the Synthetic Minority Oversampling Technique (SMOTE), which creates new examples from existing data, i.e., using an automatic sampling strategy and with a number of k (10) neighbours, it is possible to increase the data for the minority classes. This process consist of taking a tweet at random from the minority class and from the nearest k neighbours a randomly select neighbour is chosen, and a synthetic example is created at a random point between the two examples [19].

Before applying this technique, by means of the Scikit-Learn library the texts are transformed into vectorised values to enable their processing, carried out via the TF-IDF (Term Frequency Inverse Document Frequency) model and the use of the English stop words given by the NLTK library, to discard those words that are not very relevant for the word vocabulary. After the application of the SMOTE technique, a classified dataset was obtained with all its classes balanced, i.e., the minority classes increased their observations to 19,190 each. Then Machine Translation is applied to Dataset 2 through the GoogleTrans library for the mass translation of these tweets and for their vectorisation the same TF-IDF frequency model is used to vectorise the tweets of Dataset 1, the same frequency model is used to generate the same amount of characteristics in both datasets for their later use.

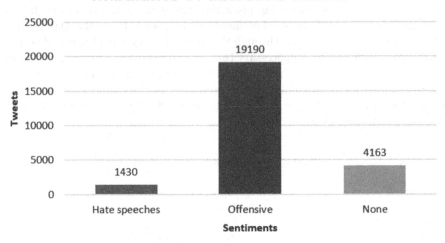

Fig. 3. Imbalance in the dataset 1 classes.

2.4   Phase 4: Model Development and Hypothesis Building

The detection of xenophobia is done in the messages that contain hate speech, the same that cover racism and hatred of foreigners, which is why, for the construction of our model as mentioned above, it is took a classified dataset that Davidson et al. [6] used to train the models, which obtained an accuracy of 91%, recall 90% and F1-score of 90%.

Before creating and applying the models for Dataset 2, it is started by creating a balanced model of Dataset 1, and then in the Discussion (4) section, we compared it with the results of this same dataset but with its initially unbalanced classes.

According to Leonardo et al. [16], it is recommended to use 80% of the data for training and 20% for testing, these datasets are created randomly through the Scikit-Learn library.

For knowing the real performance of a model before applying it, there is a very common solution, which is to use the training set to train and validate at the same time, known as cross-validation; it consists of dividing the training set in k equal parts, if k = 5 then the model is trained with the first four parts and tested with the fifth, then it is trained with the first three and the fifth and tested with the fourth, this is repeated k times, always leaving out one part for the test, then the performance in each one is averaged and thus the expected performance is obtained [5]. For the validations, it is considered to use k = 10 (number of folds), which is the number of parts into which the dataset is divided to train and evaluate the models.

Table 3 below presents the results of the cross-validation for each of the classification algorithms applied to Dataset 1.

Table 3. Cross-validation and F1-score for dataset 1

Algorithm	Cross-validation	F1-score
Logistic Regression	0.925	0.93
Support Vector Machine	0.934	0.94
Naive Bayes	0.884	0.89

The results obtained in the cross-validation in theory are the values closest to reality, which was confirmed when applying the model to a set of tests, giving values similar to those given by the cross-validation; these values are represented by the F1-scores (see Table 3).

2.5   Phase 5: Choosing and Execution of Suitable Data Mining Algorithms

For the execution of the algorithms, the models tuned in the previous phase are used to carry out the classification of Dataset 2, the update of the names of the classes of this dataset is carried out because it is created with tweets directed to Venezuelans who live in Ecuador, where the wide field of the speeches of the hate is reduced to the specific ones of rejection to the foreigners (xenophobia) and the class previously called "None" is changed for "Other" since it represents better the field of feelings that this category includes. The classification made for Dataset 2 is shown in Fig. 4.

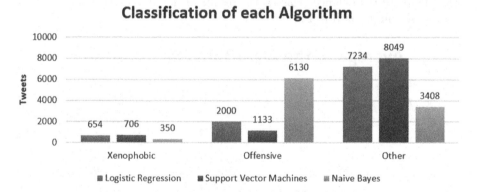

Fig. 4. Classification of dataset 2 according to each algorithm.

As can be seen in Fig. 4, through these algorithms a similar classification between each class is obtained, in contrast to the Naive Bayes algorithm that presented dissimilar results compared to the others. To create the Dataset 2 classification models with xenophobic content, the SMOTE technique is applied,

Table 4. Dataset 2 classification and the balance between its classes.

	Initial classification			SMOTE		
	Xenophobic	Offensive	Other	Xenophobic	Offensive	Other
Logistic Regression	654	2,000	7,234	7,234	7,234	7,234
Support Vector Machine	706	1,133	8,049	8,049	8,049	8,049
Naive Bayes	350	6,130	3,408	6,130	6,130	6,130

also with an automatic sampling strategy and a $k = 10$ (number of neighbours) in order to create new data for the minority classes (see Table 4)).

Once the datasets with their balanced classes are obtained, new models capable of classifying tweets with xenophobic content are created. These models are in a GitHub repository[1].

3   Results

3.1   Phase 6: Results Interpretation and Visualization

In Table 4 the classification results for each of the algorithms can be seen, values that vary between one or another algorithm, therefore, the overall percentage average for the three algorithms are also obtained, as presented in Fig. 5.

Once these classification results are obtained, a new model is trained for each algorithm with the balanced classes, the results of the tests carried out for these models are summarized in Fig. 6.

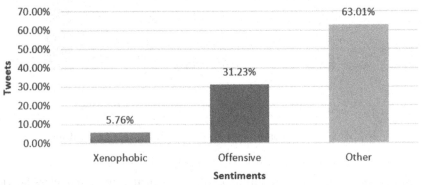

Fig. 5. Percentage average of the tweets classified, according to each sentiment.

---

[1] https://github.com/raulrrv/Deteccion_Xenofobia_TT/tree/master/modelo.

The final classification models are trained with their balanced classes, to obtain a better performance in each model, as can be seen in Fig. 6, the Support Vector Machines obtained the best performance with 98%, the Logistic Regression algorithm with 96%, and Naive Bayes with 89% of F1-score.

Training results for the new classification models

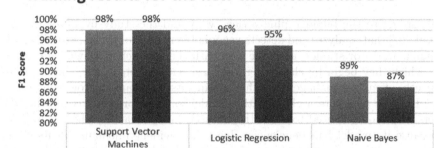

	Support Vector Machines	Logistic Regression	Naive Bayes
■ Validation Set	98%	96%	89%
■ Test Set	98%	95%	87%

Fig. 6. Training results for the new classifying models of the xenophobic sentiment.

As a way of testing the precision with which they predict the models created, a few tweets are presented in Table 5 that are classified as xenophobic.

Table 5. Examples of tweets classified as xenophobic.

Original tweet	Machine Translation	Prediction
Venezolano no te queremos en nuestro país	Venezuelan we don't want you in our country	Xenophobic
Odio las novelas venezolanas pero aquí en Ecuador se pasan contratando actores venezolanos desconocidos, malos, gays y ridículos	I hate Venezuelan novels, but here in Ecuador they go on hiring unknown, bad, gay and ridiculous Venezuelan actors	Xenophobic
Ya de una embalalos mándalos fuera de Ecuador sidosos, ladrones, maricones de más no los queremos aquí fuera venezolanos fuera	Hurry up and get them out of Ecuador, they're too thieves, faggots, we don't want them out here, Venezuelans out	Xenophobic

Finally, with the classification already performed to the Dataset 2 that is framed with content directed towards Venezuelan immigrants in Ecuador, it is possible to answer the research question: Are there tweets with xenophobic content towards Venezuelan immigrants in Ecuador? Yes, there are tweets with xenophobic content towards Venezuelan immigrants in Ecuador, with a presence of 5.76%, which is relatively low compared to 31.23% of tweets found with offensive content towards them, also the existence in 63% of other sentiments.

4   Discussion

According to the bibliographic review, we found the study by Plaza Del Arco et al. [22] that analyzes and detects xenophobia in a set of tweets, as well as other similar works or studies, as is the case with the research of Davidson et al. [6], in which they begin by classifying a dataset with tweets in the context of hate speech, offensive language and other sentiments by means of crowdsourcing[2].

In order to create a classification model to make predictions to other data sets, this model is used to make the Dataset 2 classification, which is improved because its model had deficiencies due to an evident imbalance in its classes, this is a weak point during the training of a model, making it inefficient or low performance in the accuracy of its predictions, for this reason, in the present investigation, the number of samples is increased by creating new synthetic data of the minority classes through SMOTE, which creates new classification models for each algorithm. The results of the best precision performance by the study

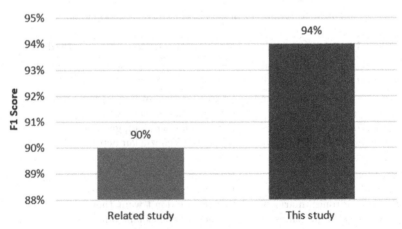

Fig. 7. Comparison of the performance of the results of the related study and the present study.

---

[2] https://github.com/raulrrv/Deteccion_Xenofobia_TT/blob/master/data/dataset_1_clasificado.csv.

of Davidson et al. are presented in Fig. 7, together with the results of the best performance by the algorithm of this research.

The results of the related study refer to the F1-score of the most efficient model by Davidson et al. with 90% accuracy, which is improved by the present research by balancing its classes, giving an F1-score of 94% of the best model, being the Support Vector Machine algorithm.

On the other hand, the related work of Plaza Del Arco et al. [22], in contrast to the present research detects xenophobia by creating lexicons of words that indicate hatred towards immigrants; uses lexicons to classify a tweet as xenophobic or not. The performance of its best algorithm is 73%. This low performance is possible due to the misclassification that occurs when using patterns based on word terms since a negative word in a positive context can be considered as a xenophobic tweet, marked as a false positive and leading to be misclassified.

5 Conclusions and Future Works

5.1 Conclusions

Through the application of the KDT methodology, it was determined that there is indeed xenophobic content in the social network Twitter directed to Venezuelan immigrants in Ecuador, although in a smaller proportion, since, out of the 9,888 tweets classified only 5.76% are xenophobic i.e. 570 tweets, however, this does not mean that the rest of the content is friendly since it is also found that 31.23% of the tweets published contain offensive messages towards them.

According to the literature review, it is determined that there is not enough information to detect more complex feelings such as xenophobia, i.e., the found studies of feelings analysis determine mostly only the polarity of a text (positive, negative or neutral), thru the development and fine-tuning of a classification model it is possible to detect xenophobic feelings in the set of tweets, these models have their importance for their use in similar or future studies.

Based on the performance tests of the classification algorithm models, it is concluded that a better performance is obtained when the classes of the training set have been balanced i.e. when the number of samples of the minority classes increases.

Comparing the results of each classification algorithm, it is concluded that the algorithm with the best performance results during the predictions with 94% F1-score is that of the Support Vector Machines, as well as it is also worth mentioning that this algorithm, unlike that of the Logistic Regression and the Naive Bayes, is the one that has taken the longest time to create the model, as it constantly searches the classes to find the best hyperplane that maximises the margin separation between these classes.

5.2 Future Work

To implement a software solution capable of automating the classification process of a given set of data or texts, since, through this research, a model with the highest performance algorithm (SVM) was trained to recognise texts with xenophobic content[3]. On the basis of this research, other algorithms can be applied to try and improve its results, including Google's relatively new BERT [8] system, which analyses and understands the context and subject matter of the whole sentence to be processed, allowing the generation of new results that can be compared with current research, which would also be a contribution to other research.

References

1. Al-Amrani, Y., Lazaar, M., Elkadiri, K.E.: Sentiment analysis using supervised classification algorithms. In: ACM International Conference Proceeding Series, vol. Part F1294 (2017). https://doi.org/10.1145/3090354.3090417
2. Al Shammari, A.S.: Real-time Twitter sentiment analysis using 3-way classifier. In: 21st Saudi Computer Society National Computer Conference, NCC 2018, pp. 1–3 (2018). https://doi.org/10.1109/NCG.2018.8593205
3. Artetxe, M., Labaka Intxauspe, G., Agirre Bengoa, E.: Unsupervised Neural Machine Translation, a new paradigm solely based on monolingual text. Procesamiento del lenguaje natural **63**, 151–154 (2019). https://doi.org/10.26342/2019-63-18
4. Chen, T., Xu, R., He, Y., Wang, X.: Improving sentiment analysis via sentence type classification using BiLSTM-CRF and CNN. Expert Syst. Appl. **72**, 221–230 (2017). https://doi.org/10.1016/j.eswa.2016.10.065
5. Cumbicus-Pineda, O.M., Ordoñez-Ordoñez, P.F., Neyra-Romero, L.A., Figueroa-Diaz, R.: Automatic categorization of Tweets on the political electoral theme using supervised classification algorithms. In: Botto-Tobar, M., Pizarro, G., Zúñiga-Prieto, M., D'Armas, M., Zúñiga Sánchez, M. (eds.) CITT 2018. CCIS, vol. 895, pp. 671–682. Springer, Cham (2019). https://doi.org/10.1007/978-3-030-05532-5_51
6. Davidson, T., Warmsley, D., Macy, M., Weber, I.: Automated hate speech detection and the problem of offensive language. In: Proceedings of the 11th International AAAI Conference on Web and Social Media, ICWSM 2017, pp. 512–515 (2017)
7. Deng, X., Liu, Q., Deng, Y., Mahadevan, S.: An improved method to construct basic probability assignment based on the confusion matrix for classification problem. Inf. Sci. **340–341**, 250–261 (2016). https://doi.org/10.1016/j.ins.2016.01.033
8. Devlin, J., Chang, M.W., Lee, K., Toutanova, K.: BERT: pre-training of deep bidirectional transformers for language understanding. arXiv preprint arXiv:1810.04805 (2018)
9. Elmenreich, W., Machado, J.A.T., Rudas, I.J.: Intelligent Systems at the Service of Mankind, vol. 1 (2016)
10. Fernández, A., García, S., Herrera, F., Chawla, N.V.: SMOTE for learning from imbalanced data: progress and challenges, marking the 15-year anniversary. J. Artif. Intell. Res. **61**, 863–905 (2018). https://doi.org/10.1613/jair.1.11192
11. Griffiths, N.: How To Fine-Tune Your Neural Network For Your Data: Image Classification (2019). https://towardsdatascience.com/how-to-fine-tune-your-neural-network-for-your-data-image-classification-d0f01c92300b

---

[3] https://github.com/raulrrv/Deteccion_Xenofobia_TT/blob/master/modelo/modelo_svm_final.pkl.

12. Herrera Flores, B.: Polaridad de las opiniones sobre un personaje público en el Ecuador. Latin Am. J. Comput. **V**(2), 27–32 (2018)
13. del Interior, M.: Migración - Ministerio de Gobierno (2019). https://www. ministeriodegobierno.gob.ec/migracion/
14. Justicia de la Torre, M.C.: Nuevas Técnicas De Minería De Textos: Aplicaciones (2017)
15. Kitchenham, B., Charters, S.: Guidelines for performing Systematic Literature Reviews in Software Engineering (2007)
16. Leonardo, P.D.: Análisis de sentimientos. Aplicación sobre textos en redes sociales (2019)
17. Luque, A., Carrasco, A., Martín, A., de las Heras, A.: The impact of class imbalance in classification performance metrics based on the binary confusion matrix. Pattern Recogn. **91**, 216–231 (2019). https://doi.org/10.1016/j.patcog.2019.02.023
18. Mahajan, D., Kumar Chaudhary, D.: Sentiment analysis using RNN and Google Translator. In: Proceedings of the 8th International Conference Confluence 2018 on Cloud Computing, Data Science and Engineering, Confluence 2018, pp. 798–802 (2018). https://doi.org/10.1109/CONFLUENCE.2018.8442924
19. Neyra-Romero, L.A., Cumbicus-Pineda, O.M., Sierra, B., Cueva-Carrion, S.P.: Automatic categorization of answers by applying supervised classification algorithms to the analysis of student responses to a series of multiple choice questions. In: Botto-Tobar, M., León-Acurio, J., Díaz Cadena, A., Montiel Díaz, P. (eds.) ICAETT 2019. AISC, vol. 1066, pp. 454–463. Springer, Cham (2020). https://doi.org/10.1007/978-3-030-32022-5_42
20. Phand, S.A., Chakkarwar, V.A.: Enhanced sentiment classification using GEO location tweets. In: 2018 2nd International Conference on Inventive Communication and Computational Technologies (ICICCT), pp. 881–886 (2018). https://doi.org/10.1109/ICICCT.2018.8473048
21. Phand, S.A., Phand, J.A.: Twitter sentiment classification using stanford NLP. In: Proceedings of the 1st International Conference on Intelligent Systems and Information Management, ICISIM 2017, 1–5 January 2017, (2017). https://doi.org/10.1109/ICISIM.2017.8122138
22. Plaza-Del-Arco, F.M., Molina-González, M.D., Ureña-López, L.A., Martín-Valdivia, M.T.: Detecting misogyny and xenophobia in Spanish tweets using language technologies. ACM Trans. Internet Technol. **20**(2), 1–19 (2020). https://doi.org/10.1145/3369869
23. Rubio Cortés, D.: Herramienta para el análisis de opiniones y sentimientos sobre Twitter (2017). http://riuma.uma.es/xmlui/bitstream/handle/10630/15422/Davidrubioc-ortesMemoria.pdf
24. Sajib, M.I., Mahmud Shargo, S., Hossain, M.A.: Comparison of the efficiency of machine learning algorithms on Twitter sentiment analysis of Pathao. In: 2019 22nd International Conference on Computer and Information Technology, ICCIT 2019, pp. 1–6 (2019). https://doi.org/10.1109/ICCIT48885.2019.9038208
25. Sebastian, R.: El peligro de la xenofobia (March) (2019). https://www.la-razon.com/voces/2020/06/02/el-peligro-de-la-narrativa/
26. Tellez, E.S., Miranda-Jiménez, S., Graff, M., Moctezuma, D., Siordia, O.S., Villaseñor, E.A.: A case study of Spanish text transformations for Twitter sentiment analysis. Exp. Syst. Appl. **81**, 457–471 (2017). https://doi.org/10.1016/j.eswa.2017.03.071

27. Valdez-Apolo, M.B.: El discurso del odio hacia migrantes y refugiados a través del tono y los marcos de los mensajes en Twitter. RAEIC **6**, 361–384 (2019)
28. Watanabe, H., Bouazizi, M., Ohtsuki, T.: Hate speech on Twitter: a pragmatic approach to collect hateful and offensive expressions and perform hate speech detection. IEEE Access **6**(c), 13825–13835 (2018). https://doi.org/10.1109/ACCESS. 2018.2806394

Sentiment Analysis Related of International Festival of Living Arts Loja-Ecuador Employing Knowledge Discovery in Text

Ramiro R. Rivera-Guamán[1]([⊠])(iD), Oscar M. Cumbicus-Pineda[1](iD),
Ruperto A. López-Lapo[1](iD), and Lisset A. Neyra-Romero[2](iD)

[1] Facultad de Energía, CIS, Universidad Nacional de Loja,
Ave. Pío Jaramillo Alvarado, La Argelia, Loja, Ecuador
`ramiro.rivera@unl.edu.ec`
[2] Departamento de Ciencias de la Computacion y Electronica, Universidad Tecnica
Particular de Loja, San Cayetano Alto, Loja, Ecuador

Abstract. Nowadays, the use of social networks is part of the daily life of most people, especially young people, to share content and opinions. Twitter is one of the most popular social networks, in which users are the first actors to generate a large amount of information. The analysis of Twitter data requires a systematic process of collection, processing and classification. The main objective of this work is to classify the data tweets in three different classes: Positive, Negative and Neutral Opinions, corresponding to the "International Festival of the Living Arts in Loja (FIAVL)" in the years between 2016 and 2019. The official account of the "FIAVL" produced a total of 18k tweets in Spanish language, which followed the different phases of the Knowledge Discovery in Text (KDT) methodology for its analysis and study. Vector Support Machines (SVM) and Naive Bayes (NB) were used to classify the classes, where an accuracy rate of 98.7% was obtained, with the neutral opinion prevailing over the rest of the classes with 57%, thus it could be concluded that there are no positive or negative opinions about the FIAVL.

Keywords: Data mining · Sentiment analysis · Tweet categorization · KDT methodology · Supervised classification · Vector Support Machines

1 Introduction

Ecuador has 17 million people, 13.6 million of whom have access to social networks. Twitter occupying the 11th place worldwide is considered among the most popular social networks, in Ecuador alone with a total of 4 million accounts and 0.8 million tweets distributed in a 33% for women and 67% for men both over 15 years old, according to the study conducted by Juan Pablo del Alcázar Ponce in 2018 [14].

© Springer Nature Switzerland AG 2021
M. Botto-Tobar et al. (Eds.): ICAT 2020, CCIS 1388, pp. 327–339, 2021.
https://doi.org/10.1007/978-3-030-71503-8_25

Twitter have the potential to provide a way to classify the opinions on the Loja International Festival of Living Arts (FIAVL), since it has a vast amount of information, and the collected tweets about the event are very helpful to this purpose. The event receives people from all over the country and abroad, having an investment of 1,642,856.79 dollars in its fourth edition with 35,573 spectators according to the Management Report of the Minister of Culture and Patrimony, Juan Fernando Velasco [14] [18], and [19]; being an annual festival of few years of validity to be precise between 2016 and 2019 it is not known with exactitude which are the opinions emitted by the attendants thus being able to categorize their opinions.

Not having a real opinion of the effect that the FIAVL has on people is an uncertainty for society. By not having an objective opinion of the event, institutions, private or public entities will not be able to make decisions that benefit them; many criticisms arise that have led to budget cuts, as the journalist Yalilé Loaiza says, mentioning in her publication that "The festival has become a political booty".

Currently, artificial intelligence techniques make it possible to organise databases to obtain information that is not visualised at first glance [17], this is the case with tweets collected through the Twitter API, this dataset has a large amount of information that can be undermined to determine useful information that is implicit. This research proposes the application of data mining algorithms in the information collected from 2016 to 2019, to determine the feeling that people give in the International Festival of Living Arts of Loja - Ecuador having three positive, negative or neutral alternatives.

In the development of this article, the objectives that allow the classification of the tweets, which are extracted from a reliable repository such as Twitter, are established. Data mining techniques are also implemented in the data sets obtained in order to extract the relevant information for their subsequent classification [11].

In the Methodology section, each of the tasks to be carried out in the stages of the KDT methodology are described, and the materials, tools and techniques needed to carry out this project are mentioned. Python is the most outstanding tool that serves as a basis for the whole operation of the source code.

In the Results section the results of the applied algorithms are presented. A large number of representative graphics are used for a better visual interpretation. Next, there is the Discussion section where a brief explanation is presented about the data obtained and how they contribute to the fulfilment of the proposed objectives.

In the Conclusions section the deductions obtained from the experience during the process of elaboration of the results are expressed. Finally, there is the section of Recommendations, where suggestions are given for a better performance of similar works as well as for future research on the improvement of the models presented in this work.

2   Methodology

For the development of this research work, the Knowledge Discovery in Text (KDT) methodology is achieved, which implies mastery in different areas of knowledge, information retrieval methods, information extraction, natural language processing, and data mining. This type of knowledge is essential for the researcher to be able to comply with each of the stages [15], to this end; the following phases are applied in data processing as shown in Fig. 1.

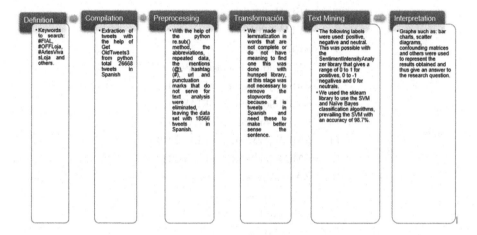

Fig. 1. The methodology used for the research

2.1   Phase 1: Definition of Concepts

For the definition of the concepts, it is used the following works related to the topic [13, 15, 21], in which it is obtained as a result the Python tool for sentiment analysis, also another results are obtained of the classification algorithms Naive Bayes and SVM that provide very good perform for this type of data.

Once the key concepts of the research are obtained, it is proceeded to define the search criteria for the extraction of tweets, which are hashtags, accounts, or words related to the Loja International Festival of Living Arts (FIAVL) as show in Table 1.

Table 1. Search terms for tweets extraction.

Nº	Criterion
1	Festival de Artes Vivas en Loja
2	@festivaloffloja
3	@FestivalDeLoja
4	#FIAVL
5	#FIAVL2016
6	#FIAVL2017
7	#FIAVL2018
8	#FIAVL2019
9	#FIAVL2020
10	#MiMejorMomentoFIAV
11	#MiMejorMomentoFIAV2016
12	#MiMejorMomentoFIAV2017
13	#MiMejorMomentoFIAV2018
14	#MiMejorMomentoFIAV2019
15	#MiMejorMomentoFIAV2020
16	#ArtesVivas
17	#artesvivas
18	#FestivalLojaMasTuyoQueNunca
19	#OFFLoja
20	#OffLoja
21	#ElArteViveEnLoja

2.2 Phase 2: Gathering Information

For the compilation of the tweets related to the Loja International Festival of Living Arts, the GetOldTweets3 library is implemented. Using only a few lines of code, it extracts the requested tweets, using as search criteria the terms in Table 1 with a time range between 2016 and 2019.

26,668 tweets are collected in Spanish, these being the independent variable; the dependent variable is the result obtained from the classification of the data, being categorised into positive, negative and neutral.

2.3 Phase 3: Pre-processing

Firstly, the text is made homogeneous, then the concepts or characters that do not allow for the detection of patterns are removed, as are abbreviations, mentions (@), hashtags (#), URLs and punctuation marks that are not useful for analysing the text.

The mention (@) and hashtag (#) columns, are of great help for the cleaning of these characters in the texts, since for each row there are mentions and hashtags that do not allow the interpretation of the text, so it is eliminated as part of the cleaning of the text.

With the help of the re and string methods of Python Language, it is possible to remove URLs and punctuation marks from texts to make them more readable and easier to interpret.

Finally, duplicate tweets in the dataset are removed with the help of panda library, collecting a total of 18,566 tweets in Spanish.

2.4   Phase 4: Transformation

In this section each word in the tweets is lemmatized or paraphrased to give a better meaning to what is being expressed, this is done thanks to the hunspell library. After lemmatizing and pre-processing the data, the column FILTER_URL_OTHERS is created which contains more readable tweets and is easier to interpret.

As a final result of this activity, the data is saved in a CSV file, for which it is necessary to use the panda library.

2.5   Phase 5: Text Mining

Once the tweets have been cleaned up, they are classified by labels. This is possible thanks to the sklearn library, which is very useful in classifying the texts, since its classifiers include Naive Bayes, SVM, and other classifiers [5].

To obtain the polarity of the tweets in Spanish, the SentimentIntensityAnalyzer library is used. This library provides the polarity of each tweet in a range of -1 to 1, having as neutral polarity the zero, all this process is made with the tweets in Spanish being its main advantage [3].

To designate the label of the tweets, a range of polarity is used as shown in Table 2.

Table 2. Class designation according to their polarity.

Class	Range
NEG (negative)	Polarity less than 0
POS (positive)	Polarity greater than 0
NEU (neutral)	Polarity = 0

– **Application of selected classifiers.**
  Once the data labeling is done, it is proceeded to divide the original dataset in 20% for test and 80% train [8,16]. The Naive Bayes and SVM algorithms can be used to obtain better results as shown in Fig. 2.

Original dataset division from 18566 tweets

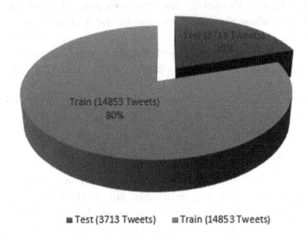

Fig. 2. Original dataset division.

- **Classification by Naive Bayes.**

As a first point, the data to be classified must be taken into account with their respective labelling as mentioned in their official documentation [2]. For this purpose, the data are divided into "X" and "Y", the data of "X" would be the tweets, and the data of "Y" would be the classes with which the model is compared. For the classification of the data, the FILTER column is used, which contains the tweets already filtered, and the FILTER column contains the designation of the labels for each tweet. For each label, a numerical value is designated to identify it. With the help of the train test division function, we proceed to divide the data which is 80% for the training and 20% for the test or trial. Once the data has been divided, it is then vectorised, with the help of the CountVectorizer function. This function allows the transformation of text data into binary matrices, this is done thanks to tokenisation [4]. According to the official documentation, the training and test data can be classified in binary form after the training and test data have been obtained, using the Multinomial NB function [4]. As every model must be evaluated, by means of the Confusion Matrix function, the confusion matrix is obtained, allowing the classification to be observed in a more detailed way. To do this, the test data designated for the training of the model are introduced, followed by the expected data and finally the matrix with the following data −1 for negatives, 0 for neutrals and 1 for positives as shown in Fig. 3.

As a final step, the model gives the following results, as shown in Fig. 4; with acceptable prediction and accuracy.

- **Classification by Support Vector Machine (SVM).**

Another widely used sorter, and above all with results of precision and accu-

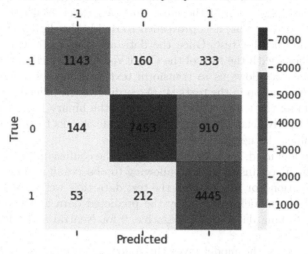

Fig. 3. Data for Naive Bayes classification

```
Data sorted by label for Naive Bayes classifier
NEU    10586
POS    5924
NEG    2056
Name: FILTRO_2_CLASE_ES, dtype: int64


Accuracy (Exactitud) score:  0.8780044435467582
Precision (Precisión) score:  0.8780044435467582
Recall (sensibilidad) score:  0.8780044435467582
F1 score:  0.8784643037635321
```

Fig. 4. Results obtained from the Naive Bayes model

racy far above the naive Bayes sorter, is the SVM sorter. This classifier gives the highest percentages of accuracy when dealing with texts, contains a set of supervised learning methods that are used for classification, regression and outlier detection [9]. As a first point, the data to be classified with their respective labelling, as mentioned in their official documentation [1], is split into two dataset "X" and "Y", the "X" data being the tweets, and the "Y" data being the classes to which the model is compared. For the classification of the data is used the column of FILTRO_1_url_otros, which contains the tweets already filtered and the column of FILTRO_3_CLASEES, this column contains the designation of the labels for each tweet. With the help of the function train test split, it is proceeded to divide the data which is 80% for training and 20% for test. Once the data are divided, it is carried out to vectorize them, with the help of the CountVectorizer function this is possible make it, since it allows us to transform text data into binary arrays, for it uses the tokenisation in the texts [4]. According to the official documentation after obtaining the training and test data in the binary form it is proceeded to their respective classification, which is made thanks to the SVM function using the linear kernel [1].

As every model needs to be evaluated, using the confusion_matrix function, it is obtained the confusion matrix, allowing to observe in a more detailed way the classification, for it is entered the test data that were designated for the training of the model, followed by the predicted data and finally the array with the following data −1 for Negative, 0 for Neutral and 1 for positive as shown figure Fig. 5.

As the last step, the model gives the following results, as shown in Fig. 6; with acceptable prediction and accuracy.

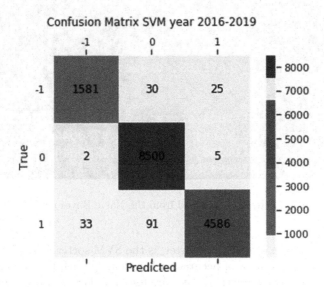

Fig. 5. Data for SVM classification.

```
Data sorted by label for SVM classifier
NEU     10586
POS      5924
NEG      2056
Name: FILTRO_2_CLASE_ES, dtype: int64


Accuracy (Exactitud) score:  0.9874772773177136
Precision (Precisión) score:  0.9874772773177136
Recall (sensibilidad) score:  0.9874772773177136
F1 score:  0.9874350708008617
```

Fig. 6. Results of the SVM model.

3   Results

For the fulfilment of this section, the results obtained from the KDT methodology are collected, being this a previous step to treat the data to evaluate and interpret them as detailed below:

3.1   Evaluation of Results

Once the evaluation is established for each year, it is carried out to make a comparison of all the tweets obtained, in this way it is checked if the supremacy of the SVM algorithm over the Naive Bayes algorithm is maintained. For this verification, the entire original dataset is used, having a total of 18,566 tweets in Spanish, as shown in Fig. 7, the results ratify that the best algorithm is the SVM with a 98.7% of precision being this a very important data in the development of the investigation.

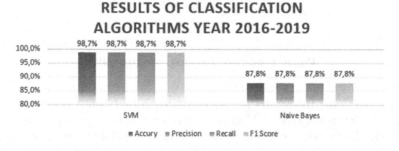

Fig. 7. Result of algorithms year 2016–2019.

3.2   Interpretation of Results

Next, the results obtained by the SMV classification algorithm are interpreted, being this the one with the best precision and thus evidencing, which is the predominant polarity over the tweets. The classification of the original dataset is performed, which contains 18,566 tweets, in a date range from 2016 to 2019. These are classified using class labels, in which neutral polarity prevailed with 11%, followed by positive polarity with 32% and lastly neutralism with 57% as shown in Fig. 8 and Fig. 9.

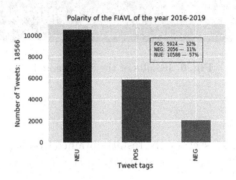

Fig. 8. Polarity bar graph 2016–2019.

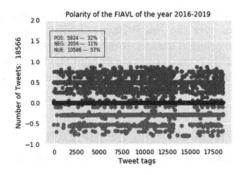

Fig. 9. Polarity scatter diagram 2016–2019.

After obtaining the results of the classification by label, it is carried out to classify the tweets with the SVM algorithm. It gave different results at the time of classifying the tweets, prevailing equally the neutral polarity with 8,500 tweets, followed by the positive polarity with 4,586 tweets and finally the negative polarity with 1,581 tweets, as shown in Fig. 10 the confusion matrix. Furthermore, the results do not vary concerning the classification by the label, as shown in Fig. 8 and Fig. 9.

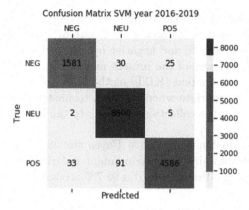

Fig. 10. Confusion matrix 2016–2019.

4 Discussion

Each of the stages of the KDT methodology is developed, which are: concept definition, information gathering, pre-processing, transformation, and text mining, obtaining a total of 18566 tweets.

The first four stages, allowed to extract the tweets and then process them and result in tweets more understandable and easy to interpret, according to [7] the use of a methodology is essential for an analysis of feelings about opinions, because if we work on social networks these data are not structured and for this reason difficult to give polarity to the commentaries.

After having the data processed, text mining is performed, for which SVM and Naive Bayes classification algorithms are implemented. These classifiers are very important, since they gave very encouraging results, leading the SVM that resulted in 98.7% accuracy, as shown in the results section, this percentage is very favourable since in some related works lower results are obtained as can be seen in the following researches [6], [10], and [20], these had results between 80% to 90% accuracy. The results shown in the graphs are made based on SVM and Naive Bayes algorithms, considering which of them obtained the highest percentages. Through these graphs, he could easily determine the predominant polarity of the tweets. As shown in Fig. 10, the confusion matrix resulted in a neutral opinion from the FIAVL viewers.

5 Conclusion and Future Work

5.1 Conclusion

– The extraction of tweets related to the FIAVL and its processing is carried out with the help of the Knowledge Discovery in Text (KDT) methodology, being the first step to follow to categorize the tweets. Moreover, with the help of the algorithms of classification Naive Bayes and Support Vector Machine opinions are classified into three different categories: positive, negative and neutral. As result, neutral opinions prevail with 57% over the other categories, positive opinions with 32% and negative opinions with 11%, giving fulfilment to the principal objective of the present article.

- Knowledge Discovery in Text (KDT) methodology played a fundamental role, being the most appropriate when it comes to unstructured data, each stage is fundamental from the collection of tweets to the final interpretation of the results.
- Support Vector Machine and Naive Bayes classification algorithms are an essential part of obtaining the predominant polarity of the tweets. Support Vector Machine algorithm obtained a 98.7% accuracy over Naive Bayes.

5.2   Future Work

- With the models already trained, a real-time sentiment analyze could be made that predicts the polarity of the FIAVL in the following years through the same social network Twitter.
- Implement the model with Google's BERT [12].

References

1. 1.4.1. Soporte de máquinas vectoriales: documentación de scikit-learn 0.23.1. https://scikit-learn.org/stable/modules/svm.html#svm-classification
2. 1.9. Naive Bayes - documentación de scikit-learn 0.23.1. https://scikit-learn.org/stable/modules/naive_bayes.html
3. Paquete nltk.sentiment - documentación de NLTK 3.5. https://www.nltk.org/api/nltk.sentiment.html
4. sklearn.feature_extraction.text.CountVectorizer - scikit-learn 0.23.1 documentation. https://scikit-learn.org/stable/modules/generated/sklearn.feature_extraction.text.CountVectorizer.html
5. User guide: contents. https://scikit-learn.org/stable/supervised_learning.html#supervised-learning
6. Anto, M.P., Antony, M., Muhsina, K.M., Johny, N., James, V., Wilson, A.: Product rating using sentiment analysis. In: International Conference on Electrical, Electronics, and Optimization Techniques, ICEEOT, vol. 2016, pp. 3458–3462 (2016). https://doi.org/10.1109/ICEEOT.2016.7755346
7. Arce García, S., Menéndez Menéndez, M.I.: Aplicaciones de la estadística al framing y la minería de texto en estudios de comunicación. Información, cultura y sociedad **39**, 61–70 (2018). https://doi.org/10.34096/ics.i39.4260
8. Arcila Calderón, C., Ortega Mohedano, F., Mateo, Á., Vicente Mariño, M.: Análisis distribuido y supervisado de sentimientos en Twitter: Integrando aprendizaje automático y analítica en tiempo real para retos de dimensión big data en investigación de comunicación y audiencias, pp. 113–136 (2018)
9. Baviera Puig, T.: Técnicas para el Análisis de Sentimiento en Twitter: Aprendizaje Automático Supervisado y SentiStrength. Dígitos. Revista de Comunicación Digital **1**, 33–50 (2017)
10. Chakraborty, P., Pria, U.S., Rony, M.R.A.H., Majumdar, M.A.: Predicting stock movement using sentiment analysis of Twitter feed, pp. 1–6 (2017)

11. Cumbicus-Pineda, O.M., Ordoñez-Ordoñez, P.F., Neyra-Romero, L.A., Figueroa-Diaz, R.: Automatic categorization of tweets on the political electoral theme using supervised classification algorithms. In: Botto-Tobar, M., Pizarro, G., Zúñiga-Prieto, M., D'Armas, M., Zúñiga Sánchez, M. (eds.) CITT 2018. CCIS, vol. 895, pp. 671–682. Springer, Cham (2019). https://doi.org/10.1007/978-3-030-05532-5_51

12. Devlin, J., Chang, M.W., Lee, K., Toutanova, K.: BERT: pre-training of deep bidirectional transformers for language understanding. arXiv preprint arXiv:1810.04805 (2018)

13. Godoy Viera, A.F.: Técnicas de aprendizaje de máquina utilizadas para la minería de texto. Investigacion Bibliotecologica **31**(71), 103–126 (2017). https://doi.org/10.22201/iibi.0187358xp.2017.71.57812

14. Juan Pablo, D.A.P.: Ecuador Estado Digital Octubre 2018. Technical report (2018). https://drive.google.com/file/d/116eZRcn-FH-cLVWmGGlt3jAn_SdG1aTL/view

15. Masiilas, J.: Knowledge Discovery in Text (2018). https://www.linkedin.com/pulse/knowledge-discovery-text-javier-mansilla/

16. Moreno Villalba, L., Avila, J., Meléndez Ramírez, A.: Análisis de sentimientos en redes sociales (Twitter) (June 2018), 17–78 (2018). http://openaccess.uoc.edu/webapps/o2/handle/10609/81435

17. Neyra-Romero, L.A., Cumbicus-Pineda, O.M., Sierra, B., Cueva-Carrion, S.P.: Automatic categorization of answers by applying supervised classification algorithms to the analysis of student responses to a series of multiple choice questions. In: Botto-Tobar, M., León-Acurio, J., Díaz Cadena, A., Montiel Díaz, P. (eds.) ICAETT 2019. AISC, vol. 1066, pp. 454–463. Springer, Cham (2020). https://doi.org/10.1007/978-3-030-32022-5_42

18. Patrimonio, M.C.: Loja unida por el Festival Internacional de Artes Vivas 2019 (2019). https://www.culturaypatrimonio.gob.ec/loja-unida-por-el-festival-internacional-de-artes-vivas-2019/

19. Patrimonio, M.C.: Informe de Rendicion Cuentas 2018. Technical report (2018). https://www.culturaypatrimonio.gob.ec/wp-content/uploads/downloads/2019/03/InformeRendicionCuentasFinal2018.pdf

20. Poornima, A.: A comparative sentiment analysis of sentence embedding using machine learning techniques, pp. 493–496 (2020). https://doi.org/10.1109/ICACCS48705.2020.9074312

21. Sharma, N.K., Rahamatkar, S., Sharma, S.: Classification of airline tweet using naïve-Bayes classifier for sentiment analysis. In: Proceedings of the 2019 International Conference on Information Technology, ICIT 2019, pp. 70–75 (2019). https://doi.org/10.1109/ICIT48102.2019.00019

Data Mining to Predict COVID-19 Patients' Recovery on a Balanced Dataset

Priscila Valdiviezo-Diaz[✉]

Departamento de Ciencias de la Computación y Electrónica,
Universidad Técnica Particular de Loja, Loja, Ecuador
pmvaldiviezo@utpl.edu.ec

Abstract. The coronavirus disease (COVID-19), has caused a considerable increase in hospitalizations of people with different symptoms caused by this disease. Currently, the world needs a quick solution to tackle the further spread of COVID-19. Data mining techniques, machine learning and other artificial intelligence techniques can provide a best patient prognosis infected by coronavirus. This paper applies data mining techniques to predict COVID-19 infected patients' recovery using open dataset with day level information on COVID-19 affected cases of China. We also use minority Downsampling technique to balance the classes we have in the dataset and thus demonstrate the importance of balancing the classes to yield better results. Additionally, the pre-processing methods and the prediction performance using evaluation metrics are presented. Logistic Regression, Decision tree, and Neural Network algorithms are applied directly on the dataset using R programming language. Experimental results show that the neural network provides a lower error and increases the classification accuracy significantly compared with other algorithms.

Keywords: Data mining · Balanced dataset · Exploratory analysis · Prediction

1 Introduction

Currently, data mining and machine learning techniques are being widely used in the health area, due these allow the processing of information from medical records and other sources, in such a way that a series of actions related to care and health management can be carried out.

On 31 December 2019, The World Health Organization (WHO) announced the current outbreak of the coronavirus disease (COVID-19) [1], first detected in Wuhan City, Hubei Province of China. Novel Coronavirus (COVID-19) is a virus identified as the cause of an outbreak of respiratory illness is rapidly spreading in humans, is believed that it was derived from bats [2]. The majority of the initial cases from the Wuhan area had been associated with visitation of a seafood/live exotic animal market or by close contact with an ill family member [3].

© Springer Nature Switzerland AG 2021
M. Botto-Tobar et al. (Eds.): ICAT 2020, CCIS 1388, pp. 340–350, 2021.
https://doi.org/10.1007/978-3-030-71503-8_26

Due to the large number of affected cases presented in the world, data mining techniques play an important role in the analysis and interpretation of available information about this pandemic, these techniques can be used for identification of patients [4], identification of the risk of infection [4], predict COVID-19 incidence [5], predict its evolution [5], etc.

Supervised learning techniques such as prediction and classification are being used to predict certain diseases, for example: [6] proposes a machine learning technique that allows a joint and fully supervised optimization of dimensionality reduction and classification models, to highlight relevant properties in the low dimensional space, to ease the classification of patients. In [7] uses algorithms machine learning for the prediction of heart disease based on the above attributes. Some researches that adopt ensemble methods for class imbalance are: [8] uses synthetic minority over-sampling technique (SMOTE) to balance the survival and non-survival classes they have in their dataset. [9] develops Cox proportional hazards elastic net logistic regression models using sampling techniques (both upsampling and downsampling), allowing to identify and select features that more accurately identify individuals at higher risk of myocardial infarction (MI).

Works related to the subject covered in this manuscript are the one presented by [10], which uses data mining models for the prediction of COVID-19 infected patients' recovery using epidemiological dataset of COVID-19 patients of South Korea. Likewise, [11] develops an outbreak prediction system for COVID-19. The prediction model forecasts the count of the new cases likely to arise for the next 5 days using different machine learning algorithms, on the other hand in [12] to better understand the growth of the number of infected cases in Taiwan, authors construct predictive models to analyze the historical data and also predict the future number of infected cases, examining some methods in time series analysis.

Unlike these studies, in this manuscript, several data mining models to predict COVID-19 infected patients' recovery, balancing the number of observations for the class variable in the dataset are developed. The models are developed with the published data by Johns Hopkins University on affected cases of COVID-19 patients. According to [9], class imbalance can present a major issue in the prediction process. This imbalance may result in inaccurate predictions for individuals who are more likely to recovery. For this reason in this study the aimed is develop an accurate prediction model of COVID-19 patients' recovery using unbiased values of class to balance predictive performance.

This paper is organized as follows. Section 2 presents material and methods used for this research, specifically, data preprocessing techniques realized to the statistical analysis and prediction. Section 3 describes in detail the experimental results and discussion. Section 4 encloses the conclusions of this paper and future work.

2 Material and Method

For this work, data published by the Johns Hopkins University are taken as reference, which makes available the affected cases data of patients, for academic and educational research purposes. This dataset has daily level information on the number of affected cases, deaths and recovery from COVID-19 coronavirus [13, 14].

The original dataset from Johns Hopkins Github repository include 1085 records with 26 attributes related to demographic information, and patients' clinical data. However, only relevant attributes were extracted from the original dataset with 825 data records, these attributes are: reporting date, gender, age, symptom_onset, symptoms and recovered. We considered two states of the patient (1: recovered and 0: non-recovered) as class values. Table 1 revealed the name and data type of the attributes used.

Table 1. Variables names and data type in the dataset extracted.

Variable	Data type	Description
Reporting date	Date	Date the patients was released or die
Gender	Object	Patient gender with two values {female, male}
Age	Numeric	Patient age
Symptom_onset	Date	Symptoms onset date
Symptoms	Object	Patient symptoms
Recovered	Numeric	State of the patient which includes two values {1, 0}

The dataset was prepared and cleaned to later be used in the experiments.

2.1 Data Processing

An exploratory analysis of the variables is carried out to analyze data using a multivariate method. According to [15], This process will allow mainly enhances and identifies the insight into our dataset, determines the correlation among the explanatory variables, identifies the anomalies and builds models. As a result of this analysis, the following is highlighted:

a) The minimum age of COVID-19 patients is 5 months, the average is 49 years, and the maximum age is 96 years.
b) 57% of the presented cases are men and 42% are women.
c) In some of the variables there are missing values which can affect the task of prediction, for example: symptom_onset, and hosp_visit_date. It probably be a big problem for the algorithm application. Therefore, a treatment for these variables is carried out.
d) The mean time from symptom onset to date patients was released is of 12 days. To get this indicator, a new attribute called no_day (Number of days) is calculated based on the symptom onset and the reporting date.
e) The most common symptoms of affected cases are: fever, cough, sore throat, difficult in breathing, chills and flu, and vomiting. There are a large number of infected cases are asymptomatic (see Fig. 1).
f) It is observed that the recovered class is imbalanced, only 19% of the data corresponds to recovered cases, the rest have a value of 0, corresponding to non-recovered patients (see Fig. 4(a)). Therefore, it is proceeds to realize a balance of the class.

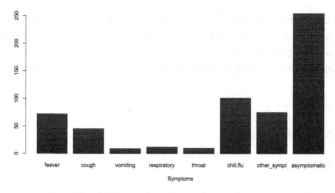

Fig. 1. Frequency of symptom attribute.

Missing Values Treatment. The existence of missing values in a dataset, according to [16] reduces the predictive power and produces biased estimates leading to an invalid results. The variables that present missing values are: asymptom_onset, and hosp_visit_date. Then, we get a new dataset without missing values.

The mode imputation technique [17] is used to handle the missing values in the dataset. This technique replaces this value with the value that occurs most frequently. The missing value in the symptom attribute represents asymptomatic cases, so this attribute is explain in the next section.

Derivation of Attributes. This task consists in the generation of new atributtes by certain calculations. In this case, a new "no_day" attribute is calculated based on the symptom onset date and the reporting date. This attribute corresponds the number of days between the symptom onset and date patient was released. Then, symptom_onset and reporting date variables are removed from the dataset and no_day is added. Figure 2 shows the sample of some instances of the dataset.

	gender	age	symptom	recovered	no_day
1	male	70.00	NA	0	8
2	male	55.00	NA	0	32
3	male	55.00	NA	0	33
4	female	45.00	NA	0	28
5	female	55.00	NA	0	28
6	female	24.00	NA	0	33
7	male	65.00	fever	0	11
8	female	55.00	fever/ cough	0	8
9	male	65.00	fever/ headache	0	22
10	female	25.00	cough/ fever/ headache/ nausea/ vomiting/ diarrhea	0	5
11	male	55.00	cough/ fever	0	2
12	male	55.00	sore throat	0	5

Fig. 2. Sample of cases in the dataset

On the other hand, considering the symptoms identified in e), a structuring of the symptoms attribute is carried out. For this process the most common symptoms that COVID-19 patients present are considered.

According to [18, 19], people with COVID-19 may have some symptoms:

- Fever
- Cough
- Difficult in breathing
- Vomiting
- Chills or Runny nose
- Sore throat
- Muscle or body aches
- Headache
- Diarrhea
- Other

Thus, for a better treatment of symptoms variable, this is divided into several sub-attributes related to the most common symptoms presented in the dataset by patients with coronavirus. Also, the "other_symptom" variable is added to group the rest of the symptoms that a patient may present. If the patient presents any of these symptoms, the value of 1 would be set and 0 if he does not present (Fig. 3).

	gender	age	no_day	feaver	cough	vomiting	respiratory	throat	chill.flu	other_sympt	asymptomatic	recovered
1	male	70.00	8	0	0	0	0	0	0	0	1	0
2	male	55.00	32	0	0	0	0	0	0	0	1	0
3	male	55.00	33	0	0	0	0	0	0	0	1	0
4	female	45.00	28	0	0	0	0	0	0	0	1	0
5	female	55.00	28	0	0	0	0	0	0	0	1	0
6	female	24.00	33	0	0	0	0	0	0	0	1	0
7	male	65.00	11	1	0	0	0	0	1	1	0	0
8	female	55.00	8	1	1	0	0	0	1	1	0	0
9	male	65.00	22	1	0	0	0	0	1	0	0	0
10	female	25.00	5	1	1	1	0	0	1	0	0	0
11	male	55.00	2	1	1	0	0	0	1	1	0	0
12	male	55.00	5	0	0	0	0	1	1	1	0	0

Fig. 3. Processed dataset

Once this transformation has been carried out, there is a new set of variables with approximately 12 attributes.

Data Balancing. By working with classification problems, there are usually drawbacks when we have only two classes or categories, mainly when they are binary. Based on this, in the present work, the option of balance the data and perform the experiments with a new dataset where the recovered class is balanced is considered.

Figure 4(a), shows the data distribution corresponding to each class (0 and 1). As we can see in this figure, the number of observations is not the same for all the classes of the dataset used for the experiment, one of the classes in the sample is extremely minority. To balance the classes, the "Downsampling" subsampling technique [20] is used, which reduces the size of the majority class, in order to improve the balance between the classes by means of assembly methods, capable of making an intelligent selection on the majority class and thus avoid eliminating important data for classification process. Figure 4(b) shows results by applying subsampling method to balance the classes in the dataset used.

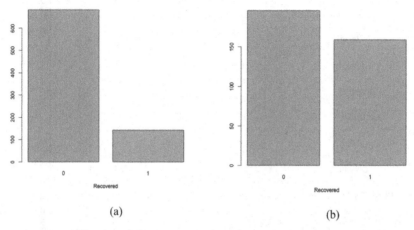

(a)   (b)

Fig. 4. (a) Imbalanced dataset and (b) Balanced dataset

When applying the assembly method to balance the classes in the dataset, the result was 380 affected cases. It can be observed that the dataset is balanced to a great extent. Considering this new dataset, the experiments are carried out.

Correlation Analysis. The recovered variable is slightly dependent on some symptoms, also there are some variables highly correlated (see Fig. 5).

Figure 5 shows the correlation coefficient of each pair of quantitative variables.

The figure evidence that there is a high negative correlation between the other_sympt and asymptomatic variables. This is probably happening because the 18% of patients present the fever symptom and the rest of them are asymptomatic patients or present another symptom. There are a large percentage of asymptomatic cases 75%. That means, that as there are more asymptomatic cases, the cases with fever or other symptoms decrease. As we observed from the correlations, fever, chill and flu, and other_sympt have strong positive correlation. There is a low negative correlation between no_day and recovered variables, which means, that if the affected number of days decreases the probability of recovery slightly increases. Likewise, age has an effect lightly on respiratory problems symptom. It was observed this symptom is more frequently in patients >40 years.

In summary, it can be observed that there is no clear dependence between the recovered variable and symptoms, which means that the recovery state of the patient does not necessarily depend on whether or not he/she presents symptoms.

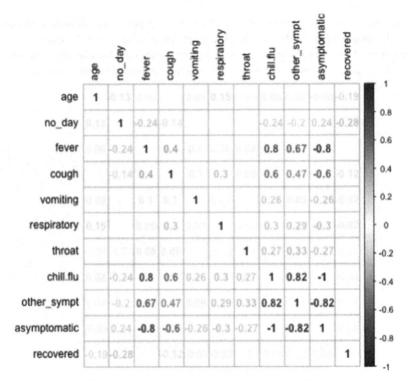

Fig. 5. Correlation coefficient among the variables

2.2 Data Mining Algorithms

Three data mining algorithms were applied to determine the model with the best results. Models were compared based on performance accuracy metrics.

Logistic Regression. This method is used for binary classification problems (with two class values, such as 0 and 1, yes and no, etc.). Logistic regression studies the association between a categorical dependent variable and a set of explanatory (independent variables) variables [21]. Also, this method is better suited for most situations because it does not assume that the independent variables are normally distributed. In this manuscript the logistic regression model is fitted using the "glm" function of R.

Decision Tree. It is a classification method in data mining, which acts in accordance with If-Then rule. Decision Tree predict a variable based on other features that are known as predictors [22]. In this work "RPART" (Recursive Partitioning And Regression Trees) package of R is used, which provides a powerful framework for growing classification and regression trees.

Neural Network. The neural network (NN) can be modeled to detect complex nonlinear relationships between the response variable and independent variables [23], These methods are based on simple mathematical models originated from brain, it can be used for classification tasks in data mining. To implement the NN model, we use the "neuralnet" package of R to fit the training data.

All models generated were evaluated using the Monte Carlo cross-validation technique [24], Accuracy metric and Root Mean Square Error (RMSE) [25] was used to evaluate the predictive accuracy of methods.

3   Results and Discussion

This section presents the data mining algorithms results and their evaluation using quality of predictions metrics. For the experiments cross-validation was used to compute the classification accuracy. The trained models were used to predict the recovered class with each algorithm selected. The performance of the models is measured in terms of accuracy, as show in Fig. 6.

Classification accuracy determines the percentage of the dataset instances correctly classified for the model developed by the data mining algorithm [10]. Figure 6 shows the classification accuracy for each algorithm.

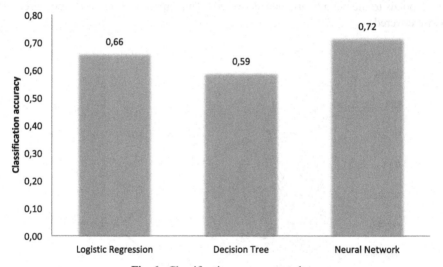

Fig. 6. Classification accuracy results.

From Fig. 6, the maximum classification accuracy of 0.72 is obtained using neural network model, compare to other developed predictions models. Accuracy for logistic regression and neural network has outperformed than Decision Tree. Decision Tree model shows lower classification accuracy (0.59). Overall, these results reveals better performance of neural network classification algorithm. This means a degree of accuracy of 72% in the predictions made. Therefore, from the purpose of prediction, it seems that the NN model may be more reliable and its results may be more satisfactory.

Additionally, the RMSE metric is also considered to evaluate the models performance (Table 2).

Table 2. RMSE results.

Model	RMSE
Logistic regression	0.5814
Decision tree	0.6391
Neural network	0.3064

Compare all methods, we find that they have fairly comparable performance with highly differences. We can see that the model developed with neural network gets the best RMSE value (0.30). The lower errors indicate that the predicted value of this method is much closer to the actual value. This means that neural network is a valuable algorithm to predict COVID-19 patients' recovery. On the other hand, the logistic regression algorithm performed poorly; with this method we obtain poor predictions.

Figure 7 shows the architecture of the neural network used. This NN is made up of 1 input layer, 2 hidden layers and 1 output layer. The input layer consists of 11 neurons that correspond to the input variables. The output layer consists of a neuron that corresponds to the output variable (recovered). This output is discrete (1: recovered, 0: non-recovered).

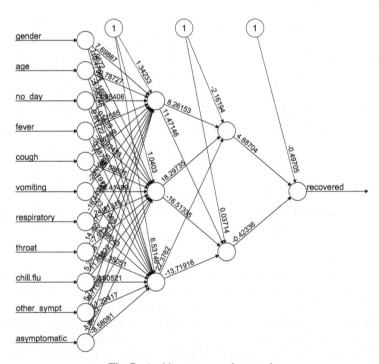

Fig. 7. Architecture neural network

This neural network topology classified correctly more cases. Specifically, this topology presented satisfactory results.

On the other hand, an experiment was carried out with the imbalanced dataset, with which higher accuracy results were obtained with the decision tree; however, when observing the confusion matrix, a bias towards the majority class is noted. That is to say, accuracy obtained a biased result, because the classes were imbalanced. For this reason, these results are not presented.

4 Conclusions

Symptoms developed by infected people with novel coronavirus (COVID-19) are very variables. In this context, data mining techniques can provide effective tools to the patients' recovery prediction based on symptoms they present, by processing affected cases datasets of patients with this virus. Also, these techniques can help the health workers to determine quickly the infected people recovery state with pandemic COVID-19.

In this manuscript, we presented data mining algorithms to predict COVID-19 patients' recovery. Logistic Regression, Decision Tree and Neural Network algorithms were applied on dataset COVID-19 patients using R programming language. Among all models considered in the experiments, we find that the NN model give relatively accurate predictions and are able to provide more reliable prediction. Neural Network application to a balanced dataset showed that their effectiveness is not biased to majority class values.

Our current results could be references for others researchers who can further develop new methods to predict coronavirus patients recovery.

In the future, it is plan to employ other approaches for data missing imputation, as k-nearest neighbor. As well as other prediction algorithms, like Naive Bayes and Support Vector Machine.

References

1. Jiang, F., Deng, L., Zhang, L., Cai, Y., Cheung, C.W., Xia, Z.: Review of the clinical characteristics of coronavirus disease 2019 (COVID-19). J. Gen. Intern. Med. **35**(5), 1545–1549 (2020). https://doi.org/10.1007/s11606-020-05762-w
2. Randhawa, G.S., Soltysiak, M.P.M., El Roz, H., de Souza, C.P.E., Hill, K.A., Kari, L.: Machine learning-based analysis of genomes suggests associations between Wuhan 2019-nCoV and bat Betacoronaviruses. bioRxiv (2020)
3. Dolin, R., Perlman, S.: Novel coronavirus from Wuhan, China 2019–2020, 9th edn. In: Mandell, Douglas, and Bennett's Principles and Practice of Infectious Diseases. Elsevier (31 January 2020)
4. Song, Z.-G., et al.: Identifying the risk of SARS-CoV-2 infection and environmental monitoring in airborne infectious isolation rooms (AIIRs). Virol. Sin. **35**(6), 785–792 (2020). https://doi.org/10.1007/s12250-020-00301-7
5. Buscema, P.M., Della Torre, F., Breda, M., Massini, G., Grossi, E.: COVID-19 in Italy and extreme data mining. Phys. A **557**, 124991 (2020)

6. Fernandes, K., Chicco, D., Cardoso, J.S., Fernandes, J.: Supervised deep learning embeddings for the prediction of cervical cancer diagnosis. PeerJ Comput. Sci. **4**(8), 1–20 (2018)
7. Haribaabu, V., Sivakumar, V., Selvakumarasamy, Dixit, V.: Prediction of heart disease risk using machine learning. Int. J. Mech. Prod. Eng. Res. Dev. **8**(Special Issue 2), 605–614 (2018)
8. Al-Bahrani, R., Agrawal, A., Choudhary, A.: Colon cancer survival prediction using ensemble data mining on SEER data. In: Proceedings of the 2013 IEEE International Conference on Big Data, pp. 9–16 (2013)
9. Datta, G., Alexander, L.E., Hinterberg, M.A., Hagar, Y.: Balanced event prediction through sampled survival analysis. Syst. Med. **2**(1), 28–38 (2019)
10. Muhammad, L.J., Islam, M.M., Usman, S.S., Ayon, S.I.: Predictive data mining models for novel coronavirus (COVID-19) infected patients' recovery. SN Comput. Sci. **1**(4), 1–7 (2020). https://doi.org/10.1007/s42979-020-00216-w
11. Li, L., et al.: Propagation analysis and prediction of the COVID-19. Infect. Dis. Model. **5**, 282–292 (2020)
12. Chen, L.-P.: Analysis and prediction of COVID-19 data in Taiwan. SSRN Electron. J. (2020)
13. Xu, B., Kraemer, M.U.G.: Open access epidemiological data from the COVID-19 outbreak. Lancet. Infect. Dis. **20**(5), 534 (2020)
14. Xu, B., et al.: Epidemiological data from the COVID-19 outbreak, real-time case information. Lancet Infect. Dis. **20**(5), 534 (2020)
15. Indrakumari, R., Poongodi, T., Jena, S.R.: Heart disease prediction using exploratory data analysis. Procedia Comput. Sci. **173**(2019), 130–139 (2020)
16. Stavseth, M.R., Clausen, T., Roislien, J.: How handling missing data may impact conclusions: a comparison of six different imputation methods for categorical questionnaire data. SAGE Open Med. **7**, 1–2 (2019)
17. Triola, M.F.: Estadística (Doceava Ed.). Pearson Educación, México (2018)
18. Zhao, D., et al.: A comparative study on the clinical features of Coronavirus 2019 (COVID-19) pneumonia with other pneumonias. Clin. Infect. Dis. **71**(15), 756–761 (2020). An Official Publication of the Infectious Diseases Society of America
19. Wiersinga, W.J., Rhodes, A., Cheng, A.C., Peacock, S.J., Prescott, H.C.: Pathophysiology, transmission, diagnosis, and treatment of Coronavirus disease 2019 (COVID-19): a review. J. Am. Med. Assoc. (JAMA) **324**, 782–793 (2019)
20. Rustogi, R., Prasad, A.: Swift imbalance data classification using SMOTE and extreme learning machine. In: Proceedings of the 2nd International Conference on Computational Intelligence in Data Science, ICCIDS 2019. Institute of Electrical and Electronics Engineers Inc. (2019)
21. Hintze, J.L.: User's Guide III. Regression and Curve Fitting. NCSS Statistical System (2007)
22. Abdar, M., Kalhori, S.R.N., Sutikno, T., Subroto, I.M.I., Arji, G.: Comparing performance of data mining algorithms in prediction heart diseases. Int. J. Electr. Comput. Eng. **5**(6), 1569–1576 (2015)
23. Paradarami, T.K., Bastian, N.D., Wightman, J.L.: A hybrid recommender system using artificial neural networks. Exp. Syst. Appl. **83**, 300–313 (2017)
24. Chlis, N.: Machine Learning Methods for Genomic Signature Extraction. Technical University of Crete, School of Electronic and Computer Engineering, Digital Signal and Image Processing Lab (2015)
25. Chai, T., Draxler, R.R.: Root mean square error (RMSE) or mean absolute error (MAE)? - Arguments against avoiding RMSE in the literature. Geosci. Model Dev. **7**(3), 1247–1250 (2014)

Topic Identification from Spanish Unstructured Health Texts

Andrea Mena and Ruth Reátegui[✉]

Universidad Técnica Particular de Loja, San Cayetano Alto, 1101608 Loja, Ecuador
{aemena3,rmreategui}@utpl.edu.ec

Abstract. Topic Models allow to extract topics from documents and classify them. In this work, Latent Dirichlet Allocation model was applied to extract topics from documents with medical information. 220 digital documents written in Spanish were used, these documents have information about different health conditions. A pre-processing was carried out, which implies tokenization, stop words elimination and lemmatization, to define the medical data or terms that will represent the documents. Subsequently, a document representation was made through a document-term matrix. An important step was to use a medical glossary based on terminology extracted from Internet to assign weights to the terms. LDA was applied and two new matrices were obtained: a document-topic matrix and a topic-term matrix. 25 topics were identified, they can be visualized by heat maps, word cloud and an interactive tool called PyL-DAvis. The application was developed in Phyton using some libraries such as Spacy, Scikit-learn, Tmtoolkit, PyLDAvis among others.

Keywords: Topic model · LDA · Medical text

1 Introduction

In the medical field exists a large number of documents such as scientific articles and medical texts that have extensive information about a disease or patients' health. Extracting information from these types of documents to identify or classify them is a difficult task due to their specialized vocabulary and an unstructured format. This task is even more aggravated if the language in which they are written is different from English because most of the tools to extract information are for English language.

Topic modeling is a method for unsupervised classification used to identify latent topics from unstructured texts. Topic modeling discovers and annotate datasets with latent "topic" , each sample piece of data is a mixture of "topics" , where a "topic" is a set of "words" occurring together across the samples [1]. These methods extract useful semantic information from many types of text such as newspapers, tweets, papers, medical text, and so on.

Latent Dirichlet Allocation (LDA) is a well-established topic model proposed in 2003 by [2] and widely used by researched from different fields. LDA represents

© Springer Nature Switzerland AG 2021
M. Botto-Tobar et al. (Eds.): ICAT 2020, CCIS 1388, pp. 351–362, 2021.
https://doi.org/10.1007/978-3-030-71503-8_27

each document as a random mixture of latent topics, which are multinomial distributions over the unique words in a corpus [3].

Recently, topic models have been applied in the health domain. In [4] applied LDA model to find associations across SNOMEDCT codes diagnoses in patients with kidney disease. Also, [5] used LDA to identify 25 phenotypes topics from information of two healthcare systems. Similarly, [6] proposed a LDA algorithm to annotate multiple phenotypes from electronic health records. In [7] applied LDA to identify topics in documents written by doctors and to carry out multi-label classification of EHRs according to the ICD-10. Also, [8] used LDA to combine information from multiple hospitals to be used in a readmission predictive model. Considering on-line information or from social media, some works used topic models to analyze behavior patterns of specific health problems such as emotional eaters [9], alcoholism [10], autism [11], diabetes [12] and so on.

This work aims to identify topics from medical text with unstructured format applying LDA model and weighing the terms according to a medical glossary. In this way, this work contributes to the automatic identification of terms, topics and the documents classification task. The data consist of 220 documents obtained from the Biomedical Abbreviation Recognition and Resolution 2nd Edition event. The documents are written in Spanish and have information of different diseases.

The paper is organized as follows: section "Materials and Methods" describes the dataset used, the data preprocessing and representation, the LDA model, the evaluation process and some tools used; section "Results and Discussion" present and discusses the results; and section "Conclusions" resume our findings and future work.

2   Materials and Methods

2.1   Dataset

The dataset consists of 220 Spanish medical abstracts, clinical case studies and clinical record sentences. The data was obtained from the event Biomedical Abbreviation Recognition and Resolution 2nd Edition[1] (BARR2) which are freely available for studies. Figure 1 shows an example of a medical abstract.

2.2   Data Preprocessing and Representation

A data preprocessing was carried out applying the following steps:

- Tokenization to divide sentences in words or tokens.
- Elimination of stop words based on a list of words not relevant to the dataset.
- Lemmatization to convert words to its lemma or dictionary form.

---

[1] https://temu.bsc.es/BARR2/.

Mujer de 68 años con antecedentes de hipertensión arterial e hipotiroidismo, que acude a Urgencias por presentar dolor en hipocondrio izquierdo de presentación aguda, sin antecedentes traumáticos, de carácter constante, irradiado a epigastrio con aproximadamente 3 horas de evolución, acompañado de mareo y debilidad. En la exploración física se evidencia hipotensión y taquicardia que se mantiene a pesar de la administración de fluidos intravenosos; el abdomen es doloroso con predominio en hipocondrio y fosa lumbar izquierda sin signos de irritación peritoneal. Se realiza Ecografía y Tomografía computarizada (TC) demostrando la presencia de una tumoración retroperitoneal redondeada de aproximadamente 10 x 12 cm por delante del polo superior del riñón izquierdo, vascularizada, con captación del contraste de forma irregular y con pequeñas calcificaciones en su interior; además, se observa un aumento de la densidad del espacio retroperitoneal compatible con sangrado. Con los hallazgos antes mencionados se decide intervenir quirúrgicamente evidenciándose un gran hematoma retroperitoneal izquierdo que se extiende hasta la línea media y la fosa iliaca izquierda y una tumoración de aproximadamente 12 cm de diámetro por encima del polo superior del riñón izquierdo, encapsulada, con sangrado activo por fisura en la misma, la cual se extrae preservando parte de la glándula suprarrenal y el riñón izquierdo. La evolución es satisfactoria. La evaluación realizada posteriormente revela la ausencia de hipertensión arterial y en la ecografía abdominal no se observan hallazgos patológicos. La biopsia describe una tumoración nodular de 10 cm de diámetro y 457 gr. de peso de coloración rojiza con margen periférico de coloración amarillenta, diagnosticándose en el estudio microscópico: Pseudoquiste endotelial suprarrenal.

Fig. 1. Example of medical abstract.

After that, a document term matrix was constructed taking account the occurrences of the words in each document. A medical glossary was constructed from three on-line dictionaries, then, if a word from the dataset exists in the glossary, the word has an extra weight. The final matrix has 220 rows that represent the documents and 5987 columns that represent words or terms.

2.3 Latent Dirichlet Allocation

Nowadays, some models permit extract topics from text. Latent Dirichlet Allocation is a model widely used to identify topics form medical documents, therefore, this work applied this model.

Latent Dirichlet Allocation (LDA) [2,13] is a generative probabilistic model for text corpora. Each document of a collection is represented as a finite mixture over an underlying set of latent topics and each topic is represented by a distribution over words [2].

This model was applied over the term-document matrix, and two new matrices were obtained: document-topic matrix and topic-term matrix. In order to select the number of topics, this work used the following metrics:

- Pair-wise cosine distance method (cao_juan_2009), proposed by [14], is based on the pairwise distances between all topics in the topic-word distribution of a model.

- Kullback-Leibler divergence method (arun_2010), proposed by [15], calculates the symmetric between the distribution of variance in the topic-word distribution and the marginal topic distribution.
- Model Coherence (cohorence_mimno_2011), proposed by [16], the pointwise mutual information is maximized when the most probable words in a given topic frequently co-occur.
- Harmonic mean method (griffiths_2004), proposed by [17], calculates the probability of the data in a set of statistical models, its purpose is to reveal the highest value of the probability.

2.4   Evaluation

Despite topic modeling is an unsupervised method without a specific variable to compare the results, in this work, was carried out a comparison between terms of topics and keywords present in some documents. The dataset used have some abstract from scientific papers, then, when the keywords were available they were used to compare with the terms of the topics.

The process is as follows: 1) the highest values (greater than or equal to 0.7) in the document-topic matrix were observed; 2) these topics were searched in the topic-term matrix; 3) then, the most relevant topics and terms were extracted for each document to create a table with the following information: name of the document, its keywords and the terms obtained from LDA. Figure 2 shows this process.

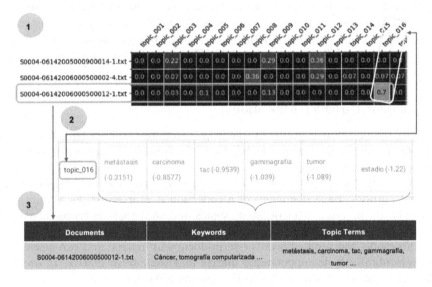

Fig. 2. Evaluation process.

2.5   Tools

This research was developed in Phyton using Jupyter Notebook. Also, some libraries were used such as:

- Spacy: It is a powerful library used for text processing in different languages. In this library tagging stands out because it uses an entity identifier for each language [18]. In addition, it allows the removal of stop words and the models can be customized to use them in a specialized way.
- Pandas: Is a library specialized in data processing, analysis and extraction. This tool is important because it creates new data structures, the data can be managed in spreadsheets and databases [19]. Its main data structures are series and data frames. It is built based on Numpy and is compatible with other modules for high-level data management.
- Scikit-learn: This library focus on supervised and unsupervised machine learning. It has a wide number of classes and methods for Natural Language Processing, Topic Modeling and data prediction.
- Tmtoolkit: It is used for text mining and for Topic Modeling. For data processing, it uses Numpy objects[2]. It has functions for the NLP such as tokenization, labeling, stemming, n-grams, etc. For Topic Modeling, the following stand out: multicore modeling, topic visualization, evaluation of topic models, graphs of evaluation metrics, among others.
- PyLDAvis: It allows to display topics and terms and it is independent of the library used for Topic Modeling [18]. This library is based on the document-topic and topic-term distributions to show the topics in circles of different sizes according to the relevance of the topic and in different quadrants due to the distances between the topics. It is useful for the interpretation of topics.
- Matplotlib: This tool is used for creating interactive graphics from data for easy interpretation and attractive data visualization. The graphics can be exported in different formats such as PNG, SVG, among others. It implements mathematical expressions in LaTex [19].

3   Results and Discussion

To select the best number of topics, for arun_2010 and cao_juan_2009 the minimum points of their curves must to be considered, while for cohorence_mimno_2011 and griffiths_2004 the maximum value should be taken. As we can see in Fig. 3, the possible values for the number of topics vary between 15 and 35, therefore, for this work the experiments were carried out considering 25 topics.

In order to see the words for each topic and the topics for each document, two matrices were obtained:

---

[2] https://tmtoolkit.readthedocs.io/en/latest/index.html.

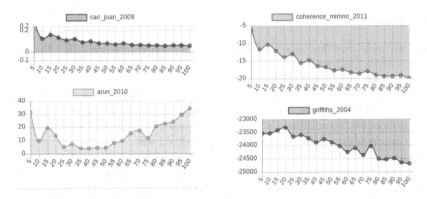

Fig. 3. Metrics to select number of topics.

- The first matrix has as rows 25 topics and as columns the 10 most relevant words by topic. The Fig. 4 presents the ranking of the 10 relevant words in topics 16 to 19. Topic 16 presents words related to cancer, topic 17 presents words related to ischemia, topic 18 has words related to blood, and topic 19 has words related to pancreas.
- The second matrix has 220 rows that represent documents and 25 columns for topics. The Fig. 5 shows a fraction of a heat map of the document-topic matrix. The relevance of the topics is highlighted by a range of colors, the most prominent being yellow, then shades of green and blue, and finally violet. As an example, the document in the third row has the topic 16 as the more important, it means that this document is about cancer.

▼	rank_1	rank_2	rank_3	rank_4	rank_5	rank_6	rank_7	rank_8	rank_9	rank_10
topic_019	pancreatitis (-0.4175)	náusea (-0.115)	fibrosis (-0.1946)	páncreas (-0.4011)	tratamiento (-0.4522)	deshidratación (-0.5346)	recurrencia (-0.971)	dermatitis (-0.971)	dermatología (-0.971)	enzima (-1.037)
topic_018	leucocito (-0.4345)	fiebre (-0.5487)	hemoglobina (-0.5744)	plaqueta (-0.9158)	linfocito (-0.9562)	tórax (-1.008)	hematocrito (-1.047)	astenia (-1.12)	ecografía (-1.124)	esplenomegalia (-1.175)
topic_017	isquemia (0.06339)	aneurisma (-0.04746)	arteria (-0.2265)	abdomen (-0.5163)	trombosis (-0.5626)	perfusión (-0.6256)	escotoma (-0.7896)	viscera (-0.7896)	epilepsia (-0.9818)	hipertensión (-1.013)
topic_016	metástasis (-0.3151)	carcinoma (-0.8577)	tac (-0.9539)	gammagrafía (-1.039)	tumor (-1.089)	estadio (-1.22)	leiomiosarcoma (-1.242)	adenocarcinoma (-1.276)	linfadenectomía (-1.517)	célula (-1.531)

Fig. 4. Some topics and relevants words.

Two widely used ways to visualize topics information is through word clouds and the PyLDAvis.

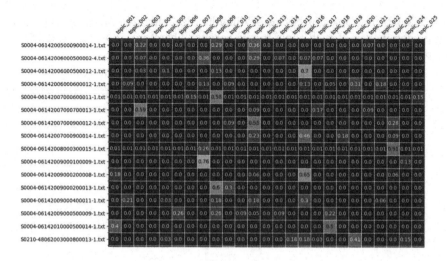

Fig. 5. Some documents and topics. (Color figure online)

For a correct interpretation of the word cloud it is important to point out that the larger the word is, the more relevant it is to the topic, on the contrary, if smaller words are observed, they are less representative for the topic. Figure 6 show 20 and 15 words for topics 16 and 18 respectively. As we can see, the words are related to cancer and blood, coinciding with the aforementioned.

Fig. 6. Word clouds for topic 16 y 18.

PyLDAvis is a Python library for interactive topic model visualization and helps to interpret topics from a LDA model[3]. The most relevant words or terms for topic 16 and 18 are present in Fig. 7 and Fig. 8, respectively. Also, both

---

[3] https://pyldavis.readthedocs.io/en/latest/.

figures show the topics in circles of different size, the area of circles represent the predominance of each topic in the corpus. Therefore, topics 16 and 18 are the predominates topics.

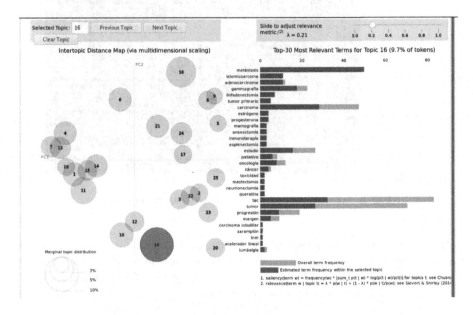

Fig. 7. PyLDAvis visualization of topic 16.

Some medical documents from the dataset used have a set of keywords that were extracted from the web link where each document was stored. Therefore, in the present work it was possible to compare the terms provided by LDA and the keywords. With this, it was possible to verify that the topics are adequate and represent in a significant way the conditions that each patient presents.

3.1   Evaluation

The evaluation shows that most of the terms in the topics correspond with the keywords of the abstracts or documents. This manual exploration was not carried out by a health professional. However a search of the medical words was done in order to relate the terms and improve the validation.

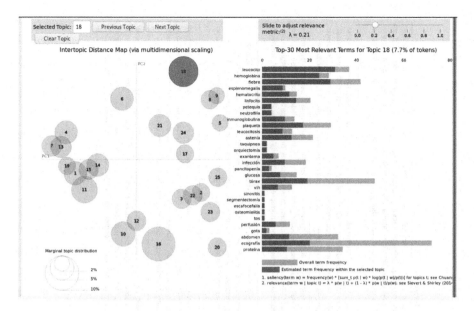

Fig. 8. PyLDAvis visualization of topic 18.

The Fig. 9 shows the comparison of some documents. Words in the second y third columns with different colors that black are related. As an example, we can see the following documents:

– The document "S1888-75462014000200009-1.txt" in the first row has the keyword "Sindrome Wolff-Parkinson-White" in red, this medical condition is related to the topic terms: "taquicardia", "arritmia", "electrofisiología" and "palpitación". The keyword "Niños" in green is related to the term "pediatria". The keyword "Diagnostico" in purple is related to "ecocardiografía" and "tomografía axial computarizada".

– The document "S1130-05582015000100004-1.txt" in the second row also shows some related word. The keyword "Reacción a un cuerpo extraño" in red is related to terms: "lesión", "epitelio", "mácula", "neurofibromatosis" and "fascitis". The keyword "Cirugía plástica" in green is related to terms "prótesis" and "blefaroplastia".

Documents	Keyword	Topic Terms
S1888-7546201400 0200009-1.txt	Síndrome Wolff-Parkinson-White, Niños. Medicina del Deporte. Diagnóstico, Ablación.	'hematoma', 'taquicardia', 'disfagia', 'subaracnoideo', 'hipotiroidismo', 'tratamiento', 'arritmia', 'edema', 'traqueostomía', 'ablación', 'radiología', 'neurocirugía', 'endocarditis', 'sistema nervioso central', 'ecocardiografía', 'anamnesis', 'hipertensión', 'esquizofrenia', 'radiofrecuencia', 'electrofisiología', 'ependimoma', 'cirugía vascular', 'serotipo', 'palpitación', 'astrocitoma', 'neuropraxia', 'blefaroplastia', 'parestesia', 'litotricia', 'ataxia', 'tomografía axial computarizada', 'gammagrafía', 'lesión', 'hematemesis', 'queratoplastia', 'espondilitis', 'astigmatismo', 'aducción', 'histocompatibilidad', 'candidiasis', 'pediatría', 'melanocito', 'incubación', 'bruxismo', 'onicofagia', 'fascitis', 'inmunodepresión', 'orquitis', 'laringe', 'amnesia'
S1130-0558201500 0100004-1.txt	Reacción a un cuerpo extraño, Cirugía plástica, Biopolímero.	'lesión', 'epitelio', 'estroma', 'catarata', 'biopsia', 'oftalmología', 'lipoma', 'ptosis', 'mácula', 'tratamiento', 'neurofibromatosis', 'hipercolesterolemia', 'fibroma', 'vestibular', 'pterigión', 'lípido', 'prótesis', 'eritema', 'célula', 'nódulo', 'astigmatismo', 'candidiasis', 'histocompatibilidad', 'pediatría', 'aducción', 'melanocito', 'espondilitis', 'hematemesis', 'queratoplastia', 'tumorectomía', 'linfocito', 'estadio', 'laringe', 'inmunodepresión', 'incubación', 'onicofagia', 'orquitis', 'enuresis', 'amnesia', 'linfocitosis', 'bruxismo', 'fascitis', 'neuropraxia', 'blefaroplastia', 'serotipo', 'esquizofrenia', 'ependimoma', 'radiofrecuencia', 'palpitación', 'astrocitoma'
S1139-7632201600 0300012-1.txt	Absceso submandibular, Caries dental	'tratamiento', 'subcutáneo', 'shock', 'suspensión', 'fiebre', 'disnea', 'flemón', 'inflamación', 'síntoma', 'síndrome', 'bacteriemia', 'congénito', 'catarro', 'neumonía', 'respuesta', 'dentista', 'linfangitis', 'osmolalidad', 'neumología', 'anticuerpo monoclonal', 'exantema', 'hepatitis', 'hipertensión', 'lactosa', 'linfadenopatía', 'leucocitosis', 'braquiterapia', 'histerectomía', 'tomografía axial computarizada', 'diabetes', 'aducción', 'pediatría', 'candidiasis', 'queratoplastia', 'histocompatibilidad', 'astigmatismo', 'hematemesis', 'melanocito', 'espondilitis', 'onicofagia', 'orquitis', 'bruxismo', 'linfocitosis', 'enuresis', 'inmunodepresión', 'fascitis', 'incubación', 'laringe', 'amnesia', 'cirugía vascular'
S1130-1473200800 0500005-2.txt	Drenaje lumbar, Hematoma de cerebelo, Hematomas a distancia, Hidrocefalia crónica del adulto, Hidrocefalia normotensiva.	'hematoma', 'taquicardia', 'disfagia', 'subaracnoideo', 'hipotiroidismo', 'tratamiento', 'arritmia', 'edema', 'traqueostomía', 'ablación', 'radiología', 'neurocirugía', 'endocarditis', 'sistema nervioso central', 'ecocardiografía', 'anamnesis', 'hipertensión', 'esquizofrenia', 'radiofrecuencia', 'electrofisiología', 'ependimoma', 'cirugía vascular', 'serotipo', 'palpitación', 'astrocitoma', 'neuropraxia', 'blefaroplastia', 'parestesia', 'litotricia', 'ataxia', 'tomografía axial computarizada', 'gammagrafía', 'lesión', 'hematemesis', 'queratoplastia', 'espondilitis', 'aducción', 'histocompatibilidad', 'candidiasis', 'pediatría', 'melanocito', 'bruxismo', 'onicofagia', 'fascitis', 'incubación', 'inmunodepresión', 'laringe', 'amnesia'
S1130-1473200500 0200003-1.txt	Cirugía del tronco del encéfalo, Cavernoma, Estimulación cortical intraoperatoria, Mapping neurofisiológico, Fosa	'catéter', 'incidencia', 'divertículo', 'angioma', 'laparotomía', 'paresia', 'hematoma', 'núcleo', 'nistagmo', 'hidrocefalia', 'parestesia', 'respuesta', 'folículo', 'fenotipo', 'ptosis', 'estreñimiento', 'vascular', 'sepsis', 'neumonía', 'diverticulitis', 'melanina', 'macrocefalia', 'tenotomía', 'obstétrica', 'osteotomía', 'episiotomía', 'hereditario', 'embolia', 'absorción', 'gammagrafía', 'litotricia', 'síndrome', 'ligamento', 'epilepsia', 'cateterismo', 'litiasis', 'colonoscopia', 'maligno', 'melanocito', 'candidiasis', 'pediatría', 'aducción', 'queratoplastia', 'histocompatibilidad', 'espondilitis', 'hematemesis', 'astigmatismo', 'enuresis', 'onicofagia'
S0365-6691200500 1100010-2.txt	Neoplasia intraepitelial corneal, displasia corneal, displasia epitelial, conjuntiva, mitomicina-C.	'lesión', 'epitelio', 'estroma', 'catarata', 'biopsia', 'oftalmología', 'lipoma', 'ptosis', 'mácula', 'tratamiento', 'neurofibromatosis', 'hipercolesterolemia', 'fibroma', 'vestibular', 'pterigión', 'lípido', 'prótesis', 'eritema', 'célula', 'nódulo', 'astigmatismo', 'candidiasis', 'histocompatibilidad', 'pediatría', 'aducción', 'melanocito', 'espondilitis', 'hematemesis', 'queratoplastia', 'tumorectomía', 'linfocito', 'estadio', 'laringe', 'inmunodepresión', 'incubación', 'onicofagia', 'orquitis', 'enuresis', 'amnesia', 'linfocitosis', 'bruxismo', 'fascitis', 'neuropraxia', 'blefaroplastia', 'serotipo', 'esquizofrenia', 'ependimoma', 'radiofrecuencia', 'palpitación', 'astrocitoma'

Fig. 9. Example of Evaluation.

4   Conclusions

Many studies had been done to identified topics in documents from different areas, in this study we focus in identified topics in Spanish medical documents.

Due to the specialized terminology used in medical documents, the use of a medical glossary to weight words helps to improve the topics identification. This approach could be applied in corpus with terminology related to the biomedical field. It also exists, vocabularies, taxonomies and ontologies that could be applied depending of the language of the documents.

The four metrics provide an idea about the number of topics to be extracted, because it represents a fundamental hyper parameter for a correct topic modeling. Therefore, visualization plays an import role in topic modeling to identify relevant words that could help to name the topics.

For future work, the terms identified in each topic and document could be used to carry out a cluster analysis and identified groups of documents with similar characteristics such as diseases, symptoms or treatments.

References

1. Liu, L., Tang, L., Dong, W., Yao, S., Zhou, W.: An overview of topic modeling and its current applications in bioinformatics. SpringerPlus **5**(1), 1–22 (2016). https://doi.org/10.1186/s40064-016-3252-8
2. Blei, D.M., Ng, A.Y., Jordan, M.I.: Latent Dirichlet allocation. J. Mach. Learn. Res. **3**(4–5), 993–1022 (2003)
3. Speier, W., Ong, M.K., Arnold, C.W.: Using phrases and document metadata to improve topic modeling of clinical reports. J. Biomed. Inform. **61**, 260–6 (2016)
4. Bhattacharya, M., Jurkovitz, C., Shatkay, H.: Co-occurrence of medical conditions: exposing patterns through probabilistic topic modeling of snomed codes. J. Biomed. Inform. **82**, 31–40 (2018)
5. Chen, Y., et al.: Building bridges across electronic health record systems through inferred phenotypic topics. J. Biomed. Inform. **55**, 82–93 (2015)
6. Ahuja, Y., et al.: sureLDA: a multidisease automated phenotyping method for the electronic health record. J. Am. Med. Inform. Assoc. **27**(8), 1235–1243 (2020)
7. Pérez, J., Pérez, A., Casillas, A., Gojenola, K.: Cardiology record multi-label classification using latent Dirichlet allocation. Comput. Methods Programs Biomed. **164**, 111–119 (2018)
8. Baechle, C., Huang, C.D., Agarwal, A., Behara, R.S., Goo, J.: Latent topic ensemble learning for hospital readmission cost optimization. Eur. J. Oper. Res. **28**, 517–531 (2020)
9. Hwang, Y., Kim, H.J., Choi, H.J., Lee, J.: Exploring abnormal behavior patterns of online users with emotional eating behavior: topic modeling study. J. Med. Internet Res. **22**(3), e15700 (2020)
10. Jelodar, H., Wang, Y., Rabbani, M., et al.: A collaborative framework based for semantic patients-behavior analysis and highlight topics discovery of alcoholic beverages in online healthcare forums. J. Med. Syst. **44**(101), 1–8 (2020)
11. Zhao, Y., Zhang, J., Wu, M.: Finding users' voice on social media: an investigation of online support groups for autism-affected users on facebook. Int. J. Environ. Res. Pub. Health **16**(23), 4804 (2019)

12. Lenzi, A., Maranghi, M., Stilo, G., Velardi, P.: The social phenotype: extracting a patient-centered perspective of diabetes from health-related blogs. Artif. Intell. Med. **101**, 101727 (2019)
13. Blei, D.M.: Probabilistic topic models. Commun. ACM **55**(4), 77–84 (2012)
14. Cao, J., Xia, T., Li, J., Zhang, Y., Tang, S.: A density-based method for adaptive LDA model selection. Neurocomputing **72**(7–9), 1775–1781 (2009)
15. Arun, R., Suresh, V., Veni Madhavan, C.E., Narasimha Murthy, M.N.: On finding the natural number of topics with latent dirichlet allocation: some observations. In: Zaki, M.J., Yu, J.X., Ravindran, B., Pudi, V. (eds.) PAKDD 2010. LNCS (LNAI), vol. 6118, pp. 391–402. Springer, Heidelberg (2010). https://doi.org/10.1007/978-3-642-13657-3_43
16. Mimno, D., Wallach, H., Talley, E., Leenders, M., Mccallum, A.: Optimizing semantic coherence in topic models. In: Proceedings of the 2011 Conference on Empirical Methods in Natural Language Processing, EMNLP 2011, pp. 262–272 (2011)
17. Griffiths, T.L., Steyvers, M.: Finding scientific topics. Proc. Nat. Acad. Sci. **101**(suppl 1), 5228 (2004)
18. Srinivasa-Desikan, B.: Natural Language Processing and Computational Linguistics. Packt Publishing, Birmingham (2018)
19. McKinney, W.: Python for Data Analysis (2nd Edn). O'Reilly Media, Inc., Sebastopol (2017)

Chatbot for Technical Support, Analysis of Critical Success Factors Using Fuzzy Cognitive Maps

Miguel Angel Quiroz Martinez(ID), Segundo Estuardo Mayorga Plua(ID),
Monica Daniela Gomez Rios(ID), Maikel Yelandi Leyva Vázquez$^{(\boxtimes)}$ (ID),
and Daniel Humberto Plua Moran(ID)

Department of Computer Science, Universidad Politécnica Salesiana Sede Guayaquil, Ecuador,
Chamber 227 y 5 de junio, USA
{mquiroz,mgomezr,mleyva,dplua}@ups.edu.ec,
smayorgap@est.ups.edu.ec

Abstract. Remote assistance needs to be automated for better coverage in time, quality, and quantity of clients. The problem is that by increasing the number of clients with the same amount of attention personnel or none, the waiting time of clients increases, and the quality of attention decreases. The objective of this research is to perform an analysis of the general critical success factors by simulating fuzzy cognitive maps applied to a chatbot for technical support. The methodology applied is exploratory, qualitative, descriptive research and de-duction to analyze the references on chatbots, technical support, critical success factors and fuzzy cognitive maps. This research resulted in a Definition of general critical success factors for a technical support chatbot, a Simulation of critical factors in a fuzzy cognitive map, an Analysis of critical success factors, and a general architecture prototype for the technical support chatbot. It was concluded that among the main critical factors for a project are important elements the knowledge of experts, expertise, and human resources; the application and analysis of CSF through FCM helps in the improvement and optimization of the factors/tasks of the chatbot project for technical support.

Keywords: Chatbots · Critical success factors · Natural language · Technical support · Fuzzy cognitive maps simulation

1 Introduction

The chatbot or bot is a conversational agent and intelligent assistant for people service to improve times and increasing productivity [1]; it is a technology that involves a conversation between software and human through intelligent comments and interactions because it uses Machine Learning (ML) and Artificial Intelligence (AI) [2]. Software that executes interaction with humans through a natural language [3].

Some chatbots use ML algorithms to reason and respond to the user without checking texts; these agents are prepared to maintain a dialogue, not resort to prediction and have

© Springer Nature Switzerland AG 2021
M. Botto-Tobar et al. (Eds.): ICAT 2020, CCIS 1388, pp. 363–375, 2021.
https://doi.org/10.1007/978-3-030-71503-8_28

an answer to user questions [4]; in a chatbot, the input and output of the platform can be voice, text or images, here the input is managed through Natural Language Processing (NLP) [5].

There are chatbots in the industrial area, homes, autonomous cars, medical support [1], social networks [2]; step to information, debates, learning [3]; education, geographic orientation, personal services [4]; robots, personal assistance, driving assistance [5]; remote assistance for clients, training, reservations [6]; recreation, commercial activities, user support [7]; sales, repetitive questions [8]; all to assist human beings.

Some properties of chatbots are text or auditory interaction, use of language processing, keyword searches, word manipulation, applied in small or large companies, it does not increase the use of human resources [7].

According to the references, in general terms chatbots are granted to support the care of people, in the medical area it is difficult for them to replace the doctor, in other areas a chatbot replaces humans because it carries out dialogues to deliver informational, transactional and talk. Some chatbot has problems to overcome such as performance, programming requirements, training, and human dependency for their beginnings; chatbot challenges include scalability, low latency, and privacy [9].

In other cases, the judgment of the environment, transfer of intentions, inspect feelings, recognize movements, and classify emotions are critical factors for the chatbot [10].

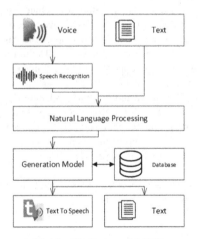

Fig. 1. Chatbot model [10].

Figure 1 presents a general model of a chatbot, these use NLP to analyze the inputs and send them to a generator.

To develop an application some activities are critical, and must be considered for the success of a project; these key activities that are necessary to achieve the objectives based on the results are Critical Success Factors (CSF) [11].

CSFs assist in prevailing the strategic organization of a project or company for the good use and exploitation of resources to obtain advantages in the face of competition [12]. Start-up, completion, time costs, monetary costs, customer satisfaction, and human resource management are crucial to influencing software development and implementation for a project.

Fuzzy Cognitive Maps (FCM) [13] are structured adaptations and quantifications of concept maps that give the direct and indirect cause, also, FCM combines features of fuzzy logic, neural networks, semantic networks, and nonlinear dynamic systems to present them inflow; it is a simpler way to present semi-quantitative modeling, these are used in various areas to understand the behavior of systems; weights between 0 and 1 are used.

The problem posed is that by increasing the number of clients with the same amount of attention personnel or none, the waiting time of clients increases and the quality of attention decreases.

Hypothesis question: Why is an analysis of critical success factors using fuzzy cognitive maps applied to a chatbot necessary for technical support?

To understand the models or architectures on chatbot that serve to maximize the hours of attention people; determine the key activities in the planning of a chatbot in technical support; understand the use and interpretation of cognitive maps.

The objective of this research is to perform an analysis of the general critical success factors by simulating fuzzy cognitive maps applied to a chatbot for technical support.

The methodology applied is exploratory, qualitative, descriptive research and deduction to analyze the references on chatbots, technical support, critical success factors and fuzzy cognitive maps.

2 Materials and Methods

2.1 Materials

Table 1 presents works related to support chabot with their success factors for implementation or operation, in addition to the model they used for the design of the chatbot.

Table 2 presents works related to CSF in software development or implementation.

2.2 Methods

Steps to Apply the Technical Support Chatbot Case

- Establish tasks for CSFs,
- Use MM software to insert CSFs,
- Update the factor weights with random values between -1 and 1,
- Get the adjacent matrix,
- Obtain and analyze the cognitive map model,
- Verify and analyze the status of the factors,
- Analyze CSFs,
- Propose an architecture for the chatbot

Table 1. Chatbot for assistance.

Ref	Proposal	Factors	Model
[1]	Incorporation of a cognitive model that captures human emotions, conversational approach	Detect and forecast the emotional states of the human being; identification and prediction of emotions; develop an NLP engine for word processing; use of emotional conversion matrix; delivery of absorbed response of emotions	Three-layer architecture, use of NLP for emotion extraction
[2]	Home automation that integrates chatbot, social network, and hardware, text input	Definition of architectural elements, design and development time, assurances, communication protocol, the place for data processing, estimated time of arrival calculations, definition of interfaces	Three-tier architecture: user-internet, cloud and home; distribution of data through provider
[3]	Dependent inquiries to the university, text entry	Process flow, programming language selection, semantics software selection, database selection	General questions in AIML format and computer application
[4]	Web platform for interaction, text input	Architecture definition, interface program selection, communication protocol selection, database selection, tests with a large number of interactions,	Architecture of: user, web access and database; application in phyton
[5]	Provide information from a specific library, conversational approach	Determine resources for assistance, correct output in understandable voice and text format, conversion methods for output, interface design, and algorithms	Architecture based on AIML files and wikipedia API, block diagram
[6]	Identification of symptoms and diagnosis in patients, conversational approach	Scope of application, selection of ML algorithms (KNN, SVM, Naive), design and implementation of algorithms, selection of data set, criteria for training and testing of each algorithm, comparison of manual versus automated tests	Use of process and sequence diagrams

(continued)

Table 1. (*continued*)

Ref	Proposal	Factors	Model
[7]	Office of admission and consultations for university students, text entry	Interface scope, network model definition, network training, database for functionality and responses, feedback functions	Use neural networks, natural language and json files
[8]	Medical attention, conversational approach	Knowledge of libraries, the definition of an internal database, search for external data, processing of voice messages, delivery time for response in text, voice and image, use of the application by users	Messaging architecture through API to databases
[9]	Create mobile applications for data generation and analysis	Planning of training and tests in different scenarios, application development route, keeping information confidential, employee participation time	Based on cognitive computing, it uses online tasks, capacity adjustments and notifications
[10]	Interpretation of user emotions and response of converted emotions, conversational approach or text input	Model selection, voice conversion processes, design of a latency and emotions compiler, storage of emotions, design of the latency and emotions structure, producer training, classifier, and compiler	Architecture for sequences of words in multiple turns of dialogues, uses database,
[14]	Recommendations and medical information, conversational approach	Testing time, advice from health experts, practices with doctors, tests with other institutions, improving practices, defining knowledge processes for the chatbot, diagnostic times for patients	Based on artificial intelligence, symptom verification
[15]	Support for student learning and material management innovations, text input	Definition of functionalities, architecture definition, programming language selection, design and implementation times, application response times	Use code to know the user's connection and minimize access to the database
[16]	Wizard to enter a programming environment without dependency on technicians, text input	Neural network training, generate data from computer professionals, use word segmentation method, data collection for training and testing	Use a neural architecture to code the questions in vectors and responses

Table 2. Critical success factors.

Ref	Proposal	Factors
[11]	Software processing through analytical category	Planning, control, team building, organization, consumer
[12]	Critical activities in banking software projects	Definition of scopes, definition of objectives, experience in software development, project management, group communication, management support, development facilities, time, organizer
[17]	Software Deployment Study	People, project, knowledge, company, experience
[18]	Recommendations for implementing planning software in companies	Staff team, Manager support, business rules, group information, management, reviews, staff training, software testing, tracking, costs, small customization
[19]	Determining student behavior	Student characteristics, pedagogical characteristics, quality measurement, learning context, information feature, dedication
[20]	Analysis of activities to manufacture software through an analytical category	Scope, monetary costs, development time, good practices, customer approval
[21]	Implementing government services in software	Project organization, human resources, strategic activities, infrastructure and technology

Tool Used for Simulation

Test software is Mental Modeler (MM) [22] that facilitates the application of FCM and is an online tool that assists in decision-making, allows to represent the assumptions in real-time; this research tool is used to evaluate mental models and is developed by Human-Environment Interactions Lab at the University of Massachusetts, Boston.

This research uses chatbot activities through FCM to facilitate and understand the dynamics of the proposed system, and this method is used as a measure of conceptual change [13].

3 Results

3.1 Definition of General Critical Success Factors for a Technical Support Chatbot

We determined the CSF for the design of a chatbot, here it was used: the analysis of the competition and experiences in software development based on the related works; the factors are as follows:

1. Definition of the scope of the chatbot
2. Definition of the process flow in technical support
3. Definition of the flow of the chatbot process
4. Definition of architecture
5. Design of common chatbot responses
6. Design of security, database, and interface
7. Design of algorithm
8. Selection of communication protocol
9. Selection of programming language
10. Implementation of database and response loading
11. Implementation of programs and processes
12. Chatbot tests with a large number of interactions
13. Meet schedule
14. User technical support practices

The factors presented were adopted from the deductions of some of the above references related to [2, 4, 5, 7, 8, 12, 15, 18] y [20].

The CSFs were built based on the related works are concepts related to definitions, design, selection, implementations and tests.

3.2 Simulation of Critical Factors in a Fuzzy Cognitive Map

MM software applies FCM and allows elements/activities and relationships between elements to be specified based on automated FCM parameters; qualitative symbologies of positive (+), negative (-) and neutral (0) are used; elements and their relationships are supposed to be an understanding for the tasks of performing the chatbot software. In this case, the array values were generated randomly.

	Defining the scope of the chatbot	Definition of the process flow in technical support	Defining the flow of the chatbot process	Definition of architecture	Design of common chatbot responses	Design of security, database and interfaces	Algorithm design	Communication protocol selection	Programming language selection	Database implementation and response loading	Implementation of programs and processes	Chatbot testing with lots of interactions	Technical support practices for users
Defining the scope of the chatbot		0.75	0.4		0.75	0.84	0.4						
Definition of the process flow in technical support	0.96				0.96	0.96	-0.48					0.39	0.4
Defining the flow of the chatbot process	0.18			0.4	0.18	0.18	-0.44					0.96	-0.44
Definition of architecture	0.4		0.44		0.64	-0.12	-0.11					-0.44	-0.7
Design of common chatbot responses						-0.91	-0.28			0.4	0.4	0.41	
Design of security, database and interfaces							0.75			0.56	0.41	0.4	
Algorithm design										0.84	0.4	-0.12	
Communication protocol selection									0.56	0.75	-0.91		
Programming language selection								-0.44		-0.48	-0.44		
Database implementation and response loading									-0.48		0.84	0.84	-0.48
Implementation of programs and processes									-0.7	0.18		0.18	0.4
Chatbot testing with lots of interactions						-0.44	0.56	0.4	-0.44	0.84	-0.44		-0.7
Technical support practices for users						-0.28	-0.28	0.41	0.75	0.84	-0.28	-0.11	

Fig. 2. Critical factors matrix for a technical support chatbot.

Figure 2 presents the mental model of activities that are in the adjacency matrix generated by MM software; in an average approach that averages values for elements and their relationships, sometimes named as a cognitive map.

Figure 3 introduces an MM-built FCM for chatbot; blue lines reveal positive relationships and red lines reveal negative relationships, directional arrows indicate that the element influences another element; the thickness of the line reveals the strength of the relationships between the elements, the thicker lines reveal stronger relationships.

In this simulation case, the factor "Definition of the scope of the chatbot" positively influences the design of algorithms through pseudocode or flow diagram, then the first factor increases in the same way with the second factor; It also has a very strong positive influence on the flow of the chatbot process, and receives a weak positive influence from this last factor. On "Definition of the scope of the chatbot" influence in a negative way: the flow of data / tasks of the technical support process, the design of the security load, the size of the database, the number of interfaces; It also has a bidirectional influence with the fulfillment of the schedule, so the development team can have new forms of testing.

The "Database Implementation and Response Loading" factor receives several strong positive influences from algorithm design, schedule adherence, user support practices, and testing of chatbot interactions; positively influences program compliance and implementation of programs, services, and components.

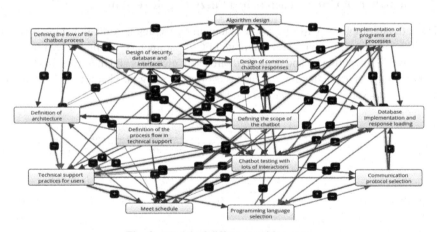

Fig. 3. Model of diffuse cognitive map.

The team has a well-established consensus and positive value in their chatbot activities; this generates knowledge among the members to review the tasks and structures of the project. The model has 14 elements, 77 connections between the model factors, 5.5 average connections per element, this serves for discussion and review of chatbot development activities; also, the team's knowledge of core activities and connections can be refined.

3.3 Analysis of Critical Success Factors

The indicator "degree of centrality" [23] cd(V) indicates the relative value of a critical factor within the FCM model, it is the sum of its absolute input and outgoing connection weights, represented in (1):

$$cd(V) = \sum (id(V) + od(V)) \tag{1}$$

Here:

id (V) = Indegree, sum of all weighted edge connections that enter factor (V), the critical factor is affected;

od (V) = Outdegree, sum of all the edge connections that leave the factor (V), the critical factor affects another factor.

For static analysis of this case, the outdegree, indegree, and centrality of critical factors that are delivered by MM software were reviewed; this list was ordered from highest to lowest (Table 3) to get the most important factors in descending order are: Implementation of database and response loading, Definition of the scope of the chatbot, and Chatbot tests with a large number of interactions; these factors will allow the performance of the project, as well as serves to guide us and focus efforts to analyze, design, develop and test the chatbot aimed at technical support.

The main factors that are most influenced (indegree) are database implementation, data relationship, response load (5.62), implementation of programs-services (4.30) and compliance with the schedule (4.26); this means that the code and data structure are influenced by other factors to achieve your goal. The main factors that influence other

Table 3. Critical success factors.

Components	Indegree	Outdegree	Centrality
Implementation of database and response loading	5.62	3.48	9.09
Definition of the scope of the chatbot	2.02	3.84	8.86
Chatbot tests with a large number of interactions	3.85	3.94	7.79
User technical support practices	3.12	3.79	6.91
Implementation of programs and processes	4.30	2.42	6.42
Design of security, database, and interface	3.73	2.12	5.85
Meet schedule	4.26	1.57	5.83
Design of common chatbot responses	2.73	2.40	5.13
Design of algorithm	3.30	1.36	4.66
Definition of the flow of the chatbot process	0.00	4.56	4.56
Definición de arquitectura	0.98	3.33	4.31
Selección de lenguaje de programación	3.93	1.36	4.29
Definición del flujo del proceso del chatbot	1.19	2.89	4.08
Selección de protocolo de comunicación	1.25	2.22	3.47

factors (outdegree) are definition of processes in support requests (4.56), chatbot tests through interactions (3.94), and the scope that can change some factors (3.84); this means that the efficiency in the tasks of the chatbot for technical support influences the factors to obtain a good tool.

3.4   General Architecture Prototype for the Technical Support Chatbot

We propose a prototype of architecture (Fig. 4), where the inputs are speech and text, for the voice you must use the recognition and transform it to text; both entries go to the NLP to understand that the user needs; the question modeler formalizes statements to the database based on keywords; the computer application selects the response from the database; feedback sends new words made by the user for storage; responses are direct about the customer's query; another process passes the text to speech for the user.

4   Discussion

Relationship of the results: the critical factors that we proposed are related in the adjacency matrix and are simulated in the cognitive map; Furthermore, the centrality of the map expresses that the implementation of databases and the load of responses to the database is the most critical factor in this simulation; the general architecture is a basic idea for a chatbot.

Our research agrees with the proposal of critical factors for software development with the following references: [11, 12, 17–20] y [21]; chatbots aimed at assistance or support: [3, 5–9, 14] y [15].

The information provided by the model is contributed by the members of the work team; there is abler to look for other options that applied; FCM assists in the evaluation of project activities, participants quantitatively and objectively measure critical factors; the process facilitates the review of the most or less successful strategies to achieve the objectives of the project.

Experts raise the Critical Success Factors that are the activities of the chatbot project; these factors arise in a mental model that uses Cognitive Map; the FCM helps determine the critical factors to be prioritized, factors that positively or negatively influence other factors. The FCM also assists in obtaining the tasks of the chatbot project, obtaining the positive or negative relationships between the tasks, the level of influence that a task can have on another task.

Exceptions: this project does not compare with other chatbot research for technical support; the Management Support task was not considered because not every project is born in a company; amounts of financial or human resources were not considered; another factor that can influence is the augmented technology existing at the time of application in the development of the software.

The results of the Mental Model are based on the values, activities, and quality of the data uploaded to the model; model adoption builds consensus on the team to improve factors in time, costs, and resources.

The theoretical consequence of our proposal is a general factor model with an emphasis on design and development activities for chatbot; and the continuous improvement of this proposal for future research.

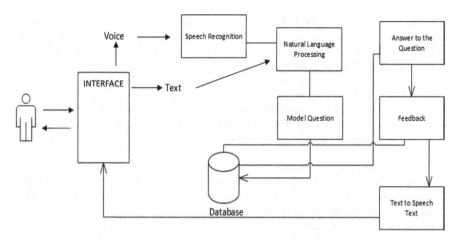

Fig. 4. Basic architecture prototype.

5   Conclusions and Future Work

It was concluded that among the main critical factors for a project are important elements the knowledge of experts, expertise, and human resources; the application and analysis of CSF through FCM helps in the improvement and optimization of the factors/tasks of the chatbot project for technical support.

The use of FCM facilitated the identification of factors to optimize the critical activities through centrality; this work is useful in decision making and planning in development projects; the use of Mental Modeler allows us to carry out various simulations to analyze possible strategies and determine their impact on software development groups; this document presented other relevant factors of references that influence development success.

We consider that the factors proposed in our research should be developed through agile methodology in web or mobile development projects or other; let's not forget that qualified personnel influence the success factors for software development and implementation.

In future work, a chatbot architecture will be proposed for medical assistance and critical success factors through fuzzy cognitive maps analysis for medical chatbots will be developed too.

Acknowledgments. This work has been supported by the GIIAR research group and the Salesian Polytechnic University of Guayaquil.

References

1. Adikari, A., De Silva, D., Alahakoon, D., Yu, X.: A cognitive model for emotion awareness in industrial chatbots. In: 2019 IEEE International Conference on Industrial Informatics, pp. 183–186 (2019). https://doi.org/10.1109/INDIN41052.2019.8972196

2. Parthornratt, T., Kitsawat, D., Putthapipat, P., Koronjaruwat, P.: A smart home automation via Facebook chatbot and raspberry Pi. In: 2018 2nd International Conference on Engineering Innovation (ICEI), pp. 52–56 (2018). https://doi.org/10.1109/ICEI18.2018.8448761
3. Ranoliya, B.R., Raghuwanshi, N., Singh, S.: Chatbot for university related FAQs. In: 2017 International Conference on Advances in Computing, Communications and Informatics (ICACCI), pp. 1525–1530 (2017). https://doi.org/10.1109/ICACCI.2017.8126057
4. Kohli, B., Choudhury, T., Sharma, S., Kumar, P.: A platform for human-chatbot interaction using python. In: Proceedings of the 2nd International Conference on Green Computing and Internet of Things (ICGCIoT), pp. 439–444 (2018). https://doi.org/10.1109/ICGCIoT.2018. 8753031
5. Naveen Kumar, M., Linga Chandar, P.C., Venkatesh Prasad, A., Sumangali, K.: Android based educational Chatbot for visually impaired people. In: 2016 IEEE International Conference on Computational Intelligence and Computing Research (ICCIC), pp. 16–19 (2017). https:// doi.org/10.1109/ICCIC.2016.7919664
6. Srivastava, P., Singh, N.: Automatized medical chatbot (Medibot), pp. 351–354 (2020). https:// doi.org/10.1109/parc49193.2020.236624
7. Singh, R., Paste, M., Shinde, N., Patel, H., Mishra, N.: Chatbot using tensorFlow for small businesses. In: Proceedings of the International Conference on Inventive Communication and Computational Technologies (ICICCT), pp. 1614–1619 (2018). https://doi.org/10.1109/ICI CCT.2018.8472998
8. Rosruen, N., Samanchuen, T.: Chatbot utilization for medical consultant system. In: 2018 3rd Technology Innovation Management and Engineering Science International Conference (TIMES-iCON) (2019). https://doi.org/10.1109/TIMES-iCON.2018.8621678
9. Bozzon, A.: Enterprise crowd computing for human aided chatbots. In: Proceedings of the International Conference on Software Engineering, pp. 29–30 (2018). https://doi.org/10.1145/ 3195555.3195566
10. Kao, C.H., Chen, C.C., Tsai, Y.T.: Model of multi-turn dialogue in emotional chatbot. In: Proceedings of the 2019 International Conference on Technologies and Applications of Artificial Intelligence (TAAI), pp. 5–9 (2019). https://doi.org/10.1109/TAAI48200.2019.8959855
11. Ribeiro, M.B., Duarte, V.D., Salgado, E.G., Castro, C.V.: Prioritization of critical success factors in the process of software development. IEEE Lat. Am. Trans. **15**, 137–144 (2017). https://doi.org/10.1109/TLA.2017.7827917
12. Priambodo, A., Handayani, P.W., Pinem, A.A.: Success factor for IT project implementation in banking industry: a case study. In: 2019 3rd International Conference on Informatics and Computational Sciences (ICICOS). Accelerators Informatics Computational Research Smarter Society Era Industry 4.0, Proceedings (2019). https://doi.org/10.1109/ICICoS48119. 2019.8982404
13. Henly-Shepard, S., Gray, S.A., Cox, L.J.: The use of participatory modeling to promote social learning and facilitate community disaster planning. Environ. Sci. Policy. **45**, 109–122 (2015). https://doi.org/10.1016/j.envsci.2014.10.004
14. Lamb, H.: News briefing - healthcare doctors slam claims that chatbot is on par with human doctors. Eng. Technol. **13**, 12 (2018). https://doi.org/10.1049/et.2018.0713
15. Murad, D.F., Fernando, E., Irsan, M., Murad, S.A., Akhirianto, P.M., Wijaya, M.H.: Learning support system using chatbot in "Kejar C Package" homeschooling program. In: 2019 International Conference on Information and Communications Technology (ICOIACT), pp. 32–37 (2019). https://doi.org/10.1109/ICOIACT46704.2019.8938479
16. Yadav, A.A., Garg, I., Mathur, P.: PACT - programming assistant chatbot. In: 2019 2nd International Conference on Intelligent Communication and Computational Techniques (ICCT), pp. 131–136 (2019). https://doi.org/10.1109/ICCT46177.2019.8969070

17. Edwita, A., Sensuse, D.I., Noprisson, H.: Critical success factors of information system development projects. In: Proceedings of the 2017 International Conference on Information Technology Systems and Innovation (ICITSI), pp. 285–290 (2017)
18. de Oliveira, E.T., Rodello, I.A.: Fatores críticos de sucesso para implantações de sistemas ERP no formato cloud computing deployment. In: 2018 13th Iberian Conference on Information Systems and Technologies, pp. 1–6 (2018)
19. Saleem, N.: Empirical analysis of critical success factors for project management in global software development. In: Proceedings of the 2019 ACM/IEEE 14th International Conference on Global Software Engineering (ICGSE), pp. 68–71 (2019). https://doi.org/10.1109/ICGSE.2019.00025
20. Octavianus, R., Mursanto, P.: The analysis of critical success factor ranking for software development and implementation project using AHP. In: 2018 International Conference on Advanced Computer Science and Information Systems (ICACSIS), pp. 313–318 (2019). https://doi.org/10.1109/ICACSIS.2018.8618147
21. Soni Fajar Surya, G., Amalia, A.: The critical success factors model for e-Government implementation in Indonesia. In: 2017 5th International Conference on Information and Communication Technology (ICoIC7) (2017). https://doi.org/10.1109/ICoICT.2017.8074711
22. University of Massachusetts: Mental Modeler Software. https://dev.mentalmodeler.com
23. Gray, S.R.J., et al.: Are coastal managers detecting the problem? Assessing stakeholder perception of climate vulnerability using Fuzzy Cognitive Mapping. Ocean Coast. Manag. **94**, 74–89 (2014). https://doi.org/10.1016/j.ocecoaman.2013.11.008

Machine Vision

Design and Construction of a Low Cost CNC Milling Machine for Woodworking

Manuel Ayala-Chauvin[1]([✉]) [ID], Fernando Saá[1] [ID], Ricardo Rodríguez[1] [ID], Carles Domènech-Mestres[2] [ID], and Genís Riba-Sanmartí[2] [ID]

[1] SISAu Research Group, Facultad de Ingeniería y Tecnologías de la Información y Comunicación, Universidad Tecnológica Indoamérica, Ambato 180103, Ecuador
{mayala,fernandosaa}@uti.edu.ec,
ricardorodriguez@indoamerica.edu.ec
[2] Centro de Diseño de Equipos Industriales, Universitat Politècnica de Catalunya-Barcelona Tech, 08034 Barcelona, Spain
domenech@cdei.upc.edu, genis.riba@upc.edu

Abstract. Computer Numeric Control (CNC) machinery were created to reduce manufacturing times for industry, but this type of machinery is costly and therefore only a few uses can recover the investment. However, the progress of electronics in the last decades has allowed to develop affordable CNC machines. This article explains the design and manufacturing process of a low budget CNC milling machine for woodworking. All the structural elements were designed and simulated using PTC CREO, as well as the manufacturing sequence. The control hardware uses commercially available electronics such as Arduino ONE, and stepper motors to move the machine, while the software uses the free open source codes Vetrica Aspire and Universal G Code. The machine was tested on different materials, obtaining good results. The result is a CNC milling machine for woodworking that costs about 50% the price of an equivalent commercial machine, an can therefore be a suitable solution for craft industries.

Keywords: CNC · Milling machine · G-code · Arduino

1 Introduction

1.1 Background

Computer numerical control (CNC) milling machines have been a great asset to manufacturing industries, since they increase manufacturing range and flexibility [1], while sustaining high milling speed and precision [2]. The advent of CNC milling machinery therefore brings reduced manufacturing times and increased quality.

One of the biggest challenges to develop a CNC milling machine is the control and synchronization of the axis (X, Y, Z) using stepper motors [3], where positioning and precision have a fundamental role. In order to maintain a high positioning precision, PID

© Springer Nature Switzerland AG 2021
M. Botto-Tobar et al. (Eds.): ICAT 2020, CCIS 1388, pp. 379–390, 2021.
https://doi.org/10.1007/978-3-030-71503-8_29

(proportional-integral-derivative) controllers, GA (genetic algorithm) or Fuzzy Logic are used to improve the dynamic characteristics of the control loop. These tools tend to keep the mathematical model simple, and find techniques to optimize the working parameters [4].

On the other hand, the controller-hardware communication is performed by microcontrollers, PC's or the systems' own cards. However, one of the most commonly used is Arduino [5], which offers great features at a very low cost. Another very common controller is Raspberry Pi, which uses an open source code [6].

CNC machines operation uses G and M codes, which are sets of instructions that define the actions and movements of the machine [7]. Some of these codes have Open-Source licenses, such as LinuxCNC. It has a very flexible configuration and interface to combine software and hardware in an inexpensive manner, but a very good performance in CNC machinery [8].

1.2 Related Works

Low cost CNC milling machines are a good way for industries in developing countries to obtain access to better technologies and results. The use of an Arduino board as a control system, together with a set of stepper motors and sensors, CAD and CAE engineering software, G and M codes, and OpenSource software results in a very robust yet flexible array of possible CNC milling machinery designs [9, 10]. Furthermore, machines built this way are very competitive compared to marketed machines, since it uses simple and modular materials that are readily available within the user's context [11].

On the other hand, their performance can be enhanced regarding precision and quality of the milled pars, by using servomotors, which increase axis speed and introduces a feedback to the control loop [12]. This is a more expensive design. Therefore, this paper will focus solely on the design of a low-cost CNC milling machine using Arduino technology and stepper motors. The rest of the contribution is organized as follows: in Sect. 2 the design method; in Sect. 3 the selection formulation; Sect. 4 describes the results; and finally the conclusions are presented in Sect. 5.

2 Design Method

The system was designed with a stage-based method to design machines and products (see Fig. 1).

It is a 4-stage method. Stage 1 is the definition of the requirements and desires of the client to generate the specifications. Stage 2 is the creation of the concept design and the definition of the working principles, as well as the selection of the main drives and the economic feasibility analysis. Stage 3 is the detail design that results in the manufacturing drawings. Finally, Stage 4 is the construction of a working prototype [14].

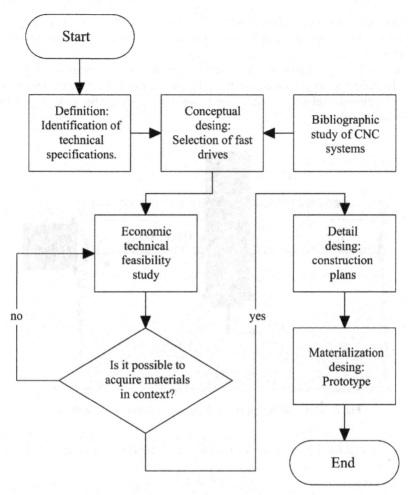

Fig. 1. Design method in context. Source: developed by the authors based on [13].

3 Selection Formulation

Linear drives transform rotational movement into lineal movement. This transformation carries a power loss, which depends on the type of bolt used and the number of entries. Therefore, the selection of the drive must take into account the work cycle.

According to that, we introduce a method to select drives for the milling machine, which studies the dynamic of the handling system using the equation for a linear angular system [15].

$$M_m = \left(J_m + \frac{J_r}{\eta i^2}\right)\alpha_m + \frac{F_r}{\eta i} \tag{1}$$

Where M_m is the torque, J_m the inertia o the motor, J_r is the inertia of the target, η is the transmission efficiency, α_m is the acceleration, F_r the force of the target and i is the gear ratio.

A trapezoidal speed profile is assumed to estimate the required power for milling wood. Therefore, the target requirements are the starting point of the calculation to obtain the acceleration α_r, velocity v_r, and force F_r needed to perform the tasks at their most demanding situation.

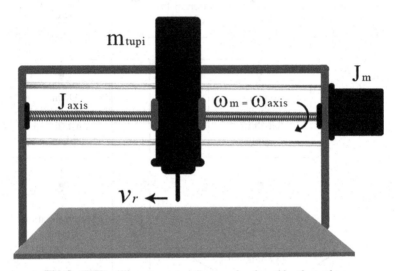

Fig. 2. CNC milling apparatus. Source: developed by the authors.

The required force F_r to move the load with a coefficient of friction $\mu = 0.01$ is.

$$F_r = F + \mu M \tag{2}$$

Where F is the working force required by the cutting tool, and M is the total mass of the mounted elements.

We use a simplified model of the milling apparatus (see Fig. 2), in which the total momentum of the system applied to the motor axis is given by:

$$J_R = J_m + J_{axis}\left(\frac{\omega_{axis}}{\omega_m}\right)^2 + m_{tupi}\left(\frac{v_r}{\omega_m}\right)^2 \tag{3}$$

Where v_r is the advance velocity of the mil or target, ω_m is the angular velocity of the motor, ω_{axis} is the velocity of the bolt, m_{tupi} is the mass of the shaper and J_{axis} is the inertia of the bolt.

The speed ratio between the bolt and the motor is direct, therefore, unity, $\frac{\omega_{axis}}{\omega_m} = 1$.

The mill speed v_r is characterized by the number of entries e of the bolt, and the pitch p:

$$v_r = \frac{pen}{60} \tag{4}$$

Where n is the turning speed in rpm.

The resulting expression for the total moment of inertia is:

$$J_R = J_m + J_{axis}\left(\frac{\omega_{axis}}{\omega_m}\right)^2 + m_{tupi}\left(\frac{pen}{\omega_m 60}\right)^2 \tag{5}$$

This method is used to find the best velocity strategy for the system, where the torque M_m and the motor speed ω_m are equal to those of the target, thus obtaining the characteristic curves of the motor and the target.

4   Results

This section shows the result of the selected drives, electronic components and the design of the milling machine for woodworking.

4.1   Actuator Selection

The motor-mill speed ratio is $\frac{v_r}{\omega_m} = 0.00127$ m/rad. Using Eq. (3) to calculate the inertia.

$$J_R = J_m + J_{axis}\left(\frac{\omega_{axis}}{\omega_m}\right)^2 + m_{tupi}\left(\frac{v_r}{\omega_m}\right)^2$$

$$J_R = 0.0003 + 0.0025(1)^2 + 10(0.00127)^2$$

$$J_R = 0.00281 \text{ Kg} \cdot \text{m}^2$$

Therefore, the inertia on the motor axis is $J_R = 0.00281$ Kg $\cdot$ m^2.

The required force F_r to move the load considering a friction coefficient with the rail $\mu = 0.01$ and $M = 60$ N.

$$F_r = F + \mu M$$

$$F_r = 119.4 + 0.01(60)$$

$$F_r = 120 \text{ N}$$

Finally, we use Eq. (1) to calculate the motor torque with a known motor acceleration $\alpha_m = 314$ rad/s^2 and the linear angular ratio $i = 785$ rad/m.

$$M_m = \left(J_m + \frac{J_r}{\eta i^2}\right)\alpha_m + \frac{F_r}{\eta i}$$

$$M_m = \left(0.0003 + \frac{0.0025}{785^2}\right)314 + \frac{120}{785}$$

$$M_m = 0.153 \text{ Nm}$$

Figure 3 depicts the stepper motor characteristics, showing the torque and the speed range between 300 and 1,000 rpm. These characteristics fit the target specifications.

Therefore, the chosen motor is a stepper NEMA 17, working at 4 V and 1.2 A, with a safety factor of 50%. The greyed area in Fig. 3 are the working conditions in terms of load torque and rotational speed.

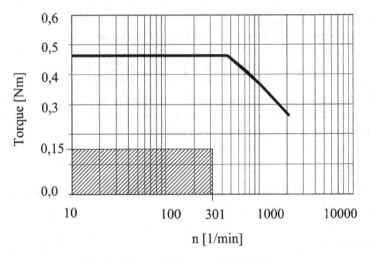

Fig. 3. Characteristic curve of a NEMA motor.

4.2 Selection of Electronic Components

The CNC milling machine operates on three axis (X, Y, Z) controlled by an Arduino UNO card, plus an integrated module CNC Shield. This setup can control the 4 stepper motors up to 2 A and 35 V.

Figure 4 shows the electronic components used to build the CNC milling machine. All modules are shelf products and relatively inexpensive, hence making it a very affordable control system for the CNC milling machine.

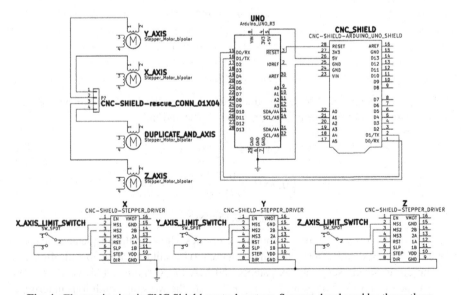

Fig. 4. Electronic circuit CNC Shield control system. Source: developed by the authors.

4.3 Machine Design

The milling machine was designed using the PTC CREO software, following the geometric requirements shown in Table 1.

Table 1. Design characteristics

Description	Size
X-axis travel	360 mm
Y-axis travel	360 mm
Z-axis travel	50 mm
Travel speed	3000 mm/min
Structure material	AISI 1020

Figure 5 shows the design of the milling machine, with the positioning of the axes and the motors.

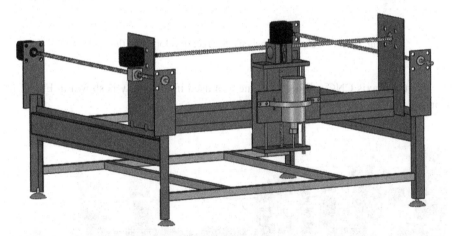

Fig. 5. CAD design of the CNC milling machine. Source: developed by the authors.

The apparatus was designed to move along the three axes (X, Y, Z), and the work bench is fixed. The workpiece is tied to the work bench using cable ties.

On the other hand, the linear movement of the axes is obtained by a 8 mm diameter and 2 mm pitch bolt system. The bolts are mounted directly on the stepper motors, so that the rotation speed of the bolt is the same as the motor's.

The assembly was also simulated using the finite elements software SIMULATE of the CREO suite. The worst case scenario used for the calculation includes simultaneous 120 N loads at the tip of the mill in the axial direction.

Figure 6 shows the Von Mises stress distribution, averaged stresses display 2.283 MPa as a maximal value with a maximum displacement of 0.0236 mm, which is negligible. It therefore satisfies the condition of resistance.

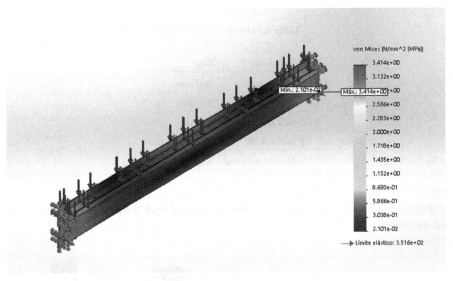

Fig. 6. Finite elements analysis. Source: developed by the authors.

The three-axis CNC milling machine tool used in this study is shown in Fig. 7. Its working volume is $360 \times 360 \times 50 \ mm^3$.

Fig. 7. CNC milling machine prototype. Source: picture taken by the authors.

4.4 Machining Process

The wood milling process begins with the placement and mounting of the work piece on the workbench, and then proceed to the milling according the previously programmed instructions.

Figure 8 shows the flow diagram of the wood milling process. The process has three main stages: mounting, programming and milling.

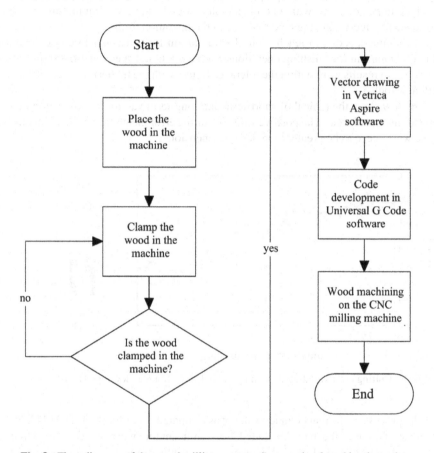

Fig. 8. Flow diagram of the wood milling process. Source: developed by the authors.

The milling stage includes three preparation steps. First, generate a vector drawing using the software Vetrica, and then the G-code of the work piece using the Universal G-code software. The last step before starting milling is verifying the zero of the machine.

4.5 Machine Construction and Testing

A prototype of the machine was built in the lab, and produced a series of test runs. The wood used for the test was Cedar and Pine, with a density of around 400 kg/m^3 and

500 kg/m^3 respectively. 50 test runs were performed on each wood type, for a total of 100 samples.

The operation is stable for feed rate to spindle speed ratios under 0.2. Furthermore, the spindle can overheat and in some cases even break during machining due to the irregular hardness of the wood.

The milling speed depends on the geometry of the cutting tools, and therefore machining times can be decreased with proper tool selection. In this case, the tool of choice was a carbide tipped end mill with a nominal diameter of 12 mm. Machining time can also be reduced by increasing the feed rate within the operation limits.

Machining speeds can reach up to 3000 mm/min for rough machining operations and 2000 mm/min for finishing operations, with a rotational speed of 14,000 rpm.

The final results were within the tolerance limits, with the highest accuracy achieved with new tools.

Figure 9 show the typical of short-term and long-term variation of the cutting error depending on tool wear. The positive value of cutting error means that the real dimension of the work piece to be greater than design dimension.

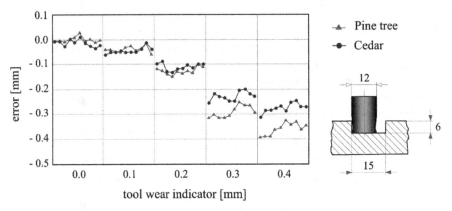

Fig. 9. Cutting error variation depending on tool wear. Source: developed by the authors.

The process performance index value was evaluated according to ISO 21747:2006. From measurements it can be concluded that significant tool wear can reduce machining accuracy from IT12 to IT14 [16]. However, the results of these evaluations show that standardized tolerances are suitable for furniture manufacturing.

4.6   Cost Analysis

A cost analysis, shown in Table 2, was performed to assess the economic viability of the CNC milling machine. It includes the materials, ancillary equipment, as well as human labour.

The CNC milling machine has a low and competitive cost, which is one of the main design specification [17]. The cost can be further reduced if larger quantities of the machine are commissioned.

Table 2. CNC milling machine manufacturing cots

Element	Total cost
Motors/Spindle turret	$210
Structural components	$199
Electronic components	$198
Human labour	$400
Total	$1007

Using shelf components, such as the Arduino CNC Shield modules, saves a lot of time and expenses when compared to printed boards created ad-hoc, which can be very costly and time consuming. In that line, open-source platforms which are also very cost-effective and flexible.

5 Conclusions

Manufacturing industry is immersed in an everlasting modernization process, and CNC machine-tools have become an essential resource for many companies to stay competitive. However, industries in developing regions often find themselves blocked from this resource due to the financial barrier of commercial CNC machinery.

This article describes a design of an affordable CNC milling machine that is flexible, and thus can be adapted to the context and the requirements of each manufacturer. It introduces a simple and reproducible system to select the components of the CNC milling machine. The formulation stems from the analysis of the dynamics of the drives, and the equations of a linear angular system.

The investment required to build this machine is low, thanks to both the use of commercial components to build the machine, and free open source software for the control. It uses stepper motors to move the spindle turret along three axes (X, Y, Z), and the control unit uses Arduino UNO and Shield CNC, which support the use of free software such as Vetrica Aspire and Universal G-code.

Machining parameters were determined, keeping in mind wood milling particularities relative to the wood properties. Besides, the proposed process flow can obtain finished parts of good quality.

On the other hand, stepper motors have low load capacities, and therefore the machine is only suitable for shallow milling. However, the selection system is reproducible and can be also used to design CNC milling machinery with better features. For instance, using servomotors would increase load capacity and precision, but also be costlier.

Lastly, since the design is modular and affordable, as well as flexible and scalable, it is an ideal solution for small craft industries, or in developing regions. Using this type of machine will both enhance the industry's quality and production time, and thus their competitiveness.

References

1. Joshi, A., Kothiyal, P.: Investigating Effect of Machining Parameters of CNC Milling on Surface Finish by Taguchi Method, pp. 60–65 (2012)
2. Amanullah, A.N.M., Saleh, T., Khan, R.: Design and development of a hybrid machine combining rapid prototyping and CNC milling operation. Procedia Eng. **184**, 163–170 (2017). https://doi.org/10.1016/j.proeng.2017.04.081
3. Madekar, K.J., Nanaware, K.R., Phadtare, P.R., Mane, V.S.: Automatic mini CNC machine for PCB drawing and drilling. Int. Res. J. Eng. Technol. (IRJET) **3**(02), 1107–1108 (2016)
4. Idrizi, F., Kacani, J.: A Fast PID Tuning Algorithm for Feed Drive Servo Loop, pp. 180–190 (2018)
5. Panchal, H.B., Vaja, M.S., Patel, P.D., Padia, U.N.: Arduino based cnc machine (2017)
6. Dimic, Z., Vorkapic, N., Mitrovic, S.: Annals of Faculty Engineering Hunedoara, pp. 57–64 (2020)
7. Sultana, N., Quader, R., Rahman, H.: SolidCAM iMachining (2D): a simulation study of a spur gear machining and G-code generation for CNC machine. Int. J. Mech. Eng. Autom. **3**, 1–9 (2016)
8. Correa, J.E., Toombs, N., Ferreira, P.M.: Open-source electronics. J. Manuf. Syst. **44**, 317–323 (2017). https://doi.org/10.1016/j.jmsy.2017.04.013
9. Quatrano, A., Control, O., De, S., Rivera, Z.B., Guida, D.: Development and implementation of a control system for a retrofitted CNC machine by using arduino. FME Trans. **45**(4), 565–571 (2017). https://doi.org/10.5937/fmet1704565Q
10. Wasif, M., Siddique, Q.M., Sakib, S., Rameez, T.M.: Design of Mini CNC using Arduino uno, pp. 3882–3884 (2019)
11. Girhe, P.: Arduino based cost effective CNC plotter machine. Int. J. Emerg. Technol. Eng. Res. (IJETER) **6**, 6–9 (2018)
12. Pahole, I., Rataj, L., Ficko, M., Brezovnik, S.: Construction and evaluation of low-cost table cnc milling machine (2010)
13. Romeva, C.R.: Diseño Concurrente. UPC, Barcelona (2010)
14. Blanco-Romero, E.: Metodología de diseño de máquinas apropiadas para contextos de comunidades en desarrollo (2018). http://hdl.handle.net/2117/121027
15. Domènech, C.: Contribució a les bases metodològiques per a la selecció i dimensionament de l'accionament i la transmissió per a moviments ràpids, en base al mètode Ṗ-K (2016). http://hdl.handle.net/2117/105138
16. Liou, F.F.: Rapid Prototyping and Engineering Applications: A Toolbox for Prototype Development. Second Edition. CRC Press, Boca Raton (2019)
17. Choudhary, R., Sambhav Titus, S.D., Akshaya, P., Mathew, J.A., Balaji, N.: CNC PCB milling and wood engraving machine. In: 2017 International Conference On Smart Technologies For Smart Nation (SmartTechCon), pp. 1301–1306 (2017). https://doi.org/10.1109/SmartTech Con.2017.8358577

Autonomous Intelligent Navigation for Mobile Robots in Closed Environments

Steven Silva Mendoza[1]([✉]), Dennys F. Paillacho Chiluiza[2], David Soque León[2], María Guerra Pintado[2], and Jonathan S. Paillacho Corredores[2]

[1] Facultad de Ingeniería en Mecánica y Ciencias de la Producción - FIMCP, ESPOL Polytechnic University, Escuela Superior Politécnica del Litoral, ESPOL, Campus Gustavo Galindo, P.O. Box 09 -01 -5863, Guayaquil, Ecuador
sasilva@espol.edu.ec
[2] Facultad de Ingeniería en Electricidad y Computación - FIEC, CIDIS, ESPOL Polytechnic University, Escuela Superior Politécnica del Litoral, ESPOL, Campus Gustavo Galindo, P.O. Box 09 -01 -5863, Guayaquil, Ecuador
{dpaillac,disoque,magaguer,jspailla}@espol.edu.ec

Abstract. Providing a map is mandatory for Autonomous Mobile Robots to be able to complete localization and navigation tasks, known as SLAM. Several SLAM algorithms which provides different quality maps have been proposed before but still issues related to map quality can appear while for accurate navigation high mapping performance is desired, therefore to be used in areas regarding health care through delivery and indoor control. For that reason, although several SLAM methods are available, the one provided by Cartographer ROS has been chosen for being one of the most recent, updated ones and has been taken into test with respect to the map quality provided. To accomplish that objective, the implementation of a simulation and experimental environment have been constructed in order to contrast between both mapping, localization and navigation results by using Turtlebot3 and Arlo Parallax platforms including LiDar and encoder sensors, with which the map created by the simulation would be the most optimum map as possible. As a result by using an RPLiDar A1, an acceptable map from the experimental procedure related to the optimized one was acquired. With which could be concluded that Cartographer ROS algorithm is satisfactory to be used for intelligent autonomous navigation purposes by providing high fidelity and effective maps even while demanding affordable computational power.

Keywords: Autonomous mobile robots · Cartographer ROS · Robotics operating system · MicroPython · ESP32 · Social navigation

1 Introduction

Several packages, navigation stacks and solution for AMR[1] have been proposed throughout both previous decade, some of them have been left outdated while

---

[1] Autonomous Mobile Robots.

© Springer Nature Switzerland AG 2021
M. Botto-Tobar et al. (Eds.): ICAT 2020, CCIS 1388, pp. 391–402, 2021.
https://doi.org/10.1007/978-3-030-71503-8_30

some of them updated continuously. An AMR corresponds to any platform that is aware of its environment and able to navigate through without colliding and finding the right trajectory for different coordinates goals without having to be overseen directly by a operator. Since it is needed for the AMR to recognize its environment, certain resources are requested by it regarding surrounding space features. These features which correspond to a map, distance array structures, and encoder values have its own quality or accuracy, from which one of the most important is a well made map. In the current project, only 2D Mapping is considered [15].

In the case of ROS[2], a map can be created by using different SLAM[3] algorithms and techniques like Gmapping, Hector SLAM and RTAB, each giving a different approach of a map solution but not a definitive one to be used without question. However not too many years ago Cartographer, a Google project which is a system that provides real-time SLAM in 2D and 3D across multiple platforms and sensor configurations was ported to ROS [6]. While seeking for one of the most optimum methods of creating a map using ROS and then use it for autonomous navigation, it was stated as an objective to test one of the SLAM methods. From the ones we researched, found Cartographer ROS to be one of the best and most promising ones, since it uses a global map optimization cycle and local probabilistic map updates which makes the system more robust to changes in the environment [2]. Having in mind that what is most important is to be able to create the map of the space experimentally, it was proposed to analyze Cartographer ROS experimental performance comparing it with simulation, considering the last one as the most precise results. In order to accomplish that, an experimental and simulated environment was needed and in both cases a 2D map were gotten with which navigation was tested.

With a definite algorithm or SLAM package with which a map can be constructed, it could enable easier AMRs implementation for indoor environments a good navigation results that conclude in solutions of automation uses for hospitals, restaurant attention, etc.

2   State of Art

Nowadays there are several SLAM methods and every of them are a different approach of a solution for autonomous navigation, some of them are dependent of some sensors like depth cameras, others might be dependent of what is called laser scan provided by a LiDar. There are many of these SLAM packages that have been with time outdated or left without any optimization. In the case of Cartographer ROS, it looks to be a well optimized and promising method to be used with other components like Move Base[4]. As a stack which is updated continuously. In terms of the results of other SLAM methods, it provides a

---

[2] Robotics Operating System [3].

[3] Simultaneous Localization and Mapping.

[4] A package provides an implementation of an action (see the actionlib package) that, given a goal in the world, will attempt to reach it with a mobile base [9].

really good algorithm in which the map that is given by it is updated by the use of submaps when it is still running, making it a real-time SLAM package capable of providing effective mapping results, as seen in other investigations and categorized as one of the most accurate [1]. In Fig. 1, it can be seen Cartographer Node structure.

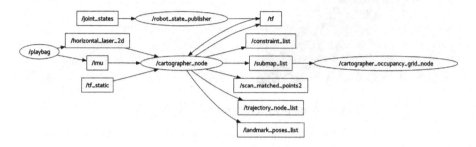

Fig. 1. Cartographer node for 2D SLAM [6].

In order to evaluate the efficiency or quality of the map, there are qualitative and quantitative ways to do it. If quantitative evaluation is requested, GT[5] data coming from simulation needs to be provided as well as the odometry from the trajectory gotten in the experimental proves, with which RMSE error can be calculated between both results as well as absolute and relative pose error [16].

Indirectly the efficiency of movement of a robot is affected by how good the map and the trajectory that in terms of ROS is here is accomplished with AMCL and Move Base. Nowadays there are already some software packages capable of this kind of analysis, one of them is a python module called EVO, a python package which can give several insight about the quality of a trajectory [4].

Qualitative analysis on the other hand can also be accomplished even of it is not as reliable as a quantitative method, and actually in the current project the maps are only analyzed in a qualitative way. One of them, corresponds to the proportion of the map, the blurrier the walls or outline of the map, the worst it is, meaning a well made map should be pretty sharp, as seen in Fig. 2.

Also, another one is the amount of corners the map has, a map with a huge amount of corners is most likely to be inconsistent unless the ones shown are actual corners. This is also related to the amount of enclosed areas, the most enclosed areas the map has, means the map is could fail for navigation in the future since the AMR shouldn't be enclosed in only one single space, taking as enclosed area a space in which the robot is surrounded completely by occupied cells. Mostly it is important to do the analysis with the before stated parameters when no ground truth is available and it is important to consider that these parameters can also be affected because of bad data sensing like odometry which could cause map shifting, for example when turning [8,11].

---

[5] Ground Truth: corresponds to the most precise trajectory or odometry recording of the robot or moving platform.

Fig. 2. A map with different proportions [1].

3   Methodology

The project was carried out in two parts; for the first part a simulation with which mapping was made using a simulated environment in Gazebo and a second part in which the same technique was implemented in the commercial ArloBot platform.

For the complete project, a repository in GitLab was established as amr-navegación. Also, in order to accomplish lots of part related to the configuration of the project, an urdf defining the ArloBot platform [7] and a wiki about Cartographer ROS with Ouster LiDar [12] were used as resources.

3.1   Simulation

Mapping Environment Setup. A navigation scene was recreated, specifically the interior of a house, trying to add details of significant size such as walls, pillars, furniture doors, dining table and chairs; by using Onshape, CAD software for collaborative drawing, supporting 3D design. Subsequently, it was necessary to carry out a conversion of the final assembly of the drawing from stl to sdf, which is one of the extensions that Gazebo handles in the software used by ROS to simulate scenarios and the interaction of the robot with it. In order to accomplish that conversion, Onshape to Robot was used. Once the stage is exported into the gazebo as a model, the settings are made to select this model as the world of our simulated robot. The resulting simulated environment exported with Onshape to Robot from Onshape can be seen in Figs. 3 and 4, according to the experimental one in Fig. 5.

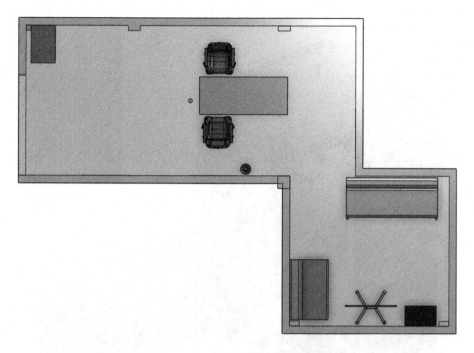

Fig. 3. Superior view of the simulated environment.

Cartographer and Robot Setup. The installation of the Cartographer ROS project was made in the workspace intended for both simulated tests and implementation. The necessary steps to follow are indicated in the GitLab repository.

Afterwards, Turtlebot3 was used as the simulated robot for the simulation. Since there wasn't a package in order to simulate ArloBot in gazebo, Tutlebot3 Burguer was considered for the purpose since it was the most similar to ArloBot.

Also other packages like `differential_drive`, `move_base` and `rplidarROS` were installed in the workspace in order to provide the data with defined messages type that Cartographer Node requests.

Launch and Config Files. In order to start the mapping, different launch files were created in which every needed node for the simulation was included. In between these is the `gazebo spawn node`, `rviz`, `move base` and `amcl`. Also `.lua` configuration files were stated to have the best result from cartographer. All the last components were needed in order to recreate, visualize, move and localize the AMR in simulation and experimental procedures [5,10].

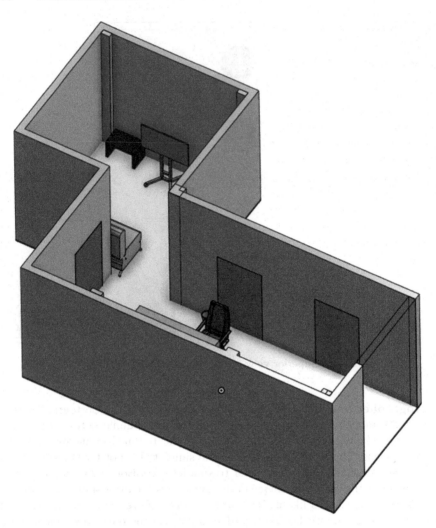

Fig. 4. Recreated experimental environment.

The structure defined in Fig. 6 was the one used in order to define all the project regarding the simulation. It was using Draw. Io including every package and middleware needed in order for the simulation to work properly. It is worth saying that red arrows correspond to *Publishers* and green arrows to *Subscribers*.

Fig. 5. Experimental physical environment.

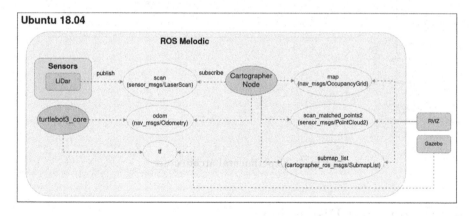

Fig. 6. Simulation architecture.

3.2 Experimental

For the experimental part, most of the launch and configuration files were copy pasted since ROS lets to use almost the same file and packages structure for simulation and experimental practices. However, it is still important to point out as defined Fig. 7, where other packages needed to be included in order to let the interaction with hardware happen.

ESP32 and MicroPython Setup. The most significant difference between the simulated and experimental part, is that in the experimental one it is needed to program a microcontroller to communicate with ROS master in order to provide information about certain sensors like encoders but also control the platform, in this case, the driver for the motors which is a DHB-10.

The ESP32 was used for this task for being a really robust and efficient microcontroller. In regard to MicroPython, it was used to rely on only one programming language since ROS is also mostly used with Python and additionally because it is a fairly easy language to use. In order to establish communication with ROS from the microcontroller, *rosserial* was proposed, with which uros[6] was used. And to control the DHB-10 driver a module called uPyArlo[7] was installed as well, which would let encoder readings and speed commands writings.

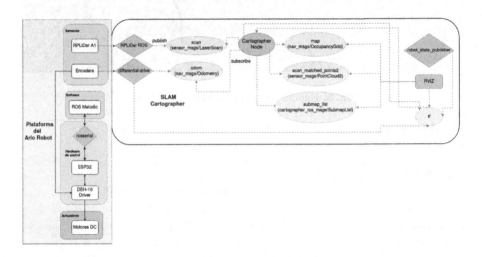

Fig. 7. Experimental architecture

4 Results and Discussion

4.1 Simulation

The resulting map obtained from simulation environment can be seen in Fig. 8. It was obtained by using **map_saver** command from the package **map_server** after

---

[6] A MicroPython module developed to be used with rosserial [14].
[7] A MicroPython module developed to control DC motors through DHB-10 driver [13].

going through the mapping process. Looking at its outline it is a fairly good result of a map. Considering the width of the walls in the map, corresponding to proportion, they show to be pretty thin, well defined and sharp, which is a good sign and helps with the accuracy of a good navigation. Some parts of the outline show to have certain anomalies in the outer part of the map, but they shouldn't affect the navigation since the robot can't actually go through that area.

Now considering the amount of corners presented in the map, there are almost none of them, the corners that are presented are mostly because the environment is actually cornered, they are really well closed and defined sufficiently. It is worth considering that some spaces were left opened because the laser from the LiDar couldn't go in such small spaces, which is then limited by hardware and not the SLAM algorithm. These opened areas should be left opened however in the current testing it is almost impossible to accomplish that matter since it is mostly a matter of how the environment was defined, for example, to not have those opened areas, the sofas from the environment should be put as close as possible to the walls.

In regard to the enclosed areas, it also shows a good sign, no enclosed areas are presented and the platform is able to go through all the map without restrictions. That is because the map doesn't show any shifting anomaly in any way. It could be said that it represents a perfect map in the context of others maps resulting from other SLAM techniques.

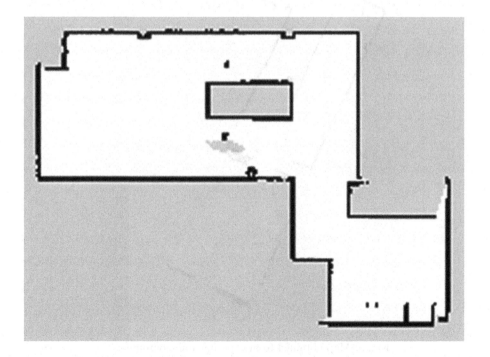

Fig. 8. Map obtained from simulated environment.

4.2   Experimental

In the case of Fig. 9, exported by using `map_server` as well, the first thing to take into account is that the map is not actually aligned with the simulated one, which is basically because of how the AMR started the mapping process. Now in terms of proportion, it is clearly that the experimental map is not as good as in the simulation, there are certain parts of it that not that neat and perfectly defined. Some of the causes could be the colors and certain disturbances from the walls, like irregular surfaces. Other than that, is shows a good sign since either way the width of the outline is thin. It should also be considered, that in this case a real LiDar was used which has a lot more errors and less accuracy than a simulated one and still the proportion of the outline is satisfying enough.

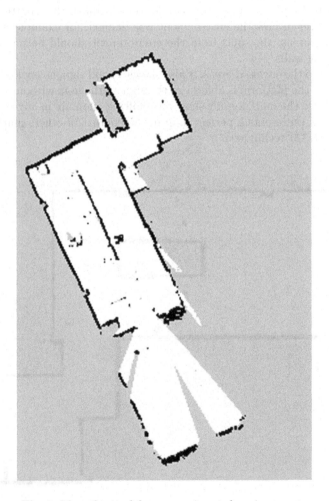

Fig. 9. Map obtained from experimental environment.

Regarding the amount of corners, this map has more corners than Fig. 8, but it does not reduces the quality of the map significantly because there aren't too much of them. Most of them can be spotted in the outline of the walls, where little spikes are shown. Also the actual corners from the environment were mapped and are shown convincing.

Related to the enclosed areas, none were created, as it can be seen from the map, it is completely open and the AMR can drive freely through it as in the simulated one. Although the map fulfills the parameters for a qualitative analysis, it has some anomalies that should be pointed out. One of them is at the inferior part, there seems to be an open part in which the map is not complete, that error is because at that area a complete window replacing a wall is placed which wasn't sensed by the LiDar leading to an open section. Another one can also bee seen at the right part, where unoccupied cells as a wide line outside the outline is shown, an error caused because of little open edges in between the door. Apart from that, the map is accurate and comparable to the simulated one, the edges and irregularities it were caused because of the hardware used and some differences between the simulated and experimental environment.

5   Conclusion

Both simulated and experimental results for mapping by the use of Cartographer ROS were shown and while analyzing the maps provided by qualitative methods, it could be concluded that Cartographer ROS is able to provide a really well made maps even when using not the most expensive hardware resources and that the efficiency doesn't vary significantly in between the simulation and experimental procedures. While using a RPLiDar A1 sensor, a considerably cheap LiDar, still no much difference was seen considering that in simulation, the laser sensor plugin from Gazebo is as accurate as possible, as well as in the best condition.

By looking at the results, it can easily be seen the maps are not of the same quality, but that doesn't mean the experimental solution can't be used nor that it can't compete with the simulated results, actually it is a really satisfying approach while the errors gotten are not enough to reduce its usefulness at all.

It is possible for the reason that this SLAM method works with submaps made while it goes through the mapping process, it is able to update the current published map and optimizing already mapped areas continuously with previous Laser Scan data samples, and without using much CPU power. Meaning that Cartographer ROS is one of the best approaches to be used when implementing a SLAM technique in order to acquire autonomous navigation.

References

1. Anton, F., Artyom, F., Kirill, K.: 2D slam quality evaluation methods, August 2017
2. Filipenko, M., Afanasyev, I.: Comparison of various slam systems for mobile robot in an indoor environment, August 2018

3. Foundation, O.S.R.: Ros documentation. https://wiki.ros.org/
4. Grupp, M.: evo: Python package for the evaluation of odometry and slam (2017). https://github.com/MichaelGrupp/evo
5. Hershberger, D., Gossow, D., Faust, J., Woodall, W.: Rviz. https://wiki.ros.org/rviz
6. Hess, W., Kohler, D., Rapp, H., Andor, D.: Real-time loop closure in 2D lidar slam. In: 2016 IEEE International Conference on Robotics and Automation (ICRA), pp. 1271–1278 (2016)
7. Lofland, C.: Arlobot. https://github.com/chrisl8/ArloBot
8. Longhi, R., Fabro, J.: Ros navigation: concepts and tutorial, February 2016
9. Marder-Eppstein, E.: Move base. https://wiki.ros.org/move_base
10. Marder-Eppstein, E.: Navigation. https://wiki.ros.org/navigation
11. Santos, J.M., Portugal, D., Rocha, R.P.: An evaluation of 2D slam techniques available in robot operating system (2013)
12. Selby, W.: Building maps using google cartographer and the os1 lidar sensor. Technical report, October 2019. https://ouster.com/blog/building-maps-using-google-cartographer-and-the-os1-lidar-sensor/
13. Silva, S.: Micropython arlorobot. https://github.com/FunPythonEC/uPyArlo
14. Silva, S.: Micropython rosserial. https://github.com/FunPythonEC/uPy-rosserial
15. Wonnacott, D., Karhumaa, M., Walker, J.: Autonomous navigation planning with ros
16. Yagfarov, R., Ivanou, M., Afanasyev, I.: Map comparison of lidar-based 2D slam algorithms using precise ground truth, November 2018

Development of a Prototype to Rehabilitate Knee and Ankle Injuries, Using a Parallel Robot with 6 Degrees of Freedom

Xavier Arias[1]($\boxtimes$), Sandro Balarezo[2]($\boxtimes$), Javier Gavilanes[3]($\boxtimes$), Miguel Aquino[3]($\boxtimes$), and Geovanny Novillo[3]($\boxtimes$)

[1] Escuela Superior Politecnica del Ejercito – ESPE, Sangolqui, Ecuador
[2] Universidad Nacional de Colombia, Bogotá D.C, Colombia
sfbalarezog@unal.edu.co
[3] Escuela Superior Politécnica de Chimborazo, Riobamba, Ecuador
{javier.gavilanes,socrates.aquino,gnovillo}@espoch.edu.ec

Abstract. The present research objective was to design and build a prototype of a robot to emulate ankle and knee rehabilitation, studying at first the types of movements that the ankle and knee need during a therapy, for which a parallel robot with a zero-rated kinematic chain was selected to facilitate the therapy that an injured lower limb needs. It was necessary to solve the problem of the inverse kinematics of the 6 degrees of freedom Stewart platform to position the prototype in the desired rehabilitation position. Finally, for the control was implemented an arduino card that is responsible for positioning the electric linear actuators of the parallel robot, to achieve the sequence of movements of restoration of the lower limb were introduced in the programming displacement values of the actuators calculated based on the solution of reverse kinematics solved by the software Matlab for each of the rehabilitation positions studied. The developed prototype allows to emulate the movements made by a physiotherapist during the movement therapy in knee and ankle injuries, for which it was validated by a physiotherapist.

Keywords: Parallel robot · Robotic rehabilitation · Stewart platform · Inverse kinematics · Knee and ankle rehabilitation

1 Introduction

Ankle sprains are one of the most common muscle-skeletal injuries in the emergency department for both the general population and athletes, with up to 30% of sports injuries reported in some series. Global epidemiologic incidence data indicate that one ankle sprain occurs for every 10,000 people per day, and approximately two million ankle sprains occur each year in the United States, resulting in a total annual health care cost of $2 billion. Medical expenses can be significantly reduced by purchasing lower extremity restoration machines to best reproduce the therapy performed by the specialist according to the patient's condition [1].

© Springer Nature Switzerland AG 2021
M. Botto-Tobar et al. (Eds.): ICAT 2020, CCIS 1388, pp. 403–416, 2021.
https://doi.org/10.1007/978-3-030-71503-8_31

The design and construction of a prototype for the rehabilitation of the knee and ankle will serve to propose a viable solution in favor of the timely care of patients in the rehabilitation area of the Hospitals. With this project, a machine capable of emulating the movements made by a physiotherapist during the knee or ankle rehabilitation process will be obtained in a reliable way. After developing this research and with the long-term implementation of this rehabilitation machine in hospitals, the direct beneficiaries will be the patients with knee or ankle injuries. The importance of the development of this research is contrasted in the fact that it promotes the use of this machine in hospitals or physical therapy and rehabilitation centers to increase the number of people attended daily and offer a greater diversity of personalized therapies; and what is more important, to reduce the recovery time of people who have suffered traumatic incidents, which will allow them to return to their daily activities faster.

1.1 Knee and Ankle Injuries

Ankle fractures are relatively common, with a bimodal age distribution that peaks in young men and older women. Ankle fractures account for 9% of all fractures, but the incidence and severity are increasing among the elderly due to increased life expectancy and the resulting poor quality of bone. The highest incidence of ankle fracture occurs in older women, although it is generally not accepted as a fragile osteoporotic fracture.

The pattern of ankle fracture depends on: the position of the foot at the time of injury; the direction of the deforming force (axial and/or rotational); age; bone quality; and the magnitude of the deforming force.

The medial collateral ligament (MCL) is one of the most commonly injured knee structures that can be managed conservatively with early protection. Therefore, a late diagnosis or neglect of such injuries can adversely affect rehabilitation after treatment of ankle fractures. It is not uncommon for the diagnosis of a combined knee injury to be delayed without additional imaging of the knee in an ankle fracture patient [2].

1.2 Rehabilitation Movements of the Lower Extremities

In the case of the ankle, the first phase of rehabilitation begins after acute pain and edema are under control and stable bone alignment is achieved for surgery. Gentle range-of-motion exercise can be initiated in each direction, preferably active rather than passive, and a gentle stretching exercise of the calf muscles can be initiated depending on the degree of stability of the fixation. If the fixation is firm and stable, the ankle range-of-motion exercise can be started as early as one week after surgery in the case of a walking boot application, the studio [3] in phase 2 presents a limited range of motion with no dorsiflexion beyond the neutral position and plantar flexion only at 5°.

1.3 Robotic Rehabilitation

It is well known that, for the realization of a mechatronic system of walking simulation, several input parameters should be considered, those that come as close as possible to reality, those that are the property of the patient. The parameters can be obtained from the measurement using non-invasive methods, generally optimal, because these parameters are individualized for each individual due to various factors such as characteristics of the body and anatomy of the person [4].

The project developed below is the result of a pre-trip research on robots, especially on parallel robot configuration, as well as on the state of the art of lower limb rehabilitation, the type of devices and/or mechanisms currently available and some prototypes under development.

3UPS + 1RPU. According to, [5, 6] and [7] the parallel robot type 3UPS + 1RPU with 4 DOF, is able to generate movements for rehabilitation of ankle and knee, and through an inverse kinematic analysis position the robot in different rehabilitation positions, positions as hip flexion, flexion-extension of the knee. The results are quantified through the calculation of the mean square error, for the servo selection the dynamic analysis was carried out, obtaining the accelerations, forces and torques using the MSC Adams software.

Four-Bar Mechanism. It is a robot for the rehabilitation of the lower limbs using a parallel structure. The aim of this robot is not only to produce soft and precise movements for the ankle, knee and hip, but also to support the tracking of the trajectory. Its parallel configuration was based on the four-bar mechanism to have a more stable and robust structure. For the kinematic analysis, the length of a bar was considered variable. This parallel robot not only showed good results, but also showed several possibilities of movement for the rehabilitation of the lower limbs [8].

Vi-RABT. It is a robotic ankle and balance trainer with virtual interface (vi-RABT) is a platform-based robot to speed up the rehabilitation of the ankle and balance. Vi-RABT is a robot with two degrees of freedom over dorsiflexion/plantarflexion and inversion/version of the ankle joint. It has a compact electromechanical design, instrumented with actuators, angle and torsion sensors and equipped with an impedance controller. Vi-RABT hosts inter-active games, designed by therapists, to make repetitive therapy more attractive. Preliminary results show that the vi-RABT can expedite ankle joint assessment and sitting training [9].

Activate Ankle. It is a new mechanism ACTIVE ANKLE presents three degrees of freedom that operate almost spherically. Compared to spherical devices, its design offers advantages such as high rigidity, simple and robust construction, and good stress distribution. In particular, the kinematic analysis of the mechanism is carried out, solving the problems of complete inversion, rotary inversion and forward kinematics. Furthermore, the working space of the manipulator is characterized and the kinematic control, which has been implemented in an ACTIVE ANKLE prototype, is presented, together with the experimental results demonstrating the possibility of use as an ankle joint in a full-body exoskeleton [10].

Assiston-Ankle. It's an exoskeleton for ankle rehabilitation. Assiston-Ankle features reconfigurable kinematics for delivery of both range of motion (RoM)/strengthening and balance/ proprioception exercises. In particular, through lockable joints, the underlying kine-matics can be configured to either a self-aligning parallel mechanism that can naturally cover the whole RoM of the human ankle, or another parallel mechanism that can support the ground reaction forces/torques transferred to the ankle [11].

Planar 1P-2P RP Hybrid Manipulator. This paper addresses a robust motion control design of a planar 1P-2PRP hybrid ma-nipulator for performing the lower limb rehabilitation treatments. The effectiveness and performances of the proposed system along with the motion control scheme is demonstrated using the real-time experiments. Further the robustness and sensitivity of the proposed control scheme is analyzed under different working conditions [12].

2 Materials and Methods

2.1 Materials

The prototype developed to rehabilitate knee and ankle injuries consists mainly of 3 parts:

Metallic Structure: A safe structure was designed and built with the help of CAD/CAE software which has the function of supporting all the main weights of the prototype during its operation such as, patient weight, robot weight, control box weight.

6 DOF Parallel Robot: This robot was built using 6 linear electric actuators joined at one end to a mobile aluminum base and at the other end to a fixed aluminum base which is attached to the metal structure mentioned in the previous point. An orthopedic shoe was adapted to the mobile base for the patient's comfort during rehabilitation.

Control Box. Within this element, all the components that allow the control and correct operation of the movements of the prototype were placed, in addition to the power supply that feeds the electrical circuit. Figure 1 shows the location of the main components of the prototype.

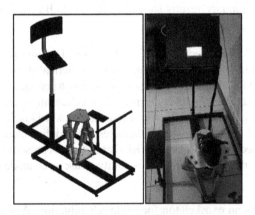

Fig. 1. Ankle and knee rehabilitation prototype.

2.2 Methods

Stewart Platform. The mechanism selected for the construction of the rehabilitation prototype for knee and ankle was the Stewart Platform that can be seen in Fig. 2. The main goal of the mechanism for the prototype is to provide rotating movements to the parallel robot moving platform through the use of six linear actuators. So it is required to provide a voltage to the linear actuators that have an internal motor where this in turn will convert it into linear displacement, which in the end will provide an angular position for the moving platform.

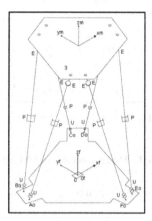

Fig. 2. Stewart platform.

Kinematic Analysis. It was made a reverse kinematic analysis which allows to find the coordinates of the joints in each of the arms of the robot, knowing the position and orientation of the mobile platform. After listing each link of the UPE chain, the coordinate axes are placed in each joint taking into account the number of degrees of freedom that has each of them [13].

It was applied the Denavit-Hartenberg method in the 6 UPE chains of the robot with coordinate system $O\_6 - X\_6\ Y\_6\ Z\_6$ which coincides with the axis of the dolly because it is joined to the last link as can be seen in Fig. 3.

Once the axes of the UPE chain are placed, we proceed to obtain the D-H parameters which will relate the coordinate systems between the joints in ascending sequential order, as can be seen in Table 1.

In order to obtain the kinematic equations of the robot, the position analysis of each arm was made independently, for it is necessary two trajectories, in the case of the first arm the trajectories converge in the point A, being the first Of – Om – A and the second Of – Ao – A, as shown in Fig. 4.

The position of Om with respect to Of was found as follows in Eq. 1

$$\begin{bmatrix} X_m \\ Y_m \\ Z_m \end{bmatrix} = [{}^f R_{A_o}{}^0 R_1(q_{11}){}^1 R_2(q_{12}){}^2 R_3(q_{13})] + \begin{bmatrix} -R\,Cos\,(7.05°) \\ -R\,Sen\,(7.05°) \\ 0 \end{bmatrix} -f_{R_m} \begin{bmatrix} -Rm\,Cos\,(49.77°) \\ -Rm\,Sen\,(49.77°) \\ 0 \end{bmatrix} \quad (1)$$

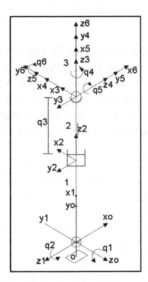

Fig. 3. Axes of the UPE chain.

Table 1. D-H parameters of UPE chain.

Degree of freedom i- esimo	α_i	a_i	d_i	θ_i
1	$-\pi/2$	0	0	$q1 + \pi/2$
2	$\pi/2$	0	0	$q2 + \pi/2$
3	0	0	q3	0
4	$\pi/2$	0	0	q4
5	$\pi/2$	0	0	q5
6	$\pi/2$	0	0	q6

Where the angle of $7.05°$ corresponds to the angle between the line defined by the center of the fixed platform and the joint of the lower end of the A-arm,, while the angle of $49.77°$ corresponds to the angle between the line defined by the center of the dolly platform and the joint of the upper end of the A-arm, as shown in Fig. 5.

In the UPE 1 arm from Eq. 1, Eqs. 2, 3 and 4 were found in function of q_11 q_12 and q_13 (coordinates of the joints):

$$X_m - \cos\vartheta\,\cos\psi\,Rm\cos(49.77°) - Rm\,sen(49.77°)(sen\,\phi\,sen\,\vartheta\,\cos\psi \\ -\cos\phi\,sen\,\psi) = q_{13}\,\cos q_{11}\,senq_{12} - R\cos(7.05°) \tag{2}$$

$$Y_m - \cos\vartheta\,sen\,\psi\,Rm\cos(49.77°) - Rm\,sen(49.77°)(sen\,\phi\,sen\,\vartheta\,sen\,\psi \\ +\cos\phi\,\cos\psi) = -q_{13}\,\cos q_{12} - R\,sen(7.05°) \tag{3}$$

$$Z_m + sen\,\vartheta\,Rm\cos(49.77°) - sen\,\phi\,\cos\vartheta\,Rm\,sen(49.77°) = q_{13}sen\,q_{11}sen\,q_{12} \tag{4}$$

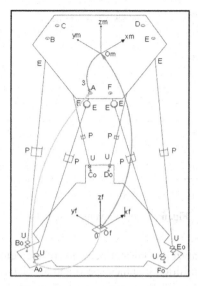

Fig. 4. Point A position trajectory.

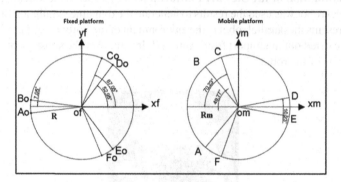

Fig. 5. Fixed and mobile robot platform.

The same process is performed to obtain the equations of motion of the 6 UPE arms of the robot, thus obtaining a system of 18 equations, for whose resolution was used Matlab software and the method of newton Raphson. Once solved the inverse kinematic movement of the robot can be positioned the mobile platform of the robot in the desired position, in this case the rehabilitation movements of knee and ankle.

The equations of speed and acceleration were obtained by deriving the equations of position and speed respectively.

To verify the equations it was carried out the kinematic simulation by means of the soft-ware Matlab being obtained this way the graph of displacement that is observed in the Fig. 6.

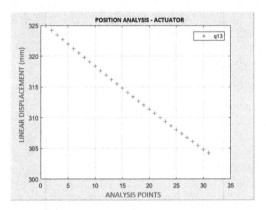

Fig. 6. Linear movement Actuator 1.

It was possible to analyze the correct behavior of the equations of the kinematics of the robot through the position graphics speed and acceleration which show a stable operation of the robot.

Dynamic simulation of the Stewart Platform. Once Resolved the kinematic problem of the parallel robot was used the results to generate the dynamic simulation of the robot, the Fig. 7 presents the parallel robot in the environment of the Software Adams View 2019 which was carried out the import from Autodesk Inventor for the subsequent simulation of movements of the robot.

Fig. 7. Imported stewart platform for Adams view.

To develop the dynamic analysis it is necessary to know all the forces present in the mechanism, as is the case of the dead weight of the leg of an average person that is equal to 17.5 kg (171.5 N) assuming an extreme case the calculation will be developed with 200 N [14].

Due to the stiffness of the injured ankle there is a force of 100 N that opposes the movement of the prototype, so the force will be placed in the X and Y axis during the entire kinetic analysis of the different rehabilitation positions, as shown in Table 2 [15].

Table 2. Forces present in dynamic analysis

Force	Location	Value
Leg weight	Z-Axis mobile platform centre	200 N
Ankle stiffness	X-Axis platform center	100 N
Ankle stiffness	Y-Axis platform center	100 N

Dynamic Forces. The Adams View software allows to find the maximum forces during the different rehabilitation movements as a function of time. In Fig. 8, a maximum force of 125 N can be observed during ankle therapies.

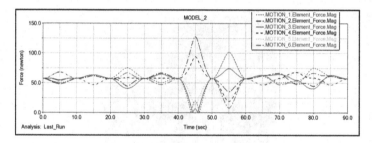

Fig. 8. Maximum strength in ankle therapy.

A maximum force of 244 N present during knee therapies can be seen in Fig. 9.

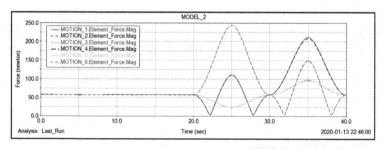

Fig. 9. Maximum strength in knee therapy.

Actuator Selection. Based on the maximum force present in the linear actuators during the dynamic analysis of the robot equal to 244 N was made the selection of linear actuators which must be electric for ease of control and must have a potentiometer for greater accuracy in the movement, then, is detailed in Table 3 characteristics of the selected actuator.

Table 3. Characteristics of the electric actuator

Linear actuator	
Input voltage	12 V DC
Speed	30 mm/s
Displacement	150 mm
Load	300 N

Construction. Finally, in Fig. 10 it can be observed the prototype of rehabilitation for ankle and knee, which allows to adjust to patients of different size.

Fig. 10. Prototype of lower limb skeletal muscle restoration

Implementation of a Control System The control system implemented for the robot was made by means of an Arduino card with all the necessary elements to control the electric actuators in the desired position. Then, it is shown in the following Fig. 11 as a diagram with all the electrical and electronic components that make possible the control of the position of the linear electric actuators.

3 Results and Discussion

3.1 Results of the Kinematic Analysis

This section will show the results obtained of mobility and precision of the ankle and knee rehabilitator when executing the therapeutic movements.

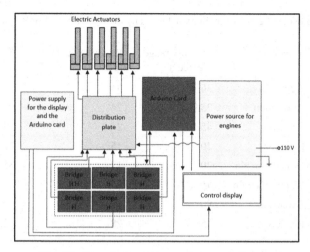

Fig. 11. Electrical and electronic control diagram

The movement of Investment of ankle is developed in the frontal transverse plane when the movement goes off the sole of the foot towards inside, this movement was not possible to develop it in previous studies that use to the robot of typology 3UPE-RPU, in this investigation the movement of inversion could be carried out thanks to the parallel robot of type platform Stewart of 6 DOF implemented, the prototype allows an angle of inclination equal to 24.9° as it is shown in the Fig. 12.

Fig. 12. Ankle restoration - inversion movement.

As can be seen in the previous figure, the tests were carried out for all knee and ankle movements, satisfying the needs of the project. The results obtained are shown in Table 4.

Figure 13 shows a comparison of the movements in degrees aligned by the prototype vs. the range of mobility allowed by the ankle and knee, taking into account that in the robot the working angles could be increased by analyzing the patient's range of

Table 4. Degrees of mobility achieved by the rehabilitation prototype

Lower limb	Movement	Mobility range (degrees)	Prototype mobility (grades)	% Movement achieved
Ankle	Aducción	36	33	91.67
	Abducción	25.9	24	92.66
	Inversión	45	24.9	55.33
	Eversión	20	15	75.00
	Dorsal Flexión	20	17	85.00
	Plantar Flexión	45	20	44.44
Knee	Extensión	90	27	30.00
	Flexión	45	28	62.22

mobility. It is important to emphasize the inversion and eversion movement of the ankle capable of performing the prototype in this research, which consists of a rotary movement around the X axis and constitutes a very important contribution in ankle rehabilitation because prototypes such as the 3UPE-RPU type robot are not capable of performing this movement.

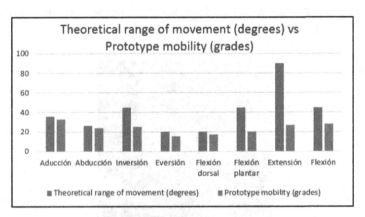

Fig. 13. Mobility range (degrees) vs. prototype mobility (degrees)

3.2 Discussion

The prototype for ankle and knee rehabilitation allowed emulating the movements performed by a physiotherapist during movement therapy in knee and ankle injuries, which was achieved by choosing as a mechanism a Stewart platform which demonstrated in the results that it is capable of performing all the movements that the ankle needs during rehabilitation being these, abduction, adduction, inversion, eversion, dorsal flexion, plantar flexion however for the case of the knee is able to generate the movements of extension and flexion that the lower limb needs but the range achieved in degrees of movement is not enough to reach the limit of the range of theoretical mobility that is needed, so it would be necessary to make a study of a prototype that allows rehabilitation specifically patients with knee injuries.

The analytical method used for the development of the investigation consists of a cognitive process that decomposes an object separating each one of the parts of the whole to study them in individual form. It was used to study all the characteristics associated to the dynamic analysis of the kinematic chains of the rehabilitation machine mechanism, for which the Denavit-Hartenberg (D-H) algorithm was used in all the extremities of the robot first in an individual way until obtaining the equations of inverse kinematics of all the Stewart platform, this was the key for the fulfillment of the investigation, since from the kinematic analysis all the later investigation starts.

As far as the machine's usefulness is concerned, an inspection of the movements was performed in order to determine its functionality, which was favorable since the physical therapy specialist stated that the machine is capable of simulating rehabilitation movements; however, there were observations for future projects such as implementing the machine's force and speed control, since these parameters vary for each patient depending on the state and progression of his injury.

4 Conclusions

The rehabilitative prototype is capable of developing ankle movements such as planar flexion, dorsiflexion, adduction, abduction, inversion, eversion, as well as knee movements such as flexion and extension within the permitted range of this form, obtaining complete mobility of these two joints. The resolution of the inverse kinematic problem of the parallel Stewart platform-type robot with 6 degrees of freedom allowed positioning the robot in the different rehabilitation positions. The parallel robot of Stewart platform type of 6 degrees of freedom used in this research, allowed to successfully generate all the therapeutic movements of the knee and ankle. The basic control developed occupying an Arduino plate and the results of the inverse kinematics, allowed to obtain the planificated movements to reach an adequate ankle and knee therapy with a low margin of error. This research presents a very relevant technical and scientific contribution as it has successfully generated the inversion and eversion movement for the ankle, a movement that according to the state of the art 3UPE-RPU type robots are not able to perform. The functioning of the restoration prototype was validated with a specialist in physical therapy to verify each of the movements that the restoration prototype develops. According to the tests performed, it was determined that the prototype is capable of generating restoration movements for the ankle, such as adduction, abduction, inversion, eversion, dorsal flexion, plantar flexion, as well as movements for the knee, such as extension and flexion. It is possible to generate future work from this research by implementing a control system that allows changing degrees of movement, speed and strength during rehabilitation, according to the state of the injury of different patients and their recovery.

References

1. Cardozo, R.: Abordaje del esguince de tobillo, Jairo Antonio Camacho Casas. Revista de la Universidad Industrial de Santander., p. 8, (2015)
2. Hwang, K.-T., Sung, I.-H., Choi, J.-H., Lee, J.K.: A higher association of medial collateral ligament injury of the knee in pronation injuries of the ankle. Arch. Orthop. Trauma Surg. **138**(6), 771–776 (2018). https://doi.org/10.1007/s00402-018-2907-z
3. Jung, H.: Rehabilitation for Foot and Ankle Disorders. In: Jung, H.G. (eds.) Foot and Ankle Disorders. Springer, Berlin (2016) https://doi.org/10.1007/978-3-642-54493-4_19
4. Abdullah, A.S., Abdullah, C.G., Alionte, C.N.: Ankle-knee rehabilitation system. In: Gheorghe, G.I. (ed.) Proceedings of the International Conference of Mechatronics and Cyber-MixMechatronics – 2018, pp. 166–172. Springer International Publishing, Cham (2019). https://doi.org/10.1007/978-3-319-96358-7_17
5. Pulloquinga, J., Aquino, M., Pozo, E., Cruz, P., Zambrano, O.: Dynamic Model of a Parallel Robot Type 3UPS + 1RPU for Knee Rehabilitation. In: IEEE (2018)
6. Aquino, M., Gavilanes, J., Novillo, G.: Kinetic analysis of an ankle rehabilitator composed of two parallel delta robots. Clawar **2018**, 109 (2018)
7. Araujo-Gómez, P., Díaz-Rodriguez, M., Mata, V., Valera, A., Page, A.: Design of a 3-UPS-RPU parallel robot for knee diagnosis and rehabilitation. In: Parenti-Castelli, V., Schiehlen, W. (eds.) ROMANSY 21 - Robot Design, Dynamics and Control, pp. 303–310. Springer International Publishing, Cham (2016). https://doi.org/10.1007/978-3-319-33714-2_34
8. Azcaray, H., et al.: Robust GPI Control of a New Parallel Rehabilitation Robot of Lower Extremities. Int. J. Control Autom. Syst. **16**(5), 2384–2392 (2018). https://doi.org/10.1007/s12555-017-0198-8
9. Farjadian, A.B., Nabian, M., Hartman, A., Yen, S.-C.: Vi-RABT: a platform-based robot for ankle and balance assessment and training. J. Med. Bio. Eng. **38**(4), 556–572 (2017). https://doi.org/10.1007/s40846-017-0332-3
10. Kumar, S.: Design and kinematic analysis of the novel almost spherical parallel mechanism active ankle. J. Intell. Robot. Syst. **94**(2), 303-325 https://doi.org/10.1007/s10846-018-0792-x
11. Erdogan, A., Celebi, B., Satici, A.C., Patoglu, V.: Assist On-Ankle: a reconfigurable ankle exoskeleton with series-elastic actuation. Auton. Robots **41**(3), 743–758 (2016)
12. Vasanthakumar, M., Vinod, B., Mohanta, J.K., Mohan, S.: Design and robust motion control of a planar 1P-2P RP hybrid manipulator for lower limb rehabilitation applications. J. Intell. Rob. Syst. **96**(1), 17–30 (2018). https://doi.org/10.1007/s10846-018-0972-8
13. Fernandez, L. A.: Análisis cinemático inverso y directo del robot paralelo. Escuela Politecnica Nacional, Quito (2016)
14. Toluna Influencers: Cuanto pesa cada Parte del cuerpo. https://es.toluna.com/opinions/245 7387/Cu%C3%A1nto-pesa-cada-parte-de-tu-cuerpo
15. Kovaleski, J.E., Norrell, P.M., Heitman, R.J., Marcus Hollis, J., Pearsall, A.W.: Knee and ankle position, anterior drawer laxity, and stiffness of the ankle complex. J. Athletic Training **43**(3), 242–248 (2008). https://doi.org/10.4085/1062-6050-43.3.242

Virtualization of a Multisensory Environment for the Treatment of Stress in Children with Autism Through Interactive Simulation

Ricardo Plasencia[✉], Gabriela Herrera[✉], Patricio Navas-Moya[✉], and Ximena López-Chico[✉]

Universidad de las Fuerzas Armadas ESPE, Sangolqui, Ecuador
{arguanoluisa1,jherrera6,mpnavas,xrlopez}@espe.edu.ec

Abstract. TEA-ROOM, is composed of interactive environments for the improvement of communication and reduction of emotional or cognitive stress states in infants with autism. Facilitating the stimulation of children due to the involvement of several aspects, movement, memory and manipulation of objects. The functioning of the system consists of two basic functions: Monitoring (Visualization) and control (manipulation). The first module shows a striking environment, accompanied by an animal (wolf) in order to fulfil certain objectives to keep the infant's attention in the course of the environment. The second module strengthens the child's motor skills through the movement of various geometrical figures, which are colored differently in order to differentiate them. Finally, the third module strengthens the child's memory. The efficiency of the application was based on successive unitary tests, which were based on evaluating the environments, sounds, characters to improve both their communication and decrease their percentage of stress.

Keywords: Interactive games · Mixed reality · Autism · Movement · Memory · Object manipulation · Skills · Attention · Environment · Stress

1 Introduction

Autism spectrum disorder (ASD) is a neurodevelopmental disorder that causes impairment in communication and social interaction. Currently, ASD affects 1% of the population worldwide [1] and, with no cure yet found, people rely on therapies and interventions to improve and overcome their impairments.

Deficiencies in social communication skills are believed to be central deficits in children with ASD [2].

Children with ASD are characterised by communication impairments, particularly with respect to the expression of affective states. However, they often experience states of emotional or cognitive stress [3]. Their social-emotional communications are limited and immature, preventing full participation in daily activities [4]. Individual and traditional behavioural interventions are the common therapeutic approaches used among children with ASD to address their social problems [5, 6]. These interventions are effective,

© Springer Nature Switzerland AG 2021
M. Botto-Tobar et al. (Eds.): ICAT 2020, CCIS 1388, pp. 417–429, 2021.
https://doi.org/10.1007/978-3-030-71503-8_32

although costly, and lead to limited rehabilitation services among low-income families or those living in rural areas [7, 8].

The Virtual Reality (VR) technologies available today are able to present users with experiences that are realistic enough to distort the mind and create a sense of presence in the environment [9]. The use of VR can be a complementary approach for children with ASD to practice their social-emotional skills [10].

RV training games have many potential benefits for autism spectrum disorder (ASD) therapy, such as increasing motivation and improving skills in performing activities of daily living [10, 11]. People with ASD often have deficits in hand-eye co-ordination, making many activities of daily living difficult [11, 12]. A virtual reality game that trains hand-eye coordination could help users with ASD improve their quality of life. In addition, incorporating users' interests into the game could be a good way to build a motivating game for ASD users [11].

A game that trains eye-hand coordination in 3D user interfaces can help users with ASD improve their 3D interaction performance [13].

The recent proliferation of applications of VR technology in autism therapy has produced optimistic results in the development of a variety of skills and abilities in them [14].

A qualitative study investigated the ideas of interested parties about the characteristics of a telerehabilitation platform among children with ASD. Through 20 interviews with doctors, parents and young people with autism, three themes were suggested, among them improving clinical features, transferring skills, and increasing motivational factors [15].

Serious games, for example, focus on learning and not on entertainment as such [9, 16]. Such games have been shown to be effective in ASD therapies, not only because they include game design techniques to keep players motivated, but also because people with ASD are often interested in computer activities [9].

ASD-ROOM is a system that provides therapies to children with attention deficit disorder on the autism spectrum. The aim of our project is to focus on a new therapy innovation based on ASD. Our approach triggers a learning process for a perfect assimilation of common behavioural skills useful in everyday life [17]. Many systems have successfully used VR in autism spectrum disorder (ASD) therapies. Most of them use virtual reality as an alternative way of performing therapies by simulating traditional therapies or real-life experiences [18].

2   State of the Art

2.1   Therapies and ICTs

With the advance of new technologies and world growth, diseases that work with different types of therapies have been evolving and thus adapting to new technologies, converting therapies that occupy specialized spaces to reduced areas and in recent years moving to virtual environments.

Obtaining equally equal results, focusing more on the medical branch, Specialized Centers in therapies for Autism and Down Syndrome, apply this type of therapy emulating a pleasant environment for the patient, who accompanied by a specialist works in the same way as in a normal therapy.

The use of computer games in the homes of patients with different disorders allows them to have a self-exposure, reducing their anxiety. Due to the high interactivity and attractive way of confronting the environment.

2.2 Microsoft Visual Studio

Microsoft Visual Studio is an integrated development environment for desktop devices or applications, either for the web or in the cloud. It allows coding for iOS, Android and Windows in the same IDE [19]. A tool that supports the design of interfaces and their interaction when developing an application focused on augmented reality, maintaining the integration between the Microsoft Visual Studio C# programming language and the Unity 3D editor.

2.3 Kinect

Kinect is a device that was initially designed as a game controller, which, thanks to the components that make it up - depth sensor, RGB camera, array of microphones and infrared sensor - is capable of capturing the human skeleton, recognising it and positioning it in the plane [20].

The Kinect incorporates a tilt motor for sensor adjustment, a microphone array and an RGB camera [21].

In particular, the Kinect, because it is affordable, ready-to-use and widely available, is considered to replicate the success of the Wiimote, which has already been adopted as a user interface for remote medical data scanning [22].

2.4 Unity3D

Engine for creating multiplatform games developed for Windows and OSX (Mac) It is widely spread in the world of videogame developers due to its set of intuitive tools that are integrated in a simple, fast and high-quality image interface. A program that configures the correlation of the objects generated in Blender, facilitating their image extrusion. Improving and correcting errors [23].

2.5 Blender

Freely distributed program for modelling, animating and creating three-dimensional objects. This tool allows the 3D modelling and its import to Unity (Unity Extension) of the different entities generated allowing to superimpose images in the corresponding marker (created in the development tool Vuforia). Configuring and incorporating the preview camera option and the directional light that facilitates viewing the 3D image and texturing it, giving a better appearance to the modelling [24].

2.6 Android Studio

Integrated development environment for creating applications on all classes of Android devices [25]. It allows the creation of the project generated in Unity 3D as an apk. By using the Build Settings option, adding the corresponding scene through the Add Current option, and then choosing and generating the platform to be created through the Build option.

2.7 Mixed Reality

Expression used for define the integration of digital content in ICT that relates those objects that are tangible and virtual in real time. Enabling users to recognise enhanced or augmented representations in the world around them. According to their interaction with users, their content and form can vary. It ranges from simple applications to complex systems [26].

3 Methodology

3.1 Figure and Table Legend

In order to design the software applied in this research, we designed the software scheme that uses the architecture design developed for VR and AR (Mixed Reality), focusing on the structure that the applications with educational model entail [27], as shown in Fig. 1, which allows us to use a colour scheme corresponding to five areas, each one with a specific function, (Blue) Users, (Light blue) Executable and execution means, (Green) Interaction means, (Yellow) Volume system, (Red) Database [28].

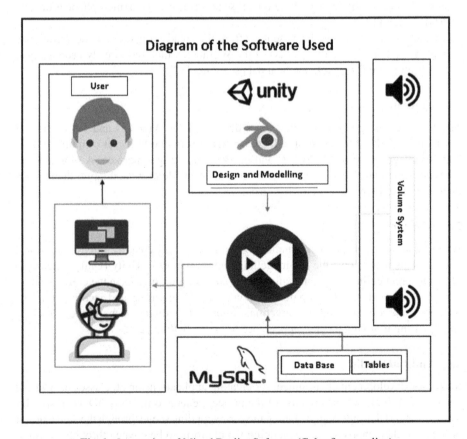

Fig. 1. Integration of Mixed Reality Software (Color figure online)

From the analysis of Fig. 1, the scheme in which the Mixed Reality software was integrated is interpreted, guided by the use of colours, so that one has a clear idea of its structure.

4 Development

4.1 Development Structure

For the construction of the software proposed in this research, a software scheme is used, which focuses on the development of applications using Augmented Reality, as shown in Fig. 1. Using six components, each one with its specific purpose (1) Kinect Configuration Environment, (2) 3D Modelling and Blender Textured Mixer, (3) Microsoft Visual Studio Development Environment, (4) Unity Development Platform, (5) Augmented Reality Application and (6) Users.

1) Kinect Development Environment: The aim of the component is to detect the movements of the person, through recognition and positioning within the plane, allowing work with the environment developed in Unity, in which the child is given the sensation of realism through augmented reality with the generation of the proposed scene in the environment.

2) Modelling and texturised 3D mixer: The purpose of this component is to model the wolf, the person and the geometric figures, which interact with the child, facilitating the creation of their skeleton and animation, using the quadrant modelling system, allowing dynamic manipulation of the characters and figures, resulting in a better finish when exporting them to Unity.

3) Microsoft Visual Studio development environment: the purpose of this component is to facilitate the creation of scripts (coding) that control the GUI (graphical user interface) and its interaction in the treatment of stress, through the use of the different stimulation environments proposed in this research. Furthermore, it reduces the development time, because it has a direct connection with Unity, simplifying the copy and paste of generated or modified scripts from one place to another, since they are in a project folder.

4) Unity's Development Platform: the aim of this component is to interrelate the objects generated in the different SDIs (integrated development environments). It allows to improve and correct errors in both animation and texture.

5) Augmented reality application: the aim of this component is the interaction of the child with the application, through the use of glasses that show a level of realism in terms of environments and characters.

6) Users: the purpose of this component is that the application allows children to reduce their stress without spending excessive resources (Fig. 2).

422   R. Plasencia et al.

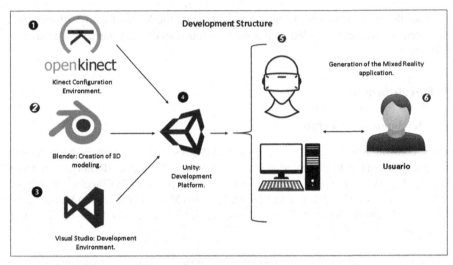

Fig. 2. Scheme to be used for the development of Interactive software through augmented reality.

The application's animation process begins by exporting the following assets to Unity: 1) Kinect: Configuration environment that detects the movements of the human being, in order to tune and position them within the plane, it is capable of detecting the movements that the child with ASD makes, being the medium between the application and the patient. 2) Modelling and Texturization 3D Blender: model where the wolf and the character are exported with their respective skeletons, textures and animations. Once both components are within Unity, the interaction of the software proposed in this research is carried out according to the level required depending on the degree of stimulation required, as shown in Fig. 3, which consists of the following steps.

A. Unity Animator: at this stage, frame animations are performed, which allows modifying existing animations, creating new ones or correcting errors.
B. Unity State Machine: Stage in which each of the wolf, person and geometric figure animation sequences are produced, with their corresponding repetition cycles or static sequences, depending on the interaction required for each level of the application.
C. Unity Coding: Stage where the application coding is developed, working with C # due to the compatibility with Unity's platform, where the execution functions in the interface and the movement of the wolf and the person are created by the environment of the corresponding scene.
D. Running application: Final stage where it is executed in the editor itself to verify errors and correct scenarios, finally passing to the creation of the APK.

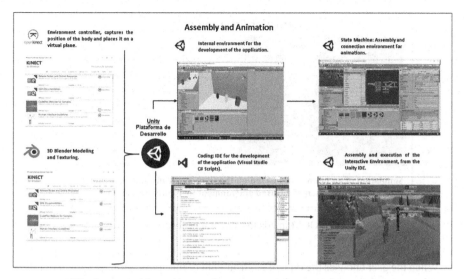

Fig. 3. Assembly and interactive software through augmented reality

5 Results

Here, we first present the results of the validation of the system to demonstrate that the TEA-ROOM system for improving communication and reducing emotional or cognitive stress states worked in a solid and stable way. Then, we present the results of the feasibility study from two aspects: the participant's experience (subjective) and the participants' performance (objective), and we also compare the results of Study 1 and Study 2 to show the advantages of the TEA-ROOM system to foster collaborative play and social communication skills in children with ASD.

The efficiency of the application was supported by successive unit tests, which were based on evaluating the environments, sounds, characters to improve their communication and decrease their percentage of stress.

5.1 System Validation Results

Next, the implementation of interactive software to mitigate the communication levels and stress states presented by children with ASD through mixed reality will be exemplified. In Fig. 4, the application consists of an environment that helps the child to relax and interact with the character, in a way that gives the sensation of touch between his hands and the environment, and also shows the level of realism of each element that is part of the environment.

In environment 2 there are 3 geometric figures, which facilitate the interaction between the child and the application thanks to the movement that can be made with each figure.

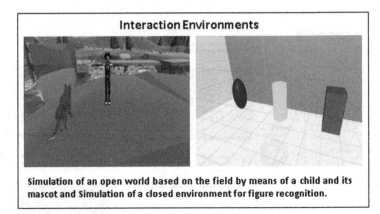

Interaction Environments

Simulation of an open world based on the field by means of a child and its mascot and Simulation of a closed environment for figure recognition.

Fig. 4. TEA-ROOM interactive environments using mixed reality

When the user chooses the type of environment of the application, as shown in Fig. 4, several activities are performed, for example in environment 1, he must go through the whole environment in the company of a wolf, this type of therapy allows the child with ASD to decrease his stress level, through the landscapes, characters and sounds that are usually a means to counteract his attention deficit problems (Table 1).

Table 1. Score delimited in the TEA-ROOM Questionnaire to determine the level of stress present in each patient and its corresponding treatment (Stage-Application)

Nivel	Nivel Estrés	Puntuación (TEA-ROOM)	Etapa TratamientO
5	Higth	109–129	1
4	Particular	91–108	2
3	Intermediate	73–90	3
2	Diffuse	37–72	4
1	Normal	19–36	4
0	Null	0–18	Anyone

As shown in Fig. 5, the treatment session begins, accessing the stage that corresponds to the patient according to the score obtained in the ASD. It allows the patient to choose the degree of virtual stimulation required, accessing each of the following levels from the application:

Level 1: the patient observes an environment with a level of realism.
Level 2: the patient can interact with the character in the environment, in this case a wolf.

Level 3: the patient observes various geometric figures in movement.
Level 4: the patient interacts with the figures by moving up, down, left and right.

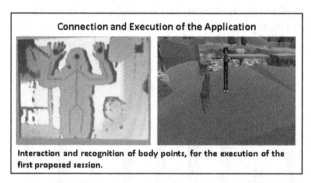

Fig. 5. Children with autism spectrum disorder (ASD) perform a therapy session according to their spontaneity and communication levels, through a computer and the kinect device that allows detecting the person's movements.

Table 2. Evaluation of implementation

Questions	Yes	No	Percentages
The designed system allows children with autism spectrum disorder (ASD) to interact correctly with environments and characters	8	2	80%
The system slows down the stress levels of children with ASD	7	3	70%
The environments made in the system are the right ones for children with ASD	7	3	60%
Children paid more attention to the system created	8	2	80%
The system is designed to help stimulate the attention and concentration of children with ASD	8	2	80%
The children were motivated using the application	8	2	80%
The dynamics of the development of each environment were easily observed	7	3	70%
Easy interaction with the application was observed	6	4	60%
The children were relaxed in the development of each game	8	2	80%
Interest was noted with the use of technological devices	9	1	90%

According to the analysis in Table 2, the indicators for the evaluation are related to "The designed system allows children with autism spectrum disorder (ASD) to interact correctly with the environments and characters," "The system decreases the stress levels of children with ASD," "The environments performed in the system are the right ones for children with ASD," "The children paid more attention with the created system," "The designed system helps stimulate attention and concentration of children with ASD," "The children were motivated using the application. The children were relaxed in the development of each game", "Interest was observed with the use of the technological devices", "Ease was observed in the dynamics of the development of each environment", "Ease was observed in the interaction with the application", "Children were relaxed in the development of each game", "Interest was observed with the use of the technological devices".

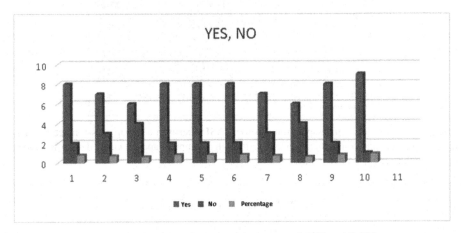

Fig. 6. Evaluation indicators with category "YES" and "NO"

Figure 6 shows the analysis of the evaluation indicators with category YES and NO, concluding that the use of the system by children with ASD with values of 8 facilitates "interaction with the environments and characters", "stimulates attention and concentration", "motivates and relaxes the children"; while the indicators that show a value lower than 7 determine that "the interaction with the application makes them difficult in some way". After the two sessions a survey was made to each apprentice according to the indicators shown in Table 2, which were validated by a professional in the area of education of people with ASD, who was also present during the development of the tests.

6 Discussion

Virtual worlds are the new path to learning, because they facilitate the development of skills and abilities in children with autism spectrum.

Based on the statutes of the American Academy of Pediatrics it was established that the limits of interaction with the system, being that a normal infant according to these statutes can remain near a television around 60 min, so taking into account the state and capabilities of those selected was established a time of 25 min with a maximum of 30.

TEA-ROOM has been very well received within the selected population, in this case children between the ages of 6 and 10. We took the data of 10 children, in which we could determine different reactions when using the TEA-ROOM application.

6 out of 10 children mentioned that the therapy was effective, because different environments are used, which not only focus on the identification of environments, but also of sounds.

The remaining 4 children had some difficulty in moving certain geometric figures, as well as having some fear of the sounds generated by the environment 2.

TEA-ROOM is a simple application that contains quiet environments, for the simple reason that children with autism spectrum require appropriate therapies for their development. The aim is not to show them something complex but rather something that they can handle and at the same time improve their skills and leave their fears behind.

7 Future Works

In the future, TEA-ROOM will be further enhanced to support a more truthful collaborative gaming platform. Haptic interfaces will be designed that can produce physical feedback for the user. The aim is to get more children with TEA from the haptic system, so that they can interact with the application, touching, feeling or manipulating the simulated objects in the virtual environments that we will provide.

Furthermore, the social-emotional and communication skills of a child with autism spectrum disorder (ASD) will be improved, from the integration of artificial intelligence regarding environments and characters, promoting a design and animation according to a level of realism.

To explore the influence of the system on the communication skills of the participants, we plan to analyse the participants' conversations in terms of game-oriented content and social content and to perform a statistical analysis of the change in the conversation content.

8 Conclusions

The interactive software proposed in this research, allowed to treat the communication skills and emotional stress faced by children with autism spectrum disorder (ASD). Demonstrating that therapies based on exposure and use of RV, promotes natural interaction.

The use of stimulation levels favours the decrease of the deterioration in communication and social interaction, contributing to the child with ASD to his correct development in society.

The dedication with respect to the time that the children invest in each session is of great importance to satisfactorily fulfill the treatment of stress in the children with autism, according to the level of intercommunication that each one has.

The use of calm and interactive environments and the insertion of augmented reality in the interaction with the application, allowed the children to improve their communication and social interaction, thus decreasing the stress caused by not being able to express their emotions. In addition, most of the children obtained an ease of use with the system.

The Kinect enabled improved interactivity between the child and the application because it has a depth sensor, RGB camera, microphone array and infrared sensor, which is capable of capturing the person's movement. This provided a controlled environment for the children, keeping them safe and not causing them any problems in their mental state.

References

1. American Psychiatric Association, Diagnostic and statistical manual of mental disorders, 5th ed. American Psychiatric Publishing, Arlington (2013)
2. American Psychiatric Association, Diagnostic and statistical manual of mental disorders: DSM-IVTR, APA, Washington (2000)
3. Lahiri, U., Welch, K.C., Warren, Z., Sarkar, N.: Developing a Client-centered Tele-rehabilitation Virtual Reality Program for Children with Autism to Address Socio-emotional Skills (2011) https://doi.org/10.1109/ICVR.2011.5971841
4. American Psychiatric Association, The diagnostic and statistical manual of mental disorders: DSM 5. bookpointUS: Oxon. (2013)
5. Kawachi, I., Berkman, L.: Social ties and mental health. J. Urban Health 78, 458–467 (2001) https://doi.org/10.1093/jurban/78.3.458
6. Parsons, S.: Authenticity in virtual reality for assessment and intervention in autism: a conceptual review. Educ. Res. Rev. 19, 138–157 (2016)
7. Alper, S., Raharinirina, S., Assistive technology for individuals with disabilities: a review and synthesis of the literature. J. Spec. Educ. Technol. 21(2), 47–64 (2006)
8. Bomber, O.: Thinking Virtual, Computer (Long Beach.Calif) 47(7), 22–23 (2014)
9. Michael, D., Chen, S.: Serious games: Games that educate, train and inform. Muska & Lipman/Premier-Trade (2005)
10. Bekele, E.: Understanding how adolescents with autism respond to facial expressions in virtual reality environments. IEEE Trans. Vis. Comput. Graph. 19, 7112–7720 (2013)
11. Ghanouni, P., Jarus, T., Zwicker, J.G., Mow, K., Ledingham, A.: The Content of a Virtual Reality Program for Children with Autism: Incorporating Stakeholders' Input. In: International Conference on Virtual Rehabilitation (ICVR), (2017) https://doi.org/10.1109/icvr.2017.800746
12. Mei, C., Mason, L., Quarles, J.: "I Built It!" - exploring the effects of customizable virtual humans on adolescents with ASD. In: IEEE Virtual Reality (VR) (2015).
13. Mei, C., Mason, L., Quarles, J.: Usability issues with 3D user interfaces for adolescents with high functioning autism. In: Proceedings of the 16th International ACM SIGACCESS Conference on Computers and Accessibility (2014)
14. Cai, Y., Chia, N., Thalmann, D., Kee, N.K., Zheng, J.: Design and development of a virtual Dolphinarium for children with autism. IEEE Trans. Neural Syst. Rehabil. Eng. 21(2), 208–217 (2013)
15. Ghanouni, P., et al.: Developing a client-centered tele-rehabilitation virtual reality program for children with autism to address socio-emotional skills. In: International Conference on Virtual Rehabilitation (ICVR) (2017)
16. Bernardes, M., Barros, F., Simoes, M., Castelo, B.: A serious game with virtual reality for travel training with autism spectrum disorder. In: Conferencia Internacional sobre Rehabilitación Virtual (ICVR) (2015)
17. Gelsomini, M., Garzotto, F., Montesano, D., Occhiuto, D.: Wildcard: a wearable virtual reality storytelling tool for children with intellectual developmental disability. In: 38th Annual International Conference of the IEEE Engineering in Medicine and Biology Society (EMBC) (2016)

18. Mei, C., Guo, R.: Enable an innovative prolonged exposure therapy of attention deficits on autism spectrum through adaptive virtual environments. In: Décima Conferencia Internacional 2018 sobre mundos virtuales y juegos para aplicaciones serias (VS-Games) (2018)
19. Microsoft Visual Studio https://msdn.microsoft.com/es-es/library/dd831853.aspx. (Octubre 2016)
20. Murillo A. ¿Qué es el dispositivo Kinect?, https://www.kinectfordevelopers.com/es/2012/11/06/que-es-el-dispositivo-kinect/. (2016)
21. Gallo, L., Pierluigi, A., Ciampi, M.: Controller-free exploration of medical image data: experiencing the Kinect, p. 12215186 (2011)
22. Gallo, L., Minutolo, A., De Pietro, G.: A user interface for VR-ready 3D medical imaging by off-the-shelf input devices. Comput. Biol. Med. **40**(3), 350–358 (2010) Unity https://unity3d.com/
23. Unity Technologies, Unity software. https://unity3d.com/es/. Junio (2017)
24. Blender Foundation, Blender software. https://www.blender.org/. Mayo (2017)
25. Android Studio. https://developer.android.com/studio/index.html?hl=es-419. Enero (2017)
26. Mazen, A.A.: Análisis de sistemas de realidad aumentada y metodología para el desarrollo de aplicaciones educativas. Trabajo fin de Máster. Universidad Rey Juan Carlos. Escuela Superior de Ingeniería Informática. Madrid, España. (2012)
27. Bautista, J.: Programacion XP. Universidad Unión Bolivariana (2018)
28. Hernández, A.: Software architecture for the development of videogames on the game engine Unity 3D. La Habana: Revista ID Tecnológico (2015)

Unicycle Mobile Robot Formation Control in *Hardware in the Loop* Environments

Manuel A. Quispe$^{(\boxtimes)}$, Martha C. Molina$^{(\boxtimes)}$, Jessica S. Ortiz$^{(\boxtimes)}$, and Víctor H. Andaluz$^{(\boxtimes)}$

Universidad de las Fuerzas Armadas ESPE, Sangolquí, Ecuador
{maquispe2,mcmolina6,jsortiz4,vhandaluz1}@espe.edu.ec

Abstract. This work presents the development of a formation control algorithm for three unicycle-type robots, to solve the problem in the implementation of controllers oriented to collaborative functions and also subject to an excessive economic cost. This leads to the approximation of the simulation technique in environments Hardware in the loop (HIL), which allow clearly visualize with a real idea and a high percentage of approximation of the behavior of mobile robots unicycle type integrating different types of advanced controllers that will allow the execution of tasks of mobile robots unicycle type the same that are determined by the trajectories that control the position and thus raises the strategy of nonlinear control with a centralized and decentralized formation in the work area, acting as a command and control management system that will in turn be able to receive input signals, process the information and deliver control signals, which will later be displayed and analyzed to help verify the control theory.

Keywords: Formation control · Unicycle type robot · Mathematical modeling · Control theory and analysis

1 Introduction

Industrial robots have been considered the most popular robots; due to the importance they have maintained in the industrial sector as a key tool in modernizing [1]. However, in recent years the need has arisen to extend the scope of application of robotics outside the area of the purely industrial sector, thus trying to make the robots perform tasks like the demanded in service robotics [1, 2]. Thus, its use has evolved both in its characteristics and in its maneuverability in the execution of high-impact actions within society. Several definitions they have been imparted around a robot of service, it is so that the International Federation of Robotics (IFR, for their initials in English), organism that is in charge to coordinate the activities in this technological area it has defined it as: A robot that operates of automatic way or semiautomatic to carry out useful services to the well-being of the humans or to their equipment, excluding the operations of manufacture. The name arises for the restlessness of the scientific community of carrying out developments destined to be to the service of the society, trying that this one recognizes and endorses their results [3].

© Springer Nature Switzerland AG 2021
M. Botto-Tobar et al. (Eds.): ICAT 2020, CCIS 1388, pp. 430–443, 2021.
https://doi.org/10.1007/978-3-030-71503-8_33

It is evident and certain at the same time that the robots, are the systems that in a future will perform most of the tasks oriented to the physical highlighting the heaviest, in this section is detailed the sectors as possible main users of these robots are: Agriculture, construction, mining, energy, space, security and defense. In all of them, and in many others [4], In the field of robotics, there are a large number of tasks that must and can be robotized, which requires the development of specific robots, a task that manufacturers are not able to perform but only research centers. As for the physical structure, there are more and more demands regarding the characteristics of these. One can speak of robots with extremely large and small dimensions capable of entering dangerous, inaccessible and complex places for humans, thus contributing to the development of various activities that benefit society. The great variety of environments and situations in which they can develop requires locomotion capabilities developed according to their purpose may be these based on wheels or legs, [5]. Among the most relevant contributions in the field of locomotion have been automatic car driving systems, underwater robots, climbing and airborne robots, as they require hostile environments as well as air and water, thus becoming a center of attraction for researchers specializing in mobile robots.

Mobile robotics is an active research area where every day the world finds new technologies to improve the intelligence of mobile robots and their respective areas of application, these robots are characterized by the ability to: roll, slide, walk, jump, etc., [6]. Among the different mobile robots, there are the following types of robots: unicycle, car-like and omnidirectional. The unicycle type mobile robots are the most used due to its good mobility and simple configuration, these robots are specialized in sectors such as: floor cleaning, surveillance and industrial charge transport using autonomous guided vehicles [6, 7], These robots consist of a structure with 3 or 4 wheels, which in turn consist of a series of rollers that allow the wheel to move flexibly in two directions (together with the wheel and together with the roller) in the coordinate frame [8] The Car-like mobile robot is composed of an electric system, *i.e.,* a motor with drive on the rear wheel and steering on the front wheel [9].

In recent years, the formation and coordination of multiple robots has been an area of intense research. Various applications in the field of robotics and automatic control allowed a great boom in the scientific community. One of the existing alternatives is the control in formation based on different methods that are classified within three conventional ones: leader follower or master/slave [10, 11], based on behavior, [12], and virtual structures. Many of the multi-vehicle coordination algorithms, such as [8], it considers only robots of punctual mass with dynamics of simple or double integrator, where the robot can be moved instantaneously in any direction on the plane. The robots uniciclo with different characteristics, require the synchronization of their movements to achieve to maintain the formation and this way to follow a predefined path [13]. In the presence of disturbances, robots must work cooperatively to recover their trajectory and formation. In addition, the robots can go in and out of the formations, so the rest of the formation must be adjusted to the maximum speed conditions that will be reached by all the members of the group. The problem of formation multiple robots has been studied through different approaches including the implementation of controllers.

Therefore, the proposal of this article is the implementation of a formation control algorithm through Hardware in the loop, in this work the formed robotic assembly moves along a path with a desired speed, simultaneously it can alter the formation of the whole assembly through the modification of the distances and orientations of the main and secondary projections. The proposed controller uses a hierarchical control structure, in order to provide scalability to the system and at the same time not saturate the processing unit, thus merging the centralized and decentralized information processors. In a high level hierarchy, a centralized computer is in charge of generating the control actions to achieve the secondary projections, while, at a local level, each member of the heterogeneous robotic assembly includes its own processing unit to achieve kinematic and dynamic control and also to provide feedback [14], which is shared through wireless communications by means of Raspberry Pi cards.

This article is divided into six sections, including the introduction. Section 2 presents the system structure, the description of the HIL and its VR environment, while Sect. 3 presents the kinematic and dynamic modeling of the unicycle robot. Section 4 presents the scheme, design and stability analysis of the formation control algorithm for three or more robots. Section 5 presents the experimental results obtained with the implementation of the HIL and finally the conclusions of this work are presented in Sect. 6.

2   System Structure

The Hardware in the Loop (HIL) environment, which is a simulation technique used for the visualization, development and testing of the behavior of complex embedded systems in real time, aims to implement an HIL environment in order to develop advanced control algorithms for the formation of three mobile robots of the unicycle type. The HIL to be implemented will consider so much the kinematic part as the dynamics of the mobile robot of type unicicle.

The system proposed in this work (to see Fig. 1) it consists of a controller advanced of centralized formation, based on a system of management of command and control, where it is considered as entrance the task desired (position) for the three robots mobile of type unicicle, where each robot follower will send signals to the robot leader the same that will process the information and it will resend signals of execution for the task assigned. In addition, with the purpose to emulate a real robot in the structure HIL it will be implemented controllers PID for each actuator of the mobile robots, that is to say, two PID that will compensate the dynamics of the mobile robot. Later, it will be developed an intuitive graphical interface that allows the user interaction with each mobile robot, in order to evaluate the behavior of the robotic system and the evolution of control errors. The HIL will be developed in a master control unit that allows bilateral wireless communication with the advanced controller and independent structures of each of the mobile robots, in order to close the control loop.

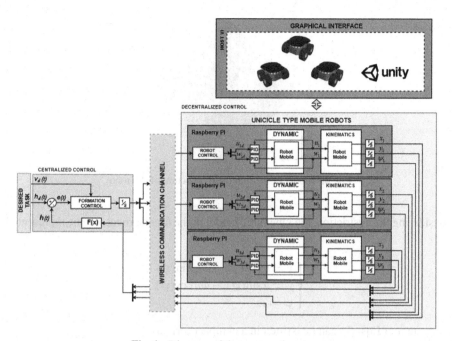

Fig. 1. Diagram of the proposed system.

3 Mobile Unicycle Robot

In the field of applied robotics both kinematic and dynamic models are widely used for the design of different control algorithms, as needed. Next, it is presented the kinematic and dynamic model of unicycle robots considering the restrictions of movement that it has.

3.1 Kinematic Model

When a mobile robot performs desired tasks or actions at low speeds and with a small load or weight in relation to its structure, the best option for controller design is the kinematic model. Figure 2 defines the geometry of the mobile robot type unicycle.

Where G represents the center of mass of the mobile robot which is at a distance a forward of the axis of the moving reference system $\{R_m\}$, considering that x and y belong to the position of the point **h** with regard to the global reference system; and finally ψ defines the orientation of the mobile robot with respect to $\{R\}$.

It is of vital importance to consider the restrictions of movement that the mobile robot presents, in this case it is considered the non-holonomic restriction which determines that the mobile robot can only be moved perpendicularly to the axis that joins the motors, and it is given by:

$$\dot{x}\sin(\psi) + \dot{y}\cos(\psi) + a\psi = 0 \tag{1}$$

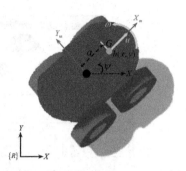

Fig. 2. Model of the kinematic structure of the robot

considering this restriction, the kinematic model of the mobile robot, can be represented by:

$$\begin{cases} \dot{x} = u\cos(\psi) - a\omega\sin(\psi) \\ \dot{y} = u\sin(\psi) + a\omega\cos(\psi) \\ \dot{\psi} = \omega \end{cases} \tag{2}$$

the system of Eqs. (2) can be written in a compact form as:

$$\begin{aligned} \dot{\mathbf{h}}(t) &= \mathbf{J}(\psi)\mathbf{v}(t) \\ \dot{\psi}(t) &= \omega(t) \end{aligned} \tag{3}$$

where $\dot{\mathbf{h}} = \begin{bmatrix} \dot{x} & \dot{y} \end{bmatrix} \in \Re^2$ represent the velocity vector of the axis; $\mathbf{J}(\psi) = \begin{bmatrix} \cos\psi & -a\sin\psi \\ \sin\psi & a\cos\psi \end{bmatrix} \in \Re^{2\times2}$ is a unique matrix; and defines the maneuverability control of the mobile robot $\mathbf{v} \in \Re^n$ and $\mathbf{v} = \begin{bmatrix} u & \omega \end{bmatrix}^T \in \Re^2$ in which u and ω represent the linear and angular speeds of the mobile robot, respectively.

3.2 Dynamic Model

Generally, the existing robots on the market have a low level in terms of reference speeds of PID controllers to monitor input speeds and which do not allow the motor voltage is directly proportional. Therefore, it is useful to express the dynamic model of the mobile robot unicycle type conveniently considering the linear and angular speed as input signals, all in order to use this model in controller design. Then, the model of the mobile robot can be expressed as [15, 16]

$$\mathbf{v_{ref}} = \mathbf{M}(\varsigma)\dot{\mathbf{v}} + \mathbf{C}(\varsigma, \mathbf{v})\mathbf{v} \tag{4}$$

where, $\mathbf{M}(\varsigma) \in \Re^{n\times n}$ with $n = 2$ and $\mathbf{M}(\varsigma) = \begin{bmatrix} \varsigma_1 & -\varsigma_7 \\ -\varsigma_8 & \varsigma_2 \end{bmatrix}$ represents the inertia of the robot-mobile system; $\mathbf{C}(\varsigma, \mathbf{v}) \in \Re^{n\times n}$ and $\mathbf{C}(\varsigma, \mathbf{v}) = \begin{bmatrix} \varsigma_4 & -\varsigma_3\omega \\ \varsigma_5\omega & \varsigma_6 \end{bmatrix}$ represents the components of the centripetal forces; $\mathbf{v} \in \Re^n$ and $\mathbf{v} = [\, u \; \omega \,]^T$ is the speed vector of the system; $\mathbf{v}_{ref} \in \Re^n$ and $\mathbf{v_{ref}} = [\, u_{ref} \; \omega_{ref} \,]^T$ is the vector of speed control signals for the mobile robot; and $\varsigma \in \Re^l$ with $l = 8$ and $\varsigma = [\, \varsigma_1 \; \varsigma_2 \ldots \varsigma_l \,]^T$ is the vector that contains the dynamic parameters of the mobile robotic system.

4   Multilayer Scheme

In this section is presented the distribution of variables that make up the cooperative control of mobile robots, which is composed of three main layers, *i.e.,* centralized, decentralized and virtual environment, see Fig. 3. The main layers are divided into six secondary layers where two of them correspond to the main layer of the centralized and the remaining four correspond to the decentralized layer. The six secondary layers are described as follows: *i) Task Planning* This layer establishes the characteristics of the environment where the desired formation task is planned to be executed either online or offline based on the configuration of the initial parameters: desired path, initial positions of the mobile robots and formation structure. *ii) Formation control* has the purpose of calculating the different control actions so that the mobile robots maintain a position so that the desired formation is satisfied. *iii) Environment* represents the communication channel which allows a closed-loop control between the centralized control and the independent structure of each of the mobile robots. *iv) Non-Linear*

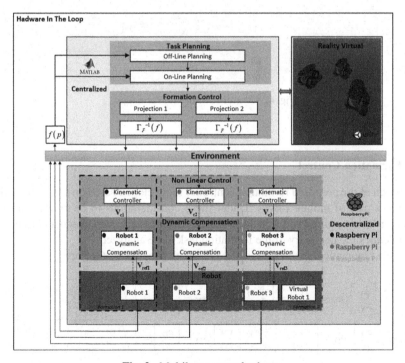

Fig. 3. Multilayer control scheme.

Control is responsible for providing maneuverability speeds to each robot that make up the system, taking as reference the control actions generated by the formation control. *v) Dynamic Compensation* Its main objective is to compensate the dynamics of each of the mobile robots, thus reducing the speed tracking error and limiting it near zero. *vi) Robots* represents the set of mobile robots considered for the formation system.

5   Control Schemes

The proposed control scheme to fulfill collaborative and trajectory tracking tasks is shown in Fig. 4, the controller design is mainly based on two main blocks. A centralized control block itself that is responsible for managing all data from the mobile robots for them to apply the control of formation of the 3 mobile robots, and on the other hand a decentralized control block which is confirmed by 3 control algorithms each for each robot, this means that each of the robots can have different dynamic characteristics.

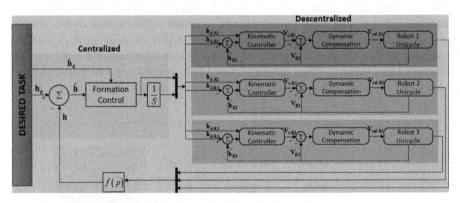

Fig. 4. Control structure for formation

5.1   Formation Control

The design of the proposed formation controller is developed based on projections given between a pair of mobile robots. Under these considerations to be able to meet the formation tasks required between three mobile robots is necessary to add a virtual robot, Fig. 5 defines the geometry of the formation task to be analyzed.

Direct kinematic transformations $f(.)$ For both projections they are given by:

$$\gamma_V = \begin{bmatrix} \mathbf{p}_V \\ \mathbf{s}_V \end{bmatrix}; \mathbf{p}_V = \begin{bmatrix} x_V \\ y_V \end{bmatrix} = \begin{bmatrix} \frac{1}{2}(x_1 + x_2) \\ \frac{1}{2}(y_1 + y_2) \end{bmatrix}; \mathbf{s}_V = \begin{bmatrix} d_V \\ \theta_V \end{bmatrix} = \begin{bmatrix} \sqrt{(x_1 - x_2)^2 + (y_1 - y_2)^2} \\ \tan^{-1}\left(\frac{y_1 - y_2}{x_1 - x_2}\right) \end{bmatrix},$$

$$\gamma_O = \begin{bmatrix} \mathbf{p}_O \\ \mathbf{s}_O \end{bmatrix}; \mathbf{p}_O = \begin{bmatrix} x_O \\ y_O \end{bmatrix} = \begin{bmatrix} \frac{1}{2}(x_V + x_3) \\ \frac{1}{2}(y_V + y_3) \end{bmatrix}; \mathbf{s}_O = \begin{bmatrix} d_O \\ \theta_O \end{bmatrix} = \begin{bmatrix} \sqrt{(x_V - x_3)^2 + (y_V - y_3)^2} \\ \tan^{-1}\left(\frac{y_V - y_3}{x_V - x_3}\right) \end{bmatrix}.$$

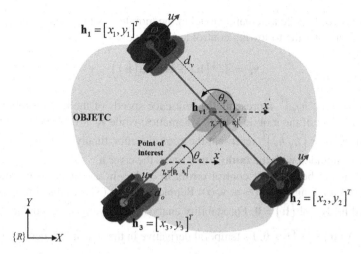

Fig. 5. Analysis of the formation of unicycle robots.

taking the time derivative of the forward and backward kinematic transformations so that the relationship between the time variations of $\dot{\mathbf{h}}(\mathbf{t})$ and $\dot{\gamma}(\mathbf{t})$, represented by the Jacobian matrix $\mathbf{J_F}$, that is given by:

$$\dot{\gamma} = \mathbf{J_F}(\mathbf{h})\dot{\mathbf{h}} \tag{5}$$

That is why the desired position and shape parameters are considered when designing the formation controller $\gamma_{\mathbf{d}} = \begin{bmatrix} \mathbf{p_d} & \mathbf{s_d} \end{bmatrix}$ and desired speed variations $\dot{\gamma}_{\mathbf{d}} = \begin{bmatrix} \dot{\mathbf{p}}_{\mathbf{d}} & \dot{\mathbf{s}}_{\mathbf{d}} \end{bmatrix}$. Therefore, the formation error can be defined as $\tilde{\gamma} = \gamma_{\mathbf{d}} - \gamma$ obtaining the time derivative denoted as $\dot{\tilde{\gamma}} = \dot{\gamma}_{\mathbf{d}} - \dot{\gamma}$. However, defining the control objective as $\tilde{\gamma}(\mathbf{t}) = \mathbf{0}$ this to demonstrate the stability of the system. To achieve this is proposed a driver based on a Lyapunov candidate function which is defined as $\mathbf{V}(\tilde{\gamma}) = \frac{1}{2}\tilde{\gamma}^T\gamma > 0$, Considering the temporal derivative of this function, is obtained $\dot{\mathbf{V}}(\tilde{\gamma}) = \tilde{\gamma}^T\gamma$.

Now, the proposed formation control law is defined as:

$$\dot{\mathbf{h}}(\mathbf{t}) = J_F^{-1}(\dot{\gamma}_{\mathbf{d}} + \mathbf{K}\tanh(\tilde{\gamma})) \tag{6}$$

where $\mathbf{K}$ is a diagonal gain matrix. Replacing (6) in the temporal derivative of $\dot{\mathbf{V}}(\tilde{\gamma})$, is obtained

$$\dot{\mathbf{V}}(\tilde{\gamma}) = -\tilde{\gamma}^T\mathbf{K}\tanh(\tilde{\gamma}) < 0 \tag{7}$$

So the law of closed-loop control (6) is asymptotically stable, *i.e.*, that formation control errors $\tilde{\gamma}(\mathbf{t}) \to 0$, is asymptotically stable with $t \to \infty$.

5.2 Kinematic Control of the I-th Robot

The purpose of implementing a control algorithm is to find the maneuverability vector to achieve the desired operational movement of the robot. Thus, the proposed control algorithm is based on the kinematic model of the mobile robot (3), that is to say, $\dot{\mathbf{h}}(t) = f(\mathbf{h})\mathbf{v}(t)$, Therefore, the following control law is proposed,

$$\mathbf{v_c} = \mathbf{J}^{-1}\left(\dot{\mathbf{h}}_{\mathbf{d}} + \mathbf{K}\tanh\left(\tilde{\mathbf{h}}\right)\right) \tag{8}$$

where, $\dot{\mathbf{h}}_{\mathbf{d}} = \begin{bmatrix} \dot{h}_{dx} & \dot{h}_{dy} \end{bmatrix}^T$ represents the reference speeds of the mobile robot; $\mathbf{J}^{-1}$ is the inverse matrix of the mobile robot's kinematics; while $\mathbf{K} > 0$ are positive diagonal gain matrices; $\tilde{\mathbf{h}} = \begin{bmatrix} \tilde{h}_x & \tilde{h}_y \end{bmatrix}^T$ represent the control errors; finally an analytical velocity saturation is included with the $\tanh(.)$ that limits the error $\tilde{\mathbf{h}}$.

However, the behavior of control errors $\tilde{\mathbf{h}} = \mathbf{h_d} - \mathbf{h}$ are analyzed considering a perfect speed tracking, $i.e.$, $\mathbf{v}(t) \equiv \mathbf{v_c}(t)$. Replacing (8) in (3) the closed-loop equation is obtained $\dot{\tilde{\mathbf{h}}} + \mathbf{K}\tanh\left(\tilde{\mathbf{h}}\right) = \mathbf{0}$. For stability analysis, the Lyapunov candidate function defined as $\mathbf{V}\left(\tilde{\mathbf{h}}\right) = \frac{1}{2}\tilde{\mathbf{h}}^T\tilde{\mathbf{h}} > 0$. Its temporal derivative in the system's trajectory is:

$$\dot{V}\left(\tilde{\mathbf{h}}\right) = \tilde{\mathbf{h}}^T\mathbf{K}\tanh\left(\tilde{\mathbf{h}}\right) < 0 \tag{9}$$

What the closed-loop system implies is asymptotically stable, so that the positioning error of the robots $\tilde{\mathbf{h}}(t) \to 0$ is asymptotically stable with $t \to \infty$.

5.3 Dynamic Compensation of the I-th Robot

On the other hand, if perfect speed tracking is not considered in the design of the kinematic controller, $i.e.$, $\mathbf{v}(t) \neq \mathbf{v_c}(t)$, the speed error is defined as $\tilde{\mathbf{v}}(t) = \mathbf{v_c}(t) - \mathbf{v}(t)$. Considering this speed error arises the need to design a dynamic compensation control, whose objective is to reduce the speed tracking error; therefore, it is proposed the following control law based on the dynamic model (4), [15, 17]

$$\mathbf{v_{ref}} = \mathbf{M}(\varsigma)(\dot{\mathbf{v}}_c + \mathbf{K}\tanh(\tilde{\mathbf{v}})) + \mathbf{C}(\varsigma, \mathbf{v})\mathbf{v} \tag{10}$$

where, $\mathbf{v_{ref}} = \begin{bmatrix} u_{ref} & \omega_{ref} \end{bmatrix}^T$ represent the control actions; $\dot{\mathbf{v}}_c = \begin{bmatrix} \dot{u}_c & \dot{\omega}_c \end{bmatrix}^T$ represent the kinematic control accelerations; finally, an analytical speed saturation is included with the function. $\tanh(.)$ that limits the error $\tilde{\mathbf{v}}$.

A Lyapunov candidate function and its temporal drift are then introduced into the system trajectories to perform the stability analysis $\mathbf{V}(\tilde{\mathbf{v}}) = \frac{1}{2}\tilde{\mathbf{v}}^T\tilde{\mathbf{v}}$. The temporal derivative of Lyapunov's candidate function is:

$$\dot{\mathbf{V}}(\tilde{\mathbf{v}}) = \tilde{\mathbf{v}}^T\dot{\tilde{\mathbf{v}}} \tag{11}$$

After introducing the control laws (4) and (10) in (11), the time derivative can be expressed as:

$$\dot{\mathbf{V}}(\tilde{\mathbf{v}}) = -\tilde{\mathbf{v}}^T\mathbf{K}_1\tanh(\tilde{\mathbf{v}}) < 0 \tag{12}$$

For the stability of the proposed control law, with $\mathbf{K}_1 > 0$, it is possible to guarantee that $\tilde{\mathbf{v}}(t) \to 0$ is asymptotically when $t \to \infty$.

6   Experimental Results

This section presents the experimental results of the HIL scheme implemented for the formation control of three unicycle-type robots. For the execution of the different tests of experimentation it was considered a computer in which it was implemented the algorithm of centralized control of formation of the three mobile robots. While, the decentralized control of each robot and kinematic and dynamic models were implemented in embedded devices, known as Raspberry Pi 4., see Fig. 6. This decentralized control consists of kinematic models represented by (3) and dynamic, represented by (4) where the values of $\varsigma_1 = 0.1951, \varsigma_2 = 0.2231, \varsigma_3 = -0.0006, \varsigma_4 = 1.0015, \varsigma_5 = 0.0027, \varsigma_6 = 0.9723,$ $\varsigma_7 = -0.0004$ and $\varsigma_8 = -0.0554$ were found based on experimental tests performed on the mobile robots available at the research laboratory in automation, robotics and intelligent systems (ARSI)

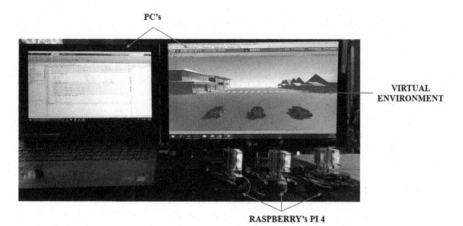

Fig. 6. Implementation of formation control in HIL environments

In addition, it is important to mention that for the virtualization of the robots' movements a 3D virtual environment was developed, see Fig. 7. In the virtual environment was incorporated physical characteristics of the real world, *e.g.,* gravity; friction forces of tires with different soil types; audio data, and other properties that simulate a real environment so as to allow the evaluation of different control algorithms.

i. First Experiment

The first experiment consists of executing the formation of three unicycle-type robots. The desired trajectory for this formation is described with: $x_{do} = 0.1t$ and $y_{do} = 2\sin(0.1t)$. Figure 8 shows the strobe movement of the trajectory execution (x_{do} and y_{do}) in which it can be observed that the movement of the robots satisfactorily fulfills the desired task, so much in orientation and distance, it is to say that the primary robot it was maintained in the path desired, the same as the second and third robot.

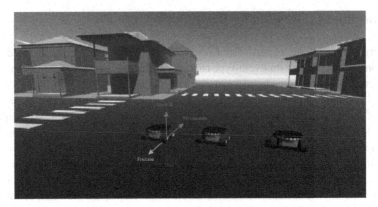

Fig. 7. Virtual environment developed for the formation of mobile robots

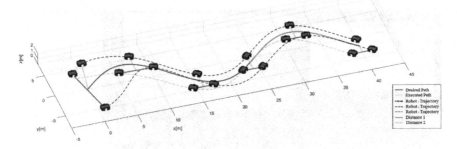

Fig. 8. Formation path, executed by unicycle type robots.

Below are the errors obtained in the execution of the trajectory (x_{do} and y_{do}) of each one of the robots type unicycle considering a null disturbance, in addition it is evident that the errors have a suitable behavior since its magnitude is almost negligible is ideal since it is concentrated in the proximities of zero (Fig. 9).

ii. Second Experiment

In this section, both position and orientation errors obtained in the same desired path are shown (see Fig. 8). Where it can be detailed that, to the beginning of the experiment, it was produced a considerable error caused by the initial positions of each robot. By means of the implementation of the control of formation, it was found the point more near to the path, where the robots it was placed of way that the position of the main robot it was in the path desired and therefore the remaining realized it same (Fig. 10).

It is necessary to emphasize that, for the developed experiment, the control of formation has as purpose to generate speeds of reference that, through the kinematic control, each robot followed a path, the same that contributes to find the expected formation.

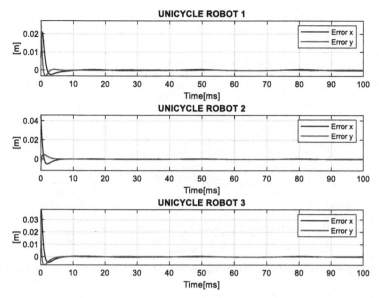

Fig. 9. Errors presented in each robot immersed in the formation system.

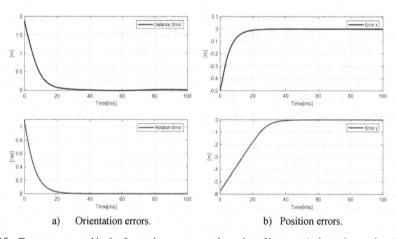

a)   Orientation errors.   b)   Position errors.

Fig. 10. Errors presented in the formation system at the point of interest (orientation and position).

iii. Third Experiment

In this section, they are presented the errors (see Fig. 11) obtained of each one of the robots type uniciclo in the trajectory already mentioned taking in consideration a disturbance in the dynamics of the same ones, where it refers to the interaction among the tires of the robot and the type of floor that is to say the force of friction that is generated among them, producing this way a representative error of speeds, but in turn these errors are limited in the neighborhoods of zero.

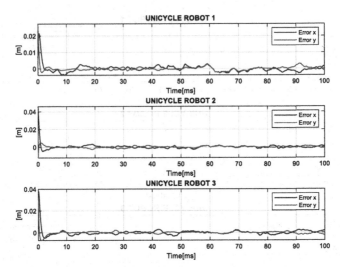

Fig. 11. Errors presented in each robot immersed in the formation system applying disturbances.

7 Conclusion

The control of formation in environments HIL that considers distance, position and angle is achieved through signals of reference emitted to the independent structures of each robot, for it three robots type unicycle were used the same ones that in turn, contributed to the evaluation of the performance of the controller implemented in this proposal in comparison to other more complex and expensive controls, that is to say, the pursuit of the trajectory for the robotic set, In addition, by means of the analysis of stability of the law of control it is de-shown that the system is asymptotically stable maintaining the errors in the proximities of zero. This work employs for its operation the processing of centralized and decentralized tasks so that a computer calculates the position, distance and angle of the path, while the processing units ensure the kinematic control added a dynamic compensation of each robot independently. Finally, it simulates the set of robots used a virtual environment to obtain the experimental results, results that demonstrate the proper functioning of the proposed controller in HIL environments for the three mechanisms. All the mentioned can be applied in different areas, sectors and strategic places oriented to collaborative tasks.

Acknowledgements. The authors would like to thank the Corporación Ecuatoriana para el Desarrollo de la Investigación y Academia-CEDIA for their contribution in innovation, through the CEPRA projects, especially the project CEPRA-XIV-2020-08RVA "Tecnologías Inmersivas Multi-Usuario Orientadas a Sistemas Sinérgicos de Enseñanza y Aprendizaje"; also the Universidad de las Fuerzas Armadas ESPE, Escuela Superior Politécnica de Chimborazo, Universidad Técnica de Ambato, Universidad tecnológica Indoamérica and the ARSI Research Group, for the support for the development of this work.

References

1. Aracil, R., et al.: "Service Robots," Revista Iberoamericana de Automática e Informática Industrial, pp. 1–4 (2008)
2. J. Engelberger, Robotics in Service, MIT Press. Cambridge (1989)
3. Kuo, C.M., Chen, L.C., Tseng, C.Y.: Investigating an innovative service with hospitality robots. Int. J. Contemp. Hospitality Manage. **29**, 4–7 (2017)
4. Decker, M., Fischer, M., Ott, I.: Service robotics and human labor: a first technology assessment of substitution and cooperation. Robot. Auton. Syst. **87**, 348–354 (2017)
5. Song, S.M., Waldron, K.J.: Machines that Walk, the Adaptive Suspension Vehicle, MIT Press, Cambridge (1989)
6. Andaluz Ortiz, G.M.: Modelación, Identificación y Control de robots móviles (2011)
7. Andaluz, V.H.: Dynamics of a unicycle-type wheeled mobile manipulator robot. Adv. Emerg. Trends Technol. **2**(1067), 24 (2019)
8. Jiang, Y., Yang, C., Wang, M., Wang, N., Liu, X.: Bioinspired control design using cerebellar model articulation controller network for omnidirectional mobile robots. Adv. Mech. Eng. **10**, 1687814018794349 (2018)
9. Valero, F., Rubio, F., Llopis-Albert, C., Cuadrado, J.I.: Influence of the friction coefficient on the trajectory performance for a car-like robot. Math. Prob. Eng. **3**, 4–5 (2017)
10. Huang, J., Farritor, S.M., Qadi, A., Goddard, S.: Localitation and follow-the-leader control for a heterogeneous group of mobile robots. IEEE/ASME Trans. Mech. **11**(2), 205–215 (2006)
11. Gustavi, T., Hu, X.: Observer-based leader-following formation control using onboard sensor information. IEEE Trans. Rob. **24**(6), 1457–1462 (2018)
12. Balch, T., Arkin, R.C.: Behavior-based formation control for multi-robot systems. IEEE Trans. Autom. Control **14**, 926–939 (1998)
13. Chu, X., Peng, Z., Wen, G., Rahmani, A.: Robust fixed-time consensus tracking with application to formation control of unicycles. IET Control Theory Appl. **12**, 53–59 (2017)
14. Acosta, J.F., Rivera, G.G.D., Andaluz, V.H., Garrido, J.: Multirobot heterogeneous control considering secondary objectives. Sensors **19**(20), 4367 (2019)
15. Andaluz V.H., et al.: Robust Control with Dynamic Compensation for Human-Wheelchair System. In: Zhang, X., Liu, H., Chen, Z., Wang, N. (eds.) Intelligent Robotics and Applications, ICIRA 2014, Part I, vol. 8917, pp. 376–389, Springer, Heidelberg (2014) https://doi.org/10.1007/978-3-319-13966-1_37
16. Andaluz, V.H., et al.: Modeling and control of a wheelchair considering center of mass lateral displacements. In: Liu, H., Kubota, N., Zhu, X., Dillmann, R. (eds.) Intelligent Robotics and Applications, ICIRA 2015, vol. 9246, pp. 254–270, Springer, Heidelberg (2015) https://doi.org/10.1007/978-3-319-22873-0_23
17. Daniel, H.: Modeling and path-following control of a wheelchair in human-shared environments. Int. J. Humanoid Rob. **15**, 33 (2018)

Control of an Omnidirectional Robot Based on the Kinematic and Dynamic Model

Luis V. Gallo$^{(\boxtimes)}$, Byron D. Paste$^{(\boxtimes)}$, Jessica S. Ortiz$^{(\boxtimes)}$,
and Víctor H. Andaluz$^{(\boxtimes)}$

Universidad de las Fuerzas Armadas ESPE, Sangolquí, Ecuador
{lvgallo,bdpaste,jsortiz4,vhandaluz1}@espe.edu.ec

Abstract. This work focuses on the proposal for the implementation and evaluation of control algorithms for the monitoring of autonomous trajectories based on the kinematic and dynamic model of an omnidirectional robotic platform in four wheel configuration type mecanum also built for the process of identification and validation of the dynamic parameters obtained from the mathematical model by means of an identification algorithm, the evaluation of these control algorithms is carried out experimentally on the Robotic Platform in real four-wheel omnidirectional configuration with which it also allows to evaluate the operation of the Hardware in the Loop control scheme (HIL), a technique that constitutes the untimely connection of external hardware with computer equipment allowing to simulate in real time the behavior of the robotic system with omnidirectional traction in four-wheel configuration type mecanum. Subsequently the data resulting from the Hardware in the Loop (HIL) control scheme will be compared to the data obtained in the experimental test for corresponding validation.

Keywords: Omnidirectional robot · Mecanum wheel · Hardware-in-the-Loop

1 Introduction

In recent years, the robotics industry has developed rapidly. A lot of technologies are implemented in various applications [1, 2], *e.g.*, mobile robots have the ability to perform specific tasks in an industrial work environment, homes, hospitals, among others [3]. Some representative mobile robots include household cleaning robots, military surveillance drones, warehouse robots and autonomous robots [4, 5]. The latter have become indispensable components in many applications, including research, warehouse management, surveillance and safety, and autonomous vehicles [6, 7].

Currently there are different types of platforms that are characterized by the type of wheels or by the mechanical structure that makes up it among the main ones can be detailed: *i) Unicycle robots,* they are formed of a mechanical structure with three degrees of freedom consisting of two conventional fixed wheels and a stable partial wheel that is independently controlled on the same axle, so it can automatically navigate in a specific work environment. This type of robot is the most commonly used in security, surveillance, transport, education and research applications [8]; *ii) robots car-like*, it has its kinematic model based on Ackerman's mobility system with its linear

© Springer Nature Switzerland AG 2021
M. Botto-Tobar et al. (Eds.): ICAT 2020, CCIS 1388, pp. 444–457, 2021.
https://doi.org/10.1007/978-3-030-71503-8_34

velocity and rotation angle, this model has a fairly large studio and is the basis for the current car [9]. Its use has increased significantly due to advances in sensors and control systems, these range from Google cars to modern automatically guided vehicles. They are used in industrial applications to transport materials in manufacturing, value-added and warehousing operations [10]; and *iii) omnidirectional robots*, A vehicle that can drive with 3 degrees of freedom in a two dimensional space and also independently control, translation and rotation can be considered as an omnidirectional robot [11]. By configuration, the omnidirectional robot can move in the desired direction from any starting position [12], because the mobile system ensures perfect mobility in any narrow space (curved, diagonal or any other space) because of its type of mecanum wheels [13]. Due to their versatility they can perform the functions of suppliers, inspectors, supervise different tasks in remote or explosive areas and provide support or bases for other robots or manipulators, because of all these features the demand for the use of omnidirectional robots has increased [12].

Among the different works carried out with omnidirectional robots we can detail: *i) construction,* the theory describes that for the construction of such omnidirectional robots with mecanum wheel the AB configuration is more used [12, 14], and the arrangement of the wheels are made rectangular or in turn commercial type robots such as KUKA Youtbot are used [15, 16]; *ii) modeling,* the previously designed models employ only the robot's kinematics regardless of the advantages provided by the dynamic model for controller stability and when the dynamic model is presented it has as inputs torques or voltages as shown in [17], where as a contribution to the dynamic model the dynamics of the engines were considered in this case the system inputs are the armature voltages of each engine; *iii) implementing control algorithms,* Several of the articles use nonlinear controllers based on linear algebra, numerical or unified-based methods in the robot's kinematics with dynamic compensation, *e.g.,* [18], it details the implementation of a kinematic controller with internal dynamic compensation that reduces the velocity tracking error.

One of the problems that exists in the field of robotics, is directly being able to experience control algorithms in which the necessary hardware is not available because of its high cost or its limitation for the number of tests, for which one of the alternatives for industrial automation processes is hardware in the loop (HIL). This is a technique in which a real time simulation environment is developed to test the behavior of its control algorithms without physical prototypes [19, 20]. It is widely used in the automotive industry to test vehicle dynamics and drivers [21], also used in aerospace and industrial automation. Therefore, this work proposes the implementation of the hardware in the loop technique in a virtual environment in real time, to evaluate control algorithms based on the kinematic and dynamic model of an omnidirectional robotic platform in four wheel configuration type mecanum, using as inputs velocities with what differs from previous jobs [12, 14, 17], will also be validated through the implementation of the control algorithm in a real omnidirectional robot.

The article is organized as follows: Sect. 2 presents the kinematic and dynamic modeling of the four-wheel omnidirectional mecanum robot; the control scheme of the HIL, control algorithm design and stability analysis are presented in Sect. 3; Experimental results are presented and discussed in Sect. 4. Finally, the conclusions are given in Sect. 5.

2 Robot Omnidirectional

Among the fundamental parts in the design of controllers for robotic systems are based on obtaining mathematical models that represent the characteristics and restrictions of movement, from a cinematic and dynamic point of view; therefore, this section presents the obtaining of *the Kinematic Model* and *the Dynamic Model* of the omnidirectional robotic platform, in which two linear velocities and an angular velocity are considered as signs of maneuverability.

2.1 Kinematic Model

Obtaining this model involves analyzing the positions and velocities required to perform autonomous tasks such as path tracking (see Fig. 1).

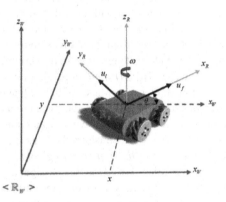

Fig. 1. Reference frames for omnidirectional robotic platform movement.

The omnidirectional platform consists of two linear velocities: Front u_f and sideways u_l found on the axes of the mobile reference system $<\mathbb{R}_R>$; in addition to an angular velocity ω that rotates around the axis Z_R. Rotation matrices are defined $\mathbf{R}_W^R(\theta)$ that rotates from the Robot frame of reference $<\mathbb{R}_R>$ to the inertial frame of reference $<\mathbb{R}_W>$ and $\mathbf{R}_W^R(\theta)$ that rotates from the inertial frame to the Robot frame, the latter is used to know the velocities of the mobile platform seen from the robot frame and represented by η performing the following process:

$$\mathbf{R}_W^R(\theta) = \begin{bmatrix} \cos\theta & \sin\theta & 0 \\ -\sin\theta & \cos\theta & 0 \\ 0 & 0 & 1 \end{bmatrix} \; ; \; \mathbf{R}_R^W(\theta) = \begin{bmatrix} \cos\theta & -\sin\theta & 0 \\ \sin\theta & \cos\theta & 0 \\ 0 & 0 & 1 \end{bmatrix} \; \eta(t) = \begin{bmatrix} u_f \\ u_l \\ \omega \end{bmatrix} = \mathbf{R}_W^R(\theta)\dot{\xi}(t)$$

$$(1)$$

Obtained as a result the kinematic model that describes the movement of the omnidirectional robot with respect to the inertial reference system.

$$\begin{cases} \dot{x} = u_f \cos(\theta) - u_l \sin(\theta) \\ \dot{y} = u_f \sin(\theta) + u_l \cos(\theta) \\ \dot{\theta} = \omega \end{cases} \tag{2}$$

Where, $\dot{\xi}$ represents the derivative of the robot's positions relative to the inertial reference system $<\mathbb{R}_W>$ with $\xi = [x\,y\,\theta]^T$ and its variation over time $\dot{\xi} = \begin{bmatrix} \dot{x}\,\dot{y}\,\dot{\theta} \end{bmatrix}^T$; also, is defined $\mathbf{W} = [W_1\,W_2\,W_3\,W_4]^T$ as the vector of the angular velocities of each wheel of the omnidirectional robotic platform that is obtained from:

$$\mathbf{W}(t) = \mathbf{E}(a,b)\,\boldsymbol{\eta}(t) \tag{3}$$

Considering that $\mathbf{E}$ is a constant transformation matrix that contains the parameters detailed below (see Fig. 2).

$$\mathbf{E} = \frac{1}{r} \begin{bmatrix} 1 & 1 & (a+b) \\ 1 & -1 & -(a+b) \\ 1 & 1 & -(a+b) \\ 1 & -1 & (a+b) \end{bmatrix}$$

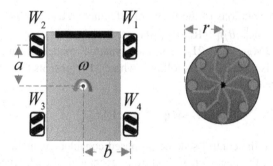

Fig. 2. Omnidirectional robotic platform parameters.

2.2 Dynamic Model

The dynamic model of the omnidirectional robotic platform is obtained from the Euler-Lagrange formulation, with the balance between the kinetic energy and potential of (4) to apply (5), where τ_i represents the generalized forces of the torques applied by the motors on each wheel.

$$L = E_C - E_P \tag{4}$$

$$\tau_i = \frac{d}{dt}\left(\frac{\partial L}{\partial \dot{q}}\right) - \frac{\partial L}{\partial q} \tag{5}$$

$$\mathbf{E_C} = \dot{\boldsymbol{\xi}}^T \mathbf{M}_{R1}\,\dot{\boldsymbol{\xi}} + \mathbf{W}^T \mathbf{I}_1\,\mathbf{W} \tag{6}$$

The sum of the robot's kinetic energies is represented by (6) where $M_{R1} = \frac{1}{2}diag\{m_R, m_R, I_R\}$ is made up of the total mass of the robotic platform, m_R; the total inertia of the robotic platform, I_R; and the matrix $I_1 = \frac{1}{2}diag\{I_W, I_W, I_W, I_W\}$ containing the inertia of the wheels, I_W. In addition, potential energy E_P of the system is equal to zero, therefore developing (6) results (7) and when applying (5) is represented compactly in (8):

$$\frac{1}{2}\left(m_R\dot{x}^2 + m_R\dot{y}^2 + I_R\dot{\theta}^2 + I_W W_1^2 + I_W W_2^2 + I_W W_3^2 + I_W W_4^2\right) = \mathbf{E}^T \boldsymbol{\tau}_i \tag{7}$$

$$\mathbf{R}_W^R(\theta)[\mathbf{E_C}]_\xi + \mathbf{E}^T[\mathbf{E_C}]_\varphi = \mathbf{E}^T \boldsymbol{\tau}_i \tag{8}$$

$$[\mathbf{E_C}]_\xi = \mathbf{M}_{R2}\ddot{\boldsymbol{\xi}}, \quad [\mathbf{E_C}]_\varphi = \mathbf{I}_2\,\dot{\mathbf{W}} \tag{9}$$

Then by replacing (9) in (8) results:

$$\mathbf{R}_W^R(\theta)\mathbf{M}_{R2}\ddot{\boldsymbol{\xi}} + \mathbf{E}^T \mathbf{I}_2\,\dot{\mathbf{W}} = \mathbf{E}^T \boldsymbol{\tau}_i \tag{10}$$

In (10) the accelerations of the frame of reference $<\mathbb{R}_W>$ to the frame $<\mathbb{R}_R>$ are defined by $\ddot{\boldsymbol{\xi}} = \mathbf{R}_R^W(\theta)\dot{\boldsymbol{\eta}} + \mathbf{R}_W^R(\theta)\boldsymbol{\eta}$; the accelerations of each wheel $\dot{\mathbf{W}} = \mathbf{E}\dot{\boldsymbol{\eta}}$; the matrices $\mathbf{M}_{R2} = 2\mathbf{M}_{R1}$, $\mathbf{I}_2 = 2\mathbf{I}_1$. So, the dynamic model of the omnidirectional robotics platform is represented as follows, where $\bar{\mathbf{M}}$ represents the mass matrix and $\bar{\mathbf{C}}$ is the matrix of centrifugal forces:

$$\bar{\boldsymbol{M}}\dot{\boldsymbol{\eta}} + \bar{\boldsymbol{C}}\boldsymbol{\eta} = \mathbf{E}^T \boldsymbol{\tau}_i \tag{11}$$

However, since the control scheme proposed considers as input velocities and not torques, can define the behavior of the torque generated in each wheel,

$$\tau_i = \frac{k_{pa}}{R_{pa}}\left(v_i - k_{pb}\mathbf{W}_i\right), \tag{12}$$

in which have the different parameters of the equations of the dynamic model of a DC engine; v_i as input voltages applied to each motor; k_{pa} is the torque constant multiplied by the reduction constant; R_{pa} is the electric resistance of the engine and k_{pb} is the product of the constant reduction and the constant electromotive. The supply voltages $v_v = v_{uf}, v_{ul}, v_\omega$, in turn can be described based on a PD controller (13), where $\mathbf{K}_P$ is the matrix of proportional constants and $\mathbf{K}_D$ the matrix of derivative constants.

$$\mathbf{v}_v = \mathbf{K}_P\left(\boldsymbol{\eta}_{ref} - \boldsymbol{\eta}\right) - \dot{\boldsymbol{\eta}}K_D \tag{13}$$

Through (10), (11), (12), (13) the compact mathematical model is obtained based on reference velocities and real velocities and accelerations:

$$\begin{bmatrix} u_{fref} \\ u_{lref} \\ \omega_{ref} \end{bmatrix} = \begin{bmatrix} \varsigma_1 & 0 & 0 \\ 0 & \varsigma_2 & 0 \\ 0 & 0 & \varsigma_3 \end{bmatrix} \begin{bmatrix} \dot{u}_f \\ \dot{u}_l \\ \dot{\omega} \end{bmatrix} + \begin{bmatrix} \varsigma_4 & -\omega\varsigma_5 & 0 \\ \omega\varsigma_6 & \varsigma_7 & 0 \\ 0 & 0 & \varsigma_8 \end{bmatrix} \begin{bmatrix} u_f \\ u_l \\ \omega \end{bmatrix}, \tag{14}$$

$$\boldsymbol{\eta}_{ref}(t) = \mathbf{M}(\varsigma)\dot{\boldsymbol{\eta}}(t) + \mathbf{C}(\varsigma, \boldsymbol{\eta})\boldsymbol{\eta}(t), \tag{15}$$

where $\varsigma \in \Re^j$ with $j = 8$ and $\varsigma = \begin{bmatrix} \varsigma_1 \varsigma_2 \dots \varsigma_j \end{bmatrix}^T$ it is the vector of the dynamic parameters of the system and the matrices that represent the inertia of the omnidirectional robotic platform and the components of centripetal forces.

3 Control Schemes

The proposed control scheme for HIL simulation consists of two blocks, in the block "Control System" is the base nonlinear mimo controller or two cascading subsystems: a) *Kinematic Controller,* where position control errors are calculated at each measurement time and are used to drive the mobile robot in *a* direction that decreases errors; and b) *Dynamic Compensation,* the objetive is to compensate for the dynamics of the omnidirectional robotic platform by reducing the velocity tracking error. This controller receives as inputs the desired velocities calculated by the kinematic controller and to its output generates velocity references that are sent through the communication channel. While the "Mathematical Model" block is the representation of the omnidirectional platform with its kinematic and dynamic mathematical model that returns the positions and velocities of the omnidirectional robotic platform (see Fig. 3).

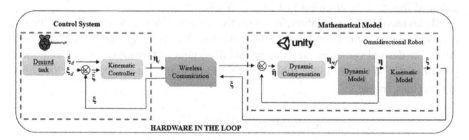

Fig. 3. Proposed HIL control scheme.

3.1 Designing the Control Algorithm

The developed control algorithm is intended to perform desired path tracking tasks.

A) Kinematic Controller the objective of the proposed cinematic controller is to calculate the position error in each sampling period and use these values to move the omnidirectional robotic platform in the direction to reduce control errors. This kinematic controller is based on the kinematic model (2) and is represented as follows:

$$\boldsymbol{\eta}_c = \mathbf{J}^{-1}\left(\dot{\boldsymbol{\xi}}_d + \mathbf{G}\tanh\left(\tilde{\boldsymbol{\xi}}\right)\right) \tag{16}$$

where, $\boldsymbol{\eta}_c$ represents the velocities of the kinematic controller; $\mathbf{J}^{-1}$ is the Jacobian matrix of the robotic platform; $\dot{\boldsymbol{\xi}}_d = \begin{bmatrix} \dot{x}_d & \dot{y}_d & \dot{\theta}_d \end{bmatrix}^T$ is the derivative of the desired trajectory; $\mathbf{G}$ is the gain matrix to compensate for control errors; and $\tanh\left(\tilde{\boldsymbol{\xi}}\right)$ is the function of saturation of position errors contained in the matrix $\tilde{\boldsymbol{\xi}} = \boldsymbol{\xi}_d - \boldsymbol{\xi}$.

In order to determine the stability of the controller, Lyapunov's candidate function of quadratic errors is determined $\mathbf{V}\left(\tilde{\boldsymbol{\xi}}\right) = \frac{1}{2}\tilde{\boldsymbol{\xi}}^T(t)\tilde{\boldsymbol{\xi}}(t)$; and applying the time derivative, is obtain.

$$\dot{\mathbf{V}}\left(\tilde{\boldsymbol{\xi}}\right) = \tilde{\boldsymbol{\xi}}^T(t)\dot{\tilde{\boldsymbol{\xi}}}(t) \tag{17}$$

It is also defined (16) compactly considering velocity errors $\dot{\tilde{\boldsymbol{\xi}}}(t) = \dot{\boldsymbol{\xi}}_d(t) - \dot{\boldsymbol{\xi}}(t)$ to get (18) and replace in (17)

$$\dot{\tilde{\boldsymbol{\xi}}}(t) = -\mathbf{G}\tanh\left(\tilde{\boldsymbol{\xi}}(t)\right) \tag{18}$$

$$\dot{\mathbf{V}}\left(\tilde{\boldsymbol{\xi}}\right) = -\tilde{\boldsymbol{\xi}}^T(t)\mathbf{G}\tanh\left(\tilde{\boldsymbol{\xi}}(t)\right) \tag{19}$$

Therefore, in order to ensure the stability of the proposed control law, it must be enforced that $\mathbf{G} > 0$, ensuring that $\tilde{\boldsymbol{\xi}}(t) \to 0$ when $t \to \infty$.

B) Dynamic Compensation, the objective of this block is to compensate for the dynamics of the omnidirectional robotic platform by reducing the velocity tracking error. The desired velocities are input $\boldsymbol{\eta}_c$ and the output of this subsystem are reference velocities $\boldsymbol{\eta}_{ref}$ to be sent to the robotic platform that in this case is located in the Unity 3D graphics engine.

$$\boldsymbol{\eta}_{ref} = \mathbf{M}\left(\dot{\boldsymbol{\eta}}_{cp} + \mathbf{K}\tanh(\tilde{\boldsymbol{\eta}})\right) + \mathbf{C}\boldsymbol{\eta} \tag{20}$$

Considering that $\dot{\boldsymbol{\eta}}_{cp}$ represents those derived from the desired velocities; $\mathbf{K}$ is the gain matrix to compensate for control errors; and $\tilde{\boldsymbol{\eta}}$ is the vector of robotic platform velocity errors.

Similarly, for the stability analysis of the compensator, the candidate Lyapunov function of quadratic errors (in this case velocities) is determined.

$$\mathbf{V}(\tilde{\boldsymbol{\eta}}) = \frac{1}{2}\tilde{\boldsymbol{\eta}}^T(t)\tilde{\boldsymbol{\eta}}(t) \tag{21}$$

$$\dot{\mathbf{V}}(\tilde{\boldsymbol{\eta}}) = \tilde{\boldsymbol{\eta}}^T(t)\dot{\tilde{\boldsymbol{\eta}}}(t) \tag{22}$$

Working with the compact form (20) where acceleration errors are considered $\dot{\tilde{\boldsymbol{\eta}}} = \dot{\boldsymbol{\eta}}_{cp} - \dot{\boldsymbol{\eta}}$, and by following the same procedure as in the previous case has:

$$\dot{\tilde{\boldsymbol{\eta}}} = -\mathbf{K}\tanh(\tilde{\boldsymbol{\eta}}) \tag{23}$$

$$\dot{\mathbf{V}}(\tilde{\boldsymbol{\eta}}) = -\tilde{\boldsymbol{\eta}}^T(t)\mathbf{K}\tanh(\tilde{\boldsymbol{\eta}}) \tag{24}$$

Consolidating the stability of the proposed control law, when $\mathbf{K} > 0$, ensuring that $\tilde{\boldsymbol{\eta}}(t) \to 0$ when $t \to \infty$.

4   Experimental Results and Discussion

This section presents the results of implementing the technique *Hardware in the Loop,* for which the construction of the omnidirectional robotic platform was carried out in order to evaluate the operation of the proposed controller, (see Fig. 4).

Fig. 4. Omnidirectional robotics platform built.

4.1   Omnidirectional Robot Construction

This sub-section describes the construction of an omnidirectional mobile robot in which the hardware is divided into four modules, (see Fig. 5).

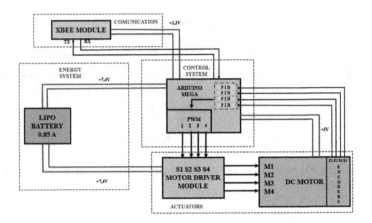

Fig. 5. Omnidirectional Robot Hardware Block Diagram.

Power System: Consists of a LIPO battery (0.85A and 7.4v) that provides power to the entire system, directly connecting its rated voltage to the control module and actuator module; *ii) Control system*: This is composed of an Arduino Mega, which receives and transmits the signal of the kinematic control performed; in addition to compensate separately the dynamics of the mobile robot is implemented internal loop controllers (PIDs), compensating for the errors resulting from the subtraction between the desired velocity and measured by each encoder located in the motors of the mecanum wheels.

Actuators: Consists of DC motors, with integrated velocity sensors and controllers (H-bridge) on each motor that support a constant current of 2 A per channel.

Communication: Manages communication between the robot and the computer. When considering the transmission velocity and distance of use of the mobile robot it was based on the IEEE 802.15.4 standard of Zigbee wireless networks.

4.2   Identification and Validation

The following expression is taken into account for the identification of dynamic model parameters:

$$\Omega(\eta)\varsigma(t) = \eta_{ref}(t) \tag{25}$$

By solving the operations of the matrices (20) and grouping the dynamic parameters, the linear parameterization in (26) required for implementation in the identification scheme (see Fig. 6).

$$
\begin{bmatrix}
\dot{u}_f & 0 & 0 & u_f & \omega u_l & 0 & 0 & 0 \\
0 & \dot{u}_l & 0 & 0 & 0 & \omega u_f & u_l & 0 \\
0 & 0 & \dot{\omega} & 0 & 0 & 0 & 0 & \omega
\end{bmatrix}
\begin{bmatrix}
\varsigma_1 \\ \varsigma_2 \\ \varsigma_3 \\ \vdots \\ \varsigma_8
\end{bmatrix}
=
\begin{bmatrix}
u_{f\,ref} \\ u_{l\,ref} \\ \omega_{ref}
\end{bmatrix}
\tag{26}
$$

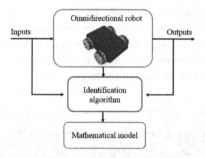

Fig. 6. Diagram for the identification of parameters of the Omnidirectional Robotic Platform.

Therefore, the identification of the parameters of the dynamic model of the robotic system was considered as excitation signals a series of steps of each velocity to be fulfilled by the omnidirectional robotic platform η_{ref}.

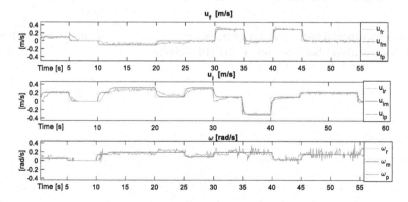

Fig. 7. Validation of dynamic parameters.

To Fig. 7 shows the results obtained from the process of identification and validation of the calculated dynamic model, where u_{fr} represents the desired reference front velocity; u_{fm} represents the front velocity calculated by the model and u_{fp} represents the real front velocity obtained from the sensors of the robotic platform built, in the same way it is considered for lateral and angular velocity. This data implements the least squares algorithm built into the schema (see Fig. 6) and the obtained parameters are as follows:

$\varsigma_1 = 0.3800$, $\varsigma_2 = 0.3800$, $\varsigma_3 = 0.1388$, $\varsigma_4 = 1.0744$, $\varsigma_5 = -1.2639$, $\varsigma_6 = 1.2639$, $\varsigma_7 = 0.8749$, $\varsigma_8 = 1.2130$

4.3   Implementation of HIL

In the Fig. 8 shows the implementation of the HIL technique in a 3D virtual environment, in order to evaluate the performance of the control laws proposed for the omnidirectional robotic platform. The control laws are implemented in a Raspberry Pi 4 card for the autonomous trajectory tracking to be fulfilled by the robot; on the other hand, the kinematic and dynamic models are included in the Unity3D graphic engine to define the behavior of the robotic platform. All this is connected by means of wireless technology that allows to close the control loop.

Fig. 8. Virtualized environment of the omnidirectional robotics platform.

For experimental testing, a circular trajectory was selected for compliance with both the robotic platform built, as well as the HIL scheme.

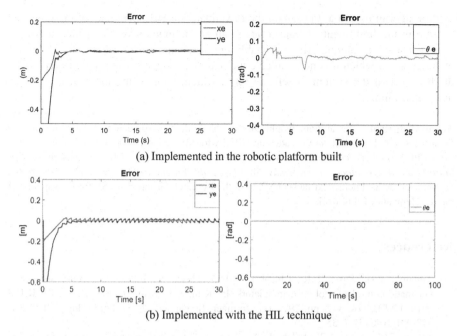

(a) Implemented in the robotic platform built

(b) Implemented with the HIL technique

Fig. 9. Autonomous path tracking control errors.

In the Fig. 9 is considered a sampling period of 100 ms, which allows to calculate the position error at each moment and uses these values to choose the direction where these errors are reduced: xe with respect to the X axis; ye with respect to the Y axis; θe with respect to the axis of the reference system $< \mathbb{R}_W >$. In the same way that in control algorithms already implemented the errors tend to zero, however in this case when considering the dynamics of the robotic platform in the HIL technique it is observed that these are not fixed at zero, because it considers in a complete way the parameters that are going to interact with the robotic platform in a real operation.

5 Conclusions

The research carried out in different scientific databases determines that the construction of the omnidirectional robot with mecanum type wheels is more convenient to be carried out in AB configuration and the arrangement of the wheels should be rectangular. In addition, obtaining the kinematic model along with the dynamic model are used to improve the stability of the system which in turn provides greater accuracy of the behavior of the mathematical model with respect to the physical system, which allows to implement and evaluate advanced control algorithms considering as input signals the velocities of the robot, prior to the stability analysis of the proposed control scheme and validation of the dynamic model with the help of an identification algorithm in conjunction with the built robotic platform. This robot allows to implement control algorithms and at the same time to validate the HIL technique of the proposed scheme in the fulfillment of trajectories in an autonomous way. For which it is concluded that the technique HIL is a viable option to implement algorithms of control in situations in which it is not available the real plant, since it is possible to reproduce the behavior of the system of reliable form, which helps to the moment to evaluate these algorithms.

Acknowledgment. The authors would like to thank the Coorporación Ecuatoriana para el Desarrollo de la Investigación y Academia- CEDIA for their contribution in innovation, through the CEPRA projects, especially the CEPRA XIV-2020-08 project, " *Tecnologías Inmersivas Multi-Usuario Orientadas a Sistemas Sinérgicos de Enseñanza-Aprendizaje*"; also to the Universidad de las Fuerzas Armadas ESPE and the Research Group at ARSI, for the support for the development of this work.

References

1. Andaluz, V.H., Sásig, E.R., Chicaiza, W.D., Velasco, P.M.: Linear algebra applied to kinematic control of mobile manipulators. In: Kim, K.J., Kim, H., Baek, N. (eds.) ICITS 2017. LNEE, vol. 449, pp. 297–306. Springer, Singapore (2018). https://doi.org/10.1007/978-981-10-6451-7_35
2. Soliman, M., Azar, A.T., Saleh, M.A., Ammar, H.H.: Path planning control for 3-omni fighting robot using PID and fuzzy logic controller. In: Hassanien, A.E., Azar, A.T., Gaber, T., Bhatnagar, R., Tolba, M.F. (eds.) AMLTA 2019. AISC, vol. 921, pp. 442–452. Springer, Cham (2020). https://doi.org/10.1007/978-3-030-14118-9_45
3. Varela-Aldás, J., Andaluz, V.H., Chicaiza, F.A.: Modelling and control of a mobile manipulator for trajectory tracking. In: International Conference on Information Systems and Computer Science (INCISCOS), pp. 69–74 (2018)
4. Guo, P., Kim, H., Virani, N., Xu, J., Zhua M., Liu, P.: RoboADS: Anomaly detection against sensor and actuator misbehaviors in mobile robots. In: Annual IEEE/IFIP International Conference on Dependable Systems and Networks, pp. 574–585 (2018)
5. Karras, G.C., Fourlas, G.K.: Model predictive fault tolerant control for omni-directional mobile robots. J. Intell. Robot. Syst. **97**, 635–655 (2019)
6. Khashayar, R. et al.: Vision-based integrated mobile robotic system for real-time applications in. Autom. Constr. **96**, 470–482 (2018)
7. Wang, C., Liu, X., Yang, X., Hu, F., Jiang, A., Yang, C.: Trajectory tracking of an omnidirectional wheeled mobile robot using a model predictive control strategy. Appl. Sci. **8**(2), 231–246 (2018)
8. Campos, J., Jaramillo, S., Morales, L., Camacho, O.: PSO tuning for fuzzy PD + I controller applied to a mobile robot trajectory control. In: International Conference on Information Systems and Computer Science (INCISCOS), pp. 62–68 (2018)
9. Vargas, M.F., Sarzosa, D.S., Andaluz, V.H.: Unified nonlinear control for car-like mobile robot 4 wheels steering. In: Mendes, A., Yan, Y., Chen, S. (eds.) Intelligent Robotics and Applications, pp. 182–194 (2018)
10. Valero, F., Rubio, F.: Assessment of the effect of energy consumption on trajectory improvement for a car-like robot. Cambridge University Press, pp. 1–12 (2019)
11. Sarmento, L., Nunes, F., Santos Martins, R., Sepúlveda, J., Sena Esteves, J.: Remote control system for a mobile platform with four Mecanum wheels. Int. J. Mech. Appl. Mech. **2017**(1), 274–281 (2017)

12. Andaluz, V.H., Carvajal, C.P., Arteaga, O., Pérez, J.A., Valencia, F.S., Solís, L.A.: Unified dynamic control of omnidirectional robots. In: Gao, Y., Fallah, S., Jin, Y., Lekakou, C. (eds.) TAROS 2017. LNCS (LNAI), vol. 10454, pp. 673–685. Springer, Cham (2017). https://doi.org/10.1007/978-3-319-64107-2_55
13. Shabalina, K., Sagitov, A., Magid, E.: Comparative analysis of mobile robot wheels design. In: 11th International Conference on Developments in eSystems Engineering (DeSE), pp. 175–179 (2018)
14. Andaluz, V.H., Carvajal, C.P., Santana, A.G., Zambrano, V.D., Pérez, J.A.: Navigation and dynamic control of omnidirectional platforms. In: Gao, Y., Fallah, S., Jin, Y., Lekakou, C. (eds.) TAROS 2017. LNCS (LNAI), vol. 10454, pp. 661–672. Springer, Cham (2017). https://doi.org/10.1007/978-3-319-64107-2_54
15. Andaluz, Víctor H., Molina, María F., Erazo, Yaritza P., Ortiz, Jessica S.: Numerical methods for cooperative control of double mobile manipulators. In: Huang, Y., Wu, H., Liu, H., Yin, Z. (eds.) ICIRA 2017. LNCS (LNAI), vol. 10463, pp. 889–898. Springer, Cham (2017). https://doi.org/10.1007/978-3-319-65292-4_77
16. Ortiz, J.S., Molina, M.F., Andaluz, V.H., Varela, J., Morales, V.: Coordinated control of a omnidirectional double mobile manipulator. In: Kim, K.J., Kim, H., Baek, N. (eds.) ICITS 2017. LNEE, vol. 449, pp. 278–286. Springer, Singapore (2018). https://doi.org/10.1007/978-981-10-6451-7_33
17. Saenz, E., Bugarin, V.S.: Kinematic and dynamic modeling of a four wheel omnidirectional mobile robot considering actuator dynamics. AMRob J. 4, 114–120 (2016). Theory and Applications
18. Andaluz, V.H., Arteaga, O., Carvajal, C.P., Zambrano, V.D.: Nonlinear control of omnidirectional mobile platforms. In: Huang, Y., Wu, H., Liu, H., Yin, Z. (eds.) ICIRA 2017. LNCS (LNAI), vol. 10464, pp. 354–364. Springer, Cham (2017). https://doi.org/10.1007/978-3-319-65298-6_33
19. Joshi, A.: Real-Time Implementation and Validation for Automated Path Following Lateral Control Using Hardware-in-the-Loop (HIL) Simulation. SAE Technical Paper 2017-01-1683 (2017)
20. Shao, Y., Zulkefli, M.A.M., Sun, Z., Huang, P.: Evaluating connected and autonomous vehicles using a hardwarein-the-loop testbed and a living lab. Transp. Res. Part C 102, 121–135 (2019)
21. Joshi, A.: Powertrain and Chassis Hardware-in-the-Loop (HIL) Simulation of Autonomous Vehicle Platform. SAE Technical Paper 2017-01-1991 (2017)

Obstacle Detection Algorithm by Means of Images with a ZED Camera Using ROS Software in a Drone

Milton Fabricio Pérez Gutiérrez[1]([✉]) [iD] and Andrea C. Córdova-Cruzatty[2]([✉]) [iD]

[1] Departamento de Eléctrica y Electrónica, Universidad de las Fuerzas Armadas ESPE,
Av. General Rumiñahui s/n, Sangolquí 171-5-231B, Ecuador
mfperez3@espe.edu.ec
[2] School of Sustainability, Arizona State University, 800S. Cady Mall, Tempe, AZ 85287, USA
accordova@asu.edu

Abstract. During flight conditions, Unmanned Air Vehicles (UAVs) can be in situations of high risk such as encountering unforeseen obstacles, thus resulting in physical damage of the device and its equipment. For this reason, an intelligent pilot system that allows the detection and evasion of obstacles is necessary for UAVs, protecting the integrity of the system without compromising the mission or the established flight plan. To implement this intelligent pilot system, a fundamental element was used, a ZED camera that acts in a similar way to people's eyes and is integrated with ROS software for depth detection through an obstacle algorithm. The interest of this research is focused on the obstacle detection algorithm using a stereoscopic camera capable of creating 3D images and software that contributes to develop applications for robots and research platforms. Once the detection algorithm was implemented, it was tested in two specific stages, the first stage was established to find the optimum detection distance through the establishment of distance ranges and a second stage included controlled and uncontrolled environments in order to carry out the algorithm validation.

Keywords: Software ROS · Camera ZED · Obstacle detection algorithm

1 Introduction

Unmanned aerial vehicles UAVs, have been constantly used as a tool in research activities given their versatility, with applications that can go from a purely recreational scope to more technical applications such as: monitoring, surveillance, security, etc. Currently, UAVs are used to work in real environments that can go from the analysis of structures of buildings to monitoring of forests or the sea [1, 2]. These environments are subject to climatological variables that are outside the control of human beings as is the case of wind, rain, etc. [3, 4], these variables depend on altitude, terrain topography, etc. In Ecuador, environments can widely range from a high mountain setting to the sea, from ravines to plains, therefore, climatological characteristics are not the same [5]. During

© Springer Nature Switzerland AG 2021
M. Botto-Tobar et al. (Eds.): ICAT 2020, CCIS 1388, pp. 458–466, 2021.
https://doi.org/10.1007/978-3-030-71503-8_35

reconnaissance flights there may be high risk situations such as finding obstacles during flight, resulting in a crash, and therefore generating damage to the UAV and its equipment [4]. For this reason, an intelligent pilot system for UAVs that detects and evades obstacles is necessary to protect its integrity without compromising the mission or the established flight plan [6]. For detection and evasion of obstacles, the type of camera to be used as well as its control algorithm are crucial because these two parameters influence in an optimal performance. The type of camera recommended for the application in the detection and evasion of obstacles are those that can generate 3D mappings [7]. The obtained image must have high resolution and detail quantity that will later be used for the construction of an orthomosaic of the monitored site. Based on this information the control algorithm will work on the detection and evasion of obstacles [8].

The interest of this research was focused on the obstacle detection algorithm using a stereoscopic camera capable of creating 3D images and software to develop applications for robots and research platforms. A StereoLabs ZED camera was used, which replicates the way human vision works, i.e. using its two "eyes" and by triangulation it generates depth data relevant to objects in 3D [9]. Robotic Operating System (ROS) was used to process information. ROS is an open source operating system that develops applications for robots or research platforms. The ZED camera and ROS software have jointly worked to enable a UAV for obstacle detection. Once the ROS detection algorithm was completed, it was tested in two specific stages. The first determined the optimum detection distance through the establishment of distance ranges by sensing in each distance range a static box and person. Afterwards, the same test was done with the person in motion to obtain a data table of how many times the test object was detected. With the information processed statistically, the algorithm successfully detected the static test subject 10% more than the dynamic test subject.

2 Methodology

UAVs require devices to help them make decisions to avoid damage or harming equipment or people. Avoiding obstacles requires a more complex control of the UAV by an intelligent pilot. Therefore, the hardware and software to be used for obstacle detection and avoidance were analyzed.

2.1 Camera

For UAVs to evade obstacles, a fundamental requirement was that the camera worked in a similar way to human eyes to detect the depth and distance of the obstacle to be evaded. Once the detection mechanism was determined, the selection variables of the camera such as robustness to the environment, weight, obstacle detection distance, acquisition speed, and sensing angle were analyzed. A scale from 5 to 1 was used, with 5 being the most desirable characteristic and 1 being the less desirable characteristic as shown in Table 1 [10].

Table 1. Variables for camera selection.

N	Measurement	Unit	LeddarTech-Vu8		Stereo Vision-ZED		Kinect	
1	Environment robustness	-	4	4	5	5	3	3
2	Weight	gr	830	4	159	5	1305	3
3	obstacle detection distance	m	100	3	200	4	3,5	1
4	Acquisition speed	Hz	50	3	100	4	16000	5
5	Detection angle	°	20	1	80	5	57	3
	Total			14		23		16

The Vision ZED stereo sensor features greater long-distance viewing capability, it can detect an obstacle that approaches from a greater distance, giving more time to the processor to take any evasive action. On the other hand, its low energy consumption and weight made it the ideal choice for the development of the application (Fig. 1).

Fig. 1. Camera ZED [11].

After choosing the camera for the UAV, the software for integrating the functionality of the camera was determined to create the detection algorithm.

2.2 Platforms or Operating Systems for Robots

One of the critical points in robot programming is the software to be used because it can be extensive and complex. A search of the appropriate platform was made, finding that the ROS platform is one of the most used platforms by developers to create applications that are currently used in study centers and in the industry [12].

ROS is a framework for control algorithm development in robotics. It contains packages that include device control libraries for actuators, sensors, engines, among other devices. ROS is a Meta open source operating system for robots that is maintained by the Open Sources Robotics Foundation (OSRF). It provides the services expected from an operating system, including hardware abstraction, low-level device control, and implementation of common-use functionality, cross-process message step, and packet management. It also provides tools and libraries for obtaining, building, writing, and executing code on multiple computers [13].

The advantage of ROS is the modularity that allows to choose which parts are useful for a specific application and which parts can be implemented separately. One advantage for developers is that they have BSD permissive open licenses of three clauses that allows reuse in commercial and closed-source products [12].

The integration of the camera with ROS software was required, for which the necessary modules were installed in the ROS software for the camera to take the images and to process them. This module is known as ZED ROS Wrapper, which provides access to the following data:

- Rectified Images/non-rectified images to the left and right
- Depth Map
- 3D color point cloud
- Visual Odometry: camera position and orientation.
- Pose Tracking: Still and fusioned camera position and orientation with IMU data (ZED mini)

Once the camera and the ROS package are integrated, an image like the one shown in Fig. 2 was obtained.

Fig. 2. Image camera ZED with ROS package [11].

2.3 Implementation of the Algorithm

Once the programs for the ROS platform were installed, the package in charge of the operation of the camera ZED was executed, it verifies its state and begins the publication of the information provided by the camera.

The "Depth image to Laser Scan" package was then executed, which captured the information obtained by the camera and converted it into a scan-type message to be used by the "RtabmapROS" package, which, after being executed in mapping mode, used the images published by the camera and the message type scan to be able to generate a map in 3D and a projection of this in 2D. This information was later used by the stack of navigation.

Once the RtabmapROS package completed the mapping phase, it was necessary to run it again, but in navigation mode to run the package "Move_base", which received the maps previously created along with information updated from the ZED camera and the Laser Scan package to detect obstacles (based on the DWA algorithm).

To carry out an autonomous navigation within the established map, the MavROS package had to be executed and ready to maneuver the aircraft. The navigation stack required a position and orientation target which was provided by the "2D-NavGoal" button located on the ROS Rviz application toolbar. Once the desired position message was published, the navigation package was responsible for publishing speeds to the Pix-Falcon driver through the MavROS package with the objective of reducing the position error between the UAV reference frame and the position Objective-selected on the map using Rviz, following the path generated by the DWA (Dynamic Window Approach) algorithm.

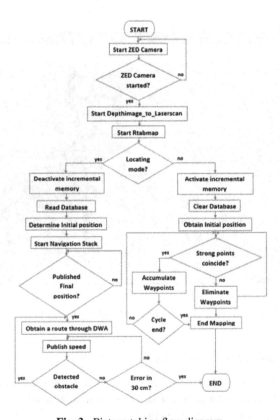

Fig. 3. Picture-taking flow diagram.

This process continued until the UAV was within a 30 cm radius of the target position (determined by the user), while the navigation stack constantly monitored the aircraft route. Meanwhile the algorithm was still looking for possible changes in the environment or new obstacles, as shown in Fig. 3.

3   Results

Once the obstacle detection algorithm was implemented, a data validation was required. For the first part, a controlled environment was used to know the behavior of the camera with the ROS software and thus to determine the optimal distance of detection using two types of obstacles: a box of dimensions 0, 5 m × 0, 6 m × 2 m and a person measuring 1.85 m high and 0.45 m wide. After verifying the optimal distance, tests were carried out in two real environments, a room, and the outdoor environment to know the functionality of the camera and software.

Executing the algorithm allowed to visualize a 3D map, and through this line of colors the obstacle distance was determined by means of the depth generated by the 2D SCANNER that is part of the algorithm. Red color represented that the obstacle is close, and Violet meant the element was further away. Lack of color described that the element distance could not be detected. Only two values were taken for the tests, detected, or not detected.

3.1   First Part. Optimal Distance Detection

In order to determine the optimum distance of detection of obstacles, a controlled environment was needed, in this case an empty room was used, making 5 reference marks on the ground, each mark at two meters starting at the value of zero and finishing at 8 m. After setting the distance ranges to be measured, the algorithm is executed to verify whether the obstacle is detected or not. For this analysis, 20 measurements were taken in each range of distance.

For the first test, a box was placed in the different ranges to evaluate how many times it was detected and how many times it was not, obtaining as result that the best distance for detection is between 2 and 4 m with a 95% effectiveness.

For the second test a still person was placed in scene, performing the same steps above. The results showed that the best detection distance is in the same range as the prior test, which was between 2 and 4 m maintaining a 95% effectiveness.

A third test was performed, where a person in movement was put on the monitored area. In this test the range was maintained between 2 and 4 m, with a difference of an 85% effectiveness.

Once the detection distance was validated, the algorithm was put to test in two real scenarios, a common room, and an external environment.

3.2 Second Part. Real Scenarios: Common Room and External Environment

First Test: Common Room

For this second part, a first test of the algorithm of detection of obstacles was performed in a normal room that had a bed, a candle and on the bed a UAV. The camera was placed at a height of 1 m, the obstacle detection algorithm was executed, generating a 3D map and the color line that represents the distance of the obstacle as shown in Fig. 4.

Fig. 4. 3d-mapped room with obstacle detection distance.

As it can be seen in the image, the map generated by the software allowed to determine the obstacle that was closer to the camera, taking as reference the height to which the camera was placed, obtaining as a result that the drone was the closest obstacle.

Second Test: External Environment

A second test of the algorithm was performed in an external environment, where a person was placed between an open space and a building. Once the mapping was done in the image, the algorithm determined that the obstacle closest to the camera was the person, but the structures that surrounded the person could also be clearly identified in the mapping, as shown in Fig. 5.

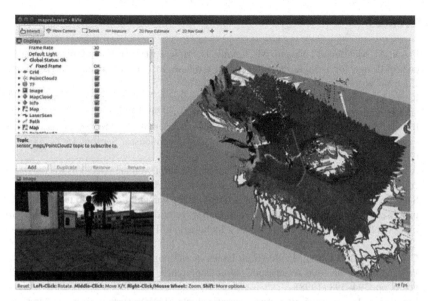

Fig. 5. 3d mapping of the external scenario.

4   Discussion and Conclusions

An algorithm of detection of obstacles using a camera ZED was implemented in ROS software ROS. Once it was implemented, different tests were carried out to determine its efficacy for detecting and avoiding obstacles in different scenarios, obtaining the following conclusions:

With the data obtained in the optimal distance detection and through first-order statistical tools, it was found that the appropriate distance range is between 2 m and 4 m, but there is a significant difference of 10% between a static object and a moving object due to different causes among the most important the computer's processing speed. One way to improve processing speed is to place embedded systems that are compatible with ROS as is the case of Beaglebone.

In the images of the two scenarios, room and external environment, one can identify two situations, the first that the 3D mapping that performs the algorithm is of very good quality, and at the same time the detection distances allows to have a reference of the object and with that the adequate evasion of obstacles can be performed.

This research contributes to scan indoor environments with a ZED camera to avoid obstacles without the aid of a GPS signal in structured environments like forest, urban zones, etc.

A future work could use the information obtained by the algorithm to perform an intelligent control for evasion of obstacles in real time.

References

1. Frank, A., McGrew, J., Valenti, M., Levine, D., How, J.: Hover, transition, and level flight control design for a single-propeller indoor airplane. In: AIAA Guidance, Navigation and Control Conference and Exhibit, pp. 20–23 (2007)
2. Khan, S., Aragao, L., Iriarte, J.: A UAV–lidar system to map Amazonian rainforest and its ancient landscape transformations. Int. J. Remote Sens. **90**, 19 (2017)
3. Roldan, J.J., Joossen, G., Sanz, D., del Cerro, J., Barrientos, A.: Mini- UAV based sensory system for measuring environmental variables in greenhouses. Sensors **15**(2), 3334–3350 (2015)
4. Adams, S., Friedland, C.J.: A survey of unmanned aerial vehicle (UAV) usage for imagery collection in disaster research and management. ResearchGate (2011)
5. Sani, J.C., Tierra Criollo, A.R., Robayo Nieto, A.A.: Vehículos aéreos no tripulados - UAV para la elaboración de cartografías escalas grandes referidas al marco de referencia SIRGAS-ECUADOR. In: X Congreso de Ciencia y Tecnología ESPE 2015, vol. 10, no. 1, pp. 112–116 (2015)
6. Chandler, P.R., Patcher, M.: Research issues in autonomous control of tactical UAVs. In: Proceedings of the 1998 American Control Conference. ACC (IEEE Cat. No.98CH36207), vol. 6, pp. 394–398 (1998)
7. Eisenbeiss, H.: A mini unmanned aerial vehicle (UAV): system overview and image acquisition. International Society for Photogrammetry and Remote Sensing (2004)
8. Niethammer, U., Rothmund, S., James, M.R., Travelletti, J., Joswig, M.: UAV-based remote sensing of landslides. In: Remote Sensing and Spatial Information Sciences, vol. XXXVIII, pp. 496–501 (2010)
9. Deris, A., Trigonis, I., Aravanis, A., Stathopoulou, E.K.: Depth cameras on UAVs: a first approach. In: Remote Sensing and Spatial Information Sciences, vol. XLII, pp. 231–236 (2017)
10. Quigley, M., et al.: ROS: an open-source robot operating system. In: ICRA Workshop on Open Source Software (2009)
11. Voos, H.: Nonlinear control of a quadrotor micro-UAV using feedback-linearization. In: 2009 IEEE International Conference on Mechatronics (2009)
12. Vachtsevanos, G., Tang, L., Drozeski, G., Gutierrez, L.: From mission planning to flight control of unmanned aerial vehicles strategies and implementation tools. Ann. Rev. Control **29**, 101–115 (2005)
13. Rivas, Control UAV, Ambato: Pio XII, 218

Security

PDUs Header-Based Online User Behavior Detection Algorithm

Darío Valarezo[1,2]([✉])[iD] and Diego Avila-Pesantez[1,3][iD]

[1] Departamento de Posgrados, Pontificia Universidad Católica del Ecuador, Ambato, Ecuador
{dario.j.valarezo.1,davila}@pucesa.edu.ec
[2] Departamento de Ciencias de la Computación y Electrónica, Universidad Técnica Particular de Loja, Loja, Ecuador
djvalarezo@utpl.edu.ec
[3] Facultad de Informática y Electrónica, Escuela Superior Politécnica de Chimborazo, Riobamba, Ecuador
davila@espoch.edu.ec

Abstract. The goal of this research is to present a detection algorithm for data interception between a Legitimate Access Point (LAP) and wireless devices employing passive eavesdropping techniques, analyzing the Protocol Data Units (PDUs) header of specific Open Systems Interconnection (OSI) protocol layers in real-time: segment (transport-layer), packet (network-layer), and frame (data link-layer). The designed algorithm takes advantage of a passive Man-in-the-Middle (MITM) system, avoiding to gather sensitive information of the users connected to the network. The system focuses on requests from web browsers and apps of wireless devices to analyze the online behavior of the users on the Internet utilizing cybersecurity techniques. The research approaches on a small-scale wireless network to implement educational environments based on parental control in educational institutions (primary, secondary and higher education), fomenting Information and Communication Technologies (ICT) security in virtual classrooms. The data acquisition process of the wireless devices uses the Dynamic Host Configuration Protocol (DHCP) and Domain Name System (DNS) services. It also analyzes the Transmission Control Protocol (TCP) control flags of the TCP three-way handshake protocol to identify requests from web browsers and apps. Finally, preliminary test results are presented, demonstrating that each wireless device can be characterized using information based on PDUs header, and these individual reports can be presented through an interactive dashboard to the teachers.

Keywords: User behavior detection algorithm · Man-in-the-Middle attack · Wireless network

1 Introduction

The inclusion of ICT in educational institutions increases the quality of the educational processes innovatively. Due to the high demand for wireless commu-

© Springer Nature Switzerland AG 2021
M. Botto-Tobar et al. (Eds.): ICAT 2020, CCIS 1388, pp. 469–483, 2021.
https://doi.org/10.1007/978-3-030-71503-8_36

nication infrastructures and the increased use of ICT to access different network services [25], wireless devices (i.e., laptops, smartphones, tablets) have become essential pedagogical support tools [3]. Therefore, massifying the use of new technologies encourages learning new skills and attitudes needed in the 21st century. With the inclusion of ICT in the virtual classroom, educational institutions have to implement strategies and policies to increase the digitalization of the education system [6,19]. However, the existing deficiency in the educational sector to control, analyze, and prevent the online behavior of the students (i.e., children, teenagers, and people with special abilities) [3], shows the need to have learning environments based on parental control.

Nevertheless, with the increased exposure to the Internet [14], teachers and students are exposed to different cybercriminal activities, where the physical and psychological integrity of the users is compromised [5,13]. Relevant examples are [1,3,5,13,15,19,25]. The similarities between networks based on the OSI model and the Transmission Control Protocol/Internet Protocol (TCP/IP) model [25] permit analyzing of the different PDUs in the common layers. Therefore, in the transport-layer, the TCP three-way handshake protocol analyzes the reliable data exchange between clients and servers [10]. TCP use control flags (9-bit) in the TCP segment header to manage the transmission of packets [8]: NS (Nonce Sum flag), CWR (Congestion Windows Reduced flag), ECE (Explicit Congestion Notification flag), URG (Urgent flag), ACK (Acknowledgment flag), PSH (Push flag), RST (Reset flag), SYN (Synchronize flag), and FIN (Fin flag). On the other hand, in the network-layer and the data link-layer, the Internet Protocol (IP) address, Media Access Control (MAC) address, and timestamp permit to identify a host employing multiple fields of the PDUs header [12,16]. Consequently, in a network, information of the wireless devices can be obtained, such as [13]: IP address, MAC address, hostname, routing information, DHCP information, DNS information, browsing information, among others.

Due to network traffic is forwarded through the router to the Internet [1,18], it is possible to gather the data of the wireless devices connected to the network [11]. A MITM attack eavesdrops and manipulates sensitive data of the users [21,23], using network traffic analysis or packet sniffing tools that intercept the incoming and outgoing network traffic [9]. A passive MITM attack sniffs information of the users connected to the Access Point (AP) in a second plane [13]. It permits to create a pattern of each wireless device to understand the online behavior of the users [22]. However, network traffic analysis tools are used for white-hat and black-hat users to implement network recognition, traffic patterns, and usage [9,13,15]. In the market, there are different open-source network traffic analysis tools. These two are the most popular: tcpdump and Wireshark [9,10]. Analyzing the requirements of this research, Wireshark has better performance than tcpdump [9,13]. Besides, Wireshark presents the information in plaintext, this helps to identify parameters quickly in real-time [9].

This paper aims to present a detection algorithm for data interception between a LAP and wireless devices utilizing passive eavesdropping techniques analyzing the PDUs header of specific OSI protocol layers. The analysis focuses on requests from web browsers and apps of wireless devices. It allows implementing parental control in educational environments to analyze the online behavior of the students. The research approaches on a small scale Wireless Local Area Network (WLAN) deployment. However, this paper does not consider active attacks. Furthermore, this work does not prevent changing the behavior of the users [3], only analyzes how online behavior is. Therefore, promoting the information universal access, it provides the freedom of navigation. On the other hand, focus on Sustainable Development Goal (SDG) 8, proposed by United Nations (UN), this research intends to contribute to the Research and Development (R&D) of the cyber defense industry.

The remainder of this paper is organized as follows. Section 2 presents an overview of relevant literature. Section 3 describes the architecture and functionalities of the designed algorithm that exploit the OSI protocol layers in a designed LAP. Section 4 submits the results of preliminary tests. Finally, Sect. 5 exhibits the conclusions and future research works.

2   Related Works

In this section, an overview of relevant literature is presented.

In [10], the authors develop a Network Scanning Detection algorithm based on Flow State (NSCDFS) for high-speed networks. Therefore, the frequency of a TCP connection request in each time slide window and the state of TCP flow according to the control flag value of each PDU is considered. Besides, experimental results for traditional scanning and distributed scanning are presented. The detection algorithm scheme based on a TCP three-way handshake protocol is used to establish a TCP/IP connection before reliable data exchange between the server and the client. Analyzing the PDU header, the state of TCP flow is classified into six connection stages: three-way handshake (3), data exchange (1), end-stage (1), other stages (1, illegal flags). Due to this system is for high-speed networks, SNORT and PFRING are used to capture the network traffic. The variables considered are source/destination IP address, source/destination port, stage of the flag, and timestamp.

In [16], a method to identify hosts behind a NAT (Network Address Translation) device is proposed. Multiple fields of IP packet and TCP segment headers to improve host identifications are used. However, different network parameters of each Operative System (OS) are considered. Furthermore, based on IP address or timestamp parameters, a classification process for existing and new devices is explained.

On the other hand, in [12], an entropy-based early detection and mitigation technique against the TCP SYN Flooding threat in SDN (Software Defined Networks) is presented. Considering the destination IP address (random variable) and TCP control flags, the entropy method is used to determine the randomness of the flow data. The architecture system consists of two major components: Detection Unit and Mitigation Unit. Also, the designed system works better in high traffic scenario (100 Mbps).

Hence, it is concluded that it is possible to implement a detection algorithm to analyze the online behavior of the users, characterizing their wireless devices connected to a designed LAP.

3 Detection Algorithm Design

In this section, the detection algorithm that exploits the OSI protocol layers is described. Besides, the architecture and functionalities of the designed algorithm are explained.

3.1 Observations

With the popularity of using the Learning Management System (LMS) platforms, the use of ICT in the classroom has increased considerably [2]. When students access to online resources and platforms on the Internet, network traffic is forwarded through the AP to the Internet [19]. It permits to create of a pattern based on requests from web browsers and apps of wireless devices used in different learning activities in the virtual classroom [25]. In this education model, teachers became passive actors who monitor online activities [19]. Besides, teachers have evidence of all the activities developed by the students in the classroom.

This research proposes a detection algorithm for data interception utilizing passive eavesdropping techniques, characterizing each wireless device to identify the online behavior of the users connected to a small scale WLAN based on IPv4 (32-bit). It allows implementing an automatic parental control system in any educational environment, analyzing the online behavior of the students on the Internet. However, it is necessary to define some network policies to avoid vulnerabilities in a WLAN. The correct functionality of the system is necessary to increase the traffic to the Internet [2]. There is no limitation of access to content or restriction of bandwidth. On the other hand, promoting the information universal access, provides the freedom of navigation on the Internet. Therefore, there is not a word list restrictions filter.

The detection algorithm is focused on a previously designed LAP known as "KAMU AP", powered by YAKOTT startup, creating a trusted network with an official AP preventing the vulnerabilities of a Rogue Access Point (RAP). It is used in small-scale WLAN deployment in educational environments to provide open and free digital educational resources (i.e., videos, documents, images, audios, among others) as sources of search and learning. The KAMU AP design has some technical characteristics that implement low latency solutions to enhance Internet connectivity.

A wide variety of OS in the market presents different request parameters (i.e., laptops, smartphones, tablets) [16,17]. This work does not consider any particular characteristics of the different OS. On the other hand, the system has to be careful with presenting terms and conditions of using the system to avoid legal risks and criminal actions recognitions [15]. Access to the personal information of each user without their consent is punishable under the laws. Besides, data of the users can be legally intercepted, if it is authorized, to protect vulnerable groups (i.e., children, teenagers, and people with special abilities) from the risks of inappropriate ICT use. Accept the conditions of the designed system depend on the users that are not forced to connect to the network. Therefore, online privacy is the responsibility of the users connected to the network [3,14,25].

This proposal considers ethical hacking techniques [4], avoiding any unethical action against the vulnerability of the user and their personal information [21]. Again, there is no intention to try different types of attacks, such as Denial-of-Service (DoS), Distributed Denial-of-Service (DDoS), session hijacking, packet injection, DNS Spoofing, Address Resolution Protocol (ARP) Poisoning, IP Spoofing, MAC Spoofing, among others. Therefore, passive monitoring is going to be implemented through the use of open-source network traffic analysis tool.

3.2 Architecture and Functionalities

The detection algorithm prioritizes the confidentiality, integrity, and availability (CIA) of the information of the users. Therefore, confidentiality is implemented by avoiding eavesdrop the sensitive data transferred through the network and encrypting the logs that store sensitive information (i.e., MAC address, user ID, DNS requests, among others). Moreover, integrity is accomplished by analyzing only PDUs header and presenting terms and conditions of browsing through the established WLAN by a captive portal. On the other hand, availability is achieved by accessing the Internet and the system services anytime.

The KAMU AP, developed using a GNU/Linux distribution, provides connectivity to the users employing the DHCP and DNS services setting, as shown in Fig. 1. Due to the KAMU AP has two Network Interface Controllers (NICs), it can forward network traffic through AP to the Internet. That is the reason to use a Gigabit Ethernet (GbE) network interface up to the Institute of Electrical and Electronics Engineers (IEEE) 802.3ab Standard to provide high-speed service to the users connected to the WLAN. Furthermore, to improve WLAN throughput, it uses a wireless network interface up to IEEE 802.11n Standard that works in the Industrial, Scientific, and Medical (ISM) Band [23].

APs have the functionality to forward network traffic from wireless network interface to the Internet over GbE network interface through masquerade configuration [7] or IP forwarding. The use of iptables rules accomplishes it [13]. This permits creating a passive MITM system inside the KAMU AP between network interfaces to eavesdrops on the communication channel between the wireless devices and the Internet connection. The purpose is to obtain network traffic information [24]. Therefore, parental control over the online behavior of the users on the Internet is a transparent service [23]. Furthermore, passive sniffing is the best option for data interception [25]. It is challenging that users identify the eavesdropping process implemented inside the AP [5].

Due that the wireless network interface works in active mode in the WLAN [23], the eavesdropping process is implemented in the GbE network interface toward the Internet connection. It is implemented through an automatic Tshark

service, a version of Wireshark for server applications, combining AP functionalities with other applications to implement all the services. In this case, TShark
is used to inspect in detail every field of the PDUs header. There is valuable
information in plaintext distributed at each OSI protocol layer: TCP segment
header, IP packet header, and Ethernet frame header. Furthermore, it is possible
to implement filters to improve the search of selective protocols in the network
traffic, avoiding data loss.

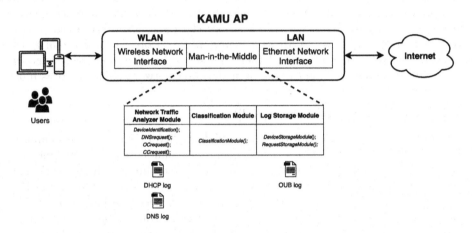

Fig. 1. System scheme.

The system adaptability and maintenance are the significant benefits of the
designed algorithm. There are not firmware modifications. The detection algorithm is configured as a passive service in a second plane. The services set in
KAMU AP generate specific information logs that are used for the detection
algorithm. In the DHCP log storages the information about wireless devices.
On the other hand, the DNS log storages the requests of the web browsers or
apps. Therefore, the network traffic information is obtained from the services
logs, filtering the required information in real-time.

The detection algorithm is implemented over the AWK programming language, a text-processing language with syntax similar to C, filtering, and classifying the information of each log mentioned above. Various passive services are
configured in the KAMU AP OS automatically in a second plane. The detection
algorithm used in the passive MITM system comprises three major components,
as shown in Fig. 1:

- The network traffic analysis module: the data is eavesdropped in real-time
  when the PDUs header satisfies the set filters. DHCP, DNS, open and close
  connection requests are analyzed.
- The classification module: the fields of TCP segment header, IP packet
  header, and Ethernet frame header are organized to create a pattern of each
  wireless device.

– The log storage module: the information is written into Online User Behavior (OUB) log, a simple formatted log, where it is necessary to encrypt sensitive data.

Network Traffic Analysis Module Algorithms: The pseudocode of the network traffic analysis modules are described below:

DHCP Request Algorithm: This algorithm is established based on the DHCP service to determine any parameter (i.e., hostname, MAC address, manufacture, web browser type, among others) related to the identification of the wireless devices. This process works for new or existence wireless devices connected to the KAMU AP. The pseudocode is shown in Algorithm 1.

Algorithm 1: DHCP Request

Input: DHCP log
Output: MAC_md_i, IP_md_i, HN_md_i, TS_md_i
1 **begin** *DeviceIdentification*(DHCP log)
2   **while** *DHCP service is available* **do**
3   **if** md_i *request a DHCP session* **then**
4   Analyze information;
5   **if** *DHCP server responds a DHCPACK packet* **then**
6   Filter information;
7   **return** MAC_md_i, IP_md_i, HN_md_i, TS_md_i;

The *DeviceIdentification*() function analyzes and filters the information of the DHCP log set by the DHCP service in real-time, identifying any wireless device (md_i) connection request, where $i = 1, 2, 3, \ldots, n$. When the DHCP server responds to md_i a DHCPACK packet, the parameters returned are: MAC address (MAC_md_i), IP address (IP_md_i), hostname (HN_md_i), and timestamp connection (TS_md_i).

The idea is to establish a relationship between the hostname and wireless devices, using the MAC addresses (48-bit) where the first 24-bit are used to obtain manufacturing information. As a unique identifier, it can be used to identify each user connected to the network. However, some devices can change their MAC address automatically. Previously, the users have to set their student ID as the hostname in their wireless devices.

DNS Request Algorithm: This algorithm is designed based on the DNS service to identify when a web browser or app requests a server (s_j), where $j = 1, 2, 3, \ldots, m$. The pseudocode is shown in Algorithm 2.

Algorithm 2: DNS Request

Input: UDP datagram header: port==53
Output: IP_s_{ij}, DM_s_{ij}, TS_s_{ij}

1 **begin** *DNSrequest*(UDP datagram header: port==53)
2   **if** *IP_md$_i$ queries a domain name to DNS resolver* **then**
3   Monitor information;
4   **if** *DNS resolver responds dns.cname* **then**
5   Filter information;
6   **return** IP_s_{ij}, DM_s_{ij}, TS_s_{ij};
7   **else**
8   **if** *DNS resolver responds dns.flags.authoritative==1* **then**
9   Filter information;
10   **return** IP_s_{ij}, DM_s_{ij}, TS_s_{ij};

The *DNSrequest*() function monitors and filters the DNS resolver responses set by the DNS service in real-time. It identifies any request from the web browser and app of each md_i with IP_md_i. The filter established is on the UDP datagram header on port 53. The variables related to each s_j are: public IP address (IP_s_{ij}), domain name (DM_s_{ij}), and timestamp query (TS_s_{ij}). Furthermore, the Canonical Name (CNAME) record is considered.

Open Connection Request Algorithm: This algorithm is designed based on the TCP three-way handshake protocol to determine when a md_i with IP_md_i opens a connection with a s_j with IP_s_{ij}, in other words, when a wireless device open a web page. The pseudocode is shown in Algorithm 3.

Algorithm 3: Open Connection Request

Input: TCP segment header: SYN==1 && ACK==0
Output: TS_oc_{ij}

1 **begin** *OCrequest*(TCP segment header: SYN==1 && ACK==0)
2   **if** *IP_md$_i$ opens a connection with IP_s$_{ij}$* **then**
3   Filter information;
4   **return** TS_oc_{ij};

The *OCrequest*() function monitors the state of the TCP flow according to the combination of control flags. The filter set is on specific TCP control flags connection stages. Understand the state of each TCP control flag is essential to implement the identification process. The variable related to the process is the timestamp open connection (TS_oc_{ij}).

The TCP segment header information analysis is based on the TCP control flag states. Therefore, the analysis is based on 9-bit TCP control flags identifying each flag by the bit set state [8]. However, the TCP control flag size depends on the network analysis characteristics. The filter process combines the value TCP control flags.

Close Connection Request Algorithm: This algorithm is designed based on the TCP three-way handshake protocol to determine when a md_i with IP_md_i close a connection with a server s_j with IP_s_{ij}, in other words, when a wireless device close a web page. The pseudocode is shown in Algorithm 4.

Algorithm 4: Close Connection Request

Input: TCP segment: FIN==1 && ACK==1
Output: TS_cc_{ij}
1 **begin** *CCrequest*(TCP segment: FIN==1 && ACK==1)
2   **if** IP_d_i *closes a connection with* IP_s_{ij} **then**
3   Filter information;
4   **return** TS_cc_{ij};

The *CCrequest*() function is similar to the *OCrequest*() function but with a different filter set in the TCP control flags connection stages. The variable related to the process is the timestamp close connection (TS_cc_{ij}).

Classification Module Algorithm: This algorithm relates all the eavesdrop information with each md_i, creating a user profile based on the online behavior on the Internet caught by the network. The pseudocode is shown in Algorithm 5.

The *ClassificationModule*() function identifies if a md_i is new or already exists in the OUB log, creating or updating the profile information through *DeviceStorageModule*() function based on MAC_md_i. Besides, the *ClassificationModule*() function classifies each md_i request to a s_j, organizing the information base on IP_md_i related to IP_s_{ij}. Then, the information is written using *RequestStorageModule*() function. Furthermore, the code filters requests by default of the devices, such as antivirus service, OS update service, dropbox service, drive service, among others. Nevertheless, the system can present the information by HN_md_i instead MAC_md_i. It permits users to connect to the network using different wearable devices. Besides, the time connection TC_{ij} of the IP_md_i with the IP_s_{ij} is calculated.

Log Storage Module Algorithm: This algorithm writes the information to the OUB log. The pseudocodes are shown in Algorithms 6 and 7.

The *DeviceStorageModule*() function creates and updates the information of the profile on each md_i in the OUB log.

The *RequestStorageModule*() function writes the browsing request of each md_i in the OUB log.

Algorithm 5: Classification Module

Input: MAC_md_i, IP_md_i, HN_md_i, TS_md_i, IP_s_{ij}, DM_s_{ij}, TS_s_{ij}, TS_oc_{ij}, TS_cc_{ij}

Output:

1 **begin** *ClassificationModule*(MAC_md_i, IP_md_i, HN_md_i, TS_md_i, IP_s_{ij}, DM_s_{ij}, TS_s_{ij}, TS_oc_{ij}, TS_cc_{ij})

2   **if** MAC_md_i *is new in the network* **then**

3   *DeviceStorageModule*(MAC_md_i, HN_md_i, IP_md_i, TS_md_i) ← Create profile;

4   **else**

5   *DeviceStorageModule*(IP_md_i, TS_md_i) ← Update information;

6   **for** IP_md_i *related with* MAC_md_i **do**

7   Classify information;

8   **for** IP_s_{ij} **do**

9   **if** *request is different from default services* **then**

10                 $TC_{ij} = TS\_cc_{ij} - TS\_oc_{ij}$;

11   RequestStorageModule(IP_s_{ij}, DM_s_{ij}, TS_s_{ij}, TC_{ij}) ← Write information;

Algorithm 6: Device Storage Module

Input: MAC_md_i, IP_md_i, HN_md_i, TS_md_i

Output: OUB log

1 **begin** *DeviceStorageModule*(MAC_md_i, IP_md_i, HN_md_i, TS_md_i)

2   **if** MAC_md_i *does not exist in OUB log* **then**

3   OUB log ← Create profile;

4   **else**

5   OUB log ← Update information;

Algorithm 7: Request Storage Module

Input: IP_s_{ij}, DM_s_{ij}, TS_s_{ij}, TS_oc_{ij}, TS_cc_{ij}

Output: OUB log

1 **begin** *RequestStorageModule*(IP_s_{ij}, DM_s_{ij}, TS_s_{ij}, TS_oc_{ij}, TS_cc_{ij})

2   **if** MAC_md_i *is located in OUB log* **then**

3   OUB log ← Write information;

4   Preliminary Tests

In this section, the results of preliminary tests are submitted. These tests contemplate the use of the detection algorithm in educational environments to implement parental control based on the online behavior of the students.

A virtual classroom of an educational institution is used as a scenario for the preliminary tests, as shown in Fig. 2. The inclusion of ICT permits students to use wireless devices as learning support tools to access online resources and platforms on the Internet. However, the teacher can create activity reports based on the analysis of the online behavior of the students. In particular, when the educational procedure involves using ICT in the learning process [3], the designed algorithm provides additional security than conventional APs do not offer to protect teachers and students [20, 22].

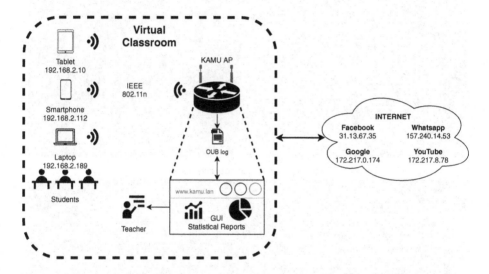

Fig. 2. Scenario for the preliminary tests.

The network traffic analysis module is implemented, eavesdropping data of each PDUs header of each wireless device. In the identification of the md_i, it is obtained: MAC_md_i, IP_md_i, HN_md_i, and TS_md_i. Then, in the identification of the s_j, as shown in Fig. 3a, it is acquired: IP_s_{ij}, DM_s_{ij}, and TS_s_{ij}. Next, in the identification of open connection requests, as shown in Fig. 3b, it is obtained: TS_oc_{ij}. Finally, in the identification of close connection requests, as shown in Fig. 3c, it is acquired: TS_cc_{ij}.

When the students access the online resources indexed on the LMS platform, the requests from web browsers and apps are stored in the OUB log by the passive MITM system. However, if the students visit social networking sites, it is registered by the system. The information stored in the OUB log permits to present browsing information of the student to the teacher through individual

```
192.168.2.112;172.217.0.174;clients3.google.com;Jan-22-23:06:17
192.168.2.112;31.13.67.35;b-graph.facebook.com;Jan-22-23:06:17
192.168.2.112;157.240.14.53;g.whatsapp.net;Jan-22-23:06:17
192.168.2.112;172.217.15.195;fonts.gstatic.com;Jan-22-23:06:21
192.168.2.112;172.217.15.194;googleads.g.doubleclick.net;Jan-22-23:06:21
192.168.2.112;186.46.72.205;r2---sn-jou-0pv6.googlevideo.com;Jan-22-23:06:22
192.168.2.112;172.217.2.134;static.doubleclick.net;Jan-22-23:06:24
192.168.2.112;172.217.15.206;www.youtube.com;Jan-22-23:06:25
192.168.2.112;216.58.192.46;www.youtube.com;Jan-22-23:06:25
192.168.2.112;172.217.8.78;www.youtube.com;Jan-22-23:06:25
192.168.2.112;172.217.8.110;www.youtube.com;Jan-22-23:06:25
192.168.2.112;172.217.8.142;www.youtube.com;Jan-22-23:06:25
192.168.2.112;172.217.2.78;www.youtube.com;Jan-22-23:06:25
192.168.2.112;172.217.2.206;www.youtube.com;Jan-22-23:06:25
192.168.2.112;172.217.0.174;www.youtube.com;Jan-22-23:06:25
192.168.2.112;172.217.1.110;www.youtube.com;Jan-22-23:06:25
```

(a) DNS requests.

```
192.168.2.112;172.217.204.188;Jan-22-23:06:17
192.168.2.112;172.217.0.174;Jan-22-23:06:17
192.168.2.112;172.217.2.131;Jan-22-23:06:17
192.168.2.112;157.240.14.53;Jan-22-23:06:17
192.168.2.112;216.58.192.36;Jan-22-23:06:17
192.168.2.112;34.224.252.124;Jan-22-23:06:17
192.168.2.112;192.168.2.1;Jan-22-23:06:17
192.168.2.112;173.194.217.114;Jan-22-23:06:21
192.168.2.112;173.194.217.114;Jan-22-23:06:21
192.168.2.112;172.217.15.204;Jan-22-23:06:21
192.168.2.112;172.217.15.195;Jan-22-23:06:21
192.168.2.112;216.58.192.42;Jan-22-23:06:21
192.168.2.112;172.217.15.204;Jan-22-23:06:21
192.168.2.112;192.168.2.1;Jan-22-23:06:22
192.168.2.112;192.168.2.1;Jan-22-23:06:22
192.168.2.112;192.168.2.1;Jan-22-23:06:22
```

(b) Open connection requests.

```
192.168.2.112;192.168.2.1;Jan-22-23:06:18
192.168.2.1;192.168.2.112;Jan-22-23:06:18
216.58.192.36;192.168.2.112;Jan-22-23:06:18
192.168.2.112;216.58.192.36;Jan-22-23:06:18
192.168.2.112;172.217.15.204;Jan-22-23:06:21
172.217.15.204;192.168.2.112;Jan-22-23:06:21
192.168.2.112;172.217.15.204;Jan-22-23:06:21
172.217.15.204;192.168.2.112;Jan-22-23:06:21
192.168.2.1;192.168.2.112;Jan-22-23:06:27
192.168.2.1;192.168.2.112;Jan-22-23:06:27
192.168.2.1;192.168.2.112;Jan-22-23:06:27
192.168.2.1;192.168.2.112;Jan-22-23:06:36
192.168.2.1;192.168.2.112;Jan-22-23:06:37
192.168.2.1;192.168.2.112;Jan-22-23:06:37
192.168.2.1;192.168.2.112;Jan-22-23:06:38
192.168.2.1;192.168.2.112;Jan-22-23:06:39
```

(c) Close connection requests.

Fig. 3. Log information.

reports in an interactive dashboard, as shown in Fig. 4. The domain name, open time, close time, and status of each request is presented. Furthermore, MAC address information of each wireless device is obfuscated.

Based on a period of one month, the teacher has real-time evidence of all the activities developed by the students in the virtual classroom. Furthermore, it permits implementing institutional security policies based on the network traffic analysis creating a more functional virtual classroom.

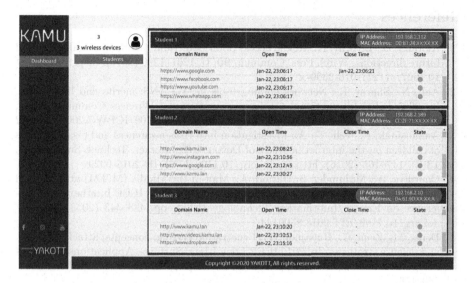

Fig. 4. System dashboard.

5   Conclusions

The detection algorithm presented in this paper takes advantage of a passive MITM attack allowing the data interception in real-time between a LAP and wireless devices in educational environments.

The online behavior detection of the users is implemented employing passive eavesdropping techniques. This detection algorithm permits the KAMU AP to provide individual browsing information of each student to the teacher, having evidence of the virtual classroom activities. It is demonstrated that the parental control implemented in educational environments is a transparent service to the students. Furthermore, the passive eavesdropping technique used by the detections algorithm is independent of the LMS platform adopted by the educational institution. However, it can be focused on dangerous activities, but it is not considered in this case study. On the other hand, if the users use a Virtual Private Network (VPN), it is impossible to detect its navigation requests because the data is encrypted on the network.

Obtaining a Minimum Viable Product (MVP) for validation on educational institutions is considered in future works. Furthermore, more elements will be incorporated into the dashboard, such as statistical charts and autonomous reports.

Acknowledgment. This Work is supported by the Research Group in Wireless Communications (GCOMIN) of the Universidad Técnica Particular de Loja under project PROY_INNOV_2019_2598. GCOMIN provides the infrastructure to implement the detection algorithm designed in this Work.

References

1. Alotaibi, B., Elleithy, K.: Rogue access point detection: taxonomy, challenges, and future directions. Wirel. Pers. Commun. **90**(3), 1261–1290 (2016). https://doi.org/10.1007/s11277-016-3390-x
2. Anh, N., Shorey, R.: Network sniffing tools for WLANS: merits and limitations. In: 2005 IEEE International Conference on Personal Wireless Communications, ICPWC 2005, pp. 389–393 (2005). https://doi.org/10.1109/ICPWC.2005.1431372
3. Annansingh, F., Veli, T.: An investigation into risks awareness and e-safety needs of children on the internet: a study of Devon, UK. Interact. Technol. Smart Educ. **13**(2), 147–165 (2016). https://doi.org/10.1108/ITSE-09-2015-0029
4. Chordiya, A., Majumder, S., Javaid, A.: Man-in-the-Middle (MITM) attack based hijacking of http traffic using open source tools. In: 2018 IEEE International Conference on Electro/Information Technology (EIT), pp. 438–443 (2018). https://doi.org/10.1109/EIT.2018.8500144
5. Denis, M., Zena, C., Hayajneh, T.: Penetration testing: concepts, attack methods, and defense strategies. In: 2016 IEEE Long Island Systems, Applications and Technology Conference (LISAT), pp. 1–6 (2016). https://doi.org/10.1109/LISAT.2016.7494156
6. Dobrovská, D., Andres, P.: Digitization and current educational changes in switzerland - inspiration for the Czech Republic? In: Auer, M.E., Hortsch, H., Sethakul, P. (eds.) ICL 2019. AISC, vol. 1135, pp. 402–408. Springer, Cham (2020). https://doi.org/10.1007/978-3-030-40271-6_40
7. Faria, D., Cheriton, D.: Detecting identity-based attacks in wireless networks using signalprints. In: Proceedings of the 5th ACM Workshop on Wireless Security, WiSE 2006, vol. 2006, pp. 43–52. Association for Computing Machinery, New York (2006). https://doi.org/10.1145/1161289.1161298
8. Fukushima, M., Goto, S.: Analysis of TCP flags in congested network. In: 1999 Internet Workshop, IWS99. (Cat. No. 99EX385), pp. 151–156 (1999). https://doi.org/10.1109/IWS.1999.811007
9. Goyal, P., Goyal, A.: Comparative study of two most popular packet sniffing tools-Tcpdump and wireshark. In: 2017 9th International Conference on Computational Intelligence and Communication Networks (CICN), pp. 77–81 (2017). https://doi.org/10.1109/CICN.2017.8319360
10. Hong, Q., Jianwei, T., Ying, Y., Zheng, T., Hongyu, Z., Shu, L.: A network scanning detection method based on TCP flow state. In: 2018 3rd International Conference on Smart City and Systems Engineering (ICSCSE), pp. 419–422 (2018). https://doi.org/10.1109/ICSCSE.2018.00089
11. Kavisankar, L., Chellappan, C.: T-RAP: (TCP reply acknowledgement packet) a resilient filtering model for DDoS attack with spoofed IP address. In: Wyld, D.C., Wozniak, M., Chaki, N., Meghanathan, N., Nagamalai, D. (eds.) NeCoM/WeST/WiMoN -2011. CCIS, vol. 197, pp. 138–148. Springer, Heidelberg (2011). https://doi.org/10.1007/978-3-642-22543-7_14

12. Kumar, P., Tripathi, M., Nehra, A., Conti, M., Lal, C.: Safety: early detection and mitigation of TCP SYN flood utilizing entropy in SDN. IEEE Trans. Netw. Serv. Manage. **15**(4), 1545–1559 (2018). https://doi.org/10.1109/TNSM.2018.2861741

13. Mandal, N., Jadhav, S.: A survey on network security tools for open source. In: 2016 IEEE International Conference on Current Trends in Advanced Computing (ICCTAC), pp. 1–6 (2016). https://doi.org/10.1109/ICCTAC.2016.7567330

14. Mcnulty, M., Kettani, H.: On cybersecurity education for non-technical learners. In: 2020 3rd International Conference on Information and Computer Technologies (ICICT), pp. 413–416 (2020). https://doi.org/10.1109/ICICT50521.2020.00072

15. van Oorschot, P.C.: Intrusion detection and network-based attacks. In: Computer Security and the Internet. Information Security and Cryptography. Springer, Cham (2020). https://doi.org/10.1007/978-3-030-33649-3_11

16. Park, H., Shin, S.H., Roh, B.H., Lee, C.: Identification of hosts behind a NAT device utilizing multiple fields of IP and TCP. In: 2016 International Conference on Information and Communication Technology Convergence (ICTC), pp. 484–486 (2016). https://doi.org/10.1109/ICTC.2016.7763518

17. Park, M.-W., Choi, Y.-H., Eom, J.-H., Chung, T.-M.: Dangerous Wi-Fi access point: attacks to benign smartphone applications. Pers. Ubiquit. Comput. **18**(6), 1373–1386 (2013). https://doi.org/10.1007/s00779-013-0739-y

18. Pingle, B., Mairaj, A., Javaid, A.: Real-world man-in-the-middle (MITM) attack implementation using open source tools for instructional use. In: 2018 IEEE International Conference on Electro/Information Technology (EIT), pp. 192–197 (2018). https://doi.org/10.1109/EIT.2018.8500082

19. Rahman, N., Sairi, I., Zizi, N., Khalid, F.: The importance of cybersecurity education in school. Int. J. Inf. Educ. Technol. **10**(5), 378–382 (2020). https://doi.org/10.18178/ijiet.2020.10.5.1393

20. Sheng, Y., Tan, K., Chen, G., Kotz, D., Campbell, A.: Detecting 802.11 mac layer spoofing using received signal strength. In: The 27th Conference on Computer Communications, IEEE INFOCOM 2008, pp. 1768–1776 (2008). https://doi.org/10.1109/INFOCOM.2007.239

21. Shrivastava, P., Jamal, M., Kataoka, K.: EvilScout: detection and mitigation of evil twin attack in SDN enabled WiFi. IEEE Trans. Netw. Serv. Manage. **17**(1), 89–102 (2020). https://doi.org/10.1109/TNSM.2020.2972774

22. Trnka, M., Rysavy, F., Cerny, T., Stickney, N.: Using Wi-Fi enabled Internet of Things devices for context-aware authentication. In: Kim, K.J., Baek, N. (eds.) ICISA 2018. LNEE, vol. 514, pp. 635–642. Springer, Singapore (2019). https://doi.org/10.1007/978-981-13-1056-0_62

23. Vanhoef, M., Piessens, F.: Advanced Wi-Fi attacks using commodity hardware. In: Proceedings of the 30th Annual Computer Security Applications Conference, pp. 256–265. Association for Computing Machinery, New York (2014). https://doi.org/10.1145/2664243.2664260

24. Yang, W., Li, X., Feng, Z., Hao, J.: TLSsem: A TLS security-enhanced mechanism against MITM attacks in public WiFis. In: 2017 22nd International Conference on Engineering of Complex Computer Systems (ICECCS), pp. 30–39 (2017). https://doi.org/10.1109/ICECCS.2017.24

25. Zou, Y., Zhu, J., Wang, X., Hanzo, L.: A survey on wireless security: technical challenges, recent advances, and future trends. Proc. IEEE **104**(9), 1727–1765 (2016). https://doi.org/10.1109/JPROC.2016.2558521

Performance and Security Evaluation in Microservices Architecture Using Open Source Containers

Diego Antonio Castillo Rivas$^{(\boxtimes)}$ and Daniel Guamán$^{(\boxtimes)}$ (iD)

Universidad Técnica Particular de Loja, Loja, Ecuador
{dacastillo11,daguaman}@utpl.edu.ec

Abstract. Nowadays, microservices architecture has increased its popularity within software development. This architecture is considered as a refinement and simplification of the service-oriented architecture (SOA). In microservices, the development approach is given by the functional decomposition into small services, where each one makes use of its own computational resources and light communication mechanisms, such as HTTP. Compared to monolithic architectures, microservices can be developed using different code bases. Therefore, performance and security are two of the quality attributes that must be taken into account when building microservices. The objective of this work is to define a DevOps Pipeline that allows us to use best practices at the development level to improve performance and security in pre-production environments. For deployment, two open-source containers are selected to evaluate under which situations it is more convenient to use Docker or Containerd, especially at the base image level.

Keywords: Microservices · Containers · Security · Performance

1 Introduction

Currently, most applications are developed using different types of architectures and architectural styles such as Layers, Client-Server, Model-View-Controller among others. However, working with monolithic architectures implies taking into account that, when incorporating new features or functionalities into the system, a complete system reconstruction and deployment must be performed in some cases, which involves significant planning, preparation, time and costs. In a monolithic architecture, all the code is embedded in an executable file, therefore, if there is a problem in the code base, it could be located anywhere within the software, which leads to the use of debugging techniques and tools, maintenance and refactoring for subsequent integration and deployment activities [1]. To mitigate these drawbacks, an alternative is a microservices architecture. This architecture is a variation of the Service Oriented architecture (SOA). It differs from its predecessor since microservices is a collection of small services for a single and specialized purpose, while SOA is a collection of services that have a broader domain and a

M. Botto-Tobar et al. (Eds.): ICAT 2020, CCIS 1388, pp. 484–498, 2021.
https://doi.org/10.1007/978-3-030-71503-8_37

considerable level of complexity at the development level [2]. The microservices architecture helps solve scalability problems, since, by having smaller components, those services that need to run other parts of the system on smaller and less powerful hardware can be scaled. For the implementation of microservices, containers are used, which allow each service to be packaged, so that the deployment process is faster and more efficient. It is important to bear in mind that the greater the number of microservices, an extra effort is required at the hardware level, which implies making use of more powerful servers, and at the software level, making use of technologies that virtualize the microservices in a better way. There are many alternatives or ecosystems that propose the use of containers, some commercial, others open source,

However, it is always important to consider the best-suited container technology when deploying microservices for a specific context. Due to the increasing use of microservices architecture, few studies refer to the virtualization technologies that best address security and performance. Therefore, in the present work, it is proposed to design and analyze a prototype based on microservices that makes use of containers and open source tools [3]. Good development practices will be applied to the prototype, performance and security will be evaluated in a pre-production environment, which will allow us to know which virtualization technology is best for deployment and integration. As a key concept in the development of microservices, a DevOps Pipeline is proposed, to carry out continuous integration and continuous deployment activities. This work has been organized as follows: in Sect. 2, the concepts and related works are presented, Sect. 3 refers to the design for the implementation of microservices, in Sect. 4 the technologies for implementing microservices are explained. In Sect. 5 the results obtained in a pre-production environment are shown. Finally, Sect. 6 summarizes the conclusions as part of the experimentation and evaluation.

2 Background and Related Works

2.1 Microservices

Microservices is an architecture that fits perfectly with the services offered by technology companies such as Amazon and Google. Microservices are like small autonomous services that work together and are responsible for solving a specific part of the work [4]. In [5] microservices architecture is defined as a cloud application design pattern that implies that the application is divided into a series of small independent services, each of which is responsible for the implementation of a certain characteristic. Each microservice works independently of another, which means that if one of them fails, it does not affect the performance of the other ones. For [6] a microservice is a small application that can be independently deployed, scaled and validated and that has a single responsibility. Scalability refers to the fact that as the microservice evolves, it should not affect the performance of the others.

2.2 Containers

Containers are defined in [7] as a mechanism that provides virtualization at the operating system level since they can isolate and control resources for a set of processes. Containers run as another process of the operating system, allowing it to run in isolation. A container uses the same resources of the operating system, and in turn does not demand as much performance, since virtual machines virtualize the entire operating system and hardware, generating more use of resources. According to [8], containers are a means to provide isolation and management of resources in a Linux environment. The term is derived from shipping containers, a standard method for storing and shipping any type of cargo. An operating system container provides a generic way to isolate a process from the rest of the system. The containers would come to be a level of virtualization of the Operating System. This technology made its debut in 1982, on UNIX operating systems, the name of this first implementation was "Chroot". It was originally created as a way to control the security of a software package [9]. Over time, many containerization technologies have emerged, so it was necessary to create a standard for the creation of these technologies. This is the reason why the Open Container Initiative [10] was established. In addition, more technologies have emerged apart from Docker which also allows this virtualization to have a positive effect on the subject of microservices.

2.3   Container Runtimes

Containers runtimes are software that runs containers and manages container images on a node. The most popular and widely used Container Runtime in Kubernetes production environments for microservices deployments in Docker [11]. However, there are other container runtimes on the market such as RKT [12], Containers [13], and CRI-O [14]. **Docker** is a platform for developing, deploying, and running containerized applications [15]. Among the most relevant features of Docker include: Flexible - even the most complex applications can be containerized. Lightweight - Containers leverage and share the host core. Interchangeable. **RKT** is part of the CoreOS project, its focus is for development in modern production environments in the Cloud. RKT is a container engine, released by CoreOS. It helps package applications, rely on portable containers, and simplify environment deployment [16]. RKT is an application container engine developed for modern cloud-native production environments. It features a native Pod approach, a pluggable runtime environment, and a well-defined surface area that makes it ideal for integration with other systems. **Containers** is an agnostic Container Runtime, which can be used by any other container orchestration platform, it works for both Linux and Windows, which is in charge of managing the complete life cycle of the container of your host system, from transfer and transfer, image storage to container execution and monitoring, image transfer, low-level storage to network attachments, process monitoring, and so on [17]. It differs from the Docker daemon in that it has a reduced feature set, and image download is not supported [18]. **CRI-O** is a Container Runtime created by Kubernetes. Its objective is to improve orchestration and performance compared to Docker. CRI-O as a Kubernetes implementation supports OCI container images and can be pulled from any container registry. Regarding its use, it is a lightweight alternative to Docker or RKT as Container Runtimes for Kubernetes [19]. **Kubernetes** is an open-source system for automating the deployment, scaling, and management of containerized applications. Groups the containers that make up an application into logical units for easy management and discovery. Additionally, they help them find the resources and tools they need to function [20].

2.4 Security in Microservices

Security is about making the software behave correctly in the presence of a malicious attack. Containers are convenient for packaging microservices and safely running an application within a virtualized environment. The containers are isolated from the host operating system and only share their resources to run the application, this does not mean that the containers are completely secure [21]. The use of these entails several security challenges, one of them is that since there are many separate parts in a microservices application; it has an even greater range of cyberattacks, in addition to the fact that the containers and images by themselves are open as well. Some good practices to implement security in microservices in what has to do with containers are proposed in NIST Special Publication 800-190 [22]. Among the practices, the following can be mentioned: analysis of vulnerabilities, images from only trusted sources, authentication and authorization, Secrets.

2.4.1 Vulnerability Scan

An analysis of the vulnerabilities prior to the deployment of the application allows us to know more about the security gaps that the containers may have in production. For this analysis, tools such as Synk [23] are used, which helps us to analyze the base image in depth to know the risks that the image may have in the future. Immutable containers help to prevent unauthorized users from entering containers. This practice arose from a bad practice that was produced by the developers since they accessed the image container to be able to repair any error when they were already in production. This is why they often exploit this access to inject malicious code. To avoid this, the most used is to create immutable containers. In the event of defects or vulnerabilities, developers can rebuild and redeploy containers [24].

2.4.2 Images from Only Trusted Sources

When transferring data between networked systems, trust is a central concern. In particular, when communicating through an untrusted medium such as the Internet, ensuring integrity is critical. Content trust allows verifying both the integrity and the publisher of all data received from a record on any channel [25]. It is important to verify that the image used has not been altered, if not checked, it would be detrimental to the system, since there is no control and it is exposed to the most important components, such as information and users.

2.4.3 Authentication and Authorization

With the arrival of microservices, the complexity of their management has increased. One of the key challenges is how to implement authentication and authorization so that security and access control can be managed. Authentication and authorization allow us to have control of the components that are part of the system, in addition to protecting information, which is a key aspect in any system [26]. Authentication and authorization are the first line of defense for APIs. Authentication refers to the validation of a user's identity while authorization occurs, once the system authenticates the identity [26].

2.4.4 Secrets

Secrets are a critical part of microservices security. This is critical information that should not be exposed when the containers are deployed. The Secrets, in the context of containers, is any information that puts your organization, customer, or application at risk if exposed to an unauthorized person or entity. As a system becomes more complex, the amount of secret information involved also increases, and the risk level involved also increases. The more moving parts there are in the system, the more susceptible it is to risk [27]. Consequently, when the system increases in complexity, it becomes a difficult issue to handle, sinceit is necessary to improve execution times and there is key information, which in a certain way must be exposed.

2.5   Performance in Microservices

Performance measurement and prediction approaches for component-based software systems help software architects evaluate their systems against component performance specifications created by component developers [28]. They are commonly evaluated at the CPU level and at the Network level.

2.5.1   CPU Level

In this type of test, computational performance is compared in different types of environments, such as the different types of containers. The CPU and RAM memory used is used as a reference point when virtualizing each container [7]. Depending on the resources used by the containers, it can generate an overhead, which can interfere with other deployed containers.

2.5.2   Network Level

Containers expose some media in multiple applications communicating with the same machine. In this type of test, the performance of the network is measured, with a focus on studying the communication overload of different technologies when it is executed [7], this by checking the concurrency within the network by the users.

2.6   Related Works

As part of the related work in [29] the analysis of microservices efficiency at the provisioning level is studied. To do this, an analytical model of performance and validation of experiments is proposed to study the provisioning of microservices platforms. As part of the design and development work, an Amazon EC2 cloud microservices platform is used using the Docker family of technology to identify important elements that contribute to the performance of the platforms. Additionally, they leveraged the results and insights from the experiments to build a manageable analytical performance model that can be used to systematically do analysis and capacity planning for large-scale microservices with minimal resources. In the work proposed by [16] a performance analysis is conducted making use of containers such as RKT and Docker. This work focuses on scaling and flexibility issues, and also makes a comparison of the execution process between these two Containers Runtime and analyze the results obtained by each execution on the Kubernetes-based containers. An analysis of the microservices architecture and commercial containers is presented in [7]. The purpose of this paper is to compare CPU and network performance, thus offering a reference analysis guide for system designers.

3 Design

In order to evaluate the security and performance metrics in the development of microservices, as part of our work, it is proposed to build a prototype where the architectural design, web services and data model used are evidenced. In addition to this, it is proposed to use a DevOps approach for integrating continuous deployment issues.

3.1 Services Definition

The prototype built with microservices is focused to be used in restaurants. The solution is designed for customers to order and pay through a Smartphone. To determine the level of granularity of the restaurant's services, a decomposition technique called Capability Map is applied. By applying this decomposition technique, five services were obtained, each of these Microservices is responsible for a part of the solution (see Fig. 1).

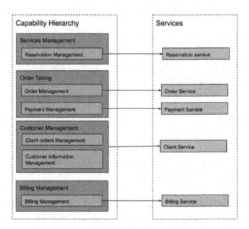

Fig. 1. Map of capacities – services

The proposed architecture for the development of microservices is detailed in Fig. 2. This architecture includes some design patterns and architectural elements such as Api Gateway, REST, event bus.

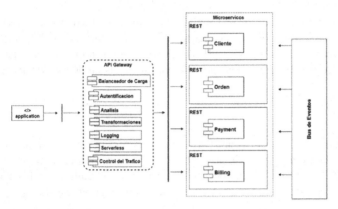

Fig. 2. Architectural design of microservices

3.2 Communication

Communication is a key factor for the operation of microservices. There are two types of communication that are regularly used, these are Synchronous and Asynchronous, in addition to the message format that microservices use to communicate, both with the client and between microservices.

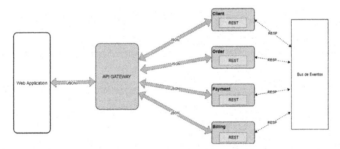

Fig. 3. Microservices communication model

In Fig. 3 the types of communication used in the prototype are observed, these are synchronous and asynchronous. For synchronous, REST is used as a communication model, which provides a simple messaging style implemented with HTTP request-response, based on resources. Therefore, most microservice implementations use HTTP in conjunction with resources (each functionality is represented by a resource and the operations performed on those resources). In asynchronous communication between services, an event-based architecture is chosen, specifically Publisher-Subscriber. With this type of communication, the client will not receive an immediate response, so it can be better applied for communication between Microservices. The REdis Serialization Protocol (RESP) is used. This protocol was designed specifically for Redis. This is so that the publishers and subscribers have all the business logic while the broker has none. A broker would come to ensure that the communication between Microservices is reliable and stable.

3.3 Decentralized Data Management

Microservices do not use the same centralized database, as it is difficult to ensure flexible coupling between services (for example, if the database schema has changed from a given Microservice, that will break several other services). Therefore, each microservice would need to have its own database. In Fig. 4 the organization of the services with their databases is observed. The data model design is in accordance with the needs of Microservices, as they are independent services, each one handles a different data model.

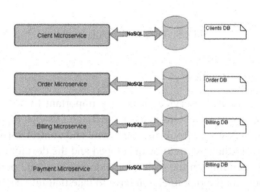

Fig. 4. Microservices data management

3.4 Microservices Register

Each microservice contains a service that must be configured correctly, the registry of these services contains some settings of interest, such as the actual locations of the servers, the ports on which they are running, etc. Microservice instances are registered with the service registration at startup and are aborted on shutdown [30]. Consumers can find available Microservices and their locations through the service registry. To know the available microservices and their location, there are currently two mechanisms to discover Microservices, these are client-side discovery and server-side discovery [30]. In this work, the discovery of services by the server are used. Using this approach, the client or API gateway sends the request to a component (such as a load balancer) that is running in a known location. This component calls the service registry and determines the location of the requested Microservice (see Fig. 5). Both client-side and server-side discovery design can leverage deployment solutions such as Kubernetes for server-side discovery. Kubernetes offers built-in service discovery and registration capabilities so that you can call your service by its logical name, and Kubernetes takes care of resolving them to real IPs and ports [30].

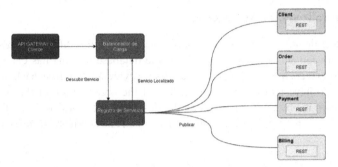

Fig. 5. Discovery by the server

3.5 DevOps Design – Pipeline

For the development of microservices it is very important to use some development methodology. For this work, DevOps is used. Next, the DevOps Pipeline design is presented, which integrates several tools that automate and control software development, these vary according to the system to be developed and the development language used [31]. Some tools, depending on the technology, do not integrate perfectly with others, for what before applying the pipeline, you have to take that into account.

Taking as reference [32] the pipeline was built, then the criteria by which the use of technologies within this ecosystem has been selected as described.

- Source Control Management: GitHub is used since it provides good support, and it allows the integration with Travis CI in an easy way, so that each time a change is made in the repository, it can be built and tested, in an automatic way.
- Build: Npm, used for Npm compilation, allows to perform any necessary construction/preparation tasks for the project before it is used in another project.
- Continuous Integration: Travis CI, is an Open Source platform that allows the code to be executed for free, the only disadvantage is that in order for the code repository to be used it must be public. The integration with GitHub is currently one of the most efficient, in addition to saving time and money in raising another free CI platform that is Jenkins, since for this you would need an instance in the cloud to be able to configure it correctly, which takes more effort. Travis has many features to help you with deployment and configuration management.
- Testing: JestJS is a JavaScript test framework with a focus on simplicity, this technology uses NodeJs own Testing packages.
- Containers: Dockeris used for many things today, both for construction, testing and for deployment, in this phase it is used to build, configure and test Microservices, in addition to having some functionalities such as Docker-Compose that allows testing the configuration, to later occupy it in the deployment of Microservices.
- Security: SonarQube takes care of its free version, this software, in addition to testing good code practices, also helps in the security aspects of the services that will be deployed.

- Orchestation & Scheduling: Kubernetes, since it is the best technology for the deployment of Microservices today per excellence, has several tools, such as the load balancer, which is very useful in the deployment of Microservices.
- Cloud: Google Cloud Platform, since it has a better integration in the Cloud than the other versions, as it can also be used natively Container Runtime Interface (CRI).
- Release Orchestration: Weave Scope is a visualization and monitoring tool for Docker and Kubernetes. It provides a top-down view into your application, as well as your entire infrastructure, and enables you to diagnose any issues with your containerized application in real-time, as it is being deployed on a cloud provider.

4 Implementation

Kong is used to connect the Microservices, which is an API Gateway. Kong makes use of API Management, which allows managing the security of REST services. Furthermore, it allows the connection of HTTP, RCP and gRPC (see Fig. 6).

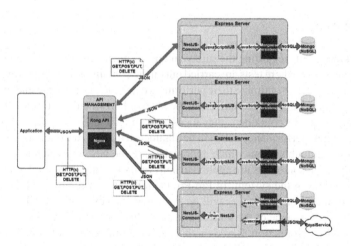

Fig. 6. API Management integration

The programming language is indifferent in the development of microservices, TypeScript [33] is chosen as the programming language, since it allows transcompilation of JavaScript, which means that, when building the application, the result is JavaScript code. To apply the REST development pattern, the Framework for the web called NestJS [34] is used. Each Microservice uses a NoSQL database called MongoDB [35], allowing it to occupy the asynchronous functionality natively. For data persistence, in the case of TypeScript, Mongoose [36] is used. PayPal [37] is used for the payment gateway. For the implementation of microservices, the technologies used are detailed in Table 1.

Table 1. Technologies used to build microservices

Name	Description	Characteristic
NestJS	Server side application	Allows applications to be modularized by applying object-oriented concepts and functional and reactive programming. Abstracts the use of JavaScript on the server
Mongoose	Database persistence	Direct solution based on schemas. Built-in type conversion. Validation and creation of queries
Swagger	RESTful services documentation	Uses a common language that everyone can understand. Easily adjustable, can be used successfully for API testing and bug fixing. You can use the same documentation to speed up various API-dependent processes
Git	Change control	Technology that allows managing changes made to the code

5 Validation

To present the results regarding the safety and performance metrics, a "Pre-Production" environment is used where tests are carried out on the containers, before putting them into production, in order to optimize their performance as much as possible and evaluate the safety of the containers. The containers at the level of known vulnerabilities. To measure the performance of the containers, they focus on scaling, both for 1, 3 and 5 clusters, from these approaches, performance data will be obtained at the CPU and Network level, which helps to resolve doubts about which approaches are the best and when to use them. At the Security level, some tests are applied to help verify the impact of implementing these security practices in the system. In Pre-Production, the considerations that are related to the performance of the images will be evaluated, two evaluations will be applied to improve the performance of the images and an evaluation to improve the security of the containers in Pre-Production. Based on this analysis, time will be obtained in the image creation, size of the image, and the vulnerability that have the containers.

5.1 Performance

Image sizes are shown in Fig. 7. It can be seen that the heaviest base images are the full ones because they have all the compilation files inserted there, even those that are not used. The smallest base images are the alpine-carbon, which are up to 3 times smaller than the full version. The slim, alpine, carbon images vary a lot according to the sizes. Up to this point it could be concluded that to have better performance and scaling, it would be the best choice to use alpine-carbon, since it is a very small image.

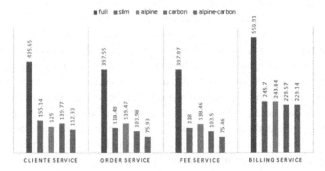

Fig. 7. Size in MB of the base images

5.2 Security

To determine security, the vulnerabilities of the base image are analyzed using the Snyk tool, as it helps to see the main vulnerabilities registered by this website, focused on security in software development. For this analysis, the images used in the previous test were analyzed; therefore, the following results were obtained asit can be seen in Fig. 8.

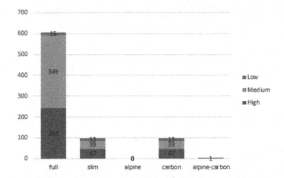

Fig. 8. Vulnerabilities in the analyzed base images

Something very important, which can be highlighted in Fig. 8, is the large number of vulnerabilities, which the full base image has, w a total of 607 vulnerabilities. This is because the base image that it deals with has all NodeJs functionalities, which we occupy and which we do not, that is why it is important to occupy only the functionalities that the image needs. In addition to the fact that the images with the least number of vulnerabilities are the alpine and the alpine-carbon, with a total of 0 vulnerabilities and 1 vulnerability, here there is a very interesting dilemma. On the one hand, we have the alpine base image, which has no vulnerabilities significant at the moment, and on the contrary this same base image weighs significantly more, compared to the alpine-carbon. Choosing which would be the most efficient decision depends a lot on the approach that the application has. If you want is to mitigate vulnerabilities significantly, the best option would be alpine, but if you want is to improve performance of the application, an optimal option would be alpine-carbon, since it only uses what is necessary to lift the image, the only disadvantage is that security in the container would be sacrificed, thus improving performance. Finally, as part of the evaluation, it was considered to use Istio, which is a service mesh (Mesh), which fits perfectly to any Microservices architecture, in addition to implementing security practices by default. As a service mesh grows in size and complexity, it can become more difficult to understand and manage. Istio provides behavioral information and operational control over the service mesh as a whole, offering a complete solution to satisfy the diverse requirements of Microservice applications [38]. In this last testing phase, the containers will be tested on this service mesh to verify which containers work best with Istio. In Fig. 9, it can be seen that for the Containerd container, a better latency was obtained compared to the Docker container. Latency remains between 300 to 350 ms, for both 1.3 and 5 clusters.

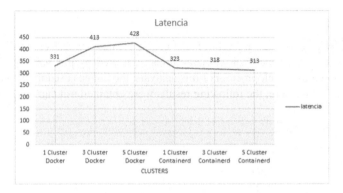

Fig. 9. Latency results with Istio

6 Conclusions

Docker and Containerd as containers allow configuring microservices deployment environments in post-production environments, where network performance, system resources (CPU and RAM) can be evaluated prior to the deployment and orchestration of microservices in the mobile application (Production). Through vertical scaling using Containerd, a significant improvement in network performance is evidenced, since the concurrency of requests remains within an acceptable range of 300 requests per second and an acceptable latency of less than 250 ms. In the present work, vertical scaling is used over horizontal scaling, because it allows dynamic scaling according to the need that each microservice requires, thus maintaining stable performance within the mobile application. At the implementation level, the maximum scaling value for each microservice was up to 5 clusters, because the cost rate of this service is related to its use and additional payments must be made to increase the clusters. The results obtained allow us to conclude that the Docker approach and its native integration with Istio is a suitable service mesh model (Service Mesh) since it improves the use of CPU and RAM resources by 20%. Through the implementation of Istio as a Service Mesh framework, some basic and advanced configurations related to security, scaling and orchestration of microservices were automated. For security issues, the container that best integrates natively with Istio is Docker, since it is the most used and validated in integration and optimization tests by Istio creators and developers. The results of the container-level experiments show that Containerd has a significant impact on CPU performance; however, there are some trade-offs in terms of network performance such as latency and requests per second compared to Docker.

The implementation of the Rate Limiting practice allows us to conclude that Docker obtains better results.This was evidenced by sending 200 requests per second for each user where the performance improved by 26% compared to Containerd who uses excessive CPU. If Docker is compared with Containerd, the implementation of microservices in the latter provides better results in metrics such as latency, the throughput of requests per second, and the CPU usage, because its implementation is more configurable and parameterizable since it does not load other services that are not necessary as Docker does. The experimentation results show that when it is necessary to increase security at the microservice level, one option is to implement the alpine base image to deploy the containers since it reduces the existence of vulnerabilities compared to images such as full, slim, carbon and alpine-carbon.

Acknowledgment. This work has been sponsored by Universidad Técnica Particular de Loja (Computer Science Department).

References

1. Smith, M., Saunders, P.R., Lyons, L.: A Practical Guide to Microservices and Containers (2018)
2. Industrial Internet Consortium: Industrial Internet Reference Architecture, p. 101 (2015)
3. Fernandez, E.B., Monge, R., Hashizume, K.: Building a security reference architecture for cloud systems. Requirements Eng. **21**(2), 225–249 (2015). https://doi.org/10.1007/s00766-014-0218-7
4. Newman, S.: Building Microservices. O'Reilly Media Inc., United States of America (2015)
5. Esposito, C., Castiglione, A., Choo, K.-K.R.: Challenges in delivering software in the cloud as microservices. IEEE Cloud Comput. **3**(5), 10–14 (2016)
6. Schwartz, A.: Microservices. Informatik-Spektrum **40**(6), 590–594 (2017). https://doi.org/10.1007/s00287-017-1078-6
7. Amaral, M., Polo, J., Carrera, D., Mohomed, I., Unuvar, M., Steinder, M.: Performance evaluation of microservices architectures using containers. In: Proceedings of the 2015 IEEE 14th International Symposium on Network Computing and Applications, NCA 2015, pp. 27–34 (2016)
8. Dua, R., Raja, A.R., Kakadia, D.: Virtualization vs containerization to support PaaS. In: Proceedings of the 2014 IEEE International Conference on Cloud Engineering, IC2E 2014, pp. 610–614 (2014)
9. Hogg, S.: Software Containers: Used More Frequently than Most Realize, 26 May 2014
10. Open Container Initiative: Open Container Initiative (2015)
11. Brown, M., Liu, L.: Containerd Brings More Container Runtime Options for Kubernetes, 2 November 2017
12. CoreOS: rkt, a security-minded, standards-based container engine (2014)

13. Containerd: containerd, an industry-standard container runtime with an emphasis on simplicity, robustness and portability (2019)
14. CRI-O: CRI-O, lightweight container runtime for Kubernetes (2018)
15. Docker: Get started, part 1: orientation and setup (2019)
16. Xie, X.L., Wang, P., Wang, Q.: The performance analysis of Docker and rkt based on Kubernetes. In: 13th International Conference on Natural Computation, Fuzzy Systems and Knowledge Discovery, ICNC-FSKD 2017, pp. 2137–2141 (2018)
17. Crosby, M.: What is containerd? 7 August 2017
18. Turnbull, J.: The Docker book: containerization is the new virtualization (2014)
19. Brown, R.: CRI-O is now our default container runtime interface, 17 September 2018
20. Vohra, D.: Kubernetes Microservices With Docker. Apress (2016)
21. Chung, M.T., Quang-Hung, N., Nguyen, M.-T., Thoai, N.: Using docker in high performance computing applications. In: 2016 IEEE 6th International Conference on Communications and Electronics (ICCE), pp. 52–57 (2016)
22. Souppaya, M., Morello, J., Scarfone, K.: NIST Special Publication 800-190 - Application container security guide. NIST Special Publication, vol. 1, p. 63 (2017)
23. Snyk: Snyk, develop fast. Stay secure (2020)
24. Liz, R.: Container Image Immutability and the Power of Metadata (2016)
25. Docker: Content trust in Docker (2019)
26. Aggarwal, B.: Authentication and Authorization in Microservices, 19 March 2019
27. Taylor, T.: 8 Best Practices for Container Secrets Management, 22 April 2019
28. Koziolek, H.: Performance evaluation of component-based software systems: a survey. Perform. Eval. **67**(8), 634–658 (2010)
29. Khazaei, H., Barna, C., Beigi-Mohammadi, N., Litoiu, M.: Efficiency analysis of provisioning microservices. In: Proceedings of the International Conference on Cloud Computing Technology and Science, CloudCom, pp. 261–268 (2017)
30. Indrasiri, B.K.: Microservices in Practice - Key Architectural Concepts of an MSA, July 2019
31. Ebert, C., Gallardo, G., Hernantes, J., Serrano, N.: DevOps. IEEE Softw. **33**(3), 94–100 (2016)
32. XebiaLabs: Periodic Table of DevOps Tools (2019)
33. TypeScript: TypeScript, JavaScript that scales (2012)
34. NestJS: Hello, nest! A progressive Node.js framework for building efficient, reliable and scalable server-side applications (2017)
35. MongoDB: The database for modern applications (2020)
36. Mongoose: Mongoose, elegant mongodb object modeling for node.js (2016)
37. Paypal Developer: Install the REST SDK (2020)
38. Istio Autores: What is Istio (2019)

Implementation of an Elliptic Curve Encryption to a Database

Erika Toro$^{(\boxtimes)}$, Carlos Romero$^{(\boxtimes)}$, and Paúl Bernal$^{(\boxtimes)}$

University of the Armed Forces ESPE, Quito, Ecuador
{eatoro,cgromero,cpbernal}@espe.edu.ec

Abstract. The encryption process is very important for various applications that cover the treatment of sensitive information since it allows the protection of information stored in databases from external agents, providing security and trust to the user. The elliptic curve encryption model has the advantage of generating shorter keys but at the same level of security as other methods with much longer key lengths. The project implements an encryption system using the elliptic curve algorithm to protect the information in a database against attacks from a mobile device. The interface allows the entry of encrypted information to the database, it also performs encryption and decryption. The application of the ISO/IEC 27001 standard allows the correct management of information security to be established, through controls and strategies based on the continuous improvement cycle. Finally, the system was subjected to information security validation tests when it is accessed from a mobile device and the information is transmitted through an insecure channel, performing the necessary number of tests to ensure that the information travels through the network is encrypted, being unreadable to the intruder even if you can access it.

Keywords: Elliptic curve cryptography · Database manager · ISO/IEC 27001

1 Introduction

1.1 Elliptic Curve Cryptography

It is an asymmetric cryptography based on the algebraic structure of elliptic curves created by Victor Miller and Neal Koblitz in 1985, where calculate the private key from the public key means solve a complex computational problem like the discrete logarithm.

The mathematical properties of elliptic curves are the basis for the development of the encryption algorithm, the finite field elliptic curve equation is represented by the Eq. 1.

$$y^2 = \left\{x^3 + ax + b\right\} mod\{p\} \tag{1}$$

Key Generation. To generate keys for an elliptic curve cryptosystem, the user must follow these steps [1]:

© Springer Nature Switzerland AG 2021
M. Botto-Tobar et al. (Eds.): ICAT 2020, CCIS 1388, pp. 499–511, 2021.
https://doi.org/10.1007/978-3-030-71503-8_38

- Generate an elliptic curve E, on the finite field F_q.
- Select a generator point G, of the elliptic curve and its order must be prime n, with $n \approx q$.
- Generate the private key d, a random number such that $1 < d < n - 1$ to compute the public key.
- Finally calculate the public key with the Eq. 2.

$$P_b = dG \qquad (2)$$

Discrete Logarithm Problem [12]. The security of elliptic curve encryption is based on the level of difficulty of the discrete logarithm problem. Let P and Q be two points of the elliptic curve such that (3), where k is a scalar.

$$kP = Q \qquad (3)$$

Given P and Q, it is computationally infeasible to obtain the value of k, if k is large enough it is called the discrete logarithm of Q to the base P [2].

ECDH [10]. The Elliptic Curve Diffie - Hellman Key Exchange anonymous key agreement scheme allows two parties, each with an elliptical curve public-private key pair, to establish a shared secret over an insecure channel.

$$alicePubKey\ bobPrivKey = bobPubKey\ alicePrivKey = Secret \qquad (4)$$

The shared secret allows you to protect a message and communicate with another user through the public key. Its calculation is based on the discrete logarithm problem that seeks to protect the private key of the encryption algorithm [2].

Once the message to be sent is encrypted with the shared secret, the user who receives it will be able to decrypt it with their private key since it is encrypted with their own public key (see Fig. 1).

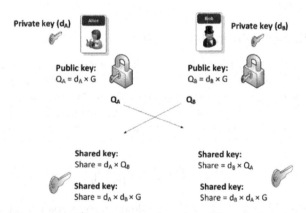

Fig. 1. Process of generating the shared secret from the public and private keys of both users.

Attack Methods [11]. The most used attacks in ECC are Pollard's Rho method and Pollard's Lambda method. The Pollard Rho method is expected to find the private key in constant time steps $\sqrt{n}$, where n is the cyclic order of the elliptic curve with G as the generator. Pollard's Lambda method is similar to Pollard's Rho method but uses many starting points to find a match. Pollard's lambda method also expects to find the private key in at most a constant time $\sqrt{n}$ steps [3].

If implemented in parallel, the execution time to find the private key can be reduced. Both methods are probabilistic, that is, they have a high probability but do not guarantee to finish in a constant time of steps $\sqrt{n}$.

1.2 ISO 27001

It is an international security standard that describes the suggested requirements to monitor and improve an information security management system, this is a set of policies to protect and manage the confidential information of a company.

The benefits of working with ISO 27001 certification include controlling access to information within an organization, reducing the risk that such information may be stolen, in addition to working with information management protocols that detail how it should be handled and transmitted [4].

Key Management. Within this context, Sect. 1.2 "Key Management" will be taken as a guide, which indicates that a policy on the use, protection and lifetime of cryptographic keys must be developed and applied.

Key management implies establishing policies that consider the complete life cycle of the key (see Fig. 2), activation and deactivation dates must be determined to reduce risks.

Fig. 2. Lifecycle gives a key generated by the elliptic curve algorithm.

1.3 Bouncy Castel

It is a collection of crypto-focused application programming interfaces developed by the "Legion of the Bouncy Castle" charity. It is freely distributed and has a version to run in java, it also focuses on the development of cryptographic applications for Android with the Spongy Castel version.

Java provides encryption support, but it is not complete, therefore the use of complementary libraries is required [5]. It facilitates the application of operations of the elliptic curve and the points that make it up, such as creating points of the curve, sum of points and obtaining the coordinates of each point.

2   Material and Method

2.1   Plain Text as Curve Point [9]

In order for the information entered by the user in the interface to be processed by the elliptic curve encryption algorithm, it must be transformed into a point on the curve (see Fig. 3).

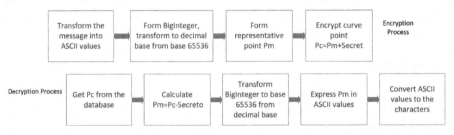

Fig. 3. Process to convert plaintext user input to a point on the generated elliptic curve.

The data must be points of the elliptic curve, in Java known as ECPoint, to be able to perform operations of this type of data such as the sum of points. The method of representing data as points on the curve encompasses block encryption, which means that a curve point will be generated for each information entered in the database fields and not a curve point for each lyrics.

2.2   Encryption

With the ASCII values of the text a BigInteger type number is formed. First, a single number is formed with the ASCII values, and then this number is transformed to a decimal base from the base 65536, because ASCII value is defined till 65535.

For the formation of the point of the curve, the number of 32 is selected as the coordinate of the abscissa axis, the number previously calculated becomes the coordinate of the ordinate axis. The point of the encrypted curve Pc, results from the sum of points between the user's shared secret and the point formed by the text entered through the interface. In this way, to know the text you must know the value of the shared secret.

$$Pc = Pm + Secret \qquad (5)$$

2.3   Decryption

The encrypted point is obtained from the database, the shared secret with the user's private and public key is calculated to obtain the point that contains the entered text Pm, like the Eq. 6.

$$Pm = Pc - Secret \qquad (6)$$

The number that forms the axis of the ordinates is taken to be transformed to base 65536 from the decimal base and obtain the number that contains the ASCII values of the original text. The whole number is divided to obtain the ASCII values of each letter and assemble the entered text.

2.4 Scene

A user wishes to encrypt the passwords of his various digital platforms for this he uses a platform that protects his information from his mobile device.

2.5 Elliptical Curve Generation

It works with the brainpoolp256r1 curve recommended by NIST (National Institute of Standards and Technology), which provides a minimum key length of 128 bits [6], with an HP Pavilion computer with Intel (R) Core processor (TM) i5 @ 2.6 GHz and 8 GB of RAM.

2.6 Key Generation [8]

The generation of the public and private keys is carried out using the KeyPairGenerator class from the Bouncy Castel library in a random way with the SecureRandom class to meet the criterion $d \in [1, n - 1]$. Where n is a prime number that represents the order of the base point of the curve, this parameter is specific to each elliptic curve.

2.7 User Interface

The mobile application presents the interface (see Fig. 4), you have the option of entering with a previously registered user or registering if you are a new user. If you are a new user, you can register by entering the fields specified in section b. and in case of authenticating with the application's own password.

Once the user is authenticated, the user can enter the passwords to be stored in an encrypted database or view the password for a specific platform.

When the user record has been created successfully, it is stored in the encrypted database so that if an intruder accesses the information on the database server, they cannot understand it.

Once the registered user has been authenticated, when writing a data to be encrypted in this case passwords of digital platforms (see Fig. 5) section a. It is evidenced that the user can safely store the passwords of Facebook, Instagram, Twitter, Google, Tinder and LinkedIn.

Similarly in section b. and c. It is observed that it displays the menu of platforms to be selected both to encrypt and save or to decrypt and display.

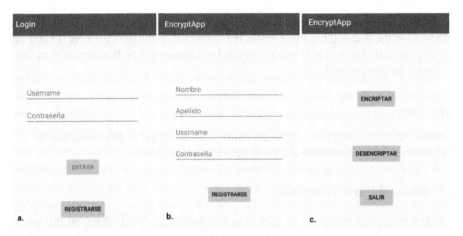

Fig. 4. The scenarios that the user interacts with on their phone. a. Home screen, b. Registration screen, c. Select activity encrypt/decrypt or exit.

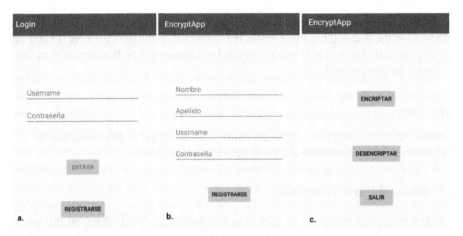

Fig. 5. Scenarios that the user interacts with when saving a key through the application. to. Deployment of platforms, b. Facebook account key registration, c. Instagram account key registration.

2.8   System Architecture

The system allows the connection from the user interface on Android with the MySQL database. The Android client through the interface of the mobile app makes an HTTP request that is received by the service layer of the Java server. In this case, since they are web services, there are no controllers (see Fig. 6), but the request goes directly to the service layer [7].

In the dependency injection service classes, the necessary repository classes are instantiated, which are classes that contain the CRUD operations that are the equivalent

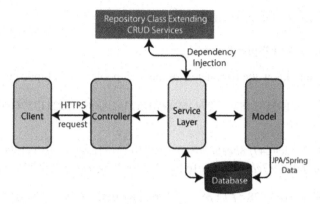

Fig. 6. Flow that follows the architecture of the Spring Boot module.

functions used by the HTTP protocol. The repository classes communicate with the database through the model classes and the persistence layer is managed with JPA which is a Java API to handle relational data structures.

2.9 Database Structure

The database is made up of the user's personal password information on the different digital platforms and user data, the tables that make it up are the following:

- User, contains the user's own information such as: name, surname, username, password and unique public key for each user, id number of user that is registered.
- Network, contains the information of each platform such as: id number of the digital platform, name of the platform, password saved by the user to enter that platform, initialization vector which allows generating different encryption of information for the same text.

The structure of the database (see Fig. 7), consists of related tables since different keys of each platform correspond to the user id.

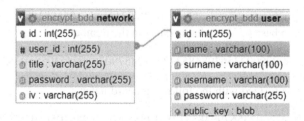

Fig. 7. Structure and correlation of the tables that make up the user databases.

3 Results and Discussions

3.1 Parameters of Elliptic Curve

First, is important know the parameters of the brainpoolp256r1 elliptic curve:

$n = 1157920892103562487626974469494075735299969552241357603424222590$
$61068512044369;$

$G = 6b17d1f2e12c4247f8bce6e563a440f277037d812deb33a0f4a13945d898c296,$
$4fe342e2fe1a7f9b8ee7eb4a7c0f9e162bce33576b315ececbb6406837bf51f5;$

$EC\ Private\ Key = [c9 : 28 : f7 : a8 : a7 : e6 : f8 : 98 : 85 : d5 : 57 : 8a : c3 : e1 : cc :$
$78 : db : 7e : 40 : 55];$

$EC\ Public\ Key :$
$X = 5ca0ae81791b1784a3fae33553cc5314373daabafc7fe896e82efab83d0f17b6;$
$Y = e63845e93d42635497b59e12b0cb64d620a3042a327daa85cc4a6ec72b3978d;$

Each elliptic curve's parameter mathematically represents:

- n, the order of the base point of the curve.
- EC Private Key, generated private key.
- G, generator point of the elliptic curve.
- Ec Public Key, generated public key.

3.2 Encryption and Decryption

Elliptical encryption works with the following steps:

- Insert the user's name: kcastillo
- The equivalent ASCII values are:

$$\{107, 99, 97, 115, 116, 105, 108, 108, 111\}$$

- Convert the number to a decimal base 10799971151161051081081111 formed by the ASCII values in base 65536, which results in the number.

$$\{113999290923567984853125612857907836245105850253422\}$$

- The point Pm is formed with the following coordinates:

$$\{113999290923567984853125612857907836245105850253422, 32\}$$

At the same time, the shared secret is calculated with the user's public and private key, Eq. 4. For the application in this project, the key of a user B will not be generated, since only one user is involved in the transmission of information.

$$Secret = EC \, PrivateKey \, ECPublicKey$$

The x coordinate that results from the mathematical operation is the shared secret.

$$Secret = 4a10ae81791b1784a3fae9e12b0cb644373daabafc7fe8965cc4a6ec72b3972e$$

Finally, to encrypt the information entered by the user, the operation described in Eq. 5 is carried out and a point on the curve is obtained as a result of the sum of points.

$$Pc = 54CF528BA53D29461493FC1370089868DC9952460158E9EB64$$

The decryption process is required to calculate or obtain the shared secret. The calculation of the shared secret is performed with the user's private key and the subtraction of points like it's shows in Eq. 6.

$$Pm = Pm + (EC \, \mathrm{Pr} \, ivateKeyECPublicKey) - (EC \, \mathrm{Pr} \, ivateKeyECPublicKey)$$

3.3 Encrypted Text Length

Table 1 records the encrypted username for different lengths of private key, in order to analyze whether it directly influences the length of the encrypted text.

Table 1. Comparison of length of encrypted text between keys of different length.

Curve type	Minimum private key length [bits]	Font size and style
brainpoolP160r1	80	760601246E21A56EA0272CD164E8DB9664611ED901A35ABD8B
brainpoolP192r1	96	D2ABD69F07AA687119E7B304FC83C6B23F88037D2041EE385D
brainpoolP224r1	112	F30AB69040C19539F84EDC96BDAB6424345117A3BCA9CC7499
brainpoolP256r1	128	0C5298EBE3E7AF6A10B906971132730001779D0AE070C623188
brainpoolP320r1	160	3228BE24DBAF02C54577AC79436ED428F9EB0DA43DFAE3C718
brainpoolP384r1	192	2FB101EAFF94C00E1594247D37C8CB6710760F8AB7F0B9A274
brainpoolP512r1	256	1399F3C6E6354A2FCD9827382A545514AEDE7DF75D2419DA4F

The security of the elliptic curve encryption algorithm does not depend on the length of the encrypted text, it only depends on the size of the private key.

3.4   Information Transmission Through Insecure Channel

For the analysis of the packets transmitted by the mobile application to the database server, the Wireshark program was used. In which we filter the transmission channel that we want to listen to, in this case, the local wireless network to which the client and the server are connected.

When you validate your username and password to access the system, the user's credentials are sent for the respective authentication and as a response, a login token is obtained, which will be different each time the user enters the platform. The token chain (see Fig. 8), allows guaranteeing that the user who makes a service request is authenticated and this process is transparent for the user.

Fig. 8. Captured packet with user registration information.

The same information travels through the channel when the information is transmitted from the database to the user (see Fig. 9), so the user can interpret the information as it is displayed legibly on the interface.

3.5   Attack Time

An issue about any encryption algorithm is the methods developing to break the algorithm. For an elliptic curve of n key length bits, the attack time is defined by the Eq. 7.

$$\sqrt{n}\ pasos \tag{7}$$

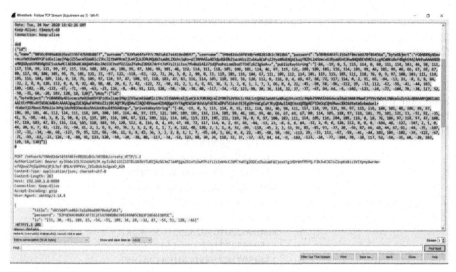

Fig. 9. A packet captured in the transmission of information over the local wireless network to the database.

Table 2 records the attack time it would take to violate the elliptical curve algorithm according to the length of the private key. It is observed that the attack time that a hacker would take using Pollard's Rho method to decrypt the passwords registered in the database is directly proportional to the number of key bits of the private key used in the encryption of the information [2].

Table 2. Attack time taken by Pollard's Rho method to find the private key.

Curve type	Minimum private key length [bits]	Value of n	Time attack [days]
brainpoolP160r1	80	1332297598440044874827085038830181364212942568457	1.335×10^{19}
brainpoolP192r1	96	47816689839061662429550018942690383081198636591198348689829	8.00×10^{23}
brainpoolP224r1	112	227216229324543527875525379959109236125675463423307571913965609666559	5.517×10^{28}
brainpoolP256r1	128	768849563970453442208097466290016490927375317844145295387555190630635363590 79	3.209×10^{33}

(continued)

Table 2. (*continued*)

Curve type	Minimum private key length [bits]	Value of n	Time attack [days]
brainpoolP320r1	160	17635933222391663541619098424460195208895127727176860637606861240167847848458434683556852582039212165927077011931617306923684233260497979611638701764860007564527482161150135851553796269511736890325222960171872394189489622076502325516566028151591534221626096440983545113445971872000570104134185283789817306435249598574513983700292805830942156138820439733543921155441169	1.537×10^{43}
brainpoolP384r1	192		5.386×10^{52}
brainpoolP512r1	256		1.094×10^{72}

3.6 Key Management Policies

For the development of this work, the following policies are established in compliance with the ISO 27001 standard, with the objective of minimizing security risks within this scenario:

- The generation of the private key must be random following the mathematical properties of elliptic curves that are explained in Sect. 1.1 of this document.
- The private key generated will not be shared, once generated on the mobile device it will be stored encrypted in the internal database of the SQLite device.
- All user information registered in the application must be saved in the encrypted database using the cryptographic algorithm.
- The information to be stored in the database must not be displayed legibly on the transmission channel to the database.
- The personal password of each user should not be transmitted by any digital means to avoid being a victim of attackers through social engineering.
- The personal password of each user in the interface must be at least 8 characters long and contain at least one special character.
- The private key must be changed within a minimum period of 8 months from the user's registration and once the first change has been made, the second change will be made in a period of 1 year.

4 Conclusion

The number of bits of the private key is proportional to the attack time required to decrypt the private key of the algorithm and break the security, therefore the length of the private key must be such that a brute force attack to reveal the information take years.

The elliptical curve encryption algorithm is based on the transmission of information between two users through an insecure channel, therefore, for the presented scenario, the existence of another user in the communication is ruled out.

The generation of the shared secret is done with the user's public and private keys and only the user transmits and receives the encrypted information, so the existence of a second user is not necessary.

The selection of the type of elliptic curve to implement must be analyzed according to the implementation of the project and the capacity and amount of computational resources available.

The implementation of the ISO27001 standard in the application framework for the encryption of information, generates the implementation of security policies and procedures that help to reinforce the security of the encryption system focused on key management.

References

1. National Cryptological Center: Employment cryptology in the national security scheme guide/tic security standard (ccn-stic-807), p. 60 (2012)
2. Singh, L.D.: Implementation of Text Encryption using Elliptic Curve Cryptography. ScienceDirect **54**, 73–82 (2015)
3. Elliptic curve Diffie Hellman (ECDH) with differing elliptic curves. https://asecuritysite.com/encryption/ecdh3. Accessed 4 Aug 2020
4. IMEPRVA. What is ISO/IEC 27001. https://www.imperva.com/learn/data-security/iso-27001/. Accessed 7 Jul 2020
5. Candel, J.M.: Seguridad en aplicaciones Web Java. RA-MA Editorial (2018)
6. Lochter, M.: Elliptic Curve Cryptography (ECC) Brainpool Standard Curves and Curve Generation. https://tools.ietf.org/html/rfc5639#section-2.1. Accessed 26 May 2020.
7. JavaTpoint: Spring Boot Architecture. https://www.javatpoint.com/spring-boot-architecture. Accessed 13 Apr 2020
8. Certicom Research: Recommended Elliptic Curve Domain Parameters, p. 51. Standards for Efficient Cryptography (SEC) (2000)
9. Reyard, O.: Text message encoding based on elliptic curve cryptography and a mapping methodology. Inf. Sci. Lett. Int. J. **7**, 7–11 (2018)
10. Svetlin Nakov, P.: ECDH Key Exchange. https://cryptobook.nakov.com/asymmetric-key-ciphers/ecdh-key-exchange. Accessed 21 Apr 2020
11. Harinath, D.: Enhancing Data Security Using Elliptic Curve. Int. J. Sci. Res. **5**, 1884–1890 (2015)
12. Polanco, R.: Algoritmos Basicos Para La Multiplicacion De Puntos En Una Curva Eliptica. Investigacion e Innovación en Ingenierias **2** (2014). https://doi.org/10.17081/invinno.2.1.2057

Adenovirus for Detection of Fecal Pollution in Santa Clara River, Rumiñahui - Ecuador

Berenice Sarmiento[1,2], Alma Koch[1,2,3], Dario Bolaños[1,4,5],
and Andres Izquierdo[1,2,3,5(✉)]

[1] Universidad de las Fuerzas Armadas - ESPE, Sangolquí, Ecuador
[2] Departamento de Ciencias de la Vida y la Agricultura, ESPE, Sangolquí, Ecuador
[3] Grupo de Investigación en Microbiología y Ambiente (GIMA), ESPE,
Sangolquí, Ecuador
[4] Departamento de Ciencias de la Tierra y la Construcción, ESPE,
Sangolquí, Ecuador
[5] Centro de Nanociencia y Nanotecnología (CENCINAT), ESPE, Sangolquí, Ecuador
arizquierdo@espe.edu.ec

Abstract. River water quality is affected by wastewater discharged and the lack of treatment plants. Contaminants include high organic loads and fecal microorganisms that may be a risk to human and animal health. Adenoviruses (AdV) are an appropriate indicator of viral contamination in water bodies due to its stability, persistence and resistance to UV light. Santa Clara River crosses Valley of the Chillos in Rumiñahui, as well as four other rivers, supporting domestic discharges, accumulation of garbage and waste. The objective of this research was to evaluate the presence of AdV as indicators of water contamination. Three water samples from Santa Clara River were taken, and molecular and bioinformatics techniques were used to identify AdV. Human AdV, serotypes 41 and 31 related to gastrointestinal diseases were found as well as porcine AdV 5, which is associated to diarrheal and respiratory diseases; and murine AdV 2, which can be asymptomatic. All these viruses are transmitted via fecal-oral route. Biochemical oxygen demand test was also performed. Results confirmed the pollution of Santa Clara River. The identification of four adenovirus species suggests fecal contamination by human and animal feces.

Keywords: Enteric viruses · Fecal pollution · Wastewater

1 Introduction

Fresh water quality has become a serious concern for costumers and researchers worldwide. The pollution by wastewater from anthropogenic activities affects ecosystems, biodiversity and human health. Projection studies suggests that in

Supported by Universidad de las Fuerzas Armadas - ESPE.

2050, the number of people affected for water pollution will be around 2.5 billion, because of increased population, livestock and sewage discharge in rivers [1,2]. Wastewater accumulates significant numbers of human and animal microbial pathogens. From 1.5 to 12 billion population around the world, pass away each year by diseases transmitted via contaminated waters. In most cases, the infectious agents have not been identified but it is suggested that these outbreaks are due to viruses [3]. The diversity and abundance of pathogenic viruses in sewage and rivers reflect the trend of infectious diseases in humans [4,5]. Urgent measures are required to ensure the quality of fresh water sources for future generations.

In industrialized countries like USA., Spain and the United Kingdom, prevalence of infectious virus in environment has been related with the discharge of wastewater in fresh water sources, leaks in septic systems, agricultural and urban runoff [4,6]. In Latin America, sewerage coverage is low, causing microbial contamination of water and increasing population diseases [7]. In Ecuador, basic sanitation coverage was 86% in 2010, but sewage treatment was less than 20% [8,9]. Rumiñahui is an inhabited zone of Pichincha province, in Ecuador (Fig. 1), its sewerage coverage is about 92%. However, most wastewater is discharged in river water [10]. Therefore, is important to diagnose rivers status, evaluating the presence or absence of contaminants.

Adenoviruses (AdV) are considered as one of the most numerous enteric viruses in water. These viruses are an appropriate indicator of viral contamination. AdV are resistant to ultraviolet light; if damaged, they use the host repair mechanisms to fix their DNA. Also, AdV can be used to differentiate animal from human contamination, they have a prevalent association with wastewater, and are resistant to some of the treatment processes [11–14].

AdV belong to Adenoviridae family, Mastadenoviridae genus, non-enveloped, icosahedral and medium sized (60–90 nm) viruses. There are 52 human AdV (HAdV) classified into seven groups (A-G) according to biochemical, biophysical, immunotypic and molecular criteria. There are five porcine (PAdV) and three murine AdV (MAdV), both divided in three groups (A-C). They have a double stranded, linear and non-segmented DNA genome [15–18]. AdV are most commonly transmitted through fecal-oral route. HAdV are responsible for multiple diseases, such as gastroenteritis, conjunctivitis, meningoencephalitis, and respiratory illness. In infected people, the concentration of HAdV in stool is around 10^2 to 10^{11} copies per gram [3,18]. PAdV and MAdV do not normally produce clinically severe pathologies [19,20].

The purpose of this study was to identify, by molecular and bioinformatic techniques, animal and human AdV in water samples collected in Santa Clara river (Rumiñahui) and correlated it with fecal pollution. In Ecuador, HAdV serotypes 40 and 41 have been reported in two urban rivers that receive the main discharges from Quito city [21]. There are currently no studies about AdV presence in rivers water of Rumiñahui.

2   Materials and Methods

2.1   Water Samples

In June 2019, in dry season, 12 L of water were taken in three points along Santa Clara River, aimed to be representative of north (P1), center (P2), and south (P3) of urban area in Sangolquí city (see Fig. 1). Each sample was harvested in a sterile bucket. An aliquot of 1 L was taken from each sample site for BOD test (standard method: APHA 5210 B), which was performed in an external laboratory. Water samples were left to settle for two hours, then 10 L of clean water were transferred to a new bucket and kept at 4 °C until the viral particles were concentrated.

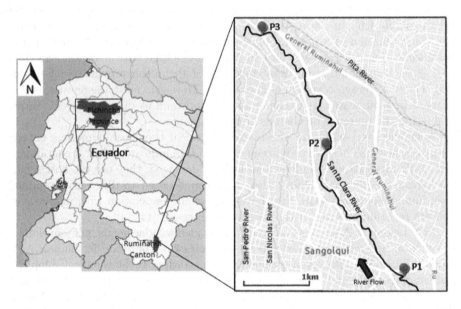

Fig. 1. Sampling locations along Santa Clara river. Coordinates: P1, 0°20'04.0"S 78°26'16.6"W; P2, 0°19'06.6"S 78°26'54.9"W; P3, 0°18'12.4"S 78°27'25.2"W.

2.2   Concentration and Viral DNA Extraction

The viral concentration was performed according Calgua et al. [4] methodology. Briefly, water samples were carefully acidified to pH 3.5 by adding HCl 1N. Then, a solution of skimmed-milk 1% in artificial seawater was added. Samples were stirred for 10 h, and the flocs were settled by gravity for 10 h. Then flocs were concentrated by centrifugation at 4000 rpm for 80 min at 4 °C. Supernatant was removed. The pellet was dissolved in phosphate buffer (pH 7.5), subsequently stored at 4 °C. Extraction of DNA was performed with PowerSoil DNA Isolation Kit (MO BIO Laboratories Inc.), using kit instructions. DNA extracts were eluted in ultrapure water and stored at 4 °C.

2.3   Nested PCR

Nucleic acid extractions were used to detect animal and human AdV as an indicator of fecal pollution [22]. Specific oligonucleotides used in this study were designed by Allard, et al. [23] for HAdV and Maluquer, et al. [19] for PAdV.

Detailed primers sets sequences are in Table 1. Nested PCR was performed in a 25 µL final volume including DreamTaq Green PCR Master Mix (Thermo-Scientific), each primer at a final concentration of 0.2 µM, and 0.4 g/µL of DNA extract. For nested reaction, 3 µL of PCR product obtained in the first reaction, were used in the master mix.

Table 1. Primers used in nested PCR.

Region	Primer	Reaction	Sequence, 5'–3'	bp	Reference
Human	Hex1deg	First left	GCCSCARTGGKCWTACATGCACATC	301	[23]
hexon	Hex2deg	First right	CAGCACSCCICGRATGTCAAA		
protein	Hex3deg	Nested left	GCCCGYGCMACIGAIACSTACTTC	171	
	Hex4deg	Nested right	CCYACRGCCAGIGTRWAICGMRCYTTGTA		
Porcine	PARF	First left	CACGGAGGAGTCRAACTGGATG	612	[19]
hexon	PALF	First right	GATGTCATGGAYAACGTCAAC		
protein	PARN	Nested left	GGAATGGAGATGGGCAGGTT	344	
	PALN	Nested right	TACTGCMAGTTYCACATCCAGGT		

PCR conditions (see Table 2 and 3) were modified from previous studies [20,24]. Amplicons were run in a 2% agarose gel stained with ethidium bromide.

Table 2. PCR conditions for HAdV primers.

Step	Temperature	Time	Cycles
Initial denaturation	95 °C	3 min	1
Denaturation	95 °C	30 s	40
Annealing	56 °C	30 s	
Extension	72 °C	30 s	
Final extension	72 °C	5 min	1

During the study, no AdV strains were available to be used as a positive control. Therefore, trials were optimized using amplified fragments previously, obtained from river water samples.

Table 3. PCR conditions for PAdV primers.

Step	Temperature	Time	Cycles
Initial denaturation	94 °C	3 min	1
Denaturation	92 °C	30 s	35
Annealing	54 °C*	30 s	
Extension	72 °C	1 min	
Final extension	72 °C	5 min	1

* For nested reaction, annealing temperature will change to 57 °C

2.4   Sanger Sequencing and Bioinformatic Analysis

Amplicons were sent for Sanger sequencing to Macrogen Inc. (Korea). Sequences obtained were compared in a database (GenBank) by using BLAST program of the NBCI (National Center of Biotechnology Information). Alignments were performed in Mega 7 program. Phylogenetic analysis was developed with maximum likelihood method based on Tamura-Ney model for nucleotide substitution.

3   Results and Discussion

3.1   BOD Analysis

Biochemical oxygen demand (BOD) is commonly used to know the amount of organic matter in a river [24]. According to Ecuadorian normative for aquatic life preservation, BOD should not exceed 20 mg/L in rivers [25]. For this analysis, the results were, in mg/L: 82.6 (P1), 5.3 (P2) and 5.9 (P3). In P2 and P3 the organic load is lower than P1; presumably because the pollutants biodegraded due to river's self-cleaning ability. Santa Clara flows into the San Pedro River that in 2015 showed BOD values between 18.5 and 33.5 were reported [26].

However, the pollution problem is not only in Rumiñahui; in Quito, rivers receive the fecal waters from 93% of the city without any treatment [21]. Therefore, wastewaters should be treated before discharging them into rivers, to comply with the environmental regulations and preserve the water quality.

3.2   Adenovirus Identification

Human Adenoviruses. HAdV were detected in the three sampling points. According to BLAST analysis, two serotypes were identified, 31 and 41 (see Table 4). HAdV-41 is the second main cause of childhood gastroenteritis in the world [11]. In Turkey, 64% of childhood gastroenteritis cases were caused by this virus [27], but in Latin America, it has low incidence. In Brazil, only 2.5% of diarrhea cases were produced by HAdV-41 [28]; while, in Colombia, 3% of acute gastroenteritis in children until five years old, was attributed to HAdV [29].

HAdV-31 is strongly involved in pathological adipogenesis, triglyceride synthesis, and lipid accumulation. Also, it could be associated with obesity [30].

Table 4. Adenoviruses identified in Santa Clara river.

Sampling point	Specie - serotype	Nucleotide homology, %	Amino acid homology, %
P1	Human adenovirus 31	95	74
	Murine adenovirus 2	85	100
P2	Human adenovirus 41	100	100
	Porcine adenovirus 5	100	89
	Murine adenovirus 2	86	96
P3	Human adenovirus 41	100	100
	Porcine adenovirus 5	98	100

The presence of this HAdV in Santa Clara river suggests health problems in population upstream and around the sampling points, and suppose a risk for people living downstream of the river. Fecal contamination is due to wastewater discharged into the water. In addition, SARS-CoV2 was also identified in Quito rivers, despite transmission of COVID-19 is mainly airborne; recent studies suggest that sewage is a potential health risk [31]. There are currently no studies about SARS-CoV2 presence in rivers water of Rumiñahui.

Animal Adenoviruses. Manure spills in rivers are an undervalued source of pollutants and potential zoonotic pathogens [32]. In Santa Clara river, PAdV were detected in P2 and P3, indicating that swine feces are constantly discharged into the water. The serotype identified was PAdV-5 by BLAST sequences analysis (see Table 4). It has been reported in rivers and slaughterhouse sewage samples in 2006 for the first time [33]. PAdV could remain at the spill site for 18 d and transported by river water at least 5.6 km downstream at the same time [32]. Although PAdV-5 is a low-grade pathogen, the possibility of disease in other pigs cannot be ruled out.

During the sampling, garbage bags and organic waste were observed on river banks, in P1. Waste disposed in illegal sites can supply a ready source of feed and habitat for rodents, promoting the spread of diseases, and environmental pollution [34]. Serotype 2 of murine AdV was detected in P1 y P2 (see Table 4).

The whole genome of the MAdV-2 was sequenced in 2011, and its only host is the domestic mouse (*Mus musculus*). The virus infect gastrointestinal tract and renal cells but is not mortal to the mice [20]. However, the presence of rodents in the river surroundings constitutes a risk for human health.

3.3 Phylogenetic Tree

AdV are usually host-specific. In consequence, they are used to differentiate sources of fecal contamination in aquatic environments [19,33,35]. To confirm the identity of the viruses detected in this study, a phylogenetic tree was built

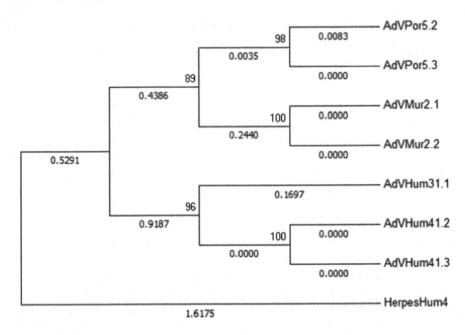

Fig. 2. Maximum likelihood phylogenetic tree. The number after the dot in each serotype represents the sampling point (P1, P2, P3). HerpesHum4: human herpesvirus serotype 4, used as outgroup. The phylogenetic distance is more than 10% between each one of the four serotypes identified.

(see Fig. 2). The conserved sequences of the capsid hexon protein gene were analyzed. This gene was recommended for the International Committee on Taxonomy of Viruses (ICTV) [36]. Human herpesvirus 4 (HerpesHum4, accession number DQ279927.1 from GenBank – NCBI) was used as outgroup to show the root of the tree. In the tree, numbers next to each node are between 89 and 100, representing a high measure of support for the node. The decimals indicate evolutionary distance between each branch.

MAdV-2 was identified according to BLAST analysis; however, no specific primers were used. Specificity (SP) and sensitivity (SE) tests have been performed on the nested PCR primer set for the detection of PAdV in human, sheep, cattle and fowl (ducks, geese and swans) feces samples, giving an SE up to 87% and SP of 100%, but it has not been evaluated with murine samples [35]. In addition, SE decreases to 5% when using wastewater samples [33,35]. More studies are necessary to confirm the presence of MAdV in Santa Clara River.

4   Conclusion

Despite of its self-cleaning ability, Santa Clara river is contaminated. The presence of human and porcine AdV showed that human sewage and animal feces are discharged into the water. The possible presence of murine AdV is correlated with wrong waste disposal. This could be a higher risk factor for human and animal health. Identification of pathogenic viruses in rivers or sewage could be used in Ecuador to know the current infections in population and prevent disease outbreaks. People must become more responsible and governments must implement better waste management systems. Fresh water sources should be taken care to ensure its long-term quality.

AdV are useful to identify fecal pollution in water; however, multiple methods need to be studied and validated for water quality studies. Also, for AdV detection, there are more advanced technologies like quantitative PCR [21] and reverse transcription PCR [31] that could be applied in Ecuador to diagnose the current state of the rivers and population health.

Acknowledgements. This study was developed with research funds from Universidad de las Fuerzas Armadas – ESPE and Grupo de Investigación en Microbiología y Ambiente (GIMA). We thank Francisco Flores Ph. D., microbiology and bioinformatic specialist. This study could not be possible without the support of the Center of Nanoscience and Nanotechnology (CENCINAT).

References

1. Wen, Y., Schoups, G., Van De Giesen, N.: Organic pollution of rivers: combined threats of urbanization, livestock farming and global climate change. Sci. Rep. **7**(43289), 1–9 (2017)
2. Dugan, P., Allison, E.H.: Water: act now to restore river health. Nature **468**(7321), 173 (2010)
3. Xagoraraki, I., O'Brien, E.: Wastewater-based epidemiology for early detection of viral outbreaks. In: O'Bannon, D.J. (ed.) Women in Water Quality. WES, pp. 75–97. Springer, Cham (2020). https://doi.org/10.1007/978-3-030-17819-2_5
4. Calgua, B., et al.: Detection and quantification of classic and emerging viruses by skimmed-milk flocculation and PCR in river water from two geographical areas. Water Res. **7**(47), 2797–2810 (2013)
5. Aizza, M., et al.: Viruses in wastewater: occurrence, abundance and detection methods. Sci. Total Environ. **745**(140910), 2797–2810 (2020)
6. Fong, T., Lipp, E.K.: Enteric viruses of humans and animals in aquatic environments: health risks, detection, and potential water quality assessment tools. Microbiol. Mol. Biol. Rev. **69**(2), 357–371 (2005)
7. UNEP: A Snapshot of the World's Water Quality: Towards a global assessment. United Nations Environment Programme, Nairobi, Kenya (2016)
8. WHO/UNICEF: Joint Monitoring Programme for Water Supply and Sanitation estimates for Ecuador (2010)
9. Rodriguez, H., Delgado, A., Nolasco, A., Saltiel, D., Gustavo, D.: From Waste to Resource: Shifting Paradigms for Smarter Wastewater Interventions in Latin America and the Caribbean. World Bank, Washington DC (2020)
10. Gobierno Municipal de Rumiñahui. Homepage. http://www.ruminahui.gob.ec. Accessed 5 Jan 2020
11. Rames, E., Roiko, A., Stratton, H., Macdonald, J.: Technical aspects of using human adenovirus as a viral water quality indicator. Water Res. **96**(2016), 308–326 (2016)

12. Jiang, S.: Human adenoviruses in water: occurrence and health implications: a critical review. Environ. Sci. Technol. **40**(23), 7132–7140 (2006)
13. Bofill-Mas, S., Rusiñol, M., Fernandez-Cassi, X., Carratalà, A., Hundesa, A., Girones, R.: Quantification of human and animal viruses to environmental samples. BioMed Res. Int. **2013**(192089), 1–11 (2013)
14. Ahmed, W., Goonetilleke, A., Gardner, T.: Human and bovine adenoviruses for the detection of source-specific fecal pollution in coastal waters in Australia. Water Res. **44**(16), 4662–4673 (2010)
15. Olalemi, A., Purnell, S., Caplin, J., Ebdon, J., Taylor, H.: The application of phage-based fecal pollution markers to predict the concentration of adenoviruses in mussels (Mytilus edulis) and their overlying waters. J. Appl. Microbiol. **121**(4), 1152–1162 (2016)
16. Benkö, M.: Adenoviruses: Pathogenesis. Elsevier Inc., Budapest (2015)
17. Iaconelli, M., et al.: Molecular characterization of human adenoviruses in urban wastewaters using next generation and Sanger sequencing. Water Res. **21**(2017), 240–247 (2017)
18. Jones, M., et al.: New adenovirus species found in a patient presenting with gastroenteritis. J. Virol. **81**(11), 5978–5984 (2007)
19. Maluquer, C., Clemente, P., Hundesa, A., Martín, M., Girones, R.: Detection of bovine and porcine adenoviruses for tracing the source of fecal contamination. Appl. Environ. Microbiol. **70**(3), 1448–1454 (2004)
20. Hemmi, S., et al.: Genomic and phylogenetic analyses of murine adenovirus 2. Virus Res. **160**(1–2), 128–135 (2011)
21. Guerrero-Latorre, L., et al.: Quito's virome: metagenomic analysis of viral diversity in urban streams of Ecuador's capital city. Sci. Total Environ. **645**(2018), 1334–1343 (2018)
22. Hernroth, B., Conden-Hanson, A., Rehnstam-Holm, A., Girones, R., Allard, A.: Environmental factors influencing human viral pathogens and their potential indicator organisms in the blue mussel, Mytilus edulis: the first Scandinavian report. Appl. Environ. Microbiol. **68**(9), 4523–4533 (2002)
23. Allard, A., Albinsson, B., Wadell, G.: Rapid typing of human adenoviruses by a general PCR combined with restriction endonuclease analysis. J. Clin. Microbiol. **39**(2), 498–505 (2001)
24. Vörösmarty, C., et al.: Global threats to human water security and river biodiversity. Nature **467**(7315), 555–561 (2010)
25. Ministerio del Ambiente de Ecuador: 097-A Refórmese el Texto Unificado de Legislación Secundaria. Registro Oficial. Año III - No 387, 6–78 Quito (2015)
26. Voloshenko-Rossin, A., et al.: Emerging pollutants in the Esmeraldas watershed in Ecuador: discharge and attenuation of emerging organic pollutants along the San Pedro-Guayllabamba-Esmeraldas rivers. Environ. Sci. Process. Impacts **17**(1), 41–53 (2015)
27. Colak, M., Bozdayi, G., Altay, A., Yalaki, Z., Ahmed, K., Ozkan, S.: Detection and molecular characterisation of adenovirus in children under 5 years old with diarrhoea. Turk. J. Med. Sci. **47**(5), 1463–1471 (2017)
28. Primo, D., Pacheco, G., Timenetsky, M., Luchs, A.: Surveillance and molecular characterization of human adenovirus in patients with acute gastroenteritis in the era of rotavirus vaccine, Brazil, 2012–2017. J. Clin. Virol. **109**, 35–40 (2018)
29. Farfán-García, A., et al.: Etiology of acute gastroenteritis among children less than 5 years of age in Bucaramanga, Colombia: a case-control study. PLoS Neglected Trop. Dis. **14**(6), e0008375 (2020)

30. Bil-Lula, I., Krzywonos-Zawadzka, A., Sawicki, G., Woźniak, M.: An infection of human adenovirus 31 affects the differentiation of preadipocytes into fat cells, its metabolic profile and fat accumulation. J. Med. Virol. **88**(3), 400–407 (2015)

31. Guerrero-Latorre, L., Ballesteros, I., Villacrés-Granda, I., Granda, M., Freire-Paspuel, B., Ríos-Touma, B.: SARS-CoV-2 in river water: implications in low sanitation countries. Sci. Total Environ. **743**, 140832 (2020)

32. Haack, S., et al.: Genes indicative of zoonotic and swine pathogens are persistent in stream water and sediment following a swine manure spill. Appl. Environ. Microbiol. **81**(10), 3430–3441 (2015)

33. Hundesa, A., Maluquer de Motes, C., Bofill-Mas, S., Albinana-Gimenez, N., Girones, R.: Identification of human and animal adenoviruses and polyomaviruses for determination of sources of fecal contamination in the environment. Appl. Environ. Microbiol. **72**(12), 7886–7893 (2006)

34. Duh, D., Hasic, S., Buzan, E.: The impact of illegal waste sites on a transmission of zoonotic viruses. Virol. J. **14**(1), 134 (2017)

35. Wong, K., Fong, T., Bibby, K., Molina, M.: Application of enteric viruses for fecal pollution source tracking in environmental waters. Environ. Int. **45**, 151–164 (2012)

36. Fauquet, C., Mayo, M., Maniloff, J., Desselberger, U., Ball, U.: Virus Taxonomy: Classification and Nomenclature of Viruses; 8th Report of the International Committee on Taxonomy of Viruses. Elsevier/Academic Press, New York (2005)

Technology Trends

Model for Supporting Decisions of Investors, Taking into Consideration Multifactoriality and Turnover

V. Lakhno[1] , V. Malyukov[1] , D. Kasatkin[1] , A. Blozva[1] , T. Zhyrova[2] ,
N. Kotenko[2(✉)], and M. Kotova[2]

[1] Department of Computer Systems and Networks, National University of Life and Environmental Sciences of Ukraine, Kyiv, Ukraine
{valss21,dm_kasat}@ukr.net, andriy.blozva@nubip.edu.ua
[2] Department of Software Engineering and Cybersecurity, Kyiv National University of Trade and Economics, Kyiv, Ukraine
{zhyrova,kotenkono,m.kotova}@knute.edu.ua

Abstract. This article describes a new analytical model for the mathematical support of decisions during the project's evaluation process. Smart City technology development projects are considered as an example of a subject area for investment. Unlike existing solutions, the new model considers the multifactorial nature of data sets. The consecutiveness of investors' steps in implementing their financial strategies was also taken into account. The model is focused on subsequent software implementation in intelligent cross-platform decision support systems. The proposed approach allows evaluating the attractiveness for investors (players) of the analyzed projects. Also, unlike the solutions previously proposed by the authors, the model considers situations in which players control a dynamic system in multidimensional project spaces. The results presented in the article were obtained based on the solution of a bilinear multistep quality game with several terminal sets. The scientific novelty of the work lies in the fact that, unlike existing solutions, this article considers a new class of bilinear multi-step games, which allows one to correctly and adequately describe investment processes, given the multifactorial nature of the problem statement. Thus, a solution for investors can be obtained analytically. The results of a computational experiment that were obtained using the prototype of decision support systems (DSS) module were described.

Keywords: Game theory · Investment strategies · Multidimensional case · Decision support system · Multistep sequential game · Bilinear equations

1 Introduction

Conceptual approaches related to the creation and development of the infrastructure of smart cities (hereinafter referred to as Smart City) were announced back in the early 2000s [1, 2]. Obviously, in order to maximize transform or adapt traditional cities (that is, cities we know today) into Smart City, it is necessary to maximize the full potential

© Springer Nature Switzerland AG 2021
M. Botto-Tobar et al. (Eds.): ICAT 2020, CCIS 1388, pp. 525–535, 2021.
https://doi.org/10.1007/978-3-030-71503-8_40

of information and communication technologies (ICT). Moreover, as many researchers note [3–6], advanced ICS are a key element for achieving the goals of such a transformation. And in addition, the use of modern ICT helps to solve other related tasks, such as improving public services, improving the efficiency and safety of the urban environment, improving urban logistics and population mobility, introducing energy-efficient and resource-saving technologies in energy and water supply systems and much more for [1, 3, 5, 6].

Currently, a large number of research initiatives to create a new Smart City and the process of improving existing ones are focused on the technical aspects of this task. Namely, technologies for the development of new touch devices, communication networks, storage and data processing systems, new cloud platforms capable of managing urban services, opening up great opportunities for companies in this sector.

However, we noted that all such innovative technologies and the ways of their implementation directly into Smart City systems require careful elaboration of financing strategies for potential investors. Many players in the investment market, including in Smart City systems and technologies, consider their ICT in the context of evaluating the uncertainty and riskiness of such financial investments. In [3, 4], the authors noted that, to increase the effectiveness and efficiency of evaluating such projects, it is advisable to use the potential of various computerized decision support systems (DSS). This problem is especially relevant for situations when several groups of investors interact in the investment market. Moreover, the interests of investors can be diametrically opposed [5–7].

The foregoing determines the relevance of the subject of our study. In terms of the need to develop new models for DSS for investing in large innovative solutions, which, of course, include Smart City ICT development projects. Such models, being implemented in the corresponding algorithmic and software development of DSS models, will reduce the discrepancy between forecasted data and the real return on investment in Smart City technologies.

Objectives of the article

– development of models for choosing rational strategies for investing by a group or groups of investors into the projects related to the implementation of ICT Smart City. Unlike the existing model, it is based on the solution of a bilinear multi-step sequential game of quality with several terminal surfaces;
– a computational experiment using the DSS software module in order to verify the model's operability, as well as its adequacy.

2 Literature Review

The relevance of the problem of increasing the efficiency of evaluating investment projects, including those related to Smart City, is evidenced by a significant number of publications on this topic. Within the scope of the article, we focused only on the analysis of publications conceptually close to the topic of our study. In [8–10], the authors showed that, relying only on traditional models and algorithms in calculating and optimizing investor options in such high-risk industries for investments as ICT, cybersecurity, Smart City, enterprise digitalization and the others, it is quite difficult to achieve an acceptable for an investor result. The models proposed by the authors, although allow one to obtain predictive assessments of investor actions, still leave many issues without due consideration. For example, in these models, the authors did not take into account the multifactorial nature of the investment process.

In [9–11], it was pointed out that for all their attractiveness, the hierarchy method (T. Saati method) [12] and expert methods [10, 11], widely used in DSS, in most cases are of little use for the synthesis of estimates so necessary for the investor. Almost all authors do not deeply touch on the multifactorial nature of the task of investing in ICT already mentioned above. It is also rare that any of the models considered in [7, 11, 12] mentions the fact that investors can act in a coordinated or non-coordinated manner. Or take action as part of an investment project in turn. As was shown in [7], this circumstance can be taken into account by applying game theory as a mathematical apparatus, namely, methods for solving bilinear multi-step quality games with several terminal surfaces.

Computer support for a decision making in evaluation of investment projects has also received sufficient attention in recent publications. For example, in [7, 9, 12], models for DSS were proposed that relate to the analysis and evaluation of investor strategies in the context of the actions of two parties (players). In accordance with [12], the general approach to the model is based on game theory. However, the models presented by the authors need to be developed, since not all of aspects of this problem are covered.

In works [1, 12], it was shown that investors in Smart City technologies can lobby in different areas of investment. For example, one group sees the development of urban logistics as promising. And the other gravitates to options for investing in security technologies. As mentioned above [7, 11], with respect to the type of problems under consideration, the most suitable for the logic that describes the behavior of a complex system are models based on game theory.

All of the factors above, in fact, determine our interest and the relevance of developing new models for DSS modules in investing in Smart City. At the same time, the ultimate goal will be the development of cross-platform DSS, which will be able to provide support for decision making procedures by a group or groups of investors who are in the search for rational investment strategies in the area of development of Smart City and taking into account multifactorial nature.

3   Methods and Models

3.1   Formulation of the Problem

Various approaches can be used to fill in the DSS of the model base (see Fig. 1). For example, as was shown above, T. Saati [12] hierarchy analysis method, models and methods of a game theory [7], discounting and compounding methods [9] and others are used to solve these problems.

Of course, to increase the reliability of estimates issued by DSS to potential investors, various methods can be combined, since each of them has both its advantages and disadvantages.

Let's assume that there are two investors (two groups can also be considered) for Smart City projects. From the point of view of the applying of the apparatus of game

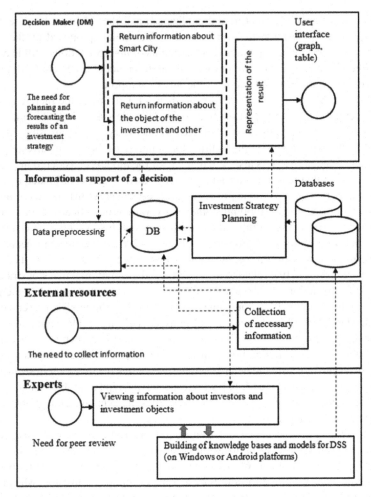

Fig. 1. Diagram of the decision-making process based on the proposed model

theory, hereinafter we are talking about players who control a dynamic system in multidimensional spaces. Let's also assume that the system controls the changes in the financial flows of players. In continuation of [7, 12], we describe the system using bilinear multistep equations. Moreover, in contrast to the cases that we previously examined, in [7, 12] in the framework of this article we speak of the dependent movements of the players and their successive steps. The task is to find many strategies of players. It is accepted U is the first player (or investor $Inv1$) and $V-$ second player (or investor $Inv2$). As in [7], we assume that terminal sets for players are given. That is, S_0 for the first player and F_0 for the second player. Players $Inv1$ and $Inv2$ are using their management strategies to try to bring a dynamic system to their terminal sets, regardless of how the opposite side acts. For example, you can imagine $Inv1$ as town council of Smart City, and $Inv2$ specific investor.

Then the goals of the players are rising to two tasks, the solution of which must be found from the point of view of the first ally player and from the point of view of the second ally player [12].

3.2 Addressing Tasks

As a methodology for solving the problem, we used the basic principles of game theory [7, 12].

This article considers only the solution to the problem from the point of view of the first ally player. This is justified by the fact that the solution to the second problem is absolutely similar to the first [7].

Let's assume that in order to solve the problem we need the following:

1) at the time instant $t = 0$ of *Inv*1 has a set of $h(0) = (h_1(0), ..., h_n(0))$, consisting of n components. Components $h_j(0)$ characterize the amount of financial resources (hereinafter *FinR*) for the development of $j - s$ new technology for Smart City;
2) In $t = 0$ we also have a set $f(0) = (f_1(0), ..., f_n(0))$ $f_i(0)$ for *Inv*2. This vector also consists on n components characterizing *FinR* aimed *Inv*2 at the development of $j - s$ Smart City technology.

Sets of $h(0)$ and $f(0)$ define the forecast, at the moment $t = 0$ of value *FinR* for *Inv*1 and *Inv*2. Unlike previous models which were proposed in [7, 12], multifactoriality in sets is taken into account.

Of course, players should interact in a process of the investment. As mentioned above, we will describe the interaction of players as a bilinear multi-step game with alternate moves and complete information.

We assume that at even times turns are made by *Inv*1 and at the odd – *Inv*2.

Let's say $t = 2 \cdot n$ and $h(t), h(t + 1)$ states of *Inv*1 at the times of $t, t + 1$. And $f(t), f(t + 1)$ – states of *Inv*2 at times $t, t + 1$. Then their states at the moments $t + 1$ and $t + 2$ are determined from the relations:

$$h(t + 1) = B_1 \times h(t) - U(t) \times B_1 \times h(t), f(t + 1)$$
$$= f(t) - S_1 \times U(t) \times B_1 \times h(t); \tag{1}$$

$$f(t + 2) = B_2 \times f(t + 1) - V(t) \times B_2 \times f(t + 1), h(t + 2)$$
$$= h(t + 1) - S_2 \times V(t + 1) \times B_2 \times f(t + 1); \tag{2}$$

where B_1, S_1, B_2, S_2 – are square matrices of order n with positive elements; $U(t), V(t + 1)$– diagonal matrices with positive elements $u_i(t) \in [0, 1]$, $v_j(t) \in [0, 1]$, respectively, on the diagonals.

Let's assume that

$$S_0 = \bigcup_{i=1}^{n} \{(h, f) : (h, f) \in R^{2n}, h \geq 0, \quad f_i < 0\}, \tag{3}$$

$$F_0 = \bigcup_{i=1}^{n} \{(h, f) : (h, f) \in R^{2n}, f \geq 0, h_i < 0\} \tag{4}$$

Where S_0, F_0 are the terminal sets for $Inv1$ and $Inv2$, respectively;
$R^{2 \cdot n} - 2 \cdot n$ dimensional extent.
The interaction of $Inv1$ and $Inv2$ will end if the following conditions are met:

$$(h(t),\ f(t)) \in F_0, t - odd, \tag{5}$$

$$(h(t),\ f(t)) \in F_0, t - even. \tag{6}$$

If the conditions (5) or (6) are met, we respectively assume that $Inv1$ and $Inv2$ do not have enough funds to continue financing procedures. If both conditions (5) and (6) are not met, we believe that the financing procedures will continue.

The solution to problem 1 is to find the sets of preferences of $Inv1$, as well as their optimal strategies. Similarly, for $Inv1$.

Let's introduce the following notation. $R^0 = S_1 \times B_1, Q^0 = E(unit\,matrix)$,

$$R^{n+1} = R^n \times B_1 + \{-R^n + [(R^n \times S_2)^+ + Q^n] \times B_2 \times S_1\}^+ \times B_1,$$

$$Q^{n+1} = [(R^n \times S_2 - Q^n)^+ + Q^n] \times B_2; L^0 = E, M^0 = S_2 \times B_2;$$

$$L^0(t_0) = L^0 \times B_1 + (M^0 \times S_1 - L^0) \times U(t_0) \times B_1, M^0(t_0) = M^0; t_0 = 0, 2, \ldots$$

$$M^0(0, 2) = M^0(2) \times B_2 + (L^0(2) \times S_2 - M^0(2))^+ \times B_2, L^2(0, 2) =$$

$$L^0(2) \times B_1 + (-L^0(2) + M^0(0, 2) \times S_1)^+ \times U(0) \times B_1,$$

$$M^{2k}(t_0, \ldots, t_k) = M^{2k-2}(t_1, \ldots, t_k) \times B_2 + (L^{2k-2}(t_1, \ldots, t_k) \times S_2$$

$$- M^{2k-2}(t_1, \ldots, t_k))^+ \times B_2,$$

$$L^{2k}(t_0, \ldots, t_k) = L^{2k-2}(t_1, \ldots, t_k) \times B_1 + (-L^{2k-2}(t_1, \ldots, t_k)$$

$$+ M^{2k}(t_1, \ldots, t_k) \times S_1)^+ \times U(t_0) \times B_1,$$

Here $t_0, \ldots, t_k$ - are even numbers in ascending order,

$$t_0 = 0,\ t_i \le 2k,\ i = 0, \ldots, k. \quad (\ll + \gg positive\ orthant)$$

The optimality equations of the first player are written as following:

$$W_1 = \bigcup_{T=1}^{\infty} W_1^T ; T = 1, \ldots, 2k + 1.$$

Where?

$$W_1^T = \bigcup_{i=1}^{n} (W_1^T)_i,$$

$(W_1^T)_i = \{(h(0), f(0)) : (h(0), f(0)) \in R_+^{2n}, [R^k \times h(0)]_i$
$> [Q^k \times f(0)]_i, L^0(0) \times h(0) \ge M^0(0) \times f(0), \ldots, L^{2k}(0, \ldots, 2k) \times h(0)$

$$\ge M^{2k}(0, \ldots, 2k) \times f(0); \}\backslash \bigcup_{j=1}^{T-2} W_1^j;$$

R_+^{2n} – is the «+» positive orthant of a $2n$– dimensional extent.

$$W_1^1 = \bigcup_{i=1}^{n} (W_1^1)_i,$$

$$(W_1^1)_i = \{(h(0), f(0)) : (h(0), f(0)) \in R_+^{2n}, [R^0 \times h(0)]_i > [Q^0 \times f(0)]_i\}.$$

Let's write optimal strategy as follows. Since optimality sets are the union of optimality sets $W_1^1 = \bigcup_{i=1}^{n} (W_1^1)_i$, then, when constructing the set $(W_1^T)_i$, each time its own optimal strategy for the first player is determined. Let's write it down. It is a diagonal matrix with the following diagonal elements:

$$u_i^j = 1, for\{-R^k + [(R^k \times S_2 - Q^k)^+ + Q^k] \times B_2 \times S_1\}_{ij} \succ 0; \ and \ 0,$$

$$otherwise; j = 1, \dots, n.$$

The following circumstance should be noted. When constructing the optimality equations $(W_1^T)_i$, we used the notation L and M, in the recording of which the record of the strategy U of the first player "participated". For these optimality sets to be constructed, it is necessary to substitute the optimal strategy, which was defined above, in the entries L and M.

4 Computational Experiment

A computational experiment was carried out using a software product written in C #. This software is essentially a prototype module for the development of DSS for the tasks of choosing rational strategies for investors in Smart City projects.

In Fig. 2, 3 and 4 shown the results for 3 – test calculations in computational experiment. On the axis – financial resources of 1 player. Axis – financial resources of 2 players. The area under the beam is (the area of "preference" of the first player). The area above the beam is (the area of "preference" of the second player).

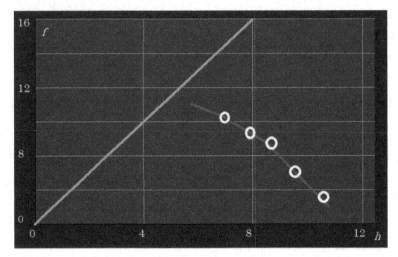

Fig. 2. Results of a computational experiment 1

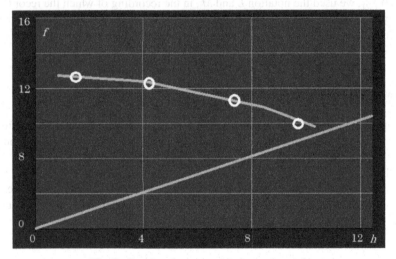

Fig. 3. Results of computational experiment 2

5 Discussion

5.1 Discussion of the Results of Computational Experiments

The calculation results were carried out for the case when investors control the distribution of finances, provided that multifactoriality is aggregated into one factor. In this case, the problem is solved with all the ratios of the game parameters.

Figure 1 is situation 1. This corresponds to the case where Inv1 has an advantage in the ratio of the initial *FinR*. That is, *FinR* are in a set of preference of *Inv1*. Then, Inv1 using his optimal strategy, will bring the systems to their "own" terminal surface.

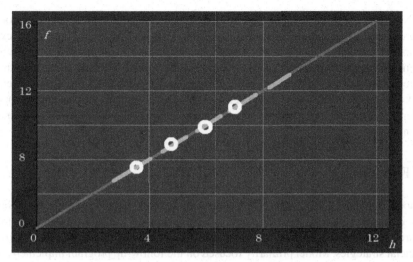

Fig. 4. Results of a computational experiment 3

Figure 2 is situation 2. This corresponds to the case when *Inv2* "brings" the state of the system to their "own" terminal surface.

Figure 3 is situation 3. A situation in which the initial state of the system is on the beam of balance. Players using their optimal strategies "move" on the line of that "satisfies" simultaneously both Inv1and *Inv2*. Therefore, this situation illustrates the "stability" of the system. We need to note, that with small deviations when choosing the implementation of the optimal strategy for *Inv*1 (see the dashed line), they will achieve their goal, but somewhat later.

The results obtained during computational experiments demonstrate the correctness of the proposed model.

Computational experiments were carried out on a computer with an i5 processor. The number of options for investment projects analyzed to choose the optimal strategy for a group of investors ranged from 5 to 9.

5.2 Prospects for Further Research

The disadvantage of the model is that the data obtained with the help of DSS, for a predictive assessment when choosing a particular development strategy for investment projects in the field of development of Smart City, will not always coincide with the actual data. However, at this stage of research, this is normal because only the model and prototype DSS has been tested. At its successful testing and confirmation of the correctness on a few real projects, a suitable second version of software product will be implemented in the form of a decision support system for groups of investors.

Based on the analysis of the results obtained using other models, for example, described in [8, 12], we can say that the proposed solution improves the efficiency and predictability for the investor by an average of 7–12%. This result was obtained by comparing the data with the results of real investment projects in Smart City technology in the city of Kiev in 2017–2018.

Note that the proposed model in most cases quite accurately describes the process of predicting the results of investment in Smart City technologies. The drawback of the model revealed in the course of testing the evaluation of real investment projects in practice is the fact that the obtained forecast evaluation data when choosing investment strategies for groups of investors did not always coincide with the actual data. Currently, work on improving the model and related software continues. In particular, work is underway to create the possibility of online modeling based on the created web service for investors.

6 Findings

A model for mathematical support of solutions during the evaluation of projects for Smart City is proposed. Unlike existing solutions, the new model considers the multifactorial nature of data sets, as well as the sequence of steps investors take to implement their financial strategies. Model primarily focused on the follow-up program implementation in intellectualized cross-platform systems for a decision support (DSS). The model allows to evaluate the attractiveness of the analyzed projects for investors (players) as part of the development of complex dynamic systems, which, for example, include Smart City. Also, unlike the solutions previously given by the authors, the model considers situations in which players control a dynamic system in multidimensional project spaces. As an example of the applied scope of the model, investment projects for Smart City were considered. The results obtained and the mathematical calculations presented in the article are obtained on the basis of the solution of a bilinear multistep quality game with several terminal sets. The scientific novelty of the work lies in the fact that, in contrast to existing solutions and conceptually close researches, the article considers a new class of multi-step bilinear games. The proposed approach and the resulting solution for the search for a multitude of players' preferences allows us to correctly and adequately describe the investment processes, given the multifactorial nature of the problem statement; the results of a computational experiment that were obtained using the prototype module of DSS are described. This module is designed to search for optimal financial investment strategies. With the results of a computational experiment, as well as with a comparative analysis with other models in this research segment, confirmed the correctness and adequacy of the results.

References

1. Pellicer, S., Santa, G., Bleda, A.L., Maestre, R., Jara, A.J., Skarmeta, A.G.: A global perspective of smart cities: a survey. In: 2013 Seventh International Conference on Innovative Mobile and Internet Services in Ubiquitous Computing, pp. 439–444 (2013)
2. Vanolo, A.: Smartmentality: the smart city as disciplinary strategy. Urban Stud. **51**(5), 883–898 (2014)
3. Albino, V., Berardi, U., Dangelico, R.M.: Smart cities: definitions, dimensions, performance, and initiatives. J. Urban Technol. **22**(1), 3–21 (2015)
4. Angelidou, M.: Smart cities: a conjuncture of four forces. Cities **47**, 95–106 (2015)
5. Glasmeier, A., Susan, C.: Thinking about smart cities, pp. 3–12 (2015)

6. Zanella, A., Bui, N., Castellani, A., Vangelista, L., Zorzi, M.: Internet of things for smart cities. IEEE Internet Things J. **1**(1), 22–32 (2014)
7. Valeriy, L., Volodymyr, M., Olena, K., Mykola, T., Alyona, D., Tetyana, M.: Model of evaluating smart city projects by groups of investors using a multifactorial approach. In: Botto-Tobar, M., Zambrano Vizuete, M., Torres-Carrión, P., Montes León, S., Pizarro Vásquez, G., Durakovic, B. (eds.) ICAT 2019. CCIS, vol. 1193, pp. 13–26. Springer, Cham (2020). https://doi.org/10.1007/978-3-030-42517-3_2
8. Paroutis, S., Bennett, M., Heracleous, L.: A strategic view on smart city technology: the case of IBM smarter cities during a recession. Technol. Forecast. Soc. Chang. **89**, 262–272 (2014)
9. Hollands, R.G.: Critical interventions into the corporate smart city. Camb. J. Reg. Econ. Soc. **8**(1), 61–77 (2015)
10. Tereikovskyi, I., Mussiraliyeva, S., Kosyuk, Y., Bolatbek, M., Tereikovska, L: An experimental investigation of infrasound influence hard drives of a computer system. Int. J. Civil Eng. Technol. **9**(6), 1558–1566 (2018)
11. Dychka, I., Chernyshev, D., Tereikovskyi, I., Tereikovska, L., Pogorelov, V.: Malware detection using artificial neural networks. In: Advances in Intelligent Systems and Computing, vol. 938, pp. 3–12. Springer, Cham (2020).https://doi.org/10.1007/978-3-030-16621-2_1
12. Akhmetov, B., Balgabayeva, L., Lakhno, V., Malyukov, V., Alenova, R., Tashimova, A.: Mobile platform for decision support system during mutual continuous investment in technology for smart city. In: Dolinina, O., Brovko, A., Pechenkin, V., Lvov, A., Zhmud, V., Kreinovich, V. (eds.) ICIT 2019. SSDC, vol. 199, pp. 731–742. Springer, Cham (2019). https://doi.org/10.1007/978-3-030-12072-6_59

A Case Study in the Banking Sector: An Ontology for the Selection of Agile and Lean Software Development Methodologies

Itza Morales⬤, Belén Bonilla-Morales⬤, and Miguel Vargas-Lombardo$^{(\boxtimes)}$ ⬤

FISC, Research Group GISES, Technological University of Panama, Panama City, Panama
{itza.morales1,belen.bonilla,miguel.vargas}@utp.ac.pa

Abstract. Nowadays, the application of methodologies that allow to guide the process of development of Software in the companies has become a fundamental aspect to achieve the suitable management of the processes in the projects. In view of the diversity of existing methodologies, there is a growing interest in defining strategies that allow the selection and application of the correct methodology, which adjusts to the characteristics of the work teams and the software projects. The aim of this work is to develop an ontology for the selection of the methodology that, according to its principles, is most appropriate and beneficial for the development of software projects. The domain of ontology is limited to the Agile and Lean approaches, without defining for Agile the specific method that it applies, but it involves any method that is governed by the agile values and principles established in the Agile manifesto. Onto-logy is applied in two organizations in the banking sector, allowing recommendations to be inferred for the use of Agile methodology in both, which will make it possible to reduce the delivery time of software products, improve communication between project participants, and facilitate the engineering of requirements. On the other hand, the ontology suggests co-regulating characteristic aspects of the Lean practices in order to minimize costs, optimize processes in the software projects and improve the organizational culture.

Keywords: Ontology · Agile software development · Lean software development · Methodologies · Risks

1 Introduction

In the field of software engineering, a growing advance has been perceived in research on methodologies and good practices of software development, which allows the efficient management and optimization of processes and resources, reduces conflicts in the assignment of routines and knowledge of the complexity of the projects [1, 2]. In this context, software development methodologies such as Agile and Lean are implemented depending on the characteristics of an organization. In fact, the authors in [3–5] discuss that the Agile methodology emerged in 2001 as an "Agile Manifesto" focused on reducing the concern about the inefficiency of iterative cycles, customer feedback, workflow

© Springer Nature Switzerland AG 2021
M. Botto-Tobar et al. (Eds.): ICAT 2020, CCIS 1388, pp. 536–551, 2021.
https://doi.org/10.1007/978-3-030-71503-8_41

visualization, which led to the evaluation of new practices to establish principles for the correct manufacturing of software products.

However, Agile was aimed at small working groups, so a new "Lean" concept was introduced. It was firstly aimed at the industrial sector and then adopted, and parameters were established to enable organizations to scale up in the software product market focusing on three bases: design thinking, Lean production, and Agile development; This reduces the waste of unnecessary processes and increases the organizational culture within the team [19, 21].

Indeed, the Agile and Lean methods have made it possible to examine aspects and factors involved in the analysis prior to the selection of methodologies. To support this approach, ontologies are constructed. They include a common and unambiguous vocabulary for a given domain. In the context of software development, their use provides organizations with an adjustment to the extent of validating their implementation because they are generally selected and adopted incorrectly due to ignorance of their principles, implying delay in the management of processes in software projects. In this sense, studies [18, 36] they emphasize that there are different ontologies focused on evaluating the Software development cycle, the processes or the communication between those involved, for the development of Agile Software and for Software development in general. Likewise, recent studies include ontologies for Agile software development methodology, but not for Lean and/or the link between the two in the Software life cycle processes and within the work team.

Therefore, the need arises for an ontology aimed at the selection of Agile or Lean Software development methodologies in the banking sector, which responds to the analysis of aspects of these two approaches. This research considers the characteristics and requirements of the methodologies for the construction of an ontology with the information supplied from the two banking organizations in Panama. In this way, the study provides organizations with a recommendation on the type of methodology to be selected for their software department and indicates the risks or points to be improved.

The general structure of this study includes: Sect. 2 presents the background that covers the Agile and/or Lean Software development methodologies; Sect. 3 describes the proposed Ontology (development and construction); Sect. 4 presents results; Sect. 5 the discussion and Sect. 6 the conclusions and future work.

2 Background

In organizations, it is essential to consolidate a stable organizational environment, and effectiveness in the delivery of the Software product. In this context, the studies related to Agile/Lean software development methodologies in organizations include characteristic aspects, advantages and risks present during the software product development cycle. Likewise, the approach of Agile and Lean are based on continuous integration and design focused on user feedback [8, 11, 29]. Indeed, Agile and Lean are related to the variables of requirements, productivity, process, and communication between team members. In addition, the authors at [2, 5, 15, 24, 26, 29, 33, 39] mention that these parameters explain that there must be organizational culture to reduce inventory operating costs, and obtain a return on investment from the use of resources, contributing to the flow of quality, and maximizing customer value. Therefore, from the IEEE 1074–1995 standard to achieve the progress of a project, the monitoring, and control of the processes must be reviewed and measured; in addition, this standard assesses the background and risk analysis, contingency planning, project management, and the record-keeping [17]. In turn, Table 1 presents in detail the aspects of the Agile and Lean approaches that are involved in the software development process. It shows the main terms, and, according to both approaches, a description is provided.

Table 1. Descriptive aspects of the Agile and Lean approaches to software development

Terms	Description	References
Risks (Weak points or failures)		
- *Agile*	-Ignorance of principles, difference in communication (planning, development, and collaboration), and there is no operational difference in the performance of the team -Requirement requests, assignment and distribution of responsibilities	[6, 10, 11, 39]
- *Lean*	-Risk management involves the organizational disposition of the client and the team, by implementing a new way of working	[19, 25, 35]
Characteristics		
- *Agile*	- Evaluate the iterations between individuals, less time in documentation, collaboration with clients, and adaptability to changes - Set requirements and resource allocation	[4, 6, 12, 20, 28]
	-Number of people less than 7 per team -Flexibility, task distribution, functionality, execution quality, process evaluation and remote communication	[3, 5, 7, 9, 15, 16, 24, 26, 27, 29, 32, 40]

(*continued*)

Table 1. (*continued*)

Terms	Description	References
- *Lean*	-Making the assumptions before the requirements -Analytical and usability reports, information on previous attempts, stakeholder analysis, and competitive analysis -Use communication strategies (roles): use of a distributed design framework maintaining multiple prototypes in parallel, adaptability to media fidelity faced with the need for communication and employ agile use cases to line up the team -Value with a robust, flexible, and iterative approach in collaboration with Agile end users -Uses a feedback loop known as "build-measure-lean" that seeks to minimize the risk of the project and uses the client's comments -Tools for the automation of process flows and more people (8–15) per teams	[2, 11, 19, 21, 25, 29, 35]
Advantage		
- *Agile*	- Reduces collaboration and/or culture at a distance and temporary distance -Offers clients project progress as soon as possible and quality software	[5, 35]

(*continued*)

Table 1. (*continued*)

Terms	Description	References
- *Lean*	-Allows the identification and elimination of waste of those unnecessary processes, facilitates an enhancement in decision -Making in the work team to simplify development time and increase learning	[31, 39]

The information presented in Table 1 describes the key elements for both approaches (Agile and Lean) and offers an overview for the construction and development of ontology.

2.1 Ontological Language (OWL)

The ontological language [22] processed for years has been transferred to the evolution of applications in the areas of software engineering. Therefore, the ontologies developed in [7, 16, 32, 40] are implemented in the sub-parts of the DS in general, which include: collaboration, workflow, process evaluation, cooperative design, and remediation. In agreement with [22, 23], the ontologies developed to ensure the traceability of the requirements in the DSA; Whereas, in [38] consider the types of requirements and their options for evaluating the time and cost of entering the data on traceability, the difference between traceability, the existence of points of view of practical benefits, problems in the organization and support of trade trusts. On the other hand, the ontology for requirements allows giving an intelligence support guide of the techniques to be used and an evaluation of the quality metrics of the traceability requirements. In essence, for [14, 36] the ontologies developed in the DSA, are used as a medium to identify the changes between external clients and the SD equipment; allow permission to improve fundamental communication in the organization and the capacity to meet the requirements Meanwhile, the [1, 21, 34, 37] risk management is focused and these were classified by levels. In this context, according to [17] the IEEE 1074 standard provides that the types of risks involved in organizations can be processed or activities, where each process derives an activity in the development of the Software.

3   Material and Methods: Proposed Ontology

This section presents the construction of an ontology focused on the selection of software development methodologies (SDM) through language-semantic web axis (OWL). This facilitates the decision-making from the analysis of the domain knowledge and gives an answer to the problem [13, 30]. The synthesis of previous studies provides support for the construction of the ontology.

This allows you to use a specific vocabulary and domain to analyze the information from two organizations in the banking sector in Panama. It also provides you with a recommendation on the most appropriate one and draws conclusions on those aspects that need to be improved.

In this manner, the seven steps that the ontology to be built must include are presented. Figure 1 shows the classification of these in two stages: the first includes the description and definition of the domain and the second the construction and results of the ontology; shown in the following diagram:

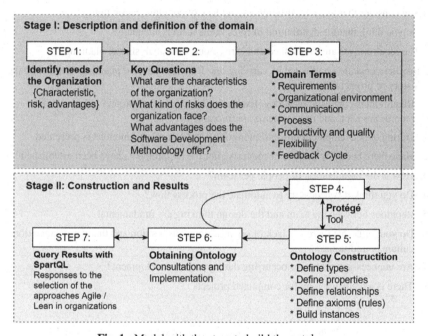

Fig. 1. Model with the steps to build the ontology

3.1 Description and Definition of the Domain

The first stage includes the description and definition of the domain, in which the identification of the organization's needs is presented with respect to the survey applied to the two Panamanian organizations in the banking sector. Likewise, Table 2 shows these 18 questions distributed as follow: questions 4 to 11 evaluate the Agile Software development methodology and from 11 to 18, the Lean approach.

Indeed, the information obtained from the two organizations was classified according to the key questions in Fig. 1; while, from these, the purpose of this study is answered through 5 research questions to classify the information. Thus, Table 3 presents an ID for each research question, discussed later in Sect. 5.

On the other hand, the results obtained from the mapping of terms, set out in Sect. 2, have been classified by the characteristics, risks and advantages of both approaches

Table 2. Survey to find out the existing level or situation of the organization

1. Is an MDS implemented in your department?
2. What kind of MDS is implemented in the Software department?
3. Do you know the benefits of applying SMD Agile or Lean?
4. Do you consider that there is a relationship between customers and the software development team?
5. Is there an organizational culture in the team?
6. You consider that there are differences and lack of communication in the team
7. Do you think that the distribution of roles in the team is adequate?
8. The requirements are established and carried out: Risk analysis and planning
9. Requirements are established by carrying out: Risk analysis and planning: Evaluating the history of project failure
10. Requirements are established by: Evaluating background of project failures: Project records are kept, and requirements are traceable
11. During the development process, monitoring and control of functions is presented
12. Have there been any failures of requests after the requirements have been established?
13. How is the organization of people per team?
14. Do you think it is necessary to automate the process flow?
15. Iterations between the team and the design thinking are fundamental
16. Do you think that there is a lack of organizational disposition and that the organizational culture is traditional?
17. Are unnecessary processes occurring during project development?
18. There is a feedback loop for completed projects

Table 3. Research questions (RQ) of ontology

ID	Research questions
RQ1	What is the scope of the ontology in the selection of Agile and Lean Software development methodologies?
RQ2	What are the most outstanding characteristics of the Agile and Lean methodologies to be inferred from the results of the ontology?
RQ3	What are the risks faced by the two banks?
RQ4	What can be inferred from the recommendation generated by the ontology?
RQ5	How can the risks and failures identified through the ontology be improved in the two banking organizations?

(Agile and Lean). Thus, the main terms to use are the following: requirements, organizational culture, communication, process, productivity and quality, flexibility, and feedback loop.

4 Results: Construction of the Ontology

This section presents the formal definition of the aspects with which the "Protégé" software tool works. Initially, a representative class diagram is defined for the ontology and the relations between them. Therefore, Fig. 2 shows the terms and their relations using the UML (Unified Modeling Language) representation of the ontology domain.

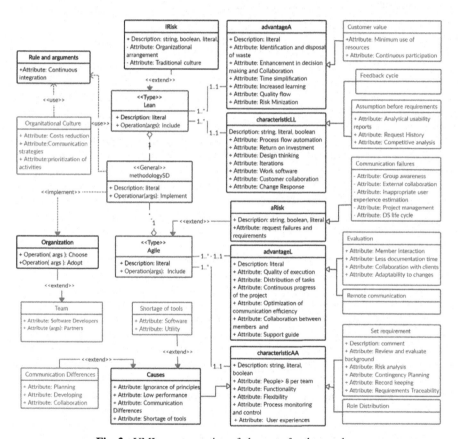

Fig. 2. UML representation of elements for the ontology

Therefore, for the ontology construction process, there are 8 named classes: methodology, risks and characteristics of Agile and Lean; recommendations, rule arguments and the organization with the subclass (teamwork).

Each of these classes constitutes the domain of the ontology, and its relations, restrictions, Object properties, Data properties and Data Types. In fact, all classes are bound to the base class < owl.Thing >, which contains the knowledge in which the information is analyzed. Thus, Fig. 3 shows the general scheme of the ontology. A short description is presented in a yellow box about the selected class and overview of the content in OWL.

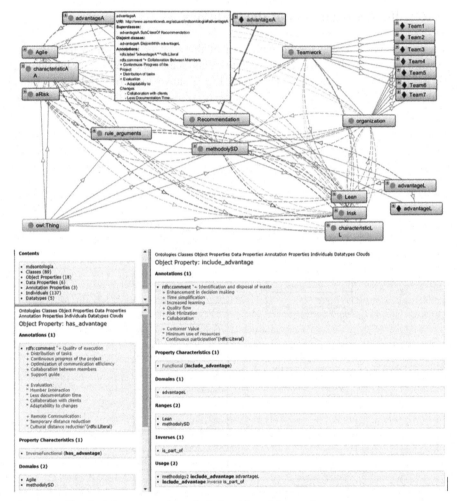

Fig. 3. Scheme overview of relationships of the ontology components.

5   Discussion

As an initial result of the survey, it states that 71% of teams use MDS while 29% it does not use them. Consequently, the 42.9% uses the Agile methodology, the 14.3% uses another type of alternative methodology, and the rest do not use any. This reveals that the Lean methodology is not used in the Software departments. On the other hand, the defined ontology analyzes theoretical knowledge through Individuals (organization's information) to generate the results through the verification queries; and using SPARQL Query check that each subject (subclass) would correspond to class (object), through the expression: SELECT? subject-object WHERE { ?subject rdfs: subClassOf?object}. For example, the logical reasoner HermiT, which incorporated Protégé, was used to analyze the entered knowledge. The analysis is implemented for 7 banking facilities. This presents in a visual way the inference by each team. Figure 4 presents two of the generated results (Left: organization 1; right: organization 2):

Fig. 4. Results for organization 1 and organization 2

From all the results inferred by the ontology, the information is synthesized in Table 4. This presents the organizations (teams), methodology to be used or maintained, as well as the suggestion of aspects to improve within the Software Development department. For its part, in the items (Name: Recommendation and fundamentals to improve) they are considered the most critical points for each organization; that is, the risks and characteristics whose level of acceptance are subject to immediate changes in the Software Development work process, and need to be improved and properly applied. Table 4 substantiates the information as follows:

The results provide conclusive support to the onto-logy proposal for the selection of the Agile or Lean methodology based on the questions. Thus, this synthesis of the information describes that organizations face challenges and risks where choosing the correct methodology becomes the greatest investment in terms of benefits for the work team and the use of resources. Therefore, the results described in this section allowed inferring in 5 questions to answer the ontology, which are discussed below:

RQ1: The proposal provided a solution window to these organizations through the knowledge inferred through the semantic web language (OWL) to consult and evaluate the profiles of the organizations before implementing a Software development methodology. In fact, the constructed ontology allows to know those weak points of the software development process and to suggest the type of methodology that should be selected. Thus, if it is implemented by the team, to indicate the aspects that represent a risk factor in its development process.

RQ2: In perspective to the scope of the ontology, it is important to highlight that the focus of this study was to initially identify the most outstanding characteristics of Agile and Lean for the two banking organizations, described in Sect. 2:

– The findings allowed them to be categorized into two groups: Agile characteristics: difference in communication, low performance, lack of knowledge of principles, scarcity of tools, functionality, monitoring and control of processes, flexibility and a team of less than 7 people.

Table 4. Recommendations to organizations in the selection of Agile and / or Lean

Name: Recommendation	Organization 1	Organization 2
Agile	**4 Team Work** (Team:1, 2, 6, 7) *Maintain: Team 6, Implement: Team 1, 2, 7*	**3 Team Work** (Team: 3, 4, 5) *Maintain: Team 5 Implement: Team 3, 4*
Fundamentals to improve	**Teams**	
* All Agile principles	Team 2	Team 3, Team 4, Team 5
* Risk analysis and requirements planning	Team 1, Team 2	Team 3, Team 5
* Monitoring and control of functions	Team 1, Team 2, Team 6	Team 4, Team 5
* Background to failures and record keeping requirements	Team 2, Team 6, Team 7	Team 5
* Communication difference	Team 7	Team 4
* Distribution of roles	---	Team 3, Team 4, Team 5
Optional: Applicability of Lean		
* Automate workflows and processes	---	Team 4
* Organizational Culture and Organizational Disposition	Team 1, Team 2, Team 6, Team 7	Team 3
* Feedback cycle	Team 1, Team 6	Team 4, Team 5
* Unnecessary processes	Team 6, Team 7	Team 5

– Characteristics of Lean: Assumption before requirements, response to change, collaboration with the customer, design thinking and the team is more than 7 people.

The analysis of the results supports the importance of these characteristics in the ontology and infers a pattern for both organizations in the seven work teams: the groups are less than 7 people. They lack the applicability of the principles and the organizational culture presents difficulties. Even the establishment of the requirements is one of the key tasks. They also present low attention from the software developers.

RQ3: This raises the question of indicating the risks for the two banks, where the following should be considered for the organization 1: improving risk analysis and requirements planning, failure background and maintenance of the requirements register, communication differences, monitoring and control of functions. While, for organization 2, an additional risk was identified and indicates the distribution of roles.

RQ4: The preceding analysis from the conceptualization of characteristics to the recommendation generated by the ontology shows that both Panamanian banking organizations are suggested to select the Agile Software development methodology, because the characteristics and risks of greater incidence are adjusted both in the number of people per team, as well as, in its principles. This implies that when implementing Agile, it must offer both organizations some advantages, such as:

– Better collaboration and interaction between team members and customers, task distribution, remote communication, improved organizational culture and reduced time distance.
– Continuous project progress and optimization of communication efficiency and provides support guidance.
– Improved evaluation of adaptability to changes and a reduced documentation time.
– In practical terms, the ontology inference used a knowledge domain manager of the team's characteristic aspects in the software development process.

RQ5: The two banking organizations can improve the weak points previously addressed and increase the team's productivity, reducing the process execution time and the practices that can be adopted afterwards. This implies that it helps in the efficiency, better planning of the requirements and fulfilling not only what is requested by the client. Also, through the ontology inference, the organizations are provided with those aspects that are within the Lean context, but that can be improved to automate and minimize risks in the Software development process execution time.

6 Conclusions and Future Work

The ontologies provide a common and unambiguous vocabulary to refer to the terms in the applied area, being able to share or reuse these among different applications that make use of the Ontology. This is the case of software agents (in the field of Web technologies), which can adequately recognize the elements of an ontology as long as the previous conditions are met. As a consequence of this, it is worth mentioning that the ontology in the framework of software development allowed the identification of:

In addition to a common vocabulary, they specify a taxonomy or inheritance of concepts that establish a categorization or classification of the domain entities. A good taxonomy is simple and easy to remember. It separates its entities in a mutually exclusive way and defines groups and subgroups without ambiguity.

The vocabulary and taxonomy represent a Conceptual Framework for the analysis, discussion or consultation of information from a domain.

An ontology includes a complete generalization/specification of its classes and subclasses, which are formally specified (including their relationships and instances) ensuring consistency in the deductive processes.

Ontologies are implemented in specific Ontology representation languages so that the specification of their classes, relations between them and their restrictions will depend on the characteristics of that language.

In consideration, the findings of our research as mentioned in Sect. 4, through the ontology in the domain of software development methodologies, have shown that the Agile approach in the banking sector solves:

It allows each of the banking institutions to identify some aspects that are fundamental during the life cycle of the software product development.

The recognition of the inference of the most outstanding characteristic risks of both organizations, reduces the incidence to failures in the establishment of requirements, communication between team members, efficiency and time of execution of the processes.

It provides team managers with an overview of the current situation in contrast to the benefits offered by the correct implementation of the Agile methodology in their projects.

Likewise, this research differs from the studies presented in Sect. 2.1, in essence, because it has a scope at the level of the selection of the most appropriate methodology, using an OWL, where the knowledge analyzed covers the phase prior to the implementation of a methodology; that is, the ontology, through the knowledge of the case study infers as a main advantage to offer, in the context of software engineering, a previous analysis to improve the failures and provide suggestions for good practices to the organizations. On the other hand, as future work, it is proposed to carry out validity by investigating specific points where a risk assessment (requirements and organizational culture) was reported from the point of view of data analysis and working with other non-banking organizations, and their evolution process at the time of implementing the methodology suggested through this study. In parallel, currently in this line of the Agile Software development methodology, we are working on the analysis of requirements, and the initial phase of the construction of an ontology that includes a general domain language for any organization based on its characteristics, offering a set of suggestions of the type of practice within Agile to be implemented.

7 Authors Contribution.

Conceptualization I.M, B.B, M.V.; methodology I.M, M.V.; formal analysis I.M, B.B, M.V; research, I.M, M.V.; original-writing I.M, M.V.; writing—review and edition I.M, B.B, M.V.; Corresponding author, M.V.

Acknowledgments. We are grateful for the support provided by the Science, Technology and Innovation National Secretariat of Panama (SENACYT), Scientific Master program TIC-UTP-FISC-2019 and to the National Research System (SNI-SENACYT) which one author is member.

References

1. Abdelghany, A.S., et al.: An agile methodology for ontology development. Int. J. Intell. Eng. Syst. **12**(2), 170–181 (2019). https://doi.org/10.22266/IJIES2019.0430.17.
2. Alahyari, H., et al.: A study of value in agile software development organizations. J. Syst. Softw. **125**, 271–288 (2017). https://doi.org/10.1016/j.jss.2016.12.007
3. Alahyari, H., et al.: An exploratory study of waste in software development organizations using agile or lean approaches: a multiple case study at 14 organizations. Inf. Softw. Technol. **105**, 78–94 (2019). https://doi.org/10.1016/j.infsof.2018.08.006
4. Batova, T.: Extended abstract: lean UX and innovation in teaching. In: IEEE International Professional Communication Conference, pp. 1–3, November 2016. https://doi.org/10.1109/IPCC.2016.7740500

5. Cagliano, R., et al.: Lean, agile and traditional supply: how do they impact manufacturing performance? J. Purch. Supply Manage. **10**(4–5) SPEC., 151–164 (2004). https://doi.org/10.1016/j.pursup.2004.11.001.

6. Ching, P.M., Mutuc, J.E.: Evaluating agile and lean software development methods from a system dynamics perspective. In: 2018 IEEE 10th International Conference on Humanoid, Nanotechnology, Information Technology Communication and Control, Environment and Management HNICEM 2018, pp. 1–6 (2019). https://doi.org/10.1109/HNICEM.2018.8666338.

7. Clarke, P.M., O'Connor, R.V., Rout, T., Dorling, A.: Erratum to: software process improvement and capability determination. In: Clarke, P.M., O'Connor, R.V., Rout, T., Dorling, A. (eds.) SPICE 2016. CCIS, vol. 609, pp. E1–E1. Springer, Cham (2016). https://doi.org/10.1007/978-3-319-38980-6_34

8. Curcio, K., et al.: Usability in agile software development: a tertiary study. Comput. Stand. Interfaces **64**(January), 61–77 (2019). https://doi.org/10.1016/j.csi.2018.12.003

9. Dingsoeyr, T., et al.: Agile development at scale: the next frontier. IEEE Softw. **36**(2), 30–38 (2019). https://doi.org/10.1109/MS.2018.2884884

10. Dingsøyr, T., et al.: Coordination in multi-team programmes: an investigation of the group mode in large-scale agile software development. In: Procedia Computer Science, pp. 123–128 Elsevier B.V. (2017). https://doi.org/10.1016/j.procs.2017.11.017.

11. Fagerholm, F., et al.: Performance alignment work : how software developers experience the continuous adaptation of team performance in lean and agile environments. Inf. Softw. Technol. (2015). https://doi.org/10.1016/j.infsof.2015.01.010

12. Fink, L., Pinchovski, B.: It is about time: bias and its mitigation in time-saving decisions in software development projects. Int. J. Proj. Manag. **38**(2), 99–111 (2020). https://doi.org/10.1016/j.ijproman.2020.01.001

13. Gennari, J.H., et al.: The evolution of Protégé: an environment for knowledge-based systems development. Int. J. Hum. Comput. Stud. **58**(1), 89–123 (2003). https://doi.org/10.1016/S1071-5819(02)00127-1

14. Gobin, B.A.: An agile and modular approach for developing ontologies (2013). https://doi.org/10.4018/978-1-4666-4900-2.ch007

15. Hajrizi, E., Bytyci, F.: Agile software development process at financial institution in Kosovo. IFAC-PapersOnLine. **48**(24), 153–156 (2015). https://doi.org/10.1016/j.ifacol.2015.12.074

16. Hsieh, S.H., Lu, M.D.: Collaborative engineering software development: Ontology-based approach. Lecture Notes in Computer Science (including Subser. Lecture Notes in Artificial Intelligence, Lecture Notes in Bioinformatics). LNAI, vol. 4200, pp. 328–342 (2006). https://doi.org/10.1007/11888598_31

17. IEEE: STD 1074–1995: IEEE Standard for Developing Software Life Cycle Processes (1995)

18. Life, S.: IEEE Standard for Developing Software Life Cycle Processes (1995)

19. Liikkanen, L.A., et al.: Lean UX - The next generation of user-centered Agile development? In: Proceedings of the NordiCHI 2014: The 8th Nordic Conference on Human-Computer Interaction: Fun, Fast, Foundational, pp. 1095–1100 (2014). https://doi.org/10.1145/2639189.2670285.

20. Liikkanen, L.A., et al.: Lean UX Applying Lean Principles to Improve User Experience (2014).https://doi.org/10.1145/2639189.2670285

21. McArthur, J.J., Bortoluzzi, B.: Lean-Agile FM-BIM: a demonstrated approach. Facilities **36**(13–14), 676–695 (2018). https://doi.org/10.1108/F-04-2017-0045

22. Murtazina, M.S., Avdeenko, T.V.: An ontology-based approach to support for requirements traceability in agile development. Procedia Comput. Sci. **150**, 628–635 (2019). https://doi.org/10.1016/j.procs.2019.02.044

23. Murtazina, M.S., Avdeenko, TV.: Ontology-based approach to the requirements engineering in agile environment. In: 2018 14th International Scientific Conference on Actual Problems of Electronic Instrument Engineering Proceedings. APEIE 2018, pp. 496–501 (2018). https://doi.org/10.1109/APEIE.2018.8546144

24. Nidagundi, P., Novickis, L.: Introducing lean canvas model adaptation in the scrum software testing. Procedia - Procedia Comput. Sci. **104**, 97–103, December 2016. https://doi.org/10.1016/j.procs.2017.01.078

25. Nudelman, G.: Lean UX communication strategies for success in large organizations. Interactions **25**(5), 80–82 (2018). https://doi.org/10.1145/3236683

26. Nurdiani, I., et al.: The impacts of agile and lean practices on project constraints: A tertiary study. J. Syst. Softw. **119**, 162–183 (2016). https://doi.org/10.1016/j.jss.2016.06.043

27. Paasivaara, M., Lassenius, C.: Communities of practice in a large distributed agile software development organization – case Ericsson. Inf. Softw. Technol. **56**(12), 1556–1577 (2014). https://doi.org/10.1016/j.infsof.2014.06.008

28. Perkusich, M., et al.: Intelligent software engineering in the context of agile software development : a systematic literature review. J. Pre-proof, 1–76 (2019). https://doi.org/10.1016/j.infsof.2019.106241.

29. Rahman, N.A.A. et al.: Lean manufacturing case study with Kanban system implementation. In: Procedia Economics and Finance, ICEBR, vol. 7, pp. 174–180 (2013). https://doi.org/10.1016/s2212-5671(13)00232-3

30. Rao, L., et al.: Building ontology based knowledge maps to assist business process re-engineering. Decis. Support Syst. **52**(3), 577–589 (2012). https://doi.org/10.1016/j.dss.2011.10.014

31. Rodríguez, P., et al.: Combining lean thinking and agile methods for software development a case study of a finnish provider of wireless embedded systems. In: Proceedings of Annual Hawaii International Conference on System Sciences, pp. 4770–4779 (2014). https://doi.org/10.1109/HICSS.2014.586.

32. Roth, W.-M., Jornet, A.: From object-oriented to fluid ontology: a case study of the materiality of design work in agile software development. Comput. Support. Coop. Work (CSCW) **27**(1), 37–75 (2017). https://doi.org/10.1007/s10606-017-9297-6

33. Secchi, R., Camuffo, A.: Lean implementation failures : the role of organizational ambidexterity. Int. J. Prod. Econ. (2019). https://doi.org/10.1016/j.ijpe.2019.01.007

34. Shrivastava, S.V., Rathod, U.: A risk management framework for distributed agile projects. Inf. Softw. Technol. **85**, 1–5 (2017). https://doi.org/10.1016/j.infsof.2016.12.005

35. da Silva, T.S., Silveira, M.S., de O. Melo, C., Parzianello, L.C.: Understanding the UX designer's role within agile teams. In: Marcus, A. (ed.) DUXU 2013. LNCS, vol. 8012, pp. 599–609. Springer, Heidelberg (2013). https://doi.org/10.1007/978-3-642-39229-0_64

36. Sitthithanasakul, S., Choosri, N.: Using ontology to enhance requirement engineering in agile software process. SKIM 2016 - 2016 10th Internationa Conference on Software, Knowledge, Information Management Application, pp. 181–186 (2017). https://doi.org/10.1109/SKIMA.2016.7916218.

37. Kruchten, P., Fraser, S., Coallier, F. (eds.): XP 2019. LNBIP, vol. 355. Springer, Cham (2019). https://doi.org/10.1007/978-3-030-19034-7

38. de Souza, P.L., do Prado, A.F., de Souza, W.L., dos Santos Forghieri Pereira, S.M., Pires, L.F.: Improving agile software development with domain ontologies. In: Latifi, S. (ed.) Information Technology – New Generations. AISC, vol. 738, pp. 267–274. Springer, Cham (2018). https://doi.org/10.1007/978-3-319-77028-4_37

39. Wang, X., et al.: "Leagile" software development: an experience report analysis of the application of lean approaches in agile software development. J. Syst. Softw. **85**(6), 1287–1299 (2012). https://doi.org/10.1016/j.jss.2012.01.061

40. Wongthongtham, P., et al.: Ontology-based multi-site software development methodology and tools. J. Syst. Archit. **52**(11), 640–653 (2006). https://doi.org/10.1016/j.sysarc.2006.06.008

Mobile App for Automation of Observational Instrument for Continuous Emotional Evaluation

Carlos Vicente-Tene[1], Pablo Torres-Carrión[1(✉)] [iD], and Carina González[2]

[1] Universidad Técnica Particular de Loja, San Cayetano Alto S/N, Loja, Ecuador
{acvicente,pvtorres}@utpl.edu.ec
[2] Universidad de La Laguna, La Laguna, Tenerife, Spain
cjgonza@ull.edu.es

Abstract. Emotions are psychophysiological expressions that are shown before a stimulus or situation, and their research in user experience environments has been growing exponentially. EMODIANA is an instrument for subjective measurement of emotions and their intensity, validated in experimental environments for academic and physical and motor rehabilitation purposes. A mobile APP is developed to automate EMODIANA, applying the ICONIX heavy-agile development methodology. For the implementation as a cross-platform hybrid application, the Ionic framework is used, and for non-relational database cloud storage, Firebase. The architecture proposed for development is based on the proposal by the Microsoft Application Architecture Guide for mobile applications, with functionalities to manage users and participants, apply EMODIANA, generate graph with interaction results, generate reports and make the prediction of the emotional state of the participant.

Keywords: Emotion · Research tool · Mobile App · Emotion predictor

1 Introduction

Emotions are psychophysiological expressions, which show living beings before some stimulus or situation for a certain time. Through emotions we show different adaptive behaviors for the organism, both positive and negative. We permanently feel emotions because they are a fundamental part of human life. Emotion is a complex state of the organism characterized by an excitation or disturbance that predisposes to action; it is generated in response to an external or internal event [1]. The emotions present in the day to day, are manifested based on our emotional intelligence [2]. In [3] they define it as the subset of social intelligence that implies the ability to control their own and other people's feelings and emotions, to discriminate between them and use this information to guide thought and actions.

About emotional evaluation, in [4] hree types of evaluative approaches to emotional intelligence are mentioned, such as: classic instruments of questionnaire-based measures and self-reports, evaluation measures of external observers based on questionnaires; and

© Springer Nature Switzerland AG 2021
M. Botto-Tobar et al. (Eds.): ICAT 2020, CCIS 1388, pp. 552–561, 2021.
https://doi.org/10.1007/978-3-030-71503-8_42

measures of ability or performance composed of various emotional tasks to be solved. n the technological context, a research field called Affective Computing arises, introduced by Rosaling Picard from MIT in 1997; Currently it is mainly supported by Artificial Intelligence models. In the last decade, it has been integrating from natural interaction environments, which include voice interaction, facial expressions, postures and body gestures, as well as wearable technologies through body sensors [5]. Other methods are based on the subjective measurement of emotions, which is carried out from the systematic and orderly observation of the user; For this, a large number of research instruments and resources have been designed.

A methodology used for the analysis of emotions is EMODIANA (see Fig. 1), an instrument for subjective measurement of emotions and their intensity [6]. For their elaboration, they focused on two specific objectives: a) to examine the graphic design for an emotional evaluation instrument, from the point of understanding of their graphic representations (faces) on emotions; and, b) the emotional intensity in front of games and videogames. In [7] an adaptation of EMODIANA is proposed, for emotional assessment from continuous observation, with a manual application, supported in a printed format; Subsequently, for analysis purposes, tabulation is performed from established time series to a digital document. This application process is the one that is proposed to automate, with the App that is detailed in this document..

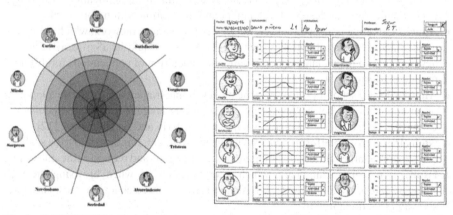

Fig. 1. a) EMODIANA Emotional Assessment Instrument [6]; b) Observational instrument for continuous emotional evaluation [7, 8].

Rosenberg's ICONIX [9] methodology is applied to develop the application. For development, the *Ionic v2* framework is used, which allows creating multiplatform hybrid applications; *Firebase* is used for storage, because it allows storing a non-relational database in the cloud. The architecture for application development is based on Microsoft's proposal for the development of mobile applications (Microsoft Corporation, 2009). The application consists of the following functionalities: a) manage users and participants; b) apply EMODIANA; c) generate graph; d) generate reports; and e) make a prediction of the participant's emotional state. This document describes the

EmoApp, from its preliminary proposal phase, to the results obtained in a production environment.

2 Method

2.1 Development Methodology

The ICONIX development methodology [9], proposed by Doug Rosenberg and Jacobson in 1993, is applied; It is a simplified methodology that helps to keep control during the product life cycle to be developed, it is between how complex and heavy RUP[1] is and how flexible and light XP[2] is, for this reason ICONIX is a heavy-type methodology-agile. It is driven by use cases, through the iterative and incremental process. ICONIX is characterized by having the following characteristics: a) iterative and incremental; b) traceability; c) UML dynamics, with the option of not requiring the development of all of these, but depending on the needs of the project to be developed.

2.2 Development Tools

- **Ionic v2** is an open source framework developed by Max Lynch, Ben Sperry and Adam Bradley in 2013 [10]. It allows to create hybrid multi-form applications, offering a good architecture for design, development and integration with mobile devices.
- **Apache Cordova** is an open source mobile development framework, which allows the use of standard web technologies such as HTML5, CSS3 and JavaScript, avoiding the development of native language, allowing the generation of applications for different mobile platforms [11].
- **AngularJS** is a set of tools to create the most suitable framework for the development of an application. Use the JavaScript programming language, and the Model View Controller (MVC) design pattern to achieve an orderly and scalable work [12].
- **Node.JS** is a cross-platform event execution environment. It is designed to be scalable and support a large number of simultaneous connections and requests efficiently [13].
- **Html5** is a markup language, which interprets content when browsing the web (images, audio, video and text). It basically provides three characteristics: structure, style and functionality [14].
- **CSS** (Cascading Style Sheets) is the language that separates the structure of a document and its presentation, to provide visual styles to the elements of the document, such as size, color, background, borders, etc. [14].
- **JavaScript** is a programming language that provides interactive features on a website, such as button events, entering data into forms, animations, etc. [15].
- **Visual Studio Code** is a lightweight but powerful source code editor that runs on your desktop and is available for Windows, macOS, and Linux. It comes with built-in support for JavaScript, TypeScript and Node.js and has a rich ecosystem of extensions for other languages [16].

---

[1] RUP: Rational Unified Process.
[2] XP: Extreme Programming.

- **Firebase** is a platform for the development of mobile and web applications in the cloud, which allows managing a non-relational database hosted in the cloud, which can be accessed from mobile applications and browsers, responding to changes in real time.

2.3 Application Architecture

The architecture proposed for the development of the application is based on the Microsoft Application Architecture Guide book [17], which gives us a global outline of the architecture for the development of mobile applications, which has been studied and implemented in order to solve an architectural solution to the problem (Fig. 2).

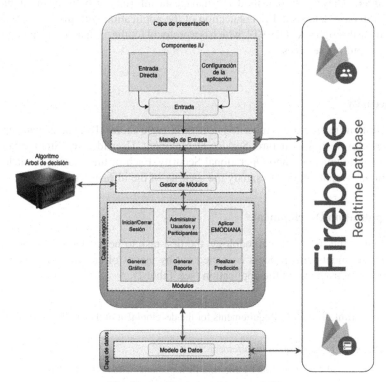

Fig. 2. Application architecture [17]

Presentation Layer. This layer is made up of the interfaces that are part of the application; It is the means of interaction between the user and the application, by which, data inputs are obtained, either of direct input type or application configuration.

- *Direct input:* These are the keystrokes made by the user on the device in order to execute a task; Emotion data record entry.

- *Application settings:* These are the keystrokes made on the device, in order to prepare a scenario for the user to access or view.
- *Entry handling:* It is in charge of managing the input data made by the user, it also serves as a link between the input data and the module manager.

Business Layer. It contains the modules that are part of the main functionalities for which the application has been designed: Start/Close session, Manage users and participants, Apply EMODIANA, Generate graph, Generate report and Make prediction. It is the component that manages the behavior of the application, it interacts with the different modules of this layer, depending on the instructions that the input handling component sent.

Data Layer. They are the data model to manage the information between the application and the Firebase database; The connection of the application with the Firebase service will be done through a API REST[3], which is a protocol for the exchange and manipulation of data in Internet services.

2.4 Security

The security infrastructure is inherited from de Google Cloud [18], and is made up of six layers: Hardware Infrastructure, Service Deployment, User Identity, Storage Services, Internet Communication and Operational Security. Each of these layers is made up of different levels that interact to satisfy the security of the infrastructure.

2.5 Application Development

According to the ICONIX methodology, the first task to be carried out is the analysis of the requirements, this process is carried out by means of an informal survey of the functional requirements of the application (see Table 1).

Table 1. List of Requirements for the development of the application

Requirement	Description of requirement
R1	User registration by entering their personal data in the database
R2	User login, to access the application functionalities
R3	User log out, to unlink the application with their user profile
R4	Edit and add additional information in the user profile
R5	Participant registration, to which the evaluation process will be applied

(continued)

---

[3] REST: Transferencia de Estado Representacional.

Table 1. (*continued*)

Requirement	Description of requirement
R6	Edit and add additional participant information
R7	Delete the participant who is registered
R8	Apply EMODIANA to the selected participant
R9	Show graphically the results obtained from the evaluation of the participant
R10	Delete the evaluations made to the participant
R11	Obtain the results of the evaluation, in a format with a CSV extension, which can be downloaded
R12	Create projects, this functionality will only be accessed by users of type Researchers
R13	Edit and add additional information to a project
R14	Delete a project, this functionality would hide the project from the User's view in order to be able to recover it at some point
R15	Add participants to a project, whether they are registered in the user profile, or also register a new participant to be part of the project
R16	Unlink the participant that has been added to the project
R17	Add users to be part of the project, the same ones who act as observers when applying the evaluation
R18	Unlink the user who has been added to the project
R19	Distribute the participant (s) with the user (s) within the project, that is, be able to assign one or more participants to one or more users for their respective evaluation.
R20	Visualize how the participants are distributed with their respective users, in order to eliminate any unwanted distribution within the project
R21	View the results of each of the participants with respect to their user (Observer) assigned within the project
R22	Visualize emotion prediction from a machine learning algorithm, to the historical data of a participant's evaluation

With the established and approved requirements, the solution is developed by means of iterations that belong to each requirement, which are made up of the following artifacts: User interface prototype, use case specification, robustness diagram, diagram sequence and class diagram.

3 Results

A mobile application was obtained, for automation of the observational instrument for continuous emotional evaluation EMODIANA, with options for user administration, project administration, evaluation visualization and generation of an emotion prediction model based on previous evaluations.

3.1 Administración De Usuarios

Exposed in the requirements R1 to R7, they include the actions of registration, income, exit of the system, update of user data. Also the corresponding to the participants (population to observe) for the entry, update and elimination (Fig. 3).

Fig. 3. Screens for entering and recording data.

3.2 Observation Record from EmoApp

It is exposed in the requirements R8–R11, including the actual application of the EMODI-ANA observational instrument in a timeline, with options to show the results of the observation in graphic format later on, as well as export the observation data in.CSV format for external analysis. In Fig. 4 you can see the sequence on screens to record the observation of emotions. A participant is selected, and then the registration process begins; when the observer identifies an emotion, she touches the option of the corresponding emotion, then indicates its level and the possible reason; then you return to the observation screen. You always have the option to pause and end the observation. Once the observation is finished, it is possible to show for each emotion, a time line of its measurement (see Fig. 5).

3.3 Project Management

The Projects allow observers (users) and participants to be organized, and even work in synchronous spaces, to carry out a collective observation. It is possible to create, edit and delete a project, if the profile is a researcher type user. In the "Distributivo" option, it is possible to assign participants to each observer, manage observers and participants (see Fig. 6.)

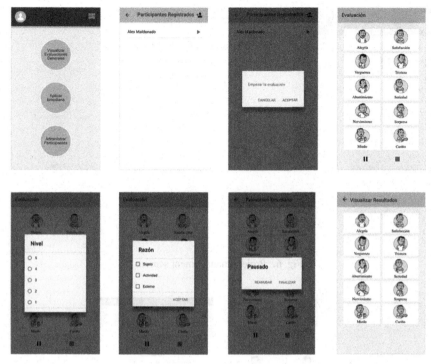

Fig. 4. Screens of the process to record the observation from EmoApp.

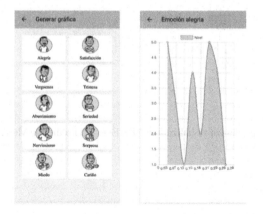

Fig. 5. Process screens to show observed emotions

3.4 Visualize Emotion Prediction Model

The mobile application allows applying a Machine Learning algorithm, specifically a prediction model using the decision tree technique on the data obtained from the evaluation of a participant (Fig. 7).

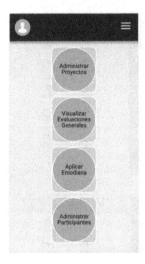

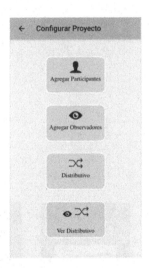

Fig. 6. Project management screens

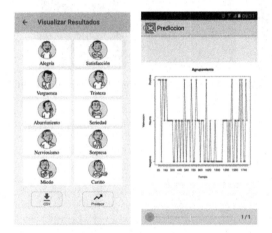

Fig. 7. Screens of the process of visualization of the Emotion Prediction Model, based on Machine Learning algorithm

4   Conclusions

The development of the mobile application EmoApp, had a positive impact on the automation of the instrument for continuous emotional evaluation EMODIANA, because it was possible to obtain a valuable reduction in time and the resources used when executing an evaluation until obtaining its results; since these are instantly generated by the application. This is a tool with great potential for scientific research.

The implementation of the application using the Iconix methodology, helped to achieve a detailed and explanatory vision of each of the requirements through its artifacts for each iteration, and is also an orderly and responsible work guide during the application development.

References

1. Bisquerra Alzina, R.: Psicopedagogía de las emociones, Madrid (2009)
2. Goleman, D.: Inteligencia emocional. Kairo's, Barcelona (2011)
3. Salovey, P., John, D.: Mayer: Emotional intelligence. Imagination, Cognition Personality. **9**, 185–211 (1990). https://doi.org/10.1016/S0962-1849(05)80058-7
4. Extremera Pacheco, N., Fernández-Berrocal, P.: La Inteligencia Emocional: Métodos de evaluación en el aula. Rev. Iberoam. Educ. **30**, 1–12 (2004).
5. Gunes, H., Piccardi, M., Pantic, M.: Affective computing: focus on emotion expression, synthesis, and recognition. From Lab to Real World Affect Recognit. using Mult. Cues Modalities. 185–218 (2008)
6. González-González, C.S., Cairós-González, M., Navarro-Adelantado, V.: EMODIANA: Un instrumento para la evaluación subjetiva de emociones en niños y niñas. Actas del XIV Congr. Int. Interacción Pers. (2013). https://doi.org/10.13140/RG.2.1.5112.2169.
7. Torres-Carrion, P., Gonzalez-Gonzalez, C.S.: Instrumento observacional para la evaluación emocional continua en videojuegos adaptada a personas con Síndrome de Down. In: González-González, C.S. (ed.) V Congreso Internacional de Videojuegos Educativos CIVE 2017. Puerto de la Cruz - Tenerife - España (2017)
8. Torres-Carrión, P.: Metodología HCI con análisis de emociones para personas con Síndrome de Down. Aplicación para procesos de aprendizaje con interacción gestual. (2017)
9. Rosenberg, D., Stephens, M., Collins-Cope, M.: Agile development with ICONIX process. New York, Editor. Apress (2005)
10. Justin, J., Jude, J.: Learn Ionic 2: Develop Multi-platform Mobile Apps. Apress (2017)
11. Camden, R.K.: Apache Cordova in action. Manning Publications Co. (2015).
12. Fain, Y., Moiseev, A.: Angular 2 Development with TypeScript. Manning Publications Co. (2016).
13. Hahn, E.: Express in Action: Writing, building, and testing Node. js applications. Manning Publications (2016)
14. Gauchat, J.D.: El gran libro de HTML5, CSS3 y Javascript. Barcelona (2012). https://doi.org/10.1017/CBO9781107415324.004.
15. Haverbeke, M.: Introduction - Eloquent JavaScript (2013)
16. Microsoft Corporation: Visual Studio Code User Guide. https://code.visualstudio.com/docs/editor/codebasics. Accessed 30 July 2020
17. Microsoft Corporation: Microsoft Application Architecture Guide, 2nd Edition (Patterns & Practices). Microsoft Corporation (2009)
18. Google Cloud: Google Infrastructure Security Design Overview | Google Cloud Platform. Whitepaper, pp. 1–14 (2017). https://doi.org/https://doi.org/10.1136/bmjopen-2016-013187.

Methodological Approach for Evaluating the Impact of Electric Vehicles on Power Distribution Networks

J. Basantes-Romero$^{(\boxtimes)}$, S. Palma-Valdivieso$^{(\boxtimes)}$, D. Ortiz-Villalba$^{(\boxtimes)}$, and J. Llanos$^{(\boxtimes)}$

Universidad de las Fuerzas Armadas ESPE, Sangolqui, Ecuador
{jabasantes2,sjpalma,ddortiz5,jdllanos1}@espe.edu.ec

Abstract. The future of transport will be based on electrical energy, but the transition from fossil fuels will not be easy and will lead to a fundamental change in power distribution networks. The insertion of plug-in-electric vehicles have become a promising solution to reduce CO_2 carbon dioxide emissions. However, the insertion of electric vehicles represents an unexpected increase in the electricity demand, this imposes new challenges for the distribution system operators, due to the uncertainties associated with the electric vehicles charging. This article proposes a practical methodological framework in order to assess the impact of plug-in-electric vehicles on power distribution networks. The proposal includes four levels of uncertainties: electric vehicle model, charging method, state of charge of the battery, and the connection node into the power distribution network. The proposal includes the calculation of power flows, to evaluate voltage regulation and determine the loading of power distribution lines. The results show that when electric vehicles are uncontrolled charge at the hour when the maximum demand occurs, this operating condition might affect the loading of power distribution lines causing the activation of over-current protection relays.

Keywords: Power distribution system · Electric vehicles · Voltage regulation

1 Introduction

The air pollution is the main source of environmental pollution in America. The World Health Organization (WHO) estimates that for every nine deaths in the world one is due to air pollution [1]. According to environmental experts, electric vehicles are able to reduce the burning of fossil fuels, the main source of transportation-induced air pollution. Indeed several governments have been promoting policies regarding electric vehicles in order to implement cost-effective innovations to ensure low pollution [2].

There are about 1200 million vehicles around the world producing 13% of total planet pollution [3]. In the large cities, the vehicles produce 52% of carbon

© Springer Nature Switzerland AG 2021
M. Botto-Tobar et al. (Eds.): ICAT 2020, CCIS 1388, pp. 562–573, 2021.
https://doi.org/10.1007/978-3-030-71503-8_43

dioxide emissions [4], this has led that most automobile companies are focused on the design and make plug-in electric vehicles (PEV) where one of its main aims is to provide to the vehicles large autonomy with short battery charge times.

The high Electric Vehicles penetration impacts the daily electricity demand and might drive to failures on the power distribution networks. There are several challenges that must be overcome in order to adapt the current power distribution networks, therefore, it is required to perform studies for evaluate the impact on the power distribution network and evaluate strategies in order to overcome the main issues regarding to the insertion of electric vehicles in the power distribution networks to establish strategies for conduct an adequate insertion.

The impacts on the power distribution networks produced by the PEVs were analyzed in [5], it is shown that the power distribution networks, might be overloaded, as well as distribution transformers, voltage droops and, power losses might be also increased.

The impact of PEVs on a low voltage power distribution network in a Budapest district in Hungary is presented in [6]. Two loading scenarios are analyzed: uncoordinated and coordinated scenarios considering three PEV penetrations levels, 20%, 40%, and 60%. The study concludes that at 60% PEV penetration level considering uncoordinated load, the power distribution transformers installed along the primary feeder are overloaded; while for the coordinated load scenario, the components of the power distribution network function normally.

The article presented in [7] analyzes the PEV penetration, proposed in the electric mobility roadmap in Singapore, to determine how the electrical network might be expanded considering the impact of electric vehicles and charging infrastructure for PEV. The research work concludes that based on the PEV penetration for the scenarios under study, until 2050, the PEV penetration considering single-phase and three-phase chargers do not represent hazard situations to the power distribution network. However, high-power DC chargers, especially those that can be used for fast PEV charging, require studies considering a more level detail.

In [8] a PEV impact study is carried out in a Seattle residential power distribution network. The study analyzes the voltage stability considering data obtained from 602 Nissan Leafs. For this research work, a PEV penetration level of about 50% was taken into consideration over 75,000 households, with different loading rates. Kernel Density Estimation (KDE) which is a no parametric density estimation technique is applied in order to estimates the battery charge level of each PEV.

In this research work, a novel methodology is presented for the PEVs impact assessment on power distribution networks considering different uncertainties levels. The uncertainties levels that are considered correspond to the randomness where the PEVs can be connected to the network, the type of PEV load (controlled or uncontrolled), vehicle model, and the battery state of charge (SOC). If the PEV battery charges occur during the peak demand, it is defined as uncontrolled load, otherwise, it is defined as a controlled load. Two types of electric vehicles models are considered in this study, with different autonomy levels, a different type of battery, and different charging time. Moreover, the model includes the SOC of the battery, e.g. at least 20% of SOC in order to preserve the battery State of Health (SOH) avoiding an accelerated level of battery degradation occurs. The methodology is implemented using MATLAB software and the MATPOWER toolbox. The paper is organized as follows, Sect. 2 describes in detail the proposed methodology, Sect. 3 presents the case study where the proposed methodology is applied and validated, Sect. 4 presents the results obtained, finally, in Sect. 5 the main conclusions of this research work are presented.

2 Methodology

The proposed methodology for the PEVs penetration analysis in a power distribution network is shown in Fig. 1.

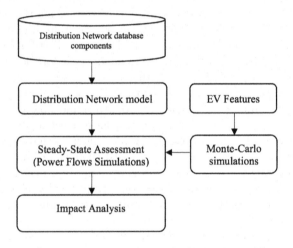

Fig. 1. Proposed methodology

The proposed methodology evaluates the PEV insertion in residential power distribution networks, under different scenarios of penetration. The proposed methodology considers some uncertainties levels, therefore Monte Carlo Simulation method is applied in order to model the uncertainties. As it was mentioned before, the uncertainties levels considered in this research work includes, the PEV connection point in the power distribution network, the PEV charging method (controlled and uncontrolled charging), the type of vehicle connected to the grid node, and finally, the state of charge (SOC) of the battery. Uncertainties levels are defined with the purpose to evaluate the impact of the PEV penetration in the power distribution network.

2.1 Power Distribution Network Database Components

In order to analyze the PEV insertion within a residential feeder in a power distribution network, charging points are added to the households. Equation 1 represents the electricity consumption in a household, including the PEV load to the electrical system. The equation incorporates the increase in electric power demand by each household where: T_D is the total required demand, F_c is the annual growth factor, DMU is the maximum unit demand of each household, and D_{PEV} is the electricity demand required by the PEV charger.

$$T_D = F_c * DMU + D_{PEV} \tag{1}$$

Each node in the distribution network has a power demand profile; the PEVs power demand in each of the nodes is added. The total electricity demand at each node is represented by Eq. 2, where P_{node}, is the total power per node D_{PEV}, is the power demand of the PEVs connected at that node, D_{system}, is the total electricity demand required by households connected at the node and n is the number of PEVs connected to this node. All values are expressed in kW.

$$P_{node} = \sum_{i=0}^{n} D_{PEV\,i} + D_{system} \tag{2}$$

2.2 Power Distribution Network Model

The power distribution network modeling is performed in MATLAB using the MATPOWER toolbox [12], the parameters considered are listed as follows: line impedance, voltage load of the substation, and transformers. The model detailed of the feeder allows to perform the power flow simulations considering PEVs insertion, as a result of the steady-state analysis the following data are obtained voltage droops, power losses, and the loading of each power distribution line. Equations 3–4 are used to obtain the parameters of the distribution network expressed in p.u. (per unit), where: Z_{base}, is the base impedance in Ohms, kV_{base} is the base voltage expressed in kV, S_{base} is the base apparent power in MVA and I_{base}, is the base current in amperes A.

$$Z_{base} = \frac{(kV_{base})^2}{MVA_{base}} \tag{3}$$

$$I_{base} = \frac{kVA_{base}}{kV_{base}} \tag{4}$$

2.3 Monte Carlo Simulations

Figure 2 shows the flowchart to implement Monte Carlo simulations in MATLAB; four uncertainties levels are considered for the PEVs insertion in the power distribution network.

The PEVs with a SOC greater than 60% is considered as a PEV not connected to the grid, the minimum SOC considered in this work is 20%, therefore the PEVs that participate in the electricity demand curve are those that have a

SOC greater than 20% and below 60%. The next uncertainty level is regarding with the PEV Model; this stochastic variable is considered due to there are PEV several models available on the electric vehicles market. Two types of PEVs are considered in this article, the first PEV with high autonomy, 5 passenger capacity, the second type, it is available for one passenger, and less autonomy (city car), the main difference between the two PEVs is the power required by the charger. The charging method is the third uncertainty level. The next paragraph describes in detail the charging methods proposed in the model.

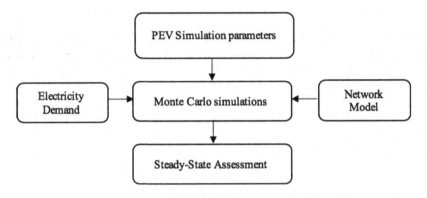

Fig. 2. Monte-Carlo simulation diagram

Non Flexible Load. PEVs start charging as soon as they are connected to the grid. Equation 5 represents the time in which the PEVs start their uncontrolled charge, where $h_{charging}$ is the hour in which the charging process begins and h_{arrive} is the hour when the PEV arrives at the household.

$$h_{charging} = h_{arrive} \tag{5}$$

The total energy consumed by this charging method is considered until the battery reaches its maximum capacity or when the PEV begins a new trip [10].

Flexible Load. The charging process is delayed by a certain time to avoid the peak power demand period. The delay in charging time is based on PEV owner configuration regarding to charge requirements and the time when the charging processing must be complete. Equation 6 represents the charging time for the PEV considering Flexible load where $h_{charging}$ is the start hour for the charging process, h_{arrive} is the PEV arrival hour at household and R is the remaining time to arrive at the time programmed by the user.

$$h_{charging} = h_{arrive} + R \tag{6}$$

The power demand of this charging method is considered until the battery reaches its maximum capacity or when the PEV is disconnected.

Monte Carlo Simulations (MCS) are performed in order to include the uncertainties levels explained above. The total number of vehicles is defined, moreover, the PEV penetration percentage in the power distribution network is defined as the scenario under analysis. The power requirements depend on the PEV model. Once the stochastic variables are defined by MCS, power flow calculations are performed using MATPOWER toolbox, the results obtained include the loading of the power distribution lines, voltage droops, and the demand increase in each node of the power distribution system. It is worth mentioning that MCS uses a uniform distribution for defining uncertainties levels.

2.4 Steady-State Assessment

As it was mentioned before, power flows are calculated by applying Newton Raphson method [9] using MATPOWER toolbox.

In order to perform the analysis, a work day load profile is considered. In addition, the analysis includes different scenarios of PEVs penetration.

The loading of the power distribution lines is calculated by Eq. 7, where $loading$ [%], is the loading of the distribution line, S_{branch}, is the apparent power of each section of the power distribution line V_{base}, is the rated voltage network.

$$loading(\%) = \frac{S_{branch}}{V_{base}} * 100 \tag{7}$$

For evaluating the global impact of PEVs penetration in a power distribution network, the following index is proposed, to evaluate the global voltage degradation, which is expressed in Eq. 8, where $\triangledown V$, is the variation of the voltage in the power distribution network V_{t0}, is the voltage droop per node without considering PEVs penetration, V_t, is the voltage droop considering PEVs insertion. This variation is related to the PEVs penetration in the power distribution network.

$$\triangledown V = \sqrt{(V_{t0} - V_t)_1^2 + (V_{t0} - V_t)_2^2 + \cdots + (V_{t0} - V_t)_n^2} \tag{8}$$

2.5 Impact Analysis

The analysis results include the calculation of the voltage droops, the power demand increase in each node, and the power distribution lines loading, to quantifying the PEVs effects on the primary feeders and their branches. For instance, overloads in the distribution lines might drive the activation of the power distribution system protections such as over-current relays, distribution fuses, and recloser, driving an economic impact on the society.

3 Case Study

3.1 PEV Characteristics

Two PEV models are implemented to analyze the impact of PEV in a power distribution network, the Nissan Leaf model [11] and Renault Twizy [12], the characteristics are summarize in Table 1. This research work considers a sample of 1200 vehicles, considering PEVs penetration index ranging from 10% to 40%, two PEVs models are selected and they are distributed randomly in the power distribution network under study.

Table 1. Electric vehicles features

Battery main features	Nissan leaf	Renault twizy
Storage capacity	24 [kWh]	6.1 [kWh]
Type of charger	220/110 [V]	220/110 [V]
Power charger	3.3 [kW]	4.6 [kW]
Time of charge	8 [Hours]	3.5/6 [Hours]
Autonomy	389 [km]	100 [km]

3.2 Charging Scenarios

Two charging scenarios are evaluated to determine the impact of PEVs on a residential power distribution network. The A scenario corresponds to uncontrolled charging, in this scenario each PEV starts its charging when the PEV is connected to the grid, without considering the load profile i.e. if all PEVs are connected to the grid considering this charging method, it will cause a significant overload in the power distribution network lines because PEVs might start its charging at the peak power demand period. Scenario B corresponds to flexible charging where the PEVs start its charging during the lower demand period (00:00 to 07:00). The main aim is to obtain a battery SOC about 100% at 07:00.

MCS method uses random distribution to place the PEVs in the test Feeder under study, considering the following penetration rates; 10%, 20%, 30%, and 40%, with the purpose to evaluate the behavior of the power distribution network under different PEVs penetration rates.

3.3 Distribution Network Characteristics

Figure 3 shows the distribution network under study, corresponding to the IEEE 34-Bus Test Feeder. The configuration of the electrical system, as well as the main grid characteristics such as conductor size, line impedance, distance, between branches, power demand by each node, among others are available in the reference [13].

Figure 4 shows a typical demand curve for the residential sector, where its maximum demand is presented from 19:00 to 21:00 h. Notice, Power Distribution networks are designed for a lifespan about 25 years [14], therefore the loading increase due to PEVs charging at peak hours period might decrease the Power Distribution networks lifespan. Moreover, it is worth mentioning that the batteries might be considered as a distributed generator, however, in this study, the power injected from the PEVs batteries is not considered.

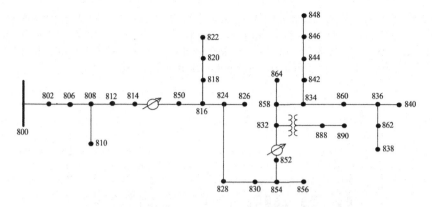

Fig. 3. IEEE 34-Bus test feeder

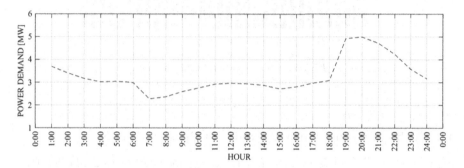

Fig. 4. Residential electricity demand curve

4 Analysis Results

This section presents the results obtained applying the proposed methodology on the IEEE 34-Bus Test Feeder considering a residential load profile using the formulation described in Sect. 2. Four uncertainty levels include; PEV charging method, electric vehicle model, battery charge level (SOC), and the distribution of PEVs in the nodes of the power distribution network. Moreover, 4 PEVs penetration scenarios are evaluated, as it was mentioning before in Sect. 3. The simulations performed take into account a total of 1200 vehicles, the number of vehicles based on fossil fuel depends on the PEVs penetration level.

4.1 Load Distribution Through Primary Feeder

Figure 5 shows the load demand increase in each node due to the insertion of PEVs in the network. As an illustrative example Fig. 5 shows the peak power demand at 20h00 for the residential network under study, considering a 10% of PEVs penetration level, the power demand increases from 5598 kW to 5956 kW. Considering a 20% of PEVs penetration level, the power demand increases about

706.1 kW, considering 30% of PEVs penetration level, the power demand increase about 1072 kW, this increased cause loading problems because the loading of line 1 is over 100%. Notice, the proposed methodology is able to distribute the PEVs load through the power distribution network in randomness way.

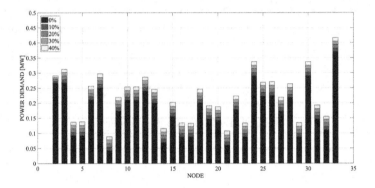

Fig. 5. Electricity demand by node

4.2   Voltage Droop Through Nodes of Primary Feeder

Figure 6 shows the voltage profile in p.u. by each node considering different PEVs penetration levels. The voltage droops must not exceed the threshold of 0.95 p.u. allowed for power distribution networks, considering 30% of PEVs penetration level, the maximum voltage droop is 0.972 in p.u. The voltage profile is not affected due to the robustness of the power distribution network, however, the method is able to identify the nodes where there are voltage droops that do not fulfill the requirements of grid codes.

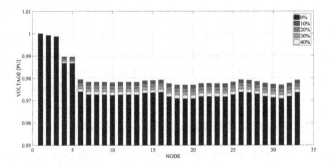

Fig. 6. Voltage droop by node

4.3   Loading of Power Distribution Lines

The power demand increase in each of the nodes causes an increase in the power flow of power distribution lines, in Fig. 7 the loading of the power lines is shown considering the PEVs penetration scenarios under study. The loading of the three first segments close to the substation without consider PEVs insertion are 85%, 81%, and 77% respectively. Considering a 10% of PEVs penetration, the loading of the power distribution line increases about 90.56% in the first section, while, considering a 20% of PEVs penetration level, the loading of the main section increases about 96.92%, when 30% of PEVs penetration level is simulated, the loading of the power distribution line exceeds its maximum capacity by 2.05%, which might cause the activation of over-current protection, therefore, expenditures occur in terms of monetary cost and, social impact.

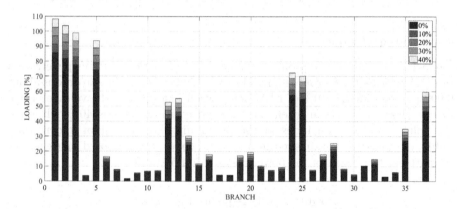

Fig. 7. Loading of power distribution lines

The power distribution network under study shows several loading problems in the power distribution lines when the index penetration is greater than 30%, at peak power demand hour, there are several PEVs connected to the power distribution network considering uncontrolled charging method, moreover, the SOC of the batteries is less than 60%. The large number of PEVs connected to the power distribution network is due to the feeder modeled contains a residential load profile.

The peak power demand hour contains the highest number of PEVs connected to the network. Because of the feeder under study, it is modeled as a residential power distribution network.

The impact of PEVs insertion is shown in Fig. 8 into the daily power demand curve, considering 30% of the penetration index. The bars in blue color represent the actual daily power demand without considering PEVs, while the bars in orange represent the increase in demand value by hour caused by the 30% insertion of PEVs in the power distribution network. Notice, there is an increment of about 1068 kW at the peak demand corresponding to PEVs insertion.

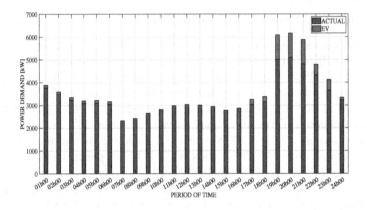

Fig. 8. Electricity demand curve considering 30% of PEVs penetration

4.4 Voltage Profile

Table 2 shows the voltage profile degradation as a function of PEVs penetration rate, considering Eq. 8 proposed in Subsect. 2.4. The Voltage profile droops about 0.992 p.u. considering 10% of PEV penetration index, while the voltage profile droops close to 0.968 p.u when the PEV penetration index is 40%. Although the voltage degradation index of the power distribution system under study fulfills the threshold established into the grid codes, the proposed index is able to represent the status of the power distribution network.

Table 2. Voltage profile degradation

PEV penetration level	Voltage profile degradation
10%	0,992 p.u.
20%	0,984 p.u.
30%	0.976 p.u.
40%	0.968 p.u.

5   Conclusions

The take-up of PEVs is expected to accelerate rapidly in the future, driven by consumer demand and government policies aimed at tackling climate change, the PEVs insertion impose several challenges in the future power distribution systems. In this context, this research work presents a practical methodological framework in order to assess the impact of PEVs in the power distribution networks. The proposal considers 4 uncertainties levels associated with randomness where the PEVs can be connected to the power distribution network, PEVs model, PEVs charging method and, the level of charge battery (SOC). The methodology is implemented and validated using the IEEE 34-Bus Test Feeder, the results demonstrate that the proposal is able to evaluate the impact of the PEVs on power distribution networks. Four PEVs penetration scenarios are considered. Considering a 30% penetration index the activation of over-current protections relays occurs. In addition, it is demonstrated that the proposed methodology is able to identify the feeder sections that need to be reinforced and allows to analyze the loading index of distribution network elements, moreover, a voltage degradation index is presented in order to determine if the voltage regulation requirements, established into the grid codes are fulfillment.

References

1. World Health Organization 2016.: Ambiente air pollution: A global assessment of exposure and burden of disease. 1rs edn. WHO, Italy (2016)
2. La contaminación del aire en latinoamérica Homepage. https://www.bcn.cl/. Accessed 2017
3. La contaminación de los vehíÂculos Homepage. https://www.elmundo.es/. Accessed 2017
4. Los vehíÂculos son los que más contaminan el aire, Homepage. https://www.eltelegrafo.com.ec/. Accessed 2017
5. Clement-Nyns, K., Haesen, E., Driesen, J.: The impact of charging plug-in hybrid electric vehicles on a residential distribution grid. IEEE Trans. Power Syst. **25**, 371–380 (2010)
6. Ramadan, H., Ali, A., Csaba, F.: Assessment of plug-in electric vehicles charging impacts on residential low voltage distribution grid in hungary. In: IEEE, International Istanbul Smart Grids and Cities Congress and Fair (ICSG), pp. 105–109 (2018)
7. Vaisambhayana, S., Tripathi, A.: Study of electric vehicles penetration in Singapore and its potential impact on distribution grid. IEEE Trans. Power Syst. (2016)
8. Días, F., Mohanpurkar, M., Medam, A.: The impact of charging plugin hybrid electric vehicles on a residential distribution grid. IEEE Trans. Power Syst. (2018)
9. C.E.M. Ray, S., Zimmerman, D.: User's manual. In: USER'S MANUAL VERSION 7.0, p. 33. Power Systems Engineering Research Center (PSerc) (2019)
10. Sadhana Shrestha, T.M.H.: Distribution feeder impacts of electric vehicles charging in an integrated traffic and power network (2016)
11. Nissan leaf Homepage. http://www.nissan.es/. Accessed 2019
12. Renault Homepage. http://www.renault.es/. Accessed 2019
13. IEEE PES amps dsas test feeder working group Homepage: https://site.ieee.org/. Accessed 2012
14. Redes de distribución de energía eléctrica Homepage. http://bibing.us.es/. Accessed 2017

IoT Management Analysis Using SDN: Survey

Manuel Montaño[1,2(✉)] ⓘ, Rommel Torres[1] ⓘ, Patricia Ludeña[1] ⓘ,
and Francisco Sandoval[1] ⓘ

[1] Universidad Técnica Particular de Loja, San Cayetano Alto, 1101608 Loja, Ecuador
mamontano5@utpl.edu.ec
[2] Instituto Superior Tecnológico Sudamericano, Miguel Riofrío, 156-26 Loja, Ecuador

Abstract. The Internet of Things (IoT) is a promising technology capable of interconnecting billions of devices over the Internet. Many challenges in IoT arise due to the increase in the number and diversity of connected devices. The heterogeneity in IoT by the presence of a variety of technologies, protocols, and data representation formats, added to the massive connection of devices, makes the administration, performance adjustments and network configuration a task that requires scalability. Technologies such as software-defined networks (SDN) help to mitigate these problems. SDNs allow simplified network administration, offer programmability, flexibility, and agility, through the SDN controller that provides a global vision of the network topology allowing to create a fully programmable scalable architecture for the management of different IoT devices. This document provides a review of the architecture of SDN and IoT, focusing on managing IoT with SDN.

Keywords: Internet of Things (IoT) · Software Defined Networks (SDN) · IoT management

1 Introduction

The increase and expansion of the Internet have allowed various objects in our environment to communicate with each other, the massive presence of interconnected devices is called the Internet of Things (IoT) or Internet of Everything (IoE). The IoT paradigm has broadened its domain field, mainly in heterogeneous applications such as medicine, agriculture, and industry, etc. IoT is considered as a massive interconnection of devices and machines that allow actions to be carried out without human manipulation, which is interconnected through different access technologies such as radio frequency identification (RFID), Bluetooth, Wifi, etc. The objective of the IoT is to support daily life through the generation of an intelligent environment where interconnected objects can in an autonomous way capture data from the physical environment and be able to send it over the Internet for processing and decision-making.

Currently, there are several proposals of IoT models such as the National Institute of Standards and Technology (NIST) model applied to Smart Grid, the ITU-T model [1], the ETSI machine to machine (M2M) model [2] among others. To achieve a total

© Springer Nature Switzerland AG 2021
M. Botto-Tobar et al. (Eds.): ICAT 2020, CCIS 1388, pp. 574–589, 2021.
https://doi.org/10.1007/978-3-030-71503-8_45

interconnection of IoT devices, a flexible architecture and a heterogeneous communication infrastructure are required. In recent years, new architecture solutions have been generated that allow the efficient management of network resources, with the aim of standardizing a global architecture for IoT.

Researchers have focused their efforts on the new paradigms of software-defined networks (SDN) to improve the capacity of resource management and mobility of IoT. SDN is a type of network technology that was created to mitigate the problems of traditional networks, it is intended to make the network more agile, flexible and programmable, through separating the control plane from the data plane, to centralize the intelligence of the network in the controller and, in turn, allowing a global vision of the network topology. Therefore, the goal of SDN is to make easier the network management to efficiently achieve network scalability.

SDNs allow monitoring, configuring, and managing traffic from any computer without having to manipulate network devices individually, they manage to supply resources and service in any part of the network, due to the controller that manages the entire topology. There are several investigations [3–9] that have proposed management frameworks to address the IoT problem.

1.1 Motivation

The exhaustive growth of devices connected to the Internet (IoT) generates greater complexity in the management of the network infrastructure. Cisco mentions that there are currently 50 billion devices connected, and in the future, according to Huawei, there will be 100 billion devices in 2025. It is indisputable that it is necessary to propose or generate innovation to improve network management more flexibly and efficiently. Software-Defined Networking (SDN) has become a promising technology to achieve these network management purposes it is drawing considerable attention from researchers and industries. To address the problems of network management, SDN has a centralized control mechanism, with this character it can provide the configuration and optimization of the IoT network devices.

The main focus of this work is the study of management frameworks for IoT through SDN, an investigation of the efforts that have been made in this area, the benefits and characteristics of SDN for the deployment of IoT is also presented. For the research, a comparison is made of the existing SDN-IoT management frameworks from 2014 to 2020, which provide mobility, resource, and network heterogeneity management services. Also, for the study of management frameworks, an analysis of the operation of the SDN and IoT architecture is presented.

The article shows a discussion about SDN systems in IoT management and current challenges in IoT. A general taxonomy of existing research in this area is presented. The aim is present to the reader the most relevant approaches with the respective characteristics and to compare all these studies according to the objective parameters: Security management, fault tolerance, energy management, and load balance.

In summary, the following sections are presented: Sect. 2 description of software-defined networks, Sect. 3 overview of IoT, Sect. 4 SDN-based IoT management frameworks and Sect. 5 the discussion.

2 Software Defined Networks

Traditional networks are based on hardware, through the use of physical equipment, entailing some limitations in terms of speed and management of the configuration of each of the network devices, such as switches or routers, essential equipment in the process of communication with end-users. Each device in a traditional network builds the flow table in its control plane and in its data plane the forwarding of traffic based on established rules, becoming a complex activity for a network administrator due to the need to configure each device individually, even more so when it comes to scheduling network scalability.

Software defined networks are different from traditional networks due to their functionality and programmability. To mitigate the problems of traditional networks, SDN relies on software, decouples the control plane and the data plane, centralizing all network intelligence on the SDN controller. SDN software can be quickly and easily modified as needed, however decoupling the control plane from the data plane is not a new concept, Multiprotocol Label Switching (MPLS) technology [10] is an example on this context; however, SDN efforts focus on the ability to provide programming interfaces on network equipment [11].

According to the Open Networking Foundation [12], software-defined networking (SDN) is an emerging technology that is dynamic, manageable, cost-effective, and adaptable, making it ideal for managing the Internet of Things. The SDN architecture facilitates management and administration, transforms network devices into simple relay elements, and links intelligence in the controller to be a centralized unit, directly programmable and managed by an operating system [13].

The SDN architecture is made up of three layers: application layer (application plane) upper level, control layer (control plane) middle level and data layer or infrastructure (data plane) lower level as shown in Fig. 1.

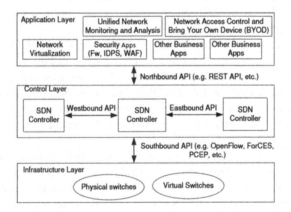

Fig. 1. SDN network architecture [12, 14].

Each layer communicates with its adjacent layer using an interface. The Northbound Interface (RESTful, Python or Java API) corresponds to the communication interface of the control plane with the application plane, and the Southbound interface for the connection of the control plane with the data plane uses protocols such as Open-Flow, Simple Network Management Protocol (SNMP), Network Configuration Protocol (NETCONF), Forwarding and Control Element Separation (forCES), Path Computation Element Communication Protocol (PCEP), among others.

The application layer is where various SDN applications are executed, it allows interaction with the entire architecture in a fast way, includes network services, tool monitoring and remote equipment configuration along with the support of Northbound APIs for the communication with the SDN controller. The control layer bases its operation on the SDN controller or on a distributed system that is composed of a group of two or more controllers that coordinate with each other, through the communication of East or Westbound interfaces, the controllers have the view global network to make decisions about forwarding devices [15]. Finally, the data plane or forwarding layer is composed of a large number of SDN switches, both physical or virtual, connected by wired or wireless means, these devices do not have a predefined functionality, but rather obey the instructions given by the data plane.

The most used protocol for the Southbound interface is OpenFlow [16], it allows the controller to manage and configure SDN switches remotely, the controller is the crucial element in the SDN architecture, in Table 1, shows a list of SDN controllers, supported programming languages and Openflow compatibility.

Table 1. SDN controllers.

Controller	Programming language	Protocol
NOX [17]	C++, REST, Python	OpenFlow 1.0, 1.3
Opendaylight [18]	Java, Python, REST	OpenFlow 1.0, 1.3
POX [19]	Python, REST	OpenFlow 1.0
ONOS [20]	Java	OpenFlow 1.0, 1.3, 1.4
Ryu [21]	Python	OpenFlow 1.0, 1.2, 1.3, 1.4, 1.5
Beacon [22]	Java	OpenFlow 1.0
HiperFlow [23]	Java, Python, REST	OpenFlow 1.0, 1.3, 1.4
Maestro [24]	Java	OpenFlow 1.0
Kandoo [25]	Python, C++, C	OpenFlow 1.0
MUL [26]	C	OpenFlow 1.0, 1.3, 1.4
Trema [27]	Ruby, C	OpenFlow 1.0
DISCO [28]	Java	OpenFlow 1.1
ElastiCon [29]	Java	OpenFlow 1.0

3 Internet of Things

IoT is an emerging technology in the field of current wired and wireless communications, its main objective is the interconnection of several things or objects that are around, such as sensors, actuators, RFID tags, and wireless devices; all connected in an intelligent environment through the Internet to achieve a common task [30]. What is interesting about this technology is that it is not only limited to industrial automation but also encompasses several applications such as smart home, smart grid, connected health, and smart city [31]. At the moment there is no specific applicable and standardized architecture for IoT [32]. There are some proposed models for IoT such as; the National Institute of Standards and Technology (NIST) project applied to Smart Grid, the ITU-T model [1], the ETSI machine to machine (M2M) model [2] among others, however, they lack a criterion specific architecture that is applicable for all fields of IoT [33, 34].

The IoT architecture of [35] describes the basic architectural design, defines three layers: perception layer, network layer, and application layer as shown in Fig. 2.

The perception layer is where physical devices like sensors, actuators, etc. are located. The main objective of this layer is to collect information from the environment such as humidity, temperature, location, movement, etc., in addition to identifying objects with the help of different elements such as RFID readers, smart cards, and sensor networks. The Network Layer has as its main objective the transmission of data from the perception layer to the application layer. To carry out the data transfer, the network layer uses different types of technologies and protocols to ensure communication, for example: cellular networks, Bluetooth, Zigbee, Wi-Fi, 6LowPAN, ad-hoc, depending on sensor devices. The main objective of the application layer is to include the IoT applications to understand, analyze, process, and store the information received from the devices that comprise the IoT network. It is the one that interacts with the end customer. IoT applications can support various services from business to industrial environments [36–38].

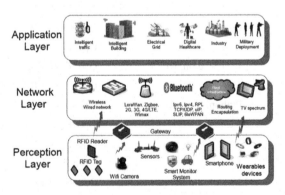

Fig. 2. IoT architecture [35].

4 IoT Management with SDN

With the use of SDN, the vast majority of critical problems or challenges of IoT can be mitigated (Table 2). The integration of SDN and IoT is implemented through an orderly management architecture, which can easily solve the configuration and reconfiguration of the system.

Table 2. SDN contributions to IoT.

SDN contributions to IoT	
Scalability	As an IoT network has many connected devices, it is expected to grow exponentially. SDN allows scalability based on its protocols that allow the management of data flows [39]
Availability	The IoT system must facilitate the installation of software and hardware at any place and time, with SDN availability is achieved based on the control layer for hardware monitoring and the application layer for configuration [14, 40]
Reliability	To have an effective IoT system requires reliable inter-layer communication, SDN improves this drawback by providing a distributed environment for controllers [40]
Interoperability	IoT has heterogeneity problems due to the various technologies, protocols, and data formats that devices handle, diversity can affect network performance. According to [41] the flexibility provided by SDN allows several devices connected to heterogeneous networks to communicate with each other
Heterogeneity	The Multiple Network Information Architecture (MINA) [7] is a middleware used to address this problem of heterogeneity in IoT environments that is very similar to the capabilities of SDN [42]
Programmability	The SDN controller has a global vision of the network, which allows configuring new functionalities and applications to the entire system without the need to configure each device [11]
Privacy and security	For IoT systems security is important to safeguard the information generated by thousands of connected devices, providers, and users, providing information security has become a problem, however, SDN can implement an identification policy in the connection phase of the controller with the router to mitigate the problem [35]
Efficiency	IoT systems need to improve communication technologies and protocols. SDN can solve this problem by incorporating a distributed control system [43]

4.1 SDN – Based IoT Management Taxonomy

The IoT device management challenges are derived from [44]. The four most relevant parameters are power management, safety, fault tolerance, and load balancing, they are generally considered critical parameters. According to their nature, IoT devices have limited resources, such as energy and memory restriction. In this way, in an IoT system, security is a significant parameter to consider, due to the large amount of information that IoT devices collect in each application. It is important to ensure data privacy. In addition to privacy, there are other security concerns [45, 46] such as routing attacks that directly interfere with IoT services. The IoT network is exposed to high failures due to power shortages and connectivity interferences, making monitoring and managing the nodes in the network a problem. To approach an effective IoT management solution security, configuration, device management, and IoT services must be considered. The studies discussed in this section are contrasted against each other according to the following four parameters.

Security Management. In an IoT system where interconnected devices send or exchange thousands of data, security becomes a fundamental parameter, data privacy, and privacy management are focused on many IoT applications.

Fault Tolerance. The problems that are generated in the IoT nodes by the transmission of the data are exposed to failures due to several factors, such as power distortion, interruption by environmental means or disasters, among others. Moreover, devices can send erroneous data captured from the environment for some unexpected reasons. Besides, ad hoc wireless networking tends to fail considerably due to topology changes causing divisions in the IoT network. These interruptions in the communication links affect the delivery of packets, however this problem is also presented by network congestion.

Energy Management. In an IoT network, the nodes are generally installed in distant areas where the main impact is energy depletion; this resource is limited in IoT. To solve the energy shortage balanced energy management between two factors, supply and load is required. Techniques such as the scheduled work period in each node for the suspension and activation of devices [47] allow the regulation of data traffic that helps to improve energy management. To build an efficient IoT network, a solution must be focused on this problem.

Load Balancing. A proper load balancing technique can improve power management in the IoT network. Clusters have become one of the most efficient methods to achieve this load balancing goal. When using clusters in an IoT system can guarantee numerous advantages such as reducing routing tables, improving bandwidth, energy management of the network, and control of packet delivery failures. For a correct IoT network performance, load balancing is a primary component in the IoT management solution.

The limitations in the resources of the IoT devices affect the management challenges, it is difficult to implement traditional techniques for IoT network management, adaptation is not possible either. This has generated multiple investigations that are detailed in this section pose challenges designing frameworks that adapt to these network management requirements.

The proposed taxonomy is presented in Fig. 3, where the IoT management frameworks with SDN are categorized into frameworks based on network function virtualization (NFV) and frameworks based on Middleware. This taxonomy is proposed to introduce the reader to the works in this field, explaining the relevant studies and comparing all the analyzed works, under the following parameters: Energy management, Security management, fault tolerance, and load management.

NFV-Based Frameworks. NFV enables network operators to manage and expand their network capabilities on demand using software-based virtual applications, it is highly compatible with SDN functions, but not directly dependent; NFV can be implemented without the need for SDN. However, concatenating these two concepts offers added value and greater potential to the network. In recent years the context of SDN-based NFV for IoT management is being addressed. The IoT network is changing and will increase its size exponentially, this change leads to difficulties for network administrators when they need to add new functions to the current network. To mitigate this problem NFV arises to connect several users without making a physical connection and avoid implementing new equipment. With NFV it is possible to virtualize different functions such as DNS, firewall, and cache, which in turn reduces the cost of implementation and network administration. In this section, the IoT frameworks based on NFV and SDN are analyzed.

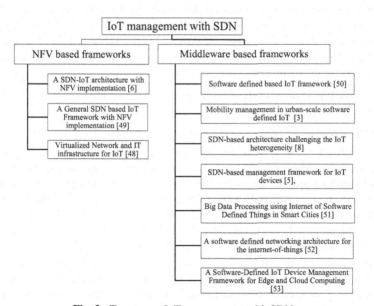

Fig. 3. Taxonomy, IoT management with SDN.

In [6], the authors present an SDN –IoT architecture with the NFV implementation, which allows the network administrator to manage the services through an SDN controller. They introduce SDN-enabled GW, which is a gateway that encompasses the heterogeneity of the network to facilitate the handling of large amounts of traffic from different IoT devices, and with the introduction of NFV, they solve the scalability problem in IoT networks.

In [48], the authors present an IoT architecture based on NFV and SDN, based on network resources and information technology (IT). This NFV architecture is used to virtualize the hardware resources of the physical part of the network. The proposed architecture consists of five layers. The first layer called the service layer is responsible for creating the functions at its level. The second global layer of the operating system places the description of each service on the network. The third layer is responsible for managing the resources to satisfy and perform the infrastructure services. The fourth layer SDN controller is in charge of the control of the network and IT resources. The virtualization layer is responsible for grouping virtual machines that contain hardware resources.

In [49], and IoT management framework based on SDN with NFV aggregation is proposed. In this architecture, NFV is responsible for virtualizing network functions through virtual machines to establish communication services. Virtual machines execute heterogeneous processes and avoid acquiring hardware devices to establish new network functions. This proposal makes use of the OpenFlow protocol to establish a secure communication path between the IoT gateway and the ONOS controller. The authors propose a three-layer framework; the infrastructure layer, which is responsible for the access of heterogeneous devices through IoT gateways with the combination of SDN switches; the control layer that is responsible for management through distributed operating systems for centralized control and total view of the network topology; and the application layer that hosts the servers to provide the IoT services and applications based on the API. This architecture with a distributed system is efficient for an environment of heterogeneity of costumers.

Frameworks Based on Middleware. In this section, the studies of middleware for IoT based on SDN are analyzed.

In [50], the authors emphasize the heterogeneity of the devices of the IoT network and IoT applications, to achieve coupling the devices and applications are based on a three-layer IoT architecture; physical layer, control layer (middleware) and application layer. The authors propose an architecture based on the integration between the cloud and IoT. The control layer is distributed in four controllers with specific functions that are: IoT controller, SDN controller, SDN storage controller, and SDN security controller (SDSec). The proposed system was built to carry out a proof of concept and explain how to collect and manage big data that is produced in an IoT network with diverse devices.

A framework called UbiFlow for ubiquitous flow control and mobility management in multiple networks is proposed in [3], it is based on distributed SDN controllers to manage heterogeneous flow control in an urban multi-network environment. UbiFlow's main function is to achieve mobility management and fault tolerance in an IoT network. The architecture has an algorithm to establish the access point for the IoT devices for each controller and thus manage the clusters that are made up of geographic partitions. The essential elements of UbiFlow are the switches, access points, servers, controllers, and devices. They conclude, based on a test bench, that UbiFlow efficiently manages to manage mobility in a scalable way in the different IoT networks.

In [8], the authors propose an SDN architecture to manage the heterogeneity of devices and IoT networks, this proposal is based on the implementation of Docker an application deployment automation for each device, they validate their proposal through the communication of different devices over the SDN network. The simulation environment was Mininet. Furthermore, with the use of a centralized SDN controller, they generate different traffics to check connectivity between heterogeneous devices linked to multiple networks.

An architecture to manage IoT devices using SDN and machine-machine technology (M2M) is presented in [5]. The architecture is based on four elements: the controller, the M2M nodes, the gateway, and the general nodes. The controller is responsible for managing and controlling network traffic. M2M nodes are terminals or networks that support M2M communications. The gateway makes use of a transfer function for protocol conversion, it is responsible for connecting the devices that cannot connect because they do not support the M2M protocol.

In [51], the authors suggest an IoT - SDN architecture applied to Smart Cities. The authors show a three-level framework, collection level, data management level, and application-level; likewise, these are connected to two intermediate sublevels according to the SDN architecture, which is event and decision management and called data network (NDN). They evaluate the architecture using Spark and GraphX with Hadoop Ecosystem, with favorable results achieving efficient data transfer over SDN for real-time processing.

Other studies propose different layers for the integration of IoT and SDN. For example, in [52], a four-layer architecture is established: tasks, services, flow, and network, based on the multiple network information architecture (MINA) The communication layer captures data from heterogeneous IoT network environments and subsequently stores it in databases. The operation of the architecture consists of first defining the task to be carried out, then specifying the devices and applications to fulfill it, and finally, the network layer routes and specifies which network is going to use to carry out the operation based on the SDN controller.

In [53], the authors present a software-defined IoT management framework (SDIM) applied to edge computing multidomain sensor networks (WSN). This architecture allows IoT devices machine-to-machine (M2M) communication, as well as the detection of operational failures for WSN. The architecture is implemented in multiple access edge computing (MEC) nodes and is concatenated with the cloud by adding multidomain topology information.

In [54–65], another investigation on middleware for managing the IoT network is shown. Efforts that have been made to achieve an architecture that is efficient for all IoT requirements.

5 Discussion

The management challenges boarded by the proposed frameworks are summarized. Table 3 shows which parameters are supported by the analyzed proposals on the SDN-IoT management framework. The methodology applied for the evaluation of the study is based on the data acquired from all the methods described in each investigation. We examine the architectures and functionalities of each of them.

The analyzed network functions virtualization (NFV) proposals address the issue of security over IoT. Safety is the most relevant factor to analyze in this field. In the different IoT scenarios, provide security services through a network with few restrictions due to the limitations in a complex work, since traditional security mechanisms and protocols are not compatible or adaptable to the IoT environment. In the proposals analyzed in [48, 49], they present a minimal approach to security services, especially in the field of attack mitigation and management. In [50], present SDSec to provide security in the IoT network, likewise in [57–59], the frameworks oriented to middleware mention a security approach.

Fault tolerance is another critical factor in the IoT environment due to its nature. To evaluate the fault-tolerance parameter the study of [3] is used as a basis, where it explains that to approach this problem, it divides the IoT network into clusters. The proposed algorithm segments traffic in different parts of the network contributing positively to load balancing, besides, fault tolerance is achieved in the first instance by identifying failed nodes in the entire IoT environment, to redirect all that traffic to the nodes that they are running normally on the network. The other proposals have approached the management of IoT based on SDN, but do not consider the fault tolerance factor.

The management of energy resources is a very important parameter in the IoT environment. SDN network can solve this problem based on the controller that can help schedule the flows in the network, with the aim of conserving energy and lowering the processing load on the devices. With this, another factor that supports this problem is to centralize the view of the network topology for energy-efficient data incorporation and management. Therefore, as a guideline for future research, it is essential to explore the potential of the SDN paradigm especially that SDN allows to centralize the network view, becoming a candidate to mitigate or solve IoT management problems. None of the frameworks analyzed contrast energy management in IoT.

The objective of load balancing the traffic in the IoT network is to distribute the traffic in different servers, computers, or virtual machines within a cluster to avoid overload and congestion of the network and in this way improve its performance. To mitigate this problem, the SDN controller, based on its complete network view, can manage and monitor the traffic, in the same way, the centralization contributes to the load balancing within the IoT network. Load balancing mechanisms and algorithms in the SDN controller manage to assess the expected load in IoT to avoid effects on the network traffic flow. Likewise, the controller can make decisions about the traffic routing of the IoT nodes. The authors in [3] suggest clustering to address this problem in the network. The other SDN-based management frameworks do not consider load balancing in their proposal.

Table 3. Comparison of current frameworks based on SDN-IoT.

Taxonomy	Existing works	Security management	Fault tolerance	Energy management	Load balance
NFV based frameworks	[48, 49]	Yes	No	No	No
	[6]	No	No	No	No
	[3]	Yes	Yes	No	Yes
Middleware based frameworks	[50, 54, 56–62, 64, 65]	Yes	No	No	No
	[5, 8, 51–53, 55, 63]	No	No	No	No

6 Conclusions

This document examines the SDN and IoT network architectures to provide an analysis of the functionalities by a layer of each architecture. A taxonomy is presented and details of all the existing software-defined network-based IoT management work search are presented. The taxonomy is classified, in frameworks based on virtualization of network functions and frameworks based on middleware, these research efforts were evaluated through the four requirements for the management of IoT that are: Security management, fault tolerance, energy management, and load balance. So far there is no evidence of any research that addresses the four critical factors for IoT management. The network functions virtualization based IoT management framework works minimally address the security service part, but lack a detailed evaluation of its effectiveness for an architecture proposal that is tailored to IoT management. However, a middleware-based management framework comprehensively addresses the software-defined security service for the Internet of Things. Likewise, there are few works that address load management and fault tolerances; the proposed UbiFlow management framework addresses this problem by including a minimum approach to security services. All the works suffer in their proposal of the energy management factor; however, they propose an IoT management framework based on SDN.

In future work, the objective is to focus on the needs and requirements of the software layer (middleware), especially the requirements of load balancing and fault tolerance. Design a management proposal that allows the control and programmability of each device in the network; the potential of software-defined networks (SDN) offers the possibility of implementing a solution for this problem. Therefore, a thorough investigation is needed on centralized control SDN in IoT, as the SDN controller can work on fault management in faulty IoT nodes and load management to balance the traffic on the network. In the same way, it is necessary to provide data reliability in the various IoT applications, addressing the security factor is a primary requirement, the SDN controller with its global network view allows implementing security services to mitigate attacks. Therefore, research on security services should be deepened through the benefits that SDN offers for IoT. These areas of IoT network management will have a lot of expansion in the future in the direction of security, fault tolerance, power management and load control aspects.

References

1. International Telecommunication Union: Overview of the Internet of things. Ser. Y Glob. Inf. infrastructure, internet Protoc. Asp. next-generation networks - Fram. Funct. Archit. Model. p. 22 (2012)
2. Alam, M., Nielsen, R.H., Prasad, N.R.: The evolution of M2M into IoT. In: 2013 First International Black Sea Conference on Communications and Networking (BlackSeaCom), pp. 112–115. IEEE (2013)
3. Wu, D., Arkhipov, D.I., Asmare, E., Qin, Z., McCann, J.A.: UbiFlow: mobility management in urban-scale software defined IoT. In: Proceedings - IEEE INFOCOM, pp. 208–216 (2015)
4. Theodorou, T., Violettas, G., Valsamas, P., Petridou, S., Mamatas, L.: A multi-protocol software-defined networking solution for the Internet of Things. IEEE Commun. Mag. 57, 42–48 (2019). https://doi.org/10.1109/MCOM.001.1900056
5. Huang, H., Zhu, J., Zhang, L.: An SDN-based management framework for IoT devices. In: IET Conference Publications, pp. 175–179. Institution of Engineering and Technology (2014)
6. Ojo, M., Adami, D., Giordano, S.: A SDN-IoT architecture with NFV implementation. In: 2016 IEEE Globecom Workshops, GC Wkshps 2016 - Proceedings. Institute of Electrical and Electronics Engineers Inc. (2016)
7. Qin, Z., Iannario, L., Giannelli, C., Bellavista, P., Denker, G., Venkatasubramanian, N.: MINA: A reflective middleware for managing dynamic multinetwork environments. In: IEEE/IFIP NOMS 2014 - IEEE/IFIP Network Operations and Management Symposium: Management in a Software Defined World (2014)
8. Bedhief, I., Kassar, M., Aguili, T.: SDN-based architecture challenging the IoT heterogeneity. In: 2016 3rd Smart Cloud Networks and Systems, SCNS 2016. Institute of Electrical and Electronics Engineers Inc. (2017)
9. Kakiz, M.T., Öztürk, E., Çavdar, T.: A novel SDN-based IoT architecture for big data. In: IDAP 2017 - International Artificial Intelligence and Data Processing Symposium. Institute of Electrical and Electronics Engineers Inc. (2017)
10. Bryant, S., Andersson, L.: Joint Working Team (JWT) Report on MPLS Architectural Considerations for a Transport Profile. RFC 5317, February 2009
11. Bizanis, N., Kuipers, F.A.: SDN and virtualization solutions for the Internet of Things: a survey. IEEE Access 4, 5591–5606 (2016)
12. ONF: Definición de redes definidas por software (SDN) - Open Networking Foundation. https://www.opennetworking.org/sdn-definition/
13. Kreutz, D., Ramos, F.M.V., Verissimo, P.E., Rothenberg, C.E., Azodolmolky, S., Uhlig, S.: Software-defined networking: a comprehensive survey. Proc. IEEE. 103, 14–76 (2015). https://doi.org/10.1109/JPROC.2014.2371999
14. Jarraya, Y., Madi, T., Debbabi, M.: A survey and a layered taxonomy of software-defined networking. IEEE Commun. Surv. Tutor. 16, 1955–1980 (2014)
15. Gong, Y., Huang, W., Wang, W., Lei, Y.: A survey on software defined networking and its applications. Front. Comput. Sci. 9, 827–845 (2015). https://doi.org/10.1007/s11704-015-3448-z
16. McKeown, N., et al.: OpenFlow. ACM SIGCOMM Comput. Commun. Rev. 38, 69–74 (2008). https://doi.org/10.1145/1355734.1355746
17. Gude, N., et al.: NOX: towards an operating system for networks. ACM SIGCOMM Comput. Commun. Rev. 38, 105–110 (2008). https://doi.org/10.1145/1384609.1384625
18. Rowshanrad, S., Abdi, V., Keshtgari, M.: Performance evaluation of SDN controllers: floodlight and OpenDaylight. IIUM Eng. J. 17, 47–57 (2016)
19. Bholebawa, I., Dalal, U.: Performance analysis of SDN/OpenFlow controllers: POX versus floodlight. Wireless Pers. Commun. 98(2), 1679–1699 (2017). https://doi.org/10.1007/s11277-017-4939-z

20. Vachuska, T.: Open Network Operating System (ONOS). Archit. Overv. ON.LAB. vol. 12, pp. 1–16 (2013)
21. COMMUNITY 2017: Ryu SDN Framework (2017)
22. Erickson, D.: The beacon OpenFlow controller. In: Proceedings of the Second ACM SIGCOMM Workshop on Hot Topics in Software Defined Networking, pp. 13–18 (2013)
23. Tootoonchian, A., Ganjali, Y.: HyperFlow: A Distributed Control Plane for OpenFlow (2010)
24. Cai, Z., Cox, A.L., Ng, T.S.E.: Maestro: a system for scalable OpenFlow control. Technical report. Rice University (2011)
25. Hassas Yeganeh, S., Ganjali, Y.: Kandoo: a framework for efficient and scalable offloading of control applications. In: Proceedings of the First Workshop on Hot Topics in Software Defined Networks, pp. 19–24 (2012)
26. Saikia, D.: MuL OpenFlow Controller. https://sourceforge.net/p/mul/wiki/Home/
27. Takamiya, Y., Karanatsios, N.: Trema OpenFlow controller framework (2012)
28. Phemius, K., Bouet, M., Leguay, J.: DISCO: distributed multi-domain SDN controllers. In: 2014 IEEE Network Operations and Management Symposium (NOMS), pp. 1–4. IEEE (2014)
29. Dixit, A., Hao, F., Mukherjee, S., Lakshman, T.V., Kompella, R.R.: ElastiCon; an elastic distributed SDN controller. In: 2014 ACM/IEEE Symposium on Architectures for Networking and Communications Systems (ANCS), pp. 17–27. IEEE (2014)
30. Gubbi, J., Buyya, R., Marusic, S., Palaniswami, M.: Internet of Things (IoT): a vision, architectural elements, and future directions. Futur. Gener. Comput. Syst. **29**, 1645–1660 (2013). https://doi.org/10.1016/j.future.2013.01.010
31. Al Hayajneh, A., Bhuiyan, M.Z.A., McAndrew, I.: Improving Internet of Things (IoT) security with software-defined networking (SDN). Computers **9**, 8 (2020). https://doi.org/10.3390/computers9010008
32. Khan, S., Ali, M., Sher, N., Asim, Y., Naeem, W., Kamran, M.: Software-defined networks (SDNs) and Internet of Things (IoTs): a qualitative prediction for 2020. Int. J. Adv. Comput. Sci. Appl. **7** (2016). https://doi.org/10.14569/ijacsa.2016.071151
33. Li, S., Xu, L.D., Zhao, S.: The Internet of Things: a survey. Inf. Syst. Front. **17**(2), 243–259 (2014). https://doi.org/10.1007/s10796-014-9492-7
34. Sethi, P., Sarangi, S.R.: Internet of Things: architectures, protocols, and applications. J. Electr. Comput. Eng. **2017** (2017). https://doi.org/10.1155/2017/9324035
35. Jing, Q., Vasilakos, A.V., Wan, J., Lu, J., Qiu, D.: Security of the Internet of Things: perspectives and challenges. Wireless Netw. **20**(8), 2481–2501 (2014). https://doi.org/10.1007/s11276-014-0761-7
36. Özbayoğlu, A.M., Sezer, Ö.B., Doğdu, E.: Context-aware computing, learning, and big data in Internet of Things: a survey. IEEE Internet Things J. **5**, 1–27 (2018)
37. Chen, S., Xu, H., Liu, D., Hu, B., Wang, H.: A vision of IoT: applications, challenges, and opportunities with china perspective. IEEE Internet Things J. **1**, 349–359 (2014)
38. Pandya, H.B., Champaneria, T.A.: Notice of retraction Internet of Things: survey and case studies. In: 2015 International Conference on Electrical, Electronics, Signals, Communication and Optimization (EESCO), pp. 1–6. IEEE (2015)
39. Karakus, M., Durresi, A.: A survey: control plane scalability issues and approaches in software-defined networking (SDN). Comput. Netw. **112**, 279–293 (2017)
40. Al-Fuqaha, A., Guizani, M., Mohammadi, M., Aledhari, M., Ayyash, M.: Internet of Things: a survey on enabling technologies, protocols, and applications. IEEE Commun. Surv. Tutor. **17**, 2347–2376 (2015). https://doi.org/10.1109/COMST.2015.2444095
41. Ganzha, M., Paprzycki, M., Pawłowski, W., Szmeja, P., Wasielewska, K.: Semantic interoperability in the Internet of Things: an overview from the INTER-IoT perspective. J. Netw. Comput. Appl. **81**, 111–124 (2017)
42. Nguyen, T.D., Khan, J.Y., Ngo, D.T.: A distributed energy-harvesting-aware routing algorithm for heterogeneous IoT networks. IEEE Trans. Green Commun. Netw. **2**, 1115–1127 (2018)

43. Flauzac, O., Gonzalez, C., Nolot, F.: Developing a distributed software defined networking testbed for IoT. Procedia Comput. Sci. **83**, 680–684 (2016)
44. Christin, D., Reinhardt, A., Mogre, P.S., Steinmetz, R.: Wireless sensor networks and the internet of things: selected challenges. In: Proceedings of the 8th GI/ITG KuVS Fachgespräch Drahtlose sensornetze, pp. 31–34 (2009)
45. Suo, H., Wan, J., Zou, C., Liu, J.: Security in the Internet of Things: a review. In: 2012 International Conference on Computer Science and Electronics Engineering, pp. 648–651. IEEE (2012)
46. Sicari, S., Rizzardi, A., Grieco, L.A., Coen-Porisini, A.: Security, privacy and trust in Internet of Things: the road ahead. Comput. Netw. **76**, 146–164 (2015)
47. Khan, J.A., Qureshi, H.K., Iqbal, A.: Energy management in wireless sensor networks: a survey. Comput. Electr. Eng. **41**, 159–176 (2015)
48. Omnes, N., Bouillon, M., Fromentoux, G., Le Grand, O.: A programmable and virtualized network & IT infrastructure for the Internet of Things: how can NFV & SDN help for facing the upcoming challenges. In: 2015 18th International Conference on Intelligence in Next Generation Networks, pp. 64–69. IEEE (2015)
49. Li, J., Altman, E., Touati, C.: A general SDN-based IoT framework with NVF implementation. ZTE Commun. **13**, 42–45 (2015)
50. Jararweh, Y., Al-Ayyoub, M., Darabseh, A., Benkhelifa, E., Vouk, M., Rindos, A.: SDIoT: a software defined based Internet of Things framework. J. Ambient Intell. Humaniz. Comput. **6**(4), 453–461 (2015). https://doi.org/10.1007/s12652-015-0290-y
51. Khan, M., Iqbal, J., Talha, M., Arshad, M., Diyan, M., Han, K.: Big data processing using internet of software defined things in smart cities. Int. J. Parallel Program. **48**(2), 178–191 (2018). https://doi.org/10.1007/s10766-018-0573-y
52. Qin, Z., Denker, G., Giannelli, C., Bellavista, P., Venkatasubramanian, N.: A software defined networking architecture for the Internet-of-Things. In: IEEE/IFIP NOMS 2014 - IEEE/IFIP Network Operations and Management Symposium: Management in a Software Defined World, pp. 1–9. IEEE Computer Society (2014)
53. Mavromatis, A., Colman-Meixner, C., Silva, A.P., Vasilakos, X., Nejabati, R., Simeonidou, D.: A software-defined IoT device management framework for edge and cloud computing. IEEE Internet Things J. **7**, 1718–1735 (2020). https://doi.org/10.1109/JIOT.2019.2949629
54. Arbiza, L.M.R., Bertholdo, L.M., dos Santos, C.R.P., Granville, L.Z., Tarouco, L.M.R.: Refactoring Internet of Things middleware through software-defined network. In: Proceedings of the 30th Annual ACM Symposium on Applied Computing, pp. 640–645 (2015)
55. Zhou, J., Jiang, H., Wu, J., Wu, L., Zhu, C., Li, W.: SDN-based application framework for wireless sensor and actor networks. IEEE Access **4**, 1583–1594 (2016)
56. Jacobsson, M., Orfanidis, C.: Using software-defined networking principles for wireless sensor networks. In: SNCNW 2015, Karlstad, Sweden, 28–29 May 2015 (2015)
57. Galluccio, L., Milardo, S., Morabito, G., Palazzo, S.: SDN-WISE: design, prototyping and experimentation of a stateful SDN solution for WIreless SEnsor networks. In: 2015 IEEE Conference on Computer Communications (INFOCOM), pp. 513–521. IEEE (2015)
58. Chakrabarty, S., Engels, D.W., Thathapudi, S.: Black SDN for the Internet of Things. In: 2015 IEEE 12th International Conference on Mobile Ad Hoc and Sensor Systems, pp. 190–198. IEEE (2015)
59. Ammar, M., Russello, G., Crispo, B.: Internet of Things: a survey on the security of IoT frameworks. J. Inf. Secur. Appl. **38**, 8–27 (2018)
60. Wan, J., et al.: Software-defined industrial Internet of Things in the context of industry 40. IEEE Sens. J. **16**, 7373–7380 (2016)
61. Li, Y., Su, X., Riekki, J., Kanter, T., Rahmani, R.: A SDN-based architecture for horizontal Internet of Things services. In: 2016 IEEE International Conference on Communications (ICC), pp. 1–7. IEEE (2016)

62. Sood, K., Yu, S., Xiang, Y.: Software-defined wireless networking opportunities and challenges for Internet-of-Things: a review. IEEE Internet Things J. **3**, 453–463 (2015)
63. Akram, H., Gokhale, A.: Rethinking the design of LR-WPAN IoT systems with software-defined networking. In: 2016 International Conference on Distributed Computing in Sensor Systems (DCOSS), pp. 238–243. IEEE (2016)
64. Orfanidis, C.: Ph.D. Forum abstract: increasing robustness in WSN using software defined network architecture. In: 2016 15th ACM/IEEE International Conference on Information Processing in Sensor Networks (IPSN), pp. 1–2. IEEE (2016)
65. Jacquenet, C., Boucadair, M.: A software-defined approach to IoT networking. ZTE Commun. **14**, 61–68 (2019)

Building an OWL Ontology Step By Step for Lean-Based Software Development

Sandra Gutierrez-Rios[1] (ID), José Manuel Gómez Pulido[2] (ID),
and Miguel Vargas-Lombardo[1](✉) (ID)

[1] FISC, Research Group GISES, Technological University of Panama, Panama City, Panama
{sandra.gutierrez,miguel.vargas}@utp.ac.pa
[2] Departamento Ciencias de la Computación, Universidad de Alcalá, Madrid, España
jose.gomez@uah.es

Abstract. Lean Software Development (LSD) is a set of principles and practices that seek to increase the value of the organization by improving quality and software development processes, through value flow mapping and waste removal. Because of LSD's contributions, many organizations are interested in implementing it; however, adopting the principles and practices of LSD without knowing the correct process leads to the premature abandonment of this methodology. Therefore, describing the implementation process through a formal and theoretical language, such as a basic ontology, allows you to have a greater perception of the elements to consider if you want to implement LSD. The objective of this research is to develop a base ontology for the implementation of Lean Software Development in an organization using a mature software development process.

Keywords: Lean Software Development · Ontology · Implementation · Companies cooperatives

1 Introduction

Lean software development is based on lean thinking, a Toyota production system that was born in the 1950s and whose principles were later adapted to software development. Lean software development (LSD) establishes seven principles aimed at software development, which are driven by a set of practices that use methods, techniques and tools focused on streamlining the development process by providing flexibility, transparency and communication to the work team and the organization so as to maximize client value by eliminating waste and offering a high-quality product. However, the process that an organization must undergo in order to adopt the LSD principles and practices is not very clear, leading organizations to apply some principles without contemplating the entire set, thereby generating results, but without an interest in continuing the process. That is why the current research develops an application ontology to illustrates LSD to the scientific community and describe the LSD implementation process within an organization. In order to provide the scientific community with information about LSD applied to cooperative companies in the Panamanian context, an ontology has been developed

© Springer Nature Switzerland AG 2021
M. Botto-Tobar et al. (Eds.): ICAT 2020, CCIS 1388, pp. 590–603, 2021.
https://doi.org/10.1007/978-3-030-71503-8_46

which describes the process of LSD implementation within an organization and its software development process flows until it reaches maturity. The research is organized as follows: Sect. 2 outlines the general concepts of lean software development and ontology engineering, Sect. 3 describes the characteristics involved in the development of the LSD ontology, Sect. 4 specifies the implementation process of the LSD ontology, and Sect. 5 highlights the conclusions and future work.

2 Background

This section describes the lean principles and practices applied to software development and the characteristics and processes that must be contemplated for the creation of ontologies focused on engineering of software.

2.1 Lean Software Development

The lean methodology has its origins in the Toyota production system (TPS) in the 1950s [30], but it was not until 1990 that lean thinking began to be associated with software development, with concepts such as the development of lean software. However, lean software development (LSD) is a different framework, created to address the problems with traditional development, which provides the theory behind agile practices. In fact, it is a necessary progression for organizations that plan to scale project or team agility to the organizational level, which agile methods fail to address adequately [6, 22, 30]. On the other hand, the lean principles are responsible for delivering or adapting the environment to the development of a product that is focused on agility, quality and value to the client. At the same time, it offers the tactical knowledge of transferable engineering experience to the next generations of collaborators on the project team through active learning [26]. In addition, value, understood from the client's perspective, is the central focus of the lean methodology, since every activity in the organization must result in value for the client. Therefore, if something absorbs resources but does not produce any value, it is considered waste and is eliminated in order to focus on the value-creating activities [1, 2, 12]. In order to provide an alternative response to the existing problem, an ontology for the implementation of lean software development is developed based on the principles of development of ontology engineering, as described in the following section.

2.2 Ontology Engineering

Ontology engineering is defined as "the set of activities concerning the development process of the ontology, the life cycle of the ontology and the methodologies, tools and languages used to build ontologies" [16]. In other words, an ontology is the representation of a vocabulary that contains a formal definition of types, properties, relationships, axioms and instances between concepts, data and entities categorized in classes and subclasses involved in a given context. This is because an ontological model is a powerful mechanism used to represent knowledge and encode its meaning in order to provide a shared understanding between people, organizations and systems by providing a formal, explicit, flexible and understandable vocabulary for anyone who wants to implement it, while avoiding ambiguity [27, 31]. This paper considers the five phases of ontology development, proposed by [18], as the basis for the creation of the LSD ontology described below:

- Specification: Identifying the purpose and scope of the ontology.
- Conceptualization: Creating a conceptual model of the ontology.
- Formalization: Translating the conceptual model into a formal one, for example, by adding axioms that restrict possible interpretations.
- Implementation: Implementing the formal model in a language for knowledge representation.
- Maintenance: Constantly evaluating, updating and correcting the implemented ontology.

Currently, ontologies have been established as one of the possible ways of presenting complex knowledge and reasoning about them, and these can be classified as application domain ontologies, ontologies that formalize the process of knowledge gathering about the application's domain and ontologies that bear knowledge about the quality attributes of the requirements [8, 13, 29]. In this specific case, for the development of the LSD ontology, the type of ontology that will be used is that of the application domain, because it creates the possibility of reducing the number of errors and problems in all the phases of the product development life cycle, from the requirements analysis to the implementation stages.

2.3   Application of Ontologies and External Investigations

Therefore, for the creation of the LSD ontological model, we will observe the guidelines set by [7, 16, 25, 29], which establish parameters and methods of creation, development and implementation of an ontology.

For this reason, for the creation of an LSD ontological model, the seven principles established by Poppendieck and Poppendieck [19, 20] are considered as fundamental concepts when implementing LSD. These concepts are described as follows:

- Eliminate Waste: Lean philosophy considers that anything that does not add value to the client is waste, in the same sense that software development contemplates seven types of waste.
- Amplify Learning: Software development is a continuous iteration-based learning process. In addition to this, lean applies short iteration cycles and increases feedback and communication within the team, allowing the increase of continuous learning for both developers and the client via awareness of the domain problems and possible solutions.
- Decide as Late as Possible: Decisions should be deferred as long as possible until they can be made based on specific facts and not on uncertain assumptions or predictions.
- Deliver as Fast as Possible: Minimize the time that between the receipt of the client's needs and the delivery of the product without defects, in order to observe and analyze the results as soon as possible, thus ensuring compliance with the client's needs.

- Empower the Team: Promote respect for people among leaders and staff, and build an expert technical workforce [8].
- Build Integrity In: The different components of a product work well in conjunction with a balance among flexibility, easy maintainability, efficiency and responsiveness, in order to establish the quality of the product as soon as possible to avoid defects in later stages.
- Optimize the Whole: The focus should be on the entire software development process; the macro tasks are divided into smaller tasks, and the different stages of the project are standardized.

Likewise, other factors to consider are lean practices, which are those techniques and/or tools designed to guarantee proper adoption of lean principles in software development [14], as described below:

- Detecting Waste: Identifies which activities add value and which do not in order to improve or eliminate them [1, 4, 9, 21, 22, 24, 30].
- Value Stream Mapping: Analyzes the current management and designs the future state of a set of events that the project has from its initial stage to its delivery, highlighting the critical steps of each process while measuring the time spent in their development, in order to reduce or eliminate waste [3, 5, 10–12, 30, 32].
- Just in Time: A set of strategies aimed at reducing the time cycle of a software project [4].
- Kanban: Describes a workflow in which all team members are updated on progress [6, 22, 30].
- Queuing Theory: Optimizes the development time of the processes by assigning tasks based on the waiting time and the appropriate personnel.
- Continuous Improvement: Focused on problem-solving, involving people in processes and solving problems present in them, and facilitating the appropriate channels of communication [14, 15, 17, 22, 23].
- Testing-Based Development: Based on the repetition of a cycle in short iterations, in which the operability of the different advances of the project is verified.
- Leveled Production: Highlights the prevalence of people with experience in the development of various types of tasks [26].

In addition, the parameters established by [18], which detail a series of steps for the creation of an ontology, are taken as a reference, and some of these characteristics are adopted to adapt them to the development needs of the LSD implementation ontology. In this way, a conceptual structure is designed offer the bases of an ontological model that allows the implementation of LSD within an organization. This model considers seven steps for the creation of the LSD ontology (see Fig. 1).

Additionally, in order to lead the implementation of LSD to a state of formality and optimization of the processes carried out within an organization, the five elements involved in the maturity scale of software development established by [28], as described below, are taken into consideration:

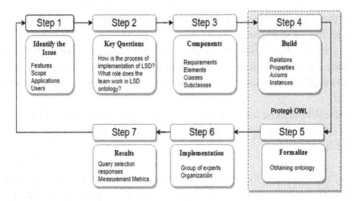

Fig. 1. Ontological model that allows the implementation of LSD within an organization

- Test Automatization (TA): Perform parallel tests and present test reports of automated security, performance, trends, unit and integration.
- Quality (Q): Apply quality policies or standards, failure tests and exploration methods, design verification, environment and production evaluation, documentation control and acceptance tests of the produced product.
- Build and Deployment (BD): Consider continuous development, continuous delivery, production processes, client and environment monitoring, documentation configuration, migration control and version control.
- Running and Monitoring (RM): Establish performance monitoring, value assessment, alert automation, server performance, work team performance control, user actions, registrations, accesses and errors records.
- Typical Lead Time (TLT): Establish a development period based on specific times depending on the project's complexity or magnitude.

2.4   Questions About Competences

As mentioned before, the ontology must be able to represent the necessary tasks for an external system if necessary. The competence questions are developed in response to these considerations, which according to [7] must be divided into basic categories, which in turn can be subdivided into domain-specific requirements to establish logical parts of the system, as defined below:

- Selection: Questions that can be answered by means of a selection of the ontology instances.
- Count: Questions that are answered by adding instances.
- Capacity: A technology or interface that the ontology must support in its design.
- Reasoning: An aspect of reasoning that is required through validating or categorizing instances.

3   Material and Methodology: Ontology-Based Lean Software Development Implementation Process

Based on the methodology detailed above, the next step is the development of an ontology focused on LSD, considering the step sequences described before:

3.1   Step 1: Identifying the Issue

To adopt LSD principles and practices, an organization must consider the different characteristics involved in implementing LSD, but many organizations apply lean methodologies without doing a prior study of the needs and/or requirements that these demand. Moreover, unawareness of the adoption, implementation and execution process of the LSD principles and practices leads to a deterioration of the development processes, thus causing dissatisfaction among the members involved and the subsequent abandonment of LSD. This happens because there is no literature that includes, in formal language, a set of actions or parameters to consider for the implementation of LSD. Taking these considerations into account, the ontology-based LSD implementation seeks to respond to this problem by allowing organizational members to have a base that enables them to better manage the adoption of LSD practices. Based on the ideas presented and the scope of the LSD ontology, we proceed to determine the key questions for the development of the ontology.

3.2   Step 2: Key Questions

The key questions are determining factors for the development of the ontology, as they help to establish research parameters that promote the discovery of LSD characteristics. This leads to the creation of an ontology based on the theory outlined above and the following key questions:

What are the established parameters to develop an LSD ontology?
How is the LSD process implemented?
What are the principles and practices to apply when implementing LSD?
What role does the organizational team have in the design, development and implementation of an LSD ontology?

3.3   Step 3: Components

Once the key questions to develop the LSD ontology have been established, the components involved in implementing LSD have to be described, considering three fundamental criteria:

- Organization: The team's network, with a culture focused on people and on producing value quickly, which works with iterative learning and decision-making processes supported by technological tools.

- Teamwork: A network of empowered and multidisciplinary autonomous people committed to continuous learning and development through communication, transparency and flexibility.
- Software development process:A defined set of steps to build a software development product and/or service, which goes from the requirements' receipt to the implementation. Furthermore, it is important to describe lean principles and practices and the relationship between the two terms in order to illustrate how lean thinking works in the software development domain, as detailed in Table 1.

Table 1. Lean Software development principles and practices

Principles	Characteristics	Practices
Eliminate waste	Work performed halfway Extra functionality Re-learning Knowledge transfer Delays Change of tasks Defects	Kanban Just-in-time Inventory Value Stream Mapping Visualizing Waste
Amplify learning	Constant code reviews Elaboration of documentation Design of informative tables subject to updates Integrate Knowledge	Continuous Improvement Theory of Constraints
Decide as late as possible	Keep all options available for as long as possible Ensure certain result when there is certainty of being able to comply with the agreement	Leveled Production Just in Time
Deliver as fast as possible	Teamwork Meet quality standards Create strategies to meet objectives Have qualified personnel	Just-in-Time. Kanban Continuous Improvement Testing-Based Development
Empower the team	Respect Motivate Acknowledgement Autonomy	Leveled Production Kanban
Build integrity in	Constant feedback Reduction of the time for delivery deadlines from one task to the next Increase of the integration frequency Automation	Continuous Improvement Continuous Integration Testing-Based Development
Optimize the whole	Task division Functions distribution	Continuous Improvement Leveled Production

Based on the information described in Table 1 and the elements of the maturity scale of software development, the principles and elements involved in each phase of LSD are outlined. It should be noted that, in this research, the elements of maturity and the LSD principles are developed together in order to build a software project that is formal and valuable to the client and the organization.

3.4 Step 4: Build

The main classes and subclasses that will be applied in the construction of the ontology-based LSD implementation are established based on the components described in the previous section. As seen in Fig. 2, the main classes are lean software development, organization, teamwork, principles, practices, and software development process, from which a set of subclasses that specify the components that have to be considered for LSD implementation are derived. In addition, the classes and subclasses are linked by means of relationships and axioms that detail a formal ontological model regarding the implementation of LSD. It must be emphasized that implementing LSD in an organization not only influences the development project, but it also affects the processes of the entire organization, thus allowing improvement in matters of value, quality, transparency, flexibility and communication.

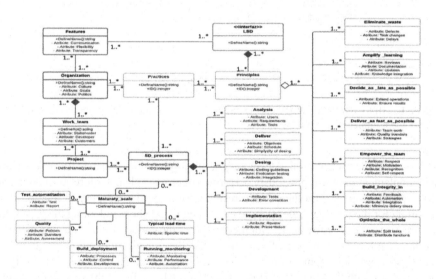

Fig. 2. Class diagram of the ontology-based lean software development implementation

3.5 Step 5: Formalize

Ontologies require logical and formal language in order to be expressed. Therefore, based on the parameters described above, this section proceeds to formalize the ontology-based LSD implementation. For its formal construction, we have used the open-source tool

Protégé, developed by Stanford University and the University of Manchester and based on the OWL (Ontology Web Language), to create, model and develop ontologies. Based on this, Fig. 3 shows an extract of the distribution of the classes and subclasses that are part of ontology-based lean software development implementation developed with the Protégé tool. It is important to emphasize that, in this illustration, the elements considered as main classes, such as lean software development in conjunction with the maturity scale, teamwork, project and organization, are observed; and at the same time, each one has subclasses that allow a complete, deep and precise implementation during the development process.

Fig. 3. Excerpt from the ontology classes and subclasses of the ontology-based lean software development implementation class diagram

A systematic review for the development of ontology-based lean software development implementation was previously performed to provide clearer, more substantial and more reliable guidance on the subject, resulting in a set of concepts and relationships important for the ontology's development. As mentioned above, adopting the principles and practices of lean software development requires the participation of the organization and the members that are part of it, as this leads the organization and its projects to a mature software development process, by involving a scalable measure of maturity in the processes with this ontology. This is the reason why in Fig. 4 the fundamental concepts for the lean software development implementation are described. This figure shows an extract from the ontology-based lean software development implementation, which generally describes, through a graph diagram, the classes, sub-classes, relationships and axioms linked to the ontology domain.

It is important to highlight that this article focuses solely on the conceptual development of ontology- based lean software development implementation to facilitate the adoption and understanding of LSD.

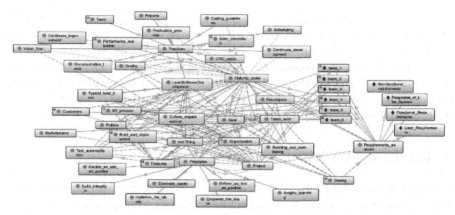

Fig. 4. Excerpt of the ontology describing the concepts extending the ontology-based lean software development implementation

3.6 Step 6: Implementation

To implement the LSD ontology, the following stages must be considered:

Analysis: Perform a preliminary study that identifies the nature and focus of the organization's policy, with the purpose of understanding its objectives, goals and needs, in order to adapt the LSD principles and practices to the organizational workflow.

Planning: Devise and design an improvement project based on the results of the previous study in order to establish a new plan with future goals that establishes the strategies, functions, roles, abilities and mentalities of all those involved in the implementation of LSD.

Implementing: From the execution of the previous stages, the ontology-based lean software development implementation is applied in the organization.

Validate: The results obtained are evaluated using measurement tools to collect behavioral, improvement or evolution metrics, with the purpose of showing relevant information for decision-making that leads to continuous improvement.

4   Validation of the Ontology

In order to validate the usefulness of the ontology, a previous study was carried out on ICT cooperative companies in Panama (cooperative companies are associations formed by natural persons, without aims of profit, who have as north plan and realize activities of work or service of economic and social benefit, directed to the production, distribution and consumption of goods and services across economic contributions of their own associates) that have qualified personnel in the development of software projects. This survey formulated 18 questions regarding the current situation (communication, organizational culture, requirements analysis, process automation, work team). As an initial result, the survey revealed significant aspects such as the presence of an adequate organizational culture and a remarkable relationship between developers and stakeholders; however, it also highlighted deficiencies in other aspects such as failures after the requirements' analysis; lack of communication in the work team; little monitoring and control of the functions, leading to unnecessary changes during the project; poor distribution of roles; and very little feedback due to the lack of optimized processes. These reasons show the need to implement a robust software development methodology and adopt a mature software development process, characteristics present in the ontology-based lean software development implementation, which would allow better results to be obtained in their projects and functional improvement of the institution.

5 Results and Discussion

As an initial result of the survey, 24 samples were obtained, which highlight important variables concerning the organizational situation: Starting with the analysis of requirements, 87% of them indicated that there were shortcomings after the analysis, 91% said that the relationship between developers and stakeholders was good, and 87% stressed that there was an organizational culture. However, when talking about communication in the work team, 54% mentioned that it was lacking, which is reflected in the distribution of roles, which 29% said was very good, but 42% said was bad. In addition, when asked about the ideal size of a working group, 58% thought that it should be fewer than 7, 34% preferred it to be between 7 and 15 people, and 8% thought that it should be composed of more than 15 people. On the other hand, when asked about the monitoring and control of functions, 75% emphasized the lack thereof, leading to unrealistic changes within the projects.

With the results described above, the need for changes in the software development process in these teams is evident, which confirms the importance of adopting an ontology-based lean software development implementation that supports the improvement of their processes. According to the results, cooperative companies in Panama have difficulties in software development processes, as well as in organizational aspects, thus hindering their efficiency and competitiveness. However, these problems can be solved by implementing the ontology-based lean software development; the cooperatives can establish new approaches by identifying the waste present in the development processes and thus increase their productivity and competitiveness, improve the conditions of the organization, and optimize and reduce the time spent on the processes, allowing them to ascend to optimal maturity levels by incorporating stages of improvement and continuous learning and identification of wastes in deeper states. Lean software development principles focus on eliminating waste from processes, behaviors and the entire value stream. The latter begins with the perception of value based on client needs together with the continuous improvement process at the business level. Poor implementation of LSD has repercussions at an organizational level, causing disinterest and abandonment of lean principles and practices. Therefore, building an ontology that describes the concepts, relationships and restrictions that are related to the implementation of LSD, elements that contribute to raising the company's and the software development project's maturity, allows the organization to perform an adequate adoption and implementation process with rapid results and an improvement in quality and processes while continuing to use LSD. Organizations that efficiently implement LSD generally follow this approach when they entrust the program's leadership and corresponding implementation to specialized managers, teams and organizational units often created or appointed for this specific purpose.

6 Conclusions and Future Work

This article, Ontology-Based Lean Software Development Implementation, proposes the conceptual development of an ontology that contains the theoretical bases for the implementation of Lean Software Development methodology in an agile environment. These theoretical bases are described by means of classes, relationships and limitations involved in implementing Lean Software development in an organization. The inadequate implementation of an Agile or Lean methodology attracts organizational repercussions, causing disinterest and abandonment of good practices in software development, as demonstrated by the results obtained from the study of cooperative enterprises in Panama. Nevertheless, by building an ontology that describes the concepts, relationships, and constraints that relate to the implementation of LSD it helps the software development organization and project scale to a higher maturity level, while its application brings improvements in the quality of project development and management within software engineering processes applied in an organization; because, by carrying out an appropriate adoption and implementation process, it will allow rapid monitoring of compliance with newly developed requirements and serve as a good tool to document the work process and performance, thus generating rapid results, improvement in quality and processes, while continuing the use of LSD. As a future work, this ontology will be implemented in a software development company, in order to verify and support with real data the workability of ontology and contribute to the process of improvement of the organization.

Acknowledgments. We are grateful for the support provided by the Science, Technology and Innovation National Secretariat of Panama (SENACYT), Scientific Master program TIC-UTP-FISC-2019 and to the National Research System (SNI-SENACYT) which one author is member.

Authors Contribution. Conceptualization S.G, M.V.; methodology S.G, MV; formal analysis S.G, JG, M.V; research S.G, J.G, M.V.; original-writing S.G, J.G, M.V.; writing—review and edition S.G, J.G, M.V.; Corresponding author, M.V.

References

1. Alahyari, H., et al.: An exploratory study of waste in software development organizations using agile or lean approaches: a multiple case study at 14 organizations. Inf. Softw. Technol. **105**, 78–94 (2019). https://doi.org/10.1016/j.infsof.2018.08.006
2. Antinyan, V., et al.: Identifying risky areas of software code in Agile/Lean software development: an industrial experience report. In: 2014 Software Evolution Week - IEEE Conference on Software Maintenance, Reengineering, and Reverse Engineering, CSMR-WCRE 2014 – Proceedings, pp. 154–163 (2014). https://doi.org/10.1109/CSMR-WCRE.2014.6747165

3. Aurelio, D., et al.: A framework for evaluating lean implementation appropriateness. In: IEEE International Conference on Industrial Engineering and Engineering Management, pp. 779–783 (2011). https://doi.org/10.1109/IEEM.2011.6118022
4. Batova, T.: Extended abstract: Lean UX and innovation in teaching. In: IEEE International Professional Communication Conference, 2016-Novem, pp. 1–3 (2016). https://doi.org/10.1109/IPCC.2016.7740500
5. Cagliano, R., et al.: Lean, Agile and traditional supply: how do they impact manufacturing performance? J. Purchasing Supply Manag. 10(4–5 Spec. Iss.), 151–164 (2004). https://doi.org/10.1016/j.pursup.2004.11.001
6. Ching, P.M., Mutuc, J.E.: Evaluating agile and lean software development methods from a system dynamics perspective. In: 2018 IEEE 10th International Conference on Humanoid, Nanotechnology, Information Technology, Communication and Control, Environment and Management, HNICEM 2018, pp. 1–6 (2019). https://doi.org/10.1109/HNICEM.2018.8666338.
7. Cummings, J., Stacey, D.: Lean ontology development: an ontology development paradigm based on continuous innovation. In: IC3K 2018 - Proceedings of the 10th International Joint Conference on Knowledge Discovery, Knowledge Engineering and Knowledge Management, IC3K, vol. 2, pp. 367–374 (2018). https://doi.org/10.5220/0006963003670374
8. Fagerholm, F., et al.: Performance Alignment Work: how software developers experience the continuous adaptation of team performance in Lean and Agile environments. Inf. Softw. Technol. 64, 132–147 (2015). https://doi.org/10.1016/j.infsof.2015.01.010
9. Hicks, B.J.: Lean information management: understanding and eliminating waste. Int. J. Inf. Manag. 27(4), 233–249 (2007). https://doi.org/10.1016/j.ijinfomgt.2006.12.001
10. Janes, A.: A guide to lean software development in action. In: 2015 IEEE 8th International Conference on Software Testing, Verification and Validation Workshops, ICSTW 2015 – Proceedings, pp. 1–2 (2015). https://doi.org/10.1109/ICSTW.2015.7107412
11. Jones, D., Womack, J.: Lean thinking-banish waste and create wealth in your corporation. J. Oper. Res. Soc. 48, 1144–1150 (1997)
12. Karvonen, T., et al.: Adapting the lean enterprise self-assessment tool for the software development domain. In: Proceedings - 38th EUROMICRO Conference on Software Engineering and Advanced Applications, SEAA 2012, pp. 266–273 (2012). https://doi.org/10.1109/SEAA.2012.51
13. Murtazina, M.S., Avdeenko, T.V.: Ontology-based approach to the requirements engineering in Agile environment. In: 2018 14th International Scientific-Technical Conference on Actual Problems of Electronic Instrument Engineering, APEIE 2018 – Proceedings, pp. 496–501 (2018). https://doi.org/10.1109/APEIE.2018.8546144
14. Nurdiani, I., et al.: The impacts of agile and lean practices on project constraints: a tertiary study. J. Syst. Softw. 119, 162–183 (2016). https://doi.org/10.1016/j.jss.2016.06.043
15. Oliveira, G.A., et al.: Lean and green approach: an evaluation tool for new product development focused on small and medium enterprises. Int. J. Prod. Econ. 205, 62–73 (2018). https://doi.org/10.1016/j.ijpe.2018.08.026
16. Ongenae, F., et al.: An ontology co-design method for the co-creation of a continuous care ontology. Appl. Ontol. 9(1), 27–64 (2014). https://doi.org/10.3233/AO-140131
17. Pearce, A., Pons, D.: Advancing lean management: the missing quantitative approach. Oper. Res. Perspect. 6, 100114 (2019). https://doi.org/10.1016/j.orp.2019.100114
18. Pinto, H.S., Martins, J.P.: Ontologies: how can they be built? Knowl. Inf. Syst. 6(4), 441–464 (2004). https://doi.org/10.1007/s10115-003-0138-1
19. Poppendieck, B.M., Poppendieck, T.: Lean Software Development: An Agile Toolkit. Tom Wesley, Publisher Addison (2003)
20. Poppendieck, M., Cusumano, M.A.: Lean software development: a tutorial. IEEE Softw. 29(5), 26–32 (2012). https://doi.org/10.1109/MS.2012.107

21. Redeker, G.A., et al.: Lean information for lean communication: analysis of concepts, tools, references, and terms. Int. J. Inf. Manag. **47**, 31–43 (2019). https://doi.org/10.1016/j.ijinfo mgt.2018.12.018

22. Rodríguez, P., et al.: Combining lean thinking and agile methods for software development a case study of a Finnish provider of wireless embedded systems. In: Proceedings of the Annual Hawaii International Conference on System Sciences, pp. 4770–4779 (2014). https://doi.org/10.1109/HICSS.2014.586

23. Secchi, R., Camuffo, A.: Lean implementation failures: the role of organizational ambidexterity. Int. J. Prod. Econ. **210**, 145–154 (2019). https://doi.org/10.1016/j.ijpe.2019.01.007

24. Sedano, T., et al.: Software development waste. In: 2017 IEEE/ACM 39th International Conference on Software Engineering (ICSE), pp. 130–140 (2017). https://doi.org/10.1109/icse.2017.20

25. Sitthithanasakul, S., Choosri, N.: Using ontology to enhance requirement engineering in agile software process. In: SKIMA 2016 - 2016 10th International Conference on Software, Knowledge, Information Management and Applications, pp. 181–186 (2017). https://doi.org/10.1109/SKIMA.2016.7916218

26. Soliman, M., et al.: The impacts of lean production on the complexity of socio-technical systems. Int. J. Prod. Econ. **197**, 342–357 (2018). https://doi.org/10.1016/j.ijpe.2018.01.024

27. de Souza, P.L., do Prado, A.F., de Souza, W.L., dos Santos Forghieri Pereira, S.M., Pires, L.F.: Improving Agile software development with domain ontologies. In: Latifi, S. (ed.) Information Technology – New Generations. AISC, vol. 738, pp. 267–274. Springer, Cham (2018). https://doi.org/10.1007/978-3-319-77028-4_37

28. Virtanen, A. et al.: On continuous deployment maturity in customer projects, pp. 1205–1212. ACM Digital Library (2017). https://doi.org/10.1145/3019612.3019777

29. Vizcaíno, A., et al.: A validated ontology for global software development. Comput. Stand. Interfaces **46**, 66–78 (2016). https://doi.org/10.1016/j.csi.2016.02.004

30. Wang, X., et al.: "Leagile" software development: an experience report analysis of the application of lean approaches in agile software development. J. Syst. Softw. **85**(6), 1287–1299 (2012). https://doi.org/10.1016/j.jss.2012.01.061

31. Yang, L., et al.: Ontology-based systems engineering: a state-of-the-art review. Comput. Ind. **111**, 148–171 (2019). https://doi.org/10.1016/j.compind.2019.05.003

32. Yilmaz, Ö.F., et al.: Lean holistic fuzzy methodology employing cross-functional worker teams for new product development projects: a real case study from high-tech industry. Eur. J. Oper. Res. (2019). https://doi.org/10.1016/j.ejor.2019.09.048

New Agile Enterprise Architecture Methodology for Small Latin American Organizations

Heber I. Mejia-Cabrera[1](✉) ⓘ, Victor A. Tuesta-Monteza[1](✉) ⓘ,
Alberto E. Samillan-Ayala[2](✉) ⓘ, and Manuel G. Forero[3](✉) ⓘ

[1] Universidad Señor de Sipán, Pimentel, Chiclayo, Peru
{hmejiac,vtuesta}@crece.uss.edu.pe
[2] Universidad Nacional Pedro Ruiz Gallo, Lambayeque, Peru
esamillan@unprg.edu.pe
[3] Universidad de Ibagué, Ibagué, Colombia
manuel.forero@unibague.edu.co

Abstract. Information technologies (IT) promise great benefits. However, companies have business alignment problems, affecting investment, performance and agility. To achieve alignment, enterprise architecture (EA) reference models called Frameworks have been developed. These proposals were born in large companies and their design has a traditional approach to these realities. However, in Peru most companies are micro-enterprises, i.e. small organizations (SOs), with their own characteristics. SOs have a low Networked Readiness Index (NRI), generating little impact on Peru's development. Therefore, this paper proposes a new business architecture methodology conceived for the reality of small Peruvian and Latin American organizations. A general method based on EA and SO criteria was developed, thus generating a metamodel, from which the elements of the methodology are instantiated, which integrates four approaches to IT management. The methodology developed was validated in a Peruvian SO and by experts. The preliminary results show that its use generates benefits with respect to the competition.

Keywords: Enterprise Architecture · IT alignment · Small organizations · IT management · Microenterprises

1 Introduction

In the past, companies performed the analysis of their data manually to generate useful information for business growth. However, with the introduction of computers and the Internet, many processes were automated and with it, the incorporation of IT resources, which should be managed according to the present and future needs of the company. To this end, IT strategic planning models were developed. However, not all companies were able to manage IT adequately, becoming a concern for entrepreneurs, due to the heavy investment required for this purpose, coupled with the lack of clarity regarding the value contribution that IT brings to the company. Thus, with this aim, in 1987, Zachman put

© Springer Nature Switzerland AG 2021
M. Botto-Tobar et al. (Eds.): ICAT 2020, CCIS 1388, pp. 604–617, 2021.
https://doi.org/10.1007/978-3-030-71503-8_47

forward a vision of how to manage IT in a different way [1]. From this work, in the following years the so-called Enterprise Architecture (EA) frameworks were developed [2], which are also known as traditional or heavy frameworks, for their broad description of the organization, covering it from end to end and including all aspects. This requires highly trained personnel and many resources to move the organization towards the target architecture [3].

One problem of the information technologies is its management, because it lacks business vision, i.e., there is a divorce between the organization's and the IT's objectives. In this way, IT rather than collaborating with the company's business objectives would be making it more difficult to achieve and, in addition, generating unnecessary expenses. Therefore, the alignment of IT with the business is the second most important issue or concern for companies [4]. There is evidence to affirm that companies require information technologies to survive, grow and expand, however, managing IT has a series of difficulties, the most important being the lack of alignment between business and IT. [5], cite four factors that influence the strategic alignment of business and information technology, which are Shared knowledge between the business manager (CEO) and the information technology manager (CIO), the success of technology implementation through user-friendly systems, the efficient communication between business executives and CIOs, and the connection between business plans and IT plans. In addition [6], assure that, if enterprise architecture is developed with traditional reference frameworks, such as TOGAF, Zachman, FEA, among others, it would represent making total changes to the architecture. These changes generate many risks of failure, however, if an enterprise architecture is developed with agile methodologies it means making small changes, since these are considered as evolutionary methods, which means that as the new architecture is consolidated the change is made and the risks are lower. Likewise [3] asserts that the agile enterprise architecture is a connector to make the alignment of the business with information technologies more efficient and less risky. Most organizations that develop enterprise architecture do so with traditional approaches. To implement these target architectures, the old system has to be shut down and the new one put into place. That is why traditional approaches contain a high rate of risk and failure affecting business processes. Because of these problems and difficulties, researchers suggest an agile approach. The benefit of this approach is that the implementation of the new architecture is quite easy compared to other approaches. [7]. To find a solution to this problem, researchers, on the one hand [8–11] and industry [12], on the other, have tested different solutions based on Enterprise Architecture, creating reference frameworks called Frameworks. [13]. Among the best known is The Open Group Architecture Framework (TOGAF) [14]. In the literature, it can be noted that the companies that participate in these studies are medium and large, so it is logical to think that EA frameworks are designed for these realities. However, the situation in Peru is different, since in 2018, 94.7% are micro companies and are the strength of the economy in Peru [15], which is also the case in most Latin American countries. Micro businesses, or small organizations (SOs), have special characteristics, where traditional frameworks are not suitable to help them grow sustainably by making intensive use of IT. Moreover, the agile frameworks proposed in the scientific literature define what should be done [6, 7, 16], but not how it should be done, besides not having been conceived according to the reality of the Latin

American SOs. For this reason, this paper proposes a new agile methodology for enterprise architecture. This methodology was conceived according to the reality of small organizations based on four approaches to IT management and was tested in a small Peruvian organization and validated by expert judgment.

2 Material and Method

2.1 Material

The architecture modeling was done in Archimate 3.0 language using the Visual Paradigm Online tool, and the business process modeling and simulation was done following the BPMN 2.0 standard implemented in Bizagi Modeler v 3.3. The microproject software was developed in Bonita Studio, Community Edition v 7.7. The application was developed on an Intel Core I7-4700MQ processor 2.40 GHz $\times$ 8, 16 GB RAM, NVidia GeForce GT 740M 2 GB graphics card, running on the x64 bits Microsoft Windows 10 platform.

2.2 Method

To generate the enterprise architecture methodology for small organizations adapted from [17], a general five-phase method called General Method for the Generation of the Enterprise Architecture Methodology for Small Organizations (GMAESO) was proposed. The first one deals with the analysis of the characteristics of the SOs and the EA developed by several researchers. Then each characteristic is analyzed, identifying criteria of the PO and the AE. In the second phase, a metamodel is developed to condense and integrate the criteria of the SO and EA into a model with a high level of abstraction to ensure that the SO and the main elements of AE remain in focus. In the third phase, an instance of the metamodel is developed and the EA methodology is built considering four approaches to IT management: business-centered, process-based, with an agile approach, and digital transformation.

To verify the designed methodology, an empirical evaluation was carried out in a PO, [18], and validated by expert judgment using the Delphi method. [19]. The team consisted of three experts, who independently analyzed the proposed methodology (Fig. 1).

Phases:

1. Analysis. In this stage the analysis of the small organization is carried out to identify its most relevant characteristics, as well as the identification of the substantial characteristics of the Enterprise Architecture, with which criteria can be established, allowing a good adjustment of the Enterprise Architecture of the Organization, which improves the efficiency and real effectiveness of the resulting methodology.
2. Metamodel. To facilitate the understanding of reality, models are built to represent the elements and relationships, similar to the plans of a construction where the elements and their organization are diagrammed. Thus, to define a new methodology, in this stage a metamodel is elaborated, which is a model of a higher level of abstraction where statements are made about the structure of the resulting model.

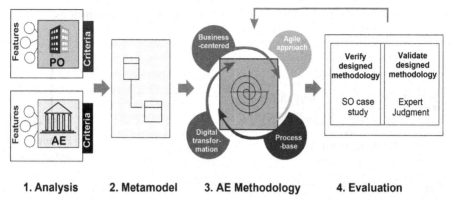

1. Analysis   2. Metamodel   3. AE Methodology   4. Evaluation

Fig. 1. General method for the generation of the enterprise architecture methodology for small organizations.

3. Enterprise Architecture Methodology. In this stage, a series of logical and well-defined steps are elaborated, thus, when used, it allows to build the EA model that fits the characteristics of a SO. This methodology has four approaches needed to better align with the SO, the business approach that is the reason for the SO's existence, the process approach to consolidate the internal organization, the agile approach that allows it to be developed quickly and collaboratively, and finally the digital transformation approach to make the core of its value proposal stand on technologies. The methodology considers the three primary drivers of digital transformation, namely: transforming business processes and models, personalizing the experience, and enhancing workforce efficiency [20]. It also used the agile approach based on the "Manifesto for Agile Software Development", which considers "Individuals and interactions on processes and tools", "Software running on extensive documentation", "Collaboration with the client on contract negotiation", "Response to change on following a plan" [21]. Also was considered the "Business Process Management (BPM) approach to combine the modeling, automation, execution, control, measurement and optimization of business activity flows in support of business objectives" [22].

4. Evaluation of the methodology. Two moments are considered at this stage. The first consists of testing the first version of the proposed methodology in a small organization and using the knowledge acquired to improve it. In the second moment, the DELPHI expert judgment validation method was used to approve the methodology.

The development of the elaborated methodology followed the principle of balance of simplicity, to provide the SO with a simple methodology according to its characteristics, but complete from the perspective of the enterprise architecture. To this end, the process of complication was used [23] (Fig. 2).

In order to identify the characteristics of the Peruvian SOs, a review of studies related to the problems faced by the SO was made, finding that Huapaya identified 18, among

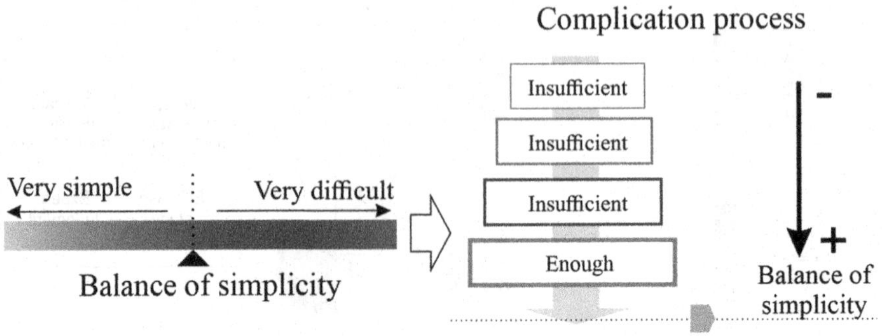

Complication process

Very simple   Very difficult

Balance of simplicity

| Insufficient |
| Insufficient |
| Insufficient |
| Enough |

−

+

Balance of simplicity

Fig. 2. Simplicity balance model and complication process to achieve the simplicity balance.

which are informality that limits management, little experience in the specific business, liquidity problems, little information to establish internal controls, manual recording for income and expense control, trust only in experience and not in planning, not considering a business plan that connects the vision, mission, objectives and goals by periods, lack of planning of purchases according to sales, not focusing on a service or product losing efficiency and effectiveness, unrealistic expectations so that unnecessary expenses and investments are incurred, lack of capacity to integrate and reach a larger domestic or foreign market [24]. Each SOs is different, however, six common characteristics, shown in Table 1, have been identified in the literature that influence IT adoption, where many of them differ from those identified in large companies [17, 24, 25].

Table 1. Characteristics of the identified SOs.

Characteristics of the SOs	
Code	Description
C1:SO	There is limited time for strategic issues so it should be simple
C2:SO	Limited advanced IT technical skills
C3:SO	Financial limitations to have workers with good IT skills
C4:SO	Knowledge and control of OP task performance required Knowledge and control of the performance of the PO's tasks
C5:SO	Dependence on the manager-owner's skills, beliefs and knowledge for strategic issues
C6:SO	Dependence on the vision of the manager-owner, who expects benefits from the adoption of an EA model

From these characteristics, some criteria can be established for the creation of an enterprise architecture methodology that can be used in the SOs, shown in Table 2.

Table 2. SOs criteria for EA methodology.

Code	Description
CR1:PO	The business model and strategic issues are a priority
CR2:PO	It must be simple so that a non-IT expert can use it
CR3:PO	It must be implementable with very little help from external IT consultants
CR4:PO	The generated artifacts should be enough to describe how to perform all tasks
CR5:PO	The manager must be involved in the development of the architecture

The EA provides several benefits to businesses, among which can be considered the creation of a common architecture, generating an overview of company areas, testing the EA model before being implemented in practice. The points of view can be used to document the basic elements of the business, the representation of the elements and their relationships of the EA. They can be used for optimization and for change impact analysis. In addition to these general advantages, EA can help to reduce problems, clearly defining a competitive strategy, facilitating the selection of IT that best suits the current business, showing the links between daily operations and strategy, facilitating the consultation of a job description from the relationships of employees with operations, maintaining the alignment of processes with the strategy and performing change impact analysis. These advantages are condensed in Table 3 [9, 13, 14]. From the definitions, descriptions and benefits of EA mentioned above, five criteria were born for the creation of the EA methodology for SOs, shown in Table 4.

Table 3. Benefits and advantages of EA

EA benefits	
Code	Description
BG1:AE	Architecture descriptions must be acceptable to all interested stakeholders (owner, employees and customers)
BG2:AE	The architectural views of each stakeholder must be available
BG3:AE	The architecture must be able to be tested before being implemented in practice
BG4:AE	The basic descriptions of the architecture should serve as documentation
BG5:AE	The representation of the elements and their EC relationships can be used for analysis and optimization
BG6:AE	The representation of EA elements and their relationships can be used to conduct change impact analysis

(continued)

Table 3. (*continued*)

EA advantages	
Code	Description
V1:AE	Help to clearly define a competitive strategy for the SO
V2:AE	Facilitate the selection of IT that best suits the current business
V3:AE	Show the links between daily operations and the business strategy
V4:AE	To facilitate the description consultations of the business operations
V5:AE	To allow maintaining the alignment of processes with the business strategy
V6:AE	To facilitate the impact analysis of the changes

Table 4. EA criteria for EA methodology.

EA criteria	
Code	Description
CR1:AE	It must be a tool to control the business complexity
CR2:AE	It must provide a high-level holistic view of the business' stable elements
CR3:AE	It must convert business strategy into daily operational activities
CR4:AE	It must be usable by a SO since its formation
CR5:AE	It must comprise all the SO to be optimized as a whole

Based on this analysis, the metamodel illustrated in Fig. 4 was developed (Fig. 3).

The metamodel considers a layer centered on the business where the main business elements are gathered such as the business model, motivation, objectives, capabilities and processes (based on processes). A second layer where the relevant applications and data are considered to support the business and a third one where the technological platform to support them is taken into account. Based on the above models, improvements are proposed and evaluated (iterative checks - controlled risks) and then converted into short projects (micro projects with controlled risks). From the metamodel, the EA methodology for SO was proposed.

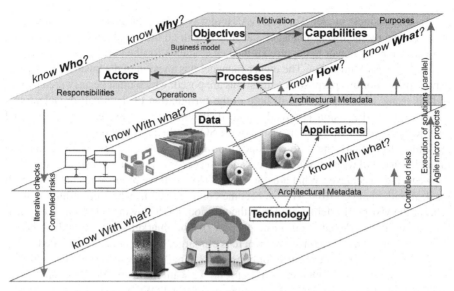

Fig. 3. Enterprise architecture metamodel for small organizations.

3   Results and Discussions

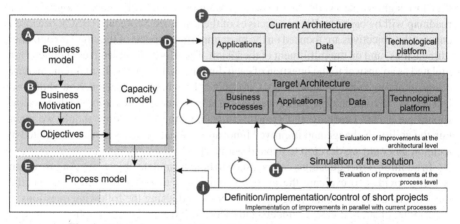

Fig. 4. Enterprise architecture methodology for small organizations.

The proposed methodology was the result of theoretical and practical development. Thus, the model was refined while it was used to improve the alignment of the business objectives with those of the technology in the Departmental Council of Lambayeque of the Association of Engineers of Peru. In this way, the model presented in this work was obtained.

A.- The business model. The CANVAS tool was selected because of its simplicity, to be developed by the owner-manager and shared with all the people in the organization, and because of its power to capture all the key elements for the success of a business.

B.- Business Motivation. The owner-manager has a vision of the business that needs to be explicit. For this purpose, ten questions are posed, which must be answered by him and his team, whose answers will help in the formulation of the small organization's vision. In case the vision is already defined, it will serve to evaluate its clarity and completeness. The writing of the vision of the SO should describe how it is visualized in the future. To this end, the following questions are posed: What do we want to do in the future?. What will we do?. Who do we want to serve? What resources will we use? What are we trying to achieve? What are our values? How will we produce results? How will we deal with change? How will we become competitive? In what time frame will we achieve the vision? To define or clarify the mission, the following questions are posed: Why do we exist? (What is our basic purpose?) What market sector should we be in? Who is our target user or consumer? where is our target user or consumer located? what is considered valuable for our user or consumer? What needs can we satisfy? how will we satisfy these needs? What market sector do we want to be in? What are our current and future products or services? What makes us different? What particular characteristic do we have or want to have? how will we measure the success of the mission?

C.- Business objectives. Defining the business objectives is fundamental, to have a reference point in measuring the progress of the SO towards the fulfillment of the vision. The objectives must be focused on achieving the fulfillment of the SO vision. The declaration of the SO objectives must be guided by a business perspective, to avoid that they lose sight of the vision, that is why a roadmap is needed to serve as a guide. This roadmap will be based on the perspectives of the Balanced Scorecard (BSC), because it ensures the objectives are focused on the most important aspects of the small organization (dimensions) and on the fulfillment of the vision. Therefore, the objectives should be formulated as an answer to the question of each dimension. Financial: To maintain/increase our profitability, what should we do, Customers: To achieve our vision, how should we be seen by customers? Internal processes: To satisfy our customers in which processes should we excel? Learning and growth: To achieve the vision, how should we maintain the ability to change and improve? Innovation: What business service facilitated by technology could we develop to expand our market?

In addition, other questions can be asked to help formulate objectives. An instrument is then provided to evaluate the proposed objectives to verify that they are specific, measurable, achievable, challenging, and time-bound, using the following questions: Is it concrete, clear, and easy to understand? Does it have explicit or implicit indicators, where it is verified if the objective was achieved? With the resources and depending on the mission of the organization, is the objective achievable? Is it relevant, does it inspire a challenge, and does it imply an effort? Does the objective explicitly or implicitly establish a time limit to obtain results?

C.1 Map of strategies. Once the objectives that need to be planned are defined, a "Strategy Map" is used that provides a concise and clear way to plan and communicate the strategy, with the members of the SO. The Strategy Map aligns the disaggregated business objectives into specific objectives with concrete actions and goals.

D.- Capacity model. A "Business Capability" is a particular skill or capacity that a business must possess or exchange to achieve a specific purpose or result (goal). A capability answers the question: What needs to be the business know how to achieve the goal? Capabilities need to be broken down to a third level of detail.

E.- Process model. The small organization needs to convert the capabilities into business processes, the business processes answer the question: How should the business do to achieve the objective? Therefore, it is necessary to define the processes that give operativity to the defined capacities. For this purpose, the following definition was used: Suppliers - Inputs - Process - Output - Customers (SIPOC), which requires answers to the following questions: Who is responsible for the process? What is the purpose of the process? Who delivers inputs to start the process? What inputs enter the process to generate the output? What activities are required to be performed with the inputs to generate the output? What outputs does the process generate? Who receives the outputs of the process? What should be measured in the process to show that the purpose of the process has been fulfilled, and what metrics should be used to measure it?

F. Current architecture. For this phase, a graphic language is used to design the process at a high level, identify the applications (components) that will support it and the most relevant data that is generated for the applications to support the processes. For the specifications of the Current and Target architectures, some basic ArchiMate 3 specifications were selected. Thus, to represent the business architecture, the definitions Actor, Business Service, Product, Process, Interface were used; for the application architecture, Component Application Service, Data and Interface were employed; for the data architecture, Data and Relationship Entity were taken; and for the technology platform architecture, Technology Service, Device, Software, Communication Network were used.

G. Goal architecture. The same reduced and adapted ArchiMate® 3.0.1 graphic language shown in the previous phase was used for this one. The aim of this phase is to have a high-level view that reflects the improvements in the organization.

H.- Solution simulation. At this stage it is necessary to analyze the target architecture against the current one. For this purpose, the methodology provides a comparison matrix.

Table 5. Service comparison matrix of the current and target architectures.

		Current architecture		
	Processes	Process 1	Process 2	Process N
Target architecture	Process 1	Equal		
	Process 2		Must be modified Modification description	
	Process N			Must be included

I.- DEFINITION AND EXECUTION OF SHORT PROJECTS. In this stage it is necessary to establish the specifications of the projects that arise from the comparison matrix and the simulation results. These specifications will be made in a succinct way, seeking to make them simple and useful. To document the projects, a format called "Microproject Profile" is used, where a brief description of the project is established, answering the questions: What is required to be done and what is wanted to be achieved?, Description of the product and service that is required to be built (Characteristics of the product/service), People in charge of the project, Schedule and project costs.

The results were submitted to expert judgment using the DELPHI [26] method. The group of experts consisted of three PhDs, two Peruvians with experience as IT managers and one Colombian, with research experience in technology management. They were given a summary of the work developed and a battery of 10 questions, presented below, to be answered based on their experience. The result of the evaluation can be seen in Table 5.

1. Do you think it is correct that the characteristics of small organizations have been analyzed to propose the Enterprise Architecture methodology according to those characteristics?
2. Do you think it is correct that the characteristics of the body of knowledge of Enterprise Architecture (EA) have been analyzed to propose the EA methodology, and thus ensure that the main elements are present in the proposed EA methodology?
3. Do you consider the elaboration of criteria based on the characteristics identified both in small organizations and in business architecture, help to establish a correct judgment to consider the elements that the proposed EA methodology will have?
4. Do you consider the elaboration of a metamodel to better describe the elements and relationships of the structure of the EA methodology at a higher level of abstraction, in such a way that it ensures that the characteristics of EA and SO are related?
5. According to your experience in IT management would you remove some element of the metamodel, to generate a methodology to be applied in a small organization? Why?
6. Which of the approaches used in the proposed EA methodology do you consider most important, to be relevant in a small organization?
7. Do you consider the nine methodology elements to comply with the structure established in the metamodel?
8. Do you consider the nine methodology elements to comply with the balance principle of simplicity, which seeks simplicity and completeness?
9. Do you think that IT management approaches are present in all nine elements of the proposed EA methodology?
10. According to Phase "I", do you consider this reduces the risk of project failure generated by the EA methodology, ensuring the success of changes in the OP?

As shown in Table 6, in six aspects (questions 1–4 and 7–8) the experts agree to give a favorable opinion of the proposed methodology, in three (questions 5, 9 and 10) two experts agree to give a positive opinion, and in question 6 all three evaluators agree that the methodology is business-centered, two that it is also process-based, and one says that it has an agile approach. These results show that it was possible to incorporate approaches based on the characteristics of the SO into the heart of the EA methodology,

Table 6. Results discussion by experts.

Question	Expected answer	Eval. 1 (Colombia) Answer	Eval. 2 (Perú) Answer	Eval. 3 (Perú) Answer	Result
Question 1	Yes	Yes	Yes	Yes	3/3
Question 2	Yes	Yes	Yes	Yes	3/3
Question 3	Yes	Yes	Yes	Yes	3/3
Question 4	Yes	Yes	Yes	Yes	3/3
Question 5	No	No	No	Yes	2/3
Question 6	4	3	2	1	2/3
Question 7	Yes	Yes	Yes	No	3/3
Question 8	Yes	Yes	Yes	Yes	3/3
Question 9	Yes	Yes	Yes	No	2/3
Question 10	Yes	Yes	Yes	No	2/3

and therefore it is very useful for small Latin American organizations to achieve their development, competitiveness and growth.

4   Conclusions

Small Latin American organizations have special characteristics due to their entrepreneurial nature and because they cannot use traditional Enterprise Architecture (EA) frameworks due to their limited resources, which imply a high consumption of time, human and financial resources. Therefore, this paper proposes a new methodology that bases its design on the influence of the characteristics of Latin American SOs, and the main elements of EA condensed into a metamodel. The methodology is a practical instance of a metamodel that allows building EA for SO. In this way, an architecture, which ensures its sustained growth, is gradually built in an agile way and on the fly. The methodology consists of nine phases called elements and each element has artifacts or instruments. A practical test made it possible to verify the practical usefulness of the methodology, which was then assessed by a second group of three experts. The results show in general the confidence of the experts in the proposed methodology, providing a unanimous verdict in 6 aspects evaluated and support for most of the remaining 4 aspects.

References

1. Zachman, J.A.: A framework for information systems architecture. IBM Syst. J. **26**(3), 454–470 (1987)
2. Schekkerman, J.: How to Survive in the Jungle of Enterprise Architecture Framework: Creating or Choosing an Enterprise Architecture Framework, 1st edn. Trafford, Victoria (2003)

3. Yuliana, R., Rahardjo, B.: Designing an agile enterprise architecture for mining company by using TOGAF framework. In: 4th International Conference on Cyber and IT Service Management on Proceedings of 2016, Bandung, pp. 1–6. IEEE (2016)
4. Kappelman, L., et al.: The 2017 SIM IT issues and trends study. MIS Q. Executive **17**(1), 53–88 (2018)
5. Chan, Y., Reich, B.: IT alignment: what have we learned? J. Inf. Technol. **22**(4), 297–315 (2007)
6. Kaddoumi, T., Watfa, M.: A proposed agile enterprise architecture framework. In: The Sixth International Conference on Innovative Computing Technology, Dubai, pp. 52–57. IEEE (20126)
7. Balcicek, O., Gundebahar, M., Cekerekli, S.: An agile approach for converting enterprise architectures. In: The International Conference on Technological Advances in Electrical, Electronics and Computer Engineering, Istambul, pp. 380–386. IEEE (2013)
8. Gampfera, F., Jürgensa, A., Müllerb, M., Buchkremera, R.: Past, current and future trends in enterprise architecture—a view beyond the horizon. Comput. Ind. **100**(2018), 70–84 (2018)
9. Niemi, E.: Enterprise architecture benefits: perceptions from literature and practice. In: Proceedings of the 7th IBIMA Conference Internet & Information Systems in the Digital, pp. 1–8. International Business Information Management Association, Brescia (2006)
10. Buckl, S., Matthes, F., Schweda, C.: A viable system perspective on enterprise architecture management. In: IEEE International Conference on Systems, Man and Cybernetics, San Antonio, pp. 1483–1488. IEEE (2009)
11. Coltman, T., Tallon, P., Sharma, R., Queiroz, M.: Strategic IT alignment: twenty-five years on. J. Inf. Technol. **30**, 91–100 (2015). https://doi.org/10.1057/jit.2014.35
12. Gartner: Hype Cycle for Enterprise Architecture 2017. Gartner, Stamford, Connecticut (2017)
13. Foorthuis, R., van Steenbergen, M., Brinkkemper, S., Bruls, W.A.G.: A theory building study of enterprise architecture practices and benefits. Inf. Syst. Front. **18**(3), 541–564 (2015). https://doi.org/10.1007/s10796-014-9542-1
14. The Open Group Standard.: The TOGAF® Standard. Version 9.2. The Open Group, San Francisco (2018)
15. Instituto Nacional de Estadística e Informática.: Demografía Empresarial en el Perú: IV trimestre 2018 Perú, 4ta. INEI, Lima (2018)
16. Aldea, A., Iacob, M., Quartel, D., Franken, H., Strategic planning and enterprise architecture. In: Proceedings of the 1st International Conference on Enterprise Systems, ES 2013, Denpasar, pp. 1–8. IEEE (2013)
17. Bernaert, M., Poels, G., Snoeck, M., De Backer, M.: Enterprise architecture for small and medium-sized enterprises: a starting point for bringing EA to SMEs, based on adoption models. In: Devos, J., van Landeghem, H., Deschoolmeester, D. (eds.) Information Systems for Small and Medium-sized Enterprises, pp. 67–90. Springer, Heidelberg (2014). https://doi.org/10.1007/978-3-642-38244-4_4
18. Moody, D.: The method evaluation model: a theoretical model for validating information systems design methods. In: Ciborra, C., Mercurio, R., De Marco, M., Martinez, M., Carignani, A. (eds.) Proceedings of the 11th European Conference on Information Systems, pp. 1327–1336. ECIS 2003 Proceedings, Naples (2003)
19. Torrado-fonseca, M., Mercedes, R.: El método Delphi. Revista d'Innovació i Recerca en Educació **9**(1), 1–20 (2016)
20. Miller, L.: Digital Transformation for Dummies®, Special Wiley , Hoboken (2017)
21. Manifiesto por el Desarrollo Ágil de Software. https://agilemanifesto.org/iso/es/manifesto.html. Accessed 06 June 2019
22. BPM. https://bpm.com/. Accessed 07 Apr 2019
23. Entusiasmado. https://entusiasmado.com/wp-content/uploads/2014/10/artflow_2014100 91144.png. Accessed 06 Oct 2019

24. Huapaya, A.: Pymes: Realidad, problemas y alternativas ineludibles de solución. Revista Alternativa Financiera **4**(4), 15–18 (2010)
25. Spillan, J., Li, X., Totten, J., Antúnez de Mayolo, C.: An exploratory analysis of market orientation of small and medium-sized businesses (SMEs) in Peru. Panorama Socioeconómico **149**(12), 136–149 (2009)

Development of a Cross-Platform Architecture for the Analysis of Vehicular Traffic in a Smart City with Machine Learning Tools

Evelyn Lomas, Priscila Cevallos, Darwin Alulema$^{(\boxtimes)}$, Verónica Alulema, and Mayerly Saenz

Universidad de Las Fuerzas Armadas ESPE, Sangolquí, Ecuador
doalulema@espe.edu.ec

Abstract. The use of the Internet today has grown by leaps and bounds both in mobile phones, appliances, televisions, computers, so the link between objects and people is more daily. Services such as cloud computing and the IoT Internet of things have had a significant advance along with machine learning for managing predictions. For this reason, this article presents a cross-platform architecture for the analysis of vehicular traffic in a smart city with machine learning tools based on model engineering to generate prediction tools. For the architecture design, MDA Model-Driven Architecture techniques were used, and services were implemented in AWS Amazon Web Service. To validate the proposal, the usability of the interface was analyzed, and load tests were applied to the services.

Keywords: Domain Specific Language (DSL) · Machine learning · Cloud computing · Vehicular traffic

1 First Section

Mobility is an important axis for the daily life of the human being and thanks to the technology with its advances, different tools and solutions have been developed to facilitate daily activities. However, the means of transport, although they have been a solution, bring with them inconveniences in circulation and transit, due to road infrastructures not planned in the future.

According to [1] for 2008, 60% of the city's roads had a ratio of traffic volume and capacity between 0 and 0.8, allowing an average travel speed of more than 50 km/h. Meanwhile, 25% of the roads had a volume/capacity ratio of more than 1, that is, they were saturated with an average travel speed of 0-10 km/h. For 2015, given the current growth conditions of the vehicle and mobilization fleet, it is expected that 44% of the roads will have a volume/capacity ratio of 0–0.8 and that 38% of the roads have a volume/capacity ratio of more than 1. This problem would be further aggravated by 2025, when only 27% of the city's roads are expected to have a volume/capacity ratio of 0–0.8 and 55% of the roads are saturated with a volume/capacity ratio greater than one.

Some initiatives to solve traffic have been focused on the information technology scenario [2], which allows, firstly, to generate data efficiently, for example, using mobile

M. Botto-Tobar et al. (Eds.): ICAT 2020, CCIS 1388, pp. 618–628, 2021.
https://doi.org/10.1007/978-3-030-71503-8_48

devices that automatically generate relevant information, and secondly, that allow to analyze the volumes of data generated. For example, PSS (Participatory Sensor Systems) are mobile applications that allow data to be shared about people's environment at any time and place. These systems contribute to the ubiquitous computing process, therefore providing potential information for the development of the vehicular traffic behavior of a city [3].

For all of the above, it is important to develop technological tools that help solve the mobility problem, for which the research addresses the issue of improving mobility through an architecture that involves the use of different platforms and tools on available services. of cloud computing. The developed system shows the vehicle traffic prediction information through Digital TV and Web interfaces. For which the architecture is based on MDA techniques [4–6] and REST Representational State Transfer services. The research provides a cross-platform architecture for the analysis of vehicular traffic through machine learning tools and cloud computing.

The first section refers to the background, introduction, motivation, scope, and general hypothesis of the project. In the second section you will find the information on the state of the art of the developed project. The third section is the design of the system, indicating in this way the technologies to be used and the fundamentals of development. The fourth section talks about the implementation of the platform, that is, a brief explanation of how the project progressed until it was completed based on the architecture. Finally, it deals with the tests carried out on the system and determining the strengths and vulnerabilities they present. Additionally, the conclusions and discussion of the project are presented.

2   Related Works

According to [7], the city of Quito is in twenty-sixth place in the world ranking with the most traffic congestion problems, as well as being the second city in the country with mobility problems. This research was carried out in 200 cities in 38 countries, based on big data analysis on traffic congestion.

The information taken from the research carried out by [8] mentions some measures that have been taken in the city of Quito to help with congestion. The peak and plate remove between 20 and 30% of private vehicles from the roads, in peak hours. Julio Puga, director of the AMT, indicates that 10 years ago there were 300,000 vehicles registered in Quito, but last year there were 448,000, although 650,000 circulate in the city, adding those that arrive from other cities. The consultant on mobility issues, Roberto Custode says that traffic problems stem from a disorderly and poorly planned development. The EPMMOP Metropolitan Public Mobility and Public Works Company reported that in the last three years works have been carried out such as the interchanges of Los Granados and Carapungo avenues, the extension of Simón Bolívar avenues and of the Ecov'ia to the south, the Charles Darwin road solution, Carapungo street, the rehabilitation of the Interoceanic avenue, the exclusive Trole corridor and the Ecovía. According to Puga, with the start of operations of the Quito Metro, the vehicular load will be alleviated because it will transport 1,500 passengers per trip and 400,000 per day. Today, in the trunk routes (Ecovía, Trolley and corridors) 700,000 are mobilized per day.

Puga affirms that the AMT carries out daily controls to reduce congestion, which include 16 counterflows and personnel organizing the vehicular flow on the roads.

The prediction of vehicular traffic obeys patterns with periodic characteristics and with seasonality. As indicated by [9] SARIMA Autoregressive automatic seasonal integrated moving average is a method that allows modeling these characteristics in a system.

In the last decade there has been a data explosion and a shift in focus on storage hardware. The research carried out by [10] indicates that NoSQL technologies have been designed with the objective of scalability in mind and present a wide range of solutions based on data models, with tolerance to faults when the volume of data and its complexity increase. Currently there is an additional cloud computing alternative, cloud storage provides flexible access from multiple locations and the ability to scale quickly and easily, as well as cheaper prices and better support based on economies of scale with an effectiveness of costs.

Traffic Detection Systems (TMS) is an active area in research, according to what is indicated in [11], there are currently several means of informing the driver of both public and private transport such as effective management of intelligent traffic lights, transport public with sensors and followed by mobile applications, models of superblocks, mobile applications for shared bike, shared car.

In the research previously studied, the existing information is analyzed to take as a reference in the development of the present project regarding machine learning, TMS, data analysis and contribute to the development of the city.

3   First Section

To make vehicle traffic predictions, the city of Quito Ecuador was taken as a reference. The type of data acquired for training and subsequent prediction is related to the time series, that is, the sampled data is periodically taken every certain time interval. As a prediction platform is being developed, an instance must be created that allows the data to be acquired, filtered, and processed. To do this, the creation of a set of tools has been proposed that allow the platform administrator to fulfill these tasks.

From having data already filtered and processed to the needs of the project, we proceed to look for a data storage tool. Next, is the prediction of vehicular traffic for this article using the knowledge of machine learning "Machine Learning". Finally, there is the user interface, where the user will request and receive the prediction requests, for which there are several alternatives to TVDigital, smartphone, web. Figure 1 shows the interaction between modules of the architecture.

4   Implementation

The platform has two software solutions that allow it to fulfill the data collection task, the Android Traffic Data application, and a data collection service from GDM API. The figure below explains the data acquisition process both in the mobile client and in the GDM API (Fig. 2).

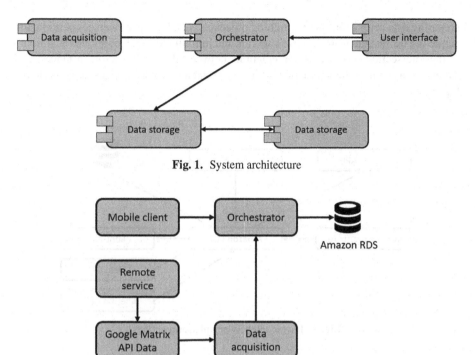

Fig. 1. System architecture

Fig. 2. Processes for acquiring vehicle traffic data

The Traffic Data application for Android is a tool for obtaining traffic data. When the application is started, the operating system renders a main template that contains a screen with an interactive map, several text spaces and buttons that allow interaction with the application services. Parallel to the rendering of screens, a service is started that checks if there is an internet connection and checks if all traffic samples stored in the internal database have been written to the cloud database. In this way it is ensured that all the data stored internally in the application is stored in the cloud. When you start the application, the device's location services are initialized, that is, you configure how often the GPS reports the location (latitude and longitude), speed, altitude, direction, etc. Using this information, it is possible to update the map shown on the device screen and relevant information can be displayed to the user. On the main screen of the application there are two buttons that allow you to start or stop the registration of traffic data. When starting the data collection service, a second service that records the vehicle traffic information and stores it in the internal database of the application is launched on the device. This service can only be stopped by the user by means of the stop button of the application. At each start or stop of the application, data, credentials, or relevant information are stored for the correct operation of the application using the shared reference file.

The Platform Master Orchestrator is described as a cloud computing instance that runs on Amazon AWS servers and performs the functions programmed in the main source code. The tasks that the server is responsible for are storing data from clients, executing, and sending responses to different clients, creating traffic data tables, and preparing data prior to automatic training processes. In addition, it oversees periodically extracting traffic data from Google's servers and initiating the task of automatic training of the intersection models. The interactions between the Orchestrator, instances, and databases, as well as the interaction with clients and additional services, are outlined in Fig. 3.

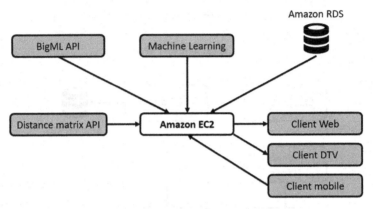

Fig. 3. Interaction between platform entities

The orchestrator feeds the database with information obtained through the Android application and data obtained through Google's Distance Matrix API. Clients issue requests and the Orchestrator responds with the requested information as HTML files or responses in JSON format. The Google Cloud Platform instance is used to train intersection models and provides prediction data to the orchestrator for it to store in the database. The BigML resource [14] is used for street classification, the orchestrator uses the BigML API to generate requests that are handled and presented to the user through the orchestrator. All traffic data, predictions, intersections, configurations, and more are stored in the Amazon RDS instance [15]. The orchestrator's programming logic has been designed so that it can be run independently of the operating system or hardware on the Python programming language. This allows the Orchestrator to be easily migrated to different platforms and improves the scalability and repeatability of its functions. The platform has been thought of as a set of distributed entities, where each instance or resource performs a task at a specific time. This allows the orchestrator not to be saturated with tasks, and it also allows unnecessary resources to not be wasted when a task that demands large processing capacities is not being carried out. The main code that runs the orchestrator has been created considering common practices in the world of software production. It has been modified and adapted so that it can be easily distributed and its implementation on other servers is more understandable for developers. In addition, the use of a repository has been implemented throughout the platform that allows the control and correction of the main code of all the applications that interact with the main orchestrator.

The elaborated web page (Fig. 4a) tries to be friendly with the user and be manageable for anyone, trying to access the complete information and with the predictions of the streets already chosen previously. It has a short menu that is understood by the end user as well as the administrators. For administrators it allows them to feed the database by adding the information and so that this information is only authorized to enter this option, it will ask us for authentication (username and password). In Fig. 4b we can see a graph by street, this graph shows the date with respect to the speed at which a driver can circulate and also shows the calculation of the RSME that it has with respect to the prediction made.

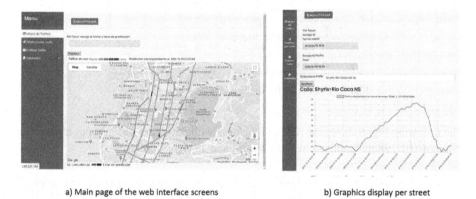

a) Main page of the web interface screens   b) Graphics display per street

Fig. 4. Screenshot of the web client

The integration with the Digital Television service is carried out by an application written in NCL and LUA [17], the program that will allow executing the display of the menu, buttons and as well as the sending of the information to the server so that it returns us the result of the prediction. The result of this prediction will be shown on the screen while the user continues to play the content on TVD; thus, having at hand at any time make inquiries of the traffic status. Below are the lines of code that will be used to make a successful connection between the server and the application made in the NCL-LUA language (Fig. 5).

5   Test

5.1   Load and Performance Testing with JMeter - Web Client Testing

Through the IP (https://3.85.227.159) it is possible to carry out tests of the elaborated architecture. JMeter [18] software is used for performance and load tests; it is performed for the case of six scenarios simulating 50, 150, 250, 350, 500 and 550 concurrent users (called threads in JMeter) making requests for a period of 60 s to the server (HTTP - GET). The settings on the main screen are done by placing the 'Server name or IP', in this case the server IP is set; also the Port number (Port: 80 for this server) and finally the number of threads or the number of users that need to be simulated to make simultaneous requests to the server. Once these parameters are configured in the program, it can be run so that it begins to show the results. Below is the test result with more emulated users.

```
hostIP= '3.85.227.159'
tcp.connect(hostIP,80)

local url = 'GET/ api/ vl/ consulta/ '.. evt. value..'
    HTTP/ 1.1\ r\n'
tcp.send(url)
tcp.send('Host:3.85.227.159\ r\n')
tcp.send('Connection: keep-alive\r\n')
tcp.send('Cache-Control:max-age=0\r\n')
tcp.send('Upgrade-Insecure-Request:1\r\n')
tcp.send('User-Agent:Mozilla/5.0(Windows NT 10.0;
    Win64; x64) AppleWebKit/537.36 (KHTML, like
    Gecko) Chrome/79.0.3945.79 Safari/537.36\r\n')
tcp.send('Accept: text/htmlapplication/xhtml+xml,
    application/xml;q=0.9,image/webp,image/apng
    ,*/*;q=0.8,application/signed-exchange;v=b3;q
    =0.9\r\n')
tcp.send('Accept-Encoding:gzip,deflate\r\n')
tcp.send('Accept-Language: es-ES,es;q=0.9,en;q=0.8\
    r\n')
tcp.send('\r\n')
```

Fig. 5. LUA code for the consumption of web services

The following Fig. 6 shows the result of the tests with 550 users and gives us an average value of 101,198 ms (equivalent to 1.68 min) and an error of 99.82%.

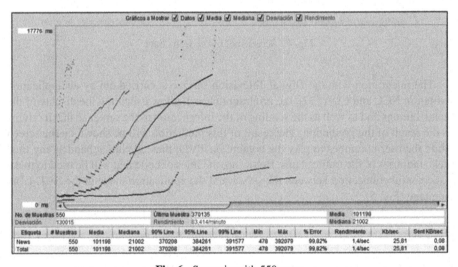

Fig. 6. Scenario with 550 users

At the end of this test with 550 users due to the error that gives us almost one hundred percent, an attempt is made to enter the server with the IP in a browser which obviously fails. In the following Table 1 there is a summary of the results of the tests carried out with the increase in users and here it can be seen that as they increase, the error increases as well as the average response time to server requests. The maximum error that is reached is 99.8% in which the server is saturated, preventing it from being accessible for a few seconds. There is a 0% error for fifty (50) users, indicating that the requests made to the server were successful during the fifty (50) samples executed and there is an average of

10651 ms (equivalent to 10 s) of time for each request. As mentioned, the mean response increases as the number of simulated users increases, reaching 1.62 min.

Table 1. Summary of test results with JMeter.

Samples	Average (ms)	Error	Performance
50	10651	0	41/min
100	85491	7	33.4/min
250	43774	78.8	1.6/s
350	72925	74	1.7/s
500	62147	87.4	1.7/s
550	101198	99.82	1.4/s

5.2   Comparison Between Actual Values and Predictive Values of Speed

The database has prediction values that were performed in the machine learning module, therefore, to carry out these tests, the data was exported in the date range: from 10/17/2019 to 24/10/2019. In addition, on the same dates, real data was taken from the Shyris - United Nations and Amazonas - Gaspar de Villarroel intersections with the GDMA API. The Shyris - United Nations is chosen for this case randomly and the intersection Amazonas - Gaspar de Villarroel empirically based on the characterization of the streets; The two intersections named above have similar parameters that are ideal for comparing speed tests with SARIMAX [19] and BIGML [20] prediction.

With the speed information, the calculation of how dispersed the data is with respect to the mean, that is, the standard deviation, was made. In the following Fig. 7, the 'X' axis represents the date and time in which the data were acquired and the 'Y' axis the vehicular speed of the intersection Shyris and United Nations, the predictive speed represented by red and colored blue the actual speed. After an analysis of the information, it was perceived that there were values outside the usual behavior of the neighboring data, so they were taken as conditions of no matter and with the remaining data the standard deviation was calculated for this case a value of 14.7% and visually the prediction graph follows the behavior pattern of the graph with real values.

For Fig. 8, which corresponds to the intersection of Amazonas and Gaspar de Villarroel, the same parameters assigned for the x-axis (date and time) and the y-axis (speed) are maintained, in this case the standard deviation is equal to 19.6% and visually the prediction plot follows the behavior of the plot of the real values, although it contains peaks outside the mean. This is due to several factors, one of them is that now of predicting and coupling the characteristics to the intersection it resembles.

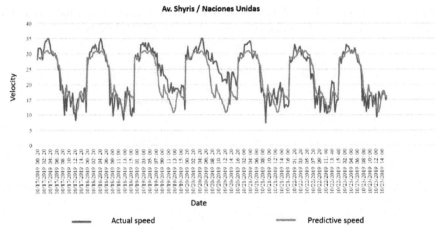

Fig. 7. Shyris y Naciones Unidas

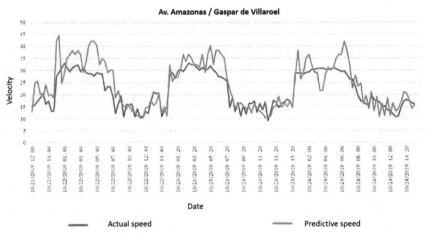

Fig. 8. Amazonas y Gaspar de Villaroel

6 Conclusions

- In the research, a cross platform architecture was designed for the analysis of vehicular traffic; composed of three platforms: a) the first the mobile client to capture the information, b) the second the Web client and c) the third the TVD client, the last two used to display the information. All the platforms use cloud computing resources to acquire, store, predict and present information, allowing the user to
- Access from multiplatform at any time or place, using the specific characteristics and capabilities of each client.
- The project is made up of a set of microservices and in turn segmented into independent modules for easy implementation. The orchestrator module establishes communication between all the services, receives requests and sends responses between the

different software and hardware devices. This allows a distributed architecture and makes the system more stable, therefore, in case of attacks, the entire system will not collapse but only the module.

- The traffic prediction system is based on MDA methodologies for the deployment and construction of the platform, since it can be adapted to other languages and scalable in time to meet needs by abstracting general characteristics of the proposal, with which it can be expand the architecture for future projects. The architecture based on metamodels separates the elements so that it is much easier to implement module by module, reducing costs and reducing complexity by choosing optimal tools that would be used to solve the problems initially raised.
- The machine learning tool has several learning methods, so prior to its use it is important to analyze the behavior of the data to have a better assertiveness in the prediction results. The project has two types of behavior in the data: a) in the first instance, the speed data is acquired by GDMA for training, from which temporal and stationary trends are obtained, for which the use of the SARIMAX model was determined, and b) secondly the
- The data are for the characterization of the streets, for which the prediction by classification is used and the decision tree algorithm was implemented in the BigML predictive analysis tool.
- When performing tests between real values and predicted values, the standard deviation of the subtraction of the two graphs was obtained in the SARIMAX prediction, the deviation was 14.7%, which is an acceptable value and has a behavior similar to the real data. Also, the deviation in the decision tree method is 19.6%. The training and learning of the decision tree were performed by qualitative characterization and the deviation increases due to the accumulation of the sum of RSME of the SARIMAX prediction and
- In addition to the characterization prediction, therefore the reliability of the trained point inherits the sum of RSME from the intersection with the classification method.
- In the qualitative comparison that was made, it was possible to see that the colors in the prediction of our Web client with that of Google Maps are similar, despite the fact that it is unknown and there is no information on the range of speeds with which Google uses to impose the status traffic (color code).
- System training depends on the quantity and quality of truthful information that is acquired for prediction and identifying the type of algorithm that must be used to process the information correctly. In this project, the sources used are the Google Distance Matrix API and the mobile client since it allows users to access and send information at any time and place.
- The use of an automatic integrator (orchestrator) allows the management, uni-fication, and coordination of the microservices for the implementation of the Model View Controller architectural pattern and thus avoid a monolithic application.
- Based on the tests carried out with the JMeter tool, the response time of the server was tested by increasing the load, reaching a saturation limit with 500 users and preventing access to the URL (Web page), this due to the specifications with those that the server has are basic due to costs.

628 E. Lomas et al.

References

1. Del Distrito, M., De Quito, M., et al.: Plan maestro de movilidad 2009–2025. Plan Maestro de Movilidad **2009**(2025), 14–18 (2009)
2. Chourabi, H., et al.: Understanding smart cities: an integrative framework. In: 2012 45th Hawaii International Conference on System Sciences, pp. 2289–2297. IEEE (2012)
3. Silva, T.H., Vaz De Melo, P.O.S., Viana, A.C., Almeida, J.M., Salles, J., Loureiro, A.A.F.: Traffic condition is more than colored lines on a map: characterization of waze alerts. In: Jatowt, A., et al. (eds.) SocInfo 2013. LNCS, vol. 8238, pp. 309–318. Springer, Cham (2013). https://doi.org/10.1007/978-3-319-03260-3_27
4. Wang, G., Wang, B., Wang, T., Nika, A., Zheng, H., Zhao, B.Y.: Defending against sybil devices in crowdsourced mapping services. In: Proceedings of the 14th Annual International Conference on Mobile Systems, Applications, and Services, pp. 179–191 (2016)
5. Modelo de aplicación de base de datos y su servicio para el descubrimiento de fármacos en la arquitectura basada en modelos. Diario de Big Data
6. Márquez, J.E.M.: Una arquitectura orientada a servicios y dirigida por eventos para el control inteligente de UAVs multipropósito. PhD thesis, Universidad de Extremadura (2018)
7. Cookson, G., Pishue, B.: Inrix global traffic scorecard. inrix research (2018)
8. Coyago, A.P.R., Ortega, S.F.C., Pinargote, A.J.P.: Análisis de la aplicación del pico y placa en la ciudad de quito. INNOVA Res. J. **2**(6), 136–142 (2017)
9. Brownlee, J.: A gentle introduction to sarima for time series forecasting in python (2018)
10. Springer, editor. Nuevos horizontes para una economía basada en datos: una hoja de ruta para el uso y la explotación de big data en Europa
11. Rodríguez, A.: Internet de las cosas contra el tráfico vehicular telcel empresas (2018)
12. Google. Google distance matrix api (2017)
13. de Madrid, A.: Portal de datos abiertos del ayuntamiento de Madrid (2020)
14. Zhou, L., Pan, S., Wang, J., Vasilakos, A.V.: Machine learning on big data: opportunities and challenges. Neurocomputing **237**, 350–361 (2017)
15. Varia, J., Mathew, S., et al.: Overview of amazon web services. Amazon Web Serv. **105**, 1–22 (2014)
16. Gunawan, A.S., Gultom, A.S.H., Manalu, S.R., et al.: Android-based framework for business expedition third party with google api: case study. In: 2017 International Conference on Information Management and Technology (ICIMTech), pp. 71–76. IEEE (2017)
17. Dávila Sacoto, M.A.: Diseño de una plataforma de software para televisión digital interactiva de un canal de deportes utilizando ginga-ncl lua. B.S. thesis (2012)
18. Halili, E.H.: Apache JMeter: A Practical Beginner's Guide to Automated Testing and Performance Measurement for Your Websites. Packt Publishing Ltd, Birmingham (2008)
19. Cools, M., Moons, E., Wets, G.: Investigating the variability in daily traffic counts through use of arimax and sarimax models: assessing the effect of holidays on two site locations. Transp. Res. Rec. **2136**(1), 57–66 (2009)
20. Kessel, M., Ruppel, P., Gschwandtner, F.: Bigml: a location model with individual waypoint graphs for indoor location-based services. PIK-Praxis der Informations verarbeitung und Kommunikation **33**(4), 261–267 (2010)
21. Aguilar, M.I.H., Villegas, A.A.G.: Análisis comparativo de la escala de usabilidad del sistema (eus) en dos versiones/Comparative analysis of the system usability scale (sus) in two versions. RECI Revista Iberoamericana de las Ciencias Computacionales e Informática **5**(10), 44–58 (2016)

Beyond Visual and Radio Line of Sight UAVs Monitoring System Through Open Software in a Simulated Environment

Miguel A. Murillo, Julio E. Alvia, and Miguel Realpe$^{(\boxtimes)}$

Facultad de Ingeniería en Electricidad y Computación, Escuela Superior Politécnica del Litoral, ESPOL, CIDIS. Gustavo Galindo Km. 30.5 Vía Perimetral, Guayaquil, Ecuador
{mianmuri,jealvia,mrealpe}@espol.edu.ec

Abstract. The problem of loss of line of sight when operating drones has become a reality with adverse effects for professional and amateur drone operators, since it brings technical problems such as loss of data collected by the device in one or more instants of time during the flight and even misunderstandings of legal nature when the drone flies over prohibited or private places. This paper describes the implementation of a drone monitoring system using the Internet as a long-range communication network in order to avoid the problem of loss of communication between the ground station and the device. For this, a simulated environment is used through an appropriate open software tool. The operation of the system is based on a client that makes requests to a server, the latter in turn communicates with several servers, each of which has a drone connected to it. In the proposed system when a drone is ready to start a flight, its server informs the main server of the system, which in turn gives feedback to the client informing it that the device is ready to carry out the flight; this way customers can send a mission to the device and keep track of its progress in real time on the screen of their web application.

Keywords: Drone · Open source · Internet · Web application · Web server · SITL · Line of sight · UAV

1 Introduction

Drones or unmanned aerial vehicles (UAV) are a technology in continuous evolution, they have different fields of application today in diverse areas such as precision agriculture [1, 2], livestock [3], fishing industry [4], among others. However, its use has been affected by different situations, such as the overflight of prohibited places, the overcoming of height limits already established in different legal frameworks, limitation of flights during the day, among others. Another potential problem consists of the loss of control of the UAV. Currently, telemetry is used to control the communication of most commercial drones with the ground station, which is a communication system that allows the transmission of data from one device to another. During these transmissions, interference may occur causing loss of control over the device and making it impossible for the user to know its status during those moments, which could cause accidents and even the possible destruction of the device.

© Springer Nature Switzerland AG 2021
M. Botto-Tobar et al. (Eds.): ICAT 2020, CCIS 1388, pp. 629–642, 2021.
https://doi.org/10.1007/978-3-030-71503-8_49

1.1 The Problem of Loss of Line of Sight

Visual line of sight (VLOS) and radio line of sight (RLOS) establish areas where it is possible to directly visualize and control drones, respectively. While using a drone, its RLOS can be lost due to various factors. For example, the drone could be located behind a large obstacle at a certain moment or there could be a partial or total loss of the data transmitted to the user caused by interference present in the electromagnetic waves that are used in wireless communication [5]. These situations do not allow the operation of long-range flights, consequently generating limitations in the applications that can be given to drones. To this is added the legal issue, since the flight of these devices over prohibited areas is not allowed, a situation that when violated could cause legal problems for the owner of the UAV.

Here are some points that must be considered in order to provide a viable and acceptable solution to the problem described above, which generates many adverse situations for drone users:

- Being able to use a drone through direct control and / or telemetry without losing line of sight.
- Have a stable direct connection alternative on the drone to avoid the problem of loss of line of sight.
- Have access to a web application that allows user-drone interaction to be handled comfortably.

1.2 Some Useful Tools for Testing Drones

The tools that allow the connection with the drones are several, one of the best known is Mission Planner (MP) [6], which provides the user with different functionalities such as creating a route by setting different appropriate parameters, to later load it into the drone and perform the mission. The different measurements of the device (height, speed, current position, current direction during the flight performed, among others) are nicely displayed on a map within MP.

MP also provides the option of simulating the flight of different UAVs with the use of an open source simulation tool known as Software In The Loop (SITL) [7]. The latter, being an open source tool, has functionalities that are not linked to MP, allowing developers to have all the benefits that it entails, such as access to the source code, the use of different libraries that allow handling the simulation data and the control of UAVs during the flight.

The use of the Internet is expanding every day, promoting technology to interconnect different devices thanks to the Internet of Things (IoT), this provides varied functionalities that help users to perform multiple tasks; such as the control of household items (appliances, security cameras, among others). Added to this are the options for data analysis offered by these devices, which give the user the possibility of making timely decisions, some examples of this are the self-adjustment of a luminaire or the temperature control of an air conditioning. This great evolution of the internet has led engineers to seek solutions that facilitate the use of different types of devices, generating interest in the technology community and expanding its use.

2 Technologies Associated with Increased Line of Sight

Laws restrictions regarding flying drones vary from country to country. However, there are many similar limitations. For example, US and many European countries, such as Spain, allow amateur drone operations only within the VLOS of the operator, which is usually define as up to 500 m horizontally and 120 m vertically [8, 9].

Extending the line of sight of drones is a very representative problem that rise many solutions such as Extended Visual Line of Sight (EVLOS), which consists of maintaining permanent contact between the drone pilot and one or more observers through radio. In Europe, one solution for extending the line of sight is VLOS fusion, that consists of positioning a pilot in a central point giving a flight radius of 500 m to the drone while another pilot stands in another central point that has an equal range radius for the same drone (the pilots' trajectories must intersect); thus widening the line of sight and allowing both to have a greater range of travel. This solution however, adds a new negative situation in a collateral way; since requires the use of more personnel to carry out a task that could be controlled by a single person through a control station that allows to maintain control of the unmanned aerial vehicle at all time.

The technologies for location awareness of drones can be classified into two main groups [10]: Direct broadcast and network publishing.

Direct broadcast applies different communication technologies using direct transmission between drones and ground stations. There are technologies that are considered relevant when managing communication between an unmanned aerial vehicle and a ground control station, such as telemetry through the use of 2.4 GHz and 5.8 GHz industrial, scientific and medical (ISM) radio communication bands; as long as the criteria analysis (communication ranges, energy consumption, costs, robustness, security, latency, interoperability between standards, among others), use cases and appropriate scenarios (applications) are carried out. This science is highly useful for one of the most common drone applications, precision agriculture (PA); both for VLOS, EVLOS and Beyond Line of Sight (BVLOS). The use of these bands in PA generates quite satisfactory results compared to other technologies, such as WI-FI, whose main problem is high energy consumption, communication range and security. Despite these statements, it is essential to emphasize the fact that this success has been proven only in this application of UAVs, there are surely many more of them [1].

In areas where BVLOS and RLOS occur, data can be sent to and received from the drone by wireless communication technologies, despite the operator cannot visualize the drone. For example, in [11] a system that realizes long-distance communication for drones using the 400 MHz frequency band and data transmission was developed where the location information is broadcasted at a constant period using a simplified protocol based on peer aware communications defined by the IEEE802.15.8 Working Group enabling location sharing in real time.

On the other hand, network publishing uses existing network infrastructure though cellular or satellite networks [12], allowing BVLOS and beyond RLOS (BRLOS) to control the drones [13, 14].

The use of mobile networks has grown even more in recent years with the birth of 5G, which allows a range of new options in different fields in the use of drones, analysis have already been carried out of the possible benefits that will be obtained thanks to its use, being one of them wide, safe and reliable connectivity. These factors favor the use of this technology in different industries since by offering economic benefits and security, governments will greatly reduce the current limitations of communications, allowing companies to make use of the technology to solve problems and needs.

2.1 An Interesting Solution

An acceptable solution for BVLOS and BRLOS is to develop a web system that allows the user to plan a flight, with the implementation of a connection between a web platform and the drone, with the MP tool as support. For the system testing, the SITL simulator is proposed, some specific objectives are described then:

- Develop a friendly interface that allows the user to select data for pre-established routes in a database, define flight routes, show feedback of the status of the drone from SITL and view them in the web application.
- Integrate the developed system and SITL to create routes that will be sent to the drone.
- Send routes from the web application to SITL for the drone flight simulation.
- Allow the use of MP as a support tool to handle more advanced operations on the drone, for example sensors calibrations.

3 Proposed Solution

The proposed solution (Fig. 1) consists of an architecture comprising a client module, a main server and an additional server called the "drone server", in addition to an administrator component and connection to open source tools. The drone server runs SITL which will be activated by an administrator using any of the TCP or UDP communication protocols. The simulated drone in SITL can optionally be calibrated via MP. Subsequently, SITL communicates with the Backend of this same server who collects the data and sends it to the main server. The latter in turn communicates with the client allowing him to perform all actions on the simulated drone as well as view its progress and status as shown in Fig. 11.

3.1 Client Component

The client component is subdivided into four components, the details of which are explained below:

- Drone module: Allows the customer to create and edit drones. It also gives the option to list the existing drones in the database (DB).
- Routes module: Allows the customer to create and edit routes.
- Mission module: Gives the option of creating and executing missions, as well as viewing their progress.
- Communication module: It communicates with the three previously mentioned modules. It allows the latter to communicate with the endpoints of the main server through messages in JavaScript Object Notation (JSON) format (Fig. 2).

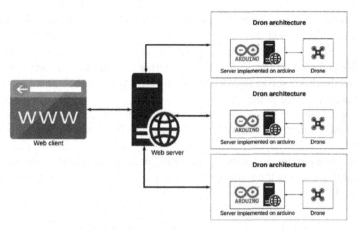

Fig. 1. Diagram of the proposed solution.

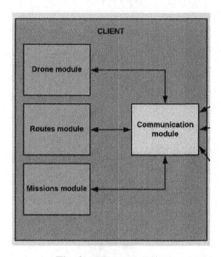

Fig. 2. Client modules.

3.2 Main Server

This component has been subdivided into five endpoints, the details of which are explained below:

- Drone endpoint: It communicates with the client's drone module through the client's communication module. Save the drones sent from the client in the DB. It also reads all the drones in the DB and returns them to the client.
- Routes endpoint: It communicates with the customer's routes module through its communication module. It saves the routes sent from the client in the DB. It is also in charge of editing the routes sent from the client in the DB.

- Mission endpoint: It communicates with the client's mission module through the client's communication module. Saves the initial data of a mission sent from the client in the DB. It also orders the execution of the mission through a connection with a suitable endpoint on the drone's server. During the mission, it receives the mission data from the drone server and stores it in the DB. At the end of the mission, save the final data of the same in the DB.
- Positioning endpoint: When a drone is being simulated, it receives its information from an endpoint on the drone's server and saves the information regarding its positions in the DB.
- Login/status endpoint: It communicates with an endpoint on the drone server and is responsible for saving the status of the drone (valid or invalid drone) simulated in the DB (Fig. 3).

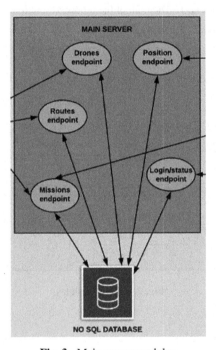

Fig. 3. Main server modules.

3.3 Drone Server

This component has three endpoints, their specifications are as follows:

- SITL connection endpoint: It communicates with an administrator module which sends the execution order through the TCP or UDP protocol. Subsequently, once the execution of the simulation begins, it takes the position data of the drone and returns it to the positioning endpoint in the main server, which saves it in the DB.

- Mission endpoint: Receives mission data continuously from SITL and sends it to the mission endpoint on the main server.
- Web connection endpoint: It communicates with the login/status endpoint present on the main server by sending data about the status of the drone. It also saves this information in the second DB (Fig. 4).

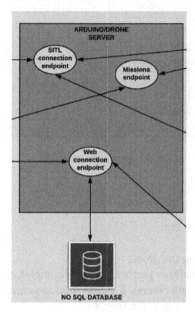

Fig. 4. Drone server modules.

3.4 Administrator Component

The administrator consists of two modules which are detailed below:

- SITL connection module: Communicates with the SITL connection endpoint on the drone server. It allows making the connection with SITL choosing a protocol between TCP and UDP, in order to set the simulator ready for the execution of a flight.
- Web connection module: Communicates with the web connection endpoint on the drone server. It allows obtaining data about the status of the simulated drone in order to know if it is suitable to use it in subsequent simulations, then it sends this data to the login/status endpoint on the main server (Fig. 5).

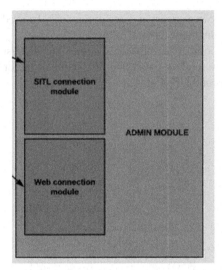

Fig. 5. Administrator modules.

3.5 Open Source Tools

The open source tools used are:

- SITL: Allows simulating the drone.
- MP: Auxiliary tool that allows performing more complex operations on the simulated drone (calibrations, among others). It is also used to generate routes quickly through a file with a "waypoints" extension (Fig. 6).

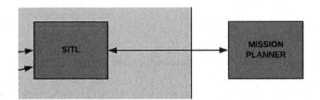

Fig. 6. Open source tools .

3.6 Tools Used for Implementation

The tools used for implementation are the following:

- Angular Framework: This Framework is currently used in large-scale projects, and it is inferred that this project is of that type. Performance issues at compile time are rare [15].

- Angular Material: Style library based on the "Material Design" design guide [16].
- JQuery Library: minimalist JavaScript library, allows you to write code quickly and easily. It has remained for years as one of the pillars of web development.
- Leaflet: It offers multiple functionalities; it is an excellent option when developing an application that includes maps since it is open-source and free [17].
- Framework Flask: Backend framework oriented towards microservices, allows the development of web applications in a simple and agile way, as well as being able to integrate with multiple Python libraries [18].
- Dronekit Library: Library implemented for Python that allows communication with drones and their simulators.
- MongoDB: It is scalable, decentralized, and its transactional costs are much lower than those of a SQL database [19].
- SITL: Open source simulator with a high learning curve and specifically implemented to work with drones.
- MP: Open source software with great documentation and relatively easy to use that allows communication with a simulator (Fig. 7).

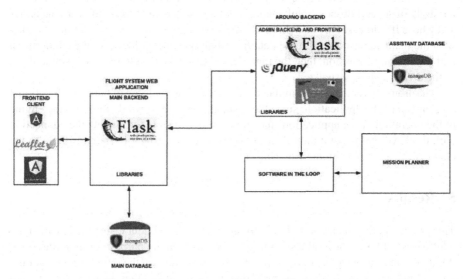

Fig. 7. Implementation architecture with chosen tools.

4   Hardware and Software Architecture

This section details the creation phase of the tests carried out on the chosen hardware and software infrastructure, as well as their real-time execution. Table 1 specifies the different physical and virtual machines used, a more specific detail on these infrastructures will be given in the next paragraphs.

The system was implemented locally on a physical machine using Pop! _OS, since it has high efficiency and high performance during the processes related to data compilation

Table 1. Description of physical and virtual machines used.

Computer	Processor	RAM	Hard disk	Operating system	Machine type
Client	AMD Ryzen 7 2700	16 GB	1 TB	Pop!_OS	Physic
Main server	AMD Ryzen 7 2700	8 GB	1 TB	Elementary-OS	Virtual
Drone server 1	AMD Ryzen 7 2700	8 GB	1 TB	Elementary-OS	Virtual
Drone server 2	AMD Ryzen 7 2700	8 GB	1 TB	Elementary-OS	Virtual

and handling. The Angular framework for client development was installed on this machine. In addition, an Elementary-OS virtual machine was used. The server that run on the drone was also implemented with Flask on an Elementary-OS virtual machine. This is done in order to be able to simulate a web server in the cloud and to simulate the flight of several drones simultaneously, which can connect from different machines and whose IP addresses are also different. These servers are in charge of communicating with the main server to send it the data regarding the current location of each drone in real time during a mission, then the main server sends the data to the client so the flight of the drones can be visualized.

The drone server that each simulated device uses is a small cog of the entire functional mechanism of the application, since these small servers as a whole make up the engine of the operation of the application since they are responsible for making the connection with the UAV and to send their data to the main server, which later sends them to the client allowing drones monitoring (Fig. 11).

5   Results

This project focuses on tracking UAVs flight in real time without losing the line of sight, which was achieved. Several tests were carried out with the purpose of monitoring the flight of drones in an Open Source simulator, below is attached the information regarding three of these scenarios. It is important to emphasize the fact that the tests were carried out on common physical and virtual machines, nevertheless, it is suggested to run the servers on several processors, as it would haven when implementing the system on real drones. The hardware architecture of the machines used was an AMD Ryzen 7 2700 processor, 8 cores, 16 threads and 16 GB RAM.

5.1   Long-Distance Flight

It consisted of a flight of 10.54 km from the Center for Research, Development and Innovation of Computer Systems (CIDIS) to the city's downtown (Fig. 8 and Table 2).

Fig. 8. Route for the long-distance flight.

Table 2. Results for flight from CIDIS to downtown Guayaquil.

Min altitude	Max altitude	Mean altitude	Mean velocity	Flight time	Battery
9.59 m	37.04m	35.013 m	2.62 m/s		3%

5.2 Short-Distance Flight

It consisted of a flight of 0.23 km at ESPOL university (Fig. 9 and Table 3).

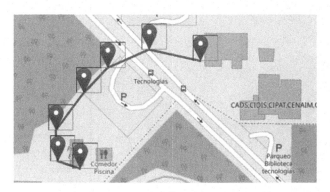

Fig. 9. Route for the short-distance flight.

Table 3. Results for flight inside ESPOL campus.

Min altitude	Max altitude	Mean altitude	Mean velocity	Flight time	Battery
9.61 m	111.07 m	103.27 m	2.44 m/s	70 s	68%

5.3 Flight with Two Drones

It was a simultaneous flight of two drones from CIDIS to two points near this research center. The first one consisted of a 0.21 km flight and the second one consisted of a flight of 0.62 km (Fig. 10).

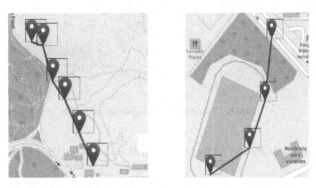

Fig. 10. Routes for simultaneous flight of two drones.

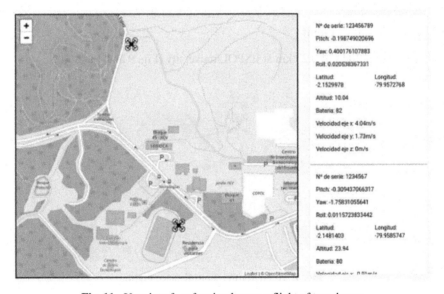

Fig. 11. User interface for simultaneous flight of two drones.

6 Conclusions

UAVs are being applied in diverse types of activities by users with different capabilities and training. However, a user-friendly system that allows flying BVLOS and BRLOS would notably increase the applications where user may operate UAVs. The implementation of a web application that allows controlling the drone through a wireless Internet network is an innovative and striking alternative to be able to dissipate the loss of line of sight of the device; also adding a pleasant human-computer interaction to the developed system. The proposed system is available on [20], it was test using SITL and virtual machines, but it can easily be implemented on real drones applying small changes in the drone server and loading it in on-board microcomputers on physical drones. Finally, some conclusions are presented:

- Communication over the Internet between the main server and the drone server allows data to be sent over long distances, even if both servers are in remote geographic locations.
- Using a NoSQL database like MongoDB provides great scalability since large amounts of data can be stored. The absence of the entity-relationship model also means that transactions are carried out at great speed.
- The use of parallelism through the threads was essential to be able to run the drone, this because the main thread of execution was the drone server itself serving the address and ports associated with it.
- In the future it is possible that the project could be put into production on servers in the cloud whose costs are convenient for the final client.

References

1. Neji, N., Mostfa, T.: Communication technology for Unmanned Aerial Vehicles: a qualitative assessment and application to Precision Agriculture. In: The 2019 International Conference on Unmanned Aircraft Systems (2019)
2. Saverio, J., Alarcón, A., Paillacho, J., Calderón, F., Realpe, M.: Open source system for identification of maize leaf chlorophyll contents based on multispectral images. In: Botto-Tobar, M., Zambrano Vizuete, M., Torres-Carrión, P., Montes León, S., Pizarro Vásquez, G., Durakovic, B. (eds.) ICAT 2019. CCIS, vol. 1194, pp. 572–581. Springer, Cham (2020). https://doi.org/10.1007/978-3-030-42520-3_45
3. Al-Thani, N., Albuainain, A., Alnaimi, F., Zorba, N.: Drones for sheep livestock monitoring. In: 2020 IEEE 20th Mediterranean Electrotechnical Conference (MELECON), Palermo, Italy, pp. 672–676 (2020). https://doi.org/10.1109/MELECON48756.2020.9140588
4. Cameron, D., et al.: The feasibility of using remotely piloted aircraft systems (RPAS) for recreational fishing surveys in Western Australia. Fisheries Occasional Publ. **137** (2019)
5. Guang, Y., et al.: A Telecom Perspective on the Internet of Drones: From LTE-Advanced to 5G (2018)
6. Mission Planner Homepage. https://ardupilot.org/planner, Accessed 9 Oct 2020
7. SITL Simulator Homepage. https://ardupilot.org/dev/docs/sitl-simulator-software-in-the-loop.html#overview, Aaccessed 9 Oct 2020
8. BOE, Real Decreto 1036/2017. https://www.seguridadaerea.gob.es/media/4629426/rd_1036_17_rpas.pdf, Accessed 02 Oct 2020, Accessed 9 Oct 2020
9. Federal Aviation Administration, Fly under the small UAS Rule. https://www.faa.gov/uas/getting_started, Accessed 9 Oct 2020
10. ARC Recommendations Final Report. UAS identification and tracking (UAS ID) Aviation Rulemaking Committee (ARC) (2017)

11. Kato, N., et al.: Location awareness system for drones flying beyond visual line of sight exploiting the 400 MHz frequency band. IEEE Wirel. Commun. **26**, 149–155 (2019)
12. Fotouhi, A., Ding, M., Hassan, M.: Flying drone base stations for macro hotspots. IEEE Access **6**, 19530–19539 (2018)
13. Jiang, T., Geller, J., Ni, D., Collura, J.: Unmanned aircraft system traffic management: concept of operation and system architecture. Int. J. Transp. Sci. Technol. **5**(3), 123–135 (2016). https://doi.org/10.1016/j.ijtst.2017.01.004
14. Davies, L., Bolam, R.C., Vagapov, Y., Anuchin, A.: review of unmanned aircraft system technologies to enable beyond visual line of sight (BVLOS) operations. In: 2018 X International Conference on Electrical Power Drive Systems (ICEPDS), Novocherkassk (2018)
15. Angular Documentation. https://angular.io/docs, Accessed 9 Oct 2020
16. Angular Material. https://material.angular.io/, Accessed 9 Oct 2020
17. Leaflet Documentation. https://leafletjs.com/reference-1.6.0.html, Accessed 9 Oct 2020
18. Flask Documentation. https://flask.palletsprojects.com/en/1.1.x/, Accessed 9 Oct 2020
19. Advantages of MongoDB. https://www.educba.com/advantages-of-mongodb/, Accessed 9 Oct 2020
20. "Sistema de monitoreo de drones", repository at Github. https://github.com/Jealvia/Sistema-de-monitoreo-de-drones.git, Accessed 9 Oct 2020

A Quality in Use Model for Ambient Assisted Living (AAL) Systems

Lenin Erazo-Garzon[1,2]([✉]), Lourdes Illescas-Peña[2], and Priscila Cedillo[1,2]

[1] Universidad del Azuay, Av. 24 de Mayo 7-77, Cuenca, Ecuador
lerazo@uazuay.edu.ec
[2] Universidad de Cuenca, Av. 12 de Abril, Cuenca, Ecuador
{lourdes.illescasp,priscila.cedillo}@ucuenca.edu.ec

Abstract. Ambient Assisted Living (AAL) aims to improve the people's quality of life, especially vulnerable groups, with the support of information technologies, increasing the autonomy, self-confidence and mobility of the users in their daily activities. Hence, it is essential to know the end-user's opinion about the perceived quality when using an AAL system in terms of the degree of satisfaction of their real needs and achieved objectives. However, since AAL is a relatively new domain, existing quality models are limited, with an incomplete set of attributes and metrics. Therefore, this research proposes a quality in use model for AAL systems focused on the followings characteristics: effectiveness, efficiency, satisfaction, freedom from risk, and context coverage; and their corresponding metrics adjusted to the AAL domain. Finally, the proposed model has been applied as a guideline during the evaluation of an intelligent pillbox. The results of this application have proven that this model is a valuable tool for evaluating the results and effects of using an AAL system from the perspectives of either a primary user (e.g., elderly people, people with special needs, patients) or a secondary user (e.g., family, caregivers). Consequently, it identifies essential aspects that contribute to improving the quality of those systems.

Keywords: AAL · Ambient Assisted Living · Quality in use · Quality of context · Quality model · Evaluation · Measurement · Metric

1 Introduction

The innovative use of information technologies to support the daily activities of people, especially vulnerable groups, has given rise to Ambient Assisted Living (AAL) [1], whose main objectives are oriented to: i) increase the autonomy, self-confidence and mobility of people in their natural living environment; ii) support the preservation of health of older people; iii) promote a healthier lifestyle for vulnerable people; iv) improve safety and prevent social isolation of older people; and, v) support carers, family members, and geriatric centers [2].

The demographic aging of the population [3] and technological convergence (communication network technologies, information technologies, detection and control technologies, software technologies, device/hardware technologies) have led to a growing

© Springer Nature Switzerland AG 2021
M. Botto-Tobar et al. (Eds.): ICAT 2020, CCIS 1388, pp. 643–660, 2021.
https://doi.org/10.1007/978-3-030-71503-8_50

market for solutions AAL aimed at improving people's life at home, in the community, and at work [4].

AAL solutions operate in real time, collecting, processing and interpreting data from sensors or other sources in order to infer contextual knowledge and react to events that occur in the user's environment [5]. However, errors in this process can infer false positive or false negative events, and consequently cause defects in the operation of the AAL system, dissatisfaction and bad experiences in the end users. Even in critical systems can endanger people's life [4].

The quality in use is the end-user's perception about quality of a system in operation and is measured and evaluated based on the results of using the system, rather than by properties of the system itself [6]. In particular, it is essential to know the degree to which an AAL system can satisfy the real needs and achieve the objectives of its end users, especially when these systems operate in highly changing scenarios, with a great variety of users, who present a diversity of cognitive and functional capacities, as well as emotional attitudes. However, the studies in this research area are scarce as it is reported in a systematic mapping [7], which concludes that it is necessary to have more complete quality models, with appropriate and specific metrics of quality for the AAL domain.

Therefore, this study proposes a quality in use model for AAL systems in order to measure and evaluate the results and impacts of its use from the perspectives of either a primary user (e.g., elderly people, people with special needs, patient) or a secondary user (e.g., family, caregivers). The intention of this paper is not to create a new quality model from scratch, but rather to incorporate a set of common and recurring characteristics among existing quality models, as well as relevant to the AAL domain and aligned with the ISO/IEC 25010 standard for quality in use.

This paper has the following structure: Sect. 2 presents a review of the related works. Section 3 specifies the methodology used for the construction of the quality in use model for AAL systems. Section 4 defines the purpose, domain, and user profiles for the evaluation of the quality in use, as well as the set of relevant characteristics and sub-characteristics that make up the model's requirements tree. Section 5 details the design of the measurement and evaluation of the quality in use. Section 6 describes the results of the assessment of the quality in use for an intelligent pillbox. Finally, Sect. 7 presents the conclusions and lines of future work.

2 Related Work

This section presents a bibliographic review of the essential quality approaches in use and context existing in the literature [8]. These approaches range from generic models, such as the ISO/IEC 25010 standard, to specific proposals for the AAL domain. The following libraries were consulted to search for quality approaches in AAL: ACM Digital Library, Science Direct, Springer Link, and IEEE Xplore. It was considered to analyze all those articles published since 2007, the year in which the "Ambient Assisted Living" initiative of the European treaty that financed the execution of research projects in this area was launched [9]. As a result of the review, six and three quality approaches in use and context were obtained for AAL systems, respectively.

In a general scope, the ISO/IEC 25010 standard [10] establishes a set of quality characteristics to evaluate the results and effects of the use of the software from the perspective of the end user. For this, the standard covers five characteristics: *effectiveness, efficiency, satisfaction, freedom from risk, and context coverage.*

Regarding the quality in use approaches, Garcés et al. [11] propose a quality model (QM4AAL) based on the ISO/IEC 25010. As a result, this model has a three-dimensional structure, made up of: constituent systems, adaptive and static properties, and quality attributes. The attributes of quality in use included in the model are: *effectiveness, efficiency, satisfaction (usefulness, trust), freedom from risk (health and safety risk mitigation), and context coverage (flexibility).* A limitation of this approach is that the formulation of quality metrics for the measurement of attributes is not included.

Salvi et al. [12] propose a methodological framework to evaluate the quality of AAL solutions at the level of the software product and in use. The methodology identifies the evaluation needs of technical and non-technical users and linking them with the quality characteristics of the ISO/IEC 25010 standard. Also, the framework includes a set of evaluation techniques, both subjective (questionnaires, focus groups, in-depth semi-structured interviews) and objective (software metrics, meta-evaluation). However, it does not detail how to apply the techniques to obtain quantitative quality indicators.

Mavridis et al. [13] define a framework to evaluate the quality of the systems resulting from R&D projects in e-health based on three levels: i) *system architecture*, determines the degree to which an architecture satisfies quality objectives; ii) *system software*, uses the ISO/IEC 14598 standard [14] that indicates how, when, who, and what should be measured, as well as the ISO/IEC 9126 - 2 & 3 standards [15] to measure the internal and external quality, and, iii) *system prototype*, applies the ISO/IEC 9126 - 4 standard [15] that provides characteristics and metrics of quality in use to evaluate the prototypes used by end users in real scenarios. A limitation of this work is that the ISO/IEC 9126 standard used has been replaced by ISO/IEC 25010.

Omerovic et al. [16] present a proposal for obtaining and weighting of the most important quality characteristics for the AAL domain. The proposal combines two approaches: i) expert judgments to assess the importance of the quality characteristics of the ISO/IEC 9126 standard concerning the AAL domain; and, ii) thematic analysis of the AAL roadmap of the AALIANCE project, to extract the categories of non-functional requirements with their respective frequencies of appearance. Regarding the quality in use, the *effectiveness, efficiency, and satisfaction* characteristics were evaluated with high weights, while the *safety* characteristic obtained a medium weight. This approach presents the same limitation as to the previous study.

Vitaletti et al. [17] define a set of functional and non-functional requirements necessary for remote healthcare systems. Within the scope of quality in use, the study is limited to evaluating only the *safety* characteristic to determine the degree to which the system mitigates the risks that could cause injury to users.

Bitelli et al. [18] present a model to evaluate the changes produced by the AAL & AT solutions (assisted living environments & assistive technology) in the lives of users and their environments (e.g., the effectiveness of the solution, user satisfaction, impact on the quality of life, saving social costs for the health system). Additionally, the model cites various instruments (questionnaires) to measure the degree of *effectiveness* and user *satisfaction* as a result of the use of AAL & AT solutions.

Regarding the context quality approaches, McNaull et al. [4] propose a multilayer quality model for AAL systems with attributes at the level of: data, information, and contextual knowledge. In particular, the attributes included at the context level are: *timeliness, probability of correctness, and consistency of the context*. This study does not explicitly detail the metrics to evaluate each of the proposed attributes.

The proposal by Nazario et al. [19] defines a context quality assessment approach for AAL systems based on five quality attributes: i) *coverage*, defines the set of all possible values for each unit of information in the context; ii) *up-to-dateness*, indicates how old the context information is; iii) *precision*, suggests the degree to which the context information represents reality; iv) *completeness*, determines the degree to which contextual information is sufficient to represent reality; and, v) *significance*, indicates the level of importance of the context information.

Finally, Sánchez et al. [20] present a user-centered evaluation method for context-aware systems under the domain of u-Health. The context quality attributes used by this approach are: i) *precision* of context information to describe reality; ii) *granularity* of context information; and, iii) *up-to-dateness* of the context information.

After reviewing the quality approaches in use and context, it is concluded that: i) the studies address quality attributes in a limited and incomplete way, leaving in evidence the non-existence of some appropriate attributes for the AAL domain; ii) the vast majority of quality approaches do not include metrics for the evaluation of their attributes, even worse they detail their formulation to obtain quantitative indicators; iii) a large part of the proposals are based on the ISO/IEC 9126 standard, therefore an effort is required to update them; and, iv) the *context coverage* characteristic of the ISO/IEC 25010 standard is directly related to the analyzed context quality approaches; therefore, it has been seen the need to specialize this standard taking advantage of the contributions of these approaches.

3 Methodology

The methodology presented in [21] was used for the construction of the quality in use model for AAL systems, being similar to that applied in a previous work [22]. In this sense, the methodology is made up of the following stages: 1) definition and specification of quality requirements; 2) design and implementation of the measurement and evaluation of the quality in use; and, 3) analysis of results, conclusion, and documentation. In the following sections, each of the indicated stages is developed.

4 Definition and Specification of Quality Requirements

The goal is to understand the quality in use of an AAL system from the perspectives of either a primary user (e.g., elderly people, people with special needs, patient) or a secondary user (e.g., family, caregivers). Hence, it is intended to design a quality model and apply it to determine the results and impacts when a primary or secondary user uses an AAL system. As a case study, the quality in use model was applied to an intelligent pillbox [23], whose objective is to improve compliance with medication programs in elderly people, people with special needs or patients with chronic diseases. Table 1 presents the definition of the domain, purpose, and user profiles for the evaluation of the quality in use.

Table 1. Domain, purpose/goal and user profile of the quality assessment.

Entity category:	AAL system
Entity:	Intelligent pillbox [23]
Measurable concept:	Quality in use
Purpose/Goal:	• Understand the quality in use of an AAL system • Propose a quality in use model for AAL systems, to serve as a guide for future developments or to improve the quality of existing AAL systems
User's point of view:	• Primary user: elderly people, people with special needs, patients • Secondary user: family, caregivers
Denomination of the quality model:	Quality in use model for AAL systems. (QiUM-AAL)

4.1 Characteristics and Sub-characteristics of the Quality in Use Model (QiUM-AAL)

The following activities were carried out to define the characteristics and sub-characteristics of the quality in use model (QiUM-AAL):

1. Bibliographic review and selection of the most relevant quality approaches in use and context (QA-x) for AAL systems (analyzed in the Related Work section), obtaining as a result:

QA1. A quality model for AAL software systems [11].
QA2. A framework to evaluate the quality of AAL technologies [12].
QA3. A framework to evaluate the quality of R&D projects in e-Health [13].
QA4. The elicitation of quality characteristics for AAL systems and services [16].
QA5. A taxonomy of functional and non-functional requirements for remote healthcare systems [17].
QA6. A quality model for service delivery through AAL and AT solutions [18].
QA7. A multilayer quality model for AAL systems [4].
QA8. A quality of context evaluating approach for AAL systems [19].
QA9. An evaluation method for context-aware systems in u-Health [20].

2. Comparative analysis between the selected quality approaches and the ISO/IEC 25010 standard for quality in use, to determine the most commonly used characteristics and sub-characteristics of this standard [8]. For the analysis, it was necessary to map the quality characteristics and sub-characteristics based on the similarity of their meaning and evaluation objective, although they have different names in the approaches. Tables 2 and 3 show the comparative tables with details of the characteristics and sub-characteristics used by the quality approaches in use and context, respectively.

Table 2. Comparative table of the quality in use approaches for AAL systems [8].

Characteristics and sub-characteristics ISO/IEC 25010	QA–1	QA–2	QA–3	QA–4	QA–5	QA–6
Effectiveness	✓	✓	✓	✓		✓
Efficiency	✓	✓	✓	✓		✓
Satisfaction	✓	✓	✓	✓		✓
Usefulness	✓					
Trust	✓					
Pleasure						
Comfort						✓
Freedom from risk	✓	✓		✓	✓	
Economic risk mitigation						
Health and safety risk mitigation	✓					
Environmental risk mitigation						
Context coverage	✓					
Context completeness						
Flexibility	✓					

Table 3. Comparative table of context quality approaches for AAL systems [8].

Attributes	QA–7	QA–8	QA–9
Accuracy	✓	✓	✓
Coverage		✓	
Completeness		✓	✓
Consistency	✓		
Significance		✓	
Currentness	✓	✓	✓

3. Selection of the characteristics to be included in the QiUM-AAL model. Regarding the level of recurrence, the following characteristics were included: *effectiveness, efficiency, and satisfaction.* Although some characteristics of the ISO/IEC 25010 standard for quality in use have been used little by the existing quality approaches, their level of relevance for the AAL domain was analyzed. In this sense, *freedom from risk and context coverage* characteristics were selected.

4. Selection of the sub-characteristics to include in the model. The quality in use approaches are minimal at the sub-characteristic level; therefore, the study aims at determining the relevance level of the sub-characteristics for the AAL domain. As a result, the following sub-characteristics were included: *satisfaction (usefulness, trust,*

and comfort), *freedom from risk (health and safety risk mitigation)* and *context coverage (accuracy, completeness, and currentness)*. The *context coverage* characteristic of the ISO/IEC 25010 standard includes the attributes most used by the context quality approaches studied.

In conclusion, the QiUM-AAL model is made up of a set of common and recurrent characteristics among the quality approaches existing in the literature, as well as relevant to the AAL domain. Additionally, the QiUM-AAL model is aligned with the ISO/IEC 25010 standard for quality in use.

5   Design of the Measurement and Evaluation of Quality in Use

For each characteristic or sub-characteristic, a metric was designed to assign a numerical percentage value as a measure. Also, the metric value was used directly to represent the satisfaction level of the characteristic or sub-characteristic, which can be interpreted in three levels of acceptability, which are presented in Table 4.

Table 4. Decision criteria.

Level of acceptability	Range	Interpretation
Unsatisfactory	$\geq$ 0% AND < 50%	Shows that it is urgent and priority to implement improvements
Marginal	$\geq$ 50% AND < 80%	Shows the need to perform improvements
Satisfactory	$\geq$ 80% AND $\leq$ 100%	Shows that it is unnecessary to implement improvements

Tables 5 and 6 present the detail of the metrics designed for the QiUM-AAL model. Regarding the questionnaire-based metrics, the questions were formulated with the participation of experts in the domain (health personnel), taking as a reference the instruments (questionnaires) presented in several quality approaches studied [12, 18]. The scoring scale for each question is as follows: i) very unsatisfactory (0 points); ii) unsatisfactory (0.25 points); iii) neutral (0.50 points); iv) satisfactory (0.75 points); and, v) very satisfactory (1 point). The questionnaire-based metrics are calculated by applying the following formula:

$$\frac{\sum_{u=1}^{NU} \sum_{i=1}^{NQ} S_{u,i}}{NQ*NU} *100 \tag{1}$$

Where: $S_{u,i}$ is the user score "u" to question "i", **NQ** is the number of questions, and **NU** is the number of end users.

In order to calculate the global satisfaction level of the quality in use for the AAL system, the importance of the sub-characteristics and characteristics was determined, assigning weights based on the expert criterion (health personnel). In turn, a step-by-step aggregation mechanism was designed, based on the weighted average (see Fig. 1).

Moreover, the flexibility of the measurement model needs to be considered since the weights can be readjusted according to the specific needs of each application domain. Likewise, the questions can be added or deleted, depending on how relevant those are to the AAL system.

Table 5. Metrics for the stated sub-characteristics.

Usefulness	
Definition:	The degree to which users are satisfied with the achievement of pragmatic goals, including results and consequences of use
Characteristics:	Satisfaction
Weight:	0,35
Metric:	**Evaluation questionnaire (to calculate metric apply Eq. 1)** **For primary users:** How satisfied were you with being able to carry out and complete all activities (functional and cognitive capacity) with the support of the AAL system? How satisfied were you with the well-being achieved with the support of the AAL system? How satisfied were you with preserving your health with the support of the AAL system? **For secondary users:** How satisfied were you with the performance of your care and monitoring activities with the support of the AAL system?
Trust	
Definition:	The degree to which users have confidence that the AAL system behaves as intended
Characteristics:	Satisfaction
Weight:	0,35
Metric:	**Evaluation questionnaire (to calculate metric apply Eq. 1)** **For primary and secondary users:** What level of self-confidence does the AAL system generate in the development of its activities? How satisfied are you that the AAL system protects you from making mistakes or oversights in your activities? How satisfied are you that the AAL system supports you in an emergency? How satisfied are you that the AAL system can recover from failure? How satisfied are you with the fact that the AAL system periodically informs you of the status of the system, the user, and the environment?

(continued)

Table 5. (*continued*)

Usefulness	
Definition:	The degree to which users are satisfied with the achievement of pragmatic goals, including results and consequences of use

Comfort	
Definition:	The degree to which users are satisfied with the physical and logical comfort of the AAL system and its devices
Characteristics:	Satisfaction
Weight:	0,30
Metric:	**Evaluation questionnaire (to calculate metric apply Eq. 1)** **For primary and secondary users:** How satisfied are you with the ease of use and handling of the AAL system? How satisfied are you with the size, weight, and shape of the AAL devices you are wearing or wearing? How satisfied are you with viewing the texts, images, videos or other objects on the screens provided by the AAL system and its devices? How satisfied are you with the audio from the AAL system and its devices? How satisfied are you with the perception that the AAL system and its devices are non-invasive? How satisfied are you that the AAL system was adequate to carry out your activities?

Health and safety risk mitigation	
Definition:	The degree to which the AAL system mitigates the potential risk concerning the physical health and safety of users
Characteristics:	Freedom from risk
Weight:	1,00
Metric:	**Evaluation questionnaire (to calculate metric apply Eq. 1)** **For primary and secondary users:** To what extent does the AAL system alert or report on emergencies, eventualities, or unusual states of the people under monitoring? To what extent does the AAL system alert if its resources or devices fails? To what extent is the AAL system resilient or self-healing in case one of its resources or devices fails?

Accuracy	
Definition:	The degree to which contextual information describes events that occur in reality
Characteristics:	Context coverage
Weight:	0,35

(*continued*)

Table 5. (*continued*)

Usefulness	
Definition:	The degree to which users are satisfied with the achievement of pragmatic goals, including results and consequences of use
Metric:	**TREC**: Total of real events concordant with the contextual information, monitored during a period **TER**: Total of real events, monitored during a period $accuracy = \frac{TREC}{TRE} * 100$ This formula can be calculated by event and then get a weighted average between all the events

Completeness	
Definition:	The degree to which contextual knowledge is sufficient for the AAL system to be used with effectiveness, efficiency, satisfaction, and freedom from risk
Characteristics:	Context coverage
Weight:	0,35
Metric:	**NCDU:** Number of contextual dimensions (e.g., time, place, activity, user profile) used by the AAL system **NCDN:** Number of contextual dimensions necessary for the AAL system to be used with effectiveness, efficiency, satisfaction, and freedom from risk $completeness = \frac{NCDU}{NCDN} * 100$

Currentness	
Definition:	Degree to which contextual information is current and available on time
Characteristics:	Context coverage
Weight:	0,30
Metric:	**TRE**: Time of occurrence of a real event **TARE**: Instant in which the system is aware or recognizes the real event **MT**: Maximum time in which contextual information becomes "old" or outdated $latency = (TRE - TARE)$ $currentness = \left(1 - \frac{(latency)}{MT}\right) * 100, \textit{ if latency} \leq \textit{MT}$ $currentness = 0\% \textit{, otherwise}$ This formula can be calculated by event and then get a weighted average between all the events

Table 6. Metrics for the stated characteristics.

Effectiveness	
Definition:	Degree of accuracy and completeness with which users achieve the proposed objectives with the support of the AAL system
Weight:	0,20
Metric:	**Evaluation questionnaire (to calculate metric apply Eq. 1)** **For primary users:** To what extent were the activities successfully completed with the support of the AAL system? To what extent did you achieve independence and autonomy in your natural living environment with the support of the AAL system? To what extent was your well-being and lifestyle improved with the support of the AAL system? To what extent did you maintain your health status with the support of the AAL system? To what extent did your functional and/or cognitive capacity increase with the support of the AAL system? **For secondary users:** To what extent were the monitoring, diagnosis and/or care of people activities carried out correctly with the support of the AAL system? To what extent were emergencies, eventualities or unusual states of the people under monitoring treated in a timely manner with the support of the AAL system?
Efficiency	
Definition:	Ability to achieve objectives optimizing resources and user time with the support of the AAL system
Weight:	0,15
Metric:	**Evaluation questionnaire (to calculate metric apply Eq. 1)** **For primary users:** To what extent did the time spent completing your activities decrease with the support of the AAL system? To what extent were the costs related to the execution of your activities reduced or optimized with the support of the AAL system? To what extent were wasted resources avoided in the execution of your activities with the support of the AAL system? **For secondary users:** To what extent was the time spent on monitoring, diagnosing, or caring for people optimized with the support of the AAL system? To what extent were resources reduced or optimized during the activities of monitoring, diagnosis and/or care of people with the support of the AAL system? In what proportion was the number of emergencies or eventualities reduced with the support of the AAL system?

(continued)

Table 6. (*continued*)

Effectiveness	
Definition:	Degree of accuracy and completeness with which users achieve the proposed objectives with the support of the AAL system

Satisfaction	
Definition:	Degree to which user needs are satisfied when the AAL system is used
Weight:	0,20
Metric:	$satisfaction = (usefulness * 0,35 + trust * 0,35 + comfort * 0,30) * 100$

Freedom from risk	
Definition:	Degree to which the AAL system mitigates the potential risk associated with users
Weight:	0,25
Metric:	$freedom\ from\ risk = health\ and\ safety\ risk\ mitigation$

Context coverage	
Definition:	Degree to which the AAL system can be used with effectiveness, efficiency, satisfaction and freedom from risk in both specified contexts of use and in contexts beyond those initially identified
Weight:	0,20
Metric:	$context\ coverage =$ $(accuracy * 0,35 + completeness * 0,35 + currentness * 0,3) * 100$

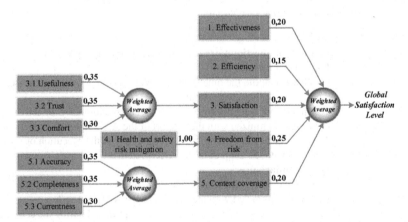

Fig. 1. Aggregation structure for calculating the global satisfaction level of the quality in use for AAL systems.

6   Results of the Application of the Quality in Use Model

The quality in use of an assistive technology (AT) system named intelligent pillbox [23] has been measured and evaluated. This example aims to demonstrate the feasibility of applying the quality in use model (QiUM-AAL) during an evaluation process.

The intelligent pillbox is composed of: i) an embedded application with a user interface to configure the dosage schedule; ii) a programmable alarm system, integrated with an automatic mechanism for opening and closing the compartments where the drugs are stored; iii) a message notification system through the GSM network; and finally, iv) a module to manage it using a mobile device. When it is time to take the medications, the system activates an alarm, sends an SMS notification to the patient, indicating that it is time for their medication; and, at the same time, it opens the door of the specific compartment that contains the medicines. There are two scenarios for closing the compartment: i) if the patient takes the medications, the system notifies the caregiver about this event and immediately closes the compartment; and, ii) if the patient does not take the medicines for 10 min, the system automatically locks the compartment. The pillbox has 21 compartments or doses distributed in three doses per day, being possible to carry out programming of up to 7 days (see Fig. 2).

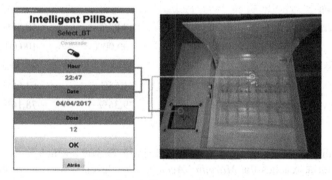

Fig. 2.   Intelligent pillbox [23].

The evaluation of the quality of use was carried out from the perspective of the end users, who interact with the pillbox: i) caregiver/family member, who configures the dosage and feeding schemes with pills in the pillbox; and, ii) patient, who uses this solution as a reminder, receiving alerts when they must take the medications.

Due to the availability of a single pillbox for the evaluation of the quality in use, the pillbox assisted ten patients older than 65 years with permanent medication (five men and five women) for a period of 50 days. Each patient used the pillbox with a dosing schedule of three times per day for 5 days. Also, two patients had visual disability and two hearing disability. Ten caregivers or family members also participated in the evaluation; that is, each patient was assigned a caregiver or relative. Before using the pillbox, training on its use was conducted, aimed at patients and caregivers, lasting 4 h.

Regarding the characteristics and sub-characteristics whose evaluation is based on questionnaires, it should be indicated that they were filled out by the participants, after having used the pillbox. Table 7 presents the results of the level of satisfaction with the quality in use by sub-characteristics, characteristics, and global (intelligent pillbox).

Table 7. Results of the satisfaction level of the quality in use for the intelligent pillbox.

Characteristic and sub-characteristics	Weight	Satisfaction level (patient)	Satisfaction level (caregiver)	Satisfaction level (total)
Effectiveness	**0,20**	**85,50%**	**88,75%**	**87,13%**
Efficiency	**0,15**	**86,67%**	**90,67%**	**88,67%**
Satisfaction	**0,20**	**76,94%**	**79,53%**	**78,23%**
Usefulness	0,35	85,83%	87,50%	**86,67%**
Trust	0,35	71,50%	74,00%	**72,75%**
Comfort	0,30	72,92%	76,67%	**74,80%**
Freedom from risk	**0,25**	**70,83%**	**73,33%**	**72,08%**
Health and safety risk Mitigation	1,00	**70,83%**	**73,33%**	**72,08%**
Context coverage	**0,20**	**68,85%**	**68,85%**	**68,85%**
Accuracy	0,35	100,00%	100,00%	100,00%
Completeness	0,35	25,00%	25,00%	25,00%
Currentness	0,30	83,65%	83,65%	83,65%
Global quality in use		**76,97%**	**79,36%**	**78,16%**

The quality in use globally has been valued at 78.16%, which, according to the decision criteria, reaches the *Marginal Acceptability* level, whose interpretation indicates the need to make improvements in the pillbox. Particularly, the *effectiveness and efficiency* characteristics present the best indicators with a *Satisfactory Acceptability* level. In turn, the characteristics of *satisfaction, freedom from risk, and context coverage* have a *Marginal Acceptability* level. The justification for some characteristics having a satisfaction level of less than 80% is that the pillbox is still in a prototype phase. Figure 3 presents a radial graph illustrating the above. The results obtained for each of the characteristics are analyzed in detail below:

Effectiveness. Concerning patients, the objective they pursue with the use of the pillbox is to independently complete the routine activity of taking the medications at the indicated times. The patients state that the objective was reached with an effectiveness of 85.50% (*Satisfactory Acceptability*). They also argue that the main causes for not completing the activity of taking medication correctly were: i) problems in sending reminders by the pillbox, as a consequence of the discharged battery or lack of balance to send SMS messages; and, ii) the patient was away from home or did not have a mobile phone at the time of notification of the pillbox. About caregivers, its objective is to monitor and control compliance with the medication program supplied to the patient. In this sense, the caregivers consider that the level of effectiveness is 88.75% (*Satisfactory Acceptability*). Therefore, to improve the perception of the end user about this characteristic, the pillbox must monitor its resources (the battery and availability of SMS messages); and, if it is below a certain threshold, send notifications about the status of these resources to the caregiver. Also, it would be convenient for the pillbox to know the location of the patient, to send advance reminders in case of being away from home.

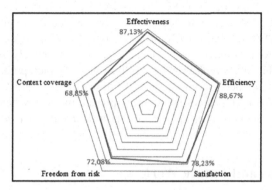

Fig. 3. Satisfaction level of the quality in use by characteristic for the intelligent pillbox.

Efficiency. As a result of the survey, a score of 86.67% was obtained by the patients, and 90.67% by the caregivers (*Satisfactory Acceptability*). Analyzing the questions, the patients valued positively (92.50%) the use of the pillbox to avoid wasting the medications due to neglect or forgetfulness. On the other hand, the caregivers consider the support of the pillbox very favorable (95.00%) to optimize their time since it will not be required (in a stable version of the pillbox) to assist the patient during the taking of medications, but rather only in the eventualities reported by the pillbox.

Satisfaction. In general terms, the degree of satisfaction achieved by patients is 76.94%, and by caregivers, it is 79.53% (*Marginal Acceptability*). Patients and caregivers have a satisfactory perception of 86.67% on the *usefulness* of the pillbox. In contrast, the satisfaction achieved about the *trust* and *comfort* provided by the pillbox is only 72.75% and 74.80%, respectively. Concerning the *trust*, the result obtained is a consequence of the fact that the reminders were not delivered in their entirety to the patients and the lack of alerts that inform or actions that mitigate issues found. About the *comfort*, users emphasize that it would be desirable to reduce the size and improve the shape of the pillbox, for it to become a mobile device. Likewise, patients with visual and hearing disabilities show the presence of difficulties in viewing the texts on the screen and listening to the audible alarms of the pillbox.

Freedom from Risk. The main risk that can affect the health of patients is that they do not receive timely reminders to take medications. Hence, the non-existence of mitigation actions to the problems related to the discharged battery and the balance lack to send

SMS messages, which caused notifications to be delivered on time, have influenced patients and caregivers to assign a score of 70.83% and 73.33%, respectively (*Marginal Acceptability*).

Context Coverage. It was necessary to observe how the pillbox operates and interacts with users to keep a record of the events that occurred and compare them with the events reported by the system, and to calculate the metrics associated with this characteristic. In turn, the metrics were calculated to obtain a single score for the two types of users (patient and caregiver), which is 68.85% (*Marginal Acceptability*). From the 300 events observed in reality, 288 were reported correctly and within the required latency limit (maximum time - MT of 5 min). Therefore, applying the metrics, a score of 96.00% and 83.65% was achieved for the *accuracy and currentness*, respectively (*Acceptability Satisfactory*). Regarding the *completeness*, the pillbox has only incorporated the contextual time dimension, being necessary to include the dimensions: location, user profile, and information technology resources (status) to represent the reality better. Applying the metric, the *completeness* reaches only 25.00% (*Unsatisfactory Acceptability*).

7   Conclusions and Future Work

The bibliographic review on the evaluation of quality in use and context for AAL systems has shown that the approaches or models found in the literature address quality attribute incompletely, leaving in evidence the non-existence of some appropriate attributes for the AAL domain. Furthermore, the vast majority of quality approaches do not include quality metrics for evaluating their attributes.

In this sense, the main contribution of this paper consists in the design of a complete quality in use model (QiUM-AAL). It is composed of a set of characteristics and sub-characteristics relevant to the AAL domain, identified from a comparative analysis between the quality approaches in use and context found in the literature and the ISO/IEC 25010 standard. In turn, the quality in use model proposes a set of metrics for all characteristics and sub-characteristics, adjusted to the operating environment of AAL systems. The application of the QiUM-AAL model to the intelligent pillbox demonstrated that it is a complete and valuable tool to evaluate the impact of the use of an AAL system. The AAL system in terms of *effectiveness, efficiency, satisfaction, freedom from risk, and context coverage,* from the perspective of the final user, allowing to identify important aspects that contribute to improve its quality.

As future work, it is proposed to delve into the design of more precise metrics for each of the attributes of the QiUM-AAL model. In turn, it is necessary to perform evaluations of other AAL applications and with different user profiles.

Acknowledgements. This study is part of the research projects: i) Run-time model-based self-awareness middleware for Internet of Things eco-systems, LIDI - Universidad del Azuay; ii) Fog Computing applied to monitoring devices used in assisted living environments; Case study: platform for the elderly, XVII DIUC Call for Research Projects. Thus, we thank Universidad del Azuay and Universidad de Cuenca for their support.

References

1. Calvaresi, D., Cesarini, D., Sernani, P., Marinoni, M., Dragoni, A., Sturm, A.: Exploring the ambient assisted living domain: a systematic review. Ambient Intell. Hum. Comput. **8**(2), 239–257 (2017)
2. AAL-Europe - Active and Assisted Living Programme. https://www.aal-europe.eu/about/, Accessed 19 May 2020
3. Department of Economic and Social Affairs Population Division: World population ageing 2015. United Nations, New York, USA (2015)
4. McNaull, J., Augusto, J., Mulvenna, M., McCullagh, P.: Data and information quality issues in ambient assisted living systems. Data Inf. Qual. **4**(1), 1–15 (2012)
5. Memon, M., Wagner, S., Pedersen, C., Beevi, F.: Ambient assisted living healthcare frameworks, platforms, standards, and quality attributes. Sensors **14**(3), 4312–4341 (2014)
6. Covella, G., Olsina, L.: Assessing quality in use in a consistent way. In: 6th International Conference on Web Engineering, pp. 1–8 (2006).
7. Garcés, L., Ampatzoglou, A., Avgeriou, P., Nakagawa, E.: Quality attributes and quality models for ambient assisted living software systems: a systematic mapping. Inf. Soft. Technol. **82**, 121–138 (2017)
8. Erazo-Garzon, L., Erraez, J., Cedillo, P., Illescas-Peña, L.: Quality assessment approaches for ambient assisted living systems: a systematic review. In: Botto-Tobar, M., Vizuete, M.Z., Torres-Carrión, P., León, S.M., Vásquez, G.P., Durakovic, B. (eds.) ICAT 2019. CCIS, vol. 1193, pp. 421–439. Springer, Cham (2020). https://doi.org/10.1007/978-3-030-42517-3_32
9. European Commission - Ambient Assisted Living - Preparation of an Art. 169-Initiative. https://cordis.europa.eu/project/rcn/71922/factsheet/en, Accessed 19 May 2020
10. ISO/IEC 25010:2011. https://iso25000.com/index.php, Accessed 19 May 2020
11. Garcés, L., Oquendo, F., Nakagawa, E.: A quality model for AAL software systems. In: 29th International Symposium on Computer-Based Medical Systems, pp. 175–180 (2016)
12. Salvi, D., Montalvá Colomer, J., Arredondo, M., Prazak-Aram, B., Mayer, C.: A framework for evaluating ambient assisted living technologies and the experience of the UniversAAL project. Ambient Intell. Smart Environ. **7**, 329–352 (2015)
13. Mavridis, A., Katriou, S.A., Koumpis, A.: An evaluation framework for EU research and development e-Health projects' systems. In: Weerasinghe, D. (ed.) eHealth 2008. LNICSSITE, vol. 0001, pp. 9–16. Springer, Heidelberg (2009). https://doi.org/10.1007/978-3-642-00413-1_2
14. ISO/IEC 14598:1998. https://www.iso.org, Accessed 19 May 2020
15. ISO/IEC 9126:2001. https://www.iso.org, Accessed 19 May 2020
16. Omerovic, A., Kofod-Petersen, A., Solhaug, B., Svagård, I.: Elicitation of quality characteristics for AAL systems and services. Ambient Intell.-Softw. Appl. **219**, 95–104 (2013)
17. Vitaletti, A., Puglia, S.: System overview of next-generation remote healthcare. In: Systems Design for Remote Healthcare, pp. 31–53 (2014)
18. Bitelli, C., Desideri, L., Malavasi, M.: A quality model for service delivery in AAL and AT provision. In: Andò, B., Siciliano, P., Marletta, V., Monteriù, A. (eds.) Ambient Assisted Living. BB, vol. 11, pp. 3–10. Springer, Cham (2015). https://doi.org/10.1007/978-3-319-18374-9_1
19. Nazário, D., Todesco, J., Dantas, M., Tromel, I., Neto, A.: A quality of context evaluating approach in an ambient assisted living e-Health system. In: 16th International Conference on e-Health Networking, Applications and Services, pp. 158–163 (2014)
20. Sanchez-Pi, N., Carbó, J., Molina, J.: An evaluation method for context–aware systems in u-Health. Ambient Intell.-Softw. Appl. **153**, 219–226 (2012)

21. Becker, P., Lew, P., Olsina, L.: Specifying process views for a measurement, evaluation, and improvement strategy. In: Advances in Software Engineering (2012)
22. Erazo-Garzon, L., Erraez, J., Illescas-Peña, L., Cedillo, P.: A Data Quality Model for AAL Systems. In: Efraín Fonseca, C., Morales, G.R., Cordero, M.O., Botto-Tobar, M., Martínez, E.C., León, A.P. (eds.) TICEC 2019. AISC, vol. 1099, pp. 137–152. Springer, Cham (2020). https://doi.org/10.1007/978-3-030-35740-5_10
23. Solís, W.V., Cedillo, P., Parra, J., Guevara, A.: Intelligent pillbox: evaluating the user perceptions of elderly people. In: 26th International Conference on Information Systems Development (2017)

Comparative Analysis of the Performance of Electric and Internal Combustion Buses in the Load and Orography Conditions of Loja City

Karen Belén Arciniega$^{(\boxtimes)}$, José Raúl Castro$^{(\boxtimes)}$, Tuesman Castillo$^{(\boxtimes)}$, and Jorge Luis Jaramillo

Universidad Técnica Particular de Loja, Loja, Ecuador
`arciniegaabelen@gmail.com, {jrcastro,tdcastillo}@utpl.edu.ec`

Abstract. Worldwide, passenger transportation by buses is one of the main sources of pollution, generating large amounts of CO2. The use of fossil fuels, global warming and environmental pollution affect the economy and the health of society. Implementing electric transportation will reduce environmental problems. Electric buses are part of a new market that is growing rapidly. Most governments have promoted new policies, incentives and laws for the massification of the electric transportation.

This work carries out a comparative mathematical analysis of the performance between electric and internal combustion buses that calculates the necessary energy and power based on the of the number of passengers (load), speed and slopes of the route. The model is validated with a simulation of two routes and its data compared with the information in the bus catalogs. The model is tested under load and orography conditions for the city of Loja and calculates the power and energy of the diesel and electric bus necessary for Loja city.

Keywords: Electric bus · Internal combustion bus · Environmental pollution

1 Introduction

In Ecuador, the "Ley orgánica de Eficiencia Energética" in Art. 14 indicates that since the year 2025, all buses that be incorporated into the urban public transport service must only be electrical [1]. Electric transport is a sustainable mobility solution to supply the high costs and lack of fossil fuels and contribute to the protection of the environment. The implementation of new clean source technologies serves to mitigate the problem of CO2 emissions.

The electric energy demanded in Ecuador is growing. By the end of 2019 it was 27,532 GWh which represents an increase of 11.20% compared to 2018 [2]. Cost reduction, greenhouse gas reduction, political support, standardization and the use of new technologies promote the increase of electric buses for urban traffic [3–5].

© Springer Nature Switzerland AG 2021
M. Botto-Tobar et al. (Eds.): ICAT 2020, CCIS 1388, pp. 661–671, 2021.
https://doi.org/10.1007/978-3-030-71503-8_51

Along the world, during the 2010 period started the introduction of the electric buses, operating 6 million units and it is expected to increase to 18 million units by the end of 2020 [6]. Electric buses are part of the new market, the same ones that have participated in debates and have become the basis for the creation of policies and laws [7]. Ecuador currently has 9 online air quality measurement centers, however, worldwide it is ranked 80th for air pollution. The parameters that govern the level of pollution and air quality result in an acceptable quality for the southern region of Ecuador [8]. Currently, the city of Loja has internal combustion buses.

This work proposes a methodology to calculate the power and energy of the internal combustion bus and the electric bus in load conditions and orography in Loja city. The mathematical model compares both buses (electric and internal combustion engine) through the operating parameters and specifications catalogs buses. Based on the equations used to obtain energy, power and performance, the parameters of the buses are established, including slopes and speeds established in the city of Loja.

2   Electric and Internal Combustion Bus

2.1   Electrical Bus

In Ecuador, the Energy Efficiency Law according to Art. 14 prioritizes a special policy for land transportation as an energy efficiency measure in public planning. By the year 2025, all vehicles incorporation to the urban public transport service must only be powered by an electric drive [9].

The INEN 2205 [10] standard established for the operation of any urban bus must provide a level of safety and comfort to the user and the NTE INEN 1668 establishes the norms requirements that passengers of public transport vehicles must require [11, 12]. The requirements like: length, width, height of the bus, passenger capacity and slope must be accomplished.

There are two types of buses according to the number of passengers. The first type with a capacity equal to or higher than 60 passengers and the second one, a minibus with a capacity of few than 60 passengers and they must have the minimum security requirements established in NTE INEN 034 [13]. The starting of a bus on a slope must be a minimum of 25% between two points with the maximum number of passengers (NTE INEN 1668 standard) [11].

The power train of an electric bus consists of a mechanical, electrical and control system. The mechanical system contains an electric motor, the inverter and the battery. The control unit that rules the electronic unit contains a governor, engine torque, and brakes depending on the vehicle's input speed [14]. So, the power train consists of the transformation of the electrochemical energy stored and fed to the motor, inverter and regeneration causing a change of mechanical energy into electrical energy.

The parameters that intervene in the power train are the environmental parameters and operating parameters defined by driving cycles, as well as necessary data from the electric motor such as power and efficiency [4, 15]. The most widely used and suitable electric motor is the induction motor because of its simplicity, reliability and low maintenance, compared to the permanent magnet motor. For the transmission system which joins the automation system with the manual system. The gearbox takes care of the gears according to the needs of the vehicle. Power consumption is reduced by 9% compared to automatic transmission to a normal gearbox [16] (Fig. 1).

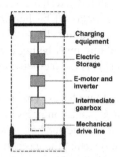

Charging equipment

Electric Storage

E-motor and inverter

Intermediate gearbox

Mechanical drive line

Fig. 1. Electric bus diagram [17].

The demand for electric buses worldwide is in an exponential development and it is hoped that this offers a high quality service for different customers. Based on statistics at a global level, it can be seen that public transport looks to migrate to clean energy. Today this technology continues facing challenges such as the development of storage systems and get the work day without interruptions [18].

The main components of the electric bus are the bodywork design, electric powertrain, power accessories, and battery charging [18]. The bodywork is important in determining the roll coefficients to optimize bus performance. The variables involved are frontal area (Af), drag coefficient (K), rolling coefficient (f_r), weight and passenger capacity (C_a).

The electric propulsion system of an electric bus consists of a mechanical, electrical and control system. The mechanical system contains the longitudinal dynamics like the differential transmission and tires. The electrical part contains an electric motor, the inverter and the battery. The control unit contains the regulator a torque and the brakes, depending on the input speed of the vehicle.

The bus working parameters and the electric motor data such as the power and efficiency curves must be known for the powertrain. Power train performance must satisfy basic characteristics such as starting torque, slow speed on a slope, confidentiality, and temperature.

Conductivity requires a physical connection between the electric bus and the charging station. All systems currently use conductive technology. Buses that have long stops can use opportunity charges. These recharges are capable of improving the autonomy limitations that electric buses have by reducing the size of the batteries, reducing the weight and cost [19, 20]. When buses have long stops, they can use opportunity charges.

The batteries that are being used for the new BYD buses are Lithium-Ion ironphosphate Fe with a charging time between 2 and 4 h and a range of around 180–200 km. They have a stored energy capacity of 300 kWh [21].

Regenerative braking system is applied in electric buses to improve energy recovery efficiency. The recovered energy is about the 50%. For the mathematical model of electric buses, a recovery of 0.5 is used [22].

2.2 Internal Combustion Bus

Currently in Ecuador, the internal combustion bus is more than 26,251 that runs on diesel engines. Public transportation has internal combustion engines that are constant pressure machines, which work is obtained by burning a certain amount of fuel. A diesel engine uses fuel spray injected into cylinders, which contain compressed air at high temperatures. The air temperature must be high enough to allow the injected fuel becomes into particles to ignite. This is the method used to carry out ignition in diesel engines [23, 24].

The principle of operation has four phases. The first phase, draws air into the combustion chamber. The second phase, is the compression of the air as it is compressed to a minimum fraction of the original volume and heated to a temperature of up to 440 °C. The third, is the mixture that burns causing the gas contained in the chamber to expand and be pushed towards the piston. Finally, the connecting rod transmits this movement to the crankshaft by changing the linear movement of the piston into a rotational movement and the fourth phase is the expulsion [25–27].

The ideal conditions that fuel injection should have is to supply each cylinder with the appropriate amount of fuel based on the engine gears. Combustion must be carried out correctly and completely by varying the injection point as the engine speed and load conditions. The injection pump is responsible for giving fuel to each injector with a precise pressure and at the right time. And finally, the pressure determines the operating condition of the engine and injectors by spraying the fuel inside the chambers on compressed air [28–30].

This system is necessary for the operation of the high pressure injection circuit and the low pressure circuit. The high-pressure circuit drives finely pulverized, high-pressure fuel to the combustion chambers. The low pressure circuit is responsible for sending the fuel from the tank to the injection pump. The circuit would be formed by the fuel tank, the feed pump, filter, injection pump and the injectors [26, 31, 32].

The engine at idling speed is the ability to run an internal combustion engine without the need for external assistance. The bus can be kept moving or by stepping on the clutch. Internal combustion buses on downgrades use 10% of energy when braking. To carry out the mathematical model, 0.1 is used in internal combustion buses when the engine at idling [23].

3 Mathematical Model

The creation of the mathematical model starts from the vehicle dynamics equations. From these equations the drag force, slope force, rolling force and total force of the bus are calculated [33].

Energy consumption is based on the importance of the bus's wheel force. Its relationship with the design of the bus leading to the design of models capable of reducing the impact of this force on it.

$$F_a = \frac{1}{2}.K.\rho_a.Af.V^2 \tag{1}$$

The drag force (F_a) is the multiplication of the drag coefficient (K), the air density (ρ_a), frontal area of the bus (Af) and the speed (V). The drag force depends on the speed at which the bus is traveling.

The force due to the slope is an additional force that opposes when the bus moves upwards, its force depends on the weight of the bus and the profile of the road. That is, when the slope is positive the force of the slope increases. When the slope is 0 there is no slope force and when the slope is downward the values are negative.

$$F_p = C.g. \sin \theta \tag{2}$$

Where F_p is the slope force, C is the weight of the bus, g is gravity, and θ is the slope.

The force that resists the movement of the bus sliding on a surface is called the rolling force. This depends on the normal force on the tire tread at low speeds. Therefore, a final expression for rolling resistance is expressed as follows, including the effect of slope on weight.

$$F_r = fr.C.g. \cos \theta \tag{3}$$

Where F_r is the rolling force, f_r rolling coefficient, C weight of the bus, g gravity and θ slope. The sum of all the resistances that oppose the propulsion of the bus can satisfy for the bus to move forward. Thus obtaining the total force of the bus as:

$$F = F_a + F_p + F_r \tag{4}$$

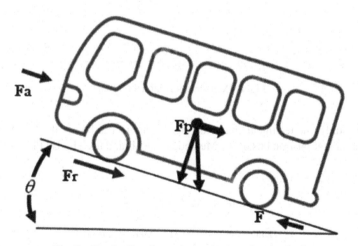

Fig. 2. Graph of mathematical representation (author)

The Fig. 2 shows representation of the Eq. 4.

Starting from the vehicle dynamics equations, the mathematical model carried out in Matlab/Simulink is obtained, the same as presented below:

Figures 3 and 4 show the subsystems used in the mathematical model for slopes and descents, both for the electric bus and the internal combustion bus. In Fig. 5, the final validation system of the mathematical model is shown.

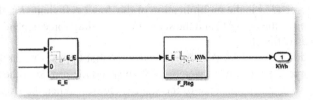

Fig. 3. Regenerative system (author)

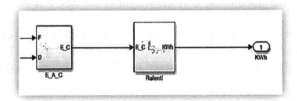

Fig. 4. Idle system (author)

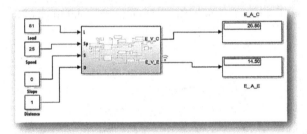

Fig. 5. Mathematical model (author)

In this study, the technical characteristics of an electric bus of the BYD brand and of an internal combustion bus of the Mercedes Benz brand used by UTPL is shown here (Table 1).

Table 1. Model of the buses.

Data	BYD	Mercedes Benz
Weigh (kg)	19500	17000
Frontal area (m)	8.5	6.3
K	0.7	0.7
Fr	0.0098	0.0098
Passengers	81	81

To validate the mathematical model, a simulated route was carried out and the results were analyzed with the values of the catalogs (Fig. 6).

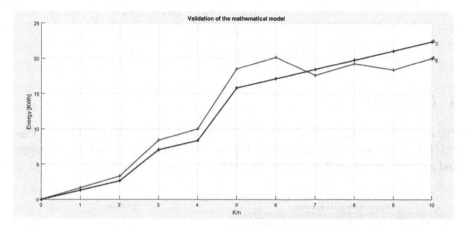

Fig. 6. Validation of the mathematical model (author) (Color figure online)

The green line is the electric bus route and the red line is the internal combustion bus route. The electric bus consumes less energy due to the recovery by the regenerative system on the descents.

Next, the graph of the power of the buses obtained by means of the mathematical model is shown. It can be seen that on a 25% slope the electric bus requires a power of 267.60 kW while the internal combustion bus requires 149.1 kW (Table 2) (Fig. 7).

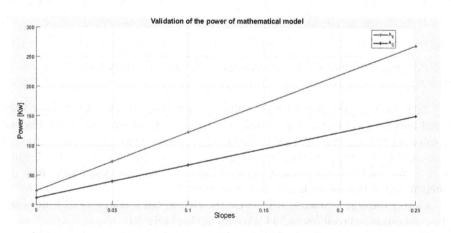

Fig. 7. Validation of the power of mathematical model (author) (Color figure online)

Table 2. Calculation of power.

Buses	Slopes			
	0%	5%	10%	25%
Electric/kW	23.80	73.10	122.25	267.60
Internal Combustion	11.84	39.59	67.26	149.10

4   Case Study

The mathematical model is applied to a real route carried out by the UTPL buses. Case 1: UTPL-Emiliano Ortega-UTPL route. Figure 8 shows the slope values in percentages and a survey carried out through Google Earth.

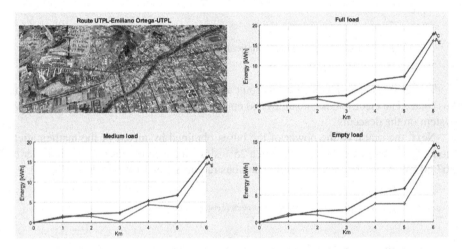

Fig. 8. Route UTPL-Emiliano Ortega-UTPL (author) (Color figure online)

Table 3 details the values obtained within the route in case 1. The route is 6 km. With a full load (81 passengers), the electric bus consumed 16.01 kWh, while the internal combustion bus required 17.73 kWh. With medium load (40 passengers) the electric bus consumed 14.47 kWh while the internal combustion bus required 16.01 kWh. Finally, with empty load (without passengers) the electric bus required less energy than the internal combustion bus under the same conditions.

Case 2: the UTPL-Solca-UTPL route. The electric bus requires 29.02 kWh while the combustion bus requires 34.58 kWh with full load (Fig. 9).

The electric bus requires 26.72 kWh while the combustion bus requires 31.15 kWh with median load (Fig. 10). Finally, the electric bus requires 24.36 kWh while the combustion bus requires 27.64 kWh without load (Fig. 11).

Table 3. Route in case 1.

Buses	Loads		
	Full	Medium	Empty
Electric/KWh	16.01	14.47	12.81
Internal combustion/KWh	17.73	16.01	14.25

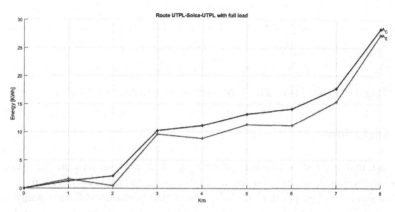

Fig. 9. Route UTPL-Solca-UTP with full load (author) (Color figure online)

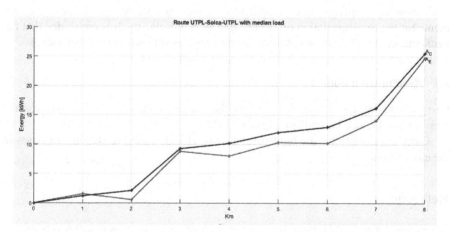

Fig. 10. Route UTPL-Solca-UTPL with median load (author) (Color figure online)

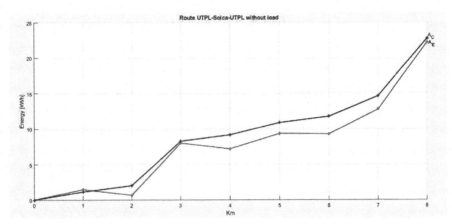

Fig. 11. Route UTPL-Solca-UTPL without load (author) (Color figure online)

5 Conclusions

This work makes possible to have a mathematical model to determine the energy and power required by buses based on route slopes, speed and passenger capacity.

This model makes possible to have a tool that performs different analyzes and comparisons between the internal combustion bus and the electric bus under the same conditions.

This work facilitates the development of feasibility studies and necessary requirements for the implementation of electric transport in Loja city. It is concluded that the mathematical model carried out is within the range established in the bus catalogs.

5.1 Recommendations

Carry out a technical-economic study for the implementation of electric buses at the Universidad Técnica Particular de Loja (UTPL).

Carry out a study for the implementation of electric charging stations for buses in the city of Loja.

References

1. Nacional, R.E.A., Barrazueta, H.P.: Ley orgánica de eficiencia energética, Quito (2019)
2. Conelec, P.M.D.E.: Plan Maestro de Electrificación II (2014)
3. Sanz Arnaiz,I.: Análisis de la evolución y el impacto de los vehículos eléctricos en la economía europea, p. 84 (2015)
4. Ríos, V., Vargas Guevara, C., Guamán Molina, J., Otorongo Cornejo, M.: Implicaciones Energéticas y Medio Ambientales de la Integración de Autobuses Eléctricos en el Sistema de Transporte Urbano de la Ciudad de Ambato, vol. 42, no. 1 (2018)
5. Teoh, L.E., Khoo, H.L., Goh, S.Y., Chong, L.M.: Scenario-based electric bus operation: a case study of Putrajaya, Malaysia. Int. J. Transp. Sci. Technol 7(1), 10–25 (2018)
6. Grütter, J.: Rendimiento Real de Buses Híbridos y Eléctricos, p. 39 (2015)

7. Santamaría Montalvo, A.: Manual de cálculo y reducción de huella de carbono para actividades de transporte por carretera, pp. 1–64 (2015)
8. World's Air Pollution: Real-time Air Quality Index (2020). https://waqi.info/#/c/0.165/-30.93/3.6z, Accessed 16 Jan 2020
9. No, A.I.I., Hugo, I.N.G., Pozo, D.E.L., Pichincha, C.: Ley orgánica de eficiencia energética (2019)
10. NTE INEN. Vehículos Automotores. Bus Urbano. Requisitos. In: Nte Inen 2 2052010, vol. 1, p. 2, 4, 12 (2010)
11. Norma INEN 1668. Ecuatoriana Nte Inen 1668. NTE INEN 1668 (2016)
12. Ckd, E.: Modificatoria 2 Pasajeros Intraprovincial (2018)
13. Inen, R.T.E., Urbano, B.U.S.: Modificatoria 3, pp. 3–7 (2018)
14. Emadi, A., Gao, D., Mi, C.: Modeling and simulation of electric and hybrid vehicles. Proc. IEEE **95**(4), 729–745 (2007)
15. Bus, T.: King County Metro Battery Electric Bus Demonstration—Preliminary Project Results Overview of NREL Work, no. April, pp. 1–6 (2016)
16. Astudillo, B.D., Cordero, R.F.: Obtención de ciclos de conducción para la flota de buses urbanos del cantón Cuenca, pp. 15–18 (2016)
17. Osses, M.: Buses eléctricos e híbridos:Riesgos tecnológicos y requerimientos de capacitación (2015)
18. G.G.G.I.: Electric Buses in India-Technology. Electr. Buses India Technol. Policy Benefits, GGGI, Seoul, Repub. Korea, vol. August, p. 82 (2016)
19. Miles, J., Potter, S.: Developing a viable electric bus service: the Milton Keynes demonstration project. Res. Transp. Econ. **48**, 357–363 (2014)
20. Zumba, W., Moreno Cordero, D.: Evaluación de la demanda energética de buses con motores de combustión interna, en rutas reales; para implementar buses eléctricos (2017)
21. Infografías.cl|Desarrollo en información visual - Buses Eléctricos BYD (2017). https://infografias.cl/buses-electricos-byd, Accessed 16 Jan 2020
22. Alegre Buj,M.S.: Vehículo Eléctrico E Híbrido Paralelo Por Medio De Matlab/Simulink Y Planificación De Estaciones De Carga Mediante Sistemas De Información Geográfica, p. 288 (2017)
23. Higuera, C., Er, E., León Cárdenas, C.E.: Estimación del consumo de combustible en buses urbanos de la ciudad de ibarra mediante equipo On Board, pp. 2–30 (2019)
24. Braun, R., Pumarino, M., Tolvett, S.: Motores Diesel : Tecnologías Para Su Futuro, no. August 2016 (2016)
25. Castillejo, A., Tutor, C.: TFG. Alejandro Castillejo Calle (2014)
26. Yolanda, M., Morales, R., Guzmán, A.: Caracterización De Un Motor De Combustión Interna Con Dos Tipos De Combustible. Imt – Sct (417) (2014)
27. Puertas, V., Proaño, F., Martínez, F.: Análisis de Los Parámetros Termodinámicos de Un Motor de Combustión Interna (2018)
28. Pacheco, S.: Motores Diesel (2007)
29. Pazarlama, A.: Antor Motor Diesel 13 HP (2007)
30. Martinez.: Capítulo I (2007)
31. Lima, B.A., Galvez, E.: Análisis de consumo de combustible de los vehículos de categoría M1 que circulan en el Centro Histórico de la ciudad de Cuenca en horas de máxima demanda en función de los ciclos de conducción, p. 62 (2016)
32. Mi, S., Stanojevic, N., Vasic, M.: Maintenance of Electric City Buses – Cost Benefit Analysis (2018)
33. Gillespie, T.D.: Fundamentals of vehicle dynamics, pp. 1–93 (1992)

Improving Software Project Management by Applying Agile Methodologies: A Case Study

Antonio Quiña-Mera[1,2](✉) ⬛, Lincon Chamorro Andrade[3], Javier Montaluisa Yugla[4], Doris Chicaiza Angamarca[4], and Cathy Pamela Guevara-Vega[1,2] ⬛

[1] Engineering in Applied Sciences Faculty, Department of Software, Universidad Técnica del Norte, 17 de Julio Avenue, 100150 Ibarra, Ecuador
[2] Network Science Research Group e-CIER, 17 de Julio Avenue, 100150 Ibarra, Ecuador
[3] Universidad de Investigación de Tecnología Experimental Yachay Tech, Urcuquí, Ecuador
lchamorro@yachaytech.edu.ec
[4] Department of Software Engineering, Universidad de Las Fuerzas Armadas ESPE, Quijano-Ordóñez Y Hermanas Páez Street, 050150 Latacunga, Ecuador
{fjmontaluisa,dkchicaiza}@espe.edu.ec

Abstract. In the industry, the demand for building custom software is continuous and pressing; this responsibility falls directly on the institutional software provider, whether internal or external. It is common to observe that development teams have problems managing work and delays in project delivery and software delivery with quality problems during the software engineering process. Thus, this study aims to implement a methodology to improve software development management and answer the research question: What success factors were found when implementing the methodology? The research structure was established as follows: 1) Comparative analysis between agile development methodologies most used in the community. 2) Conducting a case study at Yachay Tech University 3) Determine the critical success factors in adopting the methodology. 4) Statistical analysis of the results. The results obtained from the case study's critical success factors were an improvement of 60.50% in human factors, 50.27% in organizational factors, and 32.32% in other factors.

Keywords: Software engineering · Agile methodologies · Software project management · Case study

1 Introduction

The software industry's growth began in the early 90s with the incursion of emerging economy countries that focused their strategies on the development of customized software, responding to the needs of a specific market niche [1]. In this context, organizations' management allied with software information systems fundamental to support the organization's strategic leadership in the market; this generates permanent demands for software engineering, especially in terms of quality [2].

On the one hand, companies demand continuous, urgent, and high-quality custom software construction. On the other hand, software development areas

© Springer Nature Switzerland AG 2021
M. Botto-Tobar et al. (Eds.): ICAT 2020, CCIS 1388, pp. 672–685, 2021.
https://doi.org/10.1007/978-3-030-71503-8_52

must supply that demand but usually have problems delivering the requested quality at the expected time. Besides, there are difficulties in executing adequate planning of the requested projects [3].

In Ecuador, the software industry is growing [4], The implementation of agile methodologies and the automation of management processes are necessary for software projects to comply with life cycle phases and satisfy the client's functional requirements [5].

This research aim was to implement a methodology to improve software development management and answer the research question: What success factors were found when implementing the methodology? This research was carried out in the context of a case study of the Yachay Tech University.

This work is structured as follows: Sect. I. Introduction, where the problem, justification, and objective of the investigation are defined. Section 2. Materials and methods describe the research design and methodology, conceptual basis, and comparative analysis between agile development methodologies. Section 3. Case study: Implementation of the agile methodology. Section 4 Results show the results obtained from the case study, finally, Sect. 5. Conclusions and recommendations.

2 Materials and Methods

This section defines the research methodology phases, the participants, and the project's specific objectives (see Table 1).

Table 1. Research methodology phases.

First phase: Research design	(i) Define the research type, (ii) Define the research method, (iii) Population and sample
Second phase: Theoretical foundation	(i) Software life cycle, (ii) Software process, (ii) Agile Manifesto, (iii) Agile methodologies software development, (iv) Software project management
Third Phase: Comparative analysis	(i) Comparative analysis between agile development methodologies most used in the community: Scrum [6, 7]; XP [8]; Kanban [9]; Scrumban [10].
Fourth Phase: Implementation of the agile methodology - Case study	(i) Case study context, (ii) Summary of the implementation of the agile development methodology resulting from the third phase (iii) Critical success factors
Fifth Phase: Results	(i) Determine the critical success factors in adopting the methodology, (ii) Case study Results, (iii) Statistical analysis of the results

2.1 Research Design

Investigation Type. In this work, action research in the field was chosen to research an active actor in Ecuador's public institutions to find solutions to software development problems. The study was carried out in the software development area of Yachay Tech University.

Research Method. The chosen method to evaluate the research was the case study. The case study was applied to automate requesting purchases of products and services approved in the Yachay University of Technology's annual operating plan.

Population and Sample. The study population comprises four developers and a director of the software development area in five professionals who were part of the case study's implementation. The population investigated does not exceed 100 elements; we used the entire universe without drawing a representative sample.

2.2 Theoretical Foundation

This section conceptualizes the topics, software life cycle, software process, agile manifesto, agile methodologies software development, and best practices used in developing the software development management model for public institutions in Ecuador.

Software Life Cycle. It specifies the general approach of the development, processes, activities, tasks, and the order that must be carried out to generate the software products that will be delivered to the client. It also specifies the order of delivery, helping to ensure that the system meets the required functionality [11]. In this way it will formalize the structure as the software will be developed [12].

Software Process. It includes the formal procedures of elicitation, acquisition, supply, development, implantation, implementation, and maintenance of the software [13].

Agile Manifesto. It emphasizes four values and twelve principles; the values are general considerations in which the software development must be framed. The principles refer to the characteristics that differentiate between an agile and a traditional process and constitute agile development's central ideas [14].

Agile Methodologies Software Development. They manage software development giving priority to close collaboration between multidisciplinary teams. They are characterized by emphasizing communication over documentation, by the evolutionary development, and by its flexibility. They have also been criticized as undisciplined piracy. The reality depends on the fidelity to the agile philosophy with which these methodologies are implemented and on the adequacy of the implementation for the application [15].

Software Project Management. It is based on two key elements: the planning and precise estimation of the project's life cycle, and the supervision and control of the project to carry it out successfully, in terms of time, cost, and quality [16].

2.3 Comparative Analysis of Agile Development Methodologies

The purpose of this analysis was to determine which methodology fits the organizational development needs for this case study "Yachay Tech University"; we considered two approaches:

First, *the dynamics of the organization.* We began by observing the orientation of the organization's administrative management with agile methodologies. For this, we defined the scale of importance based on the study of Coronado Padilla (2007); the parameters were: none, low, medium, and high importance; to improve the objectivity of the analysis, we established a value of 0 to 3 points respectively [17]. To define the evaluation model of the organization's approach to agile and traditional methodologies, we compared each agile value and its relationship to the organization. We detail the values of the Agile Manifesto and separate between Agile and traditional orientation [18]. These values were evaluated by the organization's team of five software development professionals through a survey, see Table 4.

Second, *The characteristics of agile methodologies.* We began by verifying the degree of compliance with agile principles and selecting the methodology that suits the administrative management. To do this, we evaluated the relationship of the twelve principles of agile development with the institution's organizational and administrative management through a survey of the five professionals involved in the development team. We also considered values from 0 to 3 to measure this approach [17], see Table 5. Once the compliance values were established, we selected the agile methodology applied in the case study. In this sense, we established an evaluation matrix (forms) of the agile methodologies versus the attributes of the four agile points of view of Iacovelli (2008): use, the capacity of agility, application, processes, and products [19]. These forms were answered by the team of professionals based on the needs of the organization. We established values of 1 for true (T) and 0 for false (F). The agile methodologies for this comparison were Scrum [20], XP [21], Kanban [22], Scrumban [23] because of their importance in the software market [24], see Table 6.

2.4 Implementation of the Agile Methodology - Case Study

Implementation of the agile methodology was carried out with a case study [25] about implementing a software development project for the institution Yachay Tech University, considering the functional requirements [5]. The context of the case study is described below, see Table 2.

The architecture applied in the software project was model–view–controller (MVC), with the following tools, see Table 3. The application is unfolded in Yachay Tech's servers through the intranet; for confidentiality reasons, they were not published in the cloud.

Table 2. Case study context.

Software development project:	Automation of the process of requests for purchase of goods and services scheduled in their annual planning for Yachay Tech University
Applicant:	Purchasing and service requests
Functional requirements:	16 user stories
Application date:	01/03/2018
Start date:	02/03/2018
Execution date:	05/03/2018
Deadline:	20/06/2018
Training date:	21/06/2018
Work team:	One manager, one development director, one project leader, two developers
Sprint number:	16
Number of hours per Sprint	140 h
Smoke tests	36
Application tests	25
Load and stress test	19
Number of incidents after delivery	12

Table 3. Software Project Development Tools.

Data base:	Oracle 11g
Frontend development framework:	JavaServer Faces (JSF)
Programming language:	Java, Javascript
Viewing tools:	CSS3, BootsFaces, HTML5, Jquery

2.5 Critical Success Factors

To identify the success factors, we rely on the characterization of empirical research conducted by Misra, Kumar [26] about factors that influence agile methodologies: human and organizational factors, factors associated with project development, and the level of adoption of Scrum practices by the development team. We collected information on the experience gained in the case study and executed a validation process on the success factors raised in this research. For this purpose, we applied a survey aimed at professionals in the organization, and the evaluation criteria for these factors were based on the Likert scales [27].

3 Results

3.1 Results of the Application of the Evaluation Model Between Agile and Traditional Methodologies.

The organization presented high importance of 2.75 towards the agile orientation; this corroborated that the present investigation has more acceptance by the organization's interested parties; besides, its processes were framed in the agile methodologies' characteristics, see Table 4.

Table 4. Results of the application of the evaluation model of agile and traditional methodologies.

Agile		Traditional	
Agile values	Importance	Traditional values	Importance
Individual and team interactions	2	The process and tools	2
Develop software that works	3	Get good documentation	2
Collaboration with the client	3	Contract negotiation	2
Responding to change	3	Monitoring a plan	2
Media	**2,75**	**Media**	**2**

3.2 Results of the Evaluation of Compliance with the Agile Principles.

We obtained 31.5/36 points of evaluation in the fulfillment of the organization's agile principles; that is to say, this one is oriented in 87.5% to the fulfillment of the agile. With this evaluation, we ratify that the organization has an agile approach.

3.3 Results of the Evaluation Matrix of Agile Methodologies vs. The Attributes of Iacovelli's Four Agile Viewpoints.

The Scrum methodology obtained the highest score with 65.38%; therefore, the agile methodology best suited the organization's software development needs. Consequently, this methodology was adopted for the present case study, see Table 6 and Table 7.

Table 5. Results of the evaluation of compliance with agile principles

N°	Principles of the Agile Manifesto	Rating (average)
1	Our highest priority is to satisfy the customer through early and continuous delivery of valuable software	2
2	Welcome changing requirements, even late in development. Agile processes harness change for the customer's competitive advantage	2,5
3	Deliver working software frequently, from a couple of weeks to a couple of months, with a shorter timescale preference	2
4	Businesspeople and developers must work together daily throughout the project	2,5
5	Build projects around motivated individuals. Give them the environment and support they need and trust them to get the job done	3
6	The most efficient and effective method of conveying information to and within a development team is face-to-face conversation	3
7	Working software is the primary measure of progress	3
8	Agile processes promote sustainable development. The sponsors, developers, and users should be able to maintain a constant pace indefinitely	2,5
9	Continuous attention to technical excellence and good design enhances agility	2,5
10	Simplicity--the art of maximizing the amount of work not done--is essential	2,5
11	The best architectures, requirements, and designs emerge from self-organizing teams	3
12	At regular intervals, the team reflects on becoming more effective, then tunes and adjusts its behavior accordingly	3
	Media	**31,5**

3.4 Results of Critical Success Factors

The interviewees indicated that 68.2% fully agreed that the previous experience positively influenced the implantation. Besides, 47.6% were in total agreement with the positive experience of agility.

Concerning adaptation to Scrum practices, 50% agreed, while 65.2% expressed a commitment to personal values within the team. The development team's communication with the client was excellent (65.2%), while the client's negotiation results were very favorable (68.2%). The collaboration of the client with the development team was excellent at 63.2%. Regarding the client's level of satisfaction in using agile methodologies in development, the results were very satisfactory, with 65.2%. Another essential aspect valued by the client was the incremental delivery of the software by 68.2%. The

Table 6. The evaluation matrix of the agile methodologies *vs.* The attributes of Iacovelli's four agile points of view.

AGILE METHODOLOGIES		Software development-oriented	Project management oriented		
		XP	Scrum	Kanban	Scrumban
USE	Why use an agile method?				
	Respect for delivery dates	0	1	0	0
	Compliance with requirements	1	1	1	1
	Respect for the quality level	0	0	0	0
	End user satisfaction	0	1	0	0
	Turbulent environments	0	1	1	1
	Favourable to Off shoring	0	1	0	1
	Increase in productivity	1	1	1	1
AGILITY CAPACITY	What is the agility part included in the method?				
	Short Iterations	1	1	1	1
	Collaboration	1	1	1	1
	People-centered	1	1	1	1
	Political Refactoring	1	0	0	0
	Political test	1	1	0	1
	Integration of changes	1	1	1	1
	Lightweight	1	1	1	1
	Functional requirements may change	1	1	1	1
	Non-functional requirements may change	0	0	1	1
	The work plan can change	0	1	0	0
	Human resources can change	1	0	1	1
	Change indicators	0	1	1	1

(continued)

Table 6. (*continued*)

APPLICABILITY	When is a favorable environment to use this method?	Reactivity (at the beginning of the project, each stage, each iteration)	1	1	1	1
		Knowledge sharing (low, high)	0	1	1	1
		Project size (small, large)	0	1	0	1
		The complexity of the project (low, high)	0	1	0	1
		Project risks (low, high)	1	0	0	1
		Equipment size (small, large)	1	1	1	1
		The degree of interaction with the client (low, high)	1	1	0	0
		Degree of interaction with end users (low, high)	0	1	0	0
		Degree of interaction between team members (low, high)	1	1	0	1
		Degree of integration of novelty (low, high)	1	1	0	1
		The organization of the team (self-organization, hierarchical organization)	1	1	1	1
PROCESSES AND PRODUCTS	How are the processes of the method characterized?	**Level of abstraction of the standards and guidelines**				
		Project management	0	1	0	1
		Process description	1	0	0	0
		Specific standards and guidance on activities and products	0	1	1	1
		Activities covered by the Agile method				

(continued)

Table 6. (*continued*)

Project start-up	0	0	0	0
Definition of requirements	1	1	0	1
Modeling	0	0	1	0
Code	1	1	1	1
Unit tests	0	0	0	0
Integration tests	0	0	0	0
System test	1	1	1	1
Acceptance test	0	0	0	0
Quality control	1	1	1	1
System use	0	0	0	0
Products of Agile Method activities				
Design models	1	0	1	0
Source code commentary	1	1	1	1
Executable	1	1	1	1
Unit tests	0	0	0	0
Integration tests	0	0	0	0
System testing	1	0	1	1
Acceptance tests	0	0	1	1
Quality reports	1	1	0	0
User documentation	0	0	0	0
Total	**28**	**34**	**27**	**33**

Table 7. Results of the comparative study of agile methodologies.

Methodology	Score	Percentage
XP	28	53,85
Scrum	34	**65,38**
Kanban	27	51,92
Scrumban	33	63,46

fulfillment of the tasks planned for each Sprint was highly effective; the team was in total agreement with 65.2%.

The team stated that the project was developed to the client's satisfaction; its members mentioned that they were in total agreement by 47.6%. During the development of the project, many emphases were placed on incident management; in fact, 83.3% of the team was in total agreement. A significant factor within the development process was to carry out a permanent follow-up to make corrections in time; it was valued to be in total agreement in 65.2%; this shows excellent openness to agile methodologies.

The client's satisfaction increased as the project development progressed, mainly due to fulfilling the activities planned for each Sprint. On the other hand, the development team's level of satisfaction increased gradually throughout the project; this increase in the level of satisfaction is due to the coupling and experience that the team acquired during the project.

The following practices showed a high acceptance and adoption level by 75%: Incremental delivery, iterations, daily Stand-up Meetings, burndown chart, the definition of done, planning meeting, backlog.

Meanwhile, the following practices showed a 50% adoption level: definition of ready, planning poker, backlog meeting.

From what we have observed, we can conclude that all the team members have adopted the practices associated with Scrum by at least 50%, which indicates, in general terms, the excellent acceptance of the implementation of agile development methodologies.

According to the results obtained, it has been possible to observe as the central aspect of the client; this has been rising throughout the development by the incremental increase in the attainment of objectives in the evolution of the product. One of the aspects that most positively affect customer satisfaction is the continuous contribution of value to their business, by gradually allowing them to take advantage of new product features. Next, we will evaluate the improvement in the management of software projects for Yachay Tech University once the case study has been completed, see Table 8.

Table 8. Comparative analysis of the improvement in the management of software projects.

Critical success factors	Initial state	Final state	Improvements
Human factors	30%	90,5%	60,5%
Organizational Factors	44,53%	94,8%	50,27%
Other factors	37,53%	69,85%	32,32%
Total average			47,7%

4 Conclusions

In the comparative study of agile methodologies, using the approach proposed by Adrian Iacovelli helped determine that SCRUM is the most appropriate agile framework to solve the variable and flexible characteristics of the management of software development projects presented in the case study this research.

Applying the SCRUM agile methodology at the Yachay University of Technology found that it positively improved software development project management by 47.7%. For this reason, the hypothesis proposed in this work can be accepted.

With the results of the evaluation of the case study obtained, on the one hand, it is concluded that the adoption of development methodologies positively influenced the human factor's point of view. The study shows that more than half of the team reacts positively to Scrum's implementation with positive values (totally agree and agree); the overall evaluation has an optimistic assessment of 90.5%. On the other hand, they indicated a 94.8% satisfaction level in motivation, commitment, and willingness to work with themselves and the development team.

In general, the team's satisfaction and the client were positive, with 69.85% compliance and the development team's level of adoption of Scrum practices.

5 Recommendations

It is recommended to make the adoption incrementally with empowered and committed teams.

It is essential to sensitize the external Product Owner about the adoption of Scrum, its advantages, and improvements in the software product's development.

Involve and train the client from the beginning to the end of the project to make them aware of their team's role.

The retrospective meeting at the end of each delivery creates bonds of trust.

Do not customize Scrum to the organization's requirements.

Culture and attitude change are essential to become a more self-organized and disciplined team.

References

1. Manjavacas, A., Vizcaíno, A., Ruiz, F., Piattini, M.: Global software development governance: challenges and solutions. J. Softw. Evol. Process, pp. 1–26, March 2020
2. Masso, J., Pino, F.J., Pardo, C., García, F., Piattini, M.: Risk management in the software life cycle: a systematic literature review. Comput. Stand. Interfaces **71**, 103431 (2020)
3. García, F., Moraga, M.Á., Serrano, M., Piattini, M.: Visualisation environment for global software development management. IET Softw. **9**(2), 51–64 (2015)
4. Espinoza, M.A., del P. Gallegos, D.: La industria del software en Ecuador: evolución y situación actual The software industry in Ecuador: evolution and current situation. Revista Espacios **38**, 25 (2017)
5. Guevara-Vega, C.P., Guzmán-Chamorro, E.D., Guevara-Vega, V.A., Andrade, A.V.B., Quiña-Mera, J.A.: Functional requirement management automation and the impact on software projects: case study in ecuador. In: Rocha, Á., Ferrás, C., Paredes, M. (eds.) ICITS 2019. AISC, vol. 918, pp. 317–324. Springer, Cham (2019). https://doi.org/10.1007/978-3-030-11890-7_31
6. Bass, J.M.: Scrum master activities: process tailoring in large enterprise projects. In: Proceedings - 2014 IEEE 9th International Conference on Global Software Engineering, ICGSE 2014, no. 3, pp. 6–15 (2014)
7. Quiña-Mera, A., Barahona, S.P., Guevara-Vega, C., García-Santillán, I., Guevara-Vega, A., Yugla, J.M.: Use of gamification in the learning of children with dyseidetic disexia: a case study, RISTI - Rev. Iber. Sist. e Tecnol. Inf. **2019**(E22), 161–173 (2019)
8. Beck, K., Andres, C.: Extreme Programming Explained: Embrace Change, 2nd edn. Addison-Wesley Professional (2004)
9. Ahmad, M.O., Markkula, J., Oivo, M.: Kanban in software development: a systematic literature review. In: Proceedings - 39th Euromicro Conference Series on Software Engineering and Advanced Applications, SEAA 2013, pp. 9–16 (2013)
10. Patil, S.P., Neve, J.R.: Productivity improvement of software development process through scrumban: a practitioner's approach. In: 2018 International Conference On Advances in Communication and Computing Technology, ICACCT 2018, 2018, pp. 314–318 (2018)
11. IEEE Computer Society Sponsored by the Software & Systems Engineering Standards Committee, *IEEE Guide–Adoption of ISO/IEC TR 24748–1:2010 Systems and Software Engineering–Life Cycle Management–Part 1: Guide for Life Cycle Management.* IEEE Std 24748–1–2011, 2011.
12. G. D. Everett and R. McLeod, "The Software Development Life Cycle," in *Software Testing: Testing Across the Entire Software Development Life Cycle*, IEEE, 2007, pp. 29–58.
13. Pino, F.J., García, F., Piattini, M.: Software process improvement in small and medium software enterprises: a systematic review. Softw. Qual. J. **16**(2), 237–261 (2008)
14. Jim Highsmith Agile Alliance: Manifesto for Agile Software Development (2001). https://agilemanifesto.org/. Accessed 09 Oct 2020
15. Paulk, M.C.: Agile Methodologies and Process Discipline. Inst. Softw. Res., pp. 15–18 (2002)
16. Fitzhenry, P., Gardiner, G.: Enhanced software project management by application of metrics and cost estimation techniques. In: IEE Colloquium on Project Management for Software Engineers, pp. 4/1–4/4 (1995)
17. Coronado, J.: Escalas o niveles de medición, vol. 2, no. 2 (2007)
18. Pérez, M.J.: Guía Comparativa de Metodologías Ágiles. Universidad de Valladolid, Spain (2012)
19. Iacovelli, A., Souveyet, C.: Framework for agile methods classification. CEUR Workshop Proceedings **341**, 91–102 (2008)

20. Alsalemi, A.M., Yeoh, E.T.: A survey on product backlog change management and requirement traceability in agile (Scrum). In: 2015 9th Malaysian Softw. Eng. Conf. MySEC 2015, pp. 189–194 (2016)
21. Bertone, M.R., Pasini, A.C.A., Ramón, M.H.: Programación Extrema y Calidad . Estudio de Compatibilidad XP – CMM. In: XI Congreso Argentino de Ciencias de la Computación. II Workshop de Ingeniería de Software y Bases de Datos (WISBD), p. 11 (2005)
22. Oza, N., Fagerholm, F., Munch, J.: How does Kanban impact communication and collaboration in software engineering teams? In: 2013 6th International Workshop on Cooperative and Human Aspects of Software Engineering, CHASE 2013 - Proceedings, vol. 68, pp. 125–128 (2013)
23. Banijamali, A., Dawadi, R., Ahmad, M.O., Similä, J., Oivo, M., Liukkunen, K.: An empirical study on the impact of Scrumban on geographically distributed software development. In: MODELSWARD 2016 - Proceedings of the 4th International Conference on Model-Driven Engineering and Software Development, pp. 567–577 (2016)
24. Rujana, M., Franco, N.R., Tortosa, N., Tomaselli, G.: Análisis sobre adopción de metodologías ágiles en los equipos de desarrollo en pymes del NEA. In: XVIII Workshop de Investigadores en Ciencias de la Computación, pp. 646–650 (2016)
25. Quiña-Mera, J., Correa, L., Jácome, G., Landeta, P., Guevara-Vega, C.: Proposal for a software development project management model for public institutions in Ecuador: a case study. In: ICAETT 2020 International Conference on Advances in Emerging Trends and Technologies (2020)
26. Misra, S.C., Kumar, V., Kumar, U.: Identifying some important success factors in adopting agile software development practices. J. Syst. Softw. **82**(11), 1869–1890 (2009)
27. Likert, R.: A Technique for the Measurement of Attitudes, New York, USA, 140 (1932)

Sensor Nodes and Communication Protocols of the Internet of Things Applied to Intelligent Agriculture

Cristian Chuchico-Arcos$^{(\boxtimes)}$ (iD) and David Rivas-Lalaleo$^{(\boxtimes)}$ (iD)

Maestría en Electrónica y Automatización Mención Redes Industriales,
Departamento de Eléctrica y Electrónica, Universidad de las Fuerzas Armadas ESPE,
Av. General Rumiñahui s/n, Sangolquí 171-5-231B, Ecuador
{cpchuchico,drrivas}@espe.edu.ec

Abstract. The development of smart agriculture has presented extensive development in recent years, that is why countless proposals have been presented around the world. This high variability of technologies used in the implementation of this type of solutions has generated certain users depending on what types of equipment or communication protocols to use depending on the application case. In this article, the different jobs and technologies used in IoT applied to agriculture are analyzed, comparing their technical characteristics through documentary analysis, simulations of case studies, among others. After this study, the results obtained from the bibliographic and documentary review are described by means of tables, in addition sensor nodes are reproduced with specific technical characteristics such as their communication protocol, energy consumption, degrees of protection of the devices, security of the implemented networks, among others in the Cooja software for the simulation of the case studies. This study provides a methodology for selecting the technology that best suits each type of crop.

Keywords: IoT · Sensor node · Comunication protocol · Intelligent agriculture

1 Introduction

The trend of the Internet things (IoT) has triggered a constant development of new ways to use interconnection to help people, and in this way improve their quality of life, generating a momentum in the search of greater efficiency in management resource and cost reduction [1]. Companies, cities and different productive sectors as well as the agricultural sector are increasingly implementing IoT solutions. This rapid growth also presents challenges such as: Integration of millions devices from various suppliers using custom apps, integration of new things to existing network infrastructure, protection of new devices configured with many security levels. The agricultural sector has several challenges to overcome for the future, it is considered as a vital importance to be part of the

M. Botto-Tobar et al. (Eds.): ICAT 2020, CCIS 1388, pp. 686–703, 2021.
https://doi.org/10.1007/978-3-030-71503-8_53

primary sector for the provision of food and other basic necessities [2]. The IoT plays a leading role in enabling this sector to move forward and adapt to the changes and demands that lie ahead [3]. Smart agriculture uses the IoT to increase the process of cultivating the land through monitoring, data storage and automated evaluation to increase crop yields and reduce environmental impact [4].

Related studies agree that the assessment of the IoT is based on the analysis of the data collected. The development of low-consumption and cost sensors allows to collect a set of environmental data and send them through wireless means to a database, which can be subjected to an abstract analysis or to a deep analysis [5]; thus, modern agriculture seeks to transform traditional agriculture into intelligent agriculture, through quality improvement, in this way IoT technology, it stands as a promising approach to achieve these tasks [6]. The most common application of the use of sensor nodes in the monitoring of crop fields, is focused on the analysis of environmental data, mainly temperature, humidity, and soil quality indicators such as PH, nutrient levels, among others, which are considered as important factors in decision-making for obtaining healthy crops and harvests [6]. Optimal agricultural irrigation systems have been developed by means of sensor node and data management through smartphones and web applications, thereby ensuring that the moisture content of the soil is properly maintained for the growth of vegetables, reducing costs and increasing agricultural productivity [7,8].

On the other hand, there are also suggestions for pest detection systems through the application of wireless sensors that acquire and transmit images to a remote host station. This system is limited to detection and does not propose any pest control method [9]. On the other hand, there are also suggestions for pest detection systems through the application of wireless sensors that acquire and transmit images to a remote host station. This system is limited to detection and does not propose any pest control method [10].Thanks to technological globalization, smart agriculture projects are implemented and developed in Ecuador, whose geographic diversity is a positive factor for agricultural practice, which represents the main income of rural communities. In Cañar, an architecture was developed that allows the community of farmers, to monitor, manage and manage information on the climate and soil variables that affect the growth of the corn crop, with the aim of helping in making optimal decisions and timely based on information presented through statistical graphics [11].

Considering cacao as one of the main national export products, a low-cost IoT architecture was designed based on wireless sensor network (WSN) technology for agricultural monitoring in cocoa crops. The information acquired favors the sustainable management of the crop by means of the correct administration of resources, facilitating the quality control of the product and the prevention of protection plans against pests and diseases [12]. Within the optimization of resources we can mention the design of a rules engine and complex event processor in the context of IoT for precision agriculture which performs a prescriptive analysis that consists not only in predicting or detecting event patterns, but also in making automatic decisions. The evaluation of this project was carried out via simulation and the results obtained, demonstrate the viability of using the system in low-cost infrastructures for small and large producers [13].

With all this evidence, a number of related projects have been carried out on this topic, but it can be identified that in each project they use different technologies at the time of implementing the experimentation. This variety in the development of projects related to smart agriculture, it is important to find out what type of technology to use depending on the conditions of the crop. In addition to being able to guide producers to the use of these technologies, without focusing on issues such as Big Data, artificial intelligence (AI), communication protocols, etc., so, the IoT app should be sought as a tool to capitalize on the digitized data for making decisions, estimates and projections, to avoid having too much data but little information. With the above detailed it can be stated that there is a great variability of trends in this area and that there is no objective guide that makes it easier for users' selection of suitable components for their projects.

This research focuses on IoT applications developed for agriculture, considering technological advance and its massification as the basis for connection sensors, actuators and other intelligent technologies in order to achieve migration towards precision agriculture, taking into account that due to the incursion of the IoT in agriculture, traditional processes and procedures have been modified. The present work will become a tool that allows to counteract proven infrastructures, for the future development and implementation of projects related to agricultural technification. The analysis of the implemented solutions will allow to distinguish clearly the potentialities that each of the sensor nodes, communication equipment and protocols present for the resolution of specific problems, in a specific area, allowing to increase the efficiency in the design and dimensioning of projects, in addition it offers alternatives in projects that are already operating, to improve them according to the different conditions and needs present in the agricultural sector.

This article is divided into an Introduction that explains the problem of the topic to be treated, the Methodology, in which the basic theme that supports the subject is addressed, a section of Experimentation and Results, in which it will be explained with their corresponding results, to facilitate the reader's interpretation of them, then, the Conclusions section in which the most relevant findings of the preset work will be expressed and finally a section where future work will be discussed.

2   Methodology

The research focuses on describing four relevant characteristics: energy consumption [14] , degrees of device protection [15], security of deployed networks [16] and simulation of sensor nodes and protocols applied in intelligent agriculture as a network analysis tool, Fig. 1, describes the procedure performed to synthesize the recorded information.

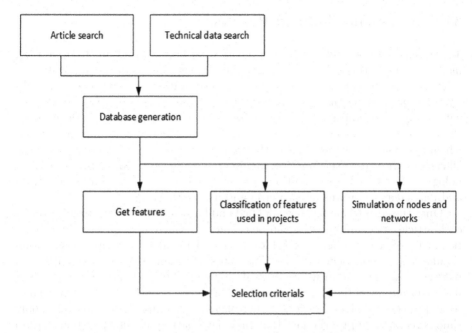

Fig. 1. Flow chart used to synthesize the recorded information.

To the searching database google and scholar Scopus were used, of which 2185 articles are obtained through the *IoT AND agriculture* search chain, a selection of recent research is subsequently carried out, considering the articles from 2015. Other selection criterial include the use of sensor nodes the description of protocols used and energy consumption; articles that clearly describe its architecture were considered as reference articles on IoT solutions applied to smart agriculture. If you do not have any of the restrictions mentioned above, the number of items would be too broad and beyond the scope of this investigation. In addition, it seeks to present the energy consumption characteristics of the microcontro- lador elements and transmission systems cited in the articles in which the average consumption of the implemented project is not required. Which the search is carried out on manufacturers' pages as well as related work on features of operation modes and energy consumption of the aforementioned elements and systems.

In order to develop this tool, three techniques were applied, the first consists of bibliometric analysis with the VOS viewer tool through which keyword search results are obtained. The second technique consists of the documentary analysis through which the extraction of the characteristics that are the subject of analysis, is carried out in this investigation. Then, through the simulation we try to expose the main tools available for the evaluation of projects, where the most common sensor nodes detected in this study are implemented. Finally, the results obtained are presented.

3   Experimentation and Results

To develop this tool, different experiments have been carried out to obtain the
most relevant in this subject. The first experiment consists of the application of
software *VOSviewer*, where a graphical interpretation is made based on bibliographic data by means of a correlated count analysis of the terms associated
with energy consumption within the *IoT + Agriculture* search chain. Figure 2
shows the terms correlated to sensor nodes and energy consumption, within
which it should also be noted that the trend of recent research focuses on energy
efficiency, whose estimation in IoT architecture is linked to communication technologies, electronic devices and sensors, as well as the environmental conditions
and particular situations of each crop and its needs [17,18].

Once the correlation has been defined and based on the specifications given in
each article, its characteristics can be extracted, which are expressed in Table 1.
It can be seen that there are solutions that demand low energy consumption
thanks to benefits special of its components, the same that accompanied by a
battery charging system using alternative energies (self charge) make the estimated autonomy of the system is hundreds of days [17,19–22]. On the other hand,
some projects developed have a higher energy consumption so their autonomy
time is reduced despite the fact that they have battery charging systems within

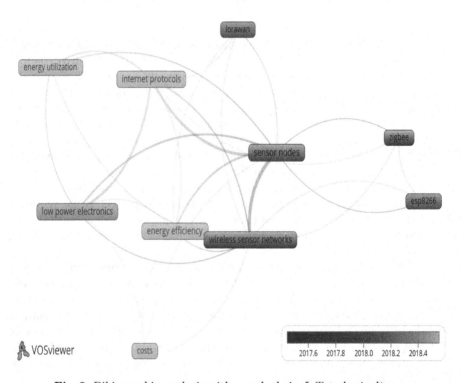

Fig. 2. Bibiographic analysis with search chain *IoT + Agriculture*.

their power supply system. This reduction in the autonomy of the systems is often linked to the incorporation of safeguards in the architectures since the computational process is increased, which demands a greater current consumption [23–26].

Other investigations do not make an estimate of the energy autonomy of the system due to the variation of modes of operation that its components would have in the field, however, emphasis is placed on the minimum consumption values that they would have during certain time intervals [12, 27–29]. It is important to point out that in the aforementioned works, the autonomy estimate is not made considering 100% battery charge, it is considered a charge of 60 to 70%. Regarding the degrees of protection of the sensor nodes, several related works do not specify the characteristics of the containers, however in the description of their research, boxes that provide protection to the sensor nodes [12, 19, 21, 24, 26]; while most research shows the importance of protecting the elements against environmental factors, which is why the design and 3D printing of waterproof casings that are coupled to the design of the sensor nodes is carried out [22, 23, 25, 27] or these in turn are introduced in housings whose degrees of protection are defined by standard IEC60529 [17, 20, 28, 29]. It can be concluded that all the works put a special emphasis in the development of the protection systems, to guarantee the optimal performance of its components conserving them within the specified characteristics for long periods of time.

Table 2 shows the power consumption of a sample sensor nodes [19, 30], while Table 3 refers to the consumption of cards used as microcontrollers for various implemented sensor nodes. [31], to provide a tool to estimate the power consumption of a solution in this area.

One of the main topics emphasized throughout the research is the energy consumption of the sensor nodes which is linked to the operation modes that present both the microcontrollers and the transmission systems, which have characteristics of ultra energy saving in moments of inactivity, through algorithms that have been developed in search of maximizing the autonomy times of the systems.

Then, the second experiment is carried out in which the same methodology of correlated count analysis of terms is applied, several communication protocols are selected which have been used in Iot solutions applied to intelligent agriculture [32] [33]. Generally these protocols are divided according to the transmission distance, for example Bluetooth [34], BLE [35] and radio frequency identification (RFID) in short distance, Wi-Fi and ZigBee [36] in medium distance, while long distance technologies can be mentioned the mobile networks (4G) and the technologies known as Low Power, Wide Area, Network or simply LPWAN which we can mention LoRA, NB-IoT and Sigfox. [37], to contain are described the applications and characteristics more relevant of each one of these technologies and its application:

Table 1. Implemented IoT solutions, energy consumption and protection features

Work	Technical contribution	Energy consumption	Autonomy estimation	Power supply	Encapsulation/Protection
[17]	An autonomous wireless device for real-time monitoring of water needs	0.069 mA	724 day	Li-Po 3.7 V 2200 mAh	Carcasa IP66
[19]	A low power IoT network for smart agriculture	NO especificado	243 day	Li-Ion 2000 mAh	Not specified
[20]	Wireless sensor networks for precision horticulture in Southern Spain	0.5 mA	223 day	AA NiMH 2700 mAh	Watertight box IP 67
[21]	SESBeacon: nodo sensor Electrónico Para Alertas Tempranas	10.63 mA	218 day	Li-Ion 3.6 V 2250 mAh	Not specified
[22]	Development of sensors-based agri-food traceability system remotely managed by a software platform for optimized farm management	10.405 mA	168 day	Li-Po 4.1 V 100 mAh	Plastic box with perforated cover
[23]	Monitoring Device for culture substrate growth parameters for precision agriculture: Acronym: MoniSen	0.4026 mA	73 day	2.4 V 2400 mAh (conv. elev. MCP1640)	3D ABS printing
[24]	Design and implementation of smart irrigation system based on LoRa	2.098 mA	57 day	3.6 V 4800 mAh	Not specified
[25]	GAIA2: A multifunctional wireless device for enhancing crop management	Not specified	56 day	NiMH 4.8 V 6000 mAh	Waterproof housing designed for the device
[26]	Characterization of a low-cost and low-power environmental monitoring system	8.71 mA	14 day	Li-Ion 7 V, 3500 mAh,	Not specified
[27]	Low-Cost LoRaWAN Node for agro-intelligence IoT	90 uA	Not specified	Not specified	3D printed housing
[12]	Iot architecture based on wireless sensor network applied to agricultural monitoring: a case of study of cacao crops in Ecuador	91 mA	Not specified	Not specified	Not specified
[28]	Design of a sensor node for IoT applications	Depending on the operating modes	Li-Po 3.7 V, 1000 mAh	Not specified	Housing IP67
[29]	An IoT monitoring system for precision viticulture	Not specified	Not specified	12 V Lead Acid 90 Ah (Solar charging system)	Housing IP66

Table 2. Power consumption characteristics of sensor nodes

Senor Node	I sleep	I active	I transmision
IITH mote	180 uA	11.58 mA	26.58 mA
M3SS	200 mA	500 mA	600 mA
DZ50 SPS mote	3.3 uA	3.25 mA	26.5 mA
MicaZ SPS	170 uA	4.35 mA	18.5 mA
TelosB PIS mote	13 uA	1.72 mA	19.12 mA
ECO	2 mA	3 mA	22 mA
Tiny Node	5 uA	3 mA	62 mA
Waspmote	7 uA	9 mA	20 mA
LOTUS	– uA	16 mA	17 mA
Sun SPOT	32 uA	206 mA	–
Tmote sky	5.1 uA	54.1 uA	195 mA

Table 3. Power consumption characteristics of micro sensor node controllers

Text controller	I Idle	I Sleep
Arduino One	49 mA	34.5 mA
Node MCU/ESP8266	15 mA	10 uA
ATmega328P	15 mA	0.36 mA

Zig Bee

Given the characteristics of this protocol, a message can be received by any device nearby. This is a disadvantage since it can lead to violations, the privacy of individuals, produce some damage or disable any system. ZigBee supports the use of standard encryption and authentication protocols. In the design of the network, the level of security, complexity and cost of the devices, it must be considered that the increase in security implies greater computing capacity and memory, which leads to an increase in energy consumption [36]. Data authentication is intended to ensure that the information is valid and that no tampering has occurred. To this, the transmitter adds a special code known as the MIC (Message Integrity Code) to the message. The MIC is generated by a method known to both, the sender and the receiver. When the receiver receives the message, it calculates the MIC and if it coincides with the MIC sent by the transmitter, the message is considered authentic. The security level in the control is increased by the number of bits in the MIC. ZigBee supports 32, 64 and 128 bit MIC. Encryption of a message provides confidentiality of the information. The MIC in ZigBee is generated using the CCM* protocol (enhanced Counter with Cipher Block Chaining Message Authentication Code). The CCM* is used in conjunction with AES (Advance Encryption Standard) 128 bit and share the same security key, the use of AES-CCM* achieves authentication and confidentiality in the message.

Bluetooth

Bluetooth technology is basically divided into two types of systems: Basic Rate (BR)/Enhanced Data Rate (DR) and Low Energy (LE). In this paper we will describe the security features of Bluetooth: Low Energy or BLE due to its performance for intelligent agriculture [38]. BLE is characterized by the implementation of security mechanisms on the host, also introduces two new features to its security model: LE privacy and data signing: LE privacy, is based on the devices modifying their address from time to time through the use of a key called IRK (Identity Resolving Key), while data signing is based on the use of a key called CSRK (Connection Signature Resolving Key) which is shared during the pairing process and it is used to sign the data and that the receiver can verify its authenticity in scenarios where the security mode activated does not allow encryption. There are currently two classes of security in BLE: LE Legacy Pairing and LE Secure Connections(V4.2). The use of either model determines the mechanisms for key generation. In both cases BLE uses the AES-CCM algorithm for encryption and message integrity services.

LoRa WAN

The fundamental properties that are supported by LoRaWAN security are: mutual authentication, integrity protection and confidentiality. Mutual authentication is established between a LoRaWAN terminal device and the network as part of the network joining procedure. This ensures that only genuine and authorized devices join to a genuine and authentic networks. In addition, the exchange of LoRa WAN messages is authenticated at the source, protected against reproduction and encrypted, this combination ensures that the network traffic has not been altered, comes from a legitimate device, that it is not comprehensible to spies and that it has not been captured and reproduced by hackers cyber criminals. LoRaWAN is one of the few IoT networks that implements end-to-end encryption [39]. The information is encrypted by AES-CTR and carries a frame counter (to avoid packet repetition) and a Message Integrity Code (MIC) calculated with AES-CMAC (to avoid packet manipulation). AES is used in the standardized CTR mode that makes use of XOR cryptographic operations (like many other modes such as CBC5). This strengthens the AES algorithm by using a unique AES key for each block cipher.

NB IoT

There are different methods to manage security in NB-IoT communication network, between the devices and the cloud server where the APN information or operator platform is reported. The operators offer for NB-IoT the possibility of which an intermediate server is assembled, that gathers the data of the own network of NB-IoT without crossing by Internet. The customer's end-center platform is typically connected by a VPN connection to the operator's platform and this makes the entire journey from the device to the customer's cloud server secure. UDP protocol security: in this case, the data travels encrypted from end to end by the same technology, and it is the cloud server that is responsible for making the authentication and final decoding of the data. Not applying security is the easiest possibility, but it is not recommended. This option should only be considered for test purposes, as in real, large-scale projects, multiple attacks could be received without any capacity to deal with them.

The Table 4 shows relevant characteristics of the protocols in question.

Table 4. General characteristics of the Iot protocols applied in intelligent agriculture

Protocol	Standard	Authentication	Encryption	Range	Speed	Power consumption
BLE	IEEE 2802.15.1	AES-CCM	AES-CCM	100 m	1 Mbps	10 mW
ZigBee	IEEE 2802.15.4	AES-CCM	AES-CCM	100 m	20,40,250 kbps	36.9 mW
LoRa	IEEE2 802.15.4g	AES-CTR	AES-ACTR	Urban 2–5 Km, Rural 15 Km m	50 kbps	100 mW
NB-IoT	3GPP release 13	DTLS APN	DTLS APN	Urban 1–8 Km, Rural 25 Km	200 kbps (UL) 250 Kbps (DL)	106 mW

The authors of the different articles agree that network security basically lies in data integrity, authentication and encryption. All the analyzed technologies present protocols that allow incorporating these safeguards. It is important to point out that the incorporation of security in the network demands the use of computing resources, which entails a higher energy consumption by the sensor node. The protocols remains the possibility of establishing a network without safeguards, which is not recommended from any point of view.

The following experiment consists of carrying out the simulations of the selected nodes using the software Contiki Cooja OS. In Fig. 3, the network topology for the simulation of the COAP protocol through 6 Lowpan can be observed. There is an edge router available which is the one in charge of translating the serial port to the internet. The transmitted data (ID = 9), which is outside the communication radius of the edge router, reaches the server through hops by the sensor nodes 5 or 7.

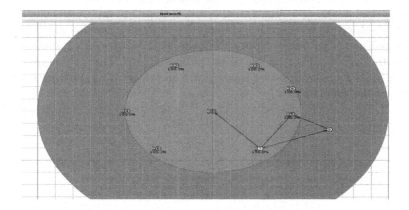

Fig. 3. Network topology for COAP simulation with the edge router ID = 1

Once the topology is established, the COAP server must be started. Its IPV6 address is aaa::212:7401:1:101 and the local link address is fe80::2121:7401:1:101. To review the established adjacencies as well as the best routes for the packages, you can access a browser and type in the search bar [IPV6 address of the server].

```
  ●  ─ □   user@instant-contiki: ~/contiki-3.0/examples/ipv6/rpl-border-router
 File  Edit  View  Search  Terminal  Help
opened tun device ``/dev/tun0''
ifconfig tun0 inet `hostname` up
ifconfig tun0 add aaaa::1/64
ifconfig tun0 add fe80::0:0:0:1/64
ifconfig tun0

tun0        Link encap:UNSPEC  HWaddr 00-00-00-00-00-00-00-00-00-00-00-00-00-00-00
-00
            inet addr:127.0.1.1  P-t-P:127.0.1.1  Mask:255.255.255.255
            inet6 addr: fe80::1/64 Scope:Link
            inet6 addr: aaaa::1/64 Scope:Global
            UP POINTOPOINT RUNNING NOARP MULTICAST  MTU:1500  Metric:1
            RX packets:0 errors:0 dropped:0 overruns:0 frame:0
            TX packets:0 errors:0 dropped:0 overruns:0 carrier:0
            collisions:0 txqueuelen:500
            RX bytes:0 (0.0 B)  TX bytes:0 (0.0 B)

*** Address:aaaa::1 => aaaa:0000:0000:0000
Got configuration message of type P
Setting prefix aaaa::
Server IPv6 addresses:
 aaaa::212:7401:1:101
 fe80::212:7401:1:101
```

Fig. 4. Establishment of COAP server, and IPV6 addresses

Once the network converges, the data analysis can be carried out using the radio messages in which there is data on the source and destination addresses, data packet size, and acknowledgments ACK Fig. 4. This information can be exported for a detailed analysis. Additionally, the data received by the server is available, Fig. 5. Figure 6 shows the radio messages exchanged by the sensor nodes, while Fig. 7 contains the data packets received at the CoAP server

Next, the implementation of a simulation of the MQTT protocol is carried out. It is one of the most widely spread protocols in IoT, for which a topology is established as shown in Fig. 8, within which there are three elements: an edge router, a subscriber representing the services or applications to which the data is directed and a publisher representing the sensor nodes. All the information reaches the server and is available on the published topic. For the example carried out, the MQTT broker or server is mosquitto and runs within the same operating system as the simulator.

```
Neighbors
fe80::212:7403:3:303
fe80::212:7404:4:404
fe80::212:7402:2:202
fe80::212:7406:6:606
Routes
aaaa::212:7405:5:505/128 (via fe80::212:7403:3:303) 16711418s
aaaa::212:7406:6:606/128 (via fe80::212:7406:6:606) 16711395s
aaaa::212:7404:4:404/128 (via fe80::212:7404:4:404) 16711394s
```

Fig. 5. Adjacencies and routes shown in the web browser

Fig. 6. Exchanged radio messages

Fig. 7. Data received on the COAP server

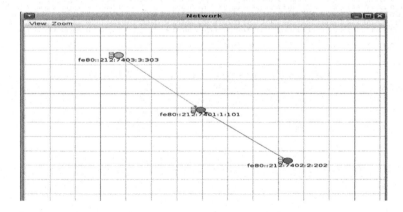

Fig. 8. Network topology for MQTT simulation

Once the MQTT server is running, the simulation ensues, Fig. 9 shows the exchange of messages between subscriber and publisher through the edge router, while in Fig. 10 shows the messages that arrive up to the mosquitto server.

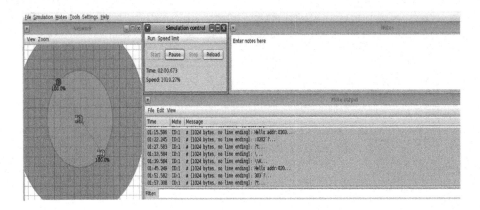

Fig. 9. MQTT swapped packages

To make a description of the other features of the simulated environment, a network topology shown in Fig. 11, is established next. In this figure we can observe a homogeneous distribution of the sensor nodes that communicate through the IEEE 802.15.4 protocol. It is important to note that the characteristics and scripts of the sensor nodes can be modified depending on the systems to be evaluated. In this particular case, the sky mote sensor node is used, while the greeting message "hello" was changed by "Smart Agriculture".

```
20201010 221420.343 4 aaaa::212:7402:2:202:1884 0012740200020202 <- MQTT-S PUBLISH msgid: 0 qos: 0 retained: 1
20201010 221425.070 4 aaaa::212:7403:3:303:1884 0012740300030303 <- MQTT-S PUBLISH msgid: 0 qos: 0 retained: 1
20201010 221434.436 4 aaaa::212:7403:3:303:1884 0012740300030303 -> MQTT-S PINGRESP (0)
20201010 221437.608 4 aaaa::212:7402:2:202:1884 0012740200020202 <- MQTT-S PUBLISH msgid: 0 qos: 0 retained: 1
20201010 221443.614 4 aaaa::212:7403:3:303:1884 0012740300030303 <- MQTT-S PUBLISH msgid: 0 qos: 0 retained: 1
20201010 221446.914 4 aaaa::212:7402:2:202:1884 0012740200020202 <- MQTT-S PUBLISH msgid: 0 qos: 0 retained: 1
20201010 221451.244 4 aaaa::212:7403:3:303:1884 0012740300030303 <- MQTT-S PUBLISH msgid: 0 qos: 0 retained: 1
20201010 221457.374 4 aaaa::212:7402:2:202:1884 0012740200020202 <- MQTT-S PUBLISH msgid: 0 qos: 0 retained: 1

20201010 221457.386 4 aaaa::212:7402:2:202:1884 0012740200020202 -> MQTT-S PINGRESP (0)
```

Fig. 10. Packages received at the MQTT server

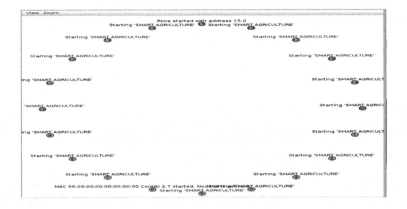

Fig. 11. Network topology for IEEE 802.15.4 simulation

Figure 12 shows the average consumption of each sensor node, with the identification corresponding to the operating modes.

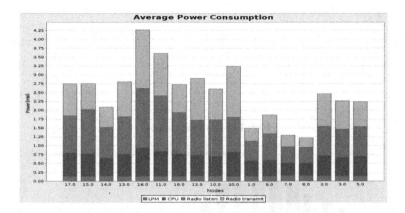

Fig. 12. Estimation of the average energy consumption of the sensor nodes

In the diagnosis of a network it is important to analyze parameters such as neighbor counters Fig. 13, routing metrics Fig. 14, network hops Fig. 15, latency Fig. 16, among others, in order to establish important characteristics such as convergence time, redundant routes, and critical points of failure. In this way, a reliable design and evaluation of the Iot solution to be implemented can be achieved.

The analysis parameters obtained from the simulated environment provide insight into both the behavior of the network (adjacencies, network hops, neighbors, radio link traffic, etc.), as well as the energy consumption of the sensor nodes (average consumption and instantaneous energy consumption). The simulator also allows incorporating sensor nodes through the programming of scripts, so the simulation is not restricted to the predefined models in it.

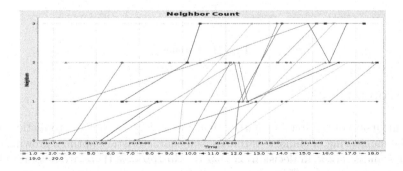

Fig. 13. Counting of adjacent nodes (neighbors)

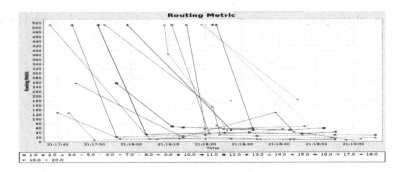

Fig. 14. Routing metrics

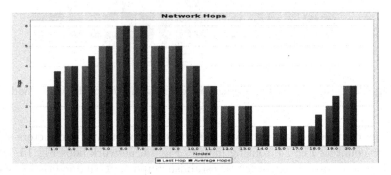

Fig. 15. Network jumps

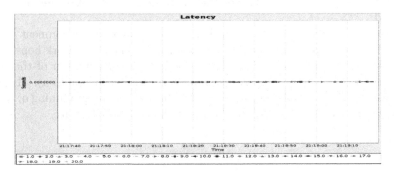

Fig. 16. Latency

4   Conclusions

The incursion of the IoT in smart agriculture seeks to optimize production, providing monitoring of climatic variables, soil characteristics, optimal growing conditions and support in decision-making. In this process there are several factors that must be analyzed such as: security in the networks, autonomy of operation, degrees of protection of sensor nodes, availability of information, among others.

This will allow heterogeneous data to converge in order to achieve the objective by facilitating decision-making or solving the proposed problem. This convergence will achieve that the immense amount of data obtained is used, turning it into information that contributes to the development of the agricultural sector. From the research carried out it can be concluded that most of the works accomplished deal with edge routers in charge of the conversion of protocols and technologies; the preferred standard in wireless communication systems is 6 LoPAN, while the most cited data transport protocol is MQTT. Projects also agree on a clear trend towards energy efficiency, network security and self-charge systems using alternative energies.

5 Future Works

As a future work, different IoT solutions focused on intelligent agriculture can be designed. They can incorporate sensor nodes that adjust to the needs of the environment. In addition, the incorporation of expert systems that collaborate in decision-making based on automatic learning can be suggested. On the other hand, the estimation of autonomy of the systems can be approached based on an analysis of the redundant power systems from the energy collection of environmental variables.

Acknowledgements. To the Universidad de las Fuerzas Armadas ESPE and to CONGOPE, for the financing of the project "Prototype of early warning systems for frost", as well as the project number 008-007-2017-07-27: "PLATANO – Intelligent Technological Support Platform for small and medium agricultural producers", carried out jointly with the Universidad Politecnica Salesiana collaboration, and the Wicom Energy Research group.

References

1. Verdouw, C., Wolfert, S., Tekinerdogan, B.: Internet of things in agriculture. CAB Rev. Perspect. Agric. Vet. Sci. Nutr. Nat. Res. **11**, 1–12 (2016)
2. Deepa, B., Anusha, C., Chaya Devi, P.: Smart agriculture using IoT. Adv. Intell. Syst. Comput **1171**, 11–19 (2021)
3. Yan, B., Yan, C., Ke, C., Tan, X.: Information sharing in supply chain of agricultural products based on the internet of things. Ind. Manag. Data Syst. **116**(7), 1397–1416 (2016)
4. Abbasi, M., Yaghmaee, M.H., Rahnama, F.: Internet of things in agriculture: a survey. In: 2019 3rd International Conference on Internet of Things and Applications (IoT), pp. 1–12. IEEE (2019)
5. Guerrero-Ibáñez, J.A., et al.: Sgreenh-IoT: Plataforma IoT para agricultura de precisión. Revista Iberoamericana de sistemas, cibernética e informática **14**(2), 53–58 (2017)
6. Khattab, A., Abdelgawad, A., Yelmarthi, K.: Design and implementation of a cloud-based iot scheme for precision agriculture. In: 2016 28th International Conference on Microelectronics (ICM), pp. 201–204. IEEE (2016)

7. Muangprathub, J., Boonnam, N., Kajornkasirat, S., Lekbangpong, N., Wanich-sombat, A., Nillaor, P.: Iot and agriculture data analysis for smart farm. Comput. Electron. Agric. **156**, 467–474 (2019)
8. Mekala, M.S., Viswanathan, P.: A survey: smart agriculture IoT with cloud computing. In: 2017 International Conference on Microelectronic Devices, Circuits and Systems (ICMDCS), pp. 1–7. IEEE (2017)
9. Priya, C.T., Praveen, K., Srividya, A.: Monitoring of pest insect traps using image sensors & DSPIC. Int. J. Eng. Trends Tech **4**(9), 4088–4093 (2013)
10. Chiluisa-Velasco, G., Lagla-Quinaluisa, J., Rivas-Lalaleo, D., Alvarez-Veintimilla, M.: Intelligent monitoring system of environmental biovariables in poultry farms. In: Arai, K., Kapoor, S., Bhatia, R. (eds.) IntelliSys 2020. AISC, vol. 1252, pp. 386–399. Springer, Cham (2021). https://doi.org/10.1007/978-3-030-55190-2_29
11. Sichiqui, F., et al.: Agricultural information management: a case study in corn crops in Ecuador. In: Botto-Tobar, M., León-Acurio, J., Díaz Cadena, A., Montiel Díaz, P. (eds.) ICAETT 2019. AISC, vol. 1066, pp. 113–124. Springer, Cham (2020). https://doi.org/10.1007/978-3-030-32022-5_11
12. Guillermo, J.C., García-Cedeño, A., Rivas-Lalaleo, D., Huerta, M., Clotet, R.: IoT architecture based on wireless sensor network applied to agricultural monitoring: a case of study of cacao crops in Ecuador. In: Corrales, J.C., Angelov, P., Iglesias, J.A. (eds.) AACC 2018. AISC, vol. 893, pp. 42–57. Springer, Cham (2019). https://doi.org/10.1007/978-3-030-04447-3_3
13. Karim, F., Karim, F.: Monitoring system using web of things in precision agriculture. Procedia Comput. Sci. **110**, 402–409 (2017)
14. Sah, D.K., Amgoth, T.: Renewable energy harvesting schemes in wireless sensor networks: a survey. Inf. Fusion **63**, 223–247 (2020)
15. Galizia, C.: os grados de protección ip en los equipos e instalaciones y su interpretación según iec y nema (2017)
16. Tzounis, A., Katsoulas, N., Bartzanas, T., Kittas, C.: Internet of things in agriculture, recent advances and future challenges. Biosyst. Eng **164**, 31–48 (2017)
17. Borrero, J.D., Zabalo, A.: An autonomous wireless device for real-time monitoring of water needs. Sensors **20**(7), 2078 (2020)
18. Marrero, D., Suárez, A., Macías, E., Mena, V.: Extending the battery life of the zigbee routers and coordinator by modifying their mode of operation. Sensors **20**(1), 30 (2020)
19. Heble, S., Kumar, A., Prasad, K.V.D., Samirana, S., Rajalakshmi, P., Desai, U.B.: A low power IoT network for smart agriculture. In: 2018 IEEE 4th World Forum on Internet of Things (WF-IoT), pp. 609–614. IEEE (2018)
20. Riquelme, J.L., Soto, F., Suardíaz, J., Sánchez, P., Iborra, A., Vera, J.: Wireless sensor networks for precision horticulture in southern Spain. Comput. Electron. Agric. **68**(1), 25–35 (2009)
21. García-Fallas, F.: Sesbeacon: Nodo sensor electrónico para alertas tempranas (2016)
22. Visconti, P., de Fazio, R., Velázquez, R., Del-Valle-Soto, C., Giannoccaro, N.I.: Development of sensors-based agri-food traceability system remotely managed by a software platform for optimized farm management. Sensors **20**(13), 3632 (2020)
23. Ilie-Ablachim, D., Pătru, G.C., Florea, I.-M., Rosner, D.: Monitoring device for culture substrate growth parameters for precision agriculture: Acronym: Monisen. In: 2016 15th RoEduNet Conference: Networking in Education and Research, pp. 1–7. IEEE (2016)

24. Zhao, W., Lin, S., Han, J., Xu, R., Hou, L.: Design and implementation of smart irrigation system based on LoRa. In: 2017 IEEE Globecom Workshops (GC Wkshps), pp. 1–6. IEEE (2017)
25. López, J.A., Navarro, H., Soto, F., Pavón, N., Suardíaz, J., Torres, R.: Gaia2: a multifunctional wireless device for enhancing crop management. Agric. Water Manag. **151**, 75–86 (2015)
26. Catelani, M., Ciani, L., Bartolini, A., Guidi, G., Patrizi, G.: Characterization of a low-cost and low-power environmental monitoring system. In: 2020 IEEE International Instrumentation and Measurement Technology Conference (I2MTC), pp. 1–6. IEEE (2020)
27. Valente, A., Silva, S., Duarte, D., Cabral Pinto, F., Soares, S.: low-cost lorawan node for agro-intelligence IoT. Electronics **9**(6), 987 (2020)
28. Estrada Mendoza, P.M.: Diseño de un nodo sensor para aplicaciones IoT (2019)
29. Pérez-Expósito, J.P., Fernández-Caramés, T.M., Fraga-Lamas, P., Castedo, L.: An IoT monitoring system for precision viticulture. In: 2017 IEEE International Conference on Internet of Things (iThings) and IEEE Green Computing and Communications (GreenCom) and IEEE Cyber, Physical and Social Computing (CPSCom) and IEEE Smart Data (SmartData), pp. 662–669. IEEE (2017)
30. Maurya, M., Shukla, S.R.: Current wireless sensor nodes (motes): performance metrics and constraints. Int. J. Adv. Res. Electron. Commun. Eng. (IJARECE) **2**(1), 45–48 (2013)
31. Rodríguez-Robles, J., Martin, Á., Martin, S., Ruipérez-Valiente, J.A., Castro, M.: Autonomous sensor network for rural agriculture environments, low cost, and energy self-charge. Sustainability **12**(15), 5913 (2020)
32. Chen, J., Hu, K., Wang, Q., Sun, Y., Shi, Z., He, S.: Narrowband internet of things: implementations and applications. IEEE Internet Things J. **4**(6), 2309–2314 (2017)
33. Raza, U., Kulkarni, P., Sooriyabandara, M.: Low power wide area networks: an overview. IEEE Commun. Surv. Tutor. **19**(2), 855–873 (2017)
34. Singelée, D., Preneel, B.: Review of the bluetooth security architecture. In: Information Security Bulletin, Citeseer (2006)
35. Tosi, J., Taffoni, F., Santacatterina, M., Sannino, R., Formica, D.: Performance evaluation of bluetooth low energy: a systematic review. Sensors **17**(12), 2898 (2017)
36. Dignani, J.P.: Análisis del protocolo ZigBee. PhD thesis, Universidad Nacional de la Plata (2012)
37. Feng, X., Yan, F., Liu, X.: Study of wireless communication technologies on internet of things for precision agriculture. Wirel. Pers. Commun **108**(3), 1785–1802 (2019)
38. Sesé Vega, E.: Estudio de las vulnerabilidades de la tecnología bluetooth (2020)
39. Alliance, L.: Lorawan security full end-to-end encryption for IoT application providers (2007). https://www.lora-alliance.org/portals/0/documents/whitepapers/LoRaWAN_Security-Whitepaper_V6_Digital.pdf

Author Index

Printed in the United States
by Baker & Taylor Publisher Services